1,001
LOW-FAT
Soups &
Stews

From elegant classics to
hearty one-pot meals

EDITED BY
SUE SPITLER

with Linda R. Yoakam, R.D., M.S.

Surrey Books
CHICAGO

1,001 LOW-FAT SOUPS AND STEWS is published by
Surrey Books, Inc., 230 E. Ohio St., Suite 120, Chicago, IL 60611.

First edition: 1 2 3 4 5

This book is manufactured in the United States of America.

Library of Congress Cataloging-in-Publication data:

Spitler, Sue
    1,001 low-fat soups and stews / edited by Sue Spitler,
with Linda R. Yoakam.
      p. cm.
    ISBN 1-57284-034-X (pbk.)
     1. Soups. 2. Stews 3. Low-fat diet—Recipes. I. Title: One
thousand and one, low-fat soups and stews. II. Yoakam, Linda R.
III. Title.

TX757 .S65 2000   00-030903
641.8'13—dc21

Editorial and production: *Bookcrafters, Inc., Chicago*
Art direction: *Joan Sommers Design, Chicago*
Nutritional analyses: *Linda R. Yoakam, R.D., M.S.*
Cover illustrations: Leigh Wells

For prices on quantity purchases or for free book catalog,
contact Surrey Books at the above address.

This title is distributed to the trade by Publishers Group West.

CONTENTS

ACKNOWLEDGMENTS

The publisher, editors, and staff of Surrey Books wish to thank the nine innovative authors who contributed to this cookbook:

> Nancy Baggett
> Ruth Glick
> Barbara Grunes
> Erica Klein
> Carole Kruppa
> Kim Lila
> Betty Marks
> Carol Munson
> Sue Spitler

Thanks and appreciation also to Editor Sue Spitler and her associate Pat Molden, Editorial Assistant Leona Pitej, Managing Editor Gene DeRoin, and Nutritionist Linda R. Yoakam, R.D.,M.S.

INTRODUCTION

Few foods are as satisfying and flavorful as delicious homemade soups and stews. They're wholesome and comforting. They're the heart and soul of the kitchen; they restore our spirit. The glorious aroma of a simmering soup or sumptuous stew is guaranteed to whet appetites and bring folks into the kitchen to check on what's cooking for dinner.

The varieties of soups and stews are nearly endless, as you'll find with the more than 1,000 creative and healthful recipes in *1,001 Low-Fat Soups and Stews*. Fifteen delectable chapters are jam-packed with stocks, chowders, chilies, supper soups, meatless soups and stews, meat, poultry, and seafood stews, and more. There are recipes for old-fashioned favorites, recipes with a foreign flair, vegetarian recipes, and recipes that highlight new trendy flavors. You'll find hearty full-flavored soups and stews, perfect for crisp fall and frosty winter seasons, and light, lovely soups and stews for the fresh days of spring and the sultry summer season. There's a soup or stew recipe for every occasion, whether a family meal, a festive celebration, or a casual evening with friends.

Recipes have been carefully created for fabulous flavors, using high-quality, low-fat, healthy ingredients that are readily available in your local supermarket—no special shopping excursions needed! Recipes are designed for cooking ease, requiring no special cooking skills or gourmet kitchen equipment. Preparation and cooking times are streamlined, too, complementing today's busy lifestyles. In fact, more than 130 recipes in Quick-and-Easy Soups and Quick-and-Easy Stews chapters can be prepared and cooked in no more than 30 to 45 minutes, and often in much less time. And, as soups and stews are perfect candidates for advance preparation, you can make them ahead to refrigerate or freeze—a great do-ahead bonus!

The Stocks chapter provides 23 homemade stocks to use for the best flavor in soups and stews. Stocks are very easy to make, as they simmer untended to flavorful goodness. Make them ahead in large quantities and freeze them if you want. Of course, a favorite canned or packaged broth can be substituted for convenience.

We've taken advantage of the fast/slow convenience that microwave ovens and slow cookers offer, with dishes that cook in minutes and others that simmer all day. Delicious accompaniments are found in Chapter 15—a trove of breads, biscuits, and muffins that will enhance your soups and stews dining experience.

NUTRITIONAL INFORMATION

In accordance with American Heart Association guidelines, virtually none of the recipes in this book exceeds 30 percent of calories from fat. Specific nutritional information is provided for each recipe (not including variations), but remember that nutritional data are not always infallible. The nutritional analyses are derived by using computer software highly regarded by nutritionists and dietitians, but they are meant to be used only as guidelines. Results may vary slightly depending upon the brand or manufacturer of an ingredient used.

Ingredients noted as "optional" or "to taste" or "as garnish" are not included in the nutritional analyses. When alternate choices or amounts of ingredients are given, the ingredient or amount listed first is used for analysis. Similarly, data is based on the first number of servings shown, where a range is given. Nutritional analyses are also based on the reduced-fat or fat-free cooking methods used in recipes; the addition of margarine, oil, or other ingredients will invalidate data.

Other factors that can affect the accuracy of nutritional data include variability in sizes, weights, and measures of fruits, vegetables, and other foods. There is also a possible 20 percent error factor in the nutritional labeling of prepared foods.

If you have any health problems that impose strict dietary requirements, it is important to consult a physician, dietitian, or nutritionist before using recipes in this or any other cookbook. Also, if you are a diabetic or require a diet that restricts calories, fat, or sodium, remember that the nutritional data may be accurate for the recipe as written but not for the food you cooked due to the variables explained above.

ONE

Stocks

QUICK SAGE CHICKEN STOCK

Make this light, fresh-tasting broth when you have just 10 minutes to simmer up a flavorful stock. The secret behind the speed? Canned broth.

makes about 2 cups

1 can (14 ounces) reduced-sodium fat-free chicken broth
1 medium onion, quartered
1/2 rib celery
2 fresh sage leaves, *or* 1/2 teaspoon dried sage leaves
2 teaspoons dry sherry

Per Cup:
Calories: 35
% Calories from fat: 1
Protein (g): 5.1
Carbohydrates (g): 1.1
Fat (g): 0
Saturated fat (g): 0
Cholesterol (mg): 0
Sodium (mg): 142
Exchanges:
Milk: 0.0
Veg.: 0.0
Fruit: 0.0
Bread: 0.0
Meat: 0.0
Fat: 0.0

1. Combine all ingredients in large saucepan; heat to boiling. Reduce heat and simmer, covered, 10 minutes. Strain; discard vegetables and seasonings.

CHICKEN STOCK

A subtly flavored, low-sodium stock with less than 1 gram of fat per cup.

makes about 2 quarts

16 ounces boneless, skinless chicken breast, cubed
1 teaspoon olive oil
2¹/2 quarts water
2 ribs celery, with leaves, halved
4 large onions, with skins, quartered
4 medium carrots, halved
1 small turnip, quartered
2 bay leaves
6 cloves garlic
8 black peppercorns
10 fresh, *or* 2 teaspoons dried, sage leaves
1 sprig thyme

Per Cup:
Calories: 15
% Calories from fat: 37
Protein (g): 1.3
Carbohydrates (g): 1.2
Fat (g): 0.7
Saturated fat (g): 0.1
Cholesterol (mg): 3.1
Sodium (mg): 6
Exchanges:
Milk: 0.0
Veg.: 0.0
Fruit: 0.0
Bread: 0.0
Meat: 0.0
Fat: 0.0

1. Saute chicken in oil in large saucepan until browned, about 10 minutes. Add remaining ingredients and heat to boiling; reduce heat and simmer, covered, 1 hour, skimming any foam from surface.

2. Strain stock through double layer of cheesecloth, discarding meat and vegetables. Cool; refrigerate. Remove congealed fat from surface of stock.

LOW-SALT CHICKEN STOCK

Save chicken bones in a plastic bag in the freezer for making chicken stock.

makes about 2 quarts

16 ounces skinless chicken breast, fat trimmed
   Chicken bones from 4 chicken breasts
2 onions, sliced
3 ribs celery, sliced
3 carrots, sliced
$^1/_2$ cup packed parsley sprigs
1 parsley root, sliced
1 large red potato, peeled, sliced
$^1/_2$ teaspoon pepper
$2^1/_2$ quarts water

Per Cup:
Calories: 8
% Calories from fat: 0
Protein (g): 1.6
Carbohydrates (g): 1.2
Fat (g): 0
Saturated fat (g): 0
Cholesterol (mg): 0
Sodium (mg): 4
Exchanges:
Milk: 0.0
Veg.: 0.0
Fruit: 0.0
Bread: 0.0
Meat: 0.0
Fat: 0.0

1. Combine all ingredients in large saucepan and heat to boiling; reduce heat and simmer, covered, 1$^1/_2$ hours, skimming any foam from surface.

2. Strain stock through double layer of cheesecloth, discarding bones, meat, and vegetables. Cool; refrigerate until cold. Remove congealed fat from surface of stock.

Variation:
Game Stock—Make stock as above, substituting **3** pounds meaty bones from rabbit, duck, goose, or other game.

RICH CHICKEN STOCK

Veal knuckle adds richness to this stock.

makes about 4 quarts

1 chicken (about 4 pounds), cut up, fat trimmed

2½ pounds chicken necks and wings

1 veal knuckle, cracked, optional

2 medium onions, studded with several whole cloves

6 medium carrots, quartered

2 medium leeks, white parts only, cut into 1-inch pieces

3 ribs celery, including leaves, cut into 1-inch pieces

½ teaspoon dried basil leaves

½ teaspoon dried thyme leaves

½ teaspoon dried tarragon leaves

1 clove garlic, peeled

2 tablespoons Spike

10 black peppercorns

6 sprigs parsley

5 quarts water

1 cup dry white wine

Per Cup:
Calories: 39
% Calories from fat: 18
Protein (g): 4.9
Carbohydrates (g): 0.8
Fat (g): 0.8
Saturated fat (g): 0.2
Cholesterol (mg): 1
Sodium (mg): 36
Exchanges:
Milk: 0.0
Veg.: 0.0
Fruit: 0.0
Bread: 0.0
Meat: 0.5
Fat: 0.0

1. Combine all ingredients in large Dutch oven or saucepan and heat to boiling. Reduce heat and simmer, covered, 3 to 4 hours, skimming any foam from surface.

2. Strain stock through double layer of cheesecloth, discarding bones, meat, and vegetables. Cool; refrigerate. Remove congealed fat from surface of stock.

Variation:
Roasted Chicken Stock—Place chicken, chicken bones, veal knuckle, and vegetables in large roasting pan. Roast at 425 degrees until well browned, about 30 minutes. Transfer to large Dutch oven and complete recipe as above.

TURKEY STOCK

The perfect ending for the Thanksgiving turkey, this stock can be used for Turkey Noodle Soup (see p. 297), or as a substitute in recipes calling for chicken stock. If you've had a goose or duck for dinner, use those bones in this recipe for another flavorful stock.

makes about 4 quarts

1	meaty turkey carcass, cut up
2	medium onions, quartered
6	medium carrots, quartered
2	medium leeks, white parts only, cut into 1-inch pieces
3	ribs celery with leaves, cut into 1-inch pieces
1	teaspoon dried thyme leaves
10	black peppercorns
6	sprigs parsley
5	quarts water
1	cup dry white wine, *or* water

Per Cup:
Calories: 29
% Calories from fat: 28
Protein (g): 2
Carbohydrates (g): 0.9
Fat (g): 0.9
Saturated fat (g): 0.2
Cholesterol (mg): 5.6
Sodium (mg): 7
Exchanges:
Milk: 0.0
Veg.: 0.0
Fruit: 0.0
Bread: 0.0
Meat: 0.0
Fat: 0.0

1. Combine all ingredients in large Dutch oven or stockpot and heat to boiling; reduce heat and simmer, covered, 3 to 4 hours, skimming any foam from surface.

2. Strain stock through double layer of cheesecloth, discarding bones and vegetables. Cool; refrigerate. Remove congealed fat from surface of stock.

BEEF STOCK

A flavorful stock that's easy to prepare in either a saucepan or a pressure cooker.

makes about 2 quarts

2¹/₂ quarts water
2 ribs from roasted beef rib roast, fat trimmed
2 ribs celery with leaves, halved
4 large onions, with skins, quartered
4 medium carrots, halved
1 parsnip, halved
2 bay leaves
8 black peppercorns
1 sprig parsley
5 sage leaves

Per Cup:
Calories: 8
% Calories from fat: **31**
Protein (g): 0.2
Carbohydrates (g): **1.3**
Fat (g): 0.3
Saturated fat (g): 0
Cholesterol (mg): **0.3**
Sodium (mg): **4**
Exchanges:
Milk: 0.0
Veg.: 0.0
Fruit: 0.0
Bread: 0.0
Meat: 0.0
Fat: 0.0

1. Combine all ingredients in a large saucepan and heat to boiling. Reduce heat; simmer, covered, 2 hours, skimming any foam from surface.

2. Strain stock through double layer of cheesecloth, discarding bones and vegetables. Cool; refrigerate. Remove congealed fat from surface of stock.

FRAGRANT BEEF STOCK

Dried mushrooms, red wine, and herbs give a rich flavor to this stock.

makes about 3¹/₂ quarts

2 pounds short ribs, *or* beef, fat trimmed
2 pounds beef marrow bones, cut into pieces
16 ounces cubed beef chuck, fat trimmed
1 large onion, chopped
1 clove garlic, peeled
¹/₂ cup dried mushrooms
4 medium carrots, quartered
2 tablespoons Spike
10 black peppercorns

Per Cup:
Calories: 16
% Calories from fat: 28
Protein (g): 2.7
Carbohydrates (g): 0.6
Fat (g): 0.5
Saturated fat (g): 0.3
Cholesterol (mg): 3
Sodium (mg): 42
Exchanges:
Milk: 0.0
Veg.: 0.0
Fruit: 0.0
Bread: 0.0
Meat: 0.0
Fat: 0.0

1 bay leaf
1 teaspoon dried basil leaves
1 teaspoon dried thyme leaves
3 sprigs parsley
3 ribs celery, quartered
4 quarts water
1 cup dry red wine, *or* water
1 tablespoon soy sauce

1. Combine all ingredients in large Dutch oven or stockpot and heat to boiling. Reduce heat and simmer, covered, 3 to 4 hours, skimming any foam from surface.

2. Strain stock through double layer of cheesecloth, discarding bones, meat, and vegetables. Cool and refrigerate; remove congealed fat from surface of stock.

Variation:
Brown Beef Stock—Place bones and meat in large roasting pan. Roast at 425 degrees until well browned; about 45 minutes. Transfer to large Dutch oven and complete recipe as above.

QUICK-SPICED BEEF STOCK

When you want a spicy stock, give this easy version a try. It's just what the broth-meister ordered for perking up a bland dish!

makes about 2 cups

1 can (14 ounces) reduced-sodium fat-free beef broth
1 medium onion, quartered
1 clove garlic
1 tablespoon dry red wine, *or* water
1 teaspoon pickling spice

Per Cup:
Calories: 25
% Calories from fat: 0
Protein (g): 4.3
Carbohydrates (g): 0.9
Fat (g): 0
Saturated fat (g): 0
Cholesterol (mg): 0
Sodium (mg): 133
Exchanges:
Milk: 0.0
Veg.: 0.0
Fruit: 0.0
Bread: 0.0
Meat: 0.0
Fat: 0.0

1. Combine broth, onion, garlic, and wine in a large saucepan. Place pickling spice in mesh tea bag or tie in cheesecloth. Add to broth and heat to boiling. Reduce heat; simmer, covered, 10 minutes. Strain; discard vegetables and seasonings.

VEAL STOCK

Veal bones and stew meat can be hard to find, so make this delicately fla-vored stock whenever you find them, and freeze it.

makes about 2 quarts

Vegetable cooking spray
1½ pounds veal stew meat
½ cup chopped onion
⅓ cup chopped carrot
⅓ cup chopped celery
1 veal knuckle, *or* veal bones (about 1¾ pounds)
2 quarts water
2 bay leaves
6 black peppercorns
3 whole cloves

Per Cup:
Calories: 17
% Calories from fat: 36
Protein (g): 2.4
Carbohydrates (g): 0.2
Fat (g): 0.6
Saturated fat (g): 0.1
Cholesterol (mg): 8.9
Sodium (mg): 6
Exchanges:
Milk: 0.0
Veg.: 0.0
Fruit: 0.0
Bread: 0.0
Meat: 0.0
Fat: 0.0

1. Spray large Dutch oven with cooking spray; heat over medium heat until hot. Cook veal stew meat until browned, 8 to 10 minutes; remove and reserve. Add vegetables and saute until browned, about 5 minutes.

2. Return veal to Dutch oven; add remaining ingredients and heat to boiling. Reduce heat and simmer, covered, 4 hours, skimming any foam from surface. Strain through double layer of cheesecloth, discarding meat, bones, and vegetables. Cool and refrigerate; remove congealed fat from stock.

FISH STOCK

Make arrangements with the fish department of your supermarket to save fish bones for you.

makes about 1¹/₂ quarts

2-3 pounds fish bones from a non-oily fish such as haddock
1 large onion, chopped
1 rib celery, sliced
2 bay leaves
7-8 black peppercorns
¹/₂ teaspoon kosher, *or* sea salt
¹/₂ teaspoon white pepper
2 quarts water

Per Cup:
Calories: 17
% Calories from fat: 0
Protein (g): 2.8
Carbohydrates (g): 0.3
Fat (g): 0.1
Saturated fat (g): 0
Cholesterol (mg): 0
Sodium (mg): 191
Exchanges:
Milk: 0.0
Veg.: 0.0
Fruit: 0.0
Bread: 0.0
Meat: 0.0
Fat: 0.0

1. Combine all ingredients in large saucepan and heat to boiling. Reduce heat and simmer 30 minutes, skimming foam from surface.

2. Strain through double layer of cheesecloth, discarding bones and vegetables. Cool; refrigerate.

EASY FISH STOCK

Any kind of mild-flavored fish will make a delicious stock; avoid strongly flavored fish such as salmon or tuna. Stock will keep in refrigerator for 2 days, or up to 2 months in the freezer.

makes about 1 quart

1¹/₂ pounds fresh, *or* frozen, fish
1 medium onion, finely chopped
3 ribs celery with leaves, halved
1 medium carrot, finely diced
3 sprigs parsley
3 slices lemon
8 black peppercorns
2 teaspoons Spike
³/₄ cup white wine, *or* water
3¹/₂ cups cold water

Per Cup:
Calories: 10
% Calories from fat: 3
Protein (g): 0.7
Carbohydrates (g): 0.2
Fat (g): 0
Saturated fat (g): 0
Cholesterol (mg): 2
Sodium (mg): 3
Exchanges:
Milk: 0.0
Veg.: 0.0
Fruit: 0.0
Bread: 0.0
Meat: 0.0
Fat: 0.0

1.   Combine all ingredients in large saucepan and heat to boiling. Reduce heat and simmer 30 minutes, skimming any foam from surface.

2.   Strain stock through double layer of cheesecloth, discarding fish and vegetables. Cool; refrigerate.

BASIC VEGETABLE STOCK

As vegetables used in stocks are later discarded, they should be scrubbed but do not need to be peeled. This basic stock can be used in any soup recipe.

makes about 2 quarts

1	large onion, coarsely chopped
1	large leek, white part only, cut into 1-inch pieces
1	large carrot, cut into 1-inch pieces
1	rib celery, cut into 1-inch pieces
1/2	teaspoon vegetable oil
2	quarts water
1	cup dry white wine or water
1	quart mixed chopped vegetables (broccoli, green beans, cabbage, potatoes, tomatoes, corn, summer or winter squash, bell peppers, mushrooms, etc.)
6-8	parsley sprigs
1	bay leaf
4	whole allspice
1	tablespoon black peppercorns
2	teaspoons bouquet garni

Per Cup:
Calories: 12
% Calories from fat: 0
Protein (g): 0.4
Carbohydrates (g): 1.8
Fat (g): 0.4
Saturated fat (g): 0
Cholesterol (mg): 0
Sodium (mg): 12
Exchanges:
Milk: 0.0
Veg.: 0.0
Fruit: 0.0
Bread: 0.0
Meat: 0.0
Fat: 0.0

1.   Saute onion, leek, carrot, and celery in oil in stock pot or large Dutch oven, 5 minutes. Add water, wine, and chopped vegetables. Tie herbs in cheesecloth bag and add to pot. Heat to boiling; reduce heat and simmer, covered, 1½ to 2 hours.

2.   Strain stock, pressing lightly on vegetables to extract all juices; discard solids. Cool; refrigerate or freeze.

VEGETABLE STOCK

This no-salt-added vegetable stock with its light onion flavor makes a perfect base for many of the soups and stews in this book.

makes about 2 quarts

2¹/₂ quarts water
5 onions with skins, quartered
3 carrots, halved
3 ribs celery with leaves, halved
2 bay leaves
¹/₄ cup packed fresh basil
10 whole white peppercorns
1 sprig parsley
1 sprig thyme

Per Cup:
Calories: 5
% Calories from fat: 0
Protein (g): 0.1
Carbohydrates (g): 1.1
Fat (g): 0
Saturated fat (g): 0
Cholesterol (mg): 0
Sodium (mg): 2
Exchanges:
Milk: 0.0
Veg.: 0.0
Fruit: 0.0
Bread: 0.0
Meat: 0.0
Fat: 0.0

1. Combine all ingredients in large saucepan and heat to boiling. Reduce heat and simmer, covered, 30 minutes.

2. Strain stock through double layer of cheesecloth, discarding vegetables. Cool; refrigerate.

CANNED VEGETABLE STOCK

A quick and easy solution for stock when you haven't the time or inclination to start from scratch.

makes about 1¹/₂ quarts

2 medium onions, coarsely chopped
2 medium leeks, white parts only, coarsely chopped
2 large carrots, cut into 1-inch pieces
2 large ribs celery, cut into 1-inch pieces
4 teaspoons minced garlic
1 teaspoon olive oil
2 cans (14¹/₂ ounces each) reduced-sodium vegetable broth
2 cups water
1 cup dry white wine, *or* water
2 medium tomatoes, quartered
4 sprigs parsley
2 bay leaves

Per Cup:
Calories: 62
% Calories from fat: 12
Protein (g): 0.8
Carbohydrates (g): 6.7
Fat (g): 0.8
Saturated fat (g): 0.1
Cholesterol (mg): 0
Sodium (mg): 55
Exchanges:
Milk: 0.0
Veg.: 1.0
Fruit: 0.0
Bread: 0.0
Meat: 0.0
Fat: 0.0

1. Saute onions, leeks, carrots, celery, and garlic in oil in Dutch oven, 5 minutes. Add broth and remaining ingredients and heat to boiling. Reduce heat and simmer, covered, 30 minutes.

2. Strain, pressing lightly on vegetables to extract all juices; discard solids. Cool; refrigerate or freeze.

LOW-SALT VEGETABLE STOCK

To store stock, pour cooked soup into ice cube tray and freeze. Dislodge the frozen cubes and store in a plastic bag in freezer until needed.

makes about 2 quarts

Vegetable cooking spray
4 cloves garlic, crushed
2 cups chopped onions
3 ribs celery, sliced
3 cups sliced carrots
1 cup sliced turnip
1 cup diced peeled potato
1/2 cup chopped parsley
2 bay leaves
1/2 teaspoon dried thyme leaves
1/2 teaspoon pepper
2 1/2 quarts water

Per Cup:
Calories: 4
% Calories from fat: 0
Protein (g): 0.1
Carbohydrates (g): 1.1
Fat (g): 0
Saturated fat (g): 0
Cholesterol (mg): 0
Sodium (mg): 3
Exchanges:
Milk: 0.0
Veg.: 0.0
Fruit: 0.0
Bread: 0.0
Meat: 0.0
Fat: 0.0

1. Spray large saucepan with cooking spray; heat over medium heat until hot. Saute garlic, onions, and celery, 5 minutes. Add remaining ingredients, except water, and cook another 5 minutes. Add water and heat to boiling. Reduce heat and simmer, covered, 1 3/4 hours.

2. Strain stock through double layer of cheesecloth, discarding vegetables. Cool; refrigerate or freeze.

RICH VEGETABLE STOCK

Keep this broth on hand to flavor dishes such as potatoes, vegetables, soup, and vegetarian dishes. The broth will keep up to a week in the refrigerator or may be frozen.

makes about 3 quarts

Vegetable cooking spray

- 3 onions, chopped
- 2 ribs celery with leaves, chopped
- 2 leeks, white and green parts, chopped
- 3 carrots, chopped
- 2 cups shredded cabbage
- 1/2 cup dried lentils
- 1 cup diced peeled potatoes
- 1/2 teaspoon dried thyme leaves
- 1/2 cup chopped fresh parsley
- 1/4 cup chopped fresh basil
- 8-10 black peppercorns
- 3 cloves garlic
- 2 bay leaves
- 1 teaspoon Spike
  Pinch ground nutmeg
- 3 1/2 quarts water

Per Cup:
Calories: 8
% Calories from fat: 4
Protein (g): 0.3
Carbohydrates (g): 1.7
Fat (g): 0
Saturated fat (g): 0
Cholesterol (mg): 0
Sodium (mg): 2
Exchanges:
Milk: 0.0
Veg.: 0.0
Fruit: 0.0
Bread: 0.0
Meat: 0.0
Fat: 0.0

1. Spray large saucepan with cooking spray; heat over medium heat until hot. Saute onions, celery, leeks, and carrots until onions begin to brown. Stir in remaining ingredients and heat to boiling. Reduce heat and simmer for 2 hours.

2. Strain stock through double layer of cheesecloth, discarding vegetables. Cool; refrigerate or freeze.

ROASTED VEGETABLE STOCK

Roasting vegetables intensifies their flavors and makes this stock very rich tasting. The beet adds a subtle sweetness to the stock, but use it only if you don't object to the pink color it creates!

makes about 2 quarts

Vegetable cooking spray
1 large onion, quartered
1 medium bulb garlic, cut crosswise in half
1 large leek, white part only, cut into 1-inch pieces
1 large carrot, quartered
1 rib celery, quartered
1 medium tomato, quartered
1/2 small butternut, *or* acorn, squash, cut into 2-inch pieces
1 small zucchini, quartered
1 small turnip, quartered
1 small beet, quartered, optional
2 quarts water
1 cup dry white wine, *or* water
3 cups coarsely chopped kale, *or* Swiss chard
6 sprigs parsley
1 bay leaf
1-2 teaspoons bouquet garni
1 teaspoon black peppercorns
4 whole allspice

Per Cup:
Calories: 25
% Calories from fat: 0
Protein (g): 0.2
Carbohydrates (g): 1.5
Fat (g): 0
Saturated fat (g): 0
Cholesterol (mg): 0
Sodium (mg): 12
Exchanges:
Milk: 0.0
Veg.: 0.0
Fruit: 0.0
Bread: 0.0
Meat: 0.0
Fat: 0.0

1. Line large jelly roll pan with aluminum foil and spray with cooking spray. Arrange vegetables on pan; spray with cooking spray. Bake at 425 degrees until vegetables are tender and browned, 35 to 40 minutes.

2. Combine vegetables and remaining ingredients in stock pot or large Dutch oven; heat to boiling. Reduce heat and simmer, covered, 1 1/2 to 2 hours.

3. Strain, pressing lightly on vegetables to extract all juices; discard solids. Cool; refrigerate or freeze.

MEDITERRANEAN VEGETABLE STOCK

A lovely stock, scented with orange, fennel, and saffron.

makes about 2 quarts

1	large onion, quartered
1	large leek, white part only, cut into 1-inch pieces
1	large carrot, quartered
1	rib celery, quartered
1	medium sweet potato, cubed
1	small zucchini, quartered
1/2	small fennel bulb, sliced
1/2	red bell pepper, coarsely chopped
2	teaspoons olive oil
2	quarts water
	Juice of 1 orange
1	cup dry white wine, *or* water
2	medium tomatoes, quartered
1	medium bulb garlic, cut crosswise in half
3	cups coarsely chopped spinach, *or* romaine lettuce
6	sprigs parsley
1	strip orange rind (3 x 1 inch)
1	bay leaf
1-2	teaspoons bouquet garni
1	teaspoon black peppercorns
4	whole allspice
	Pinch saffron

Per Cup:
Calories: 43
% Calories from fat: **25**
Protein (g): 0.5
Carbohydrates (g): **3.3**
Fat (g): 1.2
Saturated fat (g): 0.2
Cholesterol (mg): 0
Sodium (mg): 15
Exchanges:
Milk: 0.0
Veg.: 0.5
Fruit: 0.0
Bread: 0.0
Meat: 0.0
Fat: 0.5

1. Saute onion, leek, carrot, celery, sweet potato, zucchini, fennel, and bell pepper in oil in stock pot or large Dutch oven, 8 to 10 minutes. Add remaining ingredients and heat to boiling. Reduce heat and simmer, covered, 1 1/2 to 2 hours.

2. Strain, pressing lightly on vegetables to extract all juices; discard solids. Cool; refrigerate or freeze.

ORIENTAL VEGETABLE STOCK

A light, fragrant stock that can be used in many oriental soups and entrées.

makes about 2 quarts

Per Cup:
Calories: 8
% Calories from fat: 11
Protein (g): 0.6
Carbohydrates (g): 1.1
Fat (g): 0.1
Saturated fat (g): 0
Cholesterol (mg): 0
Sodium (mg): 110
Exchanges:
Milk: 0.0
Veg.: 0.0
Fruit: 0.0
Bread: 0.0
Meat: 0.0
Fat: 0.0

2	quarts water
1¹/₂	quarts shredded bok choy, *or* Chinese cabbage
1¹/₄	cups loosely packed cilantro, coarsely chopped
1	large onion, sliced
1	large carrot, sliced
¹/₂	large red bell pepper, sliced
¹/₃	cup sliced gingerroot
3	teaspoons minced garlic
3-4	dried shiitake mushrooms
4-5	teaspoons reduced-sodium tamari soy sauce
2-3	star anise
1³/₄–2	teaspoons five-spice powder
1¹/₂	teaspoons toasted Szechuan pepper

1. Combine all ingredients in small stockpot or Dutch oven; heat to boiling. Reduce heat and simmer, covered, 2 hours.

2. Strain, pressing lightly on vegetables to extract all juices; discard solids. Cool; refrigerate or freeze.

RICH MUSHROOM STOCK

The dried shiitake mushrooms, also known as Chinese black mushrooms, add richness and depth of flavor to this stock.

makes about 2 quarts

1 large onion, sliced
1 large leek, white part only, sliced
2 ribs celery, sliced
3 teaspoons minced garlic
1 teaspoon olive oil
12 ounces cremini, *or* white, mushrooms, quartered
1³/₄ quarts water
³/₄ cup dry white wine, *or* water
1¹/₂–2 ounces dried shiitake mushrooms
6 sprigs parsley
³/₄ teaspoon dried sage leaves
³/₄ teaspoon dried thyme leaves
1¹/₂ teaspoons black peppercorns

Per Cup:
Calories: 27
% Calories from fat: **23**
Protein (g): 0.4
Carbohydrates (g): **1.6**
Fat (g): 0.7
Saturated fat (g): 0.1
Cholesterol (mg): 0
Sodium (mg): 9
Exchanges:
Milk: 0.0
Veg.: 0.0
Fruit: 0.0
Bread: 0.0
Meat: 0.0
Fat: 0.0

1. Saute onion, leek, celery, and garlic in oil in small stock pot or large Dutch oven, 5 minutes. Add cremini mushrooms and cook 2 to 3 minutes longer. Add remaining ingredients and heat to boiling; reduce heat and simmer, covered, 1½ hours.

2. Strain, pressing lightly on vegetables to extract all juices; discard solids. Season to taste. Cool; refrigerate or freeze.

TWO

First-Course Soups

VERY BERRY SOUP WITH BERRY CRÈME

A garden of berries in a bowl! When fresh berries are out of season, frozen unsweetened berries can be substituted.

4 servings (about 1 cup each)

1¹/₂ cups raspberries
1¹/₂ cups quartered strawberries
1¹/₂ cups water
   ³/₄ cup dry red wine, *or* cranberry juice
     2 tablespoons sugar
   ¹/₂ cup fat-free half-and-half, *or* fat-free milk
        Mint leaves, finely chopped, as garnish
        Berry Crème (recipe follows)
   ¹/₄ cup blueberries

Per Serving
Calories: 194
% Calories from fat: 7
Protein (g): 2
Carbohydrate (g): 36.6
Fat (g): 1.5
Saturated fat (g): 1
Cholesterol (mg): 0
Sodium (mg): 37
Exchanges
Milk: 0.0
Veg.: 0.0
Fruit: 2.5
Bread: 0.0
Meat: 0.0
Fat: 1.0

1. Heat raspberries, strawberries, water, wine, and sugar to boiling in large saucepan. Reduce heat and simmer, covered, until berries are tender, 5 to 8 minutes. Remove from heat and cool.

2. Process soup in food processor or blender until smooth. Strain mixture, discarding seeds. Refrigerate until chilled, 3 to 4 hours.

3. Mix half-and-half into soup; pour into bowls and sprinkle with mint. Top each bowl with Berry Crème and sprinkle with a few blueberries.

Berry Crème

makes about ¹/₂ cup

   ¹/₂ cup light whipped topping
   ¹/₄ cup powdered sugar
     2 tablespoons seedless raspberry, *or* straw-
        berry, jam
     1 teaspoon finely grated orange rind

1. Mix all ingredients.

SUMMER FRUIT SOUP

This beautiful pink soup, lightly spiced and thickened, will cool you on a hot day.

6 servings

3 cups coarsely chopped watermelon
2 cups whole fresh strawberries
1/2 cup fresh orange juice
1 1/2 teaspoons fresh lemon juice
2 tablespoons sugar
1 tablespoon cornstarch
1/2 teaspoon ground allspice
1/4 teaspoon ground cinnamon
1/8 teaspoon ground ginger
1/8 teaspoon ground mace
3/4 cup fat-free milk
Lemon slices, as garnish

Per Serving
Calories: 83
% Calories from fat: 7
Protein (g): 2
Carbohydrate (g): 18.6
Fat (g): 0.7
Saturated fat (g): 0.1
Cholesterol (mg): 0.6
Sodium (mg): 18
Exchanges
Milk: 0.0
Veg.: 0.0
Fruit: 1.5
Bread: 0.0
Meat: 0.0
Fat: 0.0

1. Process watermelon and strawberries in food processor or blender until smooth; pour into large saucepan. Stir in combined orange juice, lemon juice, sugar, cornstarch, and spices; heat to boiling, stirring, until thickened, 1 to 2 minutes. Remove from heat; stir in milk. Refrigerate until chilled.

2. Serve soup in bowls; garnish with lemon slices.

SPICY APPLE-WINE SOUP

This sweet, spicy soup is an interesting way to serve apples, and it works well as a luncheon first course or as a dessert.

4-5 servings

6 whole cloves
2 lemon slices (1/4-inch), seeds removed
1/2 cup Burgundy wine
2 cups white grape juice, divided
2 cups coarsely chopped, peeled tart apples
1 large cinnamon stick
2 tablespoons honey
1 tablespoon sugar
1 1/2 tablespoons cornstarch
1/8 cup golden raisins
4-5 tablespoons fat-free vanilla yogurt, *or* reduced-fat sour cream, as garnish

Per Serving:
Calories: 173
% Calories from fat: 2
Protein (g): 1
Carbohydrates (g): 39.9
Fat (g): 0.4
Saturated fat (g): 0.1
Cholesterol (mg): 0
Sodium (mg): 20
Exchanges:
Milk: 0.0
Veg.: 0.0
Fruit: 3.0
Bread: 0.0
Meat: 0.0
Fat: 0.0

1. Stick cloves into lemon slices. Combine wine, 1 3/4 cups grape juice, apples, cinnamon stick, honey, sugar, and lemon slices in saucepan; heat to boiling. Reduce heat and simmer, covered, until apples are tender, about 10 minutes.

2. Remove cinnamon stick, lemon slices, and cloves. Stir in combined cornstarch and remaining 1/4 cup grape juice; simmer, stirring until soup thickens, about 2 minutes. Add raisins and simmer 2 minutes. Ladle soup into bowls and top with yogurt.

BLUEBERRY SOUP

A light and pretty soup, featuring whole blueberries in a blueberry-wine sauce.

5 servings

1 quart fresh, *or* frozen, thawed, blueberries, divided
¹/₄ cup lemon juice
¹/₂-²/₃ cup sugar, divided
2 tablespoons cornstarch
¹/₈ teaspoon ground cinnamon
1 cup cranberry juice cocktail
1 cup dry white wine
1 thick lemon slice, seeds removed
1 teaspoon vanilla extract
³/₄ cup low-fat vanilla yogurt

Per Serving:
Calories: 258
% Calories from fat: 4
Protein (g): 2.7
Carbohydrates (g): 54.3
Fat (g): 1.1
Saturated fat (g): 0.3
Cholesterol (mg): 2
Sodium (mg): 36
Exchanges:
Milk: 0.5
Veg.: 0.0
Fruit: 3.5
Bread: 0.0
Meat: 0.0
Fat: 0.0

1. Combine 2 cups blueberries and lemon juice in medium saucepan; heat to boiling. Reduce heat and simmer 2 minutes or until berries begin to exude juices. Process berry mixture in blender or food processor until smooth.

2. Combine ¹/₂ cup sugar, cornstarch, and cinnamon in saucepan; whisk in cranberry juice. Strain blueberry puree through fine sieve into saucepan. Add wine and lemon slice. Heat to boiling, stirring until thickened. Stir in vanilla and remaining sugar to taste.

3. Refrigerate until chilled. Discard lemon slice. Stir in remaining 2 cups blueberries. Serve soup in bowls; top with dollops of yogurt.

CANTALOUPE-LIME COOLER

A tangy refresher on a hot day, this soup is high in vitamin C.

4-5 servings

¹/₄ cup sugar
1 tablespoon cornstarch
Dash salt
³/₄ cup cold water
¹/₂ large cantaloupe, peeled, seeded, and cut into 1-inch chunks (about 4 cups)
Zest from 1 lime, grated
1 tablespoon fresh lime juice
Thin lime slices, as garnish

Per Serving:
Calories: 90
% Calories from fat: 3
Protein (g): 1.1
Carbohydrates (g): 22.5
Fat (g): 0.4
Saturated fat (g): 0
Cholesterol (mg): 0
Sodium (mg): 12
Exchanges:
Milk: 0.0
Veg.: 0.0
Fruit: 1.5
Bread: 0.0
Meat: 0.0
Fat: 0.0

1. Combine sugar, cornstarch, and salt in small saucepan; stir in water. Heat to boiling and cook, stirring, until mixture thickens; cool slightly.

2. Process sugar mixture and cantaloupe in blender or food processor until smooth; transfer to serving bowl. Stir in lime zest and lime juice; refrigerate until chilled. Garnish with lime slices.

SWEET CHERRY SOUP

Serve as a first course—or a dessert! For year-round enjoyment, frozen unsweetened dark sweet cherries can be substituted for the fresh.

4 servings (about 1 cup each)

1¹/₂ pounds dark sweet cherries, pitted
3-4 tablespoons sugar
 3 cups plus 3 tablespoons water, divided
 12 whole cloves
 6 whole cardamom pods
 1 large cinnamon stick, broken into pieces
1¹/₂ tablespoons cornstarch
 Freshly ground nutmeg, as garnish
 4 tablespoons fat-free sour cream

Per Serving:
Calories: 179
% Calories from fat: 8
Protein (g): 3
Carbohydrates (g): 41.9
Fat (g): 1.6
Saturated fat (g): 0.4
Cholesterol (mg): 0
Sodium (mg): 10
Exchanges:
Milk: 0.0
Veg.: 0.0
Fruit: 3.0
Bread: 0.0
Meat: 0.0
Fat: 0.0

1. Combine cherries, sugar, and 3 cups water in medium saucepan. Tie spices in cheesecloth bag and add to saucepan. Heat to boiling; reduce heat and simmer, covered, until cherries are tender, 15 to 20 minutes. Remove from heat and cool to room temperature. Discard spices.

2. Process soup mixture in food processor or blender until smooth. Strain, discarding cherry skins. Return soup to saucepan and heat to boiling. Mix cornstarch and remaining 3 tablespoons water; whisk into boiling soup. Boil, whisking constantly, until thickened, 1 to 2 minutes. Cool; refrigerate until chilled.

3. Pour soup into bowls; sprinkle lightly with nutmeg and top each with a tablespoon of sour cream.

PEAR AND MELON SOUP

Delicate flavors in a beautiful, pale green soup. Vary your garnish according to what is in season: strawberries, raspberries, or even pomegranate seeds in winter.

8 servings (about 1 cup each)

2 large ripe pears, peeled, cored, chopped
$^1/_2$ cup apple juice
$^1/_4$ cup lime juice
1 large ripe honeydew melon, peeled, seeded, cubed
$^1/_4$ teaspoon ground nutmeg
1 mango, peeled, pitted, chopped
1 cup blueberries
Honey-Lime Cream (recipe follows)
Mint sprigs, as garnish

Per Serving
Calories: 123
% Calories from fat: 3
Protein (g): 2.5
Carbohydrate (g): 30.2
Fat (g): 0.5
Saturated fat (g): 0.1
Cholesterol (mg): 0.5
Sodium (mg): 33
Exchanges
Milk: 0.0
Veg.: 0.0
Fruit: 2.0
Bread: 0.0
Meat: 0.0
Fat: 0.0

1. Heat pears, apple juice, and lime juice to boiling in medium saucepan; reduce heat and simmer, covered, until pears are tender, about 5 minutes. Cool.

2. Process pear mixture, melon, and nutmeg in food processor or blender until smooth. Refrigerate until chilled, 3 to 4 hours.

3. Ladle soup into bowls; sprinkle with mango and blueberries and top with a dollop of Honey-Lime Cream. Garnish with mint sprigs.

Honey-Lime Cream

makes 1 cup

1 cup fat-free plain yogurt
2 tablespoons honey
2 teaspoons lime juice
1 teaspoon grated lime rind

1. Combine all ingredients in small bowl; refrigerate until serving time.

ICED RED PLUM SOUP WITH BRANDY

This tangy fruit soup takes advantage of the abundance of good summer plums. For best results, choose tart, flavorful, red-skinned plums

5-6 servings

1³/₄ pounds ripe red plums (about 14 medium-sized), halved, pitted

1-1¹/₃ cups sugar, divided

¹/₂ cup cranberry juice cocktail

1¹/₂ cups low-fat vanilla yogurt

2 tablespoons cherry liqueur, *or* cranberry juice

1 teaspoon vanilla

Thinly sliced plum, as garnish

Per Serving:
Calories: 292
% Calories from fat: 5
Protein (g): 4.1
Carbohydrates (g): 65.4
Fat (g): 1.8
Saturated fat (g): 0.5
Cholesterol (mg): 3.3
Sodium (mg): 42
Exchanges:
Milk: 1.0
Veg.: 0.0
Fruit: 3.5
Bread: 0.0
Meat: 0.0
Fat: 0.0

1. Combine halved plums, 1 cup sugar, and cranberry juice in large saucepan; heat to boiling. Reduce heat and simmer, covered, until plums are soft, about 6 minutes. Process plum mixture in blender or food processor until smooth.

2. Transfer plum mixture to large bowl and stir in yogurt, liqueur, and vanilla; add additional sugar to taste, stirring until sugar dissolves.

3. Place soup in freezer 2 to 3 hours until ice crystals begin to form around edges. Stir well and ladle into small bowls; arrange several plum slices in pinwheel in center of each serving.

ICED STRAWBERRY-BUTTERMILK SOUP

Pretty, as well as zesty and refreshing, this soup is a great addition to a warm-weather brunch or luncheon menu.

4-5 servings

3 cups sliced fresh, *or* frozen, partially thawed, rhubarb

³/₄-1 cup sugar, divided

¹/₂ cup cranberry juice cocktail, divided

1 tablespoon lemon juice

1¹/₂ tablespoons cornstarch

3 tablespoons orange, *or* cherry liqueur, *or* orange juice

2²/₃ cups hulled ripe strawberries, *or* frozen, partially thawed, whole strawberries

1¹/₂ cups buttermilk, divided

1 teaspoon vanilla

Strawberry slices, as garnish

Per Serving:
Calories: 241
% Calories from fat: 4
Protein (g): 3.6
Carbohydrates (g): 52.3
Fat (g): 1.1
Saturated fat (g): 0.4
Cholesterol (mg): 2.7
Sodium (mg): 83
Exchanges:
Milk: 0.0
Veg.: 0.0
Fruit: 4.0
Bread: 0.0
Meat: 0.0
Fat: 0.0

1. Combine rhubarb, ³/₄ cup sugar, and ¹/₄ cup cranberry juice in large saucepan; heat to boiling. Reduce heat and simmer, stirring occasionally, 7 to 9 minutes or until rhubarb is very tender.

2. Combine remaining ¹/₄ cup cranberry juice, lemon juice, cornstarch, and liqueur in small bowl. Stir cornstarch mixture into rhubarb mixture; simmer, stirring until mixture thickens, 1 to 2 minutes.

3. Process rhubarb mixture in food processor or blender until smooth. Transfer to large bowl. Process strawberries, 1¹/₄ cups buttermilk, and vanilla in blender or food processor until smooth. Strain through fine sieve into rhubarb mixture; discard seeds. Add additional sugar to taste, stirring until sugar dissolves.

4. Place soup in freezer 2¹/₂ hours or until very cold and ice crystals have formed around edges; stir and ladle soup into bowls. Pour about 1 tablespoon buttermilk in center of soup in each bowl. Using a small spoon, stir once through soup and buttermilk to swirl. Garnish with strawberry slices.

CRANBERRY FRUIT SOUP

A sweet and colorful first course for holiday dining.

6 servings (about 1 cup each)

1 cup sugar
1/4 cup cornstarch
1 quart reduced-calorie cranberry juice
 Cranberry Cream (recipe follows)

Per Serving
Calories: 200
% Calories from fat: **3**
Protein (g): 0
Carbohydrate (g): 49
Fat (g): 0.7
Saturated fat (g): 0.7
Cholesterol (mg): 0
Sodium (mg): 51
Exchanges
Milk: 0.0
Veg.: 0.0
Fruit: 3.5
Bread: 0.0
Meat: 0.0
Fat: 0.0

1. Combine sugar and cornstarch in medium saucepan; whisk in cranberry juice. Heat to boiling; boil, whisking, until thickened, 1 to 2 minutes. Cool; refrigerate until chilled.

2. Serve soup in bowls; top each with Cranberry Cream.

Cranberry Cream

makes about 1/2 cup

1/2 cup light whipped topping
2-3 teaspoons powdered sugar
2-4 tablespoons chopped fresh, *or* frozen, cranberries

1. Mix all ingredients.

CIDER SOUP

An unusual soup, and a great choice for fall dining.

6 servings (about ³/₄ cup each)

¹/₂ cup thinly sliced leek, white part only
¹/₄ cup chopped celery
2 tablespoons chopped green bell pepper
2 tablespoons chopped parsley
2-3 teaspoons margarine
2 tablespoons flour
¹/₄ teaspoon dry mustard
1¹/₂ cups reduced-sodium fat-free chicken broth
2-3 teaspoons very low sodium Worcestershire sauce
1 cup (4 ounces) shredded reduced-fat Cheddar cheese
1 cup apple cider
¹/₃ cup fat-free half-and-half, *or* fat-free milk
Salt and white pepper, to taste

Per Serving
Calories: 123
% Calories from fat: **35**
Protein (g): 8.6
Carbohydrate (g): 11.4
Fat (g): 4.8
Saturated fat (g): 2.6
Cholesterol (mg): 13.5
Sodium (mg): 234
Exchanges
Milk: 0.0
Veg.: 0.0
Fruit: 1.0
Bread: 0.0
Meat: 1.0
Fat: 0.5

1. Saute leek, celery, bell pepper, and parsley in margarine in medium saucepan until tender, about 5 minutes. Stir in flour and dry mustard; cook 1 minute.

2. Stir in chicken broth and Worcestershire sauce; heat to boiling. Reduce heat and simmer, stirring, until slightly thickened, 1 to 2 minutes. Remove pan from heat; add cheese and stir until melted.

3. Process soup in food processor or blender until smooth; return to saucepan. Stir in cider and half-and-half; cook over medium heat until hot, 3 to 5 minutes. Season to taste with salt and pepper.

Variation:

Caramel Apple Soup—Make soup as above. Saute 2 cups peeled, sliced apples in 1 to 2 tablespoons margarine 2 minutes; sprinkle with ¹/₃ cup packed light brown sugar. Cook over medium heat, stirring occasionally, until apples are tender, 3 to 4 minutes. Spoon apples into bottoms of soup bowls; ladle warm soup over.

BEER SOUP

A first-course soup with spunky beer flavor. Use a flavorful micro-brewery beer.

4 servings (about ³/₄ cup each)

2 tablespoons flour

1 tablespoon sugar

2 cups fat-free half-and-half, *or* 2% reduced-fat milk

1 cup beer

1 tablespoon dark corn syrup

1 cup (4 ounces) shredded reduced-fat Swiss cheese

Ground ginger, *or* nutmeg, as garnish

Per Serving
Calories: 194
% Calories from fat: 7
Protein (g): 12.3
Carbohydrate (g): 25.1
Fat (g): 1.4
Saturated fat (g): 0.9
Cholesterol (mg): 9.5
Sodium (mg): 197
Exchanges
Milk: 0.0
Veg.: 0.0
Fruit: 0.0
Bread: 2.0
Meat: 1.0
Fat: 0.0

1. Mix flour and sugar in medium saucepan; whisk in half-and-half. Heat to boiling, whisking until thickened, 1 to 2 minutes. Reduce heat and simmer 1 minute; whisk in beer and corn syrup and simmer 1 to 2 minutes.

2. Place cheese in bottoms of soup bowls; ladle hot soup over. Sprinkle very lightly with ginger or nutmeg.

ASPARAGUS LEMON SOUP

This perfect spring luncheon soup is similar to the classic Greek egg lemon soup, with the addition of asparagus and pasta.

6 servings (about ³/₄ cup each)

1 quart Chicken Stock (see p. 2)

¹/₂ cup orzo, *or* other small soup pasta

12 ounces asparagus, sliced

2 eggs, lightly beaten

¹/₄ cup lemon juice

¹/₃ cup sliced green onions and tops

Salt and pepper, to taste

Per Serving
Calories: 105
% Calories from fat: 22
Protein (g): 6.2
Carbohydrate (g): 14.9
Fat (g): 2.6
Saturated fat (g): 0.6
Cholesterol (mg): 73
Sodium (mg): 32
Exchanges
Milk: 0.0
Veg.: 3.0
Fruit: 0.0
Bread: 0.0
Meat: 0.0
Fat: 0.5

1. Heat Chicken Stock to boiling in large saucepan. Add orzo; reduce heat and simmer 5 minutes. Stir in asparagus and heat to boiling. Reduce heat and simmer until asparagus and orzo are tender, about 7 minutes.

2. Heat soup to boiling. Whisk in eggs and cook 1 minute. Remove from heat. Add lemon juice and green onions; season to taste with salt and pepper.

FRESH BASIL SOUP

For flavor variation, try another favorite garden herb such as rosemary, oregano, lemon thyme, or marjoram. Any of your homemade stocks will make this soup even better.

6 servings (about 1 cup each)

1 quart reduced-sodium fat-free chicken broth
1 cup firmly packed basil leaves
1 cup firmly packed parsley sprigs
1/2 cup chopped onion
1 teaspoon sugar
2 cups cubed, peeled potatoes
1 cup fat-free milk
1/4 cup all-purpose flour
1 tablespoon margarine
Salt and white pepper, to taste
Finely chopped parsley, as garnish

Per Serving
Calories: 157
% Calories from fat: 13
Protein (g): 8.2
Carbohydrates (g): 25.8
Fat (g): 2.2
Saturated fat (g): 0.5
Cholesterol (mg): 0.7
Sodium (mg): 166
Exchanges
Milk: 0.0
Veg.: 2.0
Fruit: 0.0
Bread: 1.0
Meat: 0.5
Fat: 0.5

1. Heat broth, basil, parsley, onion, and sugar to boiling in medium saucepan. Simmer, covered, 30 minutes. Strain, discarding herbs and onion; return broth to saucepan.

2. Add potatoes to saucepan; heat to boiling. Reduce heat and simmer, covered, until potatoes are tender, about 15 minutes. Mix milk and flour; stir into saucepan and heat to boiling. Boil until thickened, 1 to 2 minutes, stirring constantly. Stir in margarine; season to taste with salt and white pepper.

3. Pour soup into bowls; sprinkle with parsley.

DILLED BEET SOUP

Scrub beets well, as the cooking liquid is reserved for use in the soup. It's not necessary to peel beets before cooking; the skins slip off easily after cooking.

8 servings (about 1¼ cups each)

12	medium beets, tops trimmed, scrubbed (about 3 pounds)
3	cups water
2-3	chicken bouillon cubes
¾-1	cup dry red wine *or* chicken broth
1½-2	teaspoons dried dill weed
2-3	tablespoons red wine vinegar
	Salt and pepper, to taste
8	thin lemon slices
	Finely chopped chives, as garnish

Per Serving:
Calories: 53
% Calories from fat: **2**
Protein (g): 1.4
Carbohydrates (g): 8.8
Fat (g): 0.2
Saturated fat (g): 0.1
Cholesterol (mg): 0
Sodium (mg): 319
Exchanges:
Milk: 0.0
Veg.: 2.0
Fruit: 0.0
Bread: 0.0
Meat: 0.0
Fat: 0.0

1. Heat beets, 3 cups water, and bouillon cubes to boiling in large saucepan; reduce heat and simmer, covered, until beets are tender, 30 to 40 minutes. Let stand until cool; drain, reserving cooking liquid. Slip skins off beets and cut into scant 1-inch pieces.

2. Add enough water to reserved cooking liquid to make 6 cups. Process beets, wine, reserved cooking liquid, and dill weed in food processor or blender until smooth. Season to taste with vinegar, salt, and pepper.

3. Heat soup and serve warm, or refrigerate until chilled and serve cold. Pour soup into bowls; garnish each with a lemon slice and sprinkle with chives.

BEET BORSCHT

Try this delicious beet soup, flavored in the traditional fashion with Polish sausage.

8 servings (about 1¼ cups each)

4 medium beets, peeled, julienned
8 ounces low-fat smoked Polish sausage, sliced
½-1 tablespoon margarine
6 cups reduced-sodium fat-free beef broth
1 small head red cabbage, thinly sliced or shredded
2 carrots, julienned
1 clove garlic, minced
1 bay leaf
2-3 teaspoons sugar
2 tablespoons cider vinegar
Salt and pepper, to taste
Finely chopped dill weed, *or* parsley, as garnish

Per Serving
Calories: 120
% Calories from fat: 25
Protein (g): 10.9
Carbohydrates (g): 13.1
Fat (g): 3.7
Saturated fat (g): 0.4
Cholesterol (mg): 17.2
Sodium (mg): 437
Exchanges
Milk: 0.0
Veg.: 3.0
Fruit: 0.0
Bread: 0.0
Meat: 1.0
Fat: 0.0

1. Saute beets and sausage in margarine in Dutch oven 3 to 4 minutes. Add broth, cabbage, carrots, garlic, bay leaf, sugar, and vinegar; heat to boiling. Reduce heat and simmer, covered, until vegetables are tender, 20 to 30 minutes. Discard bay leaf; season to taste with salt and pepper.

2. Pour soup into bowls; sprinkle with dill weed.

CREAM OF BROCCOLI SOUP

Fat-free half-and-half lends a wonderful richness to this soup.

6 servings (about 1 cup each)

Per Serving
Calories: 117
% Calories from fat: 5
Protein (g): 10.1
Carbohydrates (g): 18.2
Fat (g): 0.7
Saturated fat (g): 0.1
Cholesterol (mg): 0
Sodium (mg): 210
Exchanges
Milk: 0.0
Veg.: 2.0
Fruit: 0.0
Bread: 0.5
Meat: 0.5
Fat: 0.0

  2 pounds broccoli
    Vegetable cooking spray
  1 cup chopped onion
  3 cloves garlic, minced
  $^1/_2$ teaspoon dried thyme leaves
  $^1/_8$ teaspoon ground nutmeg
  $3^1/_2$ cups reduced-sodium fat-free chicken broth
  $^1/_2$ cup fat-free half-and-half, *or* fat-free milk
    Salt and white pepper, to taste
  6 tablespoons fat-free sour cream
2-3 teaspoons fat-free milk
  $1^1/_2$ cups Croutons ($^1/_2$ recipe) (see p. 784)

1. Peel broccoli stalks; cut broccoli into 1-inch pieces. Spray large saucepan with cooking spray; heat over medium heat until hot. Saute onion and garlic until tender, 3 to 5 minutes. Stir in broccoli, thyme, and nutmeg; cook 2 minutes longer.

2. Add broth to saucepan; heat to boiling. Reduce heat and simmer, covered, until broccoli is very tender, about 10 minutes.

3. Process soup in food processor or blender until smooth. Return soup to saucepan; add half-and-half and heat over medium heat until hot. Season to taste with salt and white pepper. Pour soup into bowls. Mix sour cream and milk; swirl about 1 tablespoon mixture into soup in each bowl. Sprinkle with Croutons.

Variation:
Cream of Asparagus Soup—Make soup as above, substituting 2 pounds asparagus for the broccoli, and reserving 18 small asparagus tips for garnish. Omit thyme leaves. Add 1 teaspoon dried marjoram leaves and 1 teaspoon grated lemon rind to soup. Steam reserved asparagus tips until crisp-tender, and use to garnish soup.

CREAMY BROCCOLI-POTATO SOUP

This soup can also be served cold. Just stir in 1 tablespoon lemon juice and 1/4 cup additional Chicken Stock. Chill about 5 hours and garnish servings with lemon slices.

6-8 servings

4 medium leeks (about 1 pound), white parts only, cut into 1/2-inch pieces
2 teaspoons margarine
3 cups Chicken Stock (see p. 2)
3 1/2 cups diced peeled potatoes
1 quart broccoli florets
1 1/4 cups whole milk
   Salt and white pepper, to taste
1-2 teaspoons finely chopped chives, as garnish

Per Serving
Calories: 148
% Calories from fat: 15
Protein (g): 6.3
Carbohydrates (g): 26.9
Fat (g): 2.5
Saturated fat (g): 1
Cholesterol (mg): 5.2
Sodium (mg): 175
Exchanges
Milk: 0.0
Veg.: 0.0
Fruit: 0.0
Bread: 1.5
Meat: 0.0
Fat: 0.5

1. Saute leeks in margarine in large saucepan about 10 minutes, until leeks are tender but not browned. Stir in Chicken Stock, potatoes, and broccoli; heat to boiling. Reduce heat and simmer, covered, until potatoes and broccoli are tender, about 10 minutes.

2. Process mixture in blender or food processor until smooth. Return puree to saucepan; stir in milk and heat to boiling. Reduce heat and simmer 5 minutes. Season to taste with salt and white pepper. Garnish with chives.

HERBED BROCCOLI-CAULIFLOWER BISQUE

This healthful soup combines two cancer-fighting vegetables—and it's delicious.

5-6 servings

2 medium broccoli stalks

1/2 small head cauliflower

1 cup chopped green onions and tops

2 teaspoons margarine

1 tablespoon flour

3 cups Chicken Stock (see p. 2)

1 1/3 cups coarsely chopped peeled potatoes

3 tablespoons finely chopped fresh chives, *or* 1 1/2 tablespoons dried chives

2 1/2 teaspoons dried basil leaves

1 1/2 cups 2% reduced-fat milk

Salt and pepper, to taste

Per Serving
Calories: 121
% Calories from fat: 19
Protein (g): 7
Carbohydrates (g): 18.6
Fat (g): 2.7
Saturated fat (g): 1
Cholesterol (mg): 4.5
Sodium (mg): 230
Exchanges
Milk: 0.0
Veg.: 1.0
Fruit: 0.0
Bread: 1.0
Meat: 0.0
Fat: 0.5

1. Cut broccoli and cauliflower into florets. Reserve 3/4 cup small broccoli florets and 3/4 cup small cauliflower florets; coarsely chop remaining broccoli and cauliflower.

2. Saute green onions in margarine in large saucepan until tender, about 4 minutes. Stir in flour; cook 1 minute. Stir in Chicken Stock, chopped broccoli and cauliflower, potatoes, chives, and basil; heat to boiling. Reduce heat and simmer, uncovered, until potatoes are tender, about 12 minutes.

3. Process in food processor or blender until smooth. Return puree to saucepan; add milk and reserved broccoli and cauliflower florets. Heat to boiling; reduce heat and simmer until florets are crisp-tender, about 5 minutes. Season to taste with salt and pepper.

TYROLEAN CABBAGE SOUP

This is a hearty, peasant-style soup perfect for serving with a good, dark bread.

7-8 servings

2 medium onions, chopped
2 large ribs celery, chopped
1 cup chopped rutabaga
1 medium carrot, chopped
1 large tart apple, peeled, chopped
1 tablespoon margarine
2 tablespoons flour
5 cups Beef Stock (see p. 6)
1/4 cup chopped parsley
7 cups coarsely shredded cabbage, divided
2 small pork hocks (about 1 1/4 pounds)
1/4 cup uncooked pearl barley
1 tablespoon paprika
2 large bay leaves
1/2 teaspoon dried thyme leaves
1/4 cup tomato paste
3/4 cup water
1/4 teaspoon caraway seeds
   Salt and pepper, taste

Per Serving
Calories: 120
% Calories from fat: 16
Protein (g): 6.4
Carbohydrates (g): 20.6
Fat (g): 2.3
Saturated fat (g): 0.5
Cholesterol (mg): 2.2
Sodium (mg): 230
Exchanges
Milk: 0.0
Veg.: 0.0
Fruit: 0.0
Bread: 1.5
Meat: 0.0
Fat: 0.5

1. Saute onions, celery, rutabaga, carrot, and apple in margarine in large saucepan until soft, about 10 minutes. Stir in flour; cook 1 to 2 minutes. Stir in Beef Stock, parsley, 3 1/2 cups cabbage, pork hocks, barley, paprika, bay leaves, and thyme; heat to boiling. Reduce heat and simmer, covered, 1 hour. Discard pork hocks and bay leaves. Skim fat from soup.

2. Stir in combined tomato paste and water, remaining 3 1/2 cups cabbage, and caraway seeds. Heat to boiling; reduce heat and simmer until cabbage is crisp-tender, about 10 minutes. Season to taste with salt and pepper.

CARROT SOUP WITH DILL

Steamed baby carrots, or even carrots left from dinner, can be used in this easy soup.

4 servings (about 1 cup each)

$^1/_4$ cup sliced green onions and tops

3 tablespoons chopped parsley

2 teaspoons margarine

1 tablespoon arrowroot

1$^1/_2$ cups Chicken Stock (see p. 2)

2 cups sliced carrots, steamed

$^1/_2$ cup evaporated fat-free milk

Salt and pepper, to taste

2 tablespoons chopped fresh dill weed

Per Serving
Calories: 81
% Calories from fat: 25
Protein (g): 3.7
Carbohydrate (g): 11.9
Fat (g): 2.4
Saturated fat (g): 0.5
Cholesterol (mg): 2.4
Sodium (mg): 83
Exchanges
Milk: 0.0
Veg.: 2.0
Fruit: 0.0
Bread: 0.0
Meat: 0.0
Fat: 0.5

1. Saute green onions and parsley in margarine in medium saucepan until softened. Sprinkle with arrowroot and cook 2 minutes. Stir in Chicken Stock; heat to boiling, stirring until smooth and slightly thickened.

2. Process carrots in blender or food processor with 1 cup stock mixture until smooth. Place carrot mixture in saucepan with remaining stock mixture; add evaporated milk. Heat until hot; do not boil. Season to taste with salt and pepper. Ladle into soup cups and sprinkle with dill.

GOLDEN CARROT SOUP

Orange juice adds a subtle sweetness to this carrot soup.

6 servings

8 medium carrots, peeled, cut into 1-inch pieces

1 cup coarsely chopped onion

1 tablespoon margarine

3 cups Chicken Stock (see p. 2), divided

$^1/_2$ cup fresh orange juice

1 strip orange rind

$^1/_4$ cup dry sherry, *or* orange juice

1 tablespoon sugar

Salt and white pepper, to taste

2 tablespoons snipped chives

Per Serving
Calories: 109
% Calories from fat: 20
Protein (g): 2.3
Carbohydrate (g): 18
Fat (g): 2.5
Saturated fat (g): 0.5
Cholesterol (mg): 1.7
Sodium (mg): 60
Exchanges
Milk: 0.0
Veg.: 2.0
Fruit: 0.5
Bread: 0.0
Meat: 0.0
Fat: 0.5

1. Saute carrots and onion in margarine in large saucepan, 10 minutes. Add 1 cup Chicken Stock, orange juice, and orange rind. Heat to boiling; reduce heat and simmer, covered, until carrots are tender, about 20 minutes.

2. Process carrot mixture in blender or food processor until smooth; return mixture to saucepan and stir in remaining 2 cups stock, sherry, and sugar. Heat until hot; season to taste with salt and white pepper.

3. Serve in bowls; sprinkle with chives.

Variation:
Orange Sweet Potato Soup—Make soup as above, substituting 2 medium sweet potatoes, peeled, cubed, for the carrots. Omit sherry and chives, and add ½ teaspoon ground cinnamon, pinch ground nutmeg, and pinch ground mace to the soup. Garnish with thin slices of orange.

DILLED CARROT SOUP

Carrots team with dill for a fresh, clean flavor.

6-8 servings (about 1½ cups each)

Vegetable cooking spray
1½ cups chopped onions
  2 cloves garlic, minced
1½ quarts reduced-sodium fat-free chicken broth
  1 can (16 ounces) reduced-sodium diced tomatoes, undrained
  2 pounds carrots, cut into 1/2-inch slices
  1 medium Idaho potato, peeled, cubed
2-3 tablespoons lemon juice
1-1½ teaspoons dried dill weed
    Salt and white pepper, to taste
6-8 tablespoons fat-free plain yogurt
  2 tablespoons shredded carrot
    Dill, *or* parsley, sprigs, as garnish

Per Serving
Calories: 156
% Calories from fat: 3
Protein (g): 10
Carbohydrates (g): 28.7
Fat (g): 0.5
Saturated fat (g): 0.1
Cholesterol (mg): 0.3
Sodium (mg): 245
Exchanges
Milk: 0.0
Veg.: 4.0
Fruit: 0.0
Bread: 0.5
Meat: 0.0
Fat: 0.0

1. Spray large saucepan with cooking spray; heat over medium heat until hot. Saute onions and garlic until tender, about 5 minutes. Add broth, tomatoes and liquid, sliced carrots, and potato; heat to boiling. Reduce heat and simmer, covered, until vegetables are tender, about 15 minutes.

2. Process soup in food processor or blender until smooth. Stir in lemon juice and dill weed; season to taste with salt and white pepper.

3. Serve soup warm, or refrigerate and serve chilled. Pour soup into bowls; garnish each with a tablespoon of yogurt, a teaspoon of shredded carrot, and dill sprigs.

CHILLED CAULIFLOWER SOUP

This soup is a nice way to start a summer lunch and is also good as a refreshing afternoon snack.

4-6 servings

Vegetable cooking spray
1 small onion, finely chopped
1 small garlic clove, minced
1³/₄ cups Chicken Stock (see p. 2)
³/₄ cup diced, peeled potato
2 cups chopped cauliflower
¹/₈ teaspoon dried dill weed
³/₄ cup 2% reduced-fat milk
¹/₄ teaspoon lemon juice
Salt and white pepper, to taste
Chopped chives, as garnish

Per Serving
Calories: 62
% Calories from fat: 10
Protein (g): 3.7
Carbohydrates (g): 10.7
Fat (g): 0.7
Saturated fat (g): 0.4
Cholesterol (mg): 2.3
Sodium (mg): 125
Exchanges
Milk: 0.0
Veg.: 2.0
Fruit: 0.0
Bread: 0.0
Meat: 0.0
Fat: 0.0

1. Spray large saucepan with cooking spray; heat over medium heat until hot. Saute onion and garlic until onion is tender. Stir in Chicken Stock, potato, cauliflower, and dill weed; heat to boiling. Reduce heat, and simmer, covered, until potatoes and cauliflower are tender, about 10 minutes.

2. Process mixture in blender or food processor until smooth; transfer soup to serving bowl. Stir in milk and lemon juice; season to taste with salt and white pepper. Refrigerate until chilled. Garnish with chives.

CREAM OF CAULIFLOWER SOUP WITH CHEESE

Broccoli or broccoflower can be substituted for all or part of the cauliflower.

6 servings (about 1 cup each)

Vegetable cooking spray
1/2 cup chopped onion
2 cloves garlic, minced
2 tablespoons flour
3 1/2 cups reduced-sodium fat-free chicken broth
12 ounces cauliflower, cut into florets
1 large Idaho potato, peeled, cubed
1/4-1/2 cup fat-free half-and-half, *or* fat-free milk
3/4 cup (3 ounces) shredded reduced-fat Cheddar cheese
Salt and white pepper, to taste
Ground mace, *or* nutmeg, as garnish

Per Serving
Calories: 108
% Calories from fat: 20
Protein (g): 8.8
Carbohydrates (g): 12.2
Fat (g): 2.3
Saturated fat (g): 1.1
Cholesterol (mg): 7.6
Sodium (mg): 312
Exchanges
Milk: 0.0
Veg.: 2.0
Fruit: 0.0
Bread: 0.0
Meat: 0.5
Fat: 0.5

1. Spray large saucepan with cooking spray; heat over medium heat until hot. Saute onion and garlic until tender, about 10 minutes. Stir in flour; cook 1 to 2 minutes longer. Add broth, cauliflower, and potato; heat to boiling. Reduce heat and simmer, covered, until vegetables are tender, 10 to 15 minutes.

2. Remove about half the vegetables from the soup with a slotted spoon and reserve. Process remaining soup in food processor or blender until smooth. Return soup to saucepan; stir in reserved vegetables, half-and-half, and cheese; cook over low heat until cheese is melted, 3 to 4 minutes, stirring frequently. Season to taste with salt and white pepper.

3. Pour soup into bowls; sprinkle lightly with mace or nutmeg.

Variations:
Fennel Bisque with Walnuts—Make soup as above, substituting 1 large leek, sliced, for the onion, and 2 large fennel bulbs, sliced, for the cauliflower. Complete soup as above, omitting Cheddar cheese. Ladle soup into bowls; sprinkle with 3 ounces crumbled blue cheese, and 1/4 cup chopped toasted walnuts.

Cream of Turnip Soup—Make soup as above, substituting chopped turnips for the cauliflower and reduced-fat Swiss, Gouda, or Havarti cheese for the Cheddar; add $1/2$ teaspoon dried thyme leaves.

SUMMERTIME CELERY SOUP

The livin' is easy, with this flavorful cold soup ready in the refrigerator.

5-6 servings

2/3 cup boiling water
1¼ teaspoons fennel seeds
1 teaspoon olive oil
3 cups coarsely chopped celery
8 green onions and tops, sliced
1 small garlic clove, minced
1 quart Chicken Stock (see p. 2), divided
2½ tablespoons uncooked rice
3 tablespoons finely chopped fresh chives, *or* 1½ tablespoons dried chives
Salt and white pepper, to taste
Finely chopped chives, as garnish
Fat-free plain yogurt, as garnish

Per Serving
Calories: 53
% Calories from fat: 15
Protein (g): 4.1
Carbohydrates (g): 7.7
Fat (g): 1
Saturated fat (g): 0.1
Cholesterol (mg): 0
Sodium (mg): 277
Exchanges
Milk: 0.0
Veg.: 0.0
Fruit: 0.0
Bread: 0.5
Meat: 0.0
Fat: 0.0

1. Pour boiling water over fennel seeds in small bowl; reserve.

2. Saute celery, onions, and garlic in oil in large saucepan until onions are tender, about 4 minutes. Add 2½ cups Chicken Stock, rice, and chives; heat to boiling. Reduce heat and simmer, covered, until celery and rice are tender, about 20 minutes.

3. Process soup in blender or food processor until smooth. Transfer to serving bowl. Stir in remaining 1½ cups Chicken Stock.

4. Drain fennel seeds, stirring liquid into soup; discard seeds. Season to taste with salt and white pepper. Refrigerate until chilled. Garnish with chives and yogurt.

CREAM OF CHESTNUT SOUP

What could be better for the first course of a festive holiday dinner? Roast the chestnuts on an open fire, if you like!

6 servings (about ²/₃ cup each)

1¹/₄ pounds chestnuts
  8 parsley sprigs
  2 celery leaf sprigs
  3 whole cloves
  1 bay leaf
¹/₂ teaspoon dried thyme leaves
  4 cups water
  2 cups Chicken Stock (see p. 2)
¹/₃ cup port wine, *or* Chicken Stock
¹/₂ cup fat-free half-and-half, *or* fat-free milk
    Salt and pepper, to taste

Per Serving
Calories: 221
% Calories from fat: **5**
Protein (g): 4.6
Carbohydrate (g): **44.1**
Fat (g): 1.2
Saturated fat (g): 0.2
Cholesterol (mg): 1.2
Sodium (mg): 28
Exchanges
Milk: 0.0
Veg.: 0.0
Fruit: 0.0
Bread: 3.0
Meat: 0.0
Fat: 0.0

1. Slit chestnut shells crosswise on rounded side, making an X; place in jelly roll pan. Roast at 450 degrees 8 minutes. Remove shells and skins while nuts are still warm.

2. Tie parsley sprigs, celery sprigs, cloves, bay leaf, and thyme in a cheesecloth bag. Heat chestnuts, cheesecloth bag, and water to boiling in medium saucepan; reduce heat and simmer uncovered 25 minutes. Remove cheesecloth bag.

3. Process chestnuts and cooking liquid in food processor or blender until smooth. Return mixture to saucepan and stir in Chicken Stock and port. Heat to boiling; reduce heat and stir in half-and-half. Season to taste with salt and pepper.

CUCUMBER AND SORREL SOUP

If cucumbers are mild in flavor, they do not need to be peeled. Fresh sorrel, available in the spring, gives a peppery flavor to this soup.

6 servings (about 1¹/₄ cups each)

Vegetable cooking spray
¹/₄ cup plus 2 tablespoons sliced green onions and tops, divided
1 clove garlic, minced
3 cups chopped peeled, seeded cucumbers (about 1¹/₂ pounds)
1 cup coarsely chopped sorrel, *or* spinach
2 cups fat-free milk
2 cups reduced-sodium fat-free chicken broth
1 tablespoon cornstarch
2 tablespoons water
Salt and white pepper, to taste
1¹/₂ cups Herb Croutons (¹/₂ recipe) (see p. 784)

Per Serving
Calories: 77
% Calories from fat: 8
Protein (g): 6.2
Carbohydrates (g): 11.5
Fat (g): 0.6
Saturated fat (g): 0.2
Cholesterol (mg): 1.5
Sodium (mg): 247
Exchanges
Milk: 0.0
Veg.: 3.0
Fruit: 0.0
Bread: 0.0
Meat: 0.0
Fat: 0.0

1. Spray large saucepan with cooking spray; heat over medium heat until hot. Saute ¹/₄ cup green onions and garlic until tender, 3 to 4 minutes. Add cucumbers and sorrel and cook over medium heat 5 minutes.

2. Add milk and broth to saucepan; heat to boiling. Reduce heat and simmer, covered, until cucumbers are tender, 5 to 10 minutes. Process soup in food processor or blender until smooth; return to saucepan.

3. Heat soup to boiling. Mix cornstarch and water; whisk into boiling soup. Boil, whisking constantly, until thickened, about 1 minute. Season to taste with salt and white pepper. Cool; refrigerate until chilled, 3 to 4 hours.

4. Pour soup into bowls; top with Herb Croutons and remaining 2 tablespoons green onions.

CUCUMBER VICHYSSOISE WITH ROASTED PEPPER SWIRL

Buttermilk gives this soup a refreshing tang, and roasted peppers add a flavor perk.

6 servings (about ³/₄ cup each)

1 large cucumber, peeled, seeded, sliced
1 cup chopped onion
1 cup cubed, peeled potato
1¹/₂ cups Basic Vegetable Stock (see p. 10)
1 cup water
1 teaspoon ground cumin
1 cup reduced-fat buttermilk
  Salt and white pepper, to taste
  Roasted Pepper Swirl (recipe follows)

Per Serving
Calories: 87
% Calories from fat: **7**
Protein (g): 3.3
Carbohydrate (g): 17.7
Fat (g): 0.7
Saturated fat (g): 0.3
Cholesterol (mg): 1.4
Sodium (mg): 49
Exchanges
Milk: 0.0
Veg.: 2.0
Fruit: 0.0
Bread: 0.5
Meat: 0.0
Fat: 0.0

1. Combine cucumber, onion, potato, Basic Vegetable Stock, water, and cumin in large saucepan. Heat to boiling; reduce heat and simmer, covered, until tender, about 20 minutes. Cool.

2. Process cucumber mixture in food processor or blender until smooth; pour into large bowl. Stir in buttermilk and season to taste with salt and white pepper. Refrigerate, covered, until cold.

3. Ladle soup into bowls; spoon Roasted Pepper Swirl into soup and swirl with knife.

Roasted Pepper Swirl

makes about ³/₄ cup

  Vegetable cooking spray
3 medium red bell peppers, diced
1 small serrano, *or* jalapeño, chili, chopped
¹/₂ cup water
1 clove garlic
2 teaspoons balsamic vinegar

1. Spray aluminum-foil-lined jelly roll pan with cooking spray; arrange bell pepper and serrano chili on pan. Spray with cooking spray. Roast at 425 degrees until lightly browned, about 25 minutes, stirring occasionally.

2. Process pepper mixture, water, garlic, and vinegar in food processor or blender until smooth.

Variation:

Avocado and Chipotle Vichyssoise—Make soup as above, omitting cucumber. In Step 2, add 2 medium avocados, $1/2$ small chipotle in adobo, and 2 tablespoons dry sherry to food processor. Complete soup as above; garnish with 6 tablespoons crumbled feta cheese and 2 tablespoons chopped cilantro.

DILLED CUCUMBER BUTTERMILK SOUP

A refreshing soup for the dog days of summer!

6 servings (about 1 cup each)

$3/4$ cup chopped onion

$1/2$ teaspoon minced garlic

1 tablespoon margarine

1 medium russet potato, peeled, cubed

$21/2$ cups Rich Chicken Stock (see p. 4)

2 medium cucumbers, peeled, seeded, chopped

$1/3$ cup sliced green onions and tops

$1/3$ cup chopped parsley

$1/4$ cup chopped fresh dill

1 cup reduced-fat buttermilk

Lemon juice, to taste

Salt and white pepper, to taste

Dill Sour Cream (recipe follows)

Per Serving
Calories: 116
% Calories from fat: 22
Protein (g): 6.2
Carbohydrate (g): 15.5
Fat (g): 2.8
Saturated fat (g): 0.7
Cholesterol (mg): 1.8
Sodium (mg): 103
Exchanges
Milk: 0.0
Veg.: 0.0
Fruit: 0.0
Bread: 1.0
Meat: 0.0
Fat: 1.0

1. Saute onion and garlic in margarine in large saucepan until tender, about 4 minutes. Add potato and Rich Chicken Stock and heat to boiling; reduce heat and simmer, covered, until tender, about 15 minutes. Stir in cucumbers, green onions, parsley, and dill; cool.

2. Process soup in food processor or blender until smooth; pour into large bowl. Stir in buttermilk and season to taste with lemon juice, salt, and white pepper. Refrigerate, covered, until cold.

3. Ladle soup into bowls; spoon Dill Sour Cream into soup.

Dill Sour Cream

makes 1/2 cup

> 1/2 cup fat-free sour cream
> 2 tablespoons chopped fresh dill

1. Combine sour cream and dill.

PEASANT GARLIC SOUP

Two heads of garlic may seem like a lot, but the garlic sweetens as it cooks, lending a mellow flavor to this unique soup.

6 servings (about 1 cup each)

> 1¹/2 cups cubed, peeled potatoes
> 1 cup sliced carrots
> 1 cup sliced celery
> 1/2 cup chopped onion
> 2 heads garlic, peeled
> 3 cups Chicken Stock (see p. 2)
> 1 teaspoon dried thyme leaves
> 1 slice French, *or* Italian, bread, cubed
> Salt and pepper, to taste
> Chopped parsley, *or* chives, as garnish

Per Serving
Calories: 105
% Calories from fat: 6
Protein (g): 3.4
Carbohydrate (g): 22.3
Fat (g): 0.7
Saturated fat (g): 0.1
Cholesterol (mg): 1.7
Sodium (mg): 58
Exchanges
Milk: 0.0
Veg.: 1.0
Fruit: 0.0
Bread: 1.0
Meat: 0.0
Fat: 0.0

1. Combine potatoes, carrots, celery, onion, garlic, Chicken Stock, and thyme in large saucepan. Heat to boiling; reduce heat and simmer, covered, until vegetables are very tender, about 25 minutes.

2. Process soup with bread cubes in food processor or blender until smooth. Return to saucepan; heat until hot. Season to taste with salt and pepper. Serve in bowls; garnish with parsley.

GAZPACHO WITH AVOCADO SOUR CREAM

Gazpacho is Spanish in origin but popularly served throughout Mexico and South America. Easy to make, this is a wonderful soup to keep on hand in summer months.

6 servings (about 1½ cups each)

5 large tomatoes, seeded, chopped
2 cups reduced-sodium tomato juice
2 cloves garlic
2 tablespoons lime juice
1 teaspoon dried oregano leaves
1 small seedless cucumber, coarsely chopped
1 cup chopped yellow bell pepper
1 cup chopped celery
6 green onions and tops, thinly sliced, divided
2 tablespoons finely chopped cilantro
Salt and pepper, to taste
Avocado Sour Cream (recipe follows)
Hot pepper sauce, optional

Per Serving
Calories: 76
% Calories from fat: 17
Protein (g): 3.3
Carbohydrates (g): 15.1
Fat (g): 1.6
Saturated fat (g): 0.3
Cholesterol (mg): 0.1
Sodium (mg): 46
Exchanges
Milk: 0.0
Veg.: 2.0
Fruit: 0.0
Bread: 0.0
Meat: 0.0
Fat: 0.5

1. Reserve 1 cup tomatoes; process remaining tomatoes, tomato juice, garlic, lime juice, and oregano in food processor or blender until smooth.

2. Mix tomato mixture, reserved 1 cup tomatoes, cucumber, bell pepper, celery, 5 green onions, and cilantro in large bowl; season to taste with salt and pepper. Refrigerate until chilled, 3 to 4 hours.

3. Serve soup in chilled bowls; top each with a dollop of Avocado Sour Cream and sprinkle with remaining green onion. Serve with hot pepper sauce.

Avocado Sour Cream

makes about 2/3 cup

- 1/2 medium avocado, peeled, chopped
- 1/4 cup fat-free sour cream
- 2 tablespoons fat-free milk
  Salt and white pepper, to taste

1. Process all ingredients in food processor until smooth; season to taste with salt and white pepper.

Variation:
Spicy Seafood Gazpacho—Make soup as above, adding 1/2 small chipotle in adobo, chopped, *or* 1/2 small jalapeño chili, chopped, and 1 teaspoon hot chili powder with tomatoes in Step 1. Complete soup as above, stirring in 12 ounces small cooked shrimp or crab meat.

SPANISH GAZPACHO

Make this soup with your own homemade tomato juice for that straight-from-the-garden flavor.

6 servings (about 1¼ cups each)

- 1 quart reduced-sodium tomato juice
  Juice of 1 lemon
- 2 medium green bell peppers, finely chopped
- 1/2 cup sliced green onions and tops
- 1/2 cup chopped celery
- 1 zucchini, finely chopped
- 1 small cucumber, seeded, finely chopped
- 3 cloves garlic, minced
- 2 teaspoons olive oil
- 1 teaspoon dried basil leaves
  Salt and pepper, to taste
  Hot pepper sauce, to taste

Per Serving
Calories: 63
% Calories from fat: 21
Protein (g): 2.3
Carbohydrate (g): 12.1
Fat (g): 1.8
Saturated fat (gm): 0.3
Cholesterol (mg): 0
Sodium (mg): 28
Exchanges
Milk: 0.0
Veg.: 2.0
Fruit: 0.0
Bread: 0.0
Meat: 0.0
Fat: 0.5

1. Combine all ingredients, except salt, pepper, and hot pepper sauce, in large bowl. Season to taste with salt, pepper, and hot pepper sauce. Chill several hours. Add additional tomato juice or cold water if thinner consistency is desired.

WINTER GAZPACHO

This hot version of gazpacho brings vegetable-garden flavors and a bright assortment of garnishes to the winter dinner table.

6 servings (about 1 cup each)

2 medium carrots, sliced
1 rib celery, sliced
1 cup packed spinach leaves
1 cup chopped green bell pepper, divided
1/2 cup water
4 cups reduced-sodium tomato juice, divided
2 teaspoons very low-sodium Worcestershire sauce
1 teaspoon beef bouillon crystals
1/4 teaspoon dried tarragon leaves
   Salt and cayenne pepper, to taste
   Hot pepper sauce, to taste
1 small onion, chopped
1 hard-cooked egg, chopped
1/2 small avocado, cubed
1 1/2 cups Garlic, *or* Herb, Croutons (1/2 recipe) (see pp. 784, 785)

Per Serving
Calories: 115
% Calories from fat: 27
Protein (g): 4.2
Carbohydrate (g): 18.3
Fat (g): 3.8
Saturated fat (g): 0.7
Cholesterol (mg): 35.3
Sodium (mg): 221
Exchanges
Milk: 0.0
Veg.: 2.0
Fruit: 0.0
Bread: 0.5
Meat: 0.0
Fat: 0.5

1. Place carrots, celery, spinach, 1/4 cup green pepper, and water in large saucepan. Heat to boiling; reduce heat and simmer, covered, until carrots are tender, about 10 minutes, stirring occasionally.

2. Process carrot mixture, 1 1/2 cups tomato juice, Worcestershire sauce, bouillon crystals, and tarragon in food processor or blender until smooth. Return mixture to saucepan and add remaining 2 1/2 cups tomato juice; heat until hot. Season to taste with salt, cayenne pepper, and hot pepper sauce. Serve in shallow bowls; sprinkle with remaining 3/4 cup green pepper, chopped onion, egg, avocado, and Garlic Croutons.

LENTIL SOUP

This satisfying soup is good on a cold, snowy day.

5-7 servings

1 pound dried brown lentils, picked over and rinsed
1 large onion, finely chopped
1 large rib celery, finely chopped
1 large carrot, shredded
2 quarts water
1 large smoked pork hock
2 teaspoons sugar
2 beef bouillon cubes
1/4 teaspoon dry mustard
1/2 teaspoon dried thyme leaves
   Dash cayenne pepper
   Salt and pepper, to taste

Per Serving
Calories: 89
% Calories from fat: **12**
Protein (g): 6.7
Carbohydrates (g): **16.5**
Fat (g): 1.4
Saturated fat (g): **0.3**
Cholesterol (mg): 6.5
Sodium (mg): 277
Exchanges
Milk: 0.0
Veg.: 0.0
Fruit: 0.0
Bread: 1.0
Meat: 0.0
Fat: 0.5

1. Combine all ingredients except salt and pepper in large saucepan; heat to boiling. Reduce heat and simmer, covered, until lentils are very tender and soup has thickened, about 45 minutes. Remove pork hock and discard. Skim fat from soup; season to taste with salt and pepper.

LENTIL-VEGETABLE SOUP

Because red lentils cook quickly, you can have this soup on the table in less than 35 minutes. The lentils and rice combine to make a complete protein.

6 servings

1 large onion, finely chopped
1 large rib celery, diced
1 large carrot, diced
1 large garlic clove, minced
1 teaspoon olive oil
1 quart Low-Salt Chicken Stock (see p. 3)
1 can (14¹/₂ ounces) reduced-sodium stewed tomatoes
¹/₃ cup dried red lentils, rinsed
¹/₂ large green bell pepper, diced
1¹/₂ cups cubed zucchini
3 tablespoons uncooked rice
¹/₂ teaspoon dried thyme leaves
¹/₂ teaspoon dried basil leaves
¹/₂ teaspoon sugar
¹/₄ teaspoon ground cumin
1 bay leaf
Salt and pepper, to taste

Per Serving
Calories: 115
% Calories from fat: 9
Protein (g): 7.6
Carbohydrates (g): 19.8
Fat (g): 1.2
Saturated fat (g): 0.2
Cholesterol (mg): 0
Sodium (mg): 246
Exchanges
Milk: 0.0
Veg.: 1.0
Fruit: 0.0
Bread: 1.0
Meat: 0.0
Fat: 0.0

1. Saute onion, celery, carrot, and garlic in oil in large saucepan until onion is tender, about 8 minutes. Add remaining ingredients, except salt and pepper; heat to boiling. Reduce heat and simmer, covered, until lentils are tender, about 25 minutes. Discard bay leaf. Season to taste with salt and pepper.

MUSHROOM SOUP

Fresh and dried mushrooms, accented with lemon, combine in this delicious soup.

6 servings (about 1 1/3 cups each)

1 ounce dried porcini mushrooms
1 1/2 cups hot water
    Vegetable cooking spray
3/4 cup thinly sliced onion
1 1/2 tablespoons minced garlic
2 teaspoons flour
6 tablespoons dry white wine
1 quart Rich Chicken Stock (see p. 4)
4 ounces fresh mushrooms, quartered
1 tablespoon fresh, *or* 1 teaspoon dried rosemary leaves
    Spike, to taste
    Pepper, to taste
1/2 cup chopped fresh lemon pulp
1/2 cup minced Italian parsley, divided
6 Bruschetta (1/2 recipe) (see p. 785)

Per Serving
Calories: 90
% Calories from fat: 10
Protein (g): 3.7
Carbohydrates (g): 14.9
Fat (g): 1
Saturated fat (g): 0.1
Cholesterol (mg): 0
Sodium (mg): 86
Exchanges
Milk: 0.0
Veg.: 2.0
Fruit: 0.0
Bread: 0.5
Meat: 0.0
Fat: 0.0

1. Soak porcini in hot water 20 minutes. Carefully remove mushrooms with slotted spoon. Strain liquid through double layer of cheesecloth and reserve. Pick through porcini carefully, rinsing if necessary, to remove grit. Chop coarsely.

2. Spray large saucepan with vegetable cooking spray; heat over medium heat until hot. Saute onion and garlic until translucent, about 5 minutes. Sprinkle with flour and cook 1 minute. Stir in wine, Rich Chicken Stock, porcini, 2 tablespoons reserved porcini liquid, and fresh mushrooms; heat to boiling. Reduce heat and simmer until mushrooms are tender, about 10 minutes.

3. Stir in rosemary, Spike, pepper, lemon pulp, and 1/4 cup parsley; heat until hot. Place one Bruschetta in bottom of each bowl, ladle soup over, and sprinkle with remaining 1/4 cup parsley.

FRESH MOREL SOUP

Make this elegant soup with any fragrant wild mushroom, or a mixture of mushrooms.

4 servings (about 1¹/₄ cups each)

  1¹/₂ cups chopped morel mushrooms
  1-2 teaspoons margarine
    1 quart reduced-sodium fat-free beef broth
    1 cup water
  1-2 tablespoons dry sherry, optional
      Salt and pepper, to taste
      Crumbled blue cheese, as garnish

Per Serving
Calories: 35
% Calories from fat: 26
Protein (g): 5.6
Carbohydrate (g): 1.2
Fat (g): 1.1
Saturated fat (g): 0.2
Cholesterol (mg): 0
Sodium (mg): 172
Exchanges
Milk: 0.0
Veg.: 0.0
Fruit: 0.0
Bread: 0.0
Meat: 0.5
Fat: 0.0

1. Cook mushrooms in margarine in medium saucepan over medium heat until lightly browned, about 5 minutes. Add broth and water and heat to boiling; reduce heat and simmer, uncovered, 15 minutes. Stir in sherry; season to taste with salt and pepper. Sprinkle each serving lightly with blue cheese.

MUSHROOM BARLEY SOUP WITH HERBS

This soup offers old-fashioned flavor in a true comfort food!

8 servings (about 1¹/₂ cups each)

    2 cups finely chopped onions
    1 cup diced carrots
  ¹/₂ cup finely chopped celery
    1 tablespoon vegetable oil
  16 ounces mushrooms, sliced
    1 teaspoon minced garlic
    1 teaspoon dried thyme leaves
    1 teaspoon dried basil leaves
    1 teaspoon dried tarragon leaves
  ¹/₂ teaspoon celery seeds
    2 cups Beef Stock (see p. 6)
    2 cups Chicken Stock (see p. 2)

Per Serving
Calories: 105
% Calories from fat: 20
Protein (g): 3.7
Carbohydrate (g): 18.7
Fat (g): 2.5
Saturated fat (g): 0.3
Cholesterol (mg): 0.9
Sodium (mg): 20
Exchanges
Milk: 0.0
Veg.: 2.0
Fruit: 0.0
Bread: 0.5
Meat: 0.0
Fat: 0.5

2 cups water
$^1/_2$ cup pearl barley
   Salt and pepper, to taste
3 tablespoons chopped parsley

1. Saute onions, carrots, and celery in oil in large saucepan until lightly browned, about 8 minutes. Stir in mushrooms, garlic, and herbs; saute 3 minutes. Stir in Beef Stock, Chicken Stock, water, and barley. Heat to boiling; reduce heat and simmer, covered, until barley is tender, 45 to 60 minutes. Season to taste with salt and pepper; stir in parsley.

TORTELLINI AND MUSHROOM SOUP

Porcini mushrooms, an Italian delicacy found fresh in Tuscany in fall, are available in dried form year round. Porcini impart a wonderful earthy flavor to recipes. Other dried mushrooms, such as shiitake or Chinese black mushrooms, can be substituted for a similar flavor.

6 servings (about 1 cup each)

2 ounces dried porcini mushrooms
   Vegetable cooking spray
8 ounces fresh white mushrooms, sliced
2 tablespoons finely chopped shallots, *or* green onions
2 cloves garlic, minced
$^1/_2$ teaspoon dried tarragon, *or* thyme, leaves
2 cans (15 ounces each) reduced-sodium beef broth
$^1/_4$ cup dry sherry, optional
1 package (9 ounces) fresh low-fat tomato and cheese tortellini
$^1/_4$ teaspoon salt
$^1/_4$ teaspoon pepper

Per Serving
Calories: 188
% Calories from fat: 19
Protein (g): 10.1
Carbohydrates (g): 28.8
Fat (g): 4.2
Saturated fat (g): 1.5
Cholesterol (mg): 17.7
Sodium (mg): 235
Exchanges
Milk: 0.0
Veg.: 1.0
Fruit: 0.0
Bread: 1.5
Meat: 0.5
Fat: 0.5

1. Place dried mushrooms in bowl; pour hot water over to cover. Let stand until mushrooms are soft, about 15 minutes; drain. Slice mushrooms, discarding any tough parts.

2. Spray large saucepan with cooking spray; heat over medium heat until hot. Saute dried and white mushrooms, shallots, garlic, and tarragon until mushrooms are tender, about 5 minutes.

3. Add beef broth and sherry to vegetables; heat to boiling. Add tortellini; reduce heat and simmer, uncovered, until tortellini are al dente, about 5 minutes. Stir in salt and pepper.

BLACK MUSHROOM SOUP

Chinese black mushrooms, also called shiitake mushrooms, add a fragrant, woodsy flavor to this soup.

6 servings (about 1¹/₄ cups each)

1¹/₂	ounces dried Chinese black mushrooms (shiitake)
1	ounce dried cloud ear mushrooms
2	cups boiling water
	Vegetable cooking spray
¹/₄	cup chopped onion
¹/₄	cup thinly sliced green onions and tops
1¹/₄	quarts reduced-sodium fat-free chicken broth
3	cups sliced cremini mushrooms
	Salt and white pepper, to taste
	Finely chopped parsley, as garnish

Per Serving
Calories: 72
% Calories from fat: 3
Protein (g): 7
Carbohydrates (g): 11.2
Fat (g): 0.3
Saturated fat (g): 0.1
Cholesterol (mg): 0
Sodium (mg): 145
Exchanges
Milk: 0.0
Veg.: 3.0
Fruit: 0.0
Bread: 0.0
Meat: 0.0
Fat: 0.0

1. Place dried mushrooms in bowl; pour boiling water over. Let stand until mushrooms are softened, about 15 minutes. Drain, reserving liquid. Slice mushrooms, discarding tough stems from black mushrooms.

2. Spray large saucepan with cooking spray; heat over medium heat until hot. Saute onion until tender, about 5 minutes. Add sliced dried mushrooms and reserved liquid and broth; heat to boiling. Reduce heat and simmer, covered, 20 minutes, adding cremini mushrooms during last 10 minutes. Season to taste with salt and white pepper.

3. Pour soup into bowls; sprinkle with parsley.

SHANGHAI MUSHROOM SOUP

Dried Chinese mushrooms give this light soup a very distinctive flavor. Other dried mushrooms can be substituted, if desired.

6 servings (about ³/₄ cup each)

1 package (1 ounce) dried black Chinese mushrooms
1 cup chopped onion
¹/₂ cup diced red bell pepper
1 tablespoon minced garlic
2 teaspoons minced gingerroot
2 teaspoons vegetable oil
2 cups sliced mushrooms
3¹/₂ cups Low-Salt Chicken Stock (see p. 3)
¹/₃ cup slivered lean ham
¹/₂ cup thinly sliced green onions and tops
1 tablespoon reduced-sodium soy sauce
1 tablespoon dry sherry
1 tablespoon cornstarch

Per Serving
Calories: 82
% Calories from fat: 25
Protein (g): 4.8
Carbohydrate (g): 10.5
Fat (g): 2.3
Saturated fat (g): 0.4
Cholesterol (mg): 6.3
Sodium (mg): 197
Exchanges
Milk: 0.0
Veg.: 2.0
Fruit: 0.0
Bread: 0.0
Meat: 0.0
Fat: 0.5

1. Soak dried mushrooms until softened in warm water to cover, about 20 minutes; drain well and slice, discarding tough stems.

2. Saute onion, bell pepper, garlic, and gingerroot in oil in large saucepan 1 minute; add dried and fresh mushrooms and saute 5 minutes. Add Low-Salt Chicken Stock. Heat to boiling; reduce heat and simmer, covered, 15 minutes.

3. Stir in ham and green onions; heat to boiling. Stir in combined soy sauce, sherry, and cornstarch; boil, stirring, until thickened, 1 to 2 minutes.

FRENCH ONION SOUP

This classic soup is topped with Bruschetta and fat-free cheese for health-ful low-fat dining. If you have the time, make this soup with Brown Beef Stock (see p. 7) for the very best flavor.

8 servings (about 1¼ cups each)

Vegetable cooking spray
6 cups thinly sliced Spanish onions (1½ pounds)
2 cloves garlic, minced
1 teaspoon sugar
6 cups reduced-sodium fat-free beef broth
2 bay leaves
Salt and white pepper, to taste
8 Bruschetta (²/₃ recipe) (see p. 785)
8 tablespoons (2 ounces) shredded fat-free Swiss, *or* mozzarella, cheese

Per Serving
Calories: 144
% Calories from fat: 6
Protein (g): 9
Carbohydrates (g): 24.3
Fat (g): 1
Saturated fat (g): 0.2
Cholesterol (mg): 0
Sodium (mg): 390
Exchanges
Milk: 0.0
Veg.: 3.0
Fruit: 0.0
Bread: 1.0
Meat: 0.0
Fat: 0.0

1. Spray Dutch oven with cooking spray; heat over medium heat until hot. Add onions and garlic and cook, covered, over medium-low heat until wilted, 8 to 10 minutes. Stir in sugar and cook, uncovered, over medium-low to low heat until onions are lightly browned, about 15 minutes.

2. Stir in broth and bay leaves; heat to boiling. Reduce heat and simmer, covered, 30 minutes. Discard bay leaves; season to taste with salt and white pepper.

3. Top each Bruschetta with 1 tablespoon cheese; broil 6 inches from heat source until melted. Pour soup into bowls; top each with a Bruschetta.

RED ONION AND APPLE SOUP WITH CURRY

Red onions, cooked until sweet and tender, lend a special flavor to this autumn soup.

5-6 servings (about 1¹/₄ cups each)

1¹/₄ pounds red onions (about 4 medium), thinly sliced

1 tablespoon margarine

1¹/₂ quarts Rich Chicken Stock (see p. 4)

2 cups coarsely grated, peeled tart cooking apples, divided

¹/₂ cup shredded carrots

1 large bay leaf

1 teaspoon mild curry powder

¹/₄ teaspoon chili powder

¹/₈ teaspoon dried thyme leaves

¹/₈ teaspoon ground allspice

Salt and pepper, to taste

Mango chutney, as garnish

Per Serving
Calories: 106
% Calories from fat: 18
Protein (g): 6.4
Carbohydrates (g): 16.4
Fat (g): 2.3
Saturated fat (g): 0.4
Cholesterol (mg): 0
Sodium (mg): 393
Exchanges
Milk: 0.0
Veg.: 2.0
Fruit: 0.5
Bread: 0.0
Meat: 0.0
Fat: 0.5

1. Saute onions in margarine in large sauce pan until tender and lightly browned, about 15 minutes. Stir in Rich Chicken Stock, 1 cup apples, carrots, and herbs; heat to boiling. Reduce heat and simmer, covered, until vegetables are tender, about 20 minutes.

2. Stir in remaining 1 cup apples and simmer 5 minutes. Discard bay leaf. Season to taste with salt and pepper. Serve with chutney.

THREE-ONION SOUP WITH MUSHROOMS

Mushrooms add flavor and texture interest to this soup.

6 servings (about 1¹/₂ cups each)

3 cups thinly sliced onions

1¹/₂ cups thinly sliced leeks, white parts only

¹/₂ cup chopped shallots, *or* green onions and tops

1 tablespoon margarine

1 teaspoon sugar

4 ounces mushrooms, sliced

6¹/₂ cups reduced-sodium fat-free chicken broth

Salt and pepper, to taste

Per Serving
Calories: 114
% Calories from fat: 18
Protein (g): 8.5
Carbohydrates (g): 14.7
Fat (g): 2.2
Saturated fat (g): 0.4
Cholesterol (mg): 0
Sodium (mg): 218
Exchanges
Milk: 0.0
Veg.: 3.0
Fruit: 0.0
Bread: 0.0
Meat: 0.0
Fat: 0.5

1. Cook onions, leeks, and shallots in margarine in large saucepan, covered, over medium-low heat 15 minutes. Stir in sugar; continue cooking, uncovered, until onion mixture is golden, about 10 minutes longer.

2. Stir mushrooms into onion mixture; cook over medium heat until tender, about 5 minutes. Add broth and heat to boiling; reduce heat and simmer, uncovered, 15 minutes. Season to taste with salt and pepper.

VIDALIA ONION SOUP

The mild sweetness of Vidalia onions makes this soup special, but try it with other flavorful onion varieties too. Half of the soup is pureed, resulting in a wonderful contrast of textures.

8 servings (about 1¼ cups each)

Vegetable cooking spray

1½ quarts thinly sliced Vidalia onions (1½ pounds)

2 cloves garlic, minced

1 teaspoon sugar

⅓ cup all-purpose flour

1½ quarts reduced-sodium fat-free chicken, *or* vegetable, broth

1½ teaspoons dried sage leaves

2 bay leaves

Salt, cayenne, and white pepper, to taste

Snipped chives, as garnish

Per Serving
Calories: 82
% Calories from fat: 2
Protein (g): 6.1
Carbohydrates (g): 12.7
Fat (g): 0.2
Saturated fat (g): 0
Cholesterol (mg): 0
Sodium (mg): 131
Exchanges
Milk: 0.0
Veg.: 3.0
Fruit: 0.0
Bread: 0.0
Meat: 0.0
Fat: 0.0

1. Spray Dutch oven with cooking spray; heat over medium heat until hot. Add onions and garlic and cook, covered, over medium-low heat until wilted, 8 to 10 minutes. Stir in sugar and cook, uncovered, over medium-low to low heat until onions are lightly browned, 10 to 15 minutes. Stir in flour; cook 1 to 2 minutes longer.

2. Stir in broth, sage, and bay leaves; heat to boiling. Reduce heat and simmer, covered, 30 minutes. Discard bay leaves.

3. Process half the soup in food processor or blender until smooth; return to saucepan. Season to taste with salt, cayenne, and white pepper. Serve warm, or refrigerate and serve chilled. Pour soup into bowls; sprinkle with chives.

Variation:
Baked Onion Soup with Sun-Dried Tomato Pesto—Make soup as above, adding ¼ cup dry sherry in Step 2. Spread 8 Bruschetta (see p. 785) with ½ cup Sun-Dried Tomato Pesto (see p. 814). Place in bottoms of 8 oven-proof soup bowls and sprinkle with 1 cup shredded reduced-fat Italian-blend cheese. Ladle soup over and bake at 425 degrees, 10 to 15 minutes or until cheese is melted.

POBLANO CHILI SOUP

Poblano chilies, available in most large supermarkets, give a special flavor to this Mexican-inspired soup.

6 servings (about 1 cup each)

Vegetable cooking spray
2 medium onions, chopped
4 medium poblano chilies, seeds and veins discarded, finely chopped
1/2-1 small jalapeño chili, seeds and veins discarded, finely chopped
2 cans (14 1/2 ounces each) reduced-sodium, fat-free chicken, *or* vegetable, broth
3 cups tomato juice
1/2 teaspoon ground cumin
1/2-1 cup water
Salt and pepper, to taste
Minced cilantro, as garnish

Per Serving
Calories: 88
% Calories from fat: **3**
Protein (g): 6.4
Carbohydrates (g): 18.2
Fat (g): 0.4
Saturated fat (g): **0**
Cholesterol (mg): 0
Sodium (mg): 498
Exchanges
Milk: 0.0
Veg.: 3.5
Fruit: 0.0
Bread: 0.0
Meat: 0.0
Fat: 0.5

1. Spray large saucepan with cooking spray; heat over medium heat until hot. Saute onions and chilies until onions are tender, about 5 minutes. Add broth; heat to boiling. Reduce heat and simmer, covered, until chilies are very tender, about 5 minutes.

2. Process broth mixture in food processor or blender until smooth; return to saucepan. Add tomato juice, cumin, and enough water for desired consistency; heat to boiling. Reduce heat and simmer, uncovered, 10 minutes. Season to taste with salt and pepper. Serve soup in bowls; sprinkle with cilantro.

VICHYSSOISE

Vichyssoise is one of the most popular of all potato-based soups, good served hot or cold. Leeks are very sandy, so wash them under cold running water.

8 servings (about 1¹/₂ cups each)

Vegetable cooking spray
1 quart sliced leeks, white parts only
1 cup sliced onion
4 large boiling potatoes, peeled, sliced thin
1¹/₄ quarts Low-Salt Chicken Stock (see p. 3)
1 can (13 ounces) fat-free evaporated milk
¹/₂ teaspoon white pepper
¹/₄ teaspoon salt
¹/₂ cup non-fat plain yogurt
2 tablespoons fresh mint, chopped

Per Serving
Calories: 160
% Calories from fat: 3
Protein (g): 7.9
Carbohydrate (g): 31.8
Fat (g): 0.5
Saturated fat (g): 0.2
Cholesterol (mg): 4.3
Sodium (mg): 161
Exchanges
Milk: 0.0
Veg.: 0.0
Fruit: 0.0
Bread: 2.0
Meat: 0.0
Fat: 0.0

1. Spray large saucepan with cooking spray; heat over medium heat until hot. Saute leeks, onion, and potatoes 10 minutes. Stir in Low-Salt Chicken Stock; heat to boiling. Reduce heat and simmer, covered, 15 minutes. Stir in milk; simmer 10 minutes, stirring occasionally.

2. Process soup in food processor or blender until smooth. Return soup to pan and stir in pepper, salt, and yogurt. Heat until hot, 2 to 3 minutes; do not boil. Serve hot, or refrigerate and serve chilled. Serve in bowls; sprinkle with mint.

Variation:
Celery Vichyssoise—Make soup as above, adding 3 large ribs sliced celery to the vegetables. Omit mint; garnish each bowl with a dollop of Dill Sour Cream (see p. 48) and celery leaves.

HOT CHILI VICHYSSOISE

Potato soup will never be boring if served Tex-Mex style. This version, prepared with chilies, packs a punch!

6 servings (about 1 cup each)

Mesquite-flavored vegetable cooking spray

1 pound small red potatoes, unpeeled, cut into halves

1 medium leek, cut into 3/4-inch pieces, white part only

1 large poblano chili, cut into 3/4-inch pieces

1 medium jalapeño chili, cut into 3/4-inch pieces

6 cloves garlic, peeled

1¹/2 teaspoons ground cumin

¹/2 teaspoon chili powder

¹/2 teaspoon dried oregano leaves

¹/2 teaspoon pepper

1 quart reduced-sodium fat-free chicken broth, divided

¹/2-³/4 cup fat-free half-and-half, *or* fat-free milk

¹/4 cup minced cilantro

Salt, to taste

Per Serving
Calories: 113
% Calories from fat: 2
Protein (g): 6.6
Carbohydrates (g): 20.9
Fat (g): 0.3
Saturated fat (g): 0
Cholesterol (mg): 0
Sodium (mg): 169
Exchanges
Milk: 0.0
Veg.: 1.0
Fruit: 0.0
Bread: 1.0
Meat: 0.0
Fat: 0.0

1. Spray aluminum-foil-lined jelly roll pan with cooking spray. Arrange vegetables, chilies, and garlic in single layer on pan; spray generously with cooking spray and sprinkle with herbs and pepper.

2. Roast vegetables at 425 degrees until browned and tender, about 40 minutes, removing garlic when tender, after about 20 minutes.

3. Process vegetables and 1 to 2 cups broth in food processor or blender until smooth. Place soup in large saucepan; stir in remaining broth, half-and-half, and cilantro. Cook over medium heat until hot, about 5 minutes; season with salt. Serve warm, or refrigerate and served chilled.

GINGER PUMPKIN SOUP

The crunch of red bell pepper adds a texture and flavor accent to this soup. Green or yellow bell pepper can be substituted, or use all three! Substitute 2 1/2 cups canned pumpkin if you can't get a fresh pumpkin.

6 servings (about ¾ cup each)

Per Serving
Calories: 83
% Calories from fat: 6
Protein (g): 2.8
Carbohydrate (g): 15.3
Fat (g): 0.6
Saturated fat (g): 0.2
Cholesterol (mg): 1.7
Sodium (mg): 8
Exchanges
Milk: 0.0
Veg.: 0.0
Fruit: 0.0
Bread: 1.0
Meat: 0.0
Fat: 0.0

 1 small pumpkin (3 pounds), peeled, seeded, cubed
 1 cup chopped onion
 1 tablespoon chopped gingerroot
 1 teaspoon minced garlic
 3 cups Chicken Stock (see p. 2)
 ½ cup dry white wine
 ½ teaspoon ground cloves
   Salt and pepper, to taste
 1 cup chopped red bell pepper

1. Combine all ingredients except salt, pepper, and red bell pepper in large saucepan. Heat to boiling; reduce heat and simmer, covered, until pumpkin is tender, about 20 minutes.

2. Process soup in food processor or blender until smooth. Return to saucepan and heat until hot; season to taste with salt and pepper. Serve soup in bowls; sprinkle with red bell pepper.

CREAM OF SPINACH SOUP

The evaporated milk gives a creaminess to this soup, without adding fat calories.

6 servings (about 1⅓ cups each)

Per Serving
Calories: 203
% Calories from fat: 26
Protein (g): 14.7
Carbohydrates (g): 24.2
Fat (g): 6
Saturated fat (g): 1.3
Cholesterol (mg): 7.4
Sodium (mg): 249
Exchanges
Milk: 1.5
Veg.: 1.5
Fruit: 0.0
Bread: 0.0
Meat: 0.0
Fat: 1.0

 1 large leek, white part only, thinly sliced
 2 tablespoons chopped parsley
 4 cloves garlic, minced
 2 tablespoons olive oil
16 ounces fresh spinach, torn into bite-sized pieces
 1 cup low-fat plain yogurt
 3 cups fat-free evaporated milk

2 cups Rich Chicken Stock (see p. 4)
1 tablespoon lemon juice
1 teaspoon ground nutmeg
1 teaspoon Spike
1/2 teaspoon black pepper
   Salt, to taste

1. Saute leek, parsley, and garlic in oil in large saucepan until wilted, about 5 minutes. Add spinach; saute over low heat 10 minutes, stirring frequently. Stir in yogurt, milk, Rich Chicken Stock, and lemon juice; heat to boiling. Reduce heat and simmer, covered, 30 minutes, stirring occasionally. Stir in nutmeg, Spike, and pepper; season to taste with salt.

SPINACH SOUP

This soup is best used immediately, as color will change if left standing.

10 servings (about 1 cup each)

1 large leek, white part only, thinly sliced
1 carrot, sliced
1 rib celery, sliced
1 tablespoon olive oil
2 quarts Rich Chicken Stock (see p. 4)
2 pounds fresh spinach
   Salt and pepper, to taste
1/2 cup grated Parmesan
   Croutons (see p. 784)

Per Serving
Calories: 113
% Calories from fat: 31
Protein (g): 9.1
Carbohydrate (g): 9.9
Fat (g): 3.8
Saturated fat (g): 1.2
Cholesterol (mg): 4
Sodium (mg): 229
Exchanges
Milk: 0.0
Veg.: 2.0
Fruit: 0.0
Bread: 0.0
Meat: 0.5
Fat: 0.5

1. Saute leek, carrot, and celery in oil in large saucepan until tender. Add Rich chicken Stock and heat to boiling. Add spinach and cook, uncovered, for 2 minutes, until spinach wilts.

2. Process in food processor or blender until smooth. Return soup to saucepan and heat until hot; season to taste with salt and pepper. Ladle soup into bowls; sprinkle with cheese and Croutons.

APPLE SQUASH SOUP

This soup is the perfect autumn offering.

8 servings (about 1 cup each)

1¹/₂ cups chopped onions
  2 teaspoons ground cinnamon
¹/₄ teaspoon ground ginger
¹/₄ teaspoon ground cloves
¹/₈ teaspoon ground nutmeg
1¹/₂ tablespoons margarine
  1 large butternut squash, peeled, seeded, cubed (about 2¹/₂ pounds)
  2 tart cooking apples, peeled, cored, chopped
1¹/₃ cups apple cider
  3 cups Chicken Stock (see p. 2)
    Salt and pepper, to taste
    Spiced Sour Cream (recipe follows)

Per Serving
Calories: 155
% Calories from fat: **15**
Protein (g): 3.3
Carbohydrate (g): **32.6**
Fat (g): 2.8
Saturated fat (g): 0.5
Cholesterol (mg): **1.3**
Sodium (mg): 48
Exchanges
Milk: 0.0
Veg.: 0.0
Fruit: 0.0
Bread: 2.0
Meat: 0.0
Fat: 0.5

1. Saute onions and spices in margarine in large saucepan over very low heat until onions are very tender, about 20 minutes, stirring frequently; add squash, apples, cider, and Chicken Stock. Heat to boiling; reduce heat and simmer, covered, until squash and apples are tender, about 25 minutes.

2. Process mixture in food processor or blender until smooth; return mixture to saucepan and heat to simmering. Season to taste with salt and pepper. Ladle soup into bowls and serve with Spiced Sour Cream.

Spiced Sour Cream

makes about 1 cup

¹/₂ cup fat-free sour cream
  1 teaspoon sugar
¹/₂ teaspoon ground cinnamon
¹/₈ teaspoon ground ginger
    Lemon juice, to taste

1. Combine sour cream, sugar, and spices; season to taste with lemon juice.

SUMMER SQUASH SOUP

Use zucchini or yellow summer squash in this soup.

6 servings (about 1¹/₄ cups each)

Vegetable cooking spray
¹/₂ cup chopped shallots
¹/₄ cup sliced green onions and tops
2 cloves garlic, minced
4 medium zucchini, chopped
1 cup cubed, peeled Idaho potato
1 quart reduced-sodium fat-free chicken broth
1 cup chopped kale, *or* spinach leaves
1-1¹/₂ teaspoons dried tarragon leaves
¹/₄-¹/₂ cup fat-free half-and-half, *or* fat-free milk
Salt and white pepper, to taste
6 thin slices zucchini
6 thin slices yellow summer squash
Cayenne pepper, as garnish
1¹/₂ cups Sourdough Croutons (¹/₂ recipe) (see p. 784)

Per Serving
Calories: 106
% Calories from fat: 4
Protein (g): 7.4
Carbohydrates (g): 17.9
Fat (g): 0.5
Saturated fat (g): 0.1
Cholesterol (mg): 0
Sodium (mg): 175
Exchanges
Milk: 0.0
Veg.: 2.0
Fruit: 0.0
Bread: 0.5
Meat: 0.5
Fat: 0.0

1. Spray large saucepan with cooking spray; heat over medium heat until hot. Saute shallots, green onions, and garlic until tender, about 5 minutes. Add chopped zucchini and potato; saute 5 to 8 minutes longer.

2. Add broth, kale, and tarragon to saucepan; heat to boiling. Reduce heat and simmer, covered, until vegetables are tender, 10 to 15 minutes.

3. Process soup in food processor or blender until smooth; return to saucepan. Stir in half-and-half; season to taste with salt and white pepper. Heat and serve warm, or refrigerate and serve chilled.

4. Pour soup into bowls. Garnish each with a slice of zucchini and summer squash; sprinkle lightly with cayenne pepper and Sourdough Croutons.

Variation:
Squash and Fennel Bisque—Make soup as above, adding 1 fennel bulb, sliced, and 1 cup sliced celery in Step 1, and substituting spinach for kale in Step 2. Omit tarragon. Thin with additional broth if necessary.

CHAYOTE SQUASH SOUP WITH CILANTRO CREAM

Chayote squash, often called a "vegetable pear," is native to Mexico. Readily available in supermarkets, the squash is light green in color and delicate in flavor.

6 servings (about 1 cup each)

Vegetable cooking spray
1 large onion, chopped
2 cloves garlic, minced
3 tablespoons flour
3 large chayote squash, peeled, pitted, sliced
3 cans (14¹/₂ ounces each) reduced-sodium fat-free chicken broth, divided
¹/₂ cup water
Salt and white pepper, to taste
Cilantro Cream (recipe follows)
Finely chopped cilantro, as garnish

Per Serving
Calories: 68
% Calories from fat: 4
Protein (g): 6.8
Carbohydrates (g): 10.5
Fat (g): 0.3
Saturated fat (g): 0.1
Cholesterol (mg): 0.2
Sodium (mg): 79
Exchanges
Milk: 0.0
Veg.: 2.0
Fruit: 0.0
Bread: 0.0
Meat: 0.5
Fat: 0.0

1. Spray large saucepan with cooking spray; heat over medium heat until hot. Saute onion and garlic until tender, about 5 minutes. Stir in flour; cook over medium heat 2 minutes, stirring constantly.

2. Add squash and 1 can broth to saucepan. Heat to boiling; reduce heat and simmer, covered, until squash is tender, 15 to 20 minutes. Process mixture in food processor or blender until smooth; return to saucepan. Add remaining broth and water; season to taste with salt and white pepper. Heat over medium heat and serve warm, or refrigerate and serve chilled.

3. Serve soup in bowls; drizzle with Cilantro Cream and sprinkle with cilantro.

Cilantro Cream

makes about ¹/₂ cup

¹/₃ cup fat-free sour cream
1 tablespoon finely chopped cilantro
¹/₄-¹/₃ cup fat-free milk

1. Mix sour cream and cilantro in small bowl, adding enough milk for desired consistency.

FRESH TOMATO SOUP

To peel tomatoes, place them, a few at a time, in a pan of boiling water for about 30 seconds. Remove and slip off skins. Halve the tomatoes and remove seeds.

6 servings (about 1¼ cups each)

4 green onions and tops, sliced

4 cloves garlic, minced

1 teaspoon vegetable oil

2½ pounds tomatoes, peeled, seeded, chopped, divided

2½ cups Rich Chicken Stock (see p. 4)

¼ cup chopped fresh, *or* 1½ teaspoons dried, basil leaves

1 bay leaf

2 teaspoons sugar

½ cup dry white wine

¼ cup chopped parsley

Salt and pepper, to taste

Per Serving
Calories: 87
% Calories from fat: 17
Protein (g): 4
Carbohydrate (g): 11.6
Fat (g): 1.8
Saturated fat (g): 0.3
Cholesterol (mg): 0.4
Sodium (mg): 36
Exchanges
Milk: 0.0
Veg.: 2.0
Fruit: 0.0
Bread: 0.0
Meat: 0.0
Fat: 0.5

1. Saute green onions and garlic in oil in large saucepan until transparent, about 2 minutes. Reserve 2 cups chopped tomatoes. Process remaining tomatoes in food processor or blender until smooth; stir into saucepan and cook 5 minutes. Stir in Rich Chicken Stock, basil, bay leaf, and sugar. Heat to boiling; reduce heat and simmer, uncovered, 30 minutes.

2. Stir in wine and reserved 2 cups tomatoes; heat to boiling. Reduce heat and simmer, uncovered, 15 minutes. Stir in parsley; discard bay leaf and season to taste with salt and pepper.

TOMATO BISQUE

Smoked pork hocks give a rich flavor to this tomato soup.

7-8 servings

1 large onion, chopped
2 large ribs celery, chopped
1/4 cup chopped red bell pepper
1 small carrot, chopped
2 large garlic cloves, minced
1 1/2 teaspoons margarine
2 tablespoons flour
2 1/2 cups Beef Stock (see p. 6)
2 small smoked pork hocks (about 1 1/4 pounds)
1/2 cup diced peeled potatoes
1 teaspoon dried, thyme leaves
3/4 teaspoon ground allspice
3/4 teaspoon curry powder
1 can (35 ounces) imported Italian tomatoes, undrained
1 can (6 ounces) tomato paste
1 teaspoon sugar
1 1/2 cups 1% low-fat milk
Salt and pepper, to taste
Chopped fresh chives, as garnish

Per Serving
Calories: 123
% Calories from fat: 13
Protein (g): 6.5
Carbohydrates (g): 20.1
Fat (g): 1.8
Saturated fat (g): 0.6
Cholesterol (mg): 4.1
Sodium (mg): 500
Exchanges
Milk: 0.0
Veg.: 0.0
Fruit: 0.5
Bread: 1.5
Meat: 0.0
Fat: 0.5

1. Saute onion, celery, bell pepper, carrot, and garlic in margarine in large saucepan until softened, about 5 minutes. Stir in flour; cook 1 to 2 minutes. Stir in Beef Stock, pork hocks, potatoes, thyme, allspice, and curry powder; heat to boiling. Reduce heat and simmer, covered, 15 minutes. Discard pork hocks.

2. Process in food processor or blender until smooth. Return mixture to saucepan. Blend tomatoes and liquid and tomato paste in food processor or blender until finely chopped; add to saucepan. Stir in sugar and milk. Heat to simmering over medium-high heat, stirring frequently; season to taste with salt and pepper. Garnish with chives.

TOMATO ESSENCE

With fresh tomatoes and lots of fresh herbs, this soup is the "essence" of summer. Delicious warm or chilled.

6 servings

4 tomatoes, sliced

1 medium onion, chopped

1 cup loosely packed mixed chopped herbs (oregano, dill, parsley, basil)

1 teaspoon margarine

1/2 cup reduced-sodium tomato paste

2 cups Chicken Stock (see p. 2)

1 cup fat-free milk

2 tablespoons sugar

Salt and white pepper, to taste

6 tablespoons grated Parmesan cheese

Per Serving
Calories: 110
% Calories from fat: 22
Protein (g): 5.9
Carbohydrate (g): 17
Fat (g): 3
Saturated fat (g): 1.2
Cholesterol (mg): 5.8
Sodium (mg): 153
Exchanges
Milk: 0.0
Veg.: 3.0
Fruit: 0.0
Bread: 0.0
Meat: 0.0
Fat: 0.5

1. Saute tomatoes, onion, and herbs in margarine in large saucepan until onion is soft, about 5 minutes. Stir in tomato paste.

2. Process in blender or food processor until smooth. Return to saucepan; stir in Chicken Stock, milk, and sugar. Heat until hot; do not boil. Season to taste with salt and white pepper. Ladle into bowls and sprinkle with cheese.

TOMATO-ORANGE SOUP

This light and refreshing soup requires no cooking — perfect for a hot day.

6 servings

2 small oranges

3 medium tomatoes, peeled, seeded, cubed

3/4 cup chopped onion

1 can (14 1/2 ounces) reduced-sodium fat-free chicken broth

1 cup reduced-sodium tomato juice

1/2 cup dry white wine

1 tablespoon red wine vinegar

1 tablespoon sugar

1/4 teaspoon salt

3/4 teaspoon pepper

Per Serving
Calories: 78
% Calories from fat: 3
Protein (g): 3.2
Carbohydrate (g): 13.7
Fat (g): 0.3
Saturated fat (g): 0
Cholesterol (mg): 0
Sodium (mg): 157
Exchanges
Milk: 0.0
Veg.: 3.0
Fruit: 0.0
Bread: 0.0
Meat: 0.0
Fat: 0.0

1. Remove the zest of 1 orange, cut into julienne strips, and set aside. Remove and discard peel from both oranges. Coarsely chop oranges and place in bowl; stir in tomatoes and remaining ingredients. Cover and chill for at least 1 hour to allow flavors to develop.

2. Serve soup in bowls; garnish with orange zest.

TWO-TOMATO SOUP

The concentrated flavor of sun-dried tomatoes enhances the flavor of garden-ripe tomato soup.

6 servings (about 1¼ cups each)

Olive oil cooking spray
1 cup chopped onion
½ cup sliced celery
½ cup chopped carrot
2 teaspoons minced roasted garlic
1 quart reduced-sodium fat-free chicken broth
1 quart chopped ripe tomatoes, *or* 2 cans (16 ounces each) reduced-sodium whole tomatoes, undrained, coarsely chopped
1 large Idaho potato, peeled, cubed
½ cup sun-dried tomatoes (not in oil)
1-2 teaspoons dried basil leaves
½ cup fat-free half-and-half, *or* fat-free milk
2-3 teaspoons sugar
Salt and pepper, to taste
Finely chopped basil, *or* parsley, as garnish

Per Serving
Calories: 118
% Calories from fat: 5
Protein (g): 7.5
Carbohydrates (g): 21.3
Fat (g): 0.7
Saturated fat (g): 0.1
Cholesterol (mg): 0
Sodium (mg): 255
Exchanges
Milk: 0.0
Veg.: 3.0
Fruit: 0.0
Bread: 0.5
Meat: 0.0
Fat: 0.0

1. Spray large saucepan with cooking spray; heat over medium heat until hot. Saute onion, celery, carrot, and garlic until tender; 5 to 8 minutes. Add broth, tomatoes, potato, sun-dried tomatoes, and basil; heat to boiling. Reduce heat and simmer, covered, until vegetables are tender, 10 to 15 minutes.

2. Process soup in food processor or blender until smooth; return to saucepan. Stir in half-and-half and cook over medium heat until hot through, 3 to 5 minutes. Season to taste with sugar, salt, and pepper.

3. Pour soup into bowls; sprinkle with basil or parsley.

Variation:
Baked Two-Tomato Soup—Make soup as above. Ladle into oven-proof bowls. Thaw 1 sheet ($^1/_2$ package) frozen puff pastry according to package directions. Cut 6 rounds the size of tops of bowls and place on top of soup, pressing gently to rims of bowls. Brush with beaten egg, and sprinkle with grated Parmesan cheese. Bake at 375 degrees until dough is puffed and golden, about 20 minutes.

ZESTY TOMATO-VEGETABLE SOUP

Italian tomatoes make this full-flavored vegetable soup especially good.

5-6 servings

1 medium onion, coarsely chopped
1 large rib celery, coarsely chopped
1 medium carrot, coarsely chopped
$^3/_4$ cup chopped red bell pepper
1$^1/_2$ teaspoons olive oil
1 cup Beef Stock (see p. 6)
1 can (32 ounces) imported Italian (plum) tomatoes, undrained
$^1/_4$ cup dry white wine, *or* Beef Stock
1 teaspoon lemon juice
$^3/_4$ teaspoon celery salt
Pinch crushed red pepper
Salt and pepper, to taste
Finely chopped chives, as garnish

Per Serving
Calories: 81
% Calories from fat: 15
Protein (g): 3.1
Carbohydrates (g): 11.6
Fat (g): 1.3
Saturated fat (g): 0.2
Cholesterol (mg): 0
Sodium (mg): 608
Exchanges
Milk: 0.0
Veg.: 2.0
Fruit: 0.0
Bread: 0.0
Meat: 0.0
Fat: 0.5

1. Saute onion, celery, carrot, and bell pepper in oil in large saucepan until vegetables are tender, about 10 minutes. Stir in remaining ingredients, except salt, pepper, and chives, and heat to boiling. Reduce heat and simmer, covered, 10 minutes.

2. Process soup in blender or food processor until smooth. Transfer to serving bowl; season to taste with salt and pepper. Refrigerate until chilled. Garnish with chopped chives.

SUN-DRIED TOMATO AND LINGUINE SOUP

For this skinny pasta soup, be sure to use plain sun-dried tomatoes rather than the ones packed in oil. One-half cup of uncooked orzo can be substituted for the linguine, if preferred.

4 servings (about 1 cup each)

2 sun-dried tomatoes (not in oil)
Vegetable cooking spray
1/2 cup thinly sliced celery
2 tablespoons thinly sliced green onions and tops
2 cloves garlic, minced
2 cans (15 ounces each) reduced-sodium chicken broth
2 ounces linguine, uncooked, broken into 2- to 3-inch pieces
1-2 teaspoons lemon juice
Salt and pepper, to taste

Per Serving
Calories: 68
% Calories from fat: 11
Protein (g): 3.6
Carbohydrates (g): 12.1
Fat (g): 0.9
Saturated fat (g): 0
Cholesterol (mg): 0
Sodium (mg): 71
Exchanges
Milk: 0.0
Veg.: 1.0
Fruit: 0.0
Bread: 0.5
Meat: 0.0
Fat: 0.0

1. Place sun-dried tomatoes in small bowl; pour hot water over to cover. Let tomatoes stand until softened, about 15 minutes; drain. Coarsely chop tomatoes.

2. Spray medium saucepan with cooking spray; heat over medium heat until hot. Saute celery, green onions, and garlic until tender, 5 to 7 minutes. Stir in chicken broth; heat to boiling.

3. Add linguine and sun-dried tomatoes to boiling broth. Reduce heat and simmer, uncovered, until pasta is al dente, about 10 minutes. Season with lemon juice, salt, and pepper.

LIGHTLY CREAMED VEGETABLE SOUP

Fat-free milk, whipped with an immersion blender, lends a wonderful, rich texture to this fragrant creamed soup. If you do not have an immersion blender, just stir the milk into the soup near the end of the cooking time.

6 servings (about 1¹/₃ cups each)

1	medium onion, sliced
2	medium carrots, sliced
1	medium yellow summer squash, sliced
1	medium green bell pepper, coarsely chopped
1	medium red bell pepper, coarsely chopped
2	ribs celery, sliced
1	clove garlic, minced
1¹/₂	tablespoons margarine
4	peppercorns
3	whole cloves
1	bay leaf
1	quart reduced-sodium fat-free chicken broth
¹/₃	cup all-purpose flour
²/₃	cup water
	Salt and pepper, to taste
¹/₂	cup fat-free milk
	Freshly ground nutmeg, as garnish

Per Serving
Calories: 110
% Calories from fat: 26
Protein (g): 6.5
Carbohydrates (g): 13.3
Fat (g): 3.1
Saturated fat (g): 0.6
Cholesterol (mg): 0.4
Sodium (mg): 182
Exchanges
Milk: 0.0
Veg.: 3.0
Fruit: 0.0
Bread: 0.0
Meat: 0.0
Fat: 0.5

1. Saute vegetables in margarine in large saucepan until onion is tender, 8 to 10 minutes. Tie peppercorns, cloves, and bay leaf in cheesecloth bag; add to saucepan with broth and heat to boiling. Simmer, covered, until vegetables are tender, 10 to 15 minutes. Discard bag.

2. Heat soup to boiling. Mix flour and water; stir into soup. Boil, stirring constantly, until thickened, 1 to 2 minutes. Season to taste with salt and pepper.

3. Whip milk with an immersion blender until doubled in volume and stir into soup just before serving. Pour soup into bowls; sprinkle lightly with nutmeg.

LIME-SCENTED VEGETABLE SOUP

A soup with a fresh flavor, accented with lime and cilantro. Cubed cooked chicken breast can be added, if you like.

6 servings (about 1¼ cups each)

Vegetable cooking spray
2 cups sliced carrots
1 cup chopped red bell pepper
¾ cup sliced celery
⅓ cup sliced green onions and tops
6 cloves garlic, minced
1 small jalapeño chili, finely chopped
1½ quarts reduced-sodium fat-free chicken broth
½-¾ cup lime juice
½ teaspoon ground cumin
Salt and pepper, to taste
1 cup chopped tomato
½ cup chopped, seeded cucumber
½ small avocado, peeled, chopped
3-4 tablespoons finely chopped cilantro
1½ cups Herb Croutons (½ recipe) (see p. 784)

Per Serving
Calories: 120
% Calories from fat: **23**
Protein (g): 8.3
Carbohydrates (g): **15.1**
Fat (g): 3.1
Saturated fat (g): 0.5
Cholesterol (mg): 0
Sodium (mg): 351
Exchanges
Milk: 0.0
Veg.: 4.0
Fruit: 0.0
Bread: 0.0
Meat: 0.0
Fat: 0.5

1. Spray large saucepan with cooking spray; heat over medium heat until hot. Saute carrots, bell pepper, celery, green onions, garlic, and jalapeño chili, about 5 minutes.

2. Add broth, lime juice, and cumin to saucepan; heat to boiling. Reduce heat and simmer, covered, until vegetables are tender, 10 to 15 minutes. Season to taste with salt and pepper.

3. Pour soup into bowls; add tomato, cucumber, and avocado to each bowl. Sprinkle with cilantro and Herb Croutons.

WATERCRESS SOUP

Here's a soup that celebrates the pungent, peppery taste of fresh watercress. If desired, this soup can also be served hot.

4-5 servings

1 pound leeks (about 3 medium), white parts only, cut into ¹/₂-inch pieces
1 medium onion, chopped
1 tablespoon margarine
3 cups Chicken Stock (see p. 2)
1³/₄ cups diced peeled potatoes
1 cup packed watercress leaves and tender stems, finely chopped
1 cup whole milk
1 teaspoon lemon juice
Salt and white pepper, to taste

Per Serving
Calories: 157
% Calories from fat: 23
Protein (g): 6.6
Carbohydrates (g): 24.6
Fat (g): 4.1
Saturated fat (g): 1.5
Cholesterol (mg): 6.6
Sodium (mg): 263
Exchanges
Milk: 0.0
Veg.: 0.0
Fruit: 0.0
Bread: 1.5
Meat: 0.0
Fat: 1.0

1. Saute leeks and onion in margarine in large saucepan until leeks are tender, about 5 minutes. Stir in Chicken Stock and potatoes; heat to boiling. Reduce heat and simmer, covered, until potatoes are very tender, about 12 minutes.

2. Process in blender or food processor until smooth; transfer to serving bowl. Stir in watercress, milk, and lemon juice; season to taste with salt and white pepper. Refrigerate until chilled.

TANGY ZUCCHINI SOUP

Buttermilk is a subtle addition to this unusual cold soup. For an even tangier and lower-fat version, use more buttermilk and less whole milk.

4-5 servings

  1 medium onion, finely chopped
  1 small garlic clove, minced
  2 cups diced zucchini
  1/2 cup diced, peeled potato
  3 cups Low-Salt Chicken Stock (see p. 3)
  2 tablespoons chopped parsley
  1/4 teaspoon dry mustard
    Dash cayenne pepper
  1/2 cup buttermilk
  1/2 cup whole milk
    Salt and white pepper, to taste
    Thinly sliced zucchini, as garnish

Per Serving
Calories: 77
% Calories from fat: 14
Protein (g): 5.8
Carbohydrates (g): 11.6
Fat (g): 1.2
Saturated fat (g): 0.7
Cholesterol (mg): 4.2
Sodium (mg): 243
Exchanges
Milk: 0.0
Veg.: 2.0
Fruit: 0.0
Bread: 0.0
Meat: 0.0
Fat: 0.5

1. Combine onion, garlic, zucchini, potato, Low-Salt Chicken Stock, parsley, mustard, and cayenne pepper in large saucepan; heat to boiling. Reduce heat and simmer, covered, until potato is very tender, about 15 minutes.

2. Process in blender or food processor until smooth; transfer to serving bowl. Stir in buttermilk and milk; season to taste with salt and white pepper. Refrigerate until chilled. Garnish with sliced zucchini.

CHINESE PORK AND WATERCRESS SOUP

In this recipe the watercress is stirred in, but not cooked, which helps retain its bright color and fresh, peppery taste.

5-6 servings

3 ounces boneless pork loin, fat trimmed, cut into 1 x 1/4-inch strips

1 small garlic clove, halved

1 slice fresh gingerroot, 1/4 inch thick

5 1/2 cups Chicken Stock (see p. 2), *or* fat-free chicken broth, divided

4-5 green onions and tops, quartered lengthwise and cut into 1-inch pieces

1 tablespoon dry sherry

2 teaspoons reduced-sodium soy sauce

2/3 cup cooked rice

1 1/2 cups loosely packed watercress
Salt and pepper, to taste

Per Serving
Calories: 68
% Calories from fat: 11
Protein (g): 7.4
Carbohydrates (g): 6.9
Fat (g): 0.8
Saturated fat (g): 0.3
Cholesterol (mg): 6.2
Sodium (mg): 374
Exchanges
Milk: 0.0
Veg.: 0.0
Fruit: 0.0
Bread: 1.0
Meat: 0.0
Fat: 0.0

1. Heat pork, garlic, gingerroot, and 1/2 cup Chicken Stock to boiling in large saucepan; reduce heat and simmer, covered, until pork is cooked, about 5 minutes.

2. Using a slotted spoon, transfer pork strips to a colander; rinse and reserve. Strain broth and return to saucepan; discard garlic and gingerroot.

3. Add remaining 5 cups Chicken Stock, reserved pork, green onions, sherry, soy sauce, and rice; heat to boiling. Reduce heat and simmer, covered, 2 minutes. Stir in watercress; remove from heat and let stand until watercress is wilted, about 30 seconds. Season to taste with salt and pepper; serve immediately.

GREEK LEMON SOUP

This classic soup is made extra-special with your own homemade stock, but use canned broth, if you must—it's still delicious.

4 servings (about 1¹/₄ cups each)

    1 quart Rich Chicken Stock (see p. 4)
    1 tablespoon cornstarch
  ¹/₄ cup rice, uncooked
      Salt and pepper, to taste
  ¹/₄ cup fresh lemon juice
  ³/₄ cup no-cholesterol real egg product

Per Serving
Calories: 115
% Calories from fat: 8
Protein (g): 10.3
Carbohydrate (g): 13.2
Fat (g): 0.9
Saturated fat (g): 0.3
Cholesterol (mg): 1
Sodium (mg): 119
Exchanges
Milk: 0.0
Veg.: 0.0
Fruit: 0.0
Bread: 1.0
Meat: 1.0
Fat: 0.0

1. Combine Rich Chicken Stock and cornstarch in large saucepan; heat to boiling. Stir in rice and cook, covered, until tender, 20 to 25 minutes. Season to taste with salt and pepper.

2. Combine lemon juice and egg product in medium bowl; gradually whisk in half the stock mixture. Stir mixture back into saucepan and heat, stirring, 1 to 2 minutes.

HOT SOUR SOUP

The contrast in hot and sour flavors makes this Mandarin soup a unique offering. The hot chili sesame oil and Sour Sauce are intensely flavored, so use sparingly.

6 servings (about 1 cup each)

  ¹/₂ ounce dried Chinese black mushrooms (shiitake)
  ³/₄ cup boiling water
    1 quart reduced-sodium fat-free chicken broth
  ¹/₂ cup bamboo shoots
  ¹/₄ cup white distilled vinegar
    2 tablespoons reduced-sodium tamari soy sauce

Per Serving
Calories: 106
% Calories from fat: 20
Protein (g): 10.4
Carbohydrates (g): 10.6
Fat (g): 2.3
Saturated fat (g): 0.4
Cholesterol (mg): 35.3
Sodium (mg): 483
Exchanges
Milk: 0.0
Veg.: 2.0
Fruit: 0.0
Bread: 0.0
Meat: 1.0
Fat: 0.0

 1 tablespoon finely chopped gingerroot
 1 teaspoon sugar
 1 tablespoon cornstarch
 3 tablespoons water
 1½ cups cubed light extra-firm tofu
 Salt, cayenne, and black pepper, to taste
 1 egg, lightly beaten
 1-2 teaspoons dark sesame oil
 Sliced green onion, as garnish
 12-18 drops hot chili sesame oil, *or* Szechwan chili sauce
 Sour Sauce (recipe follows)

1. Combine mushrooms and boiling water in small bowl; let stand until mushrooms are softened, 15 to 20 minutes. Drain; reserving liquid. Slice mushrooms, discarding tough stems.

2. Combine broth, mushrooms and reserved liquid, bamboo shoots, vinegar, soy sauce, gingerroot, and sugar in large saucepan; heat to boiling. Reduce heat and simmer, uncovered, 10 minutes. Heat soup to boiling; mix cornstarch and water and stir into soup. Boil until thickened, about 1 minute, stirring constantly.

3. Stir tofu into soup; simmer, covered, 5 minutes. Season to taste with salt, cayenne, and black pepper. Just before serving, stir egg slowly into soup; stir in sesame oil.

4. Pour soup into bowls; garnish with green onion. Pass the hot chili sesame oil and Sour Sauce.

Sour Sauce

makes about ¹/₃ cup

 3 tablespoons white distilled vinegar
 1 tablespoon reduced-sodium tamari soy sauce
 2 tablespoons sugar

1. Mix all ingredients; refrigerate until serving time.

INDIAN SPICED CHICKEN SOUP

This flavorful chicken soup is sometimes called Mulligatawny Soup. Delicious with Pita Breads (p. 787) for a light lunch.

8 servings (about 1 cup each)

2 quarts water
6 peppercorns
1 small chicken, cut up (about 3 1/2 pounds)
2 teaspoons ground coriander
1 teaspoon ground turmeric
1 teaspoon ground ginger
1/4 teaspoon crushed red pepper
1 1/2 teaspoons cider vinegar
1/2 cup thinly sliced onion
1 tablespoon margarine
Salt and pepper, to taste
Chopped cilantro, as garnish

Per Serving
Calories: 179
% Calories from fat: 26
Protein (g): 30.2
Carbohydrate (g): 1.4
Fat (g): 4.9
Saturated fat (g): 1.3
Cholesterol (mg): 82.1
Sodium (mg): 89
Exchanges
Milk: 0.0
Veg.: 0.0
Fruit: 0.0
Bread: 0.0
Meat: 3.0
Fat: 0.0

1. Combine water, peppercorns, and chicken in Dutch oven. Heat to boiling; reduce heat and simmer, covered, until tender, about 35 minutes. Strain broth into large bowl. Skim fat from broth. Remove meat from bones, cutting into pieces; discard bones and skin. Add meat to broth in bowl.

2. Mix coriander, turmeric, ginger, red pepper flakes, and vinegar into a paste. Saute onion in margarine in large saucepan over low heat until tender, but not brown, about 10 minutes. Stir spice paste into onion; cook 5 minutes, stirring constantly.

3. Add broth and chicken to saucepan. Heat to boiling; reduce heat and simmer, covered, 10 minutes. Season to taste with salt and pepper and garnish with chopped cilantro.

MARRAKECH SOUP

This light, clear soup, delicately flavored with Moroccan spices, makes a perfect first course for a Middle Eastern dinner. Use your richest home-made chicken stock for the best results.

8 servings (about 1¹/₄ cups each)

2¹/₂ quarts Rich Chicken Stock (see p. 4)
3 ribs celery with leaves, sliced
2 cloves garlic, halved
2 medium onions, sliced
8 sprigs parsley
2 lemons, quartered
¹/₂ teaspoon ground ginger
¹/₂ teaspoon ground turmeric
¹/₂ teaspoon ground cinnamon
Pinch saffron
Salt and pepper, to taste
8 thin lemon slices
Chopped cilantro, as garnish

Per Serving
Calories: 57
% Calories from fat: 19
Protein (g): 6.5
Carbohydrate (g): 3.6
Fat (g): 1.1
Saturated fat (g): 0.3
Cholesterol (mg): 1.3
Sodium (mg): 48
Exchanges
Milk: 0.0
Veg.: 2.0
Fruit: 0.0
Bread: 0.0
Meat: 0.0
Fat: 0.0

1. Heat all ingredients except salt, pepper, lemon slices, and cilantro, to boiling in large saucepan; reduce heat and simmer, covered, 45 minutes. Strain, discarding vegetables.

2. Heat soup to boiling; season to taste with salt and pepper. Ladle soup into bowls. Float lemon slice in each bowl and sprinkle with cilantro.

VIETNAMESE CURRIED COCONUT SOUP

Rice stick noodles, made with rice flour, can be round or flat. They must be softened in water before cooking. Angel hair pasta can be substituted.

6 servings (about 1 cup each)

Vegetable cooking spray
1 tablespoon minced garlic
3-4 tablespoons curry powder
3¹/₂ cups Basic Vegetable Stock (see p. 10)
3 cups reduced-fat coconut milk
2 tablespoons minced gingerroot
²/₃ cup sliced green onions and tops
¹/₃ cup sliced onion
1 tablespoon minced parsley
1 tablespoon grated lime rind
¹/₂-1 teaspoon oriental chili paste
¹/₄ cup lime juice
¹/₃ cup minced cilantro
Salt and white pepper, to taste
¹/₂ package (8-ounce size) rice stick noodles
Cold water
4 quarts boiling water

Per Serving
Calories: 138
% Calories from fat: 27
Protein (g): 3.4
Carbohydrates (g): 22.9
Fat (g): 4.3
Saturated fat (g): 0
Cholesterol (mg): 0
Sodium (mg): 112
Exchanges
Milk: 0.0
Veg.: 1.0
Fruit: 0.0
Bread: 1.0
Meat: 0.0
Fat: 1.0

1. Spray large saucepan with cooking spray; heat over medium heat until hot. Saute garlic 1 minute; stir in curry powder and cook, stirring, 30 seconds. Add Basic Vegetable Stock, coconut milk, gingerroot, all onions, parsley, lime rind, and chili paste; heat to boiling. Reduce heat and simmer, covered, 15 minutes.

2. Stir in lime juice and cilantro; season to taste with salt and white pepper. Simmer about 5 minutes longer.

3. Place noodles in large bowl; pour cold water over to cover. Let stand until noodles are separate and soft, about 5 minutes; drain. Stir noodles into boiling water. Reduce heat and simmer, uncovered, until tender, about 5 minutes; drain.

4. Spoon noodles into soup bowls; ladle soup over noodles.

ITALIAN GARDEN SOUP

A light, colorful soup, showcasing an appealing blend of "Italian" vegetables and herbs.

5-6 servings

1 large onion, chopped
2 large ribs celery, diced
$^1/_4$ cup diced red bell pepper
2 large garlic cloves, minced
1 tablespoon olive oil
$1^1/_2$ quarts Chicken Stock (see p. 2)
1 cup cooked, *or* canned, rinsed, drained cannellini, *or* white kidney beans
3 medium carrots, diced
1 bay leaf
$^3/_4$ teaspoon dried basil leaves
$^1/_2$ teaspoon dried marjoram leaves
$^1/_4$ teaspoon dried oregano leaves
$^1/_4$ teaspoon dried thyme leaves
1 cup diced mixed yellow squash and zucchini
2 medium plum tomatoes, peeled, seeded, diced
Salt and white pepper, to taste
Chopped chives, *or* parsley, as garnish

Per Serving
Calories: 124
% Calories from fat: 19
Protein (g): 8.8
Carbohydrates (g): 17.8
Fat (g): 2.7
Saturated fat (g): 0.4
Cholesterol (mg): 0
Sodium (mg): 366
Exchanges
Milk: 0.0
Veg.: 1.0
Fruit: 0.0
Bread: 1.0
Meat: 0.0
Fat: 0.5

1. Saute onion, celery, bell pepper, and garlic in oil in large saucepan until onion is soft, about 5 minutes. Add Chicken Stock, beans, carrots, and herbs; heat to boiling. Reduce heat and simmer, covered, 20 minutes. Add squash and tomatoes; simmer 5 to 7 minutes until tender. Discard bay leaf; season to taste with salt and white pepper. Serve in bowls; sprinkle with chives.

STRACCIATELLE WITH TINY MEATBALLS

This is a wonderful soup, with many textures and colors. Stracciatelle means "torn rags," which is what the egg whites look like when you stir them into the hot soup.

8 servings (about 1¹/₂ cups each)

1 quart Chicken Stock (see p. 2)
2 cups water
¹/₂ cup pastina, *or* other small soup pasta
1 carrot, thinly sliced
¹/₂ cup chopped celery
¹/₂ cup chopped onion
8 ounces spinach, stems removed, sliced
2 tablespoons chopped parsley
Turkey Meatballs (recipe follows)
Salt and pepper, to taste
2 egg whites, lightly beaten
Shredded Parmesan cheese, as garnish

Per Serving
Calories: 87
% Calories from fat: 28
Protein (g): 7.3
Carbohydrates (g): 8.8
Fat (g): 2.7
Saturated fat (g): 0.7
Cholesterol (mg): 10.8
Sodium (mg): 94
Exchanges
Milk: 0.0
Veg.: 1.0
Fruit: 0.0
Bread: 0.0
Meat: 1.0
Fat: 0.0

1. Combine Chicken Stock, water, pastina, vegetables, and parsley in large saucepan and heat to boiling. Drop Turkey Meatballs into boiling broth. Reduce heat and simmer 15 minutes or until meatballs and pasta are done. Season to taste with salt and pepper.

2. Slowly pour egg whites into soup, stirring gently. Ladle soup into bowls; garnish with Parmesan cheese.

Turkey Meatballs

makes 24 small meatballs

8 ounces ground lean turkey
2 tablespoons flavored bread crumbs
1 teaspoon grated Parmesan cheese
2 teaspoons chopped parsley
¹/₂ small onion, minced
2 tablespoons tomato paste

1. Mix all ingredients; form into small meatballs using about 2 teaspoons mixture for each.

PASTA SOUP WITH GREENS

Both escarole and spinach yield tasty, though very different, results in this soup. Choose the escarole for a more robust taste, spinach for a milder flavor. You can also use escarole and spinach in combination.

4 servings

1 medium leek, white part only, chopped
1 small onion, chopped
1-2 teaspoons olive oil
1 quart Low-Salt Chicken Stock (see p. 3)
1½ teaspoons dried marjoram leaves
¼ cup uncooked tiny soup pasta, such as acini de pepe or stellini
1½ cups chopped escarole, *or* spinach
Salt and pepper, to taste
2-3 tablespoons grated Parmesan cheese, as garnish

Per Serving
Calories: 88
% Calories from fat: **23**
Protein (g): 4.2
Carbohydrate (g): **13**
Fat (g): 2.3
Saturated fat (g): **0.7**
Cholesterol (mg): **5.4**
Sodium (mg): **61**
Exchanges
Milk: 0.0
Veg.: 0.0
Fruit: 0.0
Bread: 1.0
Meat: 0.0
Fat: 0.5

1. Saute leek and onion in oil in large saucepan until lightly browned.

2. Stir in Low-Salt Chicken Stock, marjoram, pasta, and escarole. Heat to boiling; reduce heat and simmer until pasta is tender, about 10 minutes. Thin soup with stock or water if necessary. Season to taste with salt and pepper. Serve sprinkled with Parmesan.

TORTELLINI SOUP

Fresh herbs enhance this soup. Use tri-color tortellini, or different flavors, for a change of pace.

10 servings (1³/₄ cups each)

Vegetable cooking spray
2 cloves garlic, minced
2 medium ribs celery, chopped
1 small onion, chopped
1 medium carrot, chopped
1 quart reduced-sodium fat-free chicken broth
1 quart water
2 packages (10 ounces each) dried cheese tortellini
2 tablespoons chopped parsley
10 fresh basil leaves, shredded
1 tablespoon chopped fresh, *or* 1 teaspoon dried, oregano leaves
1 teaspoon Spike
Salt and pepper, to taste
Shredded Parmesan cheese, as garnish

Per Serving
Calories: 109
% Calories from fat: 19
Protein (g): 5.3
Carbohydrates (g): 16.9
Fat (g): 2.4
Saturated fat (g): 2
Cholesterol (mg): 10
Sodium (mg): 136
Exchanges
Milk: 0.0
Veg.: 1.0
Fruit: 0.0
Bread: 1.0
Meat: 0.0
Fat: 0.5

1. Spray large saucepan with cooking spray; heat over medium heat until hot. Saute garlic, celery, onion, and carrot 10 minutes. Stir in chicken broth and water; heat to boiling. Stir in tortellini; reduce heat and simmer 20 minutes. Stir in parsley, basil, oregano, and Spike. Season to taste with salt and pepper. Serve in bowls; garnish with Parmesan cheese.

THREE

Chowders

PARSLEY CHOWDER

Use Italian parsley for the strongest herb flavor in this unusual chowder.

6 servings (about 3/4 cup each)

1 quart Rich Chicken Stock (see p. 4)
2 cups packed parsley sprigs, stems removed (about 4 ounces)
1/2 cup chopped onion
1/2 cup chopped celery
1 tablespoon margarine
1/4 cup all-purpose flour
2 teaspoons sugar
2 cups diced peeled potatoes
1 cup fat-free milk
2 tablespoons dry sherry, optional
1/4 cup finely chopped parsley
  Salt and pepper, to taste

Per Serving
Calories: 170
% Calories from fat: 15
Protein (g): 7.7
Carbohydrate (g): 27.4
Fat (g): 2.8
Saturated fat (g): 0.6
Cholesterol (mg): 1.4
Sodium (mg): 92
Exchanges
Milk: 0.0
Veg.: 0.0
Fruit: 0.0
Bread: 2.0
Meat: 0.0
Fat: 0.5

1. Heat Rich Chicken Stock and 2 cups parsley to boiling in large saucepan; reduce heat and simmer, covered, 30 minutes. Strain; reserve broth.

2. Saute onion and celery in margarine in large saucepan until tender, about 8 minutes. Sprinkle with flour and sugar and cook 1 minute. Stir in reserved broth and heat to boiling, stirring until thickened. Add potatoes, reduce heat and simmer, covered, until potatoes are tender, about 20 minutes. Stir in milk and sherry and simmer 2 to 3 minutes. Stir in chopped parsley and season to taste with salt and pepper.

Variation:
Pesto Chowder—Make recipe as above, substituting basil for the parsley and olive oil for the margarine; omit celery and sherry. Sprinkle each bowl of soup with freshly grated Parmesan cheese and toasted pine nuts.

LEEK CHOWDER WITH HAM

This thick, creamy chowder is brimming with leeks and ham. Horseradish mustard and Worcestershire sauce team up to give the dish a flavor that's especially pleasing and memorable.

4 servings

8 ounces lean ham, fat trimmed, cut into 1/2-inch cubes

3 leeks, white parts only, sliced

1 teaspoon olive oil

1 can (14^1/$_2$ ounces) fat-free chicken broth

2 large Idaho potatoes (about 1 pound), peeled, cut into ^{1}/$_4$-inch cubes

1 bay leaf

1 teaspoon horseradish mustard

1 teaspoon Worcestershire sauce

^{1}/$_2$ cup fat-free milk

Salt and white pepper, to taste

Per Serving
Calories: 281
% Calories from fat: 16
Protein (g): 21.2
Carbohydrate (g): 37.7
Fat (g): 5
Saturated fat (g): 1.5
Cholesterol (mg): 32.3
Sodium (mg): 881
Exchanges
Milk: 0.0
Veg.: 0.0
Fruit: 0.0
Bread: 2.5
Meat: 2.0
Fat: 0.0

1. Cook ham and leeks in oil in large saucepan over medium heat until leeks are translucent, 6 to 8 minutes. Remove from saucepan and reserve.

2. Add broth, potatoes, and bay leaf to saucepan; heat to boiling. Reduce heat and simmer, covered, until potatoes are tender, about 15 minutes; discard bay leaf. Process potatoes and broth in food processor or blender until smooth; return to saucepan.

3. Stir in mustard, Worcestershire sauce, milk, and reserved ham and leeks. Cook over medium heat until hot, about 5 minutes; season to taste with salt and white pepper.

BLACK MAGIC GARLIC CHOWDER

Garlic lovers take note: This is a colorful chowder with plenty of palate-appealing garlic flavor, which has been tamed to mild sweetness by light sauteing. The chowder is elegant enough for a dinner party and easy enough for everyday fare.

4 servings

1 can (15 ounces) black beans, rinsed, drained, divided

1 can (14 ounces) reduced-sodium vegetable broth, divided

1 garlic bulb, cloves peeled and thinly sliced

2 small serrano chilies, seeded, minced

2 teaspoons olive oil

16 ounces plum tomatoes, coarsely chopped

Salt and pepper, to taste

1¹/2 cups Chili Croutons (¹/2 recipe) (see p. 785)

¹/2 cup chopped flat-leaf parsley

¹/2 cup fat-free sour cream

Per Serving
Calories: 195
% Calories from fat: **15**
Protein (g): 9.2
Carbohydrate (g): 39.9
Fat (g): 3.9
Saturated fat (g): 0.4
Cholesterol (mg): 0
Sodium (mg): 503
Exchanges
Milk: 0.0
Veg.: 1.0
Fruit: 0.0
Bread: 2.0
Meat: 0.0
Fat: 0.5

1. Process ³/4 cup beans and ³/4 cup broth in food processor or blender until smooth.

2. Saute garlic and serrano chilies in oil in large saucepan until garlic is golden but not browned. Stir in pureed beans and broth, remaining beans, and remaining broth; heat to boiling. Reduce heat and simmer, covered, 10 minutes. Stir in tomatoes; simmer 5 minutes. Season to taste with salt and pepper.

3. Serve chowder in bowls; top each with Chili Croutons, parsley, and a dollop of sour cream.

FLORIDA AVOCADO AND TOMATO CHOWDER

In this easy recipe, corn, tomatoes, avocado, and smoked turkey create a kaleidoscope of fresh colors and flavors. Bacon, lime, and thyme complete the sensory experience.

4 servings

3 large potatoes, peeled, cut into ¹/₂-inch cubes

1 can (14 ounces) reduced-sodium fat-free chicken broth

1 teaspoon dried thyme leaves

¹/₂ pound smoked turkey breast, cut into ¹/₂-inch cubes

1 cup frozen whole-kernel corn

4 plum tomatoes, coarsely chopped

1 avocado, peeled, cut into ¹/₂-inch cubes

Juice of 1 lime

3 slices bacon, cooked, crumbled

Salt and pepper, to taste

Per Serving
Calories: 333
% Calories from fat: 26
Protein (g): 21
Carbohydrates (g): 44.7
Fat (g): 10.2
Saturated fat (g): 2.4
Cholesterol (mg): 51.1
Sodium (mg): 765
Exchanges
Milk: 0.0
Veg.: 2.0
Fruit: 0.0
Bread: 2.0
Meat: 2.0
Fat: 1.5

1. Heat potatoes, broth, and thyme to boiling in medium saucepan; reduce heat and simmer, covered, until potatoes are tender, about 15 minutes. Using slotted spoon, transfer half the potatoes to a medium bowl.

2. Process remaining broth mixture in food processor or blender until smooth; return to saucepan. Add turkey, corn, and reserved potatoes. Heat to boiling; reduce heat and simmer 5 minutes. Stir in tomatoes, avocado, lime juice, and bacon. Season to taste with salt and pepper.

FRESH TOMATO-ZUCCHINI CHOWDER

Savor summer's bounty in this lively chowder of basil, tomatoes, and zucchini. Bacon adds a delightful smoky accent.

4 servings

2	slices turkey bacon
1	cup chopped onion
1	can (14$^1/_2$ ounces) vegetable broth
1	medium potato, cut into $^3/_4$-inch cubes
1	cup cubed zucchini ($^1/_2$-inch)
1$^1/_4$	cups frozen whole-kernel corn
16	ounces plum tomatoes, sliced
$^1/_4$	teaspoon ground cayenne pepper
$^1/_4$	cup finely chopped basil leaves
	Salt, to taste

Per Serving
Calories: 138
% Calories from fat: 12
Protein (g): 4.9
Carbohydrate (g): 28.8
Fat (g): 2
Saturated fat (g): 0.4
Cholesterol (mg): 5
Sodium (mg): 463
Exchanges
Milk: 0.0
Veg.: 1.0
Fruit: 0.0
Bread: 1.5
Meat: 0.0
Fat: 0.0

1. Cook bacon in large saucepan until crisp; drain and crumble. Reserve bacon. Drain fat from saucepan; add onion and cook until translucent, 3 to 4 minutes.

2. Add remaining ingredients, except basil and salt; heat to boiling. Reduce heat and simmer, covered, until potatoes are tender, about 15 minutes. Stir in fresh basil; season to taste with salt.

3. Serve in bowls; sprinkle with crumbled bacon.

Variation:
Green Garden Chowder—Make chowder as above, adding 1$^1/_2$ cups each small broccoli florets, cut green beans, and cubed zucchini. Stir in 1 cup sliced spinach or kale during last 3 to 4 minutes cooking time. Sprinkle each bowl with crumbled bacon and grated Parmesan cheese.

SHIITAKE-PORTOBELLO CHOWDER

Celebrate a rich combination of distinctive mushrooms! The chowder features a rich broth that combines the flavors of Gruyère cheese and Marsala wine.

4 servings

4 shallots, thinly sliced

2 teaspoons margarine, divided

2 large potatoes, cut into 1/4-inch cubes

3 cups reduced-sodium vegetable broth

4 ounces shiitake mushroom caps

2 cups cubed portobello mushrooms

1/4 cup (1 ounce) shredded Gruyère, *or* Swiss, cheese

2 tablespoons Marsala wine

Salt and white pepper, to taste

Per Serving
Calories: 162
% Calories from fat: 26
Protein (g): 5.6
Carbohydrates (g): 24.7
Fat (g): 5
Saturated fat (g): 1.8
Cholesterol (mg): 7.8
Sodium (mg): 114
Exchanges
Milk: 0.0
Veg.: 2.0
Fruit: 0.0
Bread: 1.0
Meat: 0.0
Fat: 1.0

1. Saute shallots in 1 teaspoon margarine in large saucepan until tender. Add potatoes and broth. Heat to boiling; reduce heat and simmer, covered, until potatoes are tender, about 15 minutes. Process mixture in blender or food processor until smooth; return to saucepan.

2. Saute mushrooms in remaining 1 teaspoon margarine in large skillet until wilted and golden brown, about 8 minutes; stir into potato mixture. Heat to boiling; remove from heat and add cheese and wine, stirring until cheese is melted. Season to taste with salt and white pepper.

FRENCH VEGETABLE CHOWDER WITH PISTOU

A complete meal in itself, this chowder has a lively French twist: pistou. Pistou is the French version of Italy's pesto. Bon appétit!

4 servings

1 can (15 ounces) Great Northern, *or* navy, beans, rinsed, drained
1 can (14¹/₂ ounces) reduced-sodium vegetable broth, divided
1 large potato, cut into ¹/₂-inch cubes
2 carrots, thinly sliced
1 cup cut wax beans
1 cup small cauliflower florets
2 zucchini, cut into ¹/₂-inch cubes
1 cup cooked elbow macaroni
3 plum tomatoes, coarsely chopped
4 scallions, sliced
Pistou (recipe follows)
Salt and pepper, to taste

Per Serving
Calories: 254
% Calories from fat: 17
Protein (g): 12
Carbohydrate (g): 46.7
Fat (g): 5.2
Saturated fat (g): 1.8
Cholesterol (mg): 5.3
Sodium (mg): 581
Exchanges
Milk: 0.0
Veg.: 3.0
Fruit: 0.0
Bread: 2.0
Meat: 0.0
Fat: 1.0

1. Process beans and 1 cup broth in blender or food processor until smooth; reserve. Combine potato, carrots, wax beans, cauliflower, zucchini, and remaining broth in large saucepan; heat to boiling. Reduce heat and simmer, covered, until vegetables are tender, about 15 minutes.

2. Stir in macaroni, tomatoes, scallions, and reserved beans; simmer, covered, until hot, about 5 minutes. Stir in Pistou; season to taste with salt and pepper.

Pistou

makes about ²/₃ cup

1 tablespoon minced garlic
2 teaspoons olive oil
¹/₂ cup snipped fresh basil
¹/₄ cup crumbled blue cheese

1. Combine all ingredients in bowl; mash with fork.

POTATO CHOWDER

A basic chowder that is versatile—substitute any desired vegetables, such as carrots, zucchini, green beans, or corn, for part of the potatoes for a delectable vegetable chowder.

6 servings (about 1 cup each)

1 cup chopped onion
¹/₄ cup thinly sliced celery
2 tablespoons margarine
3 tablespoons flour
2 cups reduced-sodium chicken broth
3¹/₂ cups cubed, peeled Idaho potatoes
¹/₄-¹/₂ teaspoon celery seeds
2 cups fat-free milk
Salt and pepper, to taste

Per Serving
Calories: 212
% Calories from fat: 17
Protein (g): 7.5
Carbohydrates (g): 37.1
Fat (g): 4.2
Saturated fat (g): 0.9
Cholesterol (mg): 1.3
Sodium (mg): 210
Exchanges
Milk: 0.0
Veg.: 1.0
Fruit: 0.0
Bread: 2.0
Meat: 0.0
Fat: 1.0

1. Saute onion and celery in margarine in large saucepan until tender, 5 to 8 minutes. Stir in flour; cook over medium-low heat, stirring constantly, 1 minute.

2. Add broth, potatoes, and celery seeds to saucepan; heat to boiling. Reduce heat and simmer, covered, until potatoes are tender, 10 to 15 minutes. Stir in milk; cook over medium heat until hot, 2 to 3 minutes. Season to taste with salt and pepper.

Variations:
Easy Vichyssoise—Make recipe as above, substituting chopped leek for half the onion and omitting celery and celery seeds. Cool; process soup in food processor or blender until smooth. Refrigerate until chilled. Serve in bowls; sprinkle with minced fresh chives.

Potato Chowder au Gratin—Make soup as above. Process half the chowder in food processor or blender until almost smooth; return to saucepan and heat 2 to 3 minutes. Pour into 6 oven-proof bowls; top each with 2 tablespoons shredded Cheddar cheese and sprinkle lightly with ground nutmeg. Bake at 500 degrees until cheese is melted, about 5 minutes.

POTATO CURRY CHOWDER

The curry flavor in this chowder is subtle; increase the amount if you prefer.

4 servings (about 1³/₄ cups each)

Vegetable cooking spray *or* olive oil
1 cup chopped green onions and tops
3 cloves garlic, minced
3 large red potatoes, peeled, thinly sliced
1 quart Chicken Stock (see p. 2)
1 can (12 ounces) evaporated fat-free milk
1 cup fat-free milk
³/₄ teaspoon curry powder
¹/₂ teaspoon ground cumin
Salt and pepper, to taste

Per Serving
Calories: 183
% Calories from fat: 6
Protein (g): 12.2
Carbohydrate (g): 33.1
Fat (g): 1.2
Saturated fat (g): 0.3
Cholesterol (mg): 8
Sodium (mg): 186
Exchanges
Milk: 1.0
Veg.: 0.0
Fruit: 0.0
Bread: 1.5
Meat: 0.0
Fat: 0.0

1. Spray large saucepan with cooking spray; heat over medium heat until hot. Saute green onions and garlic over medium-low heat, 4 minutes. Add potatoes and Chicken Stock; heat to boiling. Reduce heat and simmer, covered, until potatoes are tender, about 15 minutes.

2. Stir in remaining ingredients, except salt and pepper, and heat to boiling. Reduce heat and simmer, covered, 10 minutes, stirring occasionally. Season to taste with salt and pepper.

IDAHO CHOWDER WITH CHEESE

You don't have to be a potato farmer to love this delicious concoction! Rosemary gives it extra flavor.

8 servings (about 1¹/₃ cups each)

Vegetable cooking spray
4 cups chopped onions
1 cup chopped celery
2 tablespoons minced garlic
¹/₂ teaspoon dried rosemary leaves
6 large Idaho potatoes, peeled, cubed (¹/₂-inch)
2 cups Chicken Stock (see p. 2)
4 cups fat-free milk
¹/₄ cup all-purpose flour
¹/₈ teaspoon ground nutmeg
2 teaspoons very-low-sodium Worcestershire sauce
1 cup (4 ounces) shredded Swiss cheese
Salt and white pepper, to taste

Per Serving
Calories: 241
% Calories from fat: 17
Protein (g): 11.9
Carbohydrate (g): 38
Fat (g): 4.7
Saturated fat (g): 2.8
Cholesterol (mg): 18.1
Sodium (mg): 111
Exchanges
Milk: 0.0
Veg.: 1.0
Fruit: 0.0
Bread: 2.0
Meat: 0.5
Fat: 1.0

1. Spray large saucepan with cooking spray; heat over medium heat until hot. Add onions, celery, garlic, and rosemary and cook over low heat, covered, until onions are golden brown, about 20 minutes.

2. Add potatoes and Chicken Stock. Heat to boiling; reduce heat and simmer, covered, until potatoes are tender, about 20 minutes. Heat to boiling; add combined milk, flour, nutmeg, and Worcestershire sauce, stirring until thickened, 1 to 2 minutes. Remove chowder from heat; add cheese, stirring until melted; season to taste with salt and white pepper.

Variation:
Three-Cheese and Potato Chowder—Make recipe as above, substituting ¹/₂ cup each reduced-fat shredded mozzarella and Cheddar cheese and 2 to 4 tablespoons crumbled blue cheese for the Swiss cheese. Sprinkle each bowl with chopped chives.

SMOKY POTATO CHOWDER

A packaged potato mix adds preparation convenience to this easy chowder.

4 servings

1	medium onion, coarsely chopped
1-2	tablespoons vegetable oil
1	package (5¹/₂ ounces) au gratin potatoes
2¹/₂	cups water
2¹/₄	cups fat-free milk, divided
2-4	ounces reduced-fat smoked sausage
¹/₄	teaspoon dried thyme leaves
	Salt and pepper, to taste
	Chopped dill weed, *or* parsley, as garnish

Per Serving
Calories: 248
% Calories from fat: **23**
Protein (g): 10.1
Carbohydrate (g): 38.5
Fat (g): 6.4
Saturated fat (g): 0.8
Cholesterol (mg): 9.1
Sodium (mg): 928
Exchanges
Milk: 0.5
Veg.: 0.0
Fruit: 0.0
Bread: 2.0
Meat: 0.0
Fat: 1.5

1. Saute onion in oil in large saucepan until tender, about 5 minutes. Stir in potatoes and sprinkle with sauce mix. Stir in water and ³/₄ cup milk; heat to boiling. Reduce heat and simmer, covered, 30 minutes or until potatoes are tender, stirring occasionally.

2. Add sausage, remaining 1¹/₂ cups milk, and thyme; simmer 5 minutes. Season to taste with salt and pepper. Serve in bowls; sprinkle with dill weed.

POTATO, CORN, AND CANADIAN BACON CHOWDER

The Canadian bacon can be sauteed in 1 teaspoon margarine or oil until crisp and "frizzled," then sprinkled on the chowder as a garnish.

5-6 servings

1 large onion, chopped
1 garlic clove, minced
2 teaspoons olive oil
3¹/₂ cups fat-free chicken broth, divided
3¹/₂ cups cubed, peeled red potatoes (¹/₂-inch)
1 large bay leaf
³/₄ teaspoon dried thyme leaves
¹/₄ teaspoon dry mustard
2¹/₂ cups 1% low-fat milk
2¹/₂ cups frozen whole-kernel corn
6 ounces Canadian bacon, julienned
Salt and white pepper, to taste

Per Serving
Calories: 374
% Calories from fat: 14
Protein (g): 21
Carbohydrate (g): 61.3
Fat (g): 6.1
Saturated fat (g): 2
Cholesterol (mg): 21.1
Sodium (mg): 624
Exchanges
Milk: 0.0
Veg.: 0.0
Fruit: 0.0
Bread: 4.0
Meat: 1.0
Fat: 0.5

1. Saute onion and garlic in oil in large saucepan until tender, about 5 minutes. Add broth, potatoes, bay leaf, thyme, and mustard; heat to boiling. Reduce heat and simmer, covered, until potatoes are tender, about 10 minutes.

2. Add milk and corn; heat to boiling. Reduce heat and simmer, covered, 5 minutes or until corn is cooked. Discard bay leaf.

3. Process half the vegetables and liquid in food processor or blender until smooth; return to saucepan. Stir in Canadian bacon and simmer, covered, 5 minutes. Season to taste with salt and white pepper.

Variation:

Colcannon Chowder—Make recipe as above, sauteing 2 cups thinly sliced cabbage with the onion and garlic, reducing milk to 2 cups, and omitting corn. Do not puree the mixture. Combine ¹/₂ cup reduced-fat sour cream and 1 tablespoon flour; stir into the chowder with the Canadian bacon.

ROASTED CORN AND POTATO CHOWDER

Perfect for summer's end, when evenings become cool.

8 servings (about 1½ cups each)

6 ears corn, in the husks
Olive oil cooking spray
2 pounds new red potatoes, unpeeled, cut into halves
1 medium red bell pepper, cut into ¾-inch pieces
1 medium onion, cut into ¾-inch pieces
3 cloves garlic, peeled
2 teaspoons dried thyme leaves
2 teaspoons dried parsley leaves
1½ quarts Canned Vegetable Stock (see p. 11), divided
⅔ cup fat-free half-and-half
Salt and pepper, to taste

Per Serving
Calories: 250
% Calories from fat: 6
Protein (g): 6.2
Carbohydrates (g): 51.1
Fat (g): 1.6
Saturated fat (g): 0.2
Cholesterol (mg): 0
Sodium (mg): 78
Exchanges
Milk: 0.0
Veg.: 1.0
Fruit: 0.0
Bread: 3.0
Meat: 0.0
Fat: 0.0

1. Soak corn in cold water to cover, 30 minutes.

2. Spray 2 aluminum-foil-lined jelly roll pans with cooking spray. Arrange corn on 1 pan. Arrange remaining vegetables on second pan; spray generously with cooking spray and sprinkle with herbs.

3. Roast corn and vegetables at 425 degrees until browned and tender, about 40 minutes, removing garlic when soft, about 20 minutes. Let vegetables stand until cool enough to handle. Remove and discard corn husks. Cut kernels off cobs.

4. Process vegetables and 2 to 3 cups Canned Vegetable Stock in food processor or blender until smooth. Heat vegetable mixture and remaining stock to boiling in large saucepan; reduce heat to medium-low. Stir in half-and-half and cook 3 to 4 minutes, until hot. Season to taste with salt and pepper.

CHEESE AND CORN CHOWDER

A satisfying whole-meal chowder, rich with sausage, cheese, and the flavor of corn. Add a tossed green salad to complete your supper.

6 servings (about 1½ cups each)

Vegetable cooking spray
8 ounces reduced-fat smoked sausage, sliced
1 medium onion, chopped
1 medium red bell pepper, chopped
1 medium potato, chopped
1 clove garlic, minced
3 tablespoons flour
3 cups fat-free milk
2-3 teaspoons chicken bouillon crystals
16 ounces frozen whole-kernel corn
1 can (16 ounces) cream-style corn
½ ¾ cup (2-3 ounces) shredded Cheddar cheese
1½ cups chopped tomatoes
Salt and pepper, to taste
1½ cups Chili Croutons (½ recipe) (see p. 785)

Per Serving
Calories: 326
% Calories from fat: 16
Protein (g): 18
Carbohydrate (g): 54.7
Fat (g): 6.2
Saturated fat (g): 2.8
Cholesterol (mg): 29.8
Sodium (mg): 786
Exchanges
Milk: 0.0
Veg.: 2.0
Fruit: 0.0
Bread: 3.0
Meat: 1.0
Fat: 0.0

1. Spray large saucepan with cooking spray; heat over medium heat until hot. Stir in sausage, onion, bell pepper, potato, and garlic and cook until sausage is lightly browned, about 5 minutes; sprinkle with flour and cook 1 to 2 minutes longer.

2. Stir in milk, bouillon crystals, and corn. Heat to boiling; reduce heat and simmer, covered, until tender, about 10 minutes. Add cheese and tomatoes, stirring until cheese is melted. Season to taste with salt and pepper. Serve in bowls; sprinkle with Chili Croutons.

BARLEY-VEGETABLE CHOWDER

A perfect dish for crisp autumn days; substitute any desired vegetables.

4 servings (about 1³/₄ cups each)

2 cans (14¹/₂ ounces each) reduced-sodium vegetable broth, divided
²/₃ cup barley
Vegetable cooking spray
2 small onions, chopped
1 leek, white part only, sliced
2 cloves garlic, minced
1 cup fresh, *or* frozen, lima beans
1 cup fresh, *or* frozen, whole-kernel corn
1 cup finely chopped cabbage
2 medium carrots, sliced
1 teaspoon dried savory leaves
¹/₂ teaspoon dried thyme leaves
1 bay leaf
2 tablespoons flour
¹/₂ cup fat-free milk
Salt and pepper, to taste

Per Serving
Calories: 322
% Calories from fat: 6
Protein (g): 12.4
Carbohydrates (g): 63.9
Fat (g): 2.3
Saturated fat (g): 1.1
Cholesterol (mg): 0
Sodium (mg): 385
Exchanges
Milk: 0.0
Veg.: 2.0
Fruit: 0.0
Bread: 3.5
Meat: 0.5
Fat: 0.0

1. Heat ¹/₂ can broth to boiling in small saucepan; stir in barley and let stand 15 to 30 minutes.

2. Spray large saucepan with cooking spray; heat over medium heat until hot. Saute onions, leek, and garlic until tender, about 5 minutes. Add remaining vegetables and herbs; saute 2 to 3 minutes. Add remaining 1¹/₂ cans broth and barley mixture; heat to boiling. Reduce heat and simmer, covered, until barley is tender, about 20 minutes.

3. Heat chowder to boiling. Mix flour and milk and stir into chowder. Boil, stirring constantly, until thickened. Discard bay leaf; season to taste with salt and pepper.

GNOCCHI CHOWDER WITH SMOKED TURKEY

Gnocchi, Italian for "dumplings," are usually topped with butter and Parmesan cheese and served as a side dish. Here, they're the main attraction in a chowder that's loaded with broccoli, cauliflower, and smoked deli turkey as well. Magnifico!

6 servings

1 cup reduced-sodium fat-free chicken broth

1 can (15 ounces) reduced-sodium crushed tomatoes, undrained

10 ounces smoked deli turkey, cut into ¹/₂-inch cubes

12 ounces frozen gnocchi

1 teaspoon poultry seasoning

2 cups broccoli florets

2 cups cauliflower florets

¹/₂ cup chopped fresh basil leaves

¹/₄ cup (1 ounce) shredded provolone cheese

Salt and pepper, to taste

Per Serving
Calories: 221
% Calories from fat: 17
Protein (g): 16.8
Carbohydrates (g): 30
Fat (g): 4.2
Saturated fat (g): 2.1
Cholesterol (mg): 24.3
Sodium (mg): 745
Exchanges
Milk: 0.0
Veg.: 1.0
Fruit: 0.0
Bread: 1.5
Meat: 2.0
Fat: 0.0

1. Combine chicken broth, tomatoes and liquid, turkey, gnocchi, and poultry seasoning in large saucepan. Heat to boiling; reduce heat and simmer, covered, 5 minutes. Stir in broccoli and cauliflower; simmer until tender, about 10 minutes longer. Add basil and cheese, stirring until cheese is melted. Season to taste with salt and pepper.

BLACK-EYED PEA AND CORN CHOWDER

Roasted red peppers and bacon enliven this fuss-free, ready-in-a-flash chowder.

4 servings

1 cup fat-free chicken broth
1 can (15 ounces) black-eyed peas, rinsed, drained
1 can (14 ounces) low-sodium cream-style corn
1 cup chopped onion
2 teaspoons minced garlic
1 teaspoon dried savory leaves
1 cup roasted red peppers, coarsely chopped
  Salt and pepper, to taste
4 slices turkey bacon, cooked, drained, crumbled

Per Serving
Calories: 153
% Calories from fat: 14
Protein (g): 11.3
Carbohydrate (g): 25.5
Fat (g): 2.7
Saturated fat (g): 0.6
Cholesterol (mg): 10
Sodium (mg): 576
Exchanges
Milk: 0.0
Veg.: 1.0
Fruit: 0.0
Bread: 1.0
Meat: 1.0
Fat: 1.0

1. Heat all ingredients, except roasted peppers, salt, pepper, and bacon, to boiling in large saucepan; reduce heat and simmer 10 minutes. Stir in roasted peppers and simmer 3 to 4 minutes longer; season to taste with salt and pepper.

2. Serve in bowls; sprinkle with bacon.

Variation:

Red Beans 'n Greens Chowder—Make recipe as above, substituting red beans for the black-eyed peas, 1¹/₂ cups frozen cut okra for the cream-style corn, and 1 cup sliced turnip greens or kale for the roasted red peppers.

PIGEON PEA CHOWDER WITH SPANISH ONIONS

This hearty chowder reflects the Spanish colonial culinary tradition that makes Cuban and Puerto Rican cooking delightfully distinctive.

4 servings

1 large Spanish onion, coarsely chopped
4 shallots, thinly sliced
2 teaspoons peanut oil
2 cups shredded zucchini
6 tomatillos, husks removed, diced
1 large potato, unpeeled, cubed
1 can (15 ounces) green pigeon peas, rinsed and drained
1 cup reduced-sodium vegetable broth
1/4 cup sofrito sauce
Salt and pepper, to taste

Per Serving
Calories: 262
% Calories from fat: 22
Protein (g): 10.7
Carbohydrate (g): 42.1
Fat (g): 6.7
Saturated fat (g): 1.7
Cholesterol (mg): 5
Sodium (mg): 350
Exchanges
Milk: 0.0
Veg.: 0.0
Fruit: 0.0
Bread: 3.0
Meat: 0.0
Fat: 1.0

1. Saute onion and shallots in oil in large saucepan until translucent, about 5 minutes. Add zucchini and saute 2 to 3 minutes longer.

2. Add remaining ingredients, except sofrito sauce, salt, and pepper; heat to boiling. Reduce heat and simmer, covered, until potatoes are tender, about 15 minutes. Stir in sofrito sauce; season to taste with salt and pepper.

CRANBERRY BEAN CHOWDER WITH ZUCCHINI

A smidgen of smoked Lebanon bologna adds a unique flavor to this heart-warming vegetable-bean chowder.

4 servings

1 medium zucchini, halved lengthwise, sliced

1 teaspoon olive oil

1¹/₂ cups fat-free beef broth

1 can (16 ounces) red cranberry beans, rinsed, drained

1 potato, cut into ¹/₂-inch cubes

1 cup flat green beans, broken into 1-inch pieces

¹/₄ teaspoon freshly ground white pepper

4 scallions, sliced

1 slice (1 ounce) smoked Lebanon beef bologna, finely chopped

Salt, to taste

Per Serving
Calories: 172
% Calories from fat: **13**
Protein (g): 11.1
Carbohydrate (g): 27.8
Fat (g): 2.5
Saturated fat (g): 0.7
Cholesterol (mg): **5**
Sodium (mg): **425**
Exchanges
Milk: 0.0
Veg.: 0.0
Fruit: 0.0
Bread: 1.5
Meat: 1.0
Fat: 0.0

1. Saute zucchini in oil in large saucepan until tender, 5 to 8 minutes. Add remaining ingredients, except scallions, bologna, and salt; heat to boiling. Reduce heat and simmer, covered, 10 minutes.

2. Stir in scallions and bologna; simmer, covered, 5 minutes. Season to taste with salt.

CARAMELIZED ONION AND BEAN CHOWDER

The onions are cooked very slowly until golden brown, giving a sweet flavor to the brew. Sprinkle each bowl with fresh grated Parmesan cheese for an extra flavor accent.

8 servings (about 1¹/₃ cups each)

1¹/₂   pounds onions, thinly sliced
2   tablespoons margarine
2   teaspoons sugar
1   quart reduced-sodium fat-free chicken broth
1   quart reduced-sodium fat-free beef broth
2   medium potatoes, peeled, cubed
³/₄   teaspoon dried thyme leaves
1   can (15¹/₂ ounces) Great Northern beans, rinsed, drained
¹/₄-¹/₂   cup dry sherry, optional
Salt and pepper, to taste
1¹/₂   cups Garlic Croutons (¹/₂ recipe) (see p. 785)

Per Serving
Calories: 159
% Calories from fat: **17**
Protein (g): 10.1
Carbohydrate (g): 25
Fat (g): 3.2
Saturated fat (g): 0.6
Cholesterol (mg): 0
Sodium (mg): 443
Exchanges
Milk: 0.0
Veg.: 2.0
Fruit: 0.0
Bread: 1.0
Meat: 0.0
Fat: 0.5

1. Saute onions in margarine in large saucepan over low heat until tender, about 15 minutes. Stir in sugar; cook until golden brown, about 20 minutes, stirring frequently.

2. Stir in chicken and beef broth, potatoes, and thyme; heat to boiling. Reduce heat and simmer, covered, until potatoes are tender, about 20 minutes. Stir in beans; simmer 5 minutes. Stir in sherry; season to taste with salt and pepper. Ladle chowder into bowls; sprinkle with Garlic Croutons.

NAVY BEAN AND BACON CHOWDER

Use 3 cans (15 1/2 ounces each) navy or Great Northern beans to speed preparation of this flavor-packed dish.

8 servings (about 1 cup each)

1¹/₂	cups dried navy beans, rinsed
2	medium carrots, chopped
1	medium onion, chopped
1	rib celery, chopped
2	large cloves garlic, minced
¹/₂	teaspoon dried oregano leaves
¹/₂	teaspoon dried basil leaves
¹/₂	teaspoon dried rosemary leaves
1¹/₂	quarts Chicken Stock (see p. 2)
1	cup fat-free half-and-half, *or* fat-free milk
	Salt and pepper, to taste
8	slices bacon, cooked, crumbled

Per Serving
Calories: 216
% Calories from fat: 18
Protein (g): 13.2
Carbohydrate (g): 31.4
Fat (g): 4.2
Saturated fat (g): 1.3
Cholesterol (mg): 7.9
Sodium (mg): 153
Exchanges
Milk: 0.0
Veg.: 0.0
Fruit: 0.0
Bread: 2.0
Meat: 1.0
Fat: 0.5

1. Cover beans with 2 inches cold water in large saucepan; heat to boiling and boil, uncovered, 2 minutes. Remove from heat and let stand, covered, 1 hour; drain.

2. Combine beans and remaining ingredients except half-and-half, salt, pepper, and bacon in large saucepan. Heat to boiling; reduce heat and simmer, covered, until beans are tender, 45 to 60 minutes.

3. Process about 2 cups of chowder mixture in food processor or blender until smooth; return to saucepan. Add half-and-half and heat to simmering; season to taste with salt and pepper. Serve in bowls; sprinkle with bacon.

Variations:
Mixed Bean Chowder—Make Steps 1 and 2 as above, substituting ¹/₂ cup each dried Great Northern, pinto, and kidney beans for the navy beans. Do not puree mixture. Heat chowder to boiling; stir in combined ¹/₂ cup Chicken Stock or water and ¹/₄ cup all-purpose flour. Boil, stirring, until thickened, 1 to 2 minutes.

EASY, CHEESY CHICKEN CORN CHOWDER

A flavorful way to have supper on the table in less than 30 minutes!

4 servings

Vegetable cooking spray

1/2 cup finely chopped onion

1 cup cooked, cubed, boneless chicken, skin removed

1 can (17 ounces) plus 1/2 can creamed corn

3 cups fat-free milk

1 1/2 cups (6 ounces) shredded reduced-fat Cheddar cheese

Salt and pepper, to taste

Per Serving
Calories: 279
% Calories from fat: 14
Protein (g): 18.2
Carbohydrates (g): 8.9
Fat (g): 6.3
Saturated fat (g): 2.9
Cholesterol (mg): 60.8
Sodium (mg): 673
Exchanges
Milk: 0.9
Veg.: 0.2
Fruit: 0.0
Bread: 1.4
Meat: 3.0
Fat: 0.0

1. Spray large saucepan with cooking spray; heat over medium heat until hot. Saute onion until tender, about 5 minutes; add chicken, creamed corn and milk and heat to boiling. Reduce heat and simmer, covered, 5 minutes. Reduce heat to low and gradually add cheese, stirring until melted. Do not boil. Season to taste with salt and pepper.

Variation:
Tex-Mex Chicken Chowder—Make recipe as above, substituting 1 cup cubed zucchini for the 1/2 can creamed corn, and reduced-fat pepper-Jack cheese for the Cheddar cheese. Serve with baked tortilla chips.

CHICKEN CORN CHOWDER

This hearty chowder is thickened in a healthful way—a portion of the ingredients are processed in a food processor until finely chopped, then added to the rest of the chowder.

8 servings (about 1¹/₄ cups each)

Vegetable cooking spray
1¹/₂ quarts frozen whole kernel corn, thawed
¹/₂ cup chopped onion
¹/₂ cup chopped green bell pepper
1-2 tablespoons water
1¹/₂ pounds boneless skinless chicken breast, cut into ¹/₂-inch pieces
1 cup chopped carrots
2 large tomatoes, chopped
1 small jalapeno chili, finely chopped
1 clove garlic, minced
¹/₂ teaspoon dried savory leaves
¹/₂ teaspoon dried thyme leaves
1¹/₂ quarts Chicken Stock (see p. 2)
2-2¹/₂ cups fat-free half-and-half, *or* fat-free milk
Salt and pepper, to taste

Per Serving
Calories: 273
% Calories from fat: 11
Protein (g): 26.1
Carbohydrate (g): 36
Fat (g): 3.4
Saturated fat (g): 0.8
Cholesterol (mg): 54.3
Sodium (mg): 124
Exchanges
Milk: 0.0
Veg.: 1.0
Fruit: 0.0
Bread: 2.0
Meat: 2.0
Fat: 0.0

1. Spray large saucepan with cooking spray; heat over medium heat until hot. Add corn, onion, and bell pepper to saucepan; saute until onion is tender, about 5 minutes. Process about 2 cups corn mixture in food processor or blender until smooth, adding water if necessary; reserve.

2. Add chicken, carrots, tomatoes, jalapeno chili, garlic, and herbs to saucepan; cook and stir until chicken begins to brown, 5 to 8 minutes.. Stir in Chicken Stock, half-and-half, and reserved corn mixture. Heat to boiling; reduce heat and simmer, covered, until chicken is tender, about 15 minutes. Season to taste with salt and pepper.

CHICKEN CORN CHOWDER WITH SWEET PEPPERS

A bright red bell pepper and a few tablespoons of picante sauce are all it takes to transform an ordinary corn chowder into an extra-special dish like this one.

4 servings

1 pound boneless, skinless chicken breast, cut into 1/2-inch pieces
1 teaspoon olive oil
1 onion, chopped
2 teaspoons minced garlic
2 cups cubed, peeled potatoes
1/2 cup reduced-sodium fat-free chicken broth
2 cans (15 ounces each) cream-style corn
1 red bell pepper, chopped
5 tablespoons mild picante sauce
Salt and pepper, to taste
Chopped black olives, as garnish

Per Serving
Calories: 437
% Calories from fat: 17
Protein (g): 33.1
Carbohydrates (g): 68.4
Fat (g): 5.9
Saturated fat (g): 1
Cholesterol (mg): 69
Sodium (mg): 804
Exchanges
Milk: 0.0
Veg.: 0.0
Fruit: 0.0
Bread: 4.0
Meat: 3.0
Fat: 0.0

1. Saute chicken in oil in large saucepan until lightly browned; add onion and garlic and saute until tender. Stir in potatoes and broth. Heat to boiling; reduce heat and simmer, covered, until potatoes are tender, about 15 minutes.

2. Stir in corn, bell pepper, and picante sauce. Cook, covered, until hot and slightly thickened, about 10 minutes. Season to taste with salt and pepper. Serve chowder in large bowls; sprinkle with olives.

Variation:
Mediterranean-Style Chicken and Shrimp Chowder—Make recipe as above, using 8 ounces chicken and substituting 1 can (19 ounces) garbanzo beans for 1 can of corn, and 1 chopped roasted red pepper for the bell pepper. Increase chicken broth to 1 cup and omit picante sauce. Add 3/4 teaspoon dried oregano leaves and 8 ounces peeled, deveined shrimp to chowder in Step 2.

CHICKEN-VEGETABLE CHOWDER

A delicious chowder, ready in less than 30 minutes using canned and frozen ingredients for convenience.

6 servings (about 1½ cups each)

16 ounces boneless, skinless chicken breast, cubed (³/₄-inch)
1 cup sliced carrots
½ cup chopped onion
2 cloves garlic, minced
1 tablespoon margarine
8 ounces small broccoli florets
½ cup frozen Mexican-style whole-kernel corn
2 cups Chicken Stock (see pg. 2)
1 can (10³/₄ ounces) reduced-sodium cream of potato soup
1 teaspoon dried thyme leaves
3 tablespoons flour
½ cup fat-free half-and-half, *or* fat-free milk
Salt and pepper, to taste

Per Serving
Calories: 207
% Calories from fat: 21
Protein (g): 21.3
Carbohydrate (g): 19.1
Fat (g): 4.8
Saturated fat (g): 1.3
Cholesterol (mg): 47.1
Sodium (mg): 107
Exchanges
Milk: 0.0
Veg.: 1.0
Fruit: 0.0
Bread: 2.0
Meat: 2.0
Fat: 0.0

1. Saute chicken, carrots, onion, and garlic in margarine in large saucepan until chicken is lightly browned. Add remaining ingredients except flour, half-and-half, and salt and pepper; heat to boiling. Reduce heat and simmer, covered, until chicken is cooked and vegetables are tender, about 10 minutes.

2. Heat mixture to boiling; add combined flour and half-and-half, stirring until thickened, 1 to 2 minutes. Season to taste with salt and pepper.

CHICKEN AND FRESH VEGETABLE CHOWDER

This delicious chowder is very fast to prepare; use a food processor to chop all the vegetables quickly.

8 servings (about 1 cup each)

Per Serving
Calories: 188
% Calories from fat: 27
Protein (g): 21.8
Carbohydrate (g): 11.3
Fat (g): 5.6
Saturated fat (g): 1.3
Cholesterol (mg): 53.5
Sodium (mg): 118
Exchanges
Milk: 0.0
Veg.: 3.0
Fruit: 0.0
Bread: 0.0
Meat: 2.0
Fat: 0.0

- 1 medium onion, chopped
- 1 medium green bell pepper, chopped
- 2 carrots, chopped
- 2 medium zucchini, chopped
- 1 rib celery, chopped
- 2 cloves garlic, minced
- 2 tablespoons margarine
- 1¹/2 pounds boneless, skinless chicken breast, cubed (1-inch)
- ¹/4 cup all-purpose flour
- 1 quart Chicken Stock (see p. 2)
- 1 teaspoon dried thyme leaves
- ¹/2 teaspoon dried marjoram leaves
- 1 bay leaf
- ³/4 cup fat-free half-and-half, *or* fat-free milk
- ¹/4 cup chopped parsley
  Salt and pepper, to taste

1. Saute vegetables in margarine in large saucepan until tender, about 8 minutes; stir in chicken and saute until lightly browned, about 5 minutes. Sprinkle with flour and cook 2 minutes longer. Stir in Chicken Stock and herbs. Heat to boiling; reduce heat and simmer until chicken is tender, about 15 minutes.

2. Stir in half-and-half and simmer until hot, 2 to 3 minutes; stir in parsley. Discard bay leaf; season to taste with salt and pepper.

CHICKEN CHOWDER HISPANIOLA

Caribbean "fusion" cuisine is hot! And so is this enticing chowder that boasts sofrito, a popular Cuban seasoning, and Spanish favorites like chicken, almonds, and olive oil.

4 servings

12 ounces boneless, skinless chicken breast, cut into 3/4-inch cubes

1 teaspoon olive oil

1 onion, chopped

1 can (15 ounces) garbanzo beans, rinsed, drained

1 can (14 1/2 ounces) reduced-sodium fat-free chicken broth

1 can (15 ounces) reduced-sodium diced tomatoes, undrained

2 cups packed fresh spinach leaves

2 tablespoons sofrito sauce, optional
   Salt and pepper, to taste

1/4 cup slivered almonds, toasted

Per Serving
Calories: 346
% Calories from fat: 29
Protein (g): 30.5
Carbohydrates (g): 28.2
Fat (g): 10.5
Saturated fat (g): 1.9
Cholesterol (mg): 54.3
Sodium (mg): 639
Exchanges
Milk: 0.0
Veg.: 3.0
Fruit: 0.0
Bread: 1.0
Meat: 3.0
Fat: 1.0

1. Saute chicken in oil in large saucepan until lightly browned. Add onion; saute until tender.

2. Add beans, broth, and tomatoes and liquid. Heat to boiling; reduce heat and simmer, covered, 10 minutes. Stir in spinach and sofrito, and simmer 10 minutes longer; season to taste with salt and pepper.

3. Spoon chowder into bowls; sprinkle with almonds.

LIME-CHICKEN AND SHRIMP CHOWDER WITH AVOCADO

Ladle up some great eating with this lively chowder. Lime provides the dominant flavor while tomatoes and avocados contribute crisp color contrasts. Tender rice gives the whole dish a creamy base.

4 servings

Per Serving
Calories: 331
% Calories from fat: 25
Protein (g): 30.9
Carbohydrate (g): 30.9
Fat (g): 9.2
Saturated fat (g): 2
Cholesterol (mg): 121.2
Sodium (mg): 290

Exchanges
Milk: 0.0
Veg.: 0.0
Fruit: 0.0
Bread: 2.0
Meat: 3.5
Fat: 0.0

- 8 ounces boneless, skinless chicken breast, cut into $3/4$-inch pieces
- 2 cans ($14^1/2$ ounces each) fat-free chicken broth
- $1/2$ cup uncooked rice
  Juice of 1 lime
- $1/8$ teaspoon celery seeds
- 8 ounces peeled, deveined shrimp, halved crosswise
- 4 scallions, sliced
- $1/2$ teaspoon crushed red pepper
- 3 plum tomatoes, coarsely chopped
- 1 teaspoon grated lime rind
- 1 avocado, cut into $3/4$-inch pieces
  Salt and pepper, to taste

1. Heat chicken, broth, rice, lime juice, and celery seeds to boiling in large saucepan; reduce heat and simmer, covered, 20 minutes.

2. Add shrimp, scallions, red pepper, tomatoes, and lime rind; simmer until rice is tender and shrimp are cooked, about 5 minutes. Stir in avocado; season to taste with salt and pepper.

BEAN AND SHRIMP CHOWDER

You can make a meal out of this high-protein chowder; just add a slice of Hearty Vegetable-Rye Bread (see p. 796).

8 servings (about 1¹/₃ cups each)

¹/₄ cup chopped onion
1 tablespoon margarine
3 tablespoons flour
¹/₂-³/₄ teaspoon dried thyme leaves
¹/₄ teaspoon dry mustard
1¹/₂ cups Chicken Stock (see p. 2)
2 cups fat-free milk
1 can (16 ounces) cream-style corn
2 cans (15¹/₂ ounces each) Great Northern beans, rinsed, drained
1¹/₂ pounds peeled, deveined medium shrimp
Salt and cayenne pepper, to taste

Per Serving
Calories: 218
% Calories from fat: 10
Protein (g): 22.9
Carbohydrate (g): 30.9
Fat (g): 2.7
Saturated fat (g): 0.6
Cholesterol (mg): 131.8
Sodium (mg): 658
Exchanges
Milk: 0.0
Veg.: 0.0
Fruit: 0.0
Bread: 2.0
Meat: 2.0
Fat: 0.0

1. Saute onion in margarine in large saucepan until tender, about 3 minutes; stir in flour, thyme, and dry mustard and cook over medium heat 1 minute. Stir in Chicken Stock and milk and heat to boiling, stirring until thickened, 1 to 2 minutes.

2. Add corn and beans, reduce heat, and simmer 10 minutes. Stir in shrimp; simmer until shrimp are tender and pink, about 5 minutes. Season to taste with salt and cayenne pepper.

LOBSTER AND SHRIMP CHOWDER

This chowder is elegant enough for a special dinner party, easy enough for a casual supper, and fast enough for a weeknight meal. Cooked lobster and shrimp can be purchased in the seafood department of many supermarkets.

4 servings

2 large Yukon gold potatoes, peeled, cut into $1/2$-inch cubes

1 Spanish onion, chopped

1 can (15 ounces) reduced-sodium diced tomatoes, undrained

1 bottle (11 ounces) clam juice

8 ounces cooked lobster, cut into small chunks

4 ounces cooked small shrimp

1 teaspoon dried tarragon leaves

1 cup 1% low-fat milk

$1/4$ cup chopped parsley

Salt and pepper, to taste

Per Serving
Calories: 210
% Calories from fat: **9**
Protein (g): 22.4
Carbohydrates (g): 25.7
Fat (g): 2.1
Saturated fat (g): 0.9
Cholesterol (mg): 100.7
Sodium (mg): 519
Exchanges
Milk: 0.0
Veg.: 1.0
Fruit: 0.0
Bread: 1.0
Meat: 2.0
Fat: 0.0

1. Combine potatoes, onion, tomatoes and liquid, and clam juice in large saucepan. Heat to boiling; reduce heat and simmer, covered, until potatoes are tender, about 12 minutes.

2. Add remaining ingredients, except salt and pepper, and simmer 5 minutes. Season to taste with salt and pepper.

Variation:
Crabmeat Chowder—Make recipe as above, substituting $1^1/2$ cups Fish Stock (p. 9) for the clam juice, $1/4$ to $1/2$ teaspoon dried thyme leaves for the tarragon, and 3 cans (4 ounces each) lump crabmeat for the lobster and shrimp; drain and remove any shells.

CURRIED SCALLOP AND POTATO CHOWDER

Create a stir with this sensational chowder. It has a lively curry flavor and bright yellow color, and takes less than half an hour to cook.

4 servings

1 bottle (11 ounces) clam juice
1/2 cup dry white wine, *or* water
16 ounces potatoes, peeled, cut into 1/2-inch cubes
1 teaspoon curry powder
1/2 teaspoon minced garlic
1 pound sea scallops
1 cup frozen peas
1/4 cup 1% low-fat milk
Salt and pepper, to taste

Per Serving
Calories: 251
% Calories from fat: **7**
Protein (g): **25.6**
Carbohydrate (g): **29.4**
Fat (g): 1.8
Saturated fat (g): 0.2
Cholesterol (mg): 49.3
Sodium (mg): 482
Exchanges
Milk: 0.0
Veg.: 0.0
Fruit: 0.0
Bread: 2.0
Meat: 2.0
Fat: 0.0

1. Heat clam juice, wine, potatoes, curry powder, and garlic to boiling in large saucepan; reduce heat and simmer, covered, 10 minutes. Add scallops; simmer until scallops are cooked and opaque, 5 to 10 minutes. Remove about half the potatoes and scallops with slotted spoon to a large bowl; keep warm.

2. Process remaining mixture in food processor or blender until smooth. Return mixture to pan. Stir in peas, milk, and reserved potatoes and scallops. Heat until peas are tender and chowder is hot through, about 5 minutes. Do not boil. Season to taste with salt and pepper.

CRAB CHOWDER WITH SNOW PEAS

This classy chowder gets its sensual, perfumy essence from jasmine rice, gingerroot, and sorrel. The crabmeat is canned, eliminating the need to pick meat from shells.

4 servings

2 cups clam juice

2¹/₂ cups water

¹/₂ cup jasmine, *or* long-grain, rice

2 scallions, sliced

1 tablespoon minced gingerroot

2 cans (4 ounces each) lump crabmeat, drained, shells removed

2 cups snow peas, halved crosswise

1 tablespoon dry sherry

¹/₂ cup 2% reduced-fat milk

2 cups torn sorrel leaves

Salt and pepper, to taste

Per Serving
Calories: 209
% Calories from fat: 8
Protein (g): 17.6
Carbohydrates (g): 28.8
Fat (g): 1.9
Saturated fat (g): 0.5
Cholesterol (mg): 52.7
Sodium (mg): 491
Exchanges
Milk: 0.0
Veg.: 1.0
Fruit: 0.0
Bread: 1.0
Meat: 2.0
Fat: 0.0

1. Heat clam juice and water to boiling in large saucepan. Stir in rice, scallions, and gingerroot; reduce heat and simmer, covered, until rice is tender, about 20 minutes.

2. Stir in crabmeat and snow peas; simmer for 1 minute. Stir in sherry, milk, and sorrel. Season to taste with salt and pepper.

SHERRIED CRAB AND MUSHROOM CHOWDER

Succulent, sweet crabmeat and fresh mushrooms complement one another nicely in this elegant dish. Although the sherry helps bring out the rich, mellow taste, it may be omitted.

5-6 servings

1¼ pounds fresh mushrooms, sliced
⅔ cup chopped onion
2 tablespoons chopped celery with leaves
2 tablespoons chopped carrot
1 tablespoon margarine
1½ tablespoons flour
2½ cups Chicken Stock (see p. 2), divided
¾ cup diced, peeled red potatoes
⅛ teaspoon dried thyme leaves
1 tablespoon tomato paste
1½ teaspoons reduced-sodium soy sauce
1⅓ cups whole milk
6 ounces fresh lump crabmeat, shells removed
1 tablespoon chopped chives
2 tablespoons dry sherry
Salt and white pepper, to taste

Per Serving
Calories: 159
% Calories from fat: 27
Protein (g): 10.8
Carbohydrates (g): 18.1
Fat (g): 5
Saturated fat (g): 1.7
Cholesterol (mg): 33.8
Sodium (mg): 371
Exchanges
Milk: 0.0
Veg.: 0.0
Fruit: 0.0
Bread: 1.0
Meat: 1.0
Fat: 0.5

1. Saute mushrooms, onion, celery, and carrot in margarine in large skillet until tender, about 8 minutes. Reserve about ⅓ mushroom mixture; transfer remaining mixture to large saucepan and stir in flour. Cook 1 to 2 minutes over medium heat.

2. Stir in 1½ cups Chicken Stock, potatoes, and thyme; heat to boiling. Reduce heat and simmer, covered, until potatoes are tender, about 10 minutes.

3. Process chowder in food processor or blender until smooth; return to saucepan. Add remaining 1 cup Chicken Stock, tomato paste, soy sauce, milk, reserved mushroom mixture, crabmeat, chives, and sherry; simmer 5 minutes. Season to taste with salt and white pepper.

SPICY CRAB AND SCALLOP CHOWDER

Ladle up some fare with flair! The flavor kick in this seafood chowder comes from pickling spice, which is readily available in supermarkets.

4 servings

1 medium onion, chopped
1 rib celery, chopped
1 tablespoon margarine
1^1/$_2$ cups clam juice
1 can (14 ounces) reduced-sodium stewed tomatoes, undrained
2 teaspoons pickling spice
1 can (4 ounces) lump crabmeat, drained
8 ounces bay scallops
^{1}/$_4$ cup 2% reduced-fat milk
Salt and pepper, to taste

Per Serving
Calories: 144
% Calories from fat: 26
Protein (g): 18.2
Carbohydrates (g): 8.9
Fat (g): 4.3
Saturated fat (g): 0.8
Cholesterol (mg): 50.4
Sodium (mg): 485
Exchanges
Milk: 0.0
Veg.: 1.0
Fruit: 0.0
Bread: 0.0
Meat: 2.0
Fat: 0.0

1. Saute onion and celery in margarine in large saucepan until softened. Add clam juice and stewed tomatoes and liquid. Place pickling spice in a mesh tea ball or tie in cheesecloth; add to mixture. Heat to boiling; simmer 2 minutes.

2. Stir in crabmeat and scallops; simmer until scallops are tender and opaque, about 3 minutes. Discard pickling spice. Stir in milk; heat until hot (do not boil). Season to taste with salt and pepper.

SEAFOOD SAMPLER

Can't decide whether to buy haddock, scallops, or shrimp? Then get some of each and simmer up this sensibly seasoned chowder. Wonderful with croutons or a chunk of crusty bread.

4 servings

1	yellow bell pepper, chopped
1	medium onion, cut into thin wedges
1	teaspoon olive oil
1	can (15 ounces) reduced-sodium diced tomatoes, undrained
2	medium potatoes, cut into 1/2-inch cubes
1/2	cup dry white wine, *or* clam juice
8	ounces haddock, cut into 1-inch cubes
4	ounces bay scallops
4	ounces shrimp, peeled, deveined
1	teaspoon herbes de Provence, *or* Italian seasoning
1/2	teaspoon celery seeds
1	teaspoon hot pepper sauce
	Salt, to taste

Per Serving
Calories: 231
% Calories from fat: 10
Protein (g): 23.7
Carbohydrates (g): 24.7
Fat (g): 2.5
Saturated fat (g): 0.4
Cholesterol (mg): 88
Sodium (mg): 172
Exchanges
Milk: 0.0
Veg.: 1.0
Fruit: 0.0
Bread: 1.0
Meat: 3.0
Fat: 0.0

1. Saute pepper and onion in oil in large saucepan until lightly browned. Add tomatoes and liquid, potatoes, and wine. Heat to boiling; reduce heat and simmer, covered, 10 minutes. Add seafood, herbes de Provence, and celery seeds. Simmer until fish is tender and flakes with a fork, 10 to 15 minutes. Stir in hot pepper sauce; season to taste with salt.

SEAFOOD CHOWDER

If you prefer, Fish Stock (see p. 9) can be used in place of the clam juice.

8 servings (about 1½ cups each)

4 slices bacon

2 medium onions, sliced

1 cup sliced celery

1 can (28 ounces) reduced-sodium whole tomatoes, undrained, chopped

4 cups chopped, peeled potatoes

2 bottles (8 ounces each) clam juice

½-1 cup tomato sauce

1 tablespoon very-low-sodium Worcestershire sauce

1 teaspoon dried rosemary leaves

⅓ cup all-purpose flour

1 cup fat-free half-and-half, *or* fat-free milk

1½ pounds fresh, *or* frozen, thawed, halibut, *or* whitefish steaks, cut into 1-inch pieces

Salt and pepper, to taste

Per Serving
Calories: 300
% Calories from fat: 12
Protein (g): 24.2
Carbohydrate (g): 41.6
Fat (g): 3.9
Saturated fat (g): 0.9
Cholesterol (mg): 29.8
Sodium (mg): 395
Exchanges
Milk: 0.0
Veg.: 2.0
Fruit: 0.0
Bread: 2.0
Meat: 2.0
Fat: 0.0

1. Fry bacon in large saucepan until crisp; drain bacon, crumble, and reserve. Pour all but 1 tablespoon bacon fat out of pan; add onions and celery and saute until tender, about 8 minutes.

2. Stir in tomatoes and liquid, potatoes, clam juice, tomato sauce, Worcestershire sauce, and rosemary; heat to boiling. Reduce heat and simmer, covered, until vegetables are tender, about 10 minutes.

3. Heat chowder to boiling. Mix flour and half-and-half; add to chowder, stirring, until thickened, about 1 minute. Add fish; reduce heat and simmer until fish is tender and flakes with a fork, about 5 minutes. Season to taste with salt and pepper. Add additional milk if chowder is too thick.

4. Serve chowder in bowls; sprinkle with reserved bacon.

Variation:

Rich Shrimp Chowder—Make recipe as above, substituting 1½ pounds peeled, deveined shrimp for the halibut. Decrease potatoes to 2 cups and add 1 cup frozen peas. Sprinkle top of each bowl with bacon and chopped chives.

FRESH SALMON CHOWDER WITH POTATOES

North Atlantic salmon and Pacific king salmon are both good choices for this recipe.

4 servings

3 cups Fish Stock (see p. 9), *or* bottled clam juice, divided
4 salmon steaks (4 ounces each)
1 cup chopped onion
2 tablespoons finely chopped celery with leaves
1 tablespoon margarine
1 tablespoon flour
$1/2$ teaspoon dry mustard powder
$1/2$ teaspoon dried marjoram leaves
$3^1/4$ cups cubed, peeled potatoes ($1/2$-inch)
1 cup whole milk
Salt and white pepper, to taste

Per Serving
Calories: 418
% Calories from fat: 20
Protein (g): 30.1
Carbohydrate (g): 50.1
Fat (g): 9.1
Saturated fat (g): 2.5
Cholesterol (mg): 70.3
Sodium (mg): 158
Exchanges
Milk: 0.0
Veg.: 0.0
Fruit: 0.0
Bread: 3.5
Meat: 3.0
Fat: 0.0

1. Heat $3/4$ cup Fish Stock to simmering in large saucepan over medium-low heat; add salmon and simmer, covered, until salmon flakes with a fork, 8 to 10 minutes. Remove to plate; break fish into bite-sized pieces, discarding skin and bones. Strain cooking liquid through fine sieve into bowl.

2. Saute onion and celery in margarine in large saucepan until onion is soft, about 5 minutes. Stir in flour; cook 1 to 2 minutes. Stir in remaining $2^1/4$ cups Fish Stock, mustered powder, marjoram, and potatoes; heat to boiling. Reduce heat and simmer, covered, until potatoes are tender, about 10 minutes.

3. Process half the broth and vegetable mixture in blender or food processor until smooth; return to saucepan. Stir in milk and salmon. Cook over medium heat until heated through; season to taste with salt and white pepper.

SALMON AND ROASTED PEPPER CHOWDER

Salmon aficionados take note—in this recipe, salmon is paired with corn and seasoned with jalapeño chilies, cumin, and oregano for a fast and fabulous feast.

4 servings

Per Serving
Calories: 259
% Calories from fat: 12
Protein (g): 20.5
Carbohydrates (g): 36.4
Fat (g): 3.4
Saturated fat (g): 0.5
Cholesterol (mg): 42.8
Sodium (mg): 197
Exchanges
Milk: 0.0
Veg.: 0.0
Fruit: 0.0
Bread: 2.0
Meat: 2.0
Fat: 0.0

2 cups frozen whole-kernel corn
2 medium potatoes, peeled, cut into
   $^1/_2$-inch cubes
2 cups reduced-sodium vegetable broth
2 jalapeño chilies, minced
2 teaspoons minced garlic
1 teaspoon cumin seeds
1 teaspoon dried oregano leaves
12 ounces salmon steak, cut into $1^1/_2$-inch
   cubes
1 cup chopped roasted red pepper
   Salt and pepper, to taste
1 tablespoon chopped parsley

1. Combine all ingredients, except salmon, roasted red pepper, salt, pepper, and parsley, in large saucepan. Heat to boiling; reduce heat and simmer, covered, 10 minutes. Add salmon and simmer until potatoes are tender and salmon flakes with a fork, about 10 minutes. Stir in roasted red pepper; season to taste with salt and pepper. Serve in bowls; sprinkle with parsley.

SHRIMP AND VEGETABLE CHOWDER

The rich flavor of this chowder comes from a combination of herbs, spices, tomato sauce, and milk.

5-6 servings

Per Serving
Calories: 270
% Calories from fat: **9**
Protein (g): 15.9
Carbohydrates (g): 45.2
Fat (g): 2.9
Saturated fat (g): 0.8
Cholesterol (mg): 72
Sodium (mg): 455
Exchanges
Milk: 0.0
Veg.: 3.0
Fruit: 0.0
Bread: 2.0
Meat: 1.0
Fat: 0.0

- 1 large onion, finely chopped
- 2 garlic cloves, minced
- 2 teaspoons olive oil
- 3 cups reduced-sodium fat-free chicken broth
- 3 cups frozen whole-kernel corn
- 2 cups diced, peeled red potatoes
- 1 large red, *or* green, bell pepper, diced
- 1/3 cup dry sherry
- 2 teaspoons Italian seasoning
- 1/4 teaspoon chili powder
- 1/4 teaspoon dry mustard
- 1/8 teaspoon pepper
- 3-4 drops hot pepper sauce
- 1 1/2 tablespoons cornstarch
- 1/4 cup cold water
- 1 1/2 cups small cooked, peeled shrimp
- 1 can (8 ounces) tomato sauce
- 1/2 cup whole milk
- Salt, to taste

1. Saute onion and garlic in oil in large saucepan until onion is soft, about 5 minutes. Add broth, corn, potatoes, bell pepper, sherry, Italian seasoning, chili powder, mustard, pepper, and hot pepper sauce; heat to boiling. Reduce heat and simmer, covered, 12 to 15 minutes.

2. Heat chowder to boiling; stir in combined cornstarch and water and boil, stirring, until chowder thickens, 1 to 2 minutes. Reduce heat and add shrimp, tomato sauce, and milk; simmer 2 to 3 minutes. Season to taste with salt.

BERMUDA FISH CHOWDER

Like Manhattan-style chowders, Bermuda chowders typically contain to-matoes. They have a wonderful flavor and robustness all their own. The following recipe makes a very savory, not to mention economical, one-pot meal.

5-7 servings

Per Serving
Calories: 267
% Calories from fat: 15
Protein (g): 19.1
Carbohydrates (g): 37.8
Fat (g): 4.5
Saturated fat (g): 0.8
Cholesterol (mg): 47.1
Sodium (mg): 781
Exchanges
Milk: 0.0
Veg.: 0.0
Fruit: 0.0
Bread: 2.0
Meat: 2.0
Fat: 0.0

  2 large onions, finely chopped

  4 medium ribs celery, including leaves, chopped

  1 tablespoon canola, safflower, *or* corn oil

  4 medium carrots, chopped

$^1/_2$ medium green bell pepper, chopped

  1 quart Fish Stock (see p. 9), *or* 2 cups bottled clam juice and 2 cups fat-free chicken broth

$2^1/_2$ teaspoons Worcestershire sauce

  2 large bay leaves

$^1/_2$ teaspoon dried thyme leaves

$^1/_4$ teaspoon pepper

  1 teaspoon mild curry powder

  2 small smoked pork hocks

$3^1/_4$ cups cubed, peeled boiled potatoes ($^1/_2$-inch)

$1^1/_2$ cups canned chopped Italian-style tomatoes, undrained

$^1/_3$ cup catsup

$^1/_2$ teaspoon salt

16 ounces fresh, *or* frozen, thawed, lean fish fillets (whitefish, flounder, haddock, cod), cut into 1-inch pieces
Pepper, to taste
Bermuda sherry peppers, as garnish

1. Saute onions and celery in oil in large saucepan until tender, about 5 minutes. Add carrots and bell pepper and saute 2 minutes more. Add Fish Stock, Worcestershire sauce, herbs and spices, pork hocks, and potatoes; heat to boiling. Reduce heat and simmer, covered, 20 minutes. Stir in tomatoes and liquid and catsup; simmer, covered, 45 minutes. Stir in salt and fish and simmer, covered, until fish flakes with a fork, about 10 minutes. Discard bay leaves and pork hocks; season to taste with pepper. Garnish with sherry peppers.

CANADIAN CHOWDER

An easy dish to prepare on one of those busy days, it can be made quickly using defrosted or fresh fish.

6 servings

Vegetable cooking spray
1 large onion, minced
2 leeks, white parts only, thinly sliced
1¹/₄ cups chopped carrots
1¹/₄ cups chopped celery
2 cups water
16 ounces cod, *or* halibut, cut into 1-inch pieces
1 can (28 ounces) crushed tomatoes, undrained
1 cup 2% reduced-fat, *or* fat-free milk
¹/₂ teaspoon white pepper
¹/₄ teaspoon ground mace
Salt, to taste
¹/₄ cup minced chives

Per Serving
Calories: 176
% Calories from fat: 8
Protein (g): 18.4
Carbohydrate (g): 22.3
Fat (g): 1.6
Saturated fat (g): 0.6
Cholesterol (mg): 35.4
Sodium (mg): 311
Exchanges
Milk: 0.0
Veg.: 2.0
Fruit: 0.0
Bread: 0.0
Meat: 2.0
Fat: 0.0

1. Spray large saucepan with cooking spray; heat over medium heat until hot. Saute onion and leeks over medium heat until soft, about 5 minutes. Add carrots, celery, and water; heat to boiling. Reduce heat and simmer, covered, until vegetables are tender, 10 to 15 minutes.

2. Add fish and tomatoes and liquid; simmer 5 minutes. Stir in milk, white pepper, and mace; simmer until chowder is hot and fish flakes with a fork, 5 to 8 minutes. Season to taste with salt. Ladle chowder into bowls and sprinkle with chives.

MONKFISH-CHEDDAR CHOWDER

One nibble and you'll be hooked on this rich-tasting, creamy chowder with monkfish, potatoes, and carrots.

4 servings

1 medium onion, chopped

2 teaspoons margarine

16 ounces potatoes, peeled, cut into
   1/2-inch cubes

2 carrots, thinly sliced

1 can (14 ounces) reduced-sodium fat-
   free chicken broth

16 ounces monkfish, membrane removed,
   cut into 3-inch cubes

1/2 cup fat-free milk

1/2 cup (2 ounces) shredded reduced-
   sodium Cheddar cheese

1 teaspoon hot pepper sauce

   Salt, to taste

1 tablespoon chopped chives

Per Serving
Calories: 274
% Calories from fat: 19
Protein (g): 24.9
Carbohydrates (g): 29.5
Fat (g): 5.9
Saturated fat (g): 1.8
Cholesterol (mg): 35.4
Sodium (mg): 344
Exchanges
Milk: 0.0
Veg.: 0.0
Fruit: 0.0
Bread: 1.5
Meat: 3.0
Fat: 0.0

1. Saute onion in margarine in large saucepan until softened; add potatoes, carrots, and broth. Heat to boiling; reduce heat and simmer, covered, until vegetables are tender, about 12 minutes. Using a slotted spoon, remove 2 cups vegetables to a bowl; reserve.

2. Process remaining vegetable mixture in blender or food processor until smooth; return to pan. Add fish; heat to boiling. Reduce heat and simmer, covered, until fish is tender and flakes with a fork, 5 to 10 minutes. Stir in milk, cheese, hot pepper sauce, and reserved vegetables. Stir over medium heat until hot, 2 to 3 minutes. Season to taste with salt. Serve in bowls; sprinkle with chives.

Variation:
Cod and Vegetable Chowder—Make recipe as above, substituting cod for the monkfish. Decrease potatoes to 2 cups; add 1 cup small broccoli florets, 1/2 cup frozen peas, and 1/2 cup julienned green beans.

NOVA SCOTIA SEAFOOD CHOWDER

Hearty chowders are a hallmark of the cuisine in Canada's Atlantic Provinces. They are milk-based like their New England counterparts. The type and combination of seafood used depend on the day's catch.

5-6 servings

1	large onion, finely chopped
1	large garlic clove, chopped
1	large rib celery, diced
2	teaspoons margarine, *or* butter
2	cups Fish Stock (see p. 9), *or* 2 cups clam juice
2	cups whole milk, divided
2¹/2	cups cubed, peeled potatoes (³/4-inch)
2	cups cauliflower pieces (³/4-inch)
1	large carrot, diced
1¹/2	teaspoons dried basil leaves
¹/2	teaspoon dried marjoram leaves
¹/4	teaspoon dried thyme leaves
¹/4	teaspoon dry mustard
¹/4	teaspoon celery seeds, crushed
¹/4	teaspoon white pepper
1	tablespoon plus 1 teaspoon cornstarch
8	ounces skinless flounder, *or* whitefish, fillets, cut into 1-inch pieces
4	ounces peeled, deveined cooked shrimp
4	ounces crabmeat
	Salt, to taste

Per Serving
Calories: 255
% Calories from fat: 19
Protein (g): 20.3
Carbohydrates (g): 31.1
Fat (g): 5.3
Saturated fat (g): 2.2
Cholesterol (mg): 80
Sodium (mg): 317
Exchanges
Milk: 0.0
Veg.: 0.0
Fruit: 0.0
Bread: 2.0
Meat: 2.0
Fat: 0.0

1. Saute onion, garlic, and celery in margarine in large saucepan until onion is tender, about 8 minutes. Add Fish Stock, 1¹/2 cups milk, potatoes, cauliflower, carrot, and herbs and spices; heat to boiling. Reduce heat and simmer, covered, until potatoes are tender, about 15 minutes.

2. Heat soup to boiling; stir in combined cornstarch and remaining ¹/2 cup of milk. Boil, stirring, until thickened, about 1 minute. Reduce heat; add seafood and simmer, covered, until flounder flakes with a fork, about 10 minutes. Season to taste with salt.

POTATO SEAFOOD CHOWDER

For a richer dish, add ¹/₂ cup clam juice.

4 servings

1	cup sliced onion
¹/₂	cup sliced celery
3	boiling potatoes, unpeeled, cubed
1	teaspoon margarine
1	quart fat-free milk
1/8	teaspoon saffron, optional
8	ounces haddock, *or* cod, fillets
¹/₄-¹/₂	cup peeled, deveined small shrimp
	Salt and white pepper, to taste

Per Serving
Calories: 254
% Calories from fat: 7
Protein (g): 22.8
Carbohydrate (g): 36.2
Fat (g): 2
Saturated fat (g): 0.6
Cholesterol (mg): 37
Sodium (mg): 245
Exchanges
Milk: 1.0
Veg.: 0.0
Fruit: 0.0
Bread: 1.0
Meat: 2.0
Fat: 0.0

1. Saute onion, celery, and potatoes in margarine in large saucepan 4 minutes; mix in milk and saffron. Heat to boiling; reduce heat and simmer, covered, 20 minutes or until vegetables are tender. Add haddock and shrimp; simmer until haddock flakes easily with a fork, about 5 minutes. Season to taste with salt and white pepper.

HALIBUT AND POTATO CHOWDER

This chunky chowder has a thick, flavorful base of pureed vegetables. For a fun change of pace, serve the chowder in a bread bowl—start with a large round loaf of crusty bread, then cut off the top and hollow it out.

4 servings

2	slices turkey bacon
1	large onion, chopped
1	rib celery, chopped
1¹/₂	cups clam juice
1	quart cubed, peeled potatoes
1	teaspoon dried savory leaves
1-2	teaspoons hot pepper sauce
1	carrot, shredded
1	pound halibut, cut into ³/₄-inch pieces
1	cup 1% low-fat milk
	Salt, to taste

Per Serving
Calories: 394
% Calories from fat: 12
Protein (g): 31.4
Carbohydrates (g): 55.4
Fat (g): 5.4
Saturated fat (g): 1.4
Cholesterol (mg): 45.7
Sodium (mg): 430
Exchanges
Milk: 0.0
Veg.: 1.0
Fruit: 0.0
Bread: 3.0
Meat: 3.0
Fat: 0.0

1. Cook bacon over medium-high heat in large saucepan until crisp. Drain on paper towels; crumble bacon and reserve.

2. Add onion and celery to saucepan; saute vegetables until tender, about 5 minutes. Stir in clam juice and potatoes. Heat to boiling; reduce heat and simmer, covered, until tender, about 15 minutes. Using a slotted spoon, transfer half the vegetables to a bowl; keep warm.

3. Using a potato masher or immersion blender, puree the vegetables in the saucepan. Return reserved vegetables to pan; stir in savory and hot pepper sauce.

4. Heat to boiling; add carrot and halibut. Reduce heat and simmer, covered, until halibut is tender and flakes with a fork, 3 to 5 minutes. Stir in milk; heat until hot. Season to taste with salt. Serve chowder in bowls; sprinkle each serving with reserved bacon.

FISH AND SWEET POTATO CHOWDER

Whitefish, cod, orange roughy, salmon, and red snapper are possible fish choices for this herb-scented chowder.

8 servings (about 1 1/2 cups each)

1 medium onion, sliced

1 green bell pepper, chopped

2 cloves garlic, minced

1-2 tablespoons margarine

1 tablespoon flour

2 cans (16 ounces each) reduced-sodium diced tomatoes, undrained

2 cups water

1 cup dry white wine, *or* clam juice

1 teaspoon dried basil leaves

1 teaspoon dried oregano leaves

1/4 teaspoon dried thyme leaves

1 quart cubed, cooked sweet potatoes (1-inch)

1/2 cup frozen whole-kernel corn

16 ounces salmon steaks or fillets, cut into 1-inch pieces

16 ounces peeled, deveined shrimp
Salt and pepper, to taste

Per Serving
Calories: 272
% Calories from fat: 14
Protein (g): 23.5
Carbohydrate (g): 31
Fat (g): 4.2
Saturated fat (g): 0.8
Cholesterol (mg): 115.2
Sodium (mg): 174
Exchanges
Milk: 0.0
Veg.: 0.0
Fruit: 0.0
Bread: 2.0
Meat: 2.0
Fat: 0.0

1. Saute onion, bell pepper, and garlic in margarine in large saucepan until tender, 3 to 4 minutes; add flour and cook 1 minute. Add tomatoes, water, wine, herbs and sweet potatoes; heat to boiling. Reduce heat and simmer, covered, 15 minutes.

2. Add remaining ingredients, except salt and pepper; simmer until fish flakes with a fork and shrimp are pink, 5 to 8 minutes. Season to taste with salt and pepper.

CHEESY CLAM CHOWDER

The cheese adds a new twist to this classic clam chowder.

8 servings (about 1¹/₂ cups each)

Vegetable cooking spray
¹/₂ cup diced carrot
¹/₂ cup chopped celery
¹/₂ cup chopped onion
3 tablespoons all-purpose flour
1 tablespoon cornstarch
3 cans (8 ounces each) minced clams, drained, liquor reserved
2 bottles (8 ounces each) clam juice
4 cups fat-free milk
1 teaspoon dried thyme leaves
1 cup cubed, cooked peeled potatoes (¹/₂-inch)
1 cup (4 ounces) shredded white Cheddar cheese
Salt and cayenne pepper, to taste
Chopped chives, as garnish
Cooked, crumbled bacon, as garnish

Per Serving
Calories: 276
% Calories from fat: 22
Protein (g): 30.6
Carbohydrate (g): 22
Fat (g): 6.7
Saturated fat (g): 3.3
Cholesterol (mg): 74
Sodium (mg): 396
Exchanges
Milk: 0.0
Veg.: 1.0
Fruit: 0.0
Bread: 1.0
Meat: 3.0
Fat: 0.0

1. Spray large saucepan with cooking spray; heat over medium heat until hot. Saute carrot, celery, and onion until tender, about 8 minutes. Sprinkle with flour and cornstarch and cook 1 to 2 minutes. Stir in clam liquor, clam juice, milk, and thyme and heat to boiling, stirring until thickened.

2. Stir in clams, potatoes, and cheese; stir until cheese is melted. Season to taste with salt and cayenne pepper. Sprinkle servings with chives and bacon.

RED CLAM CHOWDER

For variation another time, clam juice can be substituted for the tomato juice.

8 servings

1 large onion, chopped
2 cloves garlic, minced
2 ribs celery, diced
1 medium green bell pepper, chopped
2 tablespoons olive oil
4 medium potatoes, peeled and diced
4 carrots, diced
2 cans (6^1/$_2$ ounces each) chopped clams, undrained
2 bottles (6 ounces each) clam juice
1 can (14^1/$_2$ ounces) diced reduced-sodium tomatoes, undrained
2 cups tomato juice
1 bay leaf
1 tablespoon minced fresh, *or* 1 teaspoon dried, basil leaves
1 teaspoon minced fresh, *or* ^{1}/$_2$ teaspoon dried, oregano leaves
^{1}/$_2$ teaspoon sugar
^{1}/$_8$ teaspoon black pepper
Dash cayenne pepper
Salt, to taste

Per Serving
Calories: 154
% Calories from fat: 20
Protein (g): 6.3
Carbohydrates (g): 26.1
Fat (g): 3.7
Saturated fat (g): 0.5
Cholesterol (mg): 7.6
Sodium (mg): 651
Exchanges
Milk: 0.0
Veg.: 2.0
Fruit: 0.0
Bread: 2.0
Meat: 0.0
Fat: 0.5

1. Saute onion, garlic, celery, and green pepper in oil in large saucepan until onion is tender, about 8 minutes. Add potatoes and carrots to saucepan and saute 10 minutes.

2. Drain liquor from clams into a measuring cup and add enough water to make 1^3/$_4$ cups; reserve clams. Add liquor mixture, clam juice, tomatoes, and tomato juice to saucepan. Stir in herbs, sugar, and black and cayenne pepper; heat to boiling. Reduce heat and simmer, covered, until potatoes are tender, 10 to 12 minutes, stirring occasionally. Add reserved clams; simmer 5 minutes longer. Discard bay leaf; season to taste with salt.

EASY MANHATTAN CLAM CHOWDER

Here's a quick version of this always-popular clam chowder. Marjoram replaces the usual thyme, lending a subtle flavor twist.

4 servings

2 slices turkey bacon, diced

2 medium onions, chopped

2 potatoes, peeled, cut into 1/2-inch cubes

1 carrot, thinly sliced

1 can (15 ounces) reduced-sodium diced tomatoes, undrained

1 cup clam juice

1 can (6 ounces) minced clams, undrained

1/2 teaspoon dried marjoram leaves

1/4 teaspoon black pepper

Per Serving
Calories: 187
% Calories from fat: 11
Protein (g): 14.9
Carbohydrates (g): 27.5
Fat (g): 2.4
Saturated fat (g): 0.4
Cholesterol (mg): 33.4
Sodium (mg): 305
Exchanges
Milk: 0.0
Veg.: 2.0
Fruit: 0.0
Bread: 1.0
Meat: 1.0
Fat: 0.0

1. Cook bacon over medium-high heat in 4-quart saucepan until lightly browned. Add onions and saute until tender, about 5 minutes.

2. Add potatoes, carrot, tomatoes and liquid, and clam juice. Heat to boiling; reduce heat and simmer, covered, until carrot and potatoes are tender, 15 to 20 minutes. Stir in remaining ingredients and simmer 5 minutes longer.

QUICK MANHATTAN-STYLE CLAM CHOWDER

Quick, easy, and tasty!

5-6 servings

1 large onion, finely chopped

1 small clove garlic, minced

2 large ribs celery including leaves, diced

2 tablespoons margarine, *or* butter

2 cans (6¹/₂ ounces) chopped clams, undrained

Water

¹/₂ large green bell pepper, diced

1 large potato, peeled, diced

1 can (14¹/₂ ounces) stewed tomatoes, undrained

2 cups tomato juice

¹/₂ teaspoon sugar

1 bay leaf

¹/₂ teaspoon dried thyme leaves

¹/₄ teaspoon dried marjoram leaves

¹/₈ teaspoon pepper

Dash cayenne pepper

Salt, to taste

Per Serving
Calories: 106
% Calories from fat: 17
Protein (g): 7.2
Carbohydrates (g): 17.6
Fat (g): 2.2
Saturated fat (g): 0.4
Cholesterol (mg): 38.3
Sodium (mg): 519
Exchanges
Milk: 0.0
Veg.: 2.0
Fruit: 0.0
Bread: 0.5
Meat: 0.0
Fat: 0.5

1. Saute onion, garlic, and celery in margarine in large saucepan until onion is tender, about 6 minutes.

2. Drain clams, pouring liquor into a measuring cup; add enough water to make 1³/₄ cups. Add liquor mixture, clams, and remaining ingredients, except salt, to saucepan; heat to boiling. Reduce heat and simmer, covered, until potatoes are tender, 10 to 15 minutes. Discard bay leaf; season to taste with salt.

MANHATTAN-STYLE CLAM CHOWDER WITH CORN

The mild smokiness of Canadian bacon adds subtle flavor to this version of Manhattan-Style Clam Chowder.

4 servings

1 large onion, finely chopped
1 small clove garlic, minced
2 large ribs celery, including leaves, chopped
1 medium green bell pepper, chopped
2 teaspoons margarine
2 cans (6^1/$_2$ ounces each) chopped clams, undrained
1 cup fat-free chicken broth
2 medium boiling potatoes, peeled, cubed (^{1}/$_2$-inch)
2 ounces Canadian bacon, julienned
2 cans (14^1/$_2$ ounces each) reduced-sodium diced tomatoes, undrained
1 cup fresh, *or* frozen, whole-kernel corn
1 bay leaf
^{1}/$_2$ teaspoon dried thyme leaves
^{1}/$_2$ teaspoon dried basil leaves
^{1}/$_2$ teaspoon sugar
Salt, black, and cayenne pepper, to taste

Per Serving
Calories: 206
% Calories from fat: 14
Protein (g): 9.8
Carbohydrate (g): 37.3
Fat (g): 3.6
Saturated fat (g): 0.8
Cholesterol (mg): 9.5
Sodium (mg): 488
Exchanges
Milk: 0.0
Veg.: 1.0
Fruit: 0.0
Bread: 2.0
Meat: 0.5
Fat: 0.0

1. Saute onion, garlic, celery, and bell pepper in margarine in large saucepan until onion is tender, about 5 minutes.

2. Drain liquor from clams and add to saucepan; reserve clams. Add broth, potatoes, and Canadian bacon; heat to boiling. Reduce heat and simmer, covered, until potatoes are tender, 10 to 12 minutes.

3. Add reserved clams and remaining ingredients, except salt, black, and cayenne pepper; heat to boiling. Reduce heat and simmer, covered, 5 minutes. Discard bay leaf; season to taste with salt, black, and cayenne pepper.

EASY MANHATTAN-STYLE FISH CHOWDER WITH VEGETABLES

Nothing could be simpler than this fish chowder, with its flavor of the sea and vegetable-rich texture.

5-6 servings

1	large onion, finely chopped
2	ribs celery, including leaves, coarsely chopped
2	teaspoons margarine, *or* butter
2	cups reduced-sodium fat-free chicken broth
1	quart reduced-sodium tomato juice, *or* regular tomato juice
1	large carrot, very thinly sliced
1¹/₂	cups frozen French-style green beans
1¹/₂	cups frozen whole-kernel corn
1	large potato, peeled, diced
1	bay leaf
¹/₂	teaspoon dried thyme leaves
¹/₂	teaspoon dried marjoram leaves
¹/₄	teaspoon dry mustard
	Dash cayenne pepper
¹/₄	teaspoon black pepper
10-12	ounces skinless flounder, *or* halibut, fillets, cut into 3/4-inch pieces
	Salt, to taste

Per Serving
Calories: 170
% Calories from fat: 11
Protein (g): 14.4
Carbohydrates (g): 26.5
Fat (g): 2.2
Saturated fat (g): 0.4
Cholesterol (mg): 24.9
Sodium (mg): 205
Exchanges
Milk: 0.0
Veg.: 2.0
Fruit: 0.0
Bread: 1.0
Meat: 1.0
Fat: 0.0

1. Saute onion and celery in margarine in large saucepan until tender, about 8 minutes. Add broth, tomato juice, carrot, green beans, corn, potato, and herbs and spices; heat to boiling. Reduce heat and simmer, covered, until vegetables are tender, about 15 minutes.

2. Stir in fish; simmer fish until it flakes with a fork, 8 to 10 minutes. Discard bay leaf; season to taste with salt.

NEW YORK CITY CLAM CHOWDER

Serve this substantial chowder with Hearty Vegetable-Rye Bread (see p. 796).

6 servings

  36 littleneck clams, *or* other fresh small
      clams
      Olive oil cooking spray
   4 potatoes, peeled, cubed
   1 cup sliced onion
   2 carrots, chopped
   1 can (28 ounces) crushed tomatoes,
      undrained
  $1/2$ cup clam juice
  $1/3$ cup chopped parsley
  $1/2$ teaspoon dried thyme leaves
  $1/4$ teaspoon pepper
   2 bay leaves
  $1/4$ teaspoon hot pepper sauce, optional
      Salt and pepper, to taste

Per Serving
Calories: 228
% Calories from fat: **5**
Protein (g): 19
Carbohydrate (g): 34.8
Fat (g): 1.3
Saturated fat (g): 0.2
Cholesterol (mg): 38.2
Sodium (mg): 332
Exchanges
Milk: 0.0
Veg.: 1.0
Fruit: 0.0
Bread: 2.0
Meat: 1.0
Fat: 0.0

1. Wash clams and discard any that are open. Place clams in large saucepan; add 3 cups water and heat to boiling. Reduce heat and simmer, covered, 5 to 8 minutes or until clams open. Discard any clams that do not open. Strain liquid through double layer of cheesecloth and reserve.

2. Spray Dutch oven with cooking spray; heat over medium heat until hot. Saute potatoes, onion, and carrots, 5 minutes. Mix in reserved clam liquid and remaining ingredients, except salt and pepper.

3. Heat chowder to boiling; reduce heat and simmer, covered, 20 minutes or until vegetables are tender. Add clams in shells and cook 3 minutes longer. Discard bay leaves; season to taste with salt and pepper.

LIGHTHOUSE CLAM CHOWDER

Enjoy this mouth-watering New England-style chowder, creamy and load-ed with clams and potatoes.

4 servings

   1   bottle (11 ounces) clam juice
   2   cans (6¹/₂ ounces each) minced clams, drained, liquor reserved
   2   medium potatoes, cut into ¹/₂-inch cubes
   1   onion, chopped
   1   rib celery, sliced
1¹/₂   cups 2% reduced-fat milk
   1   slice (1 ounce) lean ham, fat trimmed, chopped
   2   teaspoons Worcestershire sauce
 ³/₄   teaspoon dried thyme leaves
       Salt and pepper, to taste

Per Serving
Calories: 136
% Calories from fat: 15
Protein (g): 7
Carbohydrate (g): 22.4
Fat (g): 2.3
Saturated fat (g): 1.3
Cholesterol (mg): 13.5
Sodium (mg): 568
Exchanges
Milk: 0.0
Veg.: 1.0
Fruit: 0.0
Bread: 1.0
Meat: 0.0
Fat: 0.5

1.   Heat clam juice, reserved clam liquor, potatoes, onion, and celery to boiling in large saucepan; reduce heat and simmer, cov-ered, until potatoes are tender, about 15 minutes. Using slotted spoon, remove half the vegetables; reserve.

2.   Process remaining chowder in blender or food processor un-til smooth; return to saucepan. Stir in reserved vegetables, clams, milk, ham, Worcestershire sauce, and thyme. Heat chowder until hot, about 5 minutes. Season to taste with salt and pepper.

MAINE CLAM CHOWDER

To make this chowder a day in advance for convenience, steam the clams (Step 1) and add to the chowder just before serving.

6 servings

36 littleneck clams, *or* other fresh small clams
   Vegetable cooking spray
1 cup chopped onion
$^1/_2$ cup chopped celery
1 carrot, thinly sliced
4 red potatoes, peeled, cubed
2 cups fat-free milk, divided
$^1/_2$ cup clam juice
$^1/_4$ cup all-purpose flour
$^1/_4$ teaspoon white pepper
   Salt, to taste

Per Serving
Calories: 158
% Calories from fat: **4**
Protein (g): 11.6
Carbohydrate (g): **27.5**
Fat (g): 0.8
Saturated fat (g): 0.2
Cholesterol (mg): 19.6
Sodium (mg): 164
Exchanges
Milk: 0.0
Veg.: 0.0
Fruit: 0.0
Bread: 1.5
Meat: 1.0
Fat: 0.0

1. Wash clams and discard any that are open. Place clams in saucepan with 6 cups water; heat to boiling. Reduce heat and simmer, covered, 5 to 8 minutes or until clams open. Discard any clams that do not open. Remove clams from shells, chop, and reserve. Strain liquid through double layer of cheesecloth and reserve.

2. Spray large saucepan with cooking spray; heat over medium heat until hot. Saute onion, celery, carrot, and potatoes for 5 minutes over medium heat. Add 1$^1/_2$ cups milk, reserved clam liquid, and clam juice. Cover and simmer 20 to 30 minutes or until vegetables are tender.

3. Heat chowder to boiling; whisk in combined flour and remaining $^1/_2$ cup milk. Boil, whisking, until thickened, 1 to 2 minutes. Stir in white pepper; season to taste with salt. Add reserved clams and cook 2 to 3 minutes longer.

NEW ENGLAND CLAM CHOWDER

Fresh clams can be used in this fragrant clam chowder. Soak 3 dozen clams in cold water to cover for 30 minutes. Heat clams to boiling in a covered skillet with ¹/₂ cup water; boil until clams have opened, 2 to 4 minutes. Remove clams from shells and add to chowder; discard any that did not open. Strain broth through a double layer of cheesecloth and add to chowder.

6 servings

2 slices bacon
1 cup chopped onion
1 cup chopped celery
¹/₄ cup all-purpose flour
2 cups clam juice
2 cans (6¹/₂ ounces each) diced clams, undrained
1 can (6 ounces) whole clams, undrained
1³/₄ cups cubed, peeled russet potatoes
1 teaspoon dried thyme leaves
1 bay leaf
1¹/₂-2 cups fat-free half-and-half, *or* fat-free milk
Salt and pepper, to taste

Per Serving
Calories: 195
% Calories from fat: 11
Protein (g): 13.4
Carbohydrates (g): 30.3
Fat (g): 2.3
Saturated fat (g): 0.6
Cholesterol (mg): 59.2
Sodium (mg): 261
Exchanges
Milk: 0.0
Veg.: 0.0
Fruit: 0.0
Bread: 1.5
Meat: 1.0
Fat: 0.0

1. Fry bacon in large saucepan until crisp; drain well, crumble, and reserve. Drain all fat from pan; add onion and celery and saute until tender, 5 to 8 minutes. Stir in flour; cook over medium-low heat, stirring constantly, 1 minute.

2. Stir in clam juice, undrained clams, potatoes, reserved bacon, and herbs; heat to boiling. Reduce heat and simmer, covered, until potatoes are tender, about 15 minutes. Stir in half-and-half; cook over medium heat until hot through, about 5 minutes. Discard bay leaf; season to taste with salt and pepper.

WHITE CLAM CHOWDER WITH CORN

This hearty chowder is savory and rich in flavor.

4-5 servings

1 medium onion, chopped

1 large rib celery, chopped

1 tablespoon margarine, *or* butter

1 tablespoon flour

1 cup clam juice, *or* fat-free chicken broth

1 can (10¹/₂ ounces) minced clams, undrained

1 large bay leaf

¹/₂ teaspoon dried marjoram leaves

¹/₈ teaspoon black pepper

2 cups cubed, peeled red potatoes (¹/₄-inch)

2 cups whole-kernel corn

1 cup 2% reduced-fat milk

Salt, to taste

Per Serving
Calories: 224
% Calories from fat: 15
Protein (g): 11.1
Carbohydrates (g): 39.6
Fat (g): 4.1
Saturated fat (g): 1.2
Cholesterol (mg): 40.7
Sodium (mg): 157
Exchanges
Milk: 0.0
Veg.: 0.0
Fruit: 0.0
Bread: 2.5
Meat: 1.0
Fat: 0.0

1. Saute onion and celery in margarine in large saucepan until onion is tender, about 5 minutes. Stir in flour; cook 1 minute longer. Stir in clam juice; drain minced clams and stir in liquor.

2. Stir in herbs, pepper, potatoes, and corn; heat to boiling. Reduce heat and simmer, covered, stirring occasionally, until potatoes are tender, 8 to 10 minutes. Discard bay leaf.

3. Process half the chowder in blender or food processor until smooth; return to saucepan. Stir in milk and minced clams; simmer 5 minutes. Season to taste with salt.

FLOUNDER CHOWDER

Although this dish calls for flounder, any other mild-tasting fish such as orange roughy or halibut may be substituted.

5-6 servings

1 large onion, finely chopped
1 large garlic clove, chopped
1 large rib celery, diced
2 teaspoons margarine
2 cups Fish Stock (see p. 9), *or* canned vegetable broth
2 cups 2% reduced-fat milk
2¹/2 cups cubed, peeled potatoes (³/4-inch)
1 cup frozen lima beans
1 large carrot, diced
1¹/2 teaspoons dried basil leaves
¹/2 teaspoon dried marjoram leaves
¹/4 teaspoon dried thyme leaves
¹/4 teaspoon dry mustard
¹/4 teaspoon celery seeds, crushed
1 tablespoon plus 1 teaspoon cornstarch
¹/4 cup water
1 pound skinless flounder fillets, cut into 1-inch pieces
1 cup frozen whole-kernel corn
Salt and pepper, to taste

Per Serving
Calories: 291
% Calories from fat: **13**
Protein (g): 23.1
Carbohydrates (g): 40.4
Fat (g): 4.2
Saturated fat (g): 1.5
Cholesterol (mg): 50
Sodium (mg): 277
Exchanges
Milk: 0.0
Veg.: 0.0
Fruit: 0.0
Bread: 2.5
Meat: 2.0
Fat: 0.0

1. Saute onion, garlic, and celery in margarine in large saucepan until tender, 5 to 8 minutes. Add remaining ingredients, except cornstarch, water, fish, corn, salt, and pepper; heat to boiling. Reduce heat and simmer, covered, until vegetables are tender, about 15 minutes.

2. Heat soup to boiling; stir in combined cornstarch and water; boil, stirring, until thickened, 1 to 2 minutes. Reduce heat and stir in fish and corn; simmer, uncovered, until fish is tender and flakes with a fork, about 5 minutes. Season to taste with salt and pepper.

FOUR

Chili

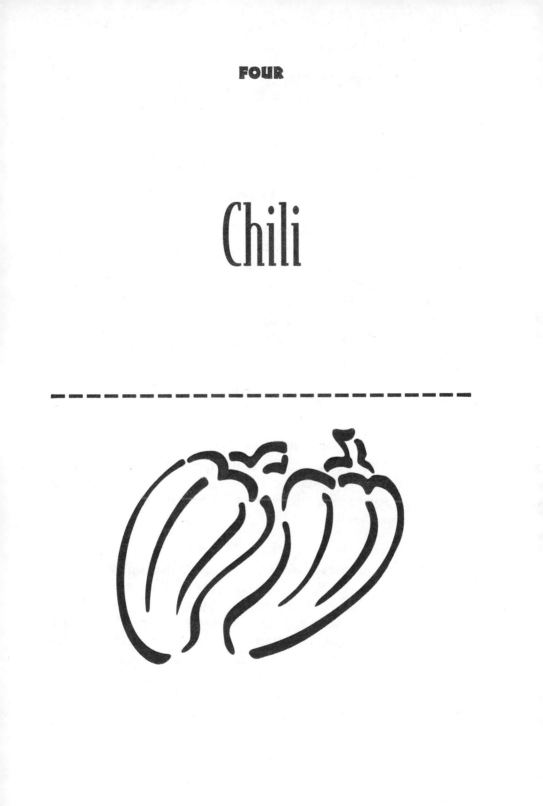

FAMILY FAVORITE CHILI

This very easy chili will appeal to all ages.

8 servings

1½ pounds lean ground beef or turkey

2 cans (15 ounces each) pinto beans, rinsed, drained

2 cans (16 ounces each) reduced-sodium stewed tomatoes, undrained

2 cups frozen whole-kernel corn

1 cup chopped onion

½ cup chopped green bell pepper

2 tablespoons taco seasoning mix

1 tablespoon light ranch salad dressing mix

Salt and pepper, to taste

Fat-free sour cream, as garnish

Tortilla chips, as garnish

Per Serving
Calories: 268
% Calories from fat: **13**
Protein (gm): 23.3
Carbohydrate (gm): **36.4**
Fat (gm): 4.1
Saturated fat (gm): **1.2**
Cholesterol (mg): **41.2**
Sodium (mg): **566**
Exchanges
Milk: 0.0
Veg.: 1.0
Fruit: 0.0
Bread: 2.0
Meat: 2.0
Fat: 0.0

1. Brown beef in large saucepan; drain well. Add remaining ingredients, except salt, pepper, sour cream, and tortilla chips, and heat to boiling. Reduce heat and simmer, covered, 20 minutes. Season to taste with salt and pepper. Garnish with sour cream and tortilla chips.

Variation:
Chili-Stuffed Potatoes—Scrub 8 medium Idaho potatoes; wrap in aluminum foil and bake at 400 degrees until tender, 45 to 60 minutes. Make chili recipe as above, cutting recipe in half and deleting tortilla chips. Split potatoes lengthwise and fluff with a fork; spoon chili over potatoes. Sprinkle each with 2 table-spoons shredded reduced-fat Cheddar cheese and garnish with dollops of sour cream.

SPEEDY CHILI

Easy for those tired mid-week evenings.

8 servings

Vegetable cooking spray
1¹/₂ pounds lean ground beef
2 pounds ground turkey breast
2 large onions, chopped
3 cloves garlic, minced
¹/₂ teaspoon pepper
1 can (6 ounces) reduced-sodium tomato paste
2 cans (10¹/₂ ounces each) zesty tomato sauce
2 cans (15¹/₂ ounces each) kidney beans, rinsed, drained
2 tablespoons chili powder
1 teaspoon dried oregano leaves
Salt and pepper, to taste
Finely chopped parsley, as garnish

Per Serving
Calories: 415
% Calories from fat: 29
Protein (gm): 43.7
Carbohydrate (gm): 28.7
Fat (gm): 13.2
Saturated fat (gm): 4.9
Cholesterol (mg): 97.5
Sodium (mg): 911
Exchanges
Milk: 0.0
Veg.: 0.0
Fruit: 0.0
Bread: 2.0
Meat: 4.0
Fat: 0.0

1. Spray large Dutch oven with cooking spray; heat oven to medium heat until hot. Add ground beef, turkey, onions, and garlic and cook until meat is browned, 10 to 12 minutes; drain fat and crumble meat with a fork. Stir in remaining ingredients, except salt, pepper, and parsley, and heat to boiling; reduce heat and simmer, covered, 15 minutes. Season to taste with salt and pepper; sprinkle each serving with parsley.

SPICY CHILI BEAN CHILI

On a cold winter's night, nothing chases the chills better than this easy-to-prepare vegetarian dish.

4 servings

1 can (14 ounces) chili beans
1 cup fat-free beef broth
1 can (14 ounces) plum tomatoes, drained, chopped
2 green bell peppers, chopped
1 cup frozen whole-kernel corn
1 medium onion, chopped
2 teaspoons minced garlic
1 teaspoon chili powder
Salt and pepper, to taste

Per Serving
Calories: 150
% Calories from fat: 7
Protein (gm): 8.8
Carbohydrate (gm): 31.5
Fat (gm): 1.3
Saturated fat (gm): 0.1
Cholesterol (mg): 0
Sodium (mg): 524
Exchanges
Milk: 0.0
Veg.: 0.0
Fruit: 0.0
Bread: 2.0
Meat: 0.0
Fat: 0.0

1. Combine all ingredients, except salt and pepper, in a large saucepan; heat to boiling. Reduce heat and simmer, covered, 15 to 20 minutes. Season to taste with salt and pepper.

CHILI CON CARNE

One of the best "bowls of red" you'll ever taste!

8 servings (about 1 cup each)

Vegetable cooking spray
1 pound 95% lean ground beef
1½ cups chopped onions
1 cup chopped green bell pepper
2 cloves garlic, minced
1-2 tablespoons chili powder
2 teaspoons dried cumin
1 teaspoon dried oregano leaves
¼ teaspoon ground cloves
2 cans (14½ ounces each) no-salt-added whole tomatoes, undrained, coarsely chopped

Per Serving
Calories: 220
% Calories from fat: 13
Protein (g): 21.9
Carbohydrates (g): 28.7
Fat (g): 3.6
Saturated fat (g): 1
Cholesterol (mg): 32.5
Sodium (mg): 224
Exchanges
Milk: 0.0
Veg.: 2.0
Fruit: 0.0
Bread: 1.0
Meat: 2.0
Fat: 0.0

   1 can (6 ounces) reduced-sodium tomato
      paste
 3/4 cup beer, *or* reduced-sodium beef broth
   1 tablespoon packed light brown sugar
2-3 teaspoons unsweetened cocoa
   1 can (15 ounces) red kidney beans,
      rinsed, drained
      Salt and pepper, to taste
 1/2 cup (2 ounces) shredded fat-free, *or*
      reduced-fat, Cheddar cheese
 1/2 cup thinly sliced green onions and tops
 1/2 cup fat-free sour cream

1. Spray large saucepan with cooking spray; heat over medium heat until hot. Add ground beef, onions, bell pepper, and garlic; cook over medium heat until meat is brown and vegetables are tender, 5 to 8 minutes. Add chili powder, cumin, oregano, and cloves; cook 1 to 2 minutes longer.

2. Add tomatoes and liquid, tomato paste, beer, brown sugar, and cocoa to beef mixture. Heat to boiling; reduce heat and simmer, covered, 1 hour. Stir in beans and simmer, uncovered, to thicken, if desired. Season to taste with salt and pepper.

3. Spoon chili into bowls; sprinkle each with equal amounts of cheese, green onions, and sour cream.

Variations:
Chili Mac—In Step 2, add 1 cup uncooked elbow macaroni, *or* chili mac pasta, and 1/2 cup water to chili after 45 minutes cooking time; heat to boiling. Reduce heat and simmer, covered, until macaroni is tender, about 15 minutes; stir in beans and simmer 5 minutes longer.

Southwest Chili—Make recipe as above, substituting poblano chili for the bell pepper, black or pinto beans for the kidney beans, and pepper-jack cheese for the Cheddar cheese.

CORN AND BEAN CON CARNE

Cornmeal Crisps are a perfect chili complement!

8 servings

12 ounces ground beef round

1 large onion, finely chopped

1 quart reduced-sodium fat-free beef broth

2 cans (14¹/₂ ounces each) reduced-sodium diced tomatoes, undrained

2 cans (15 ounces each) reduced-sodium kidney beans, rinsed, drained

2¹/₂ cups frozen whole-kernel corn

1-2 tablespoons chili powder

1 teaspoon ground cumin

1 teaspoon sugar

¹/₄ teaspoon pepper

Salt, to taste

Cornmeal Crisps (recipe follows)

Per Serving
Calories: 364
% Calories from fat: 21
Protein (gm): 22.2
Carbohydrate (gm): 52.2
Fat (gm): 8.8
Saturated fat (gm): 2
Cholesterol (mg): 21.6
Sodium (mg): 422
Exchanges
Milk: 0.0
Veg.: 1.0
Fruit: 0.0
Bread: 3.0
Meat: 2.0
Fat: 0.5

1. Cook beef and onion in large saucepan over medium heat until beef is browned, 5 to 8 minutes; drain and crumble beef with a fork. Stir in remaining ingredients, except salt and Cornmeal Crisps; heat to boiling. Reduce heat and simmer, covered, 20 to 25 minutes. Season to taste with salt. Serve with Cornmeal Crisps.

Cornmeal Crisps

makes about 12

1 cup self-rising flour

¹/₃ cup yellow cornmeal

1 tablespoon sugar

4 tablespoons cold margarine, cut into pieces

1 tablespoon distilled white vinegar

¹/₄ cup ice water

1 egg white, beaten

2-3 tablespoons grated Parmesan cheese

1. Combine flour, cornmeal, and sugar in small bowl; cut in margarine with pastry cutter until mixture resembles coarse crumbs. Mix in vinegar and enough ice water for mixture to form a dough.

2. Roll dough on floured surface to scant ¹/₄ inch thickness; cut into rounds and place on greased cookie sheet. Brush with egg white and sprinkle with Parmesan cheese. Bake at 375 degrees until golden, 7 to 10 minutes. Cool on wire rack.

BAKED CHILI CON CARNE

A colorful chili with oven-baked goodness!

6-8 servings

Per Serving
Calories: 306
% Calories from fat: 11
Protein (g): 29.3
Carbohydrates (g): 48.9
Fat (g): 4.4
Saturated fat (g): 0.9
Cholesterol (mg): 36.5
Sodium (mg): 1081
Exchanges
Milk: 0.0
Veg.: 3.0
Fruit: 0.0
Bread: 2.0
Meat: 2.0
Fat: 0.0

16 ounces beef round, *or* skirt steak, fat trimmed, cut into 1-inch pieces
1 teaspoon minced garlic
1 large onion, finely chopped
1 large green bell pepper, seeded, finely chopped
1 large red bell pepper, seeded, finely chopped
1 large yellow bell pepper, seeded, finely chopped
1 large banana pepper, seeded, finely chopped
1 large jalapeño chili, finely chopped
1 can (14¹/₂ ounces) reduced-sodium diced tomatoes, undrained
1 can (16 ounces) reduced-sodium tomato sauce
1 can (6 ounces) reduced-sodium tomato paste
1 can (15¹/₂ ounces) light red kidney beans, rinsed drained
1 can (15¹/₂ ounces) dark red kidney beans, rinsed, drained
1 teaspoon chili powder
1 teaspoon ground cumin
1 bay leaf
Salt and pepper, to taste
Condiments (not included in nutritional data): shredded reduced-fat Cheddar cheese, fat-free sour cream, chopped green onions, and tomatoes

1. Cook beef and garlic in large Dutch oven over medium heat until beef is browned, 8 to 10 minutes; drain. Stir in remaining ingredients, except salt, pepper, and condiments.

2. Bake, covered, at 350 degrees for 1¼ hours, stirring occasionally. Discard bay leaf; season to taste with salt and pepper. Serve with condiments.

CHUNKY CHILI FOR A CROWD

Make this big batch of chili for a party, and serve it with a do-it-yourself array of garnishes. Or make it for dinner, and freeze some for later use.

16 servings

4 pounds lean beef stew meat, cubed (1-inch)

1-2 tablespoons vegetable oil

2 cups sliced onions

¼ cup minced garlic

¼ cup chopped jalapeño chili

2 cans (28 ounces each) reduced-sodium whole tomatoes, undrained, chopped

3 cans (15 ounces each) pinto beans, rinsed, drained

1 can (6 ounces) reduced-sodium tomato paste

3-4 tablespoons chili powder

1 teaspoon beef bouillon crystals

2 green bell peppers, sliced

⅓ cup water

¼ cup cornstarch

Salt and pepper, to taste

Hot pepper sauce, to taste

Condiments (not included in the nutritional data): tortilla chips, oyster crackers, grated reduced-fat Cheddar cheese, fat-free sour cream, chopped tomatoes, diced avocado, pickled jalapeño chilies, sliced black olives

Per Serving
Calories: 301
% Calories from fat: 22
Protein (gm): 34.3
Carbohydrate (gm): 24.5
Fat (gm): 7.4
Saturated fat (gm): 2.3
Cholesterol (mg): 70.9
Sodium (mg): 304
Exchanges
Milk: 0.0
Veg.: 2.0
Fruit: 0.0
Bread: 1.0
Meat: 3.0
Fat: 0.0

1. Cook meat in oil in large Dutch oven until browned. Stir in onions, garlic, and jalapeño chili and cook until onions are tender, about 8 minutes.

2. Stir in tomatoes and liquid, beans, tomato paste, chili powder, and bouillon crystals. Heat to boiling and simmer, covered, until meat is very tender, about 2 hours, stirring occasionally.

3. Stir in green peppers and combined water and cornstarch; heat to boiling. Reduce heat and simmer 5 minutes. Season to taste with salt, pepper, and hot pepper sauce. Serve in bowls, garnished with condiments.

SPICED BEAN CHILI WITH FUSILLI

Use any favorite beans or shape of pasta in this versatile chili.

8 servings (about 1¼ cups each)

1 pound lean ground beef
2 cups chopped onions
½ cup sliced celery
1 cup sliced mushrooms
1-2 tablespoons vegetable oil
2 cans (14½ ounces each) diced tomatoes with roasted garlic
1 can (15½ ounces) garbanzo beans, rinsed, drained
1 can (15 ounces) dark red kidney beans, rinsed, drained
1-2 tablespoons chili powder
1-2 teaspoons ground cumin
¾ teaspoon dried oregano leaves
8 ounces fusilli, cooked, warm
Salt and pepper, to taste
3-4 tablespoons sliced green, *or* ripe, olives, optional

Per Serving
Calories: 367
% Calories from fat: 26
Protein (g): 21.3
Carbohydrates (g): 47.3
Fat (g): 10.6
Saturated fat (g): 3.2
Cholesterol (mg): 35.2
Sodium (mg): 759
Exchanges
Milk: 0.0
Veg.: 1.0
Fruit: 0.0
Bread: 3.0
Meat: 1.0
Fat: 1.5

1. Cook ground beef, onions, celery, and mushrooms in oil in large saucepan until beef is browned, about 8 minutes; drain well. Add tomatoes, beans, chili powder, and herbs. Heat to boiling. Reduce heat and simmer, covered, until vegetables are tender, about 10 minutes.

2. Stir in pasta. Season to taste with salt and pepper. Serve chili in bowls; sprinkle with olives.

CINCINNATI CHILI

5-Way Cincinnati Chili gained fame in the chili parlors of Cincinnati. The sauce is seasoned with sweet spices and generally has a hint of dark chocolate. The chili is served alone, 1 way; 2 ways, over spaghetti; 3 ways, with added beans; 4 ways, with chopped onions; 5 ways, with shredded cheese!

8 servings

12 ounces lean ground turkey, *or* beef
1/2 cup chopped onion
4 cloves garlic, minced
1 can (28 ounces) crushed tomatoes, undrained
1 can (8 ounces) reduced-sodium tomato sauce
1/2 cup water
2 tablespoons chili powder
2 teaspoons dried oregano leaves
1 teaspoon ground cinnamon
1 teaspoon ground allspice
1/2 teaspoon paprika
1 tablespoon cocoa
1/2 teaspoon salt
1/2 teaspoon pepper
16 ounces spaghetti, cooked, warm
Canned, drained pinto beans, chopped onions, shredded reduced-fat Cheddar cheese, as garnishes

Per Serving
Calories: 381
% Calories from fat: **13**
Protein (g): 19.6
Carbohydrates (g): **62**
Fat (g): 5.7
Saturated fat (g): 1.3
Cholesterol (mg): 31.6
Sodium (mg): 454
Exchanges
Milk: 0.0
Veg.: 3.0
Fruit: 0.0
Bread: 3.0
Meat: 1.0
Fat: 0.5

1. Cook ground turkey in large saucepan over medium heat until browned, 5 to 8 minutes. Remove turkey from saucepan; drain and crumble. Drain excess fat from saucepan.

2. Add onion and garlic to saucepan; saute until onion is tender, about 5 minutes. Stir in remaining ingredients except spaghetti and garnishes; heat to boiling. Reduce heat and simmer, covered, 15 minutes; simmer, uncovered, until sauce is thickened, about 15 minutes more. Serve over spaghetti; garnish with beans, onions, and shredded cheese.

MALE CHAUVINIST CHILI

A real man's chili—but women will love it too!

8 servings

8 slices reduced-sodium bacon

8 ounces reduced-fat, reduced-sodium Italian-style turkey sausage, cut into ¹/₂-inch slices

8 ounces lean ground beef eye of round

1¹/₂ cups coarsely chopped onions

1 green bell pepper, coarsely chopped

2 cloves garlic, minced

1 small jalapeño chili, minced

1 cup dry red wine, *or* tomato juice

¹/₄-¹/₂ cup very-low-sodium Worcestershire sauce

1 teaspoon dry mustard

1 teaspoon celery seeds

1-2 tablespoons chili powder

¹/₂ teaspoon ground cumin

1¹/₂ teaspoons pepper

1¹/₂ quarts chopped tomatoes

1 can (15 ounces) pinto beans, rinsed, drained

1 can (15 ounces) black beans, rinsed, drained

1 can (15 ounces) chickpeas, drained

Salt, to taste

Per Serving
Calories: 332
% Calories from fat: **21**
Protein (gm): 21.8
Carbohydrate (gm): **43.4**
Fat (gm): 8.4
Saturated fat (gm): 2.2
Cholesterol (mg): 33.9
Sodium (mg): 789
Exchanges
Milk: 0.0
Veg.: 2.0
Fruit: 0.0
Bread: 2.0
Meat: 2.0
Fat: 0.5

1. Fry bacon in large Dutch oven until crisp; drain, crumble, and reserve. Drain fat from pan. Add Italian sausage and ground beef to pan; cook over medium heat until browned, crumbling beef with a fork. Drain well.

2. Add onions, bell pepper, garlic, and jalapeño chili to pan and cook 5 minutes. Add wine and heat to boiling; reduce heat and simmer, uncovered, 5 minutes. Add reserved bacon and remaining ingredients, except salt; simmer, covered, 45 to 60 minutes. Season to taste with salt.

OLD HICKORY CHILI WITH WHITE BEANS

Holy smokes! This quick hickory-smoked turkey chili is made without wood chips or a grill. The cook's flavor trick—natural hickory seasoning.

4 servings

8 ounces ground turkey breast

1 cup chopped Spanish onion

1 cup reduced-sodium mild, *or* medium, salsa

2 cups coarsely chopped tomatoes

1 can (15 ounces) white kidney beans, rinsed, drained

2 tablespoons chili powder

1 tablespoon white wine vinegar

2 tablespoons finely chopped fresh cilantro

1 teaspoon natural hickory seasoning
    Salt and pepper, to taste

Per Serving
Calories: 212
% Calories from fat: 10
Protein (gm): 17.3
Carbohydrate (gm): 31.4
Fat (gm): 2.5
Saturated fat (gm): 0.6
Cholesterol (mg): 22.4
Sodium (mg): 630
Exchanges
Milk: 0.0
Veg.: 0.0
Fruit: 0.0
Bread: 2.0
Meat: 1.0
Fat: 0.0

1. Cook turkey in large saucepan over medium heat until browned; drain and crumble with a fork. Add onion and saute until tender, about 5 minutes. Add remaining ingredients, except cilantro, hickory seasoning, salt, and pepper; heat to boiling. Reduce heat and simmer, covered, 10 minutes. Stir in cilantro and hickory seasoning; season to taste with salt and pepper.

BLIZZARD CHILI

A great chili for snowbound winter evenings.

6 servings

16 ounces lean ground beef round
2 cups finely chopped onions
1 clove garlic, minced
2 cups cooked dry, *or* rinsed and drained canned, kidney beans
2 cups cooked dry, *or* rinsed and drained canned, black beans
2¹/₂ cups cooked dry, *or* rinsed and drained canned, cannellini beans
2 cans (15 ounces each) reduced-sodium tomato sauce
1 bay leaf
1 tablespoon chili powder
2 teaspoons sugar
1 teaspoon ground cumin
¹/₈ teaspoon pepper
Salt, to taste

Per Serving
Calories: 457
% Calories from fat: 10.4
Protein (g): 33
Carbohydrates (g): 59
Fat (g): 10.4
Saturated fat (g): 3.8
Cholesterol (mg): 47
Sodium (mg): 98
Exchanges
Milk: 0.0
Veg.: 3.0
Fruit: 0.0
Bread: 2.5
Meat: 3.0
Fat: 0.5

1. Cook ground beef, onions, and garlic in large saucepan over medium heat until beef is browned, 8 to 10 minutes; drain fat and crumble beef with a fork. Stir in remaining ingredients, except salt, and heat to boiling. Reduce heat and simmer, covered, 20 to 30 minutes. Season to taste with salt.

MICROWAVE CHILI CON CHICKEN

A perfect chili for microwave cooking—just 10 minutes from the cutting board to the dinner table!

2 servings

12 ounces boneless, skinless chicken breast
 3 tablespoons lemon juice
 1 teaspoon olive oil
 2 cloves garlic, minced
 2 medium onions, sliced
 2 bell peppers (red and green), thinly sliced
 2 teaspoons finely chopped jalapeño chili
 1 teaspoon ground cumin
1 1/2 teaspoons dried oregano leaves
     Salt and pepper, to taste
     Finely chopped parsley, as garnish

Per Serving
Calories: 153
% Calories from fat: 21
Protein (gm): 20.3
Carbohydrate (gm): 9.8
Fat (gm): 3.7
Saturated fat (gm): 0.8
Cholesterol (mg): 51.7
Sodium (mg): 49
Exchanges
Milk: 0.0
Veg.: 2.0
Fruit: 0.0
Bread: 0.0
Meat: 2.0
Fat: 0.0

1. Cut chicken into 1/2-inch strips and sprinkle with lemon juice. Set aside.

2. Combine oil, garlic, and onions in 2-quart glass casserole; microwave, uncovered, at High power, 2 minutes. Stir in remaining ingredients, except salt, pepper, and parsley. Microwave, covered, at High power 2 minutes.

3. Stir in chicken; microwave, loosely covered, at High power until chicken is cooked, 4 to 5 minutes, stirring halfway through cooking time. Season with salt and pepper and sprinkle with parsley.

MICROWAVE CHICKEN CHILI

A flavorful chili, prepared with microwave convenience.

4 servings

Per Serving
Calories: 197
% Calories from fat: 9
Protein (gm): 19.7
Carbohydrate (gm): 26
Fat (gm): 2.1
Saturated fat (gm): 0.5
Cholesterol (mg): 34.5
Sodium (mg): 555
Exchanges
Milk: 0.0
Veg.: 2.0
Fruit: 0.0
Bread: 1.0
Meat: 1.5
Fat: 0.0

  8 ounces ground chicken breast
 $1/2$ medium onion, chopped
  1 small clove garlic, minced
  1 can (16 ounces) stewed tomatoes, undrained
 $1/4$ teaspoon ground cumin
  1 teaspoon chili powder
  1 can ($15^1/2$ ounces) kidney beans, rinsed, drained
     Salt and pepper, to taste

1. Combine chicken, onion, and garlic in 2-quart glass casserole; microwave on Medium power, loosely covered, until chicken is cooked, 3 to 4 minutes. Drain; crumble chicken with a fork.

2. Stir in remaining ingredients, except salt and pepper; microwave, covered, on Medium power 10 minutes, stirring halfway through cooking time. Season to taste with salt and pepper.

MESQUITE CHICKEN CHILI

Looking for a differently delicious Tex-Mex dish that will appeal to adventurous and not-so-adventurous palates alike? This fast chili will fit the bill. It gets its unique essence from mesquite flavoring and tomatillos.

4 servings

Per Serving
Calories: 293
% Calories from fat: 15
Protein (g): 28.1
Carbohydrates (g): 36.3
Fat (g): 5.3
Saturated fat (g): 1.1
Cholesterol (mg): 51.7
Sodium (mg): 469
Exchanges
Milk: 0.0
Veg.: 2.0
Fruit: 0.0
Bread: 2.0
Meat: 2.0
Fat: 0.0

 12 ounces boneless, skinless chicken breast, cut into $1/2$-inch cubes
  1 teaspoon olive oil
  1 large onion, chopped
  1 can (28 ounces) reduced-sodium crushed tomatoes
  8 ounces tomatillos, husked, coarsely chopped
  1 can (15 ounces) red beans, rinsed, drained

1 poblano chili, chopped
2 tablespoons chili powder
2 teaspoons minced garlic
1 teaspoon mesquite smoke flavoring
   Salt and pepper, to taste

1. Saute chicken in oil in large saucepan until lightly browned; add onion and cook until tender. Add tomatoes, tomatillos, beans, poblano chili, chili powder, and garlic. Heat to boiling; reduce heat and simmer, covered, 10 minutes. Stir in smoke flavoring; season to taste with salt and pepper.

Variation:
Hominy Chili—Make chili as above, substituting boneless lean beef for the chicken and 1 can (15 ounces) hominy, drained, for the tomatillos; omit mesquite smoke flavoring. Sprinkle each serving with shredded Cheddar cheese and dollops of reduced-fat sour cream.

CHILI CON CARNE BURRITOS

We're serving this eight-ingredient chili as a knockout burrito filling. Fresh cilantro and an ancho chili boost the chili flavor to a high level.

4 servings

12 ounces ground beef sirloin steak
 1 cup chopped onion
 1 can (15 ounces) diced tomatoes, undrained
 1 ancho chili, chopped
 1 tablespoon chili powder
 1 teaspoon ground cumin
1/4 cup finely chopped fresh cilantro
     Salt and pepper, to taste
 4 flour tortillas, warm

Per Serving
Calories: 254
% Calories from fat: 24
Protein (gm): 20.1
Carbohydrate (gm): 28
Fat (gm): 6.7
Saturated fat (gm): 1.9
Cholesterol (mg): 44.6
Sodium (mg): 642
Exchanges
Milk: 0.0
Veg.: 2.0
Fruit: 0.0
Bread: 1.0
Meat: 2.0
Fat: 0.5

1. Cook beef in large skillet over medium heat until browned; drain fat and crumble with a fork. Add onion and saute until tender, about 5 minutes. Add tomatoes and liquid, ancho chili, chili powder, and cumin; heat to boiling. Reduce heat and simmer, uncovered, until hot and thickened, about 20 minutes. Stir in cilantro; season to taste with salt and pepper.

2. Spoon chili down centers of tortillas; roll up and serve immediately.

CHILI TACOS

A fun way to serve chili—in warm taco shells!

4 servings

4-6 ounces ground beef round steak
1 medium onion, chopped
2 teaspoons minced garlic
1 can (15 ounces) crushed tomatoes, undrained
2 cups low-sodium refried beans
1 tablespoon chili powder
1/4 teaspoon ground allspice
1 dried cayenne chili, seeded, minced
Salt and pepper, to taste
1 1/2 cups thinly sliced iceberg lettuce
4 reduced-sodium taco shells, warm
Condiments (not included in nutritional data): mild or medium salsa, sour cream

Per Serving
Calories: 318
% Calories from fat: 26
Protein (gm): 17.2
Carbohydrate (gm): 45.7
Fat (gm): 10
Saturated fat (gm): 1.4
Cholesterol (mg): 14
Sodium (mg): 4.5
Exchanges
Milk: 0.0
Veg.: 3.0
Fruit: 0.0
Bread: 2.0
Meat: 1.0
Fat: 1.0

1. Cook beef in large saucepan over medium heat until browned; drain fat and crumble with a fork. Add onion and garlic; saute until tender, about 5 minutes. Stir in tomatoes and liquid, beans, spices, and cayenne chili; heat to boiling. Simmer, covered, 15 to 20 minutes; season to taste with salt and pepper.

2. Spoon lettuce and chili into taco shells; serve with salsa and sour cream.

SANTA FE SKILLET CHILI WITH CHILI CHEESE DUMPLINGS

Fluffy cheese and chili-flavored dumplings top this skillet-easy chili.

6 servings

Vegetable cooking spray
1 pound ground beef round
1 cup chopped onion
1 teaspoon minced garlic
1 tablespoon chili powder
1 tablespoon ground cumin
1/2 teaspoon crushed red pepper
1 can (15 ounces) chili beans in spicy sauce, undrained
1 can (14 1/2 ounces) Mexican-style stewed tomatoes, undrained
1 can (4 ounces) chopped green chilies, undrained
Salt and pepper, to taste
Chili-Cheese Dumplings (recipe follows)

Per Serving
Calories: 307
% Calories from fat: 23
Protein (gm): 23.1
Carbohydrate (gm): 37.7
Fat (gm): 8.3
Saturated fat (gm): 2.6
Cholesterol (mg): 40.4
Sodium (mg): 909
Exchanges
Milk: 0.0
Veg.: 2.0
Fruit: 0.0
Bread: 3.0
Meat: 3.0
Fat: 0.5

1. Spray large skillet with cooking spray; heat over medium heat until hot. Cook beef, onion, garlic, and spices over medium-high heat until meat is lightly browned, about 5 minutes.

2. Stir in beans, tomatoes, and chilies; heat to boiling. Reduce heat and simmer, covered, 10 minutes, stirring occasionally. Season to taste with salt and pepper.

3. Spoon dumpling dough into mounds on top of chili. Cook, uncovered, 5 minutes; cook, covered, until dumplings are dry, 5 to 10 minutes longer.

Chili-Cheese Dumplings

makes 6 dumplings

- $2/3$ cup all-purpose flour
- $1/3$ cup yellow cornmeal
- $1^1/2$ teaspoons baking powder
- 1 teaspoon chili powder
- $1/2$ teaspoon salt
- 2 tablespoons vegetable shortening
- $1/4$ cup (1 ounce) shredded reduced-fat Monterey Jack cheese
- 1 tablespoon finely chopped cilantro
- $1/2$ cup fat-free milk

1. Combine flour, cornmeal, baking powder, chili powder, and salt in medium bowl; cut in shortening with pastry blender until mixture resembles coarse crumbs. Mix in cheese and cilantro; stir in milk, forming a soft dough.

CHILI VERDE

This "green chili" is made with tomatillos, also called Mexican green tomatoes. Use canned tomatillos if fresh are not available.

8 servings

- 1 pound boneless lean pork, cubed (1-inch)
- 2 large onions, thinly sliced
- 6-8 cloves garlic, chopped
- 1 cup water
- 2 pounds tomatillos, husks removed
- 2 cans ($14^1/2$ ounces each) reduced-sodium fat-free chicken broth
- 2 cans (4 ounces each) diced green chilies
- 2 teaspoons ground cumin
- 2 cans (15 ounces each) Great Northern beans, rinsed, drained
- $1/2$ cup lightly packed cilantro, chopped Cilantro-Chili Sour Cream (recipe follows)

Per Serving
Calories: 276
% Calories from fat: 19
Protein (gm): 24.4
Carbohydrate (gm): 31.2
Fat (gm): 5.8
Saturated fat (gm): 1.6
Cholesterol (mg): 32.2
Sodium (mg): 550
Exchanges
Milk: 0.0
Veg.: 1.0
Fruit: 0.0
Bread: 2.0
Meat: 2.0
Fat: 0.0

1. Place pork, onions, garlic, and water in large saucepan and heat to boiling. Reduce heat and simmer, covered, 30 minutes (add more water if necessary to prevent sticking). Uncover and cook over medium-high heat until meat browns.

2. Add tomatillos and broth; heat to boiling. Reduce heat and simmer, covered, until tomatillos are tender, about 20 minutes. Tear tomatillos apart with two forks. Add chilies and cumin. Simmer, covered, until meat is very tender, about 45 minutes. Add beans; heat until hot and stir in cilantro. Serve in bowls with Cilantro-Chili Sour Cream.

Cilantro-Chili Sour Cream

makes about 1/2 cup

> 1/2 cup fat-free sour cream
> 1 tablespoon chopped cilantro
> 1 teaspoon chopped pickled jalapeño chili

1. Combine all ingredients.

CHILI WITH BEANS AND BEER

This chili is very easy to make, but the longer it simmers, the better, to enhance the flavor.

6 servings

> 1 pound lean ground beef
> 1 tablespoon minced garlic
> 3 tablespoons chili powder
> 1 tablespoon ground cumin
> 1 teaspoon dried oregano leaves
> 3 tablespoons flour
> 2 cans (10 1/2 ounces each) reduced-sodium   fat-free beef broth
> 1 can (12 ounces) beer, *or* reduced-sodium beef broth
> 1 can (15 ounces) chili beans in spicy sauce, undrained
> 1 can (15 ounces) pinto beans, rinsed, drained
> Salt and pepper, to taste

Per Serving
Calories: 320
% Calories from fat: 29
Protein (gm): 25
Carbohydrate (gm): 30.8
Fat (gm): 10.7
Saturated fat (gm): 3.9
Cholesterol (mg): 47
Sodium (mg): 609
Exchanges
Milk: 0.0
Veg.: 0.0
Fruit: 0.0
Bread: 2.0
Meat: 2.5
Fat: 1.0

1. Brown ground beef in large saucepan; drain well and stir in garlic. Sprinkle with chili powder, cumin, oregano, and flour and cook 1 to 2 minutes.

2. Stir in beef broth and beer. Heat to boiling; reduce heat and simmer, covered, 1 hour. Stir in both beans and simmer 30 minutes longer. Season to taste with salt and pepper.

Variations:

Ranchero Chili—Cook ground beef as above, adding 4 ounces sliced reduced-fat smoked sausage. Add 1 cup chopped onion with the garlic; saute 3 to 4 minutes. Complete recipe as above. Serve with additional chopped onion and dollops of sour cream.

Mexican Chili Potatoes—Scrub 6 medium Idaho potatoes; cut lengthwise into quarters. Place potatoes on greased cookie sheet and spray with vegetable cooking spray; sprinkle lightly with salt and pepper. Bake at 400 degrees until golden brown and tender, 30 to 45 minutes. Make recipe as above, deleting flour, beef broth, and beer. Arrange 4 potato quarters on each of 4 oven-proof plates; spoon chili over. Sprinkle each serving with 2 to 4 tablespoons shredded reduced-fat Co-Jack cheese and return to oven until melted, about 5 minutes. Serve with fat-free sour cream; sprinkle with sliced green onions and tops.

CHILI RIO GRANDE

Lots of onions, and a combination of ground and cubed meats give this chili loads of flavor and texture.

12 servings

1 quart chopped onions
1 tablespoon vegetable oil
2 pounds lean pork, cubed
1 pound lean ground beef
2 tablespoons minced garlic
¹/₄ cup chili powder
1 tablespoon ground cumin
2 teaspoons dried oregano leaves
2 cans (16 ounces each) reduced-sodium tomatoes, undrained, chopped

Per Serving
Calories: 344
% Calories from fat: 30
Protein (gm): 32.7
Carbohydrate (gm): 25.3
Fat (gm): 11.5
Saturated fat (gm): 3.8
Cholesterol (mg): 66.4
Sodium (mg): 352
Exchanges
Milk: 0.0
Veg.: 2.0
Fruit: 0.0
Bread: 1.0
Meat: 4.0
Fat: 0.0

1³/₄ cups Quick-Spiced Beef Stock
(see p. 7)
1 can (12 ounces) beer, *or* tomato juice
1 can (4 ounces) chopped green chilies
2 cans (15 ounces each) red kidney
beans, rinsed, drained
Salt and pepper, to taste
³/₄ cup Cilantro-Chili Sour Cream
(1¹/₂ recipes) (see p. 168)

1. Saute onions in oil in large saucepan until golden brown, about 20 minutes. Add meats and cook until brown, about 10 minutes; stir in garlic, chili powder, cumin, and oregano and cook 2 minutes more.

2. Stir in tomatoes and liquid, stock, beer, and chilies. Heat to boiling; reduce heat and simmer, covered, 3 hours, stirring occasionally. Stir in beans and cook 10 minutes longer. Season to taste with salt and pepper. Serve with dollops of Cilantro-Chili Sour Cream.

FIERY PINTO BEAN CHILI

Adjust the heat in this quick chili to suit your taste. Quesadillas help quench the fire!

6 servings

1 can (15 ounces) pinto beans, rinsed, drained
2 cups shredded, cooked chicken (8 ounces)
1 clove garlic, minced
3-6 jalapeño chilies, minced
3 green onions and tops, sliced
2 medium tomatoes, chopped
1/2-1 cup tomato juice
1 teaspoon dried whole coriander
Salt, to taste
Quesadillas (recipe follows)

Per Serving
Calories: 298
% Calories from fat: 21
Protein (gm): 22.4
Carbohydrate (gm): 36.5
Fat (gm): 7.2
Saturated fat (gm): 3
Cholesterol (mg): 35.4
Sodium (mg): 564
Exchanges
Milk: 0.0
Veg.: 1.0
Fruit: 0.0
Bread: 2.0
Meat: 2.5
Fat: 0.0

1. Combine all ingredients, except salt and Quesadillas, in large saucepan; heat to boiling. Reduce heat and simmer, covered, 20 to 25 minutes. Season to taste with salt. Serve with Quesadillas.

Quesadillas

makes 6

> Vegetable cooking spray
> 1 poblano chili, thinly sliced
> 1 medium onion, finely chopped
> 1/2 teaspoon ground cumin
> 2 tablespoons finely chopped cilantro
> 1 cup (4 ounces) shredded reduced-fat
> Monterey Jack, *or* pepper-Jack cheese
> 6 flour tortillas (6-inch)

1. Spray large skillet with cooking spray; heat over medium heat until hot. Saute poblano chili and onion until tender, about 5 minutes; stir in cumin and cilantro.

2. Sprinkle cheese on half of each tortilla; spoon vegetable mixture over cheese and fold tortillas in half.

3. Spray large skillet with cooking spray; heat over medium heat until hot. Cook quesadillas over medium to medium-high heat until browned on the bottoms, 2 to 3 minutes. Spray tops of quesadillas with cooking spray; turn and cook until browned on the other side.

Variation:

Slow-Burn Chili—Make recipe as above, decreasing jalapeño chilies to 2, and adding 1/2 teaspoon each black and cayenne pepper and 1/4 to 1/2 teaspoon crushed red pepper. Season to taste with salt and hot pepper sauce.

TEXAS HOT CHILI

Hot sausage, hot chilies, and lots of spices make this chili extra good.

8 servings

3/4 pound hot Italian turkey sausage, casing removed

1 1/4 pounds boneless lean beef, coarsely ground

1 large onion, chopped

1 can (4 ounces) chopped green chilies, undrained

1 jalapeño chili, chopped

1 can (16 ounces) reduced-sodium whole tomatoes, undrained, chopped

1 can (15 ounces) reduced-sodium tomato sauce

1 can (14 1/2 ounces) reduced-sodium fat-free beef broth

2 tablespoons hot chili powder

1/2 teaspoon ground cumin

1/4 teaspoon ground coriander

1/8 teaspoon cayenne pepper

1 tablespoon very-low-sodium Worcester-shire sauce

1 can (15 ounces) red kidney beans, rinsed, drained

1 can (15 ounces) garbanzo beans, rinsed, drained

Salt, to taste

Hot pepper sauce, to taste

Per Serving
Calories: 300
% Calories from fat: 24
Protein (gm): 28.9
Carbohydrate (gm): 29.8
Fat (gm): 8.3
Saturated fat (gm): 2.2
Cholesterol (mg): 57.1
Sodium (mg): 744
Exchanges
Milk: 0.0
Veg.: 0.0
Fruit: 0.0
Bread: 2.0
Meat: 3.0
Fat: 0.0

1. Cook sausage and ground beef in large saucepan until browned; drain well. Add onion, chilies, and jalapeño and saute until tender, about 5 minutes. Stir in remaining ingredients, except salt and hot pepper sauce, and heat to boiling. Reduce heat and simmer 20 to 30 minutes or until thickened. Season to taste with salt and hot pepper sauce.

Variation:
Italian-Style Chili—Make recipe as above, deleting green chilies and jalapeño chilies and substituting 4 ounces sliced pepperoni for 4 ounces of the ground beef and 1 to 1 1/2 teaspoons dried Italian seasoning for the cumin and coriander.

POBLANO VEAL CHILI

Ground veal, a poblano chili, and purchased seasoning mix make this fast-track chili an instant favorite. Tortilla Wedges are an awesome serve-along.

4 servings

1 pound lean ground veal
1 large onion, chopped
1 rib celery, chopped
1 poblano chili, chopped
1 can (15 ounces) reduced-sodium crushed tomatoes
1 can (15 ounces) Great Northern beans, rinsed, drained
1/2-1 package (1¹/4-ounce size) chili seasoning mix
Salt and pepper, to taste
Tortilla Wedges (recipe follows)

Per Serving
Calories: 405
% Calories from fat: 18
Protein (gm): 45.4
Carbohydrate (gm): 39.5
Fat (gm): 8.5
Saturated fat (gm): 3.6
Cholesterol (mg): 124.5
Sodium (mg): 987
Exchanges
Milk: 0.0
Veg.: 2.0
Fruit: 0.0
Bread: 2.0
Meat: 4.0
Fat: 0.0

1. Cook veal in large saucepan, stirring often, until crumbly and browned; drain fat. Add onion, celery, and poblano chili; saute until tender, about 5 minutes.

2. Stir in tomatoes, beans, and seasoning mix. Heat to boiling; reduce heat and simmer, covered, 15 minutes. Season to taste with salt and pepper. Serve with Tortilla Wedges.

Tortilla Wedges

makes 12 wedges

2 flour tortillas (6-inch)
1/4 cup (1 ounce) shredded reduced-fat pepper-jack cheese
1/4 cup (1 ounce) shredded reduced-fat Cheddar cheese
1/4 cup thinly sliced green onions and tops
1/4 cup mild, *or* medium, salsa
Reduced-fat sour cream, as garnish

1. Place tortillas on baking sheet; sprinkle with combined cheeses and green onions. Bake at 450 degrees until edges of tortillas are browned and cheese is melted, 5 to 7 minutes. Cut each tortilla into 6 wedges; top each with 1 teaspoon salsa. Garnish with small dollops of sour cream.

SCOTCH BONNET CHILI

A true "hot-head's" delight, this chili gets its firepower from the redoubt-able habanero chili, often called the Scotch bonnet. Substitute jalapeño chili for a milder flavor.

4 servings

1 large onion, chopped
1 medium green bell pepper, chopped
1 habanero chili, chopped
4 ounces smoked turkey sausage, halved lengthwise, sliced
1 teaspoon olive oil
1 can (14½ ounces) reduced-sodium whole tomatoes, undrained, cut up
2 cups refried beans
1 tablespoon chili powder
1 teaspoon ground cumin
Salt, to taste
1 cup fat-free sour cream

Per Serving
Calories: 293
% Calories from fat: 18
Protein (g): 17.1
Carbohydrates (g): 43.8
Fat (g): 5.9
Saturated fat (g): 1
Cholesterol (mg): 25.6
Sodium (mg): 767
Exchanges
Milk: 0.0
Veg.: 0.0
Fruit: 0.0
Bread: 3.0
Meat: 1.0
Fat: 0.5

1. Saute onion, bell pepper, habanero chili, and sausage in oil in large saucepan until onions are tender. Stir in tomatoes and liquid, beans, chili powder, and cumin. Heat to boiling; reduce heat and simmer, uncovered, until slightly thickened, about 15 minutes. Season to taste with salt. Ladle into bowls; top with sour cream.

BIG RED CHILI

This spicy chili with red onions, red kidney beans, and red bell peppers puts a whole new light on "seeing red."

4 servings

8 ounces ground beef sirloin

1 large red onion, chopped

1 large red bell pepper, chopped

1 can (28 ounces) reduced-sodium crushed tomatoes, undrained

1 can (15 ounces) red kidney beans, rinsed, drained

2 tablespoons red wine vinegar

2 tablespoons chili powder

1/4 teaspoon ground allspice

2/3 cup mild, *or* medium, picante sauce

Salt and pepper, to taste

Per Serving
Calories: 197
% Calories from fat: 16
Protein (gm): 17.5
Carbohydrate (gm): 25.3
Fat (gm): 3.6
Saturated fat (gm): 1.1
Cholesterol (mg): 29.7
Sodium (mg): 652
Exchanges
Milk: 0.0
Veg.: 2.0
Fruit: 0.0
Bread: 1.0
Meat: 1.0
Fat: 0.5

1. Cook beef in large saucepan over medium heat until browned; drain fat and crumble with a fork. Add onion and saute until tender, about 5 minutes. Add remaining ingredients, except picante sauce, salt, and pepper; heat to boiling. Reduce heat and simmer, covered, 20 minutes. Add picante sauce; simmer, covered, 5 to 10 minutes longer. Season to taste with salt and pepper.

Variation:
Farmhouse Chili—Make recipe as above, substituting home-style turkey sausage for the ground beef and tomato juice for the picante sauce. Decrease chili powder to 1 tablespoon. Omit all-spice; add 1 to 2 tablespoons maple syrup and 1/2 teaspoon each ground cumin and dried sage leaves.

LIGHTNING-FAST TEXAS CHILI

Get Texas-size flavor in this recipe. Cilantro adds a captivating pungency.

4 servings

8 ounces lean ground pork
8 ounces ground turkey breast
1 cup sliced green onions and tops
1 pound tomatoes, chopped
1 can (15 ounces) chili beans, undrained
1 cayenne chili, seeded, chopped
  Salt and pepper, to taste
  Finely chopped cilantro, as garnish

Per Serving
Calories: 262
% Calories from fat: 19
Protein (gm): 30.5
Carbohydrate (gm): 25.3
Fat (gm): 5.9
Saturated fat (gm): 1.6
Cholesterol (mg): 54.9
Sodium (mg): 404
Exchanges
Milk: 0.0
Veg.: 2.0
Fruit: 0.0
Bread: 1.0
Meat: 2.5
Fat: 0.0

1. Cook pork and turkey in large saucepan over medium heat until browned; drain fat and crumble with a fork. Add green onions and saute 2 minutes. Stir in tomatoes, chili beans, and cayenne chili; heat to boiling. Reduce heat and simmer, covered, 15 minutes. Season to taste with salt and pepper; sprinkle each serving with cilantro.

EASY TORTILLA CHILI

Baked tortilla chips add crunch and texture to this flavorful chili.

6 servings

8 ounces ground beef round
2 cups chopped onions
3³/4 cups reduced-sodium fat-free beef broth
1 jar (16 ounces) reduced-sodium mild, *or* medium, salsa
1 can (15 ounces) kidney beans, rinsed, drained
1¹/2 cups frozen whole-kernel corn
1 teaspoon chili powder
2 cups crushed, baked tortilla chips
  Salt, to taste
¹/2 cup (2 ounces) grated reduced-fat Cheddar cheese

Per Serving
Calories: 280
% Calories from fat: 12
Protein (g): 20
Carbohydrates (g): 42
Fat (g): 3.9
Saturated fat (g): 1.1
Cholesterol (mg): 23.3
Sodium (mg): 622
Exchanges
Milk: 0.0
Veg.: 2.0
Fruit: 0.0
Bread: 2.0
Meat: 1.5
Fat: 0.0

1. Cook ground beef and onions in large saucepan over medium heat until beef is browned, about 5 minutes; drain fat and crumble beef with a fork. Stir in broth, salsa, beans, corn, and chili powder; heat to boiling. Reduce heat and simmer, covered, 15 to 20 minutes. Stir in tortillas and simmer an additional 5 minutes; season to taste with salt. Serve immediately, sprinkling each serving with cheese.

SOUTH-OF-THE-BORDER CHILI

A chili that's a little different, made with canned soup!

6 servings

- ¹/₂ cup chopped onion
- ¹/₄ cup sliced green onions and tops
- ¹/₂ cup chopped red bell pepper
- 1 small jalapeño chili, seeded, finely chopped
- 2 cloves garlic, minced
- 1-2 tablespoons vegetable oil
- 16 ounces boneless, skinless chicken breast, cut into ³/₄-inch pieces
- 1 can (10³/₄ ounces) reduced-sodium, reduced-fat cream of chicken soup
- ¹/₂ cup reduced-sodium tomato sauce
- 1-1¹/₂ cups fat-free milk
- 1 can (4 ounces) chopped green chilies, drained
- 1 tablespoon chili powder
- ¹/₂ teaspoon ground cumin
  Salt and pepper, to taste
- ¹/₂ cup shredded reduced-fat Monterey Jack cheese
  Baked Tortilla Chips (recipe follows)

Per Serving
Calories: 259
% Calories from fat: **27**
Protein (gm): 24.4
Carbohydrate (gm): **23.5**
Fat (gm): 7.8
Saturated fat (gm): 2.6
Cholesterol (mg): 59.8
Sodium (mg): 467
Exchanges
Milk: 0.0
Veg.: 2.0
Fruit: 0.0
Bread: 1.0
Meat: 2.5
Fat: 0.0

1. Saute onions, bell pepper, jalapeño chili, and garlic in oil in large saucepan 5 minutes; add chicken and cook until browned, 5 to 8 minutes.

2. Stir in remaining ingredients, except salt, pepper, cheese, and Baked Tortilla Chips; heat to boiling. Reduce heat and simmer, covered, 8 to 10 minutes. Season to taste with salt and pepper. Sprinkle each serving with cheese; serve with Baked Tortilla Chips.

Baked Tortilla Chips

makes 6 servings (8 chips each)

 6 corn tortillas (6-inch)
 Vegetable cooking spray
 1/8 teaspoon ground cumin
 1/8 teaspoon chili powder
 1/8 teaspons dried oregano leaves
 1/8 teaspoon paprika
 Salt and cayenne pepper, to taste

1. Cut each tortilla into 8 wedges; arrange in single layer on jelly roll pan. Spray tortillas with cooking spray; sprinkle lightly with herbs, salt, and cayenne pepper.

2. Bake at 350 degrees until lightly browned, 5 to 7 minutes.

CHILI MOLE

This chili boasts the intriguing flavor of traditional Mexican mole sauce; use chicken, pork, or beef or a combination of the 3 meats.

6 servings

 Vegetable cooking spray
 16 ounces lean pork, fat trimmed, cut into generous 1/2-inch cubes
 1 cup reduced-sodium fat-free chicken broth, *or* water
 1 cup chopped onion
 1 tablespoon minced roasted garlic
 1/2-1 teaspoon chopped seeded jalapeño chili
 1/4 cup slivered, blanched almonds
 1 can (15 ounces) caliente-style chili beans, undrained
 1/4 cup tomato sauce
 2-3 teaspoons very-low-sodium Worcestershire sauce
 1/4 teaspoon ground cinnamon

Per Serving
Calories: 328
% Calories from fat: 28
Protein (gm): 28.8
Carbohydrate (gm): 32.5
Fat (gm): 10.6
Saturated fat (gm): 3
Cholesterol (mg): 42.9
Sodium (mg): 671
Exchanges
Milk: 0.0
Veg.: 1.0
Fruit: 0.0
Bread: 2.0
Meat: 2.0
Fat: 1.0

1 can (16 ounces) reduced-sodium diced
   tomatoes, undrained
1 can (15 ounces) black beans, rinsed,
   drained
1/2 ounce unsweetened chocolate
   Salt and pepper, to taste
   Guacamole (recipe follows)
   Finely chopped cilantro, as garnish

1. Heat pork and chicken broth to boiling in medium sauce-pan; reduce heat and simmer, covered, until pork is tender, 20 to 30 minutes; drain, reserving liquid.

2. Saute onion, garlic, jalapeño chili, and almonds in small skillet, until onion is tender, 5 to 8 minutes. Process onion mixture, chili beans, tomato sauce, Worcestershire sauce, and cinnamon in food processor or blender until smooth; transfer to saucepan with pork.

3. Stir in tomatoes and black beans; heat to boiling. Reduce heat and simmer, covered, 10 minutes, stirring in enough reserved cooking liquid to make desired consistency. Add chocolate, stirring until melted; season to taste with salt and pepper. Top each serving with Guacamole; sprinkle generously with cilantro.

Guacamole

makes about 2/3 cup

1 medium Florida avocado (5 ounces),
   peeled, pitted
1/2 small onion, finely chopped
1/2 small jalapeño chili, seeded, minced
1 tablespoon finely chopped cilantro
   Hot pepper sauce, to taste
   Salt, to taste

1. Coarsely mash avocado in small bowl (mixture should be chunky). Mix in onion, jalapeño chili, and cilantro; season to taste with hot pepper sauce and salt.

CHORIZO CHILI

This chili begins with our flavorful low-fat version of Chorizo, to which beans, tomatoes, and onions are added. The Chorizo can be formed into patties and cooked, or used in many of your favorite Mexican recipes.

8 servings

Vegetable cooking spray
Chorizo (recipe follows)
1/2 cup chopped onion
2 cans (15 ounces each) pinto, *or* black, beans, rinsed, drained
2 cans (16 ounces each) reduced-sodium diced tomatoes, undrained
Salt and pepper, to taste

Per Serving
Calories: 229
% Calories from fat: **17**
Protein (gm): 24.4
Carbohydrate (gm): 24.2
Fat (gm): 4.3
Saturated fat (gm): 1.3
Cholesterol (mg): 49.3
Sodium (mg): 414
Exchanges
Milk: 0.0
Veg.: 2.0
Fruit: 0.0
Bread: 1.0
Meat: 2.0
Fat: 0.0

1. Spray large saucepan with cooking spray; heat over medium heat until hot. Add Chorizo and onion and cook over medium heat until Chorizo is browned, 8 to 10 minutes, crumbling with a fork. Stir in beans and tomatoes and heat to boiling; reduce heat and simmer, covered, 30 to 45 minutes. Season to taste with salt and pepper.

Chorizo

makes 1 1/2 pounds

1/2 teaspoon coriander seeds, crushed
1/2 teaspoon cumin seeds, crushed, *or* 1/8 teaspoon ground cumin
2 dried ancho chilies
11/2 pounds pork tenderloin, fat trimmed, finely chopped or ground
4 cloves garlic, minced
2 tablespoons paprika
1 teaspoon dried oregano leaves
1/2 teaspoon salt
2 tablespoons cider vinegar
2 tablespoons water

1. Spray small skillet with cooking spray; heat over medium heat until hot. Add coriander and cumin seeds; cook over medium heat, stirring frequently, until toasted. Remove from skillet; reserve.

2. Add ancho chilies to skillet; cook over medium heat until softened, about 1 minute on each side, turning so that chilies do not burn. Remove and discard stems, veins, and seeds; chop finely.

3. Combine pork tenderloin, ancho chilies, reserved coriander and cumin seeds, and remaining ingredients; refrigerate 4 hours or overnight for flavors to blend. Cook as directed in recipe.

CHEESY CHILI BLANCO WITH RED TOMATO SALSA

This white chili is made extra-creamy with the addition of sour cream and Monterey Jack cheese.

8 servings

2 cups chopped onions

1 tablespoon chopped garlic

1 tablespoon vegetable oil

1¹/₂ pounds boneless, skinless chicken breasts, cubed

2 cans (15 ounces each) Great Northern beans, rinsed, drained

1 can (14¹/₂ ounces) reduced-sodium fat-free chicken broth

1 can (4 ounces) diced green chilies, drained

1 tablespoon dried oregano leaves

1 teaspoon ground cumin

1 cup fat-free sour cream

2 cups (8 ounces) shredded reduced-fat Monterey Jack cheese

Salt and cayenne pepper, to taste

Red Tomato Salsa (recipe follows)

Per Serving
Calories: 331
% Calories from fat: 24
Protein (gm): 37.5
Carbohydrate (gm): 27.7
Fat (gm): 9.3
Saturated fat (gm): 4.4
Cholesterol (mg): 72
Sodium (mg): 674
Exchanges
Milk: 0.0
Veg.: 0.0
Fruit: 0.0
Bread: 2.0
Meat: 3.5
Fat: 0.0

1. Saute onions and garlic in oil in large saucepan until tender, about 8 minutes. Add chicken and saute until lightly browned, about 5 minutes. Stir in beans, broth, chilies, oregano, and cumin. Heat to boiling; reduce heat and simmer, covered, 30 minutes.

2. Stir in sour cream and cheese, stirring until cheese is melted. Season to taste with salt and cayenne pepper. Serve with Red Tomato Salsa.

Red Tomato Salsa

makes about 2 cups

> 2 large tomatoes, chopped
> 1 small onion, finely chopped
> 1 small poblano chili, veins and seeds discarded, chopped
> 1 clove garlic, minced
> 2 tablespoons finely chopped cilantro
> Salt, to taste

1. Mix all ingredients, except salt; season to taste with salt.

WHITE CHILI

No tomatoes, but lots of flavor in this chicken and bean chili.

8 servings

> 2 large red, *or* green, bell peppers, chopped
> 2 large onions, chopped
> 2 cloves garlic, minced
> 2 teaspoons minced gingerroot
> 2 jalapeño chilies, minced
> 1 teaspoon dried thyme leaves
> 1 teaspoon dried oregano leaves
> 1 tablespoon vegetable oil
> 1 pound boneless, skinless chicken breast, cubed (³/4-inch)
> 2 tablespoons flour
> 2 cups Chicken Stock (see p. 2)

Per Serving
Calories: 195
% Calories from fat: 16
Protein (gm): 19.6
Carbohydrate (gm): 25.1
Fat (gm): 4
Saturated fat (gm): 0.8
Cholesterol (mg): 35.4
Sodium (mg): 322
Exchanges
Milk: 0.0
Veg.: 2.0
Fruit: 0.0
Bread: 1.0
Meat: 1.5
Fat: 0.0

2 cans (15 ounces each) Great Northern
beans, rinsed, drained
Salt and pepper, to taste
Green Tomato Salsa (recipe follows)
Fat-free sour cream, as garnish

1. Saute peppers, onions, garlic, gingerroot, chilies, thyme, and oregano in oil in large saucepan until tender, about 8 minutes. Add chicken and saute 5 minutes; sprinkle with flour and cook 1 to 2 minutes longer.

2. Add Chicken Stock and beans to saucepan; heat to boiling. Reduce heat and simmer, uncovered, until chicken is tender, about 10 minutes. Season to taste with salt and pepper. Serve with Green Tomato Salsa and sour cream.

Green Tomato Salsa

makes about 1 cup

12 ounces Mexican green tomatoes
(tomatillos)
1/2 small onion, chopped
1 clove garlic, minced
1 tablespoon finely chopped cilantro
1 teaspoon minced jalapeño chili
1/4 teaspoon ground cumin
1/8 teaspoon sugar
Salt, to taste

1. Remove and discard husks from green tomatoes; simmer in water to cover in large saucepan until tender, 5 to 8 minutes. Cool; drain, reserving liquid.

2. Process tomatoes, onion, garlic, cilantro, jalapeño chili, cumin, and sugar in food processor, using pulse technique, until almost smooth, adding enough reserved liquid to make medium dipping consistency. Season to taste with salt.

BLACK AND WHITE BEAN CHILI

Made with black and white beans, this chili is uniquely accented in flavor and color with sun-dried tomatoes.

4 servings (about 1³/₄ cups each)

1/4 cup sun-dried tomatoes (not in oil)
1/2 cup boiling water
    Garlic-flavored vegetable cooking spray
12 ounces 95% lean ground beef
1 cup chopped onion
1/2 cup chopped green bell pepper
1 medium jalapeño chili, finely chopped
2 teaspoons minced garlic
2-3 tablespoons chili powder
1-1¹/₂ teaspoons ground cumin
1 teaspoon dried oregano leaves
1 bay leaf
2 cans (16 ounces each) reduced-sodium whole tomatoes, undrained, coarsely chopped
1 can (15¹/₂ ounces) Great Northern beans, rinsed, drained
1 can (15 ounces) black beans, rinsed, drained
    Salt and pepper, to taste
1/4 cup finely chopped cilantro

Per Serving
Calories: 305
% Calories from fat: 12
Protein (g): 28.9
Carbohydrates (g): 52.4
Fat (g): 4.9
Saturated fat (g): 1.2
Cholesterol (mg): 41.2
Sodium (mg): 770
Exchanges
Milk: 0.0
Veg.: 2.0
Fruit: 0.0
Bread: 2.0
Meat: 2.0
Fat: 0.0

1. Cover sun-dried tomatoes with boiling water in small bowl; let stand until softened, about 10 minutes. Drain; reserve liquid. Chop tomatoes.

2. Spray large saucepan with cooking spray; heat over medium heat until hot. Cook ground beef, onion, bell pepper, jalapeño chili, and garlic until beef is browned and vegetables are tender, 8 to 10 minutes. Stir in chili powder and herbs; cook 1 to 2 minutes longer.

3. Stir in sun-dried tomatoes and reserved liquid, and remaining ingredients, except salt, pepper, and cilantro. Heat to boiling; reduce heat and simmer, covered, 30 minutes. Discard bay leaf; season to taste with salt and pepper. Stir in cilantro.

VEGETARIAN CHILI IN BLACK AND WHITE

Black beans, white beans, and wild rice give this vegetarian chili a great texture. Its warm flavor comes from toasted cumin seeds. Toasting, a technique used by Indian cooks, enhances herb flavor.

6 servings

1 medium onion, chopped
1 teaspoon olive oil
2 cups reduced-sodium tomato juice
2 tablespoons reduced-sodium tomato paste
1 can (15 ounces) black beans, rinsed and drained
1 can (15 ounces) Great Northern, *or* navy, beans, rinsed and drained
1 cup cooked wild rice
1 anaheim chili, seeded, minced
1 teaspoon paprika
1 teaspoon cumin seeds, toasted
   Salt and pepper, to taste

Per Serving
Calories: 144
% Calories from fat: 8
Protein (gm): 8.5
Carbohydrate (gm): 33.8
Fat (gm): 1.7
Saturated fat (gm): 0.1
Cholesterol (mg): 0
Sodium (mg): 446
Exchanges
Milk: 0.0
Veg.: 0.0
Fruit: 0.0
Bread: 2.0
Meat: 0.0
Fat: 0.0

1. Saute onion in oil in large saucepan until translucent, about 5 minutes. Stir in remaining ingredients, except salt and pepper; heat to boiling. Reduce heat and simmer, covered, 5 to 10 minutes.

Variation:

Venison Chili—Cook 1 pound finely chopped lean venison with onion in 1 tablespoon vegetable oil over medium heat until browned; add 1 to 1¹/₂ cups fat-free reduced-sodium beef broth and heat to boiling; reduce heat and simmer, covered, until venison is tender, 45 to 60 minutes. Complete chili as above.

SAGEBRUSH CHILI WITH FRESH TOMATOES

For a fresh take on an old Southwestern favorite, this high-flavor chili sports ripe tomatoes and silver-green sage leaves.

4 servings

4 scallions, sliced

8 cloves garlic, thinly sliced

2 teaspoons olive oil

1 quart tomato wedges

2 cups canned pinto beans, rinsed, drained

1 large cayenne chili, roasted, seeded, minced

2 tablespoons chili powder

1 teaspoon ground cumin

1/2 teaspoon ground coriander

2 teaspoons finely chopped fresh, *or* 1/2 teaspoon dried sage leaves
   Salt and pepper, to taste

Per Serving
Calories: 197
% Calories from fat: 20
Protein (gm): 8.9
Carbohydrate (gm): 33.7
Fat (gm): 4.8
Saturated fat (gm): 0.7
Cholesterol (mg): 0
Sodium (mg): 310
Exchanges
Milk: 0.0
Veg.: 3.0
Fruit: 0.0
Bread: 1.0
Meat: 0.0
Fat: 1.0

1. Saute scallions and garlic in oil in large saucepan 3 minutes. Add remaining ingredients, except sage, salt, and pepper; heat to boiling. Reduce heat and simmer, covered, until tomatoes soften, about 5 minutes. Stir in sage; simmer, uncovered, 1 to 2 minutes; season to taste with salt and pepper.

SWEET POTATO CHIPOTLE CHILI

Chipotle chilies are dried, smoked jalapeño chilies. They are often canned in adobo sauce, which is made with ground chilies and spices. They add a distinctive smoky flavor to this robust chili; taste before adding a second chili, as they can be fiercely hot in flavor!

4 servings (about 1½ cups each)

2 cups frozen stir-fry pepper blend

1 teaspoon minced garlic

1-2 teaspoons minced gingerroot

1 teaspoon cumin seeds

1-2 tablespoons peanut, *or* vegetable, oil

3 cups cubed, peeled sweet potatoes (½-inch)

1 can (14½ ounces) reduced-sodium diced tomatoes, undrained

2 cans (15 ounces each) black beans, rinsed, drained

1-2 chipotle chilies in adobo sauce, chopped

1 cup water, *or* vegetable broth

2-3 teaspoons chili powder

½-1 teaspoon ground cumin

Salt, to taste

Per Serving
Calories: 320
% Calories from fat: 13
Protein (g): 12.5
Carbohydrates (g): 72.9
Fat (g): 5.8
Saturated fat (g): 0.7
Cholesterol (mg): 0.
Sodium (mg): 782
Exchanges
Milk: 0.0
Veg.: 2.0
Fruit: 0.0
Bread: 3.0
Meat: 0.0
Fat: 1.0

1. Saute pepper blend, garlic, gingerroot, and cumin seeds in oil in large saucepan until tender, about 5 minutes.

2. Add remaining ingredients, except salt, to saucepan; heat to boiling. Reduce heat and simmer, covered, until potatoes are tender, about 15 minutes. Season to taste with salt.

MONTEREY CHILI ACINI DE PEPE

Some vegetarian chilies call for bulgur or cracked wheat. This fuss-free and satisfying recipe uses acini de pepe, a tiny pasta that is readily available.

4 servings

1 medium onion, chopped

1 green bell pepper, chopped

1 teaspoon olive oil

1 can (15 ounces) pinto beans, rinsed, drained

1 can (14 ounces) reduced-sodium diced tomatoes, undrained

1 tablespoon chili powder

1 teaspoon dried oregano leaves

1 teaspoon unsweetened cocoa

1/2 cup acini de pepe, cooked, warm

1/4 cup chopped cilantro

Salt and pepper, to taste

3/4 cup (3 ounces) shredded Monterey Jack cheese

Per Serving
Calories: 275
% Calories from fat: 29
Protein (g): 14
Carbohydrates (g): 36
Fat (g): 9.2
Saturated fat (g): 4.5
Cholesterol (mg): 18.9
Sodium (mg): 461
Exchanges
Milk: 0.0
Veg.: 1.0
Fruit: 0.0
Bread: 2.0
Meat: 1.0
Fat: 1.0

1. Saute onion and bell pepper in oil in large saucepan until tender. Stir in beans, tomatoes and liquid, chili powder, oregano, and cocoa. Heat to boiling; reduce heat and simmer, covered, 10 minutes. Stir in acini de pepe and cilantro; season to taste with salt and pepper. Serve in bowls; top with cheese.

BLACK BEAN, RICE, AND CORN CHILI

This vegetarian chili is simple, speedy, and tastes superb. If you'd like more "heat," use cayenne pepper instead of the jalapeño.

4 servings

1¹/₂ cups chopped onions
1 tablespoon minced garlic
1 teaspoon olive oil
1 can (28 ounces) reduced-sodium crushed tomatoes, undrained
1 can (16 ounces) black beans, rinsed, drained
¹/₂ cup frozen whole-kernel corn
¹/₂ cup cooked rice
1 large red bell pepper, chopped
1 jalapeño chili, seeded and minced
1 tablespoon chili powder
1 teaspoon ground allspice
Salt and pepper, to taste

Per Serving
Calories: 219
% Calories from fat: **9**
Protein (gm): 10.1
Carbohydrate (gm): 49.2
Fat (gm): 2.7
Saturated fat (gm): 0.3
Cholesterol (mg): 0
Sodium (mg): 726
Exchanges
Milk: 0.0
Veg.: 3.0
Fruit: 0.0
Bread: 3.0
Meat: 0.0
Fat: 0.0

1. Saute onions and garlic in oil in large saucepan until tender, about 8 minutes. Stir in remaining ingredients, except salt and pepper, and heat to boiling. Reduce heat and simmer, covered, 15 minutes; season to taste with salt and pepper.

CINCINNATI CHILI WITH AN ATTITUDE

Midwesterners have a penchant for chili that's thick and spicy and served over spaghetti. Here's a vegetarian version with lentils, tomatoes, and eight easy-to-find seasonings.

6 servings

1 medium onion, chopped
1 teaspoon olive oil
2 cups cooked lentils
1 can (15 ounces) crushed tomatoes, undrained
1 tablespoon minced garlic
2 teaspoons Worcestershire sauce
1/4 teaspoon ground allspice
1/8 teaspoon ground cloves
1 tablespoon chili powder
1 teaspoon cocoa
1/4 teaspoon ground cinnamon
Salt and pepper, to taste
12 ounces linguine, cooked, warm

Per Serving
Calories: 277
% Calories from fat: **7**
Protein (gm): 13.4
Carbohydrate (gm): **53**
Fat (gm): 2.5
Saturated fat (gm): **0.2**
Cholesterol (mg): 0
Sodium (mg): 308
Exchanges
Milk: 0.0
Veg.: 2.0
Fruit: 0.0
Bread: 3.0
Meat: 0.0
Fat: 0.0

1. Saute onion in oil in large saucepan until tender, about 5 minutes. Add remaining ingredients, except salt, pepper, and linguine; heat to boiling. Reduce heat and simmer, covered, 20 minutes. Season to taste with salt and pepper. Serve over linguine.

CHILI SIN CARNE

For a Southwest version of this chili, substitute black or pinto beans for the kidney beans and add 1 minced jalapeño chili. Garnish each serving with a sprinkling of finely chopped cilantro leaves.

6 servings (about 1¹/₃ cups each)

Vegetable cooking spray
²/₃ package (12-ounce size) frozen pre-browned all-vegetable protein crumbles
1¹/₂ cups chopped onions
  1 cup chopped green bell pepper
  2 cloves garlic, minced
1-2 tablespoons chili powder
  2 teaspoons ground cumin
  1 teaspoon dried oregano leaves
¹/₄ teaspoon ground cloves
  2 cans (14¹/₂ ounces each) no-salt-added whole tomatoes, undrained, coarsely chopped
  1 can (6 ounces) reduced-sodium tomato paste
³/₄ cup beer, *or* water
  1 tablespoon packed light brown sugar
2-3 teaspoons unsweetened cocoa
  1 can (15 ounces) red kidney beans, rinsed, drained
    Salt and pepper, to taste
¹/₂ cup (2 ounces) shredded fat-free, *or* reduced-fat, Cheddar cheese
¹/₂ cup thinly sliced green onions and tops
¹/₂ cup fat-free, *or* reduced-fat, sour cream

Per Serving
Calories: 255
% Calories from fat: **5**
Protein (g): 22.5
Carbohydrates (g): **43.5**
Fat (g): 1.7
Saturated fat (g): 0.1
Cholesterol (mg): 0
Sodium (mg): 436
Exchanges
Milk: 0.0
Veg.: 4.0
Fruit: 0.0
Bread: 1.0
Meat: 1.5
Fat: 0.0

1. Spray large saucepan with cooking spray; heat over medium heat until hot. Add vegetable protein crumbles, onions, bell pepper, and garlic; cook over medium heat until vegetables are tender, 5 to 8 minutes. Add chili powder, cumin, oregano, and cloves; cook 1 to 2 minutes longer.

2. Add tomatoes, tomato paste, beer, brown sugar, and cocoa to mixture. Heat to boiling; reduce heat and simmer, covered, 1 hour. Stir in beans and simmer, uncovered, to thicken, if desired. Season to taste with salt and pepper.

3. Spoon chili into bowls; sprinkle each with 1 tablespoon cheese, green onions, and sour cream.

Variation:
Veggie Mac—In Step 2, add 1 cup uncooked elbow macaroni, *or* chili mac pasta, and 1/2 cup water to chili after 45 minutes cooking time; heat to boiling. Reduce heat and simmer, covered, until macaroni is tender, about 15 minutes; complete recipe as above.

CARIBBEAN CHILI

This hearty meatless chili with three beans, accented with Mango Salsa, would be delicious served with brown rice.

6 servings

1   cup chopped onion
2   cups chopped red, *or* green, bell peppers
1   jalapeño chili, chopped
1   tablespoon minced garlic
2   teaspoons minced gingerroot
1   tablespoon vegetable oil
2   tablespoons paprika
2   tablespoons chili powder
1   tablespoon ground cumin
1/4   teaspoon ground cloves
2   teaspoons sugar
2   cans (14 1/2 ounces each) salt-free whole tomatoes, undrained, chopped
1   can (15 ounces) pinto beans, rinsed, drained

Per Serving
Calories: 331
% Calories from fat: 13
Protein (gm): 15.2
Carbohydrate (gm): 67
Fat (gm): 5.2
Saturated fat (gm): 0.8
Cholesterol (mg): 0
Sodium (mg): 442
Exchanges
Milk: 0.0
Veg.: 3.0
Fruit: 0.0
Bread: 3.0
Meat: 0.0
Fat: 1.0

1 can (15 ounces) Great Northern beans,
  rinsed, drained
1 can (15 ounces) black beans, rinsed,
  drained
1 tablespoon lime juice
  Salt and pepper, to taste
  Mango Salsa (recipe follows)

1. Saute onion, bell peppers, jalapeño chili, garlic, and ginger-root in oil in large saucepan until tender, about 10 minutes. Add spices, herbs, and sugar; stir 1 minute.

2. Stir in tomatoes and liquid, beans, and lime juice; heat to boiling. Reduce heat and simmer, covered, 20 minutes. Season to taste with salt and pepper. Serve with Mango Salsa.

Mango Salsa

makes about 1¹/₄ cups

1 large mango, cubed
1 small banana, cubed
3 tablespoons chopped cilantro
¹/₂ small jalapeño chili, finely chopped
1 tablespoon frozen pineapple juice
  concentrate, thawed
1 teaspoon lime juice

1. Combine all ingredients.

VEGETARIAN CHILI

Cooked, crumbled vegetarian "burgers" can be added to this chili for additional texture.

6 servings

1 medium onion, chopped
1 large carrot, chopped
1 large rib celery, chopped
1 cup sliced mushrooms
1/2 green bell pepper, chopped
2 cloves garlic, minced
1-2 tablespoons olive oil
2 cans (15 ounces each) kidney beans, rinsed, drained
1 can (15 ounces) garbanzo beans, rinsed, drained
3/4 cup tomato puree
2 large tomatoes, peeled, seeded
1 teaspoon ground cumin
1-2 tablespoons chili powder
1/2 teaspoon pepper
 Salt, to taste

Per Serving
Calories: 266
% Calories from fat: **13**
Protein (gm): 12.8
Carbohydrate (gm): 47.5
Fat (gm): 4.1
Saturated fat (gm): **0.5**
Cholesterol (mg): 0
Sodium (mg): 646
Exchanges
Milk: 0.0
Veg.: 1.0
Fruit: 0.0
Bread: 3.0
Meat: 0.0
Fat: 0.5

1. Saute onion, carrot, celery, mushrooms, bell pepper, and garlic in oil in Dutch oven until tender, 5 to 8 minutes. Stir in remaining ingredients, except salt, and heat to boiling; reduce heat and simmer 30 minutes, adding water, if necessary, to prevent sticking. Season to taste with salt.

VEGETABLE-LENTIL CHILI

Lentils add great texture to this meatless chili.

5-6 servings

1 large onion, chopped
1 clove garlic, minced
2 teaspoons olive oil
1 quart vegetable broth
1 cup water
1 can (14¹/₂ ounces) reduced-sodium diced tomatoes, undrained
³/₄-1 cup brown lentils, rinsed, sorted
1 medium carrot, sliced
1 rib celery, sliced
³/₄ cup chopped red, *or* green, bell pepper
2¹/₂ teaspoons chili powder
³/₄ teaspoon ground cumin
1 bay leaf
1¹/₂ cups frozen whole-kernel corn
¹/₈ teaspoon pepper
Salt, to taste

Per Serving
Calories: 176
% Calories from fat: 11
Protein (g): 11.7
Carbohydrates (g): 30.7
Fat (g): 2.3
Saturated fat (g): 0.3
Cholesterol (mg): 0
Sodium (mg): 183
Exchanges
Milk: 0.0
Veg.: 0.0
Fruit: 0.0
Bread: 2.0
Meat: 0.0
Fat: 0.5

1. Saute onion and garlic in oil in large saucepan until tender, 3 to 4 minutes. Add remaining ingredients, except salt; heat to boiling. Reduce heat and simmer, covered, until lentils are tender, 30 to 45 minutes. Season to taste with salt.

VEGETARIAN CHILI WITH SHARP CHEDDAR

Beans and barley team up in this healthy, meatless chili.

4 servings

1 can (15¹/₂ ounces) red kidney beans, rinsed, drained
1¹/₂ cups frozen whole-kernel corn
1¹/₂ cups cooked barley
1 can (16 ounces) reduced-sodium crushed tomatoes, undrained
¹/₂ cup mild, *or* medium, salsa
2 teaspoons chili powder
1 teaspoon cocoa
¹/₂-1 teaspoon minced jalapeño chili
Salt and pepper, to taste
¹/₂ cup (2 ounces) shredded extra-sharp Cheddar cheese

Per Serving
Calories: 317
% Calories from fat: 16
Protein (gm): 14.8
Carbohydrate (gm): 55.2
Fat (gm): 5.8
Saturated fat (gm): 3.2
Cholesterol (mg): 14.9
Sodium (mg): 790
Exchanges
Milk: 0.0
Veg.: 2.0
Fruit: 0.0
Bread: 3.0
Meat: 0.0
Fat: 1.0

1. Combine all ingredients, except salt, pepper, and cheese, in large saucepan; heat to boiling. Reduce heat and simmer, covered, 10 to 15 minutes. Season to taste with salt and pepper. Sprinkle each serving with shredded cheese.

PRAIRIE CHILI WITH CHICKEN

Few dishes have snappier flavor or are simpler to prepare than this six-minute chili. Sporting ancho chilies and a mild picante sauce, it ranks low on the Scoville heat scale. Looking for a fiery punch? Just double the red pepper and use hot picante sauce.

4 servings

12 ounces cooked chicken breast, shredded
1 can (14 ounces) reduced-sodium stewed tomatoes, undrained
1 can (15¹/₂ ounces) pinto beans, rinsed, drained
³/₄ cup mild picante sauce
2 ancho chilies, softened, chopped
2 tablespoons dried onion flakes

Per Serving
Calories: 352
% Calories from fat: 29
Protein (g): 34.2
Carbohydrates (g): 28.8
Fat (g): 11.5
Saturated fat (g): 2.9
Cholesterol (mg): 70.5
Sodium (mg): 689
Exchanges
Milk: 0.0
Veg.: 3.0
Fruit: 0.0
Bread: 1.0
Meat: 4.0
Fat: 0.0

1/2 teaspoon crushed red pepper

1 teaspoon paprika

1 teaspoon dried parsley

1 cup fresh, *or* canned, rinsed, drained,
bean sprouts

Salt, to taste

1. Combine all ingredients except parsley, bean sprouts, and salt, in large saucepan. Heat to boiling; reduce heat and simmer, covered, 5 minutes. Add parsley and bean sprouts. Season to taste with salt.

TENDERLOIN CHILI

Treat your taste buds to high-on-the-hog chili! This super-easy, super-fast chili sports tender, lean pork and fresh tomatoes and has a superb taste that the usual beef chilies can't match.

4 servings

12 ounces cooked pork tenderloin, shredded

1 can (15 ounces) reduced-sodium fat-free beef broth

1 pound plum tomatoes, sliced

1 can (15 ounces) pinto beans, rinsed, drained

2 jalapeño chilies, minced

1 tablespoon chili powder

1 teaspoon cumin seeds, toasted

1 teaspoon Worcestershire sauce

Salt and pepper, to taste

Per Serving
Calories: 274
% Calories from fat: 19
Protein (g): 32.7
Carbohydrates (g): 23.4
Fat (g): 5.8
Saturated fat (g): 1.7
Cholesterol (mg): 67.1
Sodium (mg): 475
Exchanges
Milk: 0.0
Veg.: 2.0
Fruit: 0.0
Bread: 1.0
Meat: 3.0
Fat: 0.0

1. Heat all ingredients, except salt and pepper, to boiling in large saucepan; reduce heat and simmer, covered, 15 minutes. Season to taste with salt and pepper.

LENTIL CHILI WITH BACON AND BEER

Lime, beer, and bacon make this chili differently delicious. So give it a try; it's a snap to make.

4 servings

4 slices low-sodium bacon

1 medium onion, chopped

1½ cups cooked lentils

1 can (15 ounces) black beans, rinsed, drained

1 cup crushed tomatoes

1 cup beer, *or* tomato juice

1 tablespoon minced garlic

1 tablespoon chili powder

1 jalapeño chili, seeded, chopped

1 teaspoon ground cumin

1 teaspoon dried rosemary leaves, crushed

Juice of 1 lime

Salt and pepper, to taste

Per Serving
Calories: 244
% Calories from fat: 12
Protein (gm): 15
Carbohydrate (gm): 43
Fat (gm): 3.7
Saturated fat (gm): 0.9
Cholesterol (mg): 5
Sodium (mg): 631
Exchanges
Milk: 0.0
Veg.: 0.0
Fruit: 0.0
Bread: 3.0
Meat: 0.0
Fat: 0.5

1. Cook bacon in large saucepan until crisp; drain, crumble, and reserve. Add onion to saucepan; saute until tender, about 5 minutes. Stir in remaining ingredients, except bacon, lime juice, salt, and pepper; heat to boiling. Reduce heat and simmer, covered, 10 minutes. Stir in lime juice; season to taste with salt and pepper. Sprinkle each serving with reserved bacon.

ROASTED PEPPER CHILI

Here's a mild-mannered dish with a lean and healthful profile. For crunch, serve it topped with broken baked tortilla chips.

4 servings

8 ounces ground turkey breast
1 cup chopped red onion
1 can (15 ounces) stewed tomatoes, undrained
1 can (15 ounces) black beans, rinsed, drained
1 tablespoon chili powder
1/2 teaspoon ground cumin
1/4 teaspoon ground allspice
1 small jalapeño chili, seeded, minced
1/2 cup coarsely chopped roasted red peppers
Salt and pepper, to taste

Per Serving
Calories: 170
% Calories from fat: 11
Protein (gm): 15.7
Carbohydrate (gm): 29.7
Fat (gm): 2.5
Saturated fat (gm): 0.4
Cholesterol (mg): 22.4
Sodium (mg): 692
Exchanges
Milk: 0.0
Veg.: 2.0
Fruit: 0.0
Bread: 1.0
Meat: 1.0
Fat: 0.0

1. Cook turkey in large saucepan over medium heat until browned; drain and crumble with a fork. Add onion; saute until tender, about 5 minutes. Add remaining ingredients, except roasted red peppers, salt, and pepper; heat to boiling. Reduce heat and simmer, covered, 10 minutes. Stir in roasted red peppers; simmer 2 to 3 minutes. Season to taste with salt and pepper.

CHILI WITH SQUASH AND BEANS

A squeeze of lime adds a cooling touch to this spicy chili.

6 servings (about 1¹/₃ cups each)

1 pound lean ground beef
2 medium onions, cut into 1-inch pieces
2 cups chopped celery
1 red bell pepper, cut into 1-inch pieces
¹/₂ jalapeño chili, finely chopped
2 cloves garlic, minced
2 cups peeled, cubed butternut squash (1-inch)
1 can (15 ounces) reduced-sodium chunky tomato sauce
1 can (15 ounces) red kidney beans, rinsed, drained
3 cups reduced-sodium tomato juice
1 medium zucchini, cubed
1 cup sliced mushrooms
1¹/₂ teaspoons chili powder
1¹/₂ teaspoons ground cumin
Salt and pepper, to taste
6 lime wedges

Per Serving
Calories: 317
% Calories from fat: 30
Protein (g): 21.2
Carbohydrates (g): 36.1
Fat (g): 10.8
Saturated fat (g): 4
Cholesterol (mg): 46.6
Sodium (mg): 357
Exchanges
Milk: 0.0
Veg.: 1.0
Fruit: 0.0
Bread: 2.0
Meat: 2.0
Fat: 1.0

1. Cook ground beef in Dutch oven or large saucepan until browned; drain fat. Add onions, celery, bell pepper, jalapeño chili, and garlic. Saute until tender, 8 to 10 minutes.

2. Add remaining ingredients, except salt, pepper, and lime wedges, to Dutch oven; heat to boiling. Reduce heat and simmer, uncovered, until vegetables are tender and chili is thickened, 20 to 25 minutes. Season to taste with salt and pepper. Serve in bowls; squeeze lime wedge into each.

PORK CHILI WITH GREENS

Kale adds nutrients and color to this tasty chili.

8 servings

1¹/₂ pounds lean ground pork, *or* turkey

2 cans (15 ounces each) kidney beans, rinsed, drained

2 cans (16 ounces each) reduced-sodium whole tomatoes, undrained, chopped

¹/₂ cup chopped onion

¹/₂ teaspoon ground cinnamon

¹/₂ teaspoon ground cumin

8 ounces kale, *or* spinach, coarsely chopped

Salt and pepper, to taste

Per Serving
Calories: 261
% Calories from fat: **21**
Protein (gm): 28
Carbohydrate (gm): **23.8**
Fat (gm): 6.1
Saturated fat (gm): **2**
Cholesterol (mg): **48.3**
Sodium (mg): 332
Exchanges
Milk: 0.0
Veg.: 2.0
Fruit: 0.0
Bread: 1.0
Meat: 2.5
Fat: 0.0

1. Brown pork in large saucepan; drain well. Stir in beans, tomatoes and liquid, onion, cinnamon, and cumin. Heat to boiling; reduce heat and simmer, covered, 45 minutes.

2. Stir kale into chili; simmer 10 minutes. Season to taste with salt and pepper.

Variation:

Chili with Rajas—Make chili as above, substituting ground lean beef for the pork. Omit cinnamon and kale; add 1 to 2 tablespoons chili powder. Cook 2 thinly sliced poblano chilies and 1 sliced medium onion in 1 to 2 tablespoon vegetable oil in large skillet over medium to medium-low heat until chilies are very tender and onions are caramelized, 15 to 20 minutes; season to taste with salt. Serve chili in bowls; top with chili and onion mixture.

SWEET AND SPICY CHILI

Sweet potatoes and sweet spices, combined with jalapeño chili and ginger-root, make a chili that is sure to please.

6 servings

1½ cups chopped onions
8 ounces mushrooms, quartered
2 teaspoons minced garlic
2 teaspoons minced gingerroot
1 jalapeño chili, minced
1 tablespoon vegetable oil
2 tablespoons flour
1 pound boneless, skinless chicken breast, cubed (³/₄-inch)
1 can (14½ ounces) chicken broth
2 medium sweet potatoes, peeled, cubed (³/₄-inch)
2 cans (15 ounces each) Great Northern beans, rinsed, drained
1 teaspoon dried oregano leaves
1 teaspoon ground cumin
½ teaspoon ground coriander
¼ teaspoon ground cinnamon
   Salt and white pepper, to taste
   Fat-free sour cream, as garnish

Per Serving
Calories: 274
% Calories from fat: 16
Protein (gm): 26.5
Carbohydrate (gm): 36.7
Fat (gm): 5.2
Saturated fat (gm): 1
Cholesterol (mg): 46
Sodium (mg): 716
Exchanges
Milk: 0.0
Veg.: 0.0
Fruit: 0.0
Bread: 2.5
Meat: 2.0
Fat: 0.0

1. Saute onions, mushrooms, garlic, gingerroot, and jalapeño chili in oil in large saucepan until tender, about 8 minutes; sprinkle with flour and cook 1 to 2 minutes longer.

2. Add chicken, broth, sweet potatoes, beans, herbs, and spices to saucepan; heat to boiling. Reduce heat and simmer, covered, until chicken and sweet potatoes are tender, about 20 minutes. Season to taste with salt and white pepper. Serve with sour cream.

CALI-FLORIDA CHILI

With this chili, experience a regional "fusion" cuisine that traces its heritage right to the good old U.S.A.

4 servings

1 teaspoon crushed mixed peppercorns

1 pound boneless, skinless chicken breast, cut into 1-inch cubes

1 quart sliced plum tomatoes

1 cup diced sun-dried tomatoes (not in oil)

1 cup Zinfandel, *or* other dry red wine, *or* reduced-sodium chicken broth

2 dried California chilies, chopped

4 teaspoons chili powder

1 avocado, chopped

2 tablespoons sunflower seeds, toasted

Salt, to taste

6 tablespoons finely chopped fresh purple basil

Per Serving
Calories: 258
% Calories from fat: 30
Protein (g): 21.5
Carbohydrates (g): 19.7
Fat (g): 9.2
Saturated fat (g): 1.8
Cholesterol (mg): 46
Sodium (mg): 272
Exchanges
Milk: 0.0
Veg.: 4.0
Fruit: 0.0
Bread: 0.0
Meat: 2.0
Fat: 1.0

1. Sprinkle peppercorns into a medium non-stick skillet; add chicken and saute until pieces are lightly browned.

2. Combine fresh and dried tomatoes, wine, chilies, and chili powder in large saucepan; stir in chicken. Heat to boiling; reduce heat and simmer, covered, 6 minutes. Uncover and simmer until slightly thickened, about 5 minutes.

3. Stir in avocado and sunflower seeds. Season to taste with salt. Spoon into bowls; sprinkle with basil.

YELLOW SQUASH AND WHITE BEAN CHILI

Add a minced jalapeño chili, if you like your chili hot!

4 servings (about 1¹/₂ cups each)

1 pound lean ground pork
2 cups chopped onions
1 cup chopped yellow bell pepper
2 teaspoons minced garlic
2 teaspoons cumin seeds
1-2 tablespoons olive oil
1 medium yellow summer squash, cubed
2 cans (15 ounces each) Great Northern beans, rinsed, drained
2 cups reduced-sodium fat-free chicken broth
¹/₂ cup dry white wine, optional
1 teaspoon dried oregano leaves
¹/₂ teaspoon ground cinnamon
2 teaspoons chili powder
Salt and pepper, to taste
Finely chopped tomato and cilantro, as garnishes

Per Serving
Calories: 350
% Calories from fat: 23
Protein (g): 32.7
Carbohydrates (g): 41.2
Fat (g): 10
Saturated fat (g): 2.7
Cholesterol (mg): 49.3
Sodium (mg): 719
Exchanges
Milk: 0.0
Veg.: 2.0
Fruit: 0.0
Bread: 2.0
Meat: 3.0
Fat: 0.0

1. Cook pork over medium heat in medium skillet until browned, about 10 minutes; drain well.

2. Saute onions, bell pepper, garlic, and cumin seeds in oil in large saucepan 5 minutes. Add pork and remaining ingredients, except salt, pepper, and garnishes, to saucepan; heat to boiling. Reduce heat and simmer, covered, until vegetables are tender, about 15 minutes. Simmer, uncovered, until thickened, 5 to 10 minutes. Season to taste with salt and pepper.

3. Serve chili in bowls; sprinkle with tomato and cilantro.

Variation:
Med-Rim Chili—Make chili as above, substituting ground lamb or beef for the pork and adding ¹/₄ cup sliced Greek, *or* ripe, olives. Make 1 package (5.6 ounces) couscous according to package directions. Serve chili over couscous; sprinkle each serving with 1 tablespoon crumbled feta cheese.

CHICKEN CHILI WITH ORANGE CILANTRO RICE

An aromatic chili, with a perfect rice accompaniment.

6 servings

16 ounces boneless, skinless chicken breast, cut into $1/2$-inch cubes

$1/2$ cup chopped onion

1 clove garlic, minced

1-2 tablespoons vegetable oil

1 can (28 ounces) diced tomatoes, undrained

1 can (15 ounces) Great Northern beans, rinsed, drained

2 teaspoons chili powder

$1/2$ teaspoon ground cumin

$1/4$ teaspoons ground allspice

1 strip orange rind (2 inches by $1/2$ inch)

Salt and pepper, to taste

Orange Cilantro Rice (recipe follows)

Finely chopped cilantro, as garnish

Per Serving
Calories: 295
% Calories from fat: 14
Protein (gm): 24.1
Carbohydrate (gm): 41.3
Fat (gm): 4.8
Saturated fat (gm): 0.9
Cholesterol (mg): 46
Sodium (mg): 765
Exchanges
Milk: 0.0
Veg.: 2.0
Fruit: 0.0
Bread: 2.0
Meat: 2.0
Fat: 0.0

1. Saute chicken, onion, and garlic in oil in large saucepan until chicken is browned, 8 to 10 minutes. Stir in tomatoes, beans, spices, and orange rind; heat to boiling. Reduce heat and simmer, covered, 20 to 30 minutes; season to taste with salt and pepper. Serve over Orange Cilantro Rice; sprinkle with cilantro.

Orange Cilantro Rice

makes 6 servings (about $2/3$ cup each)

Vegetable cooking spray

$1/2$ cup sliced green onions and tops

1 cup long-grain rice

1-2 tablespoons finely grated orange rind

$2^1/4$ cups water

2 tablespoons finely chopped cilantro

Salt, to taste

1. Spray medium saucepan with cooking spray; heat over medium heat until hot. Saute onions until tender, 3 to 5 minutes. Add rice and orange rind; cook over medium heat until rice is lightly browned, 2 to 3 minutes.

2. Add water and heat to boiling; simmer, covered, until rice is tender, 20 to 25 minutes. Stir in cilantro; season to taste with salt.

FIVE

Lunch
or
Supper Soups

ARTICHOKE BISQUE WITH SHRIMP

This elegant soup can be made up to 3 days ahead of serving; re-heat at medium-low until hot.

6 servings (about 1 cup each)

  1/4 cup sliced green onions and tops
  1-2 tablespoons margarine
  1/4 cup all-purpose flour
    3 cups Chicken Stock (see p. 2)
 1 1/2 cups fat-free milk
    1 can (14 ounces) artichoke hearts, rinsed, drained, divided
    1 cup fat-free half-and-half, *or* fat-free milk
 8-12 ounces peeled, deveined small shrimp
      Pinch nutmeg
      Salt and cayenne pepper, to taste

Per Serving
Calories: 147
% Calories from fat: 18
Protein (gm): 12.6
Carbohydrate (gm): 15.9
Fat (gm): 2.7
Saturated fat (gm): 0.6
Cholesterol (mg): 60.6
Sodium (mg): 329
Exchanges
Milk: 0.0
Veg.: 3.0
Fruit: 0.0
Bread: 0.0
Meat: 1.0
Fat: 0.0

1. Saute green onions in margarine until tender, about 3 minutes. Sprinkle with flour and cook 2 minutes, stirring constantly. Stir in Chicken Stock and milk and heat to boiling; boil, stirring constantly, until thickened.

2. Process half the artichoke hearts in food processor or blender until smooth; stir into soup and heat until boiling.

3. Quarter remaining artichoke hearts and stir into soup; stir in half-and-half, shrimp, and nutmeg; simmer until shrimp are cooked and soup is hot, about 5 minutes. Season to taste with salt and cayenne pepper.

BEET BORSCHT WITH SMOKED SAUSAGE

For convenience, 2 cups canned, drained, shredded beets can be substitut-ed for the fresh; reduce cooking time to 10 to 15 minutes.

8 servings (about 1 1/4 cups each)

Vegetable cooking spray
2 cups julienned, peeled fresh beets (about 4 medium)
1 small head red cabbage, shredded
2 carrots, julienned
1 clove garlic, minced
1 1/2 quarts reduced-sodium fat-free beef broth
1 bay leaf
2-3 teaspoons sugar
1-2 tablespoons cider vinegar
2-4 ounces reduced-sodium, reduced-fat smoked sausage, thinly sliced
Salt and pepper, to taste
1/2 cup fat-free sour cream
Thin lemon slices, as garnish

Per Serving
Calories: 91
% Calories from fat: 4
Protein (gm): 7.5
Carbohydrate (gm): 15.1
Fat (gm): 0.4
Saturated fat (gm): 0.1
Cholesterol (mg): 3.2
Sodium (mg): 248
Exchanges
Milk: 0.0
Veg.: 3.0
Fruit: 0.0
Bread: 0.0
Meat: 0.0
Fat: 0.0

1. Spray large saucepan with cooking spray; heat over medium heat until hot. Saute beets 2 to 3 minutes; stir in cabbage, carrots, garlic, broth, bay leaf, sugar, and vinegar. Heat to boiling; reduce heat and simmer, uncovered, 30 minutes, adding sausage during last 10 minutes of cooking time. Discard bay leaf; season to taste with salt and pepper.

2. Serve soup in bowls; garnish with dollops of sour cream and lemon slices.

HERBED BROCCOLI AND PASTA SOUP

A wonderfully versatile soup, as any vegetable in season and any choice of herb can be substituted for the broccoli and thyme. If desired, 12 ounces of cubed cooked chicken breast can be added during the last 10 minutes of cooking time.

6 servings (about 1 cup each)

3 cans (15 ounces each) reduced-sodium chicken broth
4 cloves garlic, minced
2-3 teaspoons dried thyme leaves
3 cups small broccoli florets
2¹/₄ cups (6 ounces) fusilli (spirals)
2-3 tablespoons lemon juice
¹/₄ teaspoon salt
¹/₈ teaspoon pepper

Per Serving
Calories: 125
% Calories from fat: 8
Protein (g): 6.4
Carbohydrates (g): 23
Fat (g): 1.1
Saturated fat (g): 0.2
Cholesterol (mg): 0
Sodium (mg): 134
Exchanges
Milk: 0.0
Veg.: 0.5
Fruit: 0.0
Bread: 1.5
Meat: 0.0
Fat: 0.0

1. Heat chicken broth, garlic, and thyme to boiling in medium saucepan; stir in broccoli and fusilli. Reduce heat and simmer, uncovered, until broccoli is tender and pasta is al dente, about 10 minutes.

2. Stir in lemon juice, salt, and pepper.

CHEESY BROCCOLI-POTATO SOUP

To save preparation time, frozen broccoli and hash brown potatoes can be substituted for the fresh.

6 servings (about 1¹/₄ cups each)

1 cup chopped onion
³/₄ cup thinly sliced celery
¹/₂ cup finely chopped carrots
1-2 tablespoons margarine
1 quart reduced-sodium fat-free chicken, *or* beef, broth
8 ounces broccoli florets
8 ounces unpeeled Idaho potatoes, cubed

Per Serving
Calories: 299
% Calories from fat: 20
Protein (gm): 17.9
Carbohydrate (gm): 38
Fat (gm): 6.3
Saturated fat (gm): 2.5
Cholesterol (mg): 15.2
Sodium (mg): 670
Exchanges
Milk: 0.0
Veg.: 2.0
Fruit: 0.0
Bread: 2.0
Meat: 1.0
Fat: 1.0

$1/2$ teaspoon celery seeds, lightly crushed

$1/4$ teaspoon dried thyme leaves

3 cups fat-free half-and-half, *or* fat-free milk, divided

$2/3$ cup all-purpose flour

$1^1/2$-2 cups (6-8 ounces) shredded reduced-fat mild Cheddar cheese

Salt and pepper, to taste

1. Saute onion, celery, and carrots in margarine in large saucepan until onion is tender, about 5 minutes. Add broth, broccoli, potatoes, and herbs; heat to boiling. Reduce heat and simmer, covered, until vegetables are tender, 10 to 15 minutes.

2. Heat soup to boiling; stir in combined $1^1/2$ cups half-and-half and flour. Boil, stirring, until soup is thickened, 1 to 2 minutes; stir in remaining milk. Reduce heat to low; add cheese, stirring until melted. Season to taste with salt and pepper.

CHILLED PEA SOUP

A refreshing soup for hot sultry days; serve with a ripe tomato salad and crusty bread or rolls.

6 servings (about 1 cup each)

Vegetable cooking spray

$1/2$ cup chopped onion

$1/2$ teaspoon dried marjoram leaves

$1/4$ teaspoon dried thyme leaves

2 cups reduced-sodium fat-free chicken broth

2 packages (10 ounces each) frozen peas

2 cups sliced romaine lettuce

Salt and white pepper, to taste

$1/2$ cup fat-free sour cream

Paprika, as garnish

Per Serving
Calories: 257
% Calories from fat: 4
Protein (g): 17.4
Carbohydrates (g): 46.6
Fat (g): 1.1
Saturated fat (g): 0.2
Cholesterol (mg): 0
Sodium (mg): 274
Exchanges
Milk: 0.5
Veg.: 0.0
Fruit: 0.0
Bread: 3.0
Meat: 0.5
Fat: 0.0

1. Spray large saucepan with cooking spray; heat over medium heat until hot. Add onion, marjoram, and thyme and saute until onion is tender, about 5 minutes. Stir in broth, peas, and lettuce; heat to boiling. Reduce heat and simmer, covered, until peas are tender, 5 to 8 minutes.

2. Process soup in food processor or blender until smooth; season to taste with salt and pepper. Cool; refrigerate until chilled, 3 to 4 hours.

3. Stir sour cream into soup; pour into bowls and sprinkle with paprika.

EGGPLANT SOUP WITH ROASTED RED PEPPER SAUCE

Grilling gives the eggplant a distinctive smoky flavor. For indoor cooking, eggplant can be oven roasted. Pierce eggplant in several places with fork; place in baking pan and bake at 350 degrees until done, 45 to 50 minutes.

4 servings (about 1¹/₂ cups each)

   2 medium eggplant (about 2¹/₂ pounds)
  ³/₄ cup chopped onion
  ¹/₄ cup chopped green bell pepper
   2 cloves garlic, minced
   1 tablespoon extra-virgin olive oil
4-5 cups reduced-sodium fat-free chicken broth
    Salt and white pepper, to taste
    Roasted Red Pepper Sauce (recipe follows)

Per Serving
Calories: 164
% Calories from fat: 22
Protein (g): 9.1
Carbohydrates (g): 24.6
Fat (g): 4.1
Saturated fat (g): 0.6
Cholesterol (mg): 0
Sodium (mg): 180
Exchanges
Milk: 0.0
Veg.: 5.0
Fruit: 0.0
Bread: 0.0
Meat: 0.0
Fat: 1.0

1. Pierce eggplant in several places with fork. Grill over medium hot coals, turning frequently, until eggplant is very soft, about 30 minutes. Cool until comfortable to handle; cut eggplant in half, scoop out pulp, and chop coarsely.

2. Saute onion, bell pepper, and garlic in oil in large saucepan until tender, 5 to 8 minutes. Add broth and eggplant to saucepan; heat to boiling. Reduce heat and simmer, covered, 10 minutes.

3. Process soup in food processor or blender until smooth. Season to taste with salt and white pepper. Refrigerate until chilled, 4 to 6 hours.

4. Pour soup into bowls; swirl about 3 tablespoons Roasted Red Pepper Sauce into each.

Roasted Red Pepper Sauce

makes about 3/4 cup

> 2 large red bell peppers, cut into halves
> 1 teaspoon sugar

1. Place peppers, skin sides up, on broiler pan. Broil 4 to 6 inches from heat source until skins are blistered and blackened. Place peppers in plastic bag for 5 minutes; peel off skins and discard.

2. Process peppers and sugar in food processor or blender until smooth. Refrigerate until ready to use.

Note: 1 jar (12 ounces) roasted red peppers, drained, can be substituted for the peppers in the recipe.

SOUP À L'OIGNON

The flavor secret to this soup is cooking the onions slowly until they are deeply browned and caramelized.

4-6 servings

> 1 pound onions, thinly sliced
> 4 teaspoons margarine
> 1/2 teaspoon dry mustard
> 2 teaspoons flour
> 1 quart Fragrant Beef Stock (see p. 6), *or* reduced-sodium fat-free beef broth
> 3/4 cup dry white wine
> Salt and pepper, to taste
> 4-6 slices French bread, lightly toasted
> 1/2 cup shredded Parmesan cheese

Per Serving
Calories: 243
% Calories from fat: 30
Protein (gm): 10.7
Carbohydrate (gm): 25.2
Fat (gm): 8.3
Saturated fat (gm): 3.1
Cholesterol (mg): 10.9
Sodium (mg): 430
Exchanges
Milk: 0.0
Veg.: 2.0
Fruit: 0.0
Bread: 1.0
Meat: 0.5
Fat: 2.0

1. Cook onions in margarine in large saucepan over medium to medium-low heat until very soft and caramelized, 15 to 20 minutes; stir in mustard and flour and cook 1 to 2 minutes longer. Add Stock and white wine; heat to boiling. Reduce heat and simmer, covered, 30 minutes. Season to taste with salt and pepper.

2. Sprinkle French bread with cheese; broil until melted, 1 to 2 minutes. Serve soup in bowls; top with cheesy bread slices.

Variation:

Onion and White Bean Soup—Make recipe as above, adding 1 can (15 ounces) rinsed, drained navy, *or* Great Northern, beans, $1/2$ teaspoon dried savory leaves, and $1/4$ teaspoon dried thyme leaves with broth. Omit French bread and Parmesan cheese. Sprinkle top of each serving with 1 tablespoon grated Manchego cheese.

BRANDIED ONION SOUP

This soup is best if you allow it to simmer slowly so that flavors meld.

8 servings

4 cups thinly sliced onions
2-3 teaspoons margarine
2-3 teaspoons olive oil
2 tablespoons flour
$1/4$ teaspoon pepper
2 quarts Fragrant Beef Stock (see p. 6)
2-4 tablespoons brandy, optional
   Salt and pepper, to taste
8 slices French bread, toasted
1 cup grated Parmesan cheese

Per Serving
Calories: 186
% Calories from fat: 30
Protein (gm): 10.2
Carbohydrate (gm): 22.4
Fat (gm): 6.5
Saturated fat (gm): 2.7
Cholesterol (mg): 10.9
Sodium (mg): 394
Exchanges
Milk: 0.0
Veg.: 1.0
Fruit: 0.0
Bread: 1.0
Meat: 1.0
Fat: 0.5

1. Cook onions in margarine and oil in Dutch oven over medium-low heat until golden, 15 to 20 minutes. Add flour and pepper and mix well. Add Fragrant Beef Stock and heat to boiling; reduce heat and simmer, covered, 35 to 45 minutes. Add brandy; season to taste with salt and pepper.

2. Ladle soup into ovenproof bowls and top with French bread; sprinkle each with 2 tablespoons cheese. Broil 6 inches from heat source until cheese has melted and is lightly browned, 2 to 3 minutes.

Variation:

Onion and Potato Soup—Make recipe as above, adding 3 cups cubed, peeled potatoes, $1/4$ teaspoon each dried marjoram and thyme leaves with the stock; omit French bread and Parmesan cheese. Serve soup in bowls; sprinkle each with 2 tablespoons shredded Swiss cheese.

VELVET VICHYSSOISE

Serve this delicately flavored soup with a green salad and Roasted Red Pepper Bread (see p. 797).

8 servings

2 medium onions, chopped

6 leeks, sliced (white parts only)

2-3 tablespoons margarine

5 medium potatoes, peeled, sliced

1¹/₄ quarts Rich Chicken Stock (see p. 4), *or* reduced-sodium fat-free chicken broth

2 cups fat-free milk

2 cans (13 ounces each) evaporated fat-free milk

Salt and pepper, to taste

Finely chopped chives, as garnish

Per Serving
Calories: 293
% Calories from fat: 13
Protein (gm): 16.2
Carbohydrate (gm): 47.4
Fat (gm): 4.1
Saturated fat (gm): 1
Cholesterol (mg): 5.5
Sodium (mg): 230
Exchanges
Milk: 1.0
Veg.: 1.0
Fruit: 0.0
Bread: 2.0
Meat: 0.0
Fat: 1.0

1. Saute onions and leeks in margarine in large saucepan until golden. Add potatoes and Rich Chicken Stock and heat to boiling; reduce heat and simmer until potatoes are tender, about 15 minutes.

2. Process soup in blender or food processor until smooth. Cool; refrigerate until chilled.

3. Stir in fat-free and evaporated milk; season to taste with salt and pepper. Sprinkle each serving with chives.

Variation:

Creamy Cauliflower Soup—Make Step 1 as above, substituting 2 cups coarsely chopped cauliflower for 3 of the potatoes; add ¹/₃ cup grated Parmesan cheese to the soup and proceed with Steps 2 and 3. Omit chives. Sprinkle each serving lightly with ground nutmeg.

CURRIED ONION-POTATO SOUP

In summer we chill this delicious soup and sip it cold from soup cups. In winter we serve it hot.

5-6 servings

   1 garlic clove, minced
   3 cups coarsely chopped onions
1¹/₄ teaspoons ground cumin
1¹/₄ teaspoons ground turmeric
   1 teaspoon mild curry powder
 ¹/₄ teaspoon black pepper
    Dash cayenne pepper
   2 teaspoons margarine
   1 quart Chicken Stock (see p. 2), *or* fat-free chicken broth
   2 cups peeled, diced potatoes
 ³/₄ cup whole milk
    Salt, to taste
1-2 teaspoons finely chopped parsley, *or* chives, as garnish

Per Serving
Calories: 150
% Calories from fat: 16
Protein (g): 6.9
Carbohydrates (g): 25.7
Fat (g): 2.7
Saturated fat (g): 0.9
Cholesterol (mg): 4.1
Sodium (mg): 289
Exchanges
Milk: 0.0
Veg.: 0.0
Fruit: 0.0
Bread: 1.5
Meat: 0.0
Fat: 0.5

1. Saute garlic, onions, cumin, turmeric, curry powder, black and cayenne pepper in margarine in large saucepan until onions are soft, about 10 minutes. Add Chicken Stock and potatoes; heat to boiling. Reduce heat and simmer, covered, 15 minutes or until potatoes are very tender.

2. Process mixture in blender or food processor until smooth. Return to saucepan and stir in milk. Cook, covered, over low heat 5 minutes. Season to taste with salt. Serve hot, or refrigerate and serve cold. Sprinkle each serving with parsley or chives.

TUSCAN TOMATO SOUP

Every Tuscan cook has a different way of preparing this soup, but each version has two basic elements: ripe tomatoes and crusty bread.

6 servings

1 large onion, chopped

2 cloves garlic, chopped

2 tablespoons olive oil

1 quart Chicken Stock (see p. 2)

3 pounds very ripe tomatoes, peeled, seeded, coarsely chopped

1 cup chopped basil

Spike and pepper, to taste

6 slices crusty Italian bread, toasted

Per Serving
Calories: 195
% Calories from fat: **25**
Protein (g): 6.3
Carbohydrates (g): 31.4
Fat (g): 5.6
Saturated fat (g): 0.8
Cholesterol (mg): 0
Sodium (mg): 199
Exchanges
Milk: 0.0
Veg.: 3.0
Fruit: 0.0
Bread: 1.0
Meat: 0.0
Fat: 1.0

1. Saute onion and garlic in olive oil in large saucepan until tender, about 5 minutes. Add Chicken Stock and tomatoes; heat to boiling. Reduce heat and simmer, uncovered, 20 minutes.

2. Process soup in blender or food processor until coarsely pureed; return to saucepan and simmer 5 minutes. Stir in basil; season to taste with Spike and pepper.

3. Place bread slices in bottoms of bowls; ladle soup over.

TOMATO SOUP WITH PASTA

This soup is perfect when garden tomatoes are in season. You can freeze tomatoes from your garden and make this soup in the winter, too.

6 servings (about 1 cup each)

$^1/_2$ cup chopped onion
$^1/_2$ cup chopped carrot
$^1/_4$ cup chopped celery
  1 clove garlic, minced
  1 teaspoon dried basil leaves
  1 teaspoon dried oregano leaves
$^1/_2$ teaspoon anise seeds, lightly crushed
1-2 tablespoons olive oil
  3 pounds tomatoes, coarsely chopped
  3 cups Rich Chicken Stock (see p. 4)
  1 cup small soup pasta, such as stelline, orzo, *or* rings
     Salt and pepper, to taste
     Shredded Parmesan cheese, as garnish

Per Serving
Calories: 164
% Calories from fat: 20
Protein (gm): 7
Carbohydrate (gm): 26.3
Fat (gm): 3.8
Saturated fat (gm): 0.6
Cholesterol (mg): 0.5
Sodium (mg): 45
Exchanges
Milk: 0.0
Veg.: 2.0
Fruit: 0.0
Bread: 1.0
Meat: 0.0
Fat: 0.5

1. Saute onion, carrot, celery, garlic, and herbs in oil in large saucepan until tender, about 5 minutes. Add tomatoes and Rich Chicken Stock; heat to boiling. Reduce heat and simmer, covered, 25 minutes.

2. Process soup in food processor or blender until smooth. Return to saucepan and heat to boiling; stir in pasta. Simmer until tender, about 8 minutes. Season to taste with salt and pepper. Serve soup in bowls; sprinkle with Parmesan cheese.

CREAMY TOMATO SOUP WITH CHUNKY VEGETABLES

A grown-up version of that comforting soup we know so well.

5-6 servings

1 medium onion, finely chopped
1 large garlic clove, minced
2 teaspoons margarine
1 quart Chicken Stock (see p. 2)
1 large rib celery, diced
2 small new potatoes, unpeeled, cubed (^{3}/$_4$-inch)
1^1/$_2$ cups small cauliflower florets
1 cup diced zucchini
1 medium green bell pepper, diced
^{1}/$_4$ cup dry sherry, optional
^{1}/$_4$ cup finely chopped parsley
^{3}/$_4$ teaspoon dried basil leaves
^{1}/$_4$ teaspoon dried thyme leaves
^{1}/$_4$ teaspoon dried marjoram leaves
^{1}/$_8$ teaspoon dry mustard
Dash cayenne pepper
^{1}/$_8$ teaspoon black pepper
1^1/$_2$ tablespoons cornstarch
^{1}/$_4$ cup cold water
1 can (8 ounces) tomato sauce
^{3}/$_4$ cup whole milk
Salt, to taste

Per Serving
Calories: 150
% Calories from fat: 15
Protein (g): 6.3
Carbohydrates (g): 24.1
Fat (g): 2.5
Saturated fat (g): 0.9
Cholesterol (mg): 4.1
Sodium (mg): 404
Exchanges
Milk: 0.0
Veg.: 0.0
Fruit: 0.0
Bread: 1.5
Meat: 0.0
Fat: 0.5

1. Saute onion and garlic in margarine in large saucepan until onion is soft, about 5 minutes. Add Chicken Stock, vegetables, sherry, herbs, mustard, and cayenne and black pepper; heat to boiling. Reduce heat and simmer, covered, 15 to 20 minutes or until vegetables are tender.

2. Heat soup to boiling; whisk in combined cornstarch and water, boiling until thickened, 1 to 2 minutes. Reduce heat and stir in tomato sauce and milk; simmer 2 to 3 minutes. Season to taste with salt.

MATZO BALL AND VEGETABLE SOUP

We've added a variety of vegetables to this traditional Jewish soup.

6 servings

1¹/₂-2 quarts Chicken Stock (see p. 2), *or* fat-
free chicken broth
1 rib celery, sliced
1 large carrot, diced
1 cup frozen lima beans
1¹/₂ cups small cauliflower florets
¹/₈ teaspoon pepper
Matzo Balls (recipe follows)
Salt, to taste

Per Serving
Calories: 159
% Calories from fat: 26
Protein (g): 8.7
Carbohydrates (g): 20.6
Fat (g): 4.7
Saturated fat (g): 0.8
Cholesterol (mg): 44.7
Sodium (mg): 765
Exchanges
Milk: 0.0
Veg.: 0.0
Fruit: 0.0
Bread: 1.5
Meat: 0.0
Fat: 1.0

1. Combine all ingredients, except Matzo Balls and salt, in large saucepan; heat to boiling. Reduce heat and simmer, covered, 20 to 25 minutes. Add Matzo Balls to soup; simmer, covered, 5 minutes. Season to taste with salt.

Matzo Balls

makes 1 dozen

1 egg
2 egg whites
1 tablespoon canola oil
¹/₂ cup plus 1 tablespoon matzo meal
¹/₄ teaspoon salt
2¹/₂ tablespoons Chicken Stock (see p. 2), *or*
fat-free chicken broth

1. Combine all ingredients, mixing well; chill, covered, 1 hour. Form dough into 12 balls; drop into simmering water and cook 30 to 35 minutes. Remove with slotted spoon and drain.

ASIAN MUSHROOM SOUP WITH NOODLES

Thin egg noodles or thin spaghetti can be substituted for the soba noodles.

6 servings

3 cups boiling water

1 ounce dried shiitake mushrooms

1¹/₂ pounds cremini mushrooms, minced, divided

¹/₂ small onion, minced

1 clove garlic, minced

1-2 tablespoons margarine

¹/₄ teaspoon dried thyme leaves

1 quart Low-Salt Chicken Stock (see p. 3), *or* reduced-sodium fat-free chicken broth

1 cup dry white wine

¹/₄ pound soba noodles

¹/₂ pound snow peas, trimmed

¹/₂ cup sliced radishes

1 tablespoon red wine vinegar

2 tablespoons finely chopped parsley

Salt and pepper, to taste

Per Serving
Calories: 195
% Calories from fat: 10
Protein (gm): 11.3
Carbohydrate (gm): 27.7
Fat (gm): 2.3
Saturated fat (gm): 0.5
Cholesterol (mg): 2.3
Sodium (mg): 118
Exchanges
Milk: 0.0
Veg.: 3.0
Fruit: 0.0
Bread: 1.0
Meat: 0.0
Fat: 1.0

1. Pour boiling water over shiitake mushrooms in bowl and let stand until softened, about 15 minutes. Drain; strain liquid through fine strainer and reserve. Finely chop mushrooms, discarding tough stems.

2. Saute shiitake mushrooms, 1 pound cremini mushrooms, onion, and garlic in margarine in large saucepan until soft, 5 to 8 minutes. Add thyme, Low-Salt Chicken Stock, wine, and reserved mushroom liquid; heat to boiling. Reduce heat and simmer, covered, 30 minutes.

3. Strain soup, discarding mushrooms. Add remaining ¹/₂ pound cremini mushrooms, noodles, snow peas, radishes, vinegar, and parsley; simmer, uncovered, until noodles are cooked, about 5 minutes. Season to taste with salt and pepper.

EAST MEETS WEST SOUP

This creamy, hotly spiced soup is garnished with crisp Chili-Seasoned Wontons.

6 servings (about 1 cup each)

1¹/₃ cups thinly sliced onions
1 cup thinly sliced celery
1 tablespoon minced garlic
1 small jalapeño chili, minced
1 tablespoon minced gingerroot
1 teaspoon ground cumin
2 teaspoons margarine
¹/₃ cup all-purpose flour
3 cups Low-Salt Chicken Stock (see p. 3)
2¹/₂ cups fat-free milk
2 cans (4 ounces each) chopped green chilies, drained
Salt and pepper, to taste
¹/₄ cup chopped cilantro
Chili-Seasoned Wontons (recipe follows)

Per Serving
Calories: 192
% Calories from fat: 18
Protein (gm): 8.2
Carbohydrate (gm): 31.2
Fat (gm): 3.7
Saturated fat (gm): 0.7
Cholesterol (mg): 5.7
Sodium (mg): 369
Exchanges
Milk: 0.0
Veg.: 0.0
Fruit: 0.0
Bread: 2.0
Meat: 0.0
Fat: 1.0

1. Saute onions, celery, garlic, jalapeño chili, gingerroot, and cumin in margarine in large saucepan until tender, about 5 minutes. Sprinkle with flour and cook 2 minutes longer.

2. Stir in Low-Salt Chicken Stock, milk, and green chilies and heat to boiling, stirring until thickened, 1 to 2 minutes longer; reduce heat and simmer, uncovered, 5 minutes. Season to taste with salt and pepper; stir in cilantro. Serve in bowls with Chili-Seasoned Wontons.

Chili-Seasoned Wontons

makes 6 servings (6 wontons each)

1 teaspoon hot chili powder
¹/₂ teaspoon garlic powder
¹/₄ teaspoon cayenne pepper
2 teaspoons vegetable oil

2 teaspoons water
18 wonton wrappers, cut diagonally into
halves

1. Combine chili powder, garlic powder, cayenne pepper, oil, and water in small bowl. Brush both sides of wonton wrappers with mixture and place on cookie sheet. Bake at 375 degrees until crisp, about 5 minutes; cool on wire racks.

TWO-SEASON SQUASH SOUP

Winter squash and summer garden zucchini are combined in this perfect soup. Delicious with Hearty Vegetable-Rye Bread (see p. 796).

6 servings (about 1³/₄ cups each)

1 cup chopped onion
2 cloves garlic, minced
2 teaspoons margarine
3 cups Quick-Spiced Beef Stock
(see p. 7)
1 medium butternut squash, peeled, seeded, cubed
2 medium zucchini, sliced
1 can (28 ounces) reduced-sodium whole tomatoes, undrained, chopped
1 can (15 ounces) Great Northern beans, drained, rinsed
3 tablespoons minced parsley
1 bay leaf
1 teaspoon very-low-sodium Worcestershire sauce
1 teaspoon dried marjoram leaves
¹/₂ teaspoon dried rosemary leaves
Salt and pepper, to taste

Per Serving
Calories: 136
% Calories from fat: **9**
Protein (gm): **8.3**
Carbohydrate (gm): **27.3**
Fat (gm): **1.7**
Saturated fat (gm): **0.3**
Cholesterol (mg): **0**
Sodium (mg): **296**
Exchanges
Milk: **0.0**
Veg.: **3.0**
Fruit: **0.0**
Bread: **0.5**
Meat: **0.0**
Fat: **0.5**

1. Saute onion and garlic in margarine in large saucepan until tender, about 5 minutes. Add remaining ingredients, except salt and pepper, and heat to boiling. Reduce heat and simmer, covered, until squash is tender, about 25 minutes. Discard bay leaf; season to taste with salt and pepper.

FRENCH VEGETABLE SOUP

Made with a traditional French veal stock, cubes of veal, and lots of fresh vegetables, this soup is a special treat.

8 servings (about 1¹/₂ cups each)

1 pound lean veal, fat trimmed, cubed (¹/₂-inch)

¹/₂ cup chopped onion

¹/₂ cup sliced celery

¹/₂ cup sliced carrot

1 teaspoon dried thyme leaves

¹/₂ teaspoon dried savory leaves

2 teaspoons margarine

2 quarts Veal Stock (see p. 8)

1 can (16 ounces) reduced-sodium whole tomatoes, undrained, chopped

2 cups small cauliflower florets

1 cup small broccoli florets

1¹/₂ cups cubed, peeled potatoes

1 cup fresh, *or* frozen, cut green beans

²/₃ cup fresh, *or* frozen, peas

¹/₄ cup chopped parsley

Salt and pepper, to taste

Per Serving
Calories: 199
% Calories from fat: 18
Protein (gm): 21.5
Carbohydrate (gm): 19.4
Fat (gm): 4.2
Saturated fat (gm): 1.2
Cholesterol (mg): 66.1
Sodium (mg): 84
Exchanges
Milk: 0.0
Veg.: 1.0
Fruit: 0.0
Bread: 1.0
Meat: 2.0
Fat: 0.0

1. Saute veal, onion, celery, carrot, thyme, and savory in margarine in large saucepan until veal is browned, about 10 minutes. Stir in Veal Stock and heat to boiling; reduce heat and simmer, covered, until veal is tender, about 30 minutes.

2. Stir in tomatoes and liquid, cauliflower, broccoli, potatoes, green beans, and peas. Heat to boiling; reduce heat and simmer, covered, until vegetables are tender, 15 to 20 minutes. Stir in parsley; season to taste with salt and pepper.

MINESTRONE

Minestrone does not always contain pasta, nor is it always a heavy, hearty soup. Enjoy this light version of an old favorite, selecting vegetables that are freshest and most plentiful.

8 servings (about 1¼ cups each)

1 cup sliced carrots

½ cup chopped onion

½ cup chopped celery

½ cup sliced fennel bulb

2 cloves garlic, minced

1 tablespoon olive oil

5 cups reduced-sodium fat-free beef broth

1 can (19 ounces) garbanzo beans, rinsed, drained

1 cup snap peas

1 small zucchini, sliced

1 cup broccoli florets

¾-1 teaspoon dried basil leaves

¾-1 teaspoon dried oregano leaves

1 cup halved cherry tomatoes

¼ cup finely chopped parsley

Salt and pepper, to taste

1½ cups Parmesan Croutons (½ recipe) (see p. 784)

Per Serving
Calories: 146
% Calories from fat: 21
Protein (g): 7.3
Carbohydrates (g): 4.9
Fat (g): 3.5
Saturated fat (g): 0.6
Cholesterol (mg): 0.5
Sodium (mg): 447
Exchanges
Milk: 0.0
Veg.: 1.0
Fruit: 0.0
Bread: 1.0
Meat: 0.0
Fat: 0.5

1. Saute carrots, onion, celery, fennel, and garlic in oil in Dutch oven until onion is tender, 5 to 8 minutes. Add broth, beans, peas, zucchini, broccoli, and herbs; heat to boiling. Reduce heat and simmer, covered, until vegetables are tender, 10 to 15 minutes, adding tomatoes and parsley during last 5 minutes of cooking time. Season to taste with salt and pepper.

2. Pour soup into bowls; sprinkle with Parmesan Croutons.

VEGETABLE SOUP WITH ORZO

Escarole, which lends a unique taste to this hearty soup, is also a flavorful addition to green salads. Spinach leaves can be substituted for the escarole in this recipe, if desired.

4 servings (about 2 cups each)

Olive oil cooking spray
1 medium onion, coarsely chopped
2 medium carrots, sliced
2 medium ribs celery, sliced
3 cloves garlic, minced
2 medium zucchini, *or* yellow summer squash, sliced
1 cup sliced mushrooms
$^1/_2$ teaspoon dried thyme leaves
$^1/_2$ teaspoon dried oregano leaves
5 cups reduced-sodium fat-free chicken broth
$^1/_2$ cup (4 ounces) orzo, uncooked
$^1/_2$ cup frozen peas
6 medium leaves escarole, sliced, *or* coarsely chopped
$^1/_4$ teaspoon salt
$^1/_2$ teaspoon pepper
2 tablespoons grated Romano cheese

Per Serving
Calories: 221
% Calories from fat: 8
Protein (g): 15.4
Carbohydrates (g): 34.9
Fat (g): 1.9
Saturated fat (g): 0.8
Cholesterol (mg): 3.7
Sodium (mg): 453
Exchanges
Milk: 0.0
Veg.: 4.0
Fruit: 0.0
Bread: 1.0
Meat: 0.0
Fat: 0.5

1. Spray large saucepan with cooking spray; heat over medium heat until hot. Saute onion, carrots, celery, and garlic in saucepan until onion is tender, about 5 minutes. Add zucchini, mushrooms, and herbs; cook, covered, 2 to 3 minutes.

2. Add broth to saucepan; heat to boiling. Stir in orzo, peas, and escarole. Reduce heat and simmer, uncovered, until orzo is al dente, about 7 minutes. Season with salt and pepper. Spoon soup into bowls; sprinkle with cheese.

GARDEN HARVEST SOUP

Vary the vegetables according to your garden or greengrocer's bounty.

6 servings (about 1¹/₂ cups each)

2 small onions, sliced

2 cloves garlic, minced

1 tablespoon olive oil

2 carrots, sliced

1 small red bell pepper, sliced

1 small yellow bell pepper, sliced

2 cups whole-kernel corn

5 cups reduced-sodium fat-free chicken broth

1 cup cut green beans (1-inch)

1 medium zucchini, sliced

1 yellow summer squash, sliced

¹/₂-³/₄ teaspoon dried basil leaves

¹/₂ teaspoon dried oregano leaves

Salt and pepper, to taste

¹/₃ cup fat-free milk, optional

Finely chopped parsley, as garnish

Per Serving
Calories: 136
% Calories from fat: 17
Protein (g): 8.4
Carbohydrates (g): 21.3
Fat (g): 2.8
Saturated fat (g): 0.4
Cholesterol (mg): 0
Sodium (mg): 161
Exchanges
Milk: 0.0
Veg.: 4.0
Fruit: 0.0
Bread: 0.0
Meat: 0.0
Fat: 0.5

1. Saute onions and garlic in oil in large saucepan until tender, about 5 minutes. Add carrots, bell peppers, and corn and saute 5 minutes more. Add broth, green beans, zucchini, squash, and herbs; heat to boiling. Reduce heat and simmer, covered, until vegetables are tender, about 15 minutes. Season to taste with salt and pepper.

2. Whip milk until thick and foamy with immersion blender; stir into soup just before serving. Pour soup into bowls; sprinkle with parsley.

SPICY CURRIED CREAM OF VEGETABLE SOUP

This is no ordinary cream of vegetable soup! A careful blend of vegetables, apples, herbs, and spices makes it full-flavored and zesty.

7-9 servings

1 cup chopped red bell pepper
2 cups coarsely chopped onions
1 tablespoon margarine
1^1/$_2$ tablespoons flour
1 cup chopped carrot
^{1}/$_2$ cup chopped celery
3^1/$_2$ cups chopped, peeled tart cooking apples
2^1/$_2$ cups Chicken Stock (see p. 2), *or* reduced-sodium fat-free chicken broth
1^1/$_2$ tablespoons mild curry powder
^{1}/$_2$ teaspoon ground allspice
^{1}/$_2$ teaspoon dried thyme leaves
2^1/$_3$ cups diced, peeled, baking potatoes
^{1}/$_4$ cup golden raisins
^{1}/$_4$ cup tomato sauce
2 cups Beef Stock (see p. 6), *or* fat-free beef broth
2 cups whole milk
^{1}/$_2$ teaspoon salt
Chopped fresh cilantro, *or* parsley, as garnish

Per Serving
Calories: 195
% Calories from fat: **16**
Protein (g): 6.8
Carbohydrates (g): **36.3**
Fat (g): 3.7
Saturated fat (g): **1.5**
Cholesterol (mg): **7.3**
Sodium (mg): 316
Exchanges
Milk: 0.0
Veg.: 1.0
Fruit: 0.0
Bread: 2.0
Meat: 0.0
Fat: 0.5

1. Saute bell pepper and onions in margarine in large saucepan over medium heat until soft, 8 to 10 minutes. Stir in flour; cook 1 minute. Add carrot, celery, and apples, and saute 7 to 10 minutes longer. Add Chicken Stock, curry powder, allspice, thyme, potatoes, and raisins; heat to boiling. Reduce heat and simmer, covered, until potatoes are tender, about 15 minutes.

2. Remove and reserve 1 cup vegetables. Process soup in blender or food processor until smooth; return to saucepan. Add reserved vegetables, tomato sauce, Beef Stock, and milk. Simmer, uncovered, 5 minutes. Season to taste with salt; sprinkle each serving with cilantro.

HIGH SUMMER SOUP WITH SALSA

This festive, seasonal soup and Salsa features vegetables bountiful in high summer—yellow squash, corn, and tomatoes.

4-5 servings

2 large onions, coarsely chopped
1/4 cup chopped carrot
1 large garlic clove, chopped
1 tablespoon margarine
1 tablespoon white flour
1 quart Chicken Stock (see p. 2), *or* fat-free chicken broth
1 1/4 pounds yellow squash, chopped
1/2 cup diced, peeled boiling potato
1/4 teaspoon dry mustard
1/8 teaspoon white pepper
1 1/2 cups whole-kernel corn, divided
1/2 cup whole milk
1 1/2 teaspoons lemon juice
Finely chopped cilantro, as garnish
Salsa (recipe follows)

Per Serving
Calories: 169
% Calories from fat: 18
Protein (g): 7.6
Carbohydrates (g): 29.7
Fat (g): 3.7
Saturated fat (g): 1.1
Cholesterol (mg): 3.3
Sodium (mg): 357
Exchanges
Milk: 0.0
Veg.: 2.0
Fruit: 0.0
Bread: 2.0
Meat: 0.0
Fat: 0.5

1. Saute onions, carrot, and garlic in margarine in large saucepan until onions are tender, 8 to 10 minutes. Stir in flour and cook 1 minute longer. Add Chicken Stock, squash, potato, mustard, white pepper, and 1 cup corn; heat to boiling. Reduce heat and simmer, uncovered, 10 minutes, or until potato is tender.

2. Process mixture in blender or food processor until smooth; return to saucepan. Stir in remaining 1/2 cup corn, milk, and lemon juice; simmer, uncovered, 5 minutes. Sprinkle each serving with cilantro; serve with Salsa to stir into soup.

Salsa

1 large, ripe tomato, peeled, seeded, finely diced
1 tablespoon finely chopped chives
1 teaspoon red wine vinegar, *or* apple cider vinegar
1/4 teaspoon salt

1. Combine all ingredients in a non-corrosive bowl, tossing until mixed.

SPANISH-STYLE VEGETABLE SOUP

The combination of ingredients is unusual, but it yields very flavorful results.

9-11 servings

1 large onion, finely chopped

2 large garlic cloves, minced

1 medium leek, white part only, chopped

2 teaspoons olive oil

3 quarts water

2 pounds beef soup bones

4 beef bouillon cubes

1 package (8 ounces) country ham, fat trimmed, cut into bite-sized pieces

1/2 cup dried lima beans, *or* navy beans, rinsed, picked over

3 large romaine lettuce leaves, coarsely shredded

1/2 cup finely chopped parsley

2 medium carrots, thinly sliced

2 large ribs celery, including leaves, thinly sliced

2 large bay leaves

1 teaspoon dried thyme leaves

1/4 teaspoon pepper

1 large boneless, skinless chicken breast half, fat removed

2 large red potatoes, cut into 3/4-inch cubes

6-7 medium asparagus spears, cut into 1-inch pieces

1 1/2 cups fresh-cut green beans
Salt, to taste

Per Serving
Calories: 141
% Calories from fat: 18
Protein (g): 12.5
Carbohydrates (g): 17.2
Fat (g): 2.9
Saturated fat (g): 0.6
Cholesterol (mg): 18.7
Sodium (mg): 602
Exchanges
Milk: 0.0
Veg.: 0.0
Fruit: 0.0
Bread: 1.0
Meat: 1.0
Fat: 0.0

1. Saute onion, garlic, and leek in olive oil in Dutch oven until onion is tender, about 5 minutes. Add water, beef bones, bouillon cubes, ham, lima beans, lettuce, parsley, carrots, celery, bay leaves, thyme, and pepper; heat to boiling. Reduce heat and simmer, covered, 1 hour.

2. Add chicken breast and simmer until cooked, about 20 minutes. Remove chicken; cut into bite-sized pieces and return to soup. Add potatoes, asparagus, and green beans; simmer, covered, until vegetables are tender, 15 to 20 minutes. Discard beef bones and bay leaves; skim fat from surface of soup. Season to taste with salt.

LIMA BEAN AND BARLEY SOUP

An excellent winter soup, with robust seasonings.

5-6 servings

1 large onion, finely chopped
1 large rib celery, thinly sliced
2 teaspoons canola oil
1¹/₂ quarts Chicken Stock (see p. 2) *or* reduced-sodium chicken broth
1 medium pork hock
1 can (14¹/₂ ounces) diced tomatoes, undrained
1 large carrot, thinly sliced
1 cup frozen lima beans
¹/₂ cup finely chopped parsley
¹/₄ cup pearl barley
¹/₂ cup diced, peeled turnip
1 bay leaf
¹/₂-1 teaspoon sugar
³/₄ teaspoon dried thyme leaves
¹/₂ teaspoon dried marjoram leaves
¹/₈ teaspoon ground celery seed
¹/₈ teaspoon black pepper
Pinch cayenne pepper
Salt, to taste

Per Serving
Calories: 138
% Calories from fat: 14
Protein (g): 9.2
Carbohydrates (g): 21.7
Fat (g): 2.2
Saturated fat (g): 0.3
Cholesterol (mg): 1.8
Sodium (mg): 477
Exchanges
Milk: 0.0
Veg.: 1.0
Fruit: 0.0
Bread: 1.0
Meat: 0.0
Fat: 0.5

1. Saute onion and celery in oil in large saucepan until onion is tender, about 5 minutes. Add remaining ingredients, except salt, and heat to boiling. Reduce heat and simmer, covered, until barley is tender, about 1 hour. Discard pork hock and bay leaf; skim fat from top of soup. Season to taste with salt.

SPICY OATMEAL SOUP

Oatmeal adds interesting texture to this vegetable soup; fresh bread crumbs can be substituted.

4-6 servings

2 large leeks, white parts only, thinly sliced
1-2 teaspoons margarine
1-2 teaspoons peanut oil
4 carrots, cut into 1/2-inch slices
2 medium potatoes, unpeeled, diced
2 medium zucchini, sliced
2 ribs celery, thinly sliced
1¹/2 quarts Rich Chicken Stock (see p. 4), *or* reduced-sodium fat-free chicken broth
1 tablespoon dried chives
1 tablespoon dried shallots
1 tablespoon Spike
1¹/2 teaspoons dried basil leaves
2-4 drops hot pepper sauce
¹/2 cup quick-cooking oatmeal
1 cup dry white wine
Salt and pepper, to taste

Per Serving
Calories: 299
% Calories from fat: 14
Protein (gm): 12.9
Carbohydrate (gm): 40.2
Fat (gm): 4.4
Saturated fat (gm): 0.9
Cholesterol (mg): 1.5
Sodium (mg): 129
Exchanges
Milk: 0.0
Veg.: 2.0
Fruit: 0.0
Bread: 2.0
Meat: 0.0
Fat: 2.0

1. Saute leeks in margarine and peanut oil in large saucepan until tender, about 5 minutes. Add remaining ingredients, except oatmeal, wine, salt, and pepper; heat to boiling. Reduce heat and simmer, covered, 20 minutes. Stir in oatmeal and wine and simmer, uncovered, 20 minutes; season to taste with salt and pepper.

MILANESE VEGETABLE RISOTTO SOUP

This vegetable soup is enriched with Risotto Milanese for a unique touch.

10 servings

1 cup chopped onion

1 cup finely diced carrots

2 tablespoons olive oil

2 quarts Chicken Stock (see p. 2)

2 cups spinach, torn into small pieces

1/2 pound green beans, trimmed and cut into 1-inch pieces

1 cup finely diced zucchini

1/2 cup peas

1/2 cup diced tomato

1 teaspoon pepper
Risotto Milanese (recipe follows)
Grated Parmesan cheese

Per Serving
Calories: 230
% Calories from fat: 14
Protein (g): 5.6
Carbohydrates (g): 43.9
Fat (g): 3.5
Saturated fat (g): 0.5
Cholesterol (mg): 0
Sodium (mg): 44
Exchanges
Milk: 0.0
Veg.: 1.0
Fruit: 0.0
Bread: 2.5
Meat: 0.0
Fat: 0.5

1. Saute onion and carrots in large saucepan in oil until tender. Add Chicken Stock and heat to boiling; add remaining ingredients, except Risotto Milanese and Parmesan cheese, and simmer, uncovered, 30 minutes.

2. Stir in Risotto Milanese; simmer, uncovered, 4 to 5 minutes. Sprinkle each serving with Parmesan cheese.

Risotto Milanese

Vegetable cooking spray

1/2 cup diced onion

1 pound arborio rice

2 quarts Chicken Stock (see p. 2)

1. Spray large saucepan with cooking spray; heat over medium heat until hot. Add onion and saute until tender, about 5 minutes. Add rice; saute 2 to 3 minutes, stirring occasionally.

2. Heat Chicken Stock just to boiling in large saucepan; reduce heat to medium-low to keep stock hot. Add stock to rice, 1 cup at a time, stirring constantly until Stock is absorbed before adding next cup. Continue process until rice is al dente and mixture is creamy, about 20 minutes.

VEGETABLE SOUP WITH PESTO

In Italy, minestrone means something different to everyone, but the literal name, "big soup," implies a recipe generously laden with vegetables, grains, beans, and herbs. In the basil-loving town of Genoa, the addition of pungent pesto distinguishes the local version.

12 servings

2 large leeks, white parts only, chopped

3 quarts Chicken Stock (see p. 2)

2 large carrots, sliced

3 ribs celery, thinly sliced

2 cans (15 ounces each) cannellini beans, rinsed, drained

2 cups elbow macaroni

1 pound yellow summer squash, cut into 1/2-inch cubes

1 large yellow bell pepper, seeded, chopped

1 cup fresh, *or* frozen, peas
No-Fat Pesto (recipe follows), divided
Salt and pepper, to taste
Shredded Parmesan cheese, as garnish
Pine nuts, as garnish

Per Serving
Calories: 224
% Calories from fat: 19
Protein (g): 14
Carbohydrates (g): 37.6
Fat (g): 5.2
Saturated fat (g): 5
Cholesterol (mg): 23.8
Sodium (mg): 1269
Exchanges
Milk: 0.0
Veg.: 1.0
Fruit: 0.0
Bread: 2.0
Meat: 1.0
Fat: 0.0

1. Combine leeks, Chicken Stock, carrots, and celery in large stock pot; heat to boiling. Reduce heat and simmer, covered, until vegetables are tender, about 15 minutes.

2. Add beans, macaroni, squash, bell pepper, and peas; simmer, covered, until macaroni is tender, about 10 minutes. Stir in 1/2 cup No-Fat Pesto; season to taste with salt and pepper. Sprinkle each serving with Parmesan cheese and pine nuts; pass remaining No-Fat Pesto.

No-Fat Pesto

makes about 1¹/₄ cups

> 2 cups loosely packed basil leaves
> 4 large cloves garlic
> ¹/₂ cup reduced-sodium chicken broth
>   Salt and pepper, to taste

1. Process basil and garlic in food processor or blender until finely chopped; with machine running, gradually pour in chicken broth. Season to taste with salt and pepper.

SWEET-AND-SOUR CABBAGE SOUP

Here's a rich, tangy soup that evokes the flavor of stuffed cabbage, but it's much quicker and easier to make.

8 servings

> 8 ounces ground beef round
> 6 ounces ground turkey breast
> 1 large onion, chopped
> 2 garlic cloves, minced
> 2 quarts Fragrant Beef Stock (see p. 6)
> 1 can (15 ounces) tomato sauce
> 2 tablespoons cider vinegar
> 2 tablespoons brown sugar
> 1 bay leaf
> 1 teaspoon dried thyme leaves
> ¹/₄ teaspoon pepper
> ¹/₈ teaspoon ground cinnamon
>   Dash ground cloves
> 4 cups thinly sliced green cabbage
> 6 baby carrots, sliced
> ¹/₃ cup raisins
> ¹/₂ cup uncooked white rice
>   Salt, to taste

Per Serving
Calories: 202
% Calories from fat: 18
Protein (g): 16.1
Carbohydrates (g): 26.2
Fat (g): 1.2
Saturated fat (g): 1.7
Cholesterol (mg): 25.8
Sodium (mg): 425
Exchanges
Milk: 0.0
Veg.: 1.0
Fruit: 0.0
Bread: 1.0
Meat: 2.0
Fat: 0.0

1. Saute meats, onion, and garlic in Dutch oven until meat is browned. Add remaining ingredients, except rice and salt; heat to boiling. Reduce heat and simmer, covered, 20 minutes. Add rice and simmer, covered, until tender, 20 to 25 minutes. Discard bay leaf; skim fat from surface of soup. Season to taste with salt.

RUSSIAN CABBAGE SOUP

Use red or green cabbage, fresh or canned beets in this savory soup.

8 servings (about 1½ cups each)

2 medium onions, sliced
1 tablespoon margarine
7 cups reduced-sodium fat-free beef broth
1 can (16 ounces) reduced-sodium whole tomatoes, undrained, coarsely chopped
6 cups thinly sliced red cabbage
4 large beets, peeled, cubed
1 tablespoon cider vinegar
2 large carrots, sliced
1 turnip, peeled, cubed
1 large Idaho potato, peeled, cubed
    Salt and pepper, to taste
8 tablespoons fat-free sour cream
    Finely chopped parsley, as garnish

Per Serving
Calories: 121
% Calories from fat: 13
Protein (g): 8
Carbohydrates (g): 20.1
Fat (g): 1.8
Saturated fat (g): 0.3
Cholesterol (mg): 0
Sodium (mg): 218
Exchanges
Milk: 0.0
Veg.: 3.0
Fruit: 0.0
Bread: 0.5
Meat: 0.0
Fat: 0.0

1. Saute onions in margarine in Dutch oven until tender, about 5 minutes. Add broth, tomatoes, cabbage, beets, and vinegar; heat to boiling. Reduce heat and simmer, uncovered, 30 minutes; add carrots, turnip, and potato and simmer 15 minutes longer. Season to taste with salt and pepper.

2. Pour soup into bowls; spoon 1 tablespoon sour cream into each and sprinkle with parsley.

SPICY BEEF AND CABBAGE SOUP

The combination of cabbage, vinegar, sugar, and spices gives this easy soup its zest. If you like, substitute brown rice for white, and add the rice along with the beef broth.

6-8 servings

12 ounces ground beef round
1 large onion, finely chopped
1 large garlic clove, minced
1 quart beef broth
3 cups water
2 ribs celery, including leaves, thinly sliced
2 large carrots, thinly sliced
3 bay leaves
1 can (15 ounces) reduced-sodium tomato sauce
3 cups shredded cabbage
1/2 teaspoon dry mustard
2 tablespoons cider vinegar
2 tablespoons sugar
1/2 teaspoon dried thyme leaves
1/2 teaspoon dried marjoram leaves
1/4 teaspoon ground cinnamon
1/8 teaspoon ground cloves
1/2 teaspoon pepper
1/3 cup uncooked rice
   Salt, to taste

Per Serving
Calories: 136
% Calories from fat: 13
Protein (g): 10.5
Carbohydrates (g): 20.2
Fat (g): 2
Saturated fat (g): 0.5
Cholesterol (mg): 20.5
Sodium (mg): 518
Exchanges
Milk: 0.0
Veg.: 2.0
Fruit: 0.0
Bread: 0.5
Meat: 1.0
Fat: 0.0

1. Cook beef, onion, and garlic in large saucepan over medium heat until meat is browned, 5 to 8 minutes. Drain fat. Add remaining ingredients except rice and salt; heat to boiling. Reduce heat and simmer, covered, 15 minutes.

2. Add rice; simmer, covered, until rice is tender, 20 to 25 minutes. Skim fat from top of soup; discard bay leaves. Season to taste with salt.

MEATBALL AND VEGETABLE SOUP

Browning the meatballs in the oven makes preparation easier, and it cooks off some of the fat.

6-8 servings

1 medium onion, finely chopped
1 garlic clove, minced
2 ribs celery, diced
1 can (14¹/2 ounces) reduced-sodium crushed tomatoes, undrained
1 quart Beef Stock (see p. 6), *or* fat-free beef broth
2 cups water
1 can (8 ounces) tomato sauce
2 large carrots, thinly sliced
2 cups frozen whole-kernel corn
2 cups cut green beans
2 cups coarsely chopped cauliflower
¹/4 cup pearl barley
2 bay leaves
2 teaspoons sugar
1 teaspoon dried basil leaves
¹/2 teaspoon dried thyme leaves
¹/2 teaspoon dry mustard
¹/2 teaspoon chili powder
Dash ground cloves
¹/4 teaspoon black pepper
Meatballs (recipe follows)
Salt, to taste

Per Serving
Calories: 188
% Calories from fat: **13**
Protein (g): 10
Carbohydrates (g): 29.6
Fat (g): 2.1
Saturated fat (g): 0.6
Cholesterol (mg): 20.5
Sodium (mg): 351
Exchanges
Milk: 0.0
Veg.: 2.0
Fruit: 0.0
Bread: 1.0
Meat: 1.0
Fat: 0.0

1. Combine all ingredients, except Meatballs and salt, in large saucepan; heat to boiling. Reduce heat and simmer, covered, 1 hour, or until barley is tender. Add meatballs and simmer, covered 10 to 15 minutes. Skim fat from surface of soup; discard bay leaves. Season to taste with salt.

Meatballs

makes 1¹/₂ dozen

- 16 ounces ground beef round
- 2 teaspoons dried minced onions
- 1 egg white
- ¹/₄ cup quick-cooking oats
- 2 tablespoons catsup
- ¹/₈ teaspoon dried thyme leaves
- ¹/₈ teaspoon dry mustard
- ¹/₄ teaspoon salt
- ¹/₈ teaspoon pepper

1. Combine all ingredients; roll into 18 meatballs. Bake in baking pan at 350 degrees until nicely browned, about 10 minutes.

BOURBON STREET BEEF SOUP

Okra, rice, and tomatoes accent this vegetable beef soup.

6 servings (about 1¹/₂ cups each)

Per Serving
Calories: 264
% Calories from fat: 15
Protein (gm): 24.1
Carbohydrate (gm): **34.5**
Fat (gm): 4.4
Saturated fat (gm): **1.4**
Cholesterol (mg): **47.3**
Sodium (mg): 77
Exchanges
Milk: 0.0
Veg.: 1.0
Fruit: 0.0
Bread: 2.0
Meat: 2.0
Fat: 0.0

- 1 pound lean beef stew meat, fat trimmed, cut into 1-inch cubes
- 1 small beef soup bone
- 1 quart water
- 1¹/₂ cups chopped onions
- ³/₄ cup chopped green bell pepper
- 3 cloves garlic, minced
- 1 can (28 ounces) reduced-sodium whole tomatoes, undrained, chopped
- 1 can (16 ounces) reduced-sodium stewed tomatoes, undrained
- 1 teaspoon dried thyme leaves
- ¹/₂ teaspoon crushed red pepper
- 1 bay leaf
- 1¹/₂ cups whole-kernel corn
- 1¹/₂ cups sliced okra
- ¹/₃ cup rice
  Salt and pepper, to taste
  Hot pepper sauce, to taste

1. Place stew meat, soup bone, water, onions, bell pepper, garlic, whole tomatoes and liquid, stewed tomatoes and liquid, thyme, crushed red pepper, and bay leaf in large saucepan. Heat to boiling; reduce heat and simmer, covered, until meat is very tender, 1 to 1½ hours.

2. Stir in corn, okra, and rice and simmer until rice is tender, about 20 minutes. Discard soup bone and bay leaf; season to taste with salt, pepper, and hot pepper sauce.

BEEF, VEGETABLE, AND BARLEY SOUP

Thick and hearty, this soup will warm you up on a cold winter day.

6-7 servings

Vegetable cooking spray
12 ounces lean ground beef round
1 large onion, chopped
2 large garlic cloves, minced
3 cups shredded cabbage
2 large ribs celery, sliced
2 large carrots, sliced
⅓ cup pearl barley
1 cup cubed, peeled potato (¾-inch)
1½ quarts Fragrant Beef Stock (see p. 6)
2 teaspoons dried thyme leaves
1 teaspoon dried basil leaves
1 teaspoon chili powder
1 teaspoon paprika
½ teaspoon dry mustard
2 bay leaves
¼ teaspoon pepper
1 can (14½ ounces) reduced-sodium stewed tomatoes, undrained
Salt, to taste

Per Serving
Calories: 176
% Calories from fat: 11
Protein (g): 16.2
Carbohydrates (g): 24.3
Fat (g): 2.2
Saturated fat (g): 0.7
Cholesterol (mg): 23.4
Sodium (mg): 118
Exchanges
Milk: 0.0
Veg.: 2.0
Fruit: 0.0
Bread: 1.0
Meat: 1.0
Fat: 0.0

1. Spray medium saucepan with cooking spray; heat over medium heat until hot. Add beef, onion, and garlic and cook over medium heat until beef is browned, about 5 minutes. Drain fat.

2. Combine all ingredients, except tomatoes and salt, in large saucepan; heat to boiling. Reduce heat and simmer, covered, 40 minutes; add tomatoes and liquid and simmer 10 minutes or until barley is tender. Season to taste with salt.

VEGETABLE OXTAIL SOUP

Long simmering brings out the rich flavor of oxtails, making this vegetable soup a real treat.

6 servings (1¹/₂ cups each)

	Per Serving
1 pound oxtails, cut into 2-inch pieces	Calories: 219
	% Calories from fat: 28
1 tablespoon vegetable oil	Protein (gm): 12.4
	Carbohydrate (gm): 28.1
3 tablespoons flour	Fat (gm): 1.7
1¹/₂ quarts Beef Stock (see p. 6)	Saturated fat (gm): 0.4
	Cholesterol (mg): 0.3
1 teaspoon dried thyme leaves	Sodium (mg): 35
1 bay leaf	**Exchanges**
	Milk: 0.0
2 large tomatoes, chopped	Veg.: 2.0
1 cup sliced celery	Fruit: 0.0
	Bread: 1.0
³/₄ cup chopped onion	Meat: 1.0
³/₄ cup sliced carrot	Fat: 1.0

³/₄ cup diced parsnip
³/₄ cup diced potato
¹/₃ cup quick-cooking barley
     Salt and pepper, to taste

1. Brown oxtails in oil in large saucepan; drain excess oil. Sprinkle with flour and cook 2 minutes.

2. Stir in Beef Stock, thyme, and bay leaf; heat to boiling. Reduce heat and simmer, covered, 2¹/₂ hours or until oxtails are very tender; remove oxtails from soup. Remove meat from bones and return to soup; discard bones.

3. Add vegetables and barley to soup; simmer until vegetables and barley are tender, 15 to 20 minutes. Discard bay leaf; season to taste with salt and pepper.

PORTUGUESE SOUP

This flavorful kale soup is a simplified version of the Portuguese favorite, Caldo Verde. Linguica, a Portuguese sausage, can be used for most authentic flavor; just brown it and drain well.

4 servings

1 cup chopped onion

$^1/_2$ cup chopped red bell pepper

2 tablespoons minced garlic

2 teaspoons olive oil

1 quart Beef Stock (see p. 6)

3 medium potatoes, peeled, cubed

3 cups sliced kale, *or* spinach

8 ounces reduced-fat smoked sausage, sliced, browned, drained

1 can (15 ounces) red kidney beans, rinsed, drained

$^1/_4$ cup tomato sauce

Salt and pepper, to taste

Hot pepper sauce, to taste

Per Serving
Calories: 326
% Calories from fat: 15
Protein (gm): 18.7
Carbohydrate (gm): 53
Fat (gm): 5.7
Saturated fat (gm): 1.2
Cholesterol (mg): 26.8
Sodium (mg): 850
Exchanges
Milk: 0.0
Veg.: 2.0
Fruit: 0.0
Bread: 3.0
Meat: 1.0
Fat: 0.5

1. Saute onion, bell pepper, and garlic in oil in large saucepan until tender, about 8 minutes. Stir in Beef Stock, potatoes, and kale. Heat to boiling; reduce heat and simmer, covered, until potatoes are tender, about 20 minutes.

2. Stir in sausage, beans, and tomato sauce; simmer, uncovered, 10 minutes. Season to taste with salt, pepper, and hot pepper sauce.

POZOLE

Traditionally, this soup is made with a pig's head or pork hocks; our version contains lean pork tenderloin and chicken breast instead. The soup always contains hominy and is served with a variety of crisp vegetable garnishes.

6 servings

- 2 ancho chilies, stems, seeds, and veins discarded
- 1 cup boiling water
  Vegetable cooking spray
- $^1/_2$ cup chopped onion
- 1 clove garlic, minced
- 2 cans (14$^1/_2$ ounces each) reduced-sodium fat-free chicken broth
- 8 ounces pork tenderloin, cut into 1-inch pieces
- 8 ounces boneless, skinless chicken breast, cut into 1-inch pieces
- 1 can (15$^1/_2$ ounces) hominy, rinsed, drained
- 1 can (14$^1/_2$ ounces) reduced-sodium tomatoes, undrained, coarsely chopped
- $^1/_2$ teaspoon dried oregano leaves
- $^1/_4$ teaspoon dried thyme leaves
  Salt and pepper, to taste
- 6 lime wedges
- $^1/_4$ cup each thinly sliced lettuce, cabbage, green onions, radishes, and carrots

Per Serving
Calories: 181
% Calories from fat: 16
Protein (g): 21.2
Carbohydrates (g): 16.7
Fat (g): 3.2
Saturated fat (g): 0.9
Cholesterol (mg): 44.8
Sodium (mg): 244
Exchanges
Milk: 0.0
Veg.: 1.0
Fruit: 0.0
Bread: 1.0
Meat: 2.5
Fat: 0.0

1. Cover chilies with boiling water in small bowl; let stand until softened, about 10 minutes. Process chilies and water in food processor or blender until smooth; reserve.

2. Spray large saucepan with cooking spray; heat over medium heat until hot. Add onion and garlic and saute until tender, about 5 minutes. Add chicken broth and meats and heat to boiling. Reduce heat and simmer, covered, until meats are tender, 10 to 15 minutes. Remove meats and shred with a fork; return to saucepan.

3. Add reserved chilies, hominy, tomatoes and liquid, oregano, and thyme to saucepan; simmer, covered, 10 to 15 minutes. Season to taste with salt and pepper.

4. Serve soup in bowls; squeeze juice from one lime wedge into each bowl. Pass fresh vegetables for each person to add to soup.

OLD-FASHIONED CHICKEN-VEGETABLE SOUP

A homey, heartwarming soup like grandma used to make.

6 -7 servings

6-8 scallions, coarsely chopped
1/3 cup chopped parsley
2 medium ribs celery, finely chopped
1 tablespoon margarine
1 cup shredded green cabbage
1 1/2 quarts Chicken Stock (see p. 2), *or* fat-free chicken broth
1 1/2 pounds bony chicken parts (wings, backs, etc.)
1 pound boneless, skinless chicken breast, cut into 3/4-inch pieces
3 medium carrots, thinly sliced
1 large rib celery, thinly sliced
1 small rutabaga, peeled, cut into 1/4-inch cubes
2 cups coarsely chopped cauliflower
1 cup diced, peeled red potatoes
1/4 teaspoon pepper
1 1/4 cups cooked medium egg noodles
Salt to taste

Per Serving
Calories: 197
% Calories from fat: 18
Protein (g): 18.2
Carbohydrates (g): 22.9
Fat (g): 3.9
Saturated fat (g): 0.9
Cholesterol (mg): 38.2
Sodium (mg): 401
Exchanges
Milk: 0.0
Veg.: 0.0
Fruit: 0.0
Bread: 2.0
Meat: 1.0
Fat: 0.0

1. Saute scallions, parsley, and chopped celery in margarine in large saucepan until vegetables are tender, about 5 minutes. Add cabbage, Chicken Stock, chicken breast, and chicken parts and heat to boiling. Reduce heat and simmer, covered, 1 1/4 hours. Skim fat from surface. Remove chicken bones.

2. Add remaining ingredients, except egg noodles and salt. Simmer, covered, until vegetables are tender, about 15 minutes, adding noodles during last 5 minutes. Season to taste with salt.

CLASSIC CHICKEN NOODLE SOUP

A favorite of kids and adults alike.

5-6 servings

Per Serving
Calories: 273
% Calories from fat: 40
Protein (g): 25.7
Carbohydrates (g): 14.4
Fat (g): 12
Saturated fat (g): 3.3
Cholesterol (mg): 71.6
Sodium (mg): 431
Exchanges
Milk: 0.0
Veg.: 0.0
Fruit: 0.0
Bread: 1.0
Meat: 3.0
Fat: 0.5

- 3 pounds bony chicken parts (wings, backs, etc.)
- 1¹/₂ quarts Chicken Stock (see p. 2), *or* fat-free chicken broth
- 1 large onion, finely diced
- 1 large carrot, finely diced
- 1 large rib celery, finely diced
- 1 small turnip, peeled, halved, optional
- 1 large bay leaf
- ¹/₂-³/₄ teaspoon pepper
- ¹/₄ teaspoon dried thyme leaves
- ¹/₄ teaspoon dried marjoram leaves
- 3 tablespoons chopped parsley
- 2 cups cooked egg noodles
  Salt, to taste
  Finely chopped parsley, as garnish

1. Combine all ingredients, except noodles, salt, and parsley, in large saucepan; heat to boiling. Reduce heat and simmer, covered, 50 to 60 minutes. Discard turnip and bay leaf. Skim fat from surface. Remove chicken; remove meat from bones, cut into bite-sized pieces, and return to soup.

2. Add noodles and simmer, uncovered, 5 minutes. Discard bay leaf; season to taste with salt. Sprinkle each serving with parsley.

ALPHABET CHICKEN SOUP

Kids like the alphabet letters in this traditional chicken soup—adults may prefer another small pasta shape!

5-6 servings

1 medium onion, finely chopped

1 large garlic clove, minced

2 teaspoons canola oil

2 quarts Chicken Stock (see p. 2), *or* reduced-sodium fat-free chicken broth

2 large chicken breast halves, skin removed

2 large carrots, thinly sliced

2 large ribs celery, thinly sliced

2 tablespoons finely chopped fresh parsley

1 large bay leaf

1/2 teaspoon dried thyme leaves

1/8 teaspoon ground celery seed

1/4 teaspoon pepper

1/2 cup alphabet pasta

Salt, to taste

Per Serving
Calories: 195
% Calories from fat: **15**
Protein (g): 19.7
Carbohydrates (g): **21.1**
Fat (g): 3.3
Saturated fat (g): 0.5
Cholesterol (mg): 30.5
Sodium (mg): 440
Exchanges
Milk: 0.0
Veg.: 1.0
Fruit: 0.0
Bread: 1.0
Meat: 2.0
Fat: 0.0

1. Saute onion and garlic in canola oil in large saucepan until onion is tender, about 5 minutes. Add remaining ingredients, except pasta and salt; heat to boiling. Reduce heat and simmer, covered, 30 minutes or until chicken is cooked. Skim fat from top of soup.

2. Remove chicken; remove meat from bones, cut into bite-sized pieces, and reserve. Heat soup to boiling and add pasta; reduce heat and simmer, uncovered, 8 to 10 minutes until pasta is al dente. Return chicken to saucepan; season to taste with salt.

VEGETABLE NOODLE SOUP

This chicken noodle soup is loaded with vegetables for extra goodness and nutrition.

6 servings (about 1 ³/⁴ cups each)

   1 cup chopped celery
   1 cup julienned carrots
   1 cup chopped parsnip
   1 cup chopped onion
 1-2 tablespoons margarine
   2 quarts Rich Chicken Stock (see p. 4)
   1 cup small broccoli florets
   1 cup cut green beans
 ¹/₂ cup frozen peas
   1 tablespoon minced parsley
 ¹/₂ teaspoon dried thyme leaves
 ¹/₂ teaspoon dried rosemary leaves
   1 teaspoon balsamic vinegar
   4 ounces no-yolk noodles
1¹/₂ cups shredded cooked chicken breast
     Salt and pepper, to taste

Per Serving
Calories: 262
% Calories from fat: 18
Protein (gm): 22.2
Carbohydrate (gm): 28.7
Fat (gm): 4.9
Saturated fat (gm): 1.1
Cholesterol (mg): 28.3
Sodium (mg): 147
Exchanges
Milk: 0.0
Veg.: 3.0
Fruit: 0.0
Bread: 1.0
Meat: 2.0
Fat: 0.0

1. Saute celery, carrots, parsnip, and onion in margarine in large saucepan until tender, about 8 minutes. Stir in Rich Chicken Stock, broccoli, green beans, peas, herbs, and vinegar; heat to boiling.

2. Stir in noodles and chicken; reduce heat and cook until noodles are tender, 7 to 10 minutes. Season to taste with salt and pepper.

CHICKEN-RICE SOUP

Tarragon, along with shredded turnip and parsnip, helps give this soup its rich flavor. The shredded white vegetables masquerade as additional rice.

7-8 servings

1 large onion, finely chopped
1 large garlic clove, minced
2 teaspoons canola oil
2 quarts Chicken Stock (see p. 2), *or* reduced-sodium fat-free chicken broth
1 medium parsnip, peeled, shredded
1 medium turnip, peeled, shredded
2 medium carrots, thinly sliced
2 ribs celery, thinly sliced
2 bay leaves
3/4 teaspoon dried thyme leaves
1/2 teaspoon dried tarragon leaves
1/4 teaspoon ground celery seed
1/4 teaspoon pepper
1 1/2-2 pounds chicken breasts, skin removed
1/2 cup white rice
Salt, to taste

Per Serving
Calories: 182
% Calories from fat: 14
Protein (g): 19.5
Carbohydrates (g): 19.3
Fat (g): 2.9
Saturated fat (g): 0.5
Cholesterol (mg): 34.3
Sodium (mg): 435
Exchanges
Milk: 0.0
Veg.: 2.0
Fruit: 0.0
Bread: 0.5
Meat: 2.0
Fat: 0.0

1. Saute onion and garlic in oil in large saucepan until onion is tender, about 5 minutes. Add remaining ingredients except rice and salt. Heat to boiling; reduce heat and simmer, covered, 30 minutes. Add rice and simmer, covered, until rice is tender, 20 to 25 minutes. Skim fat from top of soup.

2. Remove chicken; remove meat from bones, cut into bite-sized pieces, and return to soup. Discard bay leaf; season to taste with salt.

CHICKEN AND BARLEY SOUP

This soup is perfect for a slow-cooker: Combine all ingredients, except salt, and cook, covered, at High 1 hour. Reduce heat to Low and cook until barley is tender, 7 to 8 hours. Season to taste with salt.

6-7 servings

1 large boneless, skinless chicken breast, cut into 3/4-inch pieces
1 quart Chicken Stock (see p. 2), *or* fat-free chicken broth
1 cup water
1/3 cup pearl barley
1 large onion, finely chopped
1 garlic clove, minced
1 large carrot, shredded
1 large rib celery, finely chopped
1/4 cup chopped parsley
1/2 teaspoon dried thyme leaves
1/8 teaspoon celery seed, finely crushed
1 bay leaf
1/4 teaspoon pepper
Salt, to taste

Per Serving
Calories: 145
% Calories from fat: 16
Protein (g): 18.1
Carbohydrates (g): 12
Fat (g): 2.5
Saturated fat (g): 0.7
Cholesterol (mg): 45.9
Sodium (mg): 327
Exchanges
Milk: 0.0
Veg.: 0.0
Fruit: 0.0
Bread: 0.5
Meat: 2.0
Fat: 0.0

1. Combine all ingredients, except salt, in large saucepan; heat to boiling. Reduce heat and simmer, covered, until barley is tender, 50 to 60 minutes. Season to taste with salt.

CHICKEN MEATBALL SOUP

Tiny meatballs are simmered in homemade Rich Chicken Stock. Serve with warm whole-grain rolls and crisp vegetable relishes.

8 servings

2 pounds ground chicken breast
4 slices whole wheat bread, crumbled
1/3 cup grated Parmesan cheese
2 tablespoons chopped parsley
3 egg whites, lightly beaten
2 teaspoons minced garlic
2 teaspoons grated lemon rind
1/4 teaspoon ground nutmeg
1 teaspoon salt
1/2 teaspoon pepper
2 1/2 quarts Rich Chicken Stock (see p. 4)

Per Serving
Calories: 238
% Calories from fat: **23**
Protein (gm): 35.4
Carbohydrate (gm): 6.6
Fat (gm): 5.5
Saturated fat (gm): 1.9
Cholesterol (mg): 72.9
Sodium (mg): 545
Exchanges
Milk: 0.0
Veg.: 0.0
Fruit: 0.0
Bread: 0.5
Meat: 3.5
Fat: 0.0

1. Combine all ingredients, except Rich Chicken Stock, in bowl and mix well. Form into small meatballs.

2. Heat Rich Chicken Stock to boiling in large saucepan; carefully drop in meatballs. Reduce heat and simmer, covered, until meatballs are cooked in the center, 6 to 8 minutes.

Variation:
Garden Meatball Soup—Make meatballs as above, substituting lean ground beef for the chicken breast, and Beef Stock (see p. 6) for the Rich Chicken Stock. Stir 1 can (15 ounces) rinsed, drained kidney beans, 1 can (15 ounces) stewed tomatoes, 1 cup each sliced carrots, zucchini, and cabbage into Beef Stock; simmer, covered, 10 minutes. Add meatballs and complete as above.

RAVIOLI SOUP

Wonton wrappers, found in the produce section of your supermarket, make ravioli easy to prepare.

6 servings (about 1¹/₂ cups each)

¹/₂	cup julienned carrots
¹/₄	cup sliced green onions and tops
1	teaspoon margarine
2¹/₂	quarts Rich Chicken Stock (see p. 4)
3	cups thinly sliced bok choy, *or* Napa cabbage
	Chicken Ravioli (recipe follows)
	Salt and pepper, to taste

Per Serving
Calories: 267
% Calories from fat: 14
Protein (gm): 22.2
Carbohydrate (gm): 29.9
Fat (gm): 3.8
Saturated fat (gm): 0.9
Cholesterol (mg): 29
Sodium (mg): 420
Exchanges
Milk: 0.0
Veg.: 0.0
Fruit: 0.0
Bread: 2.0
Meat: 2.0
Fat: 0.0

1. Saute carrots and green onions in margarine in large saucepan until tender, about 5 minutes. Add Rich Chicken Stock and heat to boiling; reduce heat and simmer, covered, 5 minutes.

2. Stir in bok choy and Chicken Ravioli and heat to boiling; reduce heat and simmer, uncovered, 2 to 3 minutes or until ravioli are tender and rise to top of soup. Season to taste with salt and pepper.

Chicken Ravioli

makes 18 ravioli

8	ounces ground chicken breast
1	tablespoon minced green onion
1	teaspoon minced garlic
1	teaspoon grated gingerroot
¹/₈	teaspoon salt
¹/₈	teaspoon pepper
36	wonton wrappers

1. Combine all ingredients, except wonton wrappers, in small bowl. Place rounded teaspoon of chicken mixture in center of each of 18 wonton wrappers. Moisten edges of wrappers with water. Top with remaining wrappers; press edges to seal. Refrigerate, covered, until ready to cook.

INDIAN-STYLE POTATO-SPINACH SOUP WITH CHICKEN

An unusual combination of herbs and spices gives this hearty soup an exotic flavor and aroma.

5-7 servings

1 boneless, skinless chicken breast, diced
1 large onion, chopped
1/2 teaspoon caraway seeds
1 teaspoon canola oil
2 large garlic cloves, minced
1 1/2 tablespoons mild, *or* hot, curry powder
2 teaspoons ground coriander
1/2 teaspoon ground cardamom
1 1/2 quarts Chicken Stock (see p. 2), *or* reduced-sodium fat-free chicken broth
3 cups coarsely cubed, peeled baking potatoes
1 package (10 ounces) frozen chopped spinach, thawed
1 cup chopped canned tomatoes, with liquid
Salt and pepper, to taste

Per Serving
Calories: 187
% Calories from fat: 12
Protein (g): 15
Carbohydrates (g): 27.1
Fat (g): 2.7
Saturated fat (g): 0.4
Cholesterol (mg): 20.9
Sodium (mg): 392
Exchanges
Milk: 0.0
Veg.: 0.0
Fruit: 0.0
Bread: 2.0
Meat: 1.0
Fat: 0.0

1. Saute chicken, onion, and caraway seeds in oil in large saucepan until onion begins to brown, about 5 minutes. Add garlic and spices and saute 1 minute longer. Add Chicken Stock and potatoes; heat to boiling. Reduce heat and simmer until potatoes are tender, 10 to 15 minutes. Add spinach and tomatoes with liquid; simmer, covered, 5 minutes. Season to taste with salt and pepper.

MULLIGATAWNY

Colorful and lightly spiced with curry powder, this popular soup originated in India. Today, however, versions can be found from the British Isles to the Bahamas.

4-6 servings

2 large onions, coarsely chopped

2 large ribs celery, coarsely chopped

1 large garlic clove, minced

2 large Winesap, *or* other tart, apples, peeled, chopped

2 medium carrots, coarsely chopped

1/4 cup coarsely chopped parsley

2 tablespoons chopped red bell pepper

2 teaspoons canola oil

1 quart Chicken Stock (see p. 2), *or* fat-free chicken broth

1 cup water

1/2 cup diced, peeled red potatoes

2 1/2 teaspoons curry powder

1 teaspoon chili powder

1/2 teaspoon ground allspice

1/2 teaspoon dried thyme leaves

1/4 teaspoon pepper

1 1/2 pounds bony chicken parts (wings, backs, etc.)

1 pound boneless, skinless chicken breast halves

1 1/4 cups chopped canned tomatoes, with liquid

Salt, to taste

Finely chopped parsley, as garnish

Per Serving
Calories: 189
% Calories from fat: 19
Protein (g): 17.4
Carbohydrates (g): 22.3
Fat (g): 4
Saturated fat (g): 0.7
Cholesterol (mg): 33.5
Sodium (mg): 363
Exchanges
Milk: 0.0
Veg.: 0.0
Fruit: 0.5
Bread: 1.5
Meat: 1.0
Fat: 0.0

1. Saute onions, celery, garlic, apples, carrots, parsley, and bell pepper in oil in large saucepan. Add remaining ingredients, except salt and parsley; heat to boiling. Reduce heat and simmer, covered, 1 hour. Skim fat from surface. Remove chicken; discard bony pieces, cut breast meat into bite-sized pieces, and reserve.

2. Process soup in blender or food processor until smooth; return puree to saucepan. Return chicken; simmer 5 minutes. Season to taste with salt; sprinkle each serving with parsley.

SPICY NORTH AFRICAN-STYLE CHICKEN SOUP

The tangy flavors and hearty textures of North African cuisine combine in this chicken soup.

6-7 servings

3 cups coarsely chopped onions
2 large garlic cloves, minced
2 teaspoons olive oil
1¹/₂ quarts Chicken Stock (see p. 2), *or* reduced-sodium fat-free chicken broth
2 boneless, skinless chicken breast halves, fat trimmed, cut into ¹/₂-inch pieces
¹/₂ cup bulgur wheat
2 large ribs celery, thinly sliced
1 can (14¹/₂ ounce) reduced-sodium stewed tomatoes, undrained
1 cinnamon stick
2 large bay leaves
³/₄ teaspoon dried marjoram
³/₄ teaspoon dried thyme leaves
¹/₈ teaspoon ground cloves
¹/₄ teaspoon pepper
Salt, to taste

Per Serving
Calories: 165
% Calories from fat: **16**
Protein (g): 17.5
Carbohydrates (g): 18.1
Fat (g): 3
Saturated fat (g): 0.6
Cholesterol (mg): 29.6
Sodium (mg): 335
Exchanges
Milk: 0.0
Veg.: 1.0
Fruit: 0.0
Bread: 1.0
Meat: 1.0
Fat: 0.0

1. Saute onions and garlic in oil in large saucepan until onions are soft, about 12 minutes. Add remaining ingredients, except salt, and heat to boiling. Reduce heat, and simmer, covered, 25 to 30 minutes or until bulgur is tender. Discard cinnamon stick and bay leaves and skim fat from top of soup; season to taste with salt.

WEST AFRICAN CURRIED CHICKEN SOUP

Pineapple and curry team up to give this soup its pleasing flavor.

4-5 servings

2 ribs celery, diced

1 small onion, finely chopped

1 garlic clove, minced

2 teaspoons margarine

1-2 teaspoons mild curry powder

3^1/$_2$ tablespoons flour

1 quart Chicken Stock (see p. 2), *or* fat-free chicken broth

1 can (8 ounces) crushed pineapple, drained

1 boneless, skinless chicken breast half, cooked, cut into ^{1}/$_2$-inch pieces

^{3}/$_4$ cup whole milk

Per Serving
Calories: 168
% Calories from fat: **22**
Protein (g): 16.6
Carbohydrates (g): **16.3**
Fat (g): 4.1
Saturated fat (g): **1.4**
Cholesterol (mg): **34.2**
Sodium (mg): 310
Exchanges
Milk: 0.0
Veg.: 0.0
Fruit: 0.0
Bread: 1.0
Meat: 2.0
Fat: 0.0

1. Saute celery, onion, and garlic in margarine in large saucepan over medium heat until onion is soft, about 5 minutes; stir in combined curry powder and flour and stir over medium heat 1 minute. Add Chicken Stock and heat to boiling; reduce heat and simmer, covered, 20 minutes.

2. Stir in pineapple, chicken, and milk; remove from heat and cool. Refrigerate soup until chilled.

ORIENTAL SOUP WITH NOODLES AND CHICKEN

The dried chow mein noodles in this soup are not the fried ones we have seen with chop suey for many years. Be sure the correct noodles are used.

4 servings (about 1 cup each)

1 ounce dried cloud ear mushrooms, *or*
   ¹/₂ ounce dried shiitake mushrooms
   Olive oil cooking spray
¹/₂ cup julienned carrots
2 cans (14¹/₂ ounces each) reduced-sodium chicken broth
2 tablespoons dry sherry, optional
1¹/₂ teaspoons light soy sauce
¹/₄ teaspoon five-spice powder
8 ounces boneless, skinless chicken breast, cooked, shredded
¹/₂ cup sliced white mushrooms
¹/₂ package (5-ounce size) dried chow mein noodles
2 ounces snow peas, trimmed
   Salt and pepper, to taste

Per Serving
Calories: 213
% Calories from fat: 30
Protein (g): 16.4
Carbohydrates (g): 19.7
Fat (g): 7.6
Saturated fat (g): 1.2
Cholesterol (mg): 29.2
Sodium (mg): 259
Exchanges
Milk: 0.0
Veg.: 0.5
Fruit: 0.0
Bread: 1.0
Meat: 1.5
Fat: 1.0

1. Place dried cloud ear mushrooms in bowl; pour hot water over to cover. Let stand until mushrooms are soft, about 15 minutes; drain. Slice mushrooms, discarding any tough parts.

2. Spray large saucepan with cooking spray; heat over medium heat until hot. Saute cloud ear mushrooms and carrots 3 to 4 minutes. Add chicken broth, sherry, soy sauce, and five-spice powder. Heat to boiling; reduce heat and simmer, covered, 10 minutes. Stir in chicken and white mushrooms; simmer, covered, about 4 minutes.

3. Add noodles to saucepan; cook until noodles are just tender, about 10 minutes, adding snow peas during last 5 minutes. Season to taste with salt and pepper.

SOPA DE CASA

Chicken, green chilies, and Monterey Jack cheese offer a pleasing flavor combination.

6 servings (about 1 cup each)

3 cups frozen whole-kernel corn, thawed, divided

1 can (14¹/₂ ounces) reduced-sodium fat-free chicken broth

1 cup chopped onion

¹/₂ jalapeño chili, minced

2 large cloves garlic, minced

1-2 tablespoons margarine

16 ounces boneless, skinless chicken breast, cut into scant ³/₄-inch pieces

1 cup fat-free half-and-half, *or* fat-free milk

1 can (4 ounces) chopped green chilies, undrained

1 large tomato, chopped

³/₄ teaspoon dried oregano leaves

¹/₄ teaspoon ground cumin

1 cup (4 ounces) shredded reduced-fat Monterey-Jack cheese

Salt and pepper, to taste

Per Serving
Calories: 281
% Calories from fat: 24
Protein (gm): 28.8
Carbohydrate (gm): 24.5
Fat (gm): 7.7
Saturated fat (gm): 3.4
Cholesterol (mg): 59.5
Sodium (mg): 376
Exchanges
Milk: 0.0
Veg.: 2.0
Fruit: 0.0
Bread: 1.0
Meat: 3.0
Fat: 0.0

1. Process 1¹/₂ cups corn and chicken broth in food processor or blender until smooth; reserve.

2. Saute onion, jalapeño chili, and garlic in margarine in large saucepan until tender; add chicken and cook over medium heat until chicken is browned, 8 to 10 minutes. Stir in reserved corn puree, remaining 1¹/₂ cups corn, half-and-half, chilies, tomato, and herbs and heat to boiling. Reduce heat and simmer, covered, 5 to 10 minutes; add cheese, stirring until melted. Season to taste with salt and pepper.

MEXICAN-STYLE CHICKEN AND LIME SOUP

Lightly seasoned with lime, this soup has an abundance of chicken and vegetables.

8 servings (about 1²/₃ cups each)

Per Serving
Calories: 215
% Calories from fat: 18
Protein (gm): 23.1
Carbohydrate (gm): 21.8
Fat (gm): 4.4
Saturated fat (gm): 0.9
Cholesterol (mg): 55.2
Sodium (mg): 94
Exchanges
Milk: 0.0
Veg.: 1.0
Fruit: 0.0
Bread: 1.0
Meat: 2.0
Fat: 0.0

1	medium onion, chopped
1	medium green bell pepper, chopped
2	teaspoons vegetable oil
2	quarts Low-Salt Chicken Stock (see p. 3)
1¹/₂	pounds boneless, skinless chicken breast, cut into ³/₄-inch pieces
2	large tomatoes, peeled, seeded, chopped
1	cup whole-kernel corn
1	cup diced zucchini
¹/₄	cup chopped cilantro
¹/₄-¹/₃	cup lime juice
	Salt and pepper, to taste
	Vegetable cooking spray
8	corn tortillas, each cut into 10 wedges
8	thin lime slices

1. Saute onion and bell pepper in oil in large saucepan until tender, about 5 minutes. Add Low-Salt Chicken Stock, chicken, tomatoes, corn, and zucchini; heat to boiling. Reduce heat and simmer, covered, 20 minutes. Add cilantro and lime juice; season to taste with salt and pepper.

2. Spray large skillet with cooking spray; heat over medium heat until hot. Add tortilla wedges and spray with cooking spray; cook over medium heat, tossing occasionally, until crisp, about 5 minutes. Place in soup bowls; ladle soup over. Float lime slices on top of soup.

TORTILLA SOUP

Add tortilla strips to the soup just before serving so they are crisp. If desired, tortilla strips can be baked on a cookie sheet at 350 degrees until browned and crisp, about 5 minutes. The soup should be slightly piquant—add additional lime juice to taste.

6 servings

Vegetable cooking spray

3 corn, *or* flour, tortillas, cut into 2 x $^1/_4$-inch strips

1 small onion, chopped

1 cup chopped celery

1 medium tomato, coarsely chopped

$^1/_2$ teaspoon dried basil leaves

$^1/_2$ teaspoon ground cumin

1$^1/_4$ quarts reduced-sodium fat-free chicken broth

1 can (15$^1/_2$ ounces) pinto beans, rinsed, drained

6 ounces cooked chicken breast, shredded

2 teaspoons finely chopped cilantro

1-2 teaspoons lime juice

Salt and cayenne pepper, to taste

Per Serving
Calories: 176
% Calories from fat: 10
Protein (g): 19.1
Carbohydrates (g): 22.6
Fat (g): 2
Saturated fat (g): 0.3
Cholesterol (mg): 24.1
Sodium (mg): 386
Exchanges
Milk: 0.0
Veg.: 1.0
Fruit: 0.0
Bread: 1.0
Meat: 2.0
Fat: 0.0

1. Spray medium skillet with cooking spray; heat over medium heat until hot. Add tortillas; spray tortillas with cooking spray and cook over medium heat, tossing occasionally, until browned and crisp, about 5 minutes. Reserve.

2. Spray large saucepan with cooking spray; heat over medium heat until hot. Saute onion, celery, tomato, basil, and cumin until onion is tender. Add chicken broth, beans, and chicken; heat to boiling. Reduce heat and simmer, uncovered, 3 to 5 minutes. Stir in cilantro; season with lime juice, salt, and cayenne pepper to taste.

3. Add tortilla strips to soup bowls and ladle soup over.

CHICKEN AND CHILIES SOUP

The green chilies add extra zip and give the soup its spicy South-of-the-Border flavor.

6-7 servings

1 medium onion, finely chopped
1 large garlic clove, minced
1 large rib celery, diced
1 teaspoon margarine
1 quart Chicken Stock (see p. 2), *or* fat-free chicken broth
3/4 cup cubed skinless cooked chicken breast (1/2-inch)
1 can (4 ounces) chopped green chilies, drained
1 1/2 cups small cauliflower florets
1 cup cooked kidney beans
2 tablespoons cornstarch
1/4 cup cold water
1/2 cup (2 ounces) shredded mild Cheddar cheese
1/2 cup (2 ounces) shredded fat-free Cheddar cheese
Chopped chives, as garnish

Per Serving
Calories: 139
% Calories from fat: 22
Protein (g): 12.5
Carbohydrates (g): 14.2
Fat (g): 3.4
Saturated fat (g): 1.8
Cholesterol (mg): 17.9
Sodium (mg): 471
Exchanges
Milk: 0.0
Veg.: 0.0
Fruit: 0.0
Bread: 1.0
Meat: 1.0
Fat: 0.0

1. Saute onion, garlic, and celery in margarine in large saucepan until onion is tender, about 5 minutes. Add Chicken Stock, chicken, chilies, cauliflower, and beans; heat to boiling. Reduce heat and simmer, covered, 10 minutes.

2. Heat soup to boiling; stir in combined cornstarch and water. Boil, stirring, until thickened, about 1 minute. Reduce heat to low; add cheeses, stirring until melted. Sprinkle each serving with chives.

EASY TORTILLA SOUP

This quick version of Tortilla Soup uses many canned ingredients for speedy preparation.

6 servings (about 1¹/₄ cups each)

3/4 cup chopped onion

1 clove garlic, minced

¹/₂ teaspoon crushed red pepper

1 teaspoon vegetable oil

1 can (4 ounces) chopped green chilies, drained

2 cans (14¹/₂ ounces each) reduced-sodium fat-free chicken broth

1 can (16 ounces) reduced-sodium whole tomatoes, undrained, chopped

1 can (15 ounces) spicy chili beans, undrained

2 teaspoons red wine vinegar

¹/₄ cup chopped cilantro

Salt, to taste

6 corn tortillas

Vegetable cooking spray

¹/₂ small avocado, peeled, cubed

Per Serving
Calories: 181
% Calories from fat: 18
Protein (gm): 10
Carbohydrate (gm): 30.2
Fat (gm): 4.1
Saturated fat (gm): 0.6
Cholesterol (mg): 0
Sodium (mg): 530
Exchanges
Milk: 0.0
Veg.: 0.0
Fruit: 0.0
Bread: 2.0
Meat: 0.0
Fat: 1.0

1. Saute onion, garlic, and crushed red pepper in oil in large saucepan until tender, about 5 minutes. Add chilies, broth, tomatoes and liquid, beans, and vinegar; heat to boiling. Reduce heat and simmer, covered, 10 minutes. Stir in cilantro and season to taste with salt.

2. Cut tortillas into ¹/₂-inch strips; place on baking sheet. Spray with cooking spray and bake at 375 degrees until crisp, about 5 minutes. Place tortilla strips and avocado in each bowl; ladle soup over.

HAM AND SPLIT PEA SOUP

Thick and satisfying, this soup is a meal in a bowl.

7-9 servings

2 large garlic cloves, minced
2 large onions, finely chopped
2¼ quarts water
1 meaty ham bone, *or* 2 large ham hocks
2 cups dried green split peas, sorted, rinsed
2 beef bouillon cubes
2 bay leaves
2 large carrots, thinly sliced
¼ cup finely chopped parsley
2 large ribs celery, including leaves, thinly sliced
½ teaspoon dried thyme leaves
½ teaspoon dried marjoram leaves
½ teaspoon celery salt
½ teaspoon pepper
Salt, to taste

Per Serving
Calories: 165
% Calories from fat: 25
Protein (g): 10.5
Carbohydrates (g): 21.5
Fat (g): 4.6
Saturated fat (g): 1.5
Cholesterol (mg): 23.2
Sodium (mg): 570
Exchanges
Milk: 0.0
Veg.: 0.0
Fruit: 0.0
Bread: 1.5
Meat: 1.0
Fat: 0.0

1. Combine all ingredients, except salt, in Dutch oven; heat to boiling. Reduce heat and simmer, covered, stirring occasionally, until split peas are tender and have thickened the soup, about 1½ hours. Remove ham bone, cut meat into small pieces, and return to soup. Discard bone. Skim fat from top of soup; discard bay leaves. Season to taste with salt.

CREAM OF PEA SOUP

Dried split peas and fresh peas are combined in this rich-flavored soup.

12 servings

3 small carrots, shredded

2 small onions, finely chopped

1 large leek, chopped, white part only

1-2 tablespoons margarine

3 quarts Rich Chicken Stock (see p. 4)

1¹/₂ pounds dried split peas, sorted, rinsed

1¹/₂ teaspoons sugar

2 cups fresh, *or* frozen, peas

1 can (13 ounces) evaporated fat-free milk

Salt and pepper, to taste

1¹/₂ cups Rye-Caraway Croutons (¹/₂ recipe) (see p. 784)

Per Serving
Calories: 322
% Calories from fat: 8
Protein (gm): 23.8
Carbohydrate (gm): 49.4
Fat (gm): 2.8
Saturated fat (gm): 0.6
Cholesterol (mg): 2.2
Sodium (mg): 131
Exchanges
Milk: 0.0
Veg.: 2.0
Fruit: 0.0
Bread: 3.0
Meat: 1.0
Fat: 0.0

1. Saute carrots, onions, and leek in margarine in Dutch oven 5 minutes; add Rich Chicken Stock, split peas, and sugar and heat to boiling. Reduce heat and simmer, covered, until peas are tender, about 2 hours, adding fresh peas during last 20 minutes.

2. Process soup in blender or food processor until smooth; return to saucepan. Add evaporated milk and cook over medium heat until hot, about 5 minutes. Season to taste with salt and pepper. Top each serving with Rye-Caraway Croutons.

HEARTY SPLIT PEA, BEAN, AND BARLEY SOUP

We love this stick-to-the-ribs soup for its variety of textures.

12-14 servings

4 quarts water
1 meaty ham bone, *or* 2 large smoked pork hocks
2 cups dried green split peas, sorted, rinsed
1/2 cup pearl barley
1/2 cup dried black-eyed peas, sorted, rinsed
1/2 cup dried navy beans, sorted, rinsed
3 bay leaves
2-5 beef bouillon cubes
2 large onions, coarsely chopped
2 large carrots, thinly sliced
2 large ribs celery, including leaves, thinly sliced
2 garlic cloves, minced
1/2 teaspoon dried thyme leaves
1/2 teaspoon ground celery seed
1/2 teaspoon pepper
Salt, to taste

Per Serving
Calories: 153
% Calories from fat: 10
Protein (g): 8.4
Carbohydrates (g): 27.4
Fat (g): 1.8
Saturated fat (g): 0.5
Cholesterol (mg): 5.9
Sodium (mg): 205
Exchanges
Milk: 0.0
Veg.: 0.0
Fruit: 0.0
Bread: 2.0
Meat: 0.0
Fat: 0.0

1. Combine all ingredients, except salt, in stockpot and heat to boiling. Reduce heat and simmer, covered, 2 to 2^1/$_2$ hours, stirring occasionally, until beans are tender. Remove ham bone, cut meat into bite-sized pieces, and return to soup. Discard bone. Skim fat from top of soup; discard bay leaves. Season to taste with salt.

DOWN HOME GREEN BEAN SOUP

Green beans, smoked pork hock, black-eyed peas, and barley combine to give this soup its down-home flavor and richness.

5-6 servings

1 large onion, chopped

1 large garlic clove, minced

2 teaspoons olive oil

2 quarts Chicken Stock (see p. 2), *or* reduced-sodium fat-free chicken broth

1 large carrot, sliced

1 large rib celery, finely chopped

1/2 cup dried black-eyed peas, sorted, rinsed

3 tablespoons pearl barley

2 small pork hocks

1 bay leaf

2 1/2 cups cut green beans (2-inch)

2 teaspoons dried basil leaves

1/2 teaspoon dried thyme leaves

1/4 teaspoon black pepper

Pinch crushed red pepper

1 can (14 1/2 ounces) reduced-sodium diced tomatoes, undrained

Salt, to taste

Per Serving
Calories: 143
% Calories from fat: 13
Protein (g): 9.4
Carbohydrates (g): 23.2
Fat (g): 2.3
Saturated fat (g): 0.4
Cholesterol (mg): 1.2
Sodium (mg): 415
Exchanges
Milk: 0.0
Veg.: 2.0
Fruit: 0.0
Bread: 1.0
Meat: 0.0
Fat: 0.5

1. Saute onion and garlic in oil in large saucepan until onion is tender, about 5 minutes. Add Chicken Stock, carrot, celery, black-eyed peas, barley, pork hocks, and bay leaf and heat to boiling; reduce heat and simmer, covered, until black-eyed peas are almost tender, about 40 minutes.

2. Add green beans, basil, thyme, and black and red pepper; heat to boiling. Reduce heat and simmer, covered, until green beans are tender, about 10 minutes. Add tomatoes and liquid and simmer 5 minutes longer. Discard bay leaf and pork hocks. Skim fat from soup; season to taste with salt.

BLACK-EYED PEA AND LENTIL SOUP

This soup is flavorful, economical, and full of protein. Use the food processor to chop the vegetables quickly.

10 servings (1¼ cups each)

3 medium carrots, chopped

2 ribs celery, chopped

1 medium onion, chopped

2 cloves garlic, chopped

2 teaspoons olive oil

8 ounces lean smoked ham, cut into ½-inch cubes

1 can (16 ounces) reduced-sodium whole tomatoes, undrained, chopped

2 quarts Beef Stock (see p. 6)

1½ cups dried lentils

1 cup dried black-eyed peas

½ teaspoon dried thyme leaves

½ teaspoon dried rosemary leaves

Salt and pepper, to taste

Per Serving
Calories: 219
% Calories from fat: 12
Protein (gm): 15.4
Carbohydrate (gm): 33.9
Fat (gm): 3
Saturated fat (gm): 0.7
Cholesterol (mg): 12.3
Sodium (mg): 300
Exchanges
Milk: 0.0
Veg.: 1.0
Fruit: 0.0
Bread: 2.0
Meat: 1.0
Fat: 0.0

1. Saute carrots, celery, onion, and garlic in oil in large saucepan until tender, about 10 minutes. Stir in remaining ingredients, except salt and pepper, and heat to boiling. Reduce heat and simmer, covered, until black-eyed peas are tender, about 1 hour, stirring occasionally. Season to taste with salt and pepper.

RED LENTIL SOUP

Red lentils have a milder taste and finer texture than brown lentils.

6-7 servings

1¹/₂ cups dried red lentils, sorted, rinsed
  1 large onion, finely chopped
  1 rib celery, diced
  1 green bell pepper, diced
  1 garlic clove, minced
1¹/₂ quarts Low-Salt Chicken Stock
     (see p. 3)
  1 teaspoon chili powder
  1 teaspoon paprika
  1 bay leaf
 ¹/₄ teaspoon pepper
1¹/₂ cups reduced-fat spaghetti sauce
1-2 teaspoons sugar
     Salt, to taste

Per Serving
Calories: 210
% Calories from fat: 4
Protein (g): 17
Carbohydrates (g): 34.6
Fat (g): 1
Saturated fat (g): 0.1
Cholesterol (mg): 5
Sodium (mg): 335
Exchanges
Milk: 0.0
Veg.: 1.0
Fruit: 0.0
Bread: 2.0
Meat: 0.5
Fat: 0.0

1. Combine ingredients, except spaghetti sauce, sugar, and salt, in large saucepan and heat to boiling. Reduce heat and simmer, covered, until lentils are tender, about 30 minutes. Stir in spaghetti sauce and simmer, uncovered, 10 to 15 minutes. Discard bay leaf; season to taste with sugar and salt.

LENTIL-VEGETABLE SOUP WITH HAM

Unlike many legumes, lentils don't require pre-soaking or any attention during cooking. They lend a wonderful homey flavor and heartiness to this simple soup.

4 servings

1/2 cup chopped onion

1/2 cup chopped carrot

1/2 cup chopped celery

1/3 cup chopped smoked ham

1 tablespoon olive oil

2/3 cup dried lentils

1 quart Rich Chicken Stock (see p. 4), *or* reduced-sodium fat-free chicken broth

1/8-1/4 teaspoon crushed red pepper

1 small smoked pork hock (8 ounces)

1 can (14 1/2 ounce) stewed tomatoes, undrained

Salt and pepper, to taste

Per Serving
Calories: 237
% Calories from fat: 24
Protein (gm): 16.9
Carbohydrate (gm): 27.3
Fat (gm): 6.4
Saturated fat (gm): 1.4
Cholesterol (mg): 11.6
Sodium (mg): 414
Exchanges
Milk: 0.0
Veg.: 2.0
Fruit: 0.0
Bread: 1.0
Meat: 2.0
Fat: 0.0

1. Saute onion, carrot, celery, and ham in oil in Dutch oven until onion is browned, 8 to 10 minutes. Stir in lentils, Rich Chicken Stock, crushed red pepper, and pork hock; heat to boiling. Reduce heat and simmer 35 to 40 minutes or until lentils are tender.

2. Add tomatoes and liquid; simmer 8 minutes more. Discard pork hock; season to taste with salt and pepper.

TUSCAN LENTIL SOUP

A basic lentil soup at its best—a real cold weather comfort food!

10 servings

1 pound dried lentils

1 quart Chicken Stock (see p. 2)

3 cups water

1 large onion, diced

1 red bell pepper, diced

2 cloves garlic, chopped

2 tablespoons olive oil

4 carrots, diced

1 can (16 ounces) crushed tomatoes, undrained

Spike, to taste

Pepper, to taste

Grated Parmesan cheese, as garnish

Per Serving
Calories: 211
% Calories from fat: 15
Protein (g): 13.3
Carbohydrates (g): 33.6
Fat (g): 3.6
Saturated fat (g): 0.5
Cholesterol (mg): 0
Sodium (mg): 409
Exchanges
Milk: 0.0
Veg.: 1.5
Fruit: 0.0
Bread: 1.5
Meat: 1.0
Fat: 0.5

1. Heat lentils, Chicken Stock, and water to boiling in large saucepan; reduce heat and simmer, covered, 1 hour.

2. Saute onion, bell pepper, and garlic in oil in skillet until tender, about 5 minutes; add to saucepan with carrots and tomatoes and liquid and simmer, covered, 30 minutes. Season to taste with Spike and pepper; sprinkle each serving with Parmesan cheese.

RICH BEEF AND LENTIL SOUP

Browned beef and caramelized onions add richness to a favorite lentil soup.

10 servings

16 ounces lean beef stew cubes, fat trimmed

1¹/2 cups finely chopped onions

1-2 tablespoons vegetable oil

2 tablespoons flour

3 quarts reduced-sodium fat-free beef broth

3 cups dried lentils, sorted, rinsed

1 medium leek, white part only, finely chopped

3 large carrots, finely chopped

¹/2 cup chopped celery

¹/4 cup dry white wine, *or* beef broth

Salt and pepper, to taste

Per Serving
Calories: 313
% Calories from fat: **12**
Protein (gm): 31.7
Carbohydrate (gm): **37.3**
Fat (gm): 4.2
Saturated fat (gm): 1.1
Cholesterol (mg): 28.4
Sodium (mg): 234
Exchanges
Milk: 0.0
Veg.: 1.0
Fruit: 0.0
Bread: 2.0
Meat: 2.5
Fat: 0.0

1. Cook beef and onions in oil in large saucepan over medium to medium-high heat until beef is browned and crusty and onions are well browned, about 10 minutes; stir in flour.

2. Add beef broth, lentils, leek, carrots, and celery; heat to boiling. Reduce heat and simmer, covered, until beef is tender, 1 to 1 ¹/2 hours, stirring in wine during last 15 minutes. Season to taste with salt and pepper.

SPICY LENTIL-TOMATO SOUP WITH HAM

This easy, spicy lentil soup is seasoned with ham, tomatoes, and a lively blend of herbs.

6-7 servings

3 cups chopped onions

2 large garlic cloves, minced

1 tablespoon olive oil

1¹/₂ quarts Chicken Stock (see p. 2), *or* reduced-sodium fat-free chicken broth

2 pork hocks

1 cup finely chopped celery with leaves

1 cup finely chopped carrots

¹/₂ cup dried red, *or* brown, lentils, sorted, rinsed

1 tablespoon dried basil leaves

¹/₂ teaspoon dried oregano leaves

¹/₂ teaspoon dried thyme leaves

¹/₈ teaspoon cayenne pepper

¹/₈ teaspoon black pepper

¹/₂ cup finely diced very lean ham

1 can (28 ounces) Italian-style tomatoes, coarsely chopped, undrained

1 cup shredded green cabbage

1 cup rinsed and drained canned garbanzo beans

Salt, to taste

Per Serving
Calories: 204
% Calories from fat: 16
Protein (g): 14.3
Carbohydrates (g): 28.6
Fat (g): 3.7
Saturated fat (g): 0.6
Cholesterol (mg): 5
Sodium (mg): 671
Exchanges
Milk: 0.0
Veg.: 3.0
Fruit: 0.0
Bread: 1.0
Meat: 1.0
Fat: 0.0

1. Saute onions and garlic in olive oil in large saucepan until onions are soft, 8 to 10 minutes. Add Chicken Stock, pork hocks, celery, carrots, lentils, herbs, and cayenne and black pepper; heat to boiling. Reduce heat and simmer, covered, 45 minutes. Skim fat from top of soup; discard pork hocks.

2. Add ham, tomatoes and liquid, cabbage, and beans; simmer, covered, 15 minutes. Season to taste with salt.

WHITE BEAN SOUP

Great Northern or navy beans can be substituted for the cannellini beans.

4 servings

2   cups chopped celery
1   medium onion, chopped
3   scallions, chopped
3   cloves garlic, chopped
1-2 tablespoons canola oil
2   cans (15 ounces each) cannellini beans,
     rinsed, drained
2   tablespoons oat bran
1   cup Quick Sage Chicken Stock
     (see p. 2)
1   cup water
1/2 teaspoon dried dill weed
1/8 teaspoon dried thyme leaves
3   whole allspice
     Dash cayenne pepper
     Juice of 1 lemon
     Salt and pepper, to taste
     Finely chopped parsley, as garnish

Per Serving
Calories: 238
% Calories from fat: 17
Protein (gm): 11
Carbohydrate (gm): 38.3
Fat (gm): 4.6
Saturated fat (gm): 0.3
Cholesterol (mg): 0
Sodium (mg): 399
Exchanges
Milk: 0.0
Veg.: 0.0
Fruit: 0.0
Bread: 2.5
Meat: 0.0
Fat: 1.0

1. Saute celery, onion, scallions, and garlic in oil in large saucepan until tender, about 5 minutes. Add remaining ingredients, except salt, pepper, and parsley, and heat to boiling; reduce heat and simmer, covered, 15 minutes.

2. Process soup in blender or food processor until smooth; return to saucepan and simmer, uncovered, 5 minutes. Season to taste with salt and pepper; sprinkle each serving with parsley.

WHITE BEAN AND ANGEL HAIR PASTA SOUP

We fell in love with this wonderful soup about eight years ago in a little restaurant in New York and have been making it frequently ever since.

6-8 servings

1¹/₂ cups dried Great Northern beans, sorted, rinsed
1 large onion, chopped
2 garlic cloves, chopped
2 teaspoons olive oil
2 quarts Chicken Stock (see p. 2), *or* reduced-sodium fat-free chicken broth
2 small pork hocks
2 large carrots, sliced
2 large ribs celery, including leaves, sliced
¹/₂ cup chopped parsley
2 large bay leaves
1¹/₂ tablespoons Italian seasoning
Dash cayenne pepper
¹/₄ teaspoon black pepper
2 cups broken angel hair pasta (3-inch)
1 can (8 ounces) tomato sauce
Salt, to taste

Per Serving
Calories: 189
% Calories from fat: **17**
Protein (g): 13.9
Carbohydrates (g): 26.3
Fat (g): 3.5
Saturated fat (g): **0.9**
Cholesterol (mg): **23.3**
Sodium (mg): 416
Exchanges
Milk: 0.0
Veg.: 2.0
Fruit: 0.0
Bread: 1.0
Meat: 1.0
Fat: 0.0

1. Place beans in large saucepan and cover with 2 inches water; heat to boiling. Boil 2 minutes; let stand, covered, 1 hour. Drain.

2. Saute onion and garlic in oil in Dutch oven until onion is tender, about 5 minutes. Add beans and remaining ingredients, except pasta, tomato sauce, and salt; heat to boiling. Reduce heat and simmer, covered, until beans are tender, about 1 hour. Skim fat from soup; discard pork hocks and bay leaves.

3. Heat soup to boiling and add pasta; reduce heat and simmer until pasta is al dente, 2 to 3 minutes. Add tomato sauce and simmer 5 minutes more. Season to taste with salt.

WHITE BEAN SOUP PROVENÇAL

Serve Focaccia (see p. 788) as a perfect accompaniment to this herb-infused soup.

8 servings

1 pound dried cannellini, *or* navy, beans
Olive oil cooking spray
1 cup chopped onion
1 cup chopped celery
3 cloves garlic, minced
2 teaspoons dried sage leaves
1¹/₂ quarts Low-Salt Chicken Stock
(see p. 3), *or* reduced-sodium fat-free chicken broth
2 cups water
3 large plum tomatoes, chopped
2 teaspoons lemon juice
Salt and pepper, to taste
Mixed Herb Pesto (recipe follows)

Per Serving
Calories: 283
% Calories from fat: 21
Protein (gm): 16.2
Carbohydrate (gm): 41.9
Fat (gm): 6.9
Saturated fat (gm): 1.2
Cholesterol (mg): 3.6
Sodium (mg): 199
Exchanges
Milk: 0.0
Veg.: 2.0
Fruit: 0.0
Bread: 2.0
Meat: 1.0
Fat: 1.0

1. Cover beans with 2 inches water in large saucepan and heat to boiling; boil, uncovered, 2 minutes. Remove from heat and let stand, covered, 1 hour; drain.

2. Spray large saucepan with cooking spray; heat over medium heat until hot. Saute onion, celery, and garlic 3 to 4 minutes. Stir in beans, sage, Low-Salt Chicken Stock, and water; heat to boiling. Reduce heat and simmer, covered, until beans are tender, 45 to 60 minutes.

3. Process in food processor or blender until smooth; return to saucepan. Stir in tomatoes and lemon juice; season to taste with salt and pepper.

4. Serve soup in bowls; stir 1 tablespoon Mixed Herb Pesto into each bowl.

Mixed Herb Pesto

makes about 1/2 cup

> 1/2 cup packed basil leaves
> 1/2 cup packed parsley sprigs
> 1/4 cup packed oregano leaves
> 3 cloves garlic
> 2 tablespoons grated Parmesan cheese
> 1 ounce walnuts
> 2 tablespoons olive oil
> 2 teaspoons lemon juice
> 1/2 teaspoon salt
> 1/4 teaspoon pepper

1. Combine herbs, garlic, Parmesan cheese, and walnuts in food processor or blender. Process, adding oil and lemon juice gradually, until mixture is very finely chopped. Stir in salt and pepper.

WHITE BEAN SOUP WITH SPINACH

This soup is a meal in a bowl. Serve with warm crusty bread and a crisp green salad.

8 servings

> 1 1/2 cups dried Great Northern beans
> 1 large onion, chopped
> 2 cloves garlic, minced
> 2 teaspoons olive oil
> 1 1/2 quarts Chicken Stock (see p. 2)
> 2 cups water
> 1/4 cup pearl barley
> 2 large carrots, sliced
> 2 large ribs celery, sliced
> 2 bay leaves
> 1 teaspoon dried marjoram leaves
> 1 teaspoon dried basil leaves
> 1/2 teaspoon dried thyme leaves
> Dash cayenne pepper

Per Serving
Calories: 115
% Calories from fat: 14
Protein (g): 5.4
Carbohydrates (g): 20.9
Fat (g): 1.9
Saturated fat (g): 1
Cholesterol (mg): 0
Sodium (mg): 806
Exchanges
Milk: 0.0
Veg.: 3.0
Fruit: 0.0
Bread: 0.5
Meat: 0.0
Fat: 0.0

1 can (16 ounces) diced tomatoes, undrained
1 package (10 ounces) frozen chopped spinach, thawed, drained
   Spike, to taste

1. Cover beans with 2 inches of water in large saucepan; heat to boiling. Boil 2 minutes; remove from heat and let stand, covered, 1 hour. Drain.

2. Saute onion and garlic in oil in large saucepan oven until tender, about 5 minutes. Add beans and remaining ingredients, except tomatoes, spinach, and Spike; heat to boiling. Reduce heat and simmer, covered, until beans are tender, about 1 hour. Discard bay leaves. Skim fat from top of soup.

3. Add tomatoes and liquid and spinach; simmer, uncovered, 5 minutes. Season to taste with Spike.

HEARTY BEAN AND BARLEY SOUP

Bean and barley soup is one of my fondest childhood memories.

9 servings

2 cups dried Great Northern beans, sorted, rinsed
2¹/4 quarts water
1 meaty ham bone, *or* 2 pork hocks
1/4 cup pearl barley
2 cups chopped onions
2 large carrots, peeled, sliced
2 large ribs celery, including leaves, sliced
3-5 beef bouillon cubes
2 garlic cloves, minced
3 bay leaves
1¹/2 teaspoons dried thyme leaves
¹/4 teaspoon ground celery seeds
¹/4 teaspoon pepper
3 cups thinly sliced cabbage
1 can (8 ounces) reduced-sodium tomato sauce
   Salt, to taste

Per Serving
Calories: 180
% Calories from fat: 8
Protein (g): 12
Carbohydrates (g): 31
Fat (g): 1.7
Saturated fat (g): 2.3
Cholesterol (mg): 8
Sodium (mg): 523
Exchanges
Milk: 0.0
Veg.: 5.0
Fruit: 0.0
Bread: 0.5
Meat: 0.5
Fat: 0.0

1. Cover beans with 2 inches of water in Dutch oven and heat to boiling; boil 2 minutes. Remove from heat and let stand, covered, 1 hour. Drain.

2. Return beans to Dutch oven with remaining ingredients except cabbage, tomato sauce, and salt; heat to boiling. Reduce heat and simmer, covered, 30 minutes. Add cabbage and simmer 30 to 40 minutes or until beans are very tender.

3. Remove ham bone and cut meat into small pieces; return to soup. Discard bone and bay leaves; skim fat from surface of soup. Add tomato sauce and simmer 10 minutes. Season to taste with salt.

EASY BARLEY AND GARBANZO SOUP

A 1-step soup—what could be easier?

6-7 servings

1 smoked pork hock
1¹/₂ quarts very hot water
3 beef bouillon cubes
¹/₃ cup pearl barley
1 can (15 ounces) reduced-sodium tomato sauce
1 rib celery, finely chopped
1 large carrot, finely chopped
2 tablespoons dried minced onion
2 teaspoons sugar
¹/₂ teaspoon dry mustard
¹/₄ teaspoon celery seed, finely crushed
¹/₄ teaspoon dried thyme leaves
¹/₄ teaspoon black pepper
Dash cayenne pepper
1 can (15 ounces) garbanzo beans, rinsed, drained
1 can (16 ounces) reduced-sodium cut green beans, drained
Salt, to taste

Per Serving
Calories: 169
% Calories from fat: 12
Protein (g): 7.8
Carbohydrates (g): 31.3
Fat (g): 2.3
Saturated fat (g): 0.3
Cholesterol (mg): 3
Sodium (mg): 460
Exchanges
Milk: 0.0
Veg.: 0.0
Fruit: 0.0
Bread: 2.0
Meat: 0.0
Fat: 0.5

1. Combine all ingredients except salt in large saucepan; heat to boiling. Reduce heat and simmer, covered, until barley is tender, 50 to 60 minutes. Discard pork hock; skim fat from top of soup. Season to taste with salt.

ITALIAN BREAD SOUP

Although this delicious recipe comes from humble origins, we first encountered it in a trendy Italian restaurant in Washington, D.C.

8 servings

1 large onion, chopped

1 large garlic clove, minced

2 teaspoons olive oil

1¹/₂ quarts Rich Chicken Stock (see p. 4), *or* reduced-sodium fat-free chicken broth

1 can (15 ounces) reduced-sodium tomato sauce

2 large carrots, peeled, chopped

1 can (19 ounces) cannellini beans, rinsed, drained

1 package (16 ounces) frozen mixed broccoli, corn, and red bell peppers

1¹/₂ cups chopped cabbage

1 teaspoon Italian seasoning

1 teaspoon dried basil leaves

¹/₄ teaspoon pepper
    Salt, to taste

2 cups low-fat seasoned crouton stuffing mix

Per Serving
Calories: 178
% Calories from fat: 9
Protein (g): 12.5
Carbohydrates (g): 33.9
Fat (g): 2.1
Saturated fat (g): 0.2
Cholesterol (mg): 0
Sodium (mg): 529
Exchanges
Milk: 0.0
Veg.: 3.0
Fruit: 0.0
Bread: 1.0
Meat: 0.0
Fat: 0.5

1. Saute onion and garlic in olive oil in Dutch oven until onion is tender, about 5 minutes. Add remaining ingredients, except salt and stuffing mix; heat to boiling. Reduce heat and simmer, covered, 30 minutes, stirring occasionally. Season to taste with salt.

2. Spoon ¹/₄ cup stuffing mix into each soup bowl and ladle soup over.

PINTO PASTA FAGIOLI

A traditional Pasta Fagioli, with some Mexican-style flavor twists!

6 servings

1 cup dried pinto beans, sorted, rinsed
3 cups Low-Salt Chicken Stock (see p. 3)
2¹/₂ cups diced tomatoes
1¹/₄ cups chopped onions
1¹/₄ cups sliced carrots
¹/₂ cup chopped celery
1 cup diced green bell pepper
1 clove garlic, minced
1 medium jalapeño chili, finely chopped
2 teaspoons dried oregano leaves
1-1¹/₂ cups cooked elbow macaroni
¹/₄ teaspoon cayenne pepper
Salt, to taste
¹/₄ cup finely chopped cilantro

Per Serving
Calories: 205
% Calories from fat: 5
Protein (gm): 10.5
Carbohydrate (gm): 40.5
Fat (gm): 1.2
Saturated fat (gm): 0.2
Cholesterol (mg): 1.7
Sodium (mg): 33
Exchanges
Milk: 0.0
Veg.: 2.0
Fruit: 0.0
Bread: 2.0
Meat: 0.0
Fat: 0.0

1. Cover beans with water in large saucepan and heat to boiling; boil, uncovered, 2 minutes. Let stand, covered, 1 hour; drain.

2. Heat Low-Salt Chicken Stock and beans to boiling in large saucepan; reduce heat and simmer, covered, 20 minutes. Add remaining vegetables and oregano; simmer, covered, until beans are tender, about 30 minutes, adding macaroni during last 5 minutes. Stir in cayenne pepper; season to taste with salt. Stir in cilantro.

SHRIMP AND BLACK BEAN SOUP

In Mexico, leaves from the avocado tree are used for seasoning in this favorite Oaxacan soup. We've substituted a bay leaf, which is somewhat stronger in flavor.

6 servings (about 1¹/₂ cups each)

Vegetable cooking spray

2 medium onions, chopped

4 cloves garlic, minced

2 medium tomatoes, peeled, cut into wedges

3 cans (14¹/₂ ounces each) reduced-sodium fat-free chicken broth, divided

¹/₂ cup water

3 cups cooked dried black beans *or* 2 cans (15 ounces each) black beans, rinsed, drained

1 teaspoon ground cumin

1 teaspoon dried oregano leaves

1 teaspoon dried thyme leaves

1 bay leaf

8 ounces peeled, deveined shrimp

Salt and pepper, to taste

Finely chopped cilantro, as garnish

Per Serving
Calories: 190
% Calories from fat: 5
Protein (g): 19.1
Carbohydrates (g): 27
Fat (g): 1.1
Saturated fat (g): 0.3
Cholesterol (mg): 58.3
Sodium (mg): 136
Exchanges
Milk: 0.0
Veg.: 1.0
Fruit: 0.0
Bread: 1.5
Meat: 1.5
Fat: 0.0

1. Spray large saucepan with cooking spray; heat over medium heat until hot. Saute onions and garlic until tender, about 5 minutes. Process onion mixture, tomatoes, and 1 can chicken broth until smooth; return to saucepan.

2. Add remaining 2 cans broth, water, black beans, and herbs to saucepan; heat to boiling. Reduce heat and simmer, uncovered, 10 minutes, adding shrimp during last 5 minutes. Discard bay leaf and season to taste with salt and pepper.

3. Serve soup in bowls; sprinkle with cilantro.

PASILLA BLACK BEAN SOUP

Pasilla chilies are dried chilies that can be found in the produce or ethnic foods sections of most large supermarkets. They add a distinctive flavor to this soup.

8 servings (about 1¹/₃ cups each)

1 cup chopped onion
1 cup chopped carrots
1 jalapeño chili, chopped
4 cloves garlic, chopped
1 tablespoon vegetable oil
6 pasilla chilies, stems and seeds removed, torn into pieces
³/₄ teaspoon dried oregano leaves
¹/₂ teaspoon ground cumin
¹/₄ teaspoon dried thyme leaves
1 quart Chicken Stock (see p. 2)
1 can (14¹/₂ ounces) reduced-sodium diced tomatoes, undrained
2 cans (15 ounces each) black beans, rinsed, drained
Salt and pepper, to taste
Chopped cilantro, as garnish

Per Serving
Calories: 124
% Calories from fat: **19**
Protein (gm): 6.5
Carbohydrate (gm): **26.3**
Fat (gm): 3.5
Saturated fat (gm): 0.3
Cholesterol (mg): **1.7**
Sodium (mg): 400
Exchanges
Milk: 0.0
Veg.: 1.0
Fruit: 0.0
Bread: 1.0
Meat: 0.0
Fat: 0.5

1. Saute onion, carrots, jalapeño chili, and garlic in oil in large saucepan until onion is tender, about 5 minutes. Add pasilla chilies, oregano, cumin, and thyme; cook, covered, 5 minutes.

2. Add Chicken Stock, tomatoes and liquid, and beans to saucepan; heat to boiling. Reduce heat and simmer, covered, 10 minutes. Process soup in food processor or blender until smooth. Season to taste with salt and pepper. Sprinkle each serving with cilantro.

SIX

Melting-Pot Soups

CHICKEN-NOODLE SOUP

A hearty, entrée soup that's quick and easy to make, using reduced-sodium fat-free chicken broth. If using homemade chicken broth, refrigerate it until chilled, then skim and discard fat before proceeding with the soup.

4 servings

Vegetable cooking spray

4 ounces boneless, skinless chicken breast, fat trimmed, cut into ³/₄-inch pieces

4 ounces boneless, skinless chicken thighs, fat trimmed, cut into ³/₄-inch pieces

2 cups sliced celery, including some leaves

1 cup sliced carrots

1 cup sliced onion

2 cans (14¹/₂ ounces each) reduced-sodium fat-free chicken broth

1 teaspoon dried marjoram leaves

1 bay leaf

1 cup uncooked no-yolk broad noodles

1 tablespoon minced parsley leaves

Salt and pepper, to taste

Per Serving
Calories: 307
% Calories from fat: 14
Protein (g): 22.8
Carbohydrates (g): 44.3
Fat (g): 5
Saturated fat (g): 0.8
Cholesterol (mg): 32.9
Sodium (mg): 409
Exchanges
Milk: 0.0
Veg.: 1.0
Fruit: 0.0
Bread: 2.5
Meat: 2.0
Fat: 0.0

1. Spray large saucepan with cooking spray; heat over medium heat until hot. Saute chicken until browned, about 5 minutes. Add celery, carrots, and onion and saute until tender, 5 to 7 minutes.

2. Add chicken broth and herbs to saucepan; heat to boiling. Reduce heat and simmer, covered, until chicken and vegetables are tender, 15 to 20 minutes.

3. Heat soup to boiling; add noodles. Cook, uncovered, until noodles are tender, 7 to 10 minutes. Discard bay leaf. Stir in parsley; season to taste with salt and white pepper.

COUNTRY CHICKEN-NOODLE SOUP

Made with a stewing hen, slowly simmered until tender, and homemade egg noodles, this chicken soup tastes just like the one Grandma used to make.

10 servings

1 stewing chicken, cut up (about 4 pounds)
3 quarts water
1 onion, quartered
1 teaspoon dried marjoram leaves
1 bay leaf
2 cups sliced carrots
2 cups frozen whole-kernel corn
1 cup frozen peas
  Country Noodles (recipe follows)
¹/₄ cup chopped parsley
  Salt and pepper, to taste

Per Serving
Calories: 232
% Calories from fat: 22
Protein (gm): 23.2
Carbohydrate (gm): 22.1
Fat (gm): 5.6
Saturated fat (gm): 1.5
Cholesterol (mg): 79
Sodium (mg): 138
Exchanges
Milk: 0.0
Veg.: 2.0
Fruit: 0.0
Bread: 1.0
Meat: 2.0
Fat: 0.0

1. Place chicken, water, onion, marjoram, and bay leaf in large saucepan. Heat to boiling; reduce heat and simmer, covered, until chicken is tender, about 1 hour. Strain broth and return to saucepan; skim off fat. Remove meat from chicken, discarding skin and bones; cut meat into small cubes and return to pan. Discard onion and herbs.

2. Stir carrots, corn, and peas into saucepan; heat to boiling. Reduce heat and simmer, covered, until carrots are almost tender, about 10 minutes. Uncoil Country Noodles dough and drop into soup; simmer until noodles are tender, 3 to 5 minutes. Stir in parsley; season to taste with salt and pepper.

Country Noodles

    1 cup all-purpose flour
    1 egg
    1 tablespoon water
    1/4 teaspoon salt

1. Place flour in medium bowl. Make a well in center and add egg, water, and salt. Gradually mix in flour with a fork until dough is formed. Knead dough on floured surface until smooth, kneading in additional flour if dough is sticky. Let dough stand, covered, at room temperature 1 hour.

2. Roll out dough on lightly floured surface to 1/8 inch thickness. Loosely roll up dough like a jelly roll; cut into 1/2-inch-wide coils.

CHUNKY CHICKEN SOUP

Here's a flavorful Italian-style chicken soup, with chunky vegetables for added texture. The rice helps thicken the broth.

5-6 servings

    1 large onion, chopped
    2 ribs celery, thinly sliced
    2 large carrots, thinly sliced
    2 cups coarsely chopped cauliflower
    1 large boneless, skinless chicken breast,
       cut into 3/4-inch pieces
 1 1/2 quarts reduced-sodium fat-free chicken
       broth
    2 cups cooked, *or* rinsed, drained canned,
       garbanzo beans
  1/2 cup uncooked long-grain white rice
 1 1/2 teaspoons dried thyme leaves
    1 teaspoon dried basil leaves
    1 teaspoon dried marjoram leaves
    2 bay leaves
  1/4 teaspoon black pepper
    1 can (14 1/2 ounces) stewed tomatoes,
       undrained
       Salt, to taste

Per Serving
Calories: 310
% Calories from fat: 11
Protein (g): 29.4
Carbohydrates (g): 40.5
Fat (g): 3.8
Saturated fat (g): 0.8
Cholesterol (mg): 45.7
Sodium (mg): 585
Exchanges
Milk: 0.0
Veg.: 2.0
Fruit: 0.0
Bread: 2.0
Meat: 2.0
Fat: 0.0

1. Combine all ingredients, except tomatoes and salt, in large saucepan; heat to boiling. Reduce heat and simmer, covered, until beans are tender, about 1 hour. Stir in tomatoes and liquid; simmer 5 to 10 minutes longer. Season to taste with salt.

SAVORY CHICKEN SOUP

The vegetables that cook with the chicken are used to help thicken this lightly curried soup.

6 servings

1 chicken, cut up (about 3 pounds)
3 cups sliced carrots, divided
1 cup sliced celery with tops
1 cup sliced onion
2¹/₂ quarts water
1 bay leaf
2 tablespoon finely chopped shallots
8 ounces mushrooms, sliced
1 tablespoon margarine
3 tablespoons flour
1 teaspoon curry powder
¹/₂ cup quick-cooking barley
1 cup fat-free half-and-half, *or* fat-free milk
¹/₄ cup dry sherry
Salt and pepper, to taste
Avocado slices, as garnish

Per Serving
Calories: 316
% Calories from fat: 25
Protein (gm): 28.4
Carbohydrate (gm): 27.7
Fat (gm): 8.6
Saturated fat (gm): 2.1
Cholesterol (mg): 72.3
Sodium (mg): 171
Exchanges
Milk: 0.0
Veg.: 3.0
Fruit: 0.0
Bread: 1.0
Meat: 3.0
Fat: 0.0

1. Place chicken, 1 cup carrots, celery, onion, water, and bay leaf in large Dutch oven. Heat to boiling; reduce heat and simmer, covered, until chicken is tender, about 45 minutes.

2. Strain soup; reserve stock. Remove chicken from bones; reserve meat; discard bones. Process vegetables with 1 cup stock in food processor or blender until smooth; reserve.

3. Saute shallots and mushrooms in margarine in large saucepan until tender, about 8 minutes. Sprinkle with flour and curry powder; cook 2 minutes longer. Stir in reserved stock, remaining 2 cups carrots, and barley; heat to boiling. Reduce heat and simmer until barley is tender, about 15 minutes.

4. Stir in reserved vegetable puree and chicken, half-and-half, and sherry; simmer 5 minutes. Season to taste with salt and pepper. Serve in bowls; garnish with avocado.

CHICKEN-VEGETABLE SOUP WITH ENDIVE

The flavor of endive mellows as it cooks, which adds a pleasing leafy-vegetable taste but no bitterness to the soup.

6 servings

1 large onion, chopped
1 large rib celery, diced
1 large carrot, diced
2 large garlic cloves, minced
1 tablespoon olive oil
1¹/₂ quarts reduced-sodium fat-free chicken broth
2 pounds boneless, skinless chicken breast, cut into ³/₄-inch pieces
1¹/₂ teaspoons dried marjoram leaves
¹/₂ teaspoon dried basil leaves
¹/₂ teaspoon pepper
2 medium red potatoes, peeled, coarsely diced
¹/₄ cup uncooked orzo
5-6 cups coarsely chopped curly endive
1 can (14¹/₂ ounces) reduced-sodium chopped tomatoes, undrained
Salt, to taste
2-3 tablespoons grated Parmesan cheese, as garnish

Per Serving
Calories: 284
% Calories from fat: 17
Protein (g): 31
Carbohydrates (g): 27.9
Fat (g): 5.5
Saturated fat (g): 1.1
Cholesterol (mg): 61
Sodium (mg): 404
Exchanges
Milk: 0.0
Veg.: 2.0
Fruit: 0.0
Bread: 1.0
Meat: 3.0
Fat: 0.0

1. Saute onion, celery, carrot, and garlic in oil in Dutch oven until vegetables are browned, about 8 minutes. Add broth, chicken, marjoram, basil, and pepper and heat to boiling; reduce heat and simmer, covered, 20 minutes. Add potatoes, orzo, and endive; simmer 5 minutes. Add tomatoes and liquid; simmer until potatoes and orzo are tender, about 10 minutes. Season to taste with salt. Sprinkle each serving with Parmesan cheese.

SOUTHERN GUMBO

Have a Mardi Gras party and serve this soup with an assortment of hot sauces for a "hot" time.

8 servings

2 cups cubed lean ham
2 cups chopped onions
2 cups chopped celery
2 cups chopped green bell peppers
1 tablespoon minced garlic
1 teaspoon dried thyme leaves
1 tablespoon margarine
1/2 cup all-purpose flour
1 1/2 quarts Rich Chicken Stock (see p. 4)
1 can (28 ounces) reduced-sodium tomatoes, undrained, chopped
1 cup uncooked rice
2 bay leaves
2 cups cubed cooked chicken
8 ounces small shrimp, peeled, deveined
2 teaspoons very-low-sodium Worcestershire sauce
2 teaspoons gumbo file powder
Salt, to taste
Hot pepper sauce, to taste

Per Serving
Calories: 373
% Calories from fat: **22**
Protein (gm): 32.4
Carbohydrate (gm): **37.9**
Fat (gm): 8.9
Saturated fat (gm): **2.4**
Cholesterol (mg): **92.3**
Sodium (mg): 630
Exchanges
Milk: 0.0
Veg.: 2.0
Fruit: 0.0
Bread: 2.0
Meat: 3.0
Fat: 0.0

1. Saute ham, onions, celery, bell peppers, garlic, and thyme in margarine in large saucepan until lightly browned, about 10 minutes. Sprinkle with flour; cook 1 to 2 minutes longer. Stir in Rich Chicken Stock, tomatoes and liquid, rice, and bay leaves. Heat to boiling; reduce heat and simmer, covered, 20 minutes.

2. Stir in chicken, shrimp, Worcestershire sauce, and file powder. Heat to boiling; reduce heat and simmer until shrimp are cooked, about 5 minutes. Discard bay leaves; season to taste with salt and hot pepper sauce.

SLOW-COOKER CHICKEN GUMBO

Black-eyed peas, okra, and succotash, all Southern favorites, combine nicely in this nourishing gumbo.

5-6 servings

1 package (10 ounces) frozen black-eyed peas, rinsed under hot water to partially thaw

2 large onions, finely chopped

1 medium pork hock

16 ounces boneless, skinless chicken breast, fat trimmed

2 large ribs celery, chopped

1/2 cup diced sweet red, or green, bell pepper

3 tablespoons uncooked long-grain rice

1 bay leaf

1 package (10 ounces) frozen succotash, rinsed under hot water to partially thaw

1 cup frozen sliced okra, rinsed under cool water, drained

1 quart fat-free chicken broth

1 can (14 1/2 ounces) whole tomatoes, undrained, chopped

2 tablespoons chopped parsley

1/4 teaspoon dried thyme leaves

1/4 teaspoon pepper

Salt, to taste

Per Serving
Calories: 279
% Calories from fat: 10
Protein (g): 28.4
Carbohydrates (g): 35.7
Fat (g): 3.2
Saturated fat (g): 0.8
Cholesterol (mg): 47.8
Sodium (mg): 367
Exchanges
Milk: 0.0
Veg.: 1.0
Fruit: 0.0
Bread: 2.0
Meat: 2.0
Fat: 0.0

1. Place all ingredients, except tomatoes, parsley, thyme, pepper, and salt, in slow cooker. Cover and cook on High 30 minutes. Continue cooking on High for 3 hours or change setting to Low and cook 7 hours.

2. Remove chicken breast, cut meat into bite-sized pieces, and return to slow cooker. Discard pork hock and bay leaf. Add tomatoes and liquid, parsley, thyme, and pepper; cook on Low 15 minutes longer or until soup is heated through. Season to taste with salt.

CHICK 'N PEA SOUP

This easy variation on split-pea soup uses chicken instead of ham.

8 servings

2 cups cubed, cooked boneless, skinless chicken breast

2 quarts reduced-sodium fat-free chicken broth

1 package (16 ounces) dried green split peas

2 carrots, cubed

1 cup chopped onion

Salt and pepper, to taste

Per Serving
Calories: 282
% Calories from fat: 5
Protein (gm): 28.6
Carbohydrate (gm): 37.8
Fat (gm): 1.6
Saturated fat (gm): 0.3
Cholesterol (mg): 21.8
Sodium (mg): 203
Exchanges
Milk: 0.0
Veg.: 0.0
Fruit: 0.0
Bread: 2.5
Meat: 2.0
Fat: 0.0

1. Combine all ingredients, except salt and pepper, in large saucepan; heat to boiling. Reduce heat and simmer, covered, 1 hour, stirring occasionally. Season to taste with salt and pepper.

CHICKEN-VEGETABLE SOUP WITH ORZO

This hearty vegetable soup is perfect for a light supper—just serve with a crusty bread.

4 servings (about 2 cups each)

Olive oil cooking spray

12 ounces boneless, skinless chicken breast, cut into 1/2-inch pieces

1 medium onion, coarsely chopped

2 medium carrots, sliced

2 ribs celery, sliced

3 cloves garlic, minced

1/2 teaspoon dried thyme leaves

1/2 teaspoon dried oregano leaves

2 cans (15 ounces each) reduced-sodium chicken broth

1 cup water

1/2 cup (4 ounces) uncooked orzo

Per Serving
Calories: 260
% Calories from fat: 15
Protein (g): 24
Carbohydrates (g): 29.9
Fat (g): 4.1
Saturated fat (g): 1.3
Cholesterol (mg): 47.1
Sodium (mg): 281
Exchanges
Milk: 0.0
Veg.: 1.5
Fruit: 0.0
Bread: 1.5
Meat: 2.0
Fat: 0.0

$^1/_2$ cup frozen peas

4 medium leaves escarole, sliced or
coarsely chopped

$^1/_4$ teaspoon salt

$^1/_2$ teaspoon pepper

2 tablespoons grated Romano cheese

1. Spray large saucepan with cooking spray; heat over medium heat until hot. Cook chicken until no longer pink in the center, about 8 minutes; remove from saucepan. Add onion, carrots, celery, garlic, and herbs to saucepan; saute until onion is tender, about 5 minutes. Return chicken to saucepan.

2. Add chicken broth and water to saucepan; heat to boiling. Stir in orzo, peas, and escarole. Reduce heat and simmer, uncovered, until orzo is al dente, about 7 minutes. Stir in salt and pepper. Spoon soup into bowls; sprinkle with cheese.

TORTELLINI CHICKEN SOUP

The homemade tortellini make this soup extra-special. Tortellini can be made ahead of time and frozen until ready to use.

12 servings (about 1 cup each)

2 small chickens (about 2$^1/_2$ pounds each), cut up

2 quarts water

1 onion, quartered

2 carrots, sliced

1 rib celery, sliced

1 teaspoon dried oregano leaves

1 bay leaf
Chicken Tortellini (recipe follows)

$^1/_4$ cup chopped parsley
Salt and pepper, to taste

$^1/_4$-$^1/_2$ cup (2 ounces) grated fat-free Parmesan cheese

Per Serving
Calories: 227
% Calories from fat: 27
Protein (gm): 23.9
Carbohydrate (gm): 15.7
Fat (gm): 6.7
Saturated fat (gm): 1.7
Cholesterol (mg): 95.7
Sodium (mg): 294
Exchanges
Milk: 0.0
Veg.: 0.0
Fruit: 0.0
Bread: 1.0
Meat: 3.0
Fat: 0.0

1. Place chickens, water, onion, carrots, celery, oregano, and bay leaf in large saucepan. Heat to boiling; reduce heat and simmer, covered, until chicken is tender, about 40 minutes. Strain broth and reserve. Remove meat from chicken bones, separating dark meat. Chop enough dark meat to measure 3/4 cup and reserve for tortellini; dice remaining meat and place in broth. Discard bones, vegetables, and bay leaf. Cool broth; refrigerate, covered, until ready to use.

2. Remove all fat from surface of broth. Heat to boiling; add Chicken Tortellini and simmer until they float to the top and are al dente, 5 to 7 minutes. Stir in parsley; season to taste with salt and pepper. Sprinkle each serving with Parmesan cheese.

Chicken Tortellini

makes 48 tortellini

> 1¹/₂ cups all-purpose flour
> 1 egg
> 1 egg white
> 2 teaspoons olive oil
> 1 teaspoon salt, divided
> 3/4 cup chopped dark chicken meat (reserved in Step 1 above)
> 2 tablespoons grated fat-free Parmesan cheese
> 1 egg yolk
> 1/2 teaspoon grated lemon rind
> Pinch ground nutmeg
> Dash white pepper

1. Place flour in large bowl. Make well in center; add egg, egg white, oil, and 3/4 teaspoon salt. Mix until dough can be formed into a ball. Knead on lightly floured pastry board or counter until very smooth and elastic, about 10 minutes. Let stand, covered, 10 minutes.

2. Mix chicken, Parmesan cheese, egg yolk, lemon rind, remaining 1/4 teaspoon salt, nutmeg, and pepper.

3. Divide dough in half. Roll one half on lightly floured board into 10-inch round. Cut into twenty-four 2-inch circles. Place 1/4 teaspoon chicken mixture in center of each circle. Moisten edges with water. Fold in half; seal edges. Shape into rings, stretching slightly and shaping around finger. Press tips together to seal. Repeat with remaining dough and filling. Refrigerate, covered, until ready to use, up to 24 hours, or freeze no longer than 2 months.

CHICKEN WONTON SOUP

Delicately spiced chicken-filled wontons are a delicious addition to this soup. The wontons can be filled several hours ahead of time, and refrigerated until ready to cook.

6 servings (about 1¹/₂ cups each)

1/2 cup chopped red bell pepper
1/2 cup julienned carrot
  2 teaspoons minced gingerroot
  1 teaspoon sesame oil
  1 quart Chicken Stock (see p. 2)
  1 can (8 ounces) baby corn, rinsed, drained
  1 cup packed spinach leaves, sliced
2-3 teaspoons reduced-sodium soy sauce
    Salt and cayenne pepper, to taste
    Chicken Wontons (recipe follows)

Per Serving
Calories: 187
% Calories from fat: **13**
Protein (gm): 14.5
Carbohydrate (gm): 25.1
Fat (gm): 2.8
Saturated fat (gm): 0.6
Cholesterol (mg): 28.2
Sodium (mg): 430
Exchanges
Milk: 0.0
Veg.: 2.0
Fruit: 0.0
Bread: 1.0
Meat: 1.0
Fat: 0.0

1. Saute bell pepper, carrot, and gingerroot in sesame oil in large saucepan 2 to 3 minutes; stir in Chicken Stock and heat to boiling. Stir in corn, spinach, and soy sauce; season to taste with salt and cayenne pepper.

2. Heat to boiling; stir in Chicken Wontons and simmer until wontons are tender, about 5 minutes.

Chicken Wontons

makes 24 wontons

  8 ounces, boneless, skinless chicken breast
1/4 cup sliced green onions and tops
  1 teaspoon minced gingerroot
24 wonton wrappers

1. Process all ingredients, except wonton wrappers, in food processor until finely chopped. Place 1 mounded teaspoon chicken mixture on each wonton wrapper; moisten edges with water, and fold in half diagonally to create triangles, sealing edges.

CHINESE HOT POT

Oriental vegetables and seasonings and chicken blend perfectly in this fragrant soup.

6 servings

4 cans (14¹/₂ ounces each) reduced-sodium fat-free chicken broth
1 cup dry white wine
¹/₄ cup reduced-sodium Tamari soy sauce
2 tablespoons sugar
2 packages (3¹/₂ ounces each) oriental-style noodles, broken in half, seasoning packet discarded
¹/₂ cup small broccoli florets
¹/₂ cup sliced mushrooms
¹/₂ sliced carrots
1 can (4 ounces) baby corn, drained
1 pound boneless, skinless chicken breast, cut into bite sized pieces
1 cup snow peas, trimmed
1 bunch watercress, trimmed
4 green onions and tops, cut into 1-inch pieces
Salt and pepper, to taste

Per Serving
Calories: 330
% Calories from fat: 8
Protein (gm): 30.2
Carbohydrate (gm): 36.5
Fat (gm): 2.9
Saturated fat (gm): 0.6
Cholesterol (mg): 46
Sodium (mg): 850
Exchanges
Milk: 0.0
Veg.: 1.0
Fruit: 0.0
Bread: 2.0
Meat: 3.0
Fat: 0.0

1. Heat broth, wine, soy sauce, and sugar to boiling in large saucepan. Add noodles, broccoli, mushrooms, carrots, corn, and chicken; reduce heat and simmer, covered, until vegetables are just tender and chicken is cooked, 8 to 10 minutes, adding snow peas during last 3 to 4 minutes.

2. Stir in watercress and green onions; season to taste with salt and pepper. Serve immediately.

VIETNAMESE CURRIED CHICKEN AND COCONUT SOUP

Rice noodles, made with rice flour, can be round or flat. They must be softened in water before cooking. Angel hair pasta can be substituted.

6 servings

Vegetable cooking spray
1 tablespoon minced garlic
3-4 tablespoons curry powder
2 cans (14 1/2 ounces each) reduced-sodium fat-free chicken broth
3 cups reduced-fat coconut milk
2 tablespoons minced gingerroot
2/3 cup sliced green onions and tops
1 tablespoon minced parsley
1 tablespoon grated lime rind
1/2-1 teaspoon oriental chili paste
16 ounces boneless, skinless chicken breast
1/4 cup lime juice
1/3 cup minced cilantro
Salt and white pepper, to taste
1/2 package (8-ounce size) rice noodles

Per Serving
Calories: 261
% Calories from fat: 29
Protein (g): 23
Carbohydrates (g): 23.4
Fat (g): 8.5
Saturated fat (g): 0.6
Cholesterol (mg): 46
Sodium (mg): 347
Exchanges
Milk: 0.0
Veg.: 1.0
Fruit: 0.0
Bread: 1.0
Meat: 2.5
Fat: 0.5

1. Spray large saucepan with cooking spray; heat over medium heat until hot. Saute garlic 1 minute; stir in curry powder and cook, stirring constantly, 30 seconds. Add chicken broth, coconut milk, gingerroot, onions, parsley, lime rind, and chili paste; heat to boiling.

2. Add chicken breast and return to boiling. Reduce heat and simmer, covered, until chicken is cooked, about 20 minutes. Remove chicken and shred with 2 forks; return to saucepan. Stir in lime juice and cilantro; season to taste with salt and white pepper. Simmer, uncovered, 5 minutes longer.

3. Place noodles in large bowl; pour cold water over to cover. Let stand until noodles are separate and soft, about 5 minutes; drain. Stir noodles into 4 quarts boiling water. Reduce heat and simmer, uncovered, until tender, about 5 minutes; drain.

4. Spoon noodles into soup bowls; ladle soup over noodles.

TURKEY-NOODLE SOUP

The perfect soup for utilizing that leftover holiday turkey!

6 servings

1 cup diced carrots

1 cup chopped celery

1 cup chopped onion

1 cup sliced mushrooms

1 tablespoon minced garlic

2 tablespoons margarine

3 tablespoons flour

2¹/₂ quarts Turkey Stock (see p. 5)

1 teaspoon dried marjoram leaves

1 teaspoon dried basil leaves

¹/₂ teaspoon dried thyme leaves

4 ounces no-yolk egg noodles

4 cups diced, cooked turkey

1 cup frozen peas

Salt and pepper, to taste

¹/₄ cup finely chopped parsley

Per Serving
Calories: 376
% Calories from fat: **26**
Protein (gm): 36.7
Carbohydrate (gm): **28.5**
Fat (gm): 10.4
Saturated fat (gm): **2.7**
Cholesterol (mg): **80.1**
Sodium (mg): 182
Exchanges
Milk: 0.0
Veg.: 0.0
Fruit: 0.0
Bread: 1.0
Meat: 4.0
Fat: 0.0

1. Saute carrots, celery, onion, mushrooms, and garlic in margarine in large saucepan until tender, about 10 minutes; sprinkle with flour and cook 1 to 2 minutes longer. Stir in Turkey Stock and herbs and heat to boiling; reduce heat and simmer, covered, 15 minutes.

2. Heat soup to boiling; stir in noodles, turkey, and peas. Reduce heat and simmer, uncovered, until noodles are tender, 7 to 10 minutes. Season to taste with salt and pepper; stir in parsley.

Variation:
Turkey-Wild Rice Soup—Make soup as above, omitting noodles and peas, and adding 2 cups cooked wild rice and 1 cup diced cooked turnips, *or* parsnips, with the turkey in Step 2.

HOME-STYLE TURKEY-VEGETABLE SOUP

The recipe is designed to yield a lot of soup since it's great reheated.

9-11 servings

4 pounds turkey wings
3 cups water
1³/4 quarts reduced-sodium fat-free chicken broth
3 large onions, coarsely chopped
1 cup diced, peeled rutabaga, *or* turnip
1 cup chopped celery
1 cup chopped cabbage
¹/4 cup chopped parsley
¹/4 cup pearl barley
4 carrots, cut crosswise into ¹/8-inch slices
¹/4 cup dry elbow macaroni
¹/2 teaspoon salt
¹/2 teaspoon pepper
¹/4 teaspoon dried marjoram leaves
¹/4 teaspoon dried thyme leaves
1¹/2 cups frozen whole-kernel corn
1 can (14¹/2 ounces) whole tomatoes, undrained, coarsely chopped
1 can (16 ounces) white beans, *or* cannellini beans, rinsed, drained

Per Serving
Calories: 336
% Calories from fat: 28
Protein (g): 31
Carbohydrates (g): 29.9
Fat (g): 10.6
Saturated fat (g): 2.8
Cholesterol (mg): 65.1
Sodium (mg): 610
Exchanges
Milk: 0.0
Veg.: 2.0
Fruit: 0.0
Bread: 1.0
Meat: 4.0
Fat: 0.0

1. Combine turkey, water, broth, onions, rutabaga, celery, cabbage, parsley, and barley in large saucepan; heat to boiling. Reduce heat and simmer, covered, 1 hour. Remove turkey wings; remove meat, cut into bite-sized pieces, and return to soup; discard bones. Skim fat from soup.

2. Add carrots, macaroni, salt, pepper, and herbs; simmer, covered, until macaroni is al dente, 10 to 12 minutes. Add corn, tomatoes and liquid, and beans; simmer 5 minutes longer.

MEAL-IN-A-BOWL TURKEY SOUP WITH TARRAGON

This is a chunky, stew-like soup that makes a great one-dish meal.

4-5 servings

16 ounces boneless, skinless turkey breast, cut into ¹/₂-inch cubes

2 tablespoons flour

1¹/₂ tablespoons olive oil

1 large onion, coarsely chopped

2 large carrots, sliced

1 large rib celery, thinly sliced

1 tablespoon dried tarragon leaves

¹/₄ teaspoon pepper

2 large potatoes, peeled, cubed (¹/₄-inch)

1 quart reduced-sodium fat-free chicken broth

1¹/₂ tablespoons Dijon-style mustard

Salt, to taste

Per Serving
Calories: 229
% Calories from fat: 26
Protein (g): 21.7
Carbohydrates (g): 20.9
Fat (g): 6.6
Saturated fat (g): 1.2
Cholesterol (mg): 35.2
Sodium (mg): 381
Exchanges
Milk: 0.0
Veg.: 0.0
Fruit: 0.0
Bread: 1.5
Meat: 2.0
Fat: 0.0

1. Coat turkey cubes lightly with flour. Cook in oil in Dutch oven over medium heat until lightly browned. Add onion, carrots, celery, tarragon, and pepper; cook until onion is tender, about 5 minutes.

2. Add remaining ingredients, except salt, and heat to boiling. Reduce heat and simmer, covered, 25 to 30 minutes. Season to taste with salt.

DINNER-IN-A-BOWL SOUP

This soup is made easy with use of packaged and frozen ingredients.

6 servings (about 2 cups each)

12-16 ounces reduced-sodium smoked
      sausage, cut into ¹/₂-inch slices
  2 ribs celery, sliced
  3 carrots, sliced
  1 small green bell pepper, chopped
1¹/₂ quarts water
  1 package (1.5 ounces) low-sodium
      onion soup mix
  1 can (28 ounces) reduced-sodium
      tomatoes, undrained, chopped
8-12 ounces frozen hash brown potatoes
  1 package (10 ounces) frozen sliced okra
1-2 tablespoons sugar
  1 teaspoon dried oregano leaves
¹/₂ teaspoon dried thyme leaves
      Salt and pepper, to taste
      Hot pepper sauce, to taste

Per Serving
Calories: 282
% Calories from fat: **9**
Protein (gm): 15.2
Carbohydrate (gm): 53.4
Fat (gm): 2.9
Saturated fat (gm): 0.8
Cholesterol (mg): 26.5
Sodium (mg): 617
Exchanges
Milk: 0.0
Veg.: 2.0
Fruit: 0.0
Bread: 2.5
Meat: 1.0
Fat: 0.0

1. Combine sausage, celery, carrots, bell pepper, water, and on-ion soup mix in large saucepan; heat to boiling. Reduce heat and simmer, covered, 10 minutes. Add remaining ingredients, except salt, pepper, and hot pepper sauce. Heat to boiling; reduce heat and simmer, covered, until vegetables are tender, about 20 min-utes. Season to taste with salt, pepper, and hot pepper sauce.

PAY DAY SOUP

My Italian neighbor created this soup about 20 years ago when we entered a contest to see who could produce the least expensive meal to serve before payday, when no one had any money.

8 servings

2 cloves garlic, minced

2 tablespoons olive oil

2 medium onions, chopped

2 large potatoes, peeled, diced

2 cups arborio rice

2 cups dried garbanzo beans

1 quart reduced-sodium fat-free chicken broth

1 quart water

2 tablespoons chopped parsley

2 tablespoons grated Parmesan cheese

Salt and pepper, to taste

Per Serving
Calories: 359
% Calories from fat: 21
Protein (g): 9.5
Carbohydrates (g): 61
Fat (g): 8.5
Saturated fat (g): 2
Cholesterol (mg): 4.3
Sodium (mg): 206
Exchanges
Milk: 0.0
Veg.: 3.0
Fruit: 0.0
Bread: 3.0
Meat: 0.0
Fat: 1.5

1. Saute garlic in oil in large saucepan until golden brown. Add remaining ingredients, except Parmesan cheese, salt, and pepper, and heat to boiling. Reduce heat and simmer, covered, 1 hour, stirring occasionally. Just before serving, stir in the grated cheese; season to taste with salt and pepper.

SLOW-COOKER HAMBURGER AND VEGETABLE SOUP

This sweet-sour favorite simmers all day in a slow cooker.

5-6 servings

12	ounces ground beef round
1	large onion, finely chopped
2	large garlic cloves, minced
1	can (15 ounces) reduced-sodium tomato sauce
2	ribs celery, diced
1	medium potato, diced
1	large carrot, thinly sliced
2	tablespoons pearl barley
1¹/₄	quarts very hot water
2	beef bouillon cubes
1	cup frozen whole-kernel corn
1	cup frozen baby lima beans
2	tablespoons packed light brown sugar
2	tablespoons apple cider vinegar
³/₄	teaspoon dry mustard
³/₄	teaspoon dried thyme leaves
1	large bay leaf
¹/₄	teaspoon pepper
	Salt to taste

Per Serving
Calories: 217
% Calories from fat: **10**
Protein (g): 16.1
Carbohydrates (g): **34.6**
Fat (g): 2.5
Saturated fat (g): 0.7
Cholesterol (mg): **27.4**
Sodium (mg): 383
Exchanges
Milk: 0.0
Veg.: 0.0
Fruit: 0.0
Bread: 2.5
Meat: 1.0
Fat: 0.0

1. Cook beef, onion, and garlic in large saucepan over medium heat until browned; drain. Add remaining ingredients, except salt, and heat to boiling; transfer to slow cooker. Cover and cook on Low 7 to 9 hours or until barley has thickened the soup and vegetables are tender. Skim fat from soup. Discard bay leaf; season to taste with salt.

EASY BARBECUED BEEF AND VEGETABLE SOUP

A cold weather recipe to remind you of lazy backyard barbecues.

6-7 servings

16 ounces beef round, fat trimmed, cut into 1/2-inch cubes

1 tablespoon vegetable oil

3 large onions, coarsely chopped

3 cups Beef Stock (see p. 6)

1/2 cup water

1 cup diced, peeled rutabaga, *or* turnip

1 cup coarsely chopped celery

1 tablespoon chili powder

3/4 teaspoon dried thyme leaves

3/4 teaspoon dry mustard

3/4 teaspoon ground allspice

1/4 teaspoon pepper

4 cups cubed, peeled potatoes (1/2-inch)

2 cups sliced carrots

1 cup fresh, *or* frozen, cut green beans

1 can (15 ounces) tomato sauce

2 1/2 tablespoons packed light brown sugar

1 tablespoon cider vinegar

Salt to taste

Per Serving
Calories: 307
% Calories from fat: **15**
Protein (g): **17.7**
Carbohydrates (g): **50**
Fat (g): **5.3**
Saturated fat (g): **1.2**
Cholesterol (mg): **33.1**
Sodium (mg): **639**
Exchanges
Milk: 0.0
Veg.: 2.0
Fruit: 0.0
Bread: 2.5
Meat: 1.0
Fat: 0.5

1. Saute beef in oil in large saucepan over medium-high heat until lightly browned, 4 to 5 minutes. Add onions and saute until tender. Add Beef Stock, water, rutabaga, celery, chili powder, thyme, mustard, allspice, and pepper; heat to boiling. Reduce heat and simmer, covered, 20 minutes. Add potatoes, carrots, and green beans; simmer until beef is tender, about 30 minutes.

2. Stir tomato sauce, brown sugar, and vinegar into soup and simmer 15 minutes. Season to taste with salt.

BEEF AND BARLEY SOUP

After the bones have flavored the soup and before most of the vegetables are added, we recommend refrigerating the soup so that solidified fat can be removed.

8-9 servings

4 pounds beef soup bones
2 1/2 quarts water
2 ribs celery, including leaves, thinly sliced
2 medium carrots, thinly sliced
1 large Spanish onion, finely chopped
16 ounces beef round, fat trimmed, cut into 3/4-inch cubes
1/2 cup pearl barley
3 bay leaves
2 garlic cloves, minced
4 beef bouillon cubes
1 can (15 ounces) reduced-sodium tomato sauce
1/2 cup finely chopped parsley
3 medium potatoes, peeled, cubed (3/4-inch)
2 cups green beans
2 cups thinly sliced cabbage
2 teaspoons dried thyme leaves
2 teaspoons sugar
3/4 teaspoons dried marjoram leaves
3/4 teaspoons dried basil leaves
1/2 teaspoon chili powder
1/4 teaspoon celery seeds, crushed
1/4 teaspoon pepper
Salt, to taste

Per Serving
Calories: 190
% Calories from fat: 11
Protein (g): 13.6
Carbohydrates (g): 30.3
Fat (g): 2.4
Saturated fat (g): 0.7
Cholesterol (mg): 24.3
Sodium (mg): 472
Exchanges
Milk: 0.0
Veg.: 2.0
Fruit: 0.0
Bread: 1.5
Meat: 1.0
Fat: 0.0

1. Combine beef bones, water, celery, carrots, onion, beef, barley, bay leaves, garlic, and bouillon cubes in stock pot; heat to boiling. Reduce heat and simmer, covered, 1 1/2 hours. Discard bones and bay leaves. Skim fat from soup.

2. Add remaining ingredients; heat to boiling. Reduce heat and simmer, covered, 30 minutes; season to taste with salt.

BEEF, BARLEY, AND VEGETABLE SOUP

A tasty soup that is even better if made a day or so in advance. Leftover soup will thicken, so thin with beef broth or water.

8 servings (about 1 cup each)

Vegetable cooking spray
1 pound lean beef stew meat, fat trimmed
1 cup chopped onion
2/3 cup sliced celery
2/3 cup chopped carrots
1 clove garlic, minced
1 tablespoon flour
1 quart water
1 can (14¹/₂ ounces) reduced-sodium beef broth
¹/₂ teaspoon dried marjoram leaves
¹/₂ teaspoon dried thyme leaves
1 bay leaf
1 can (14¹/₂ ounces) diced tomatoes, undrained
1 cup cut green beans (1-inch)
1 cup cubed parsnips, *or* potatoes
¹/₂ cup frozen peas
¹/₂ cup quick-cooking barley
Salt and pepper, to taste

Per Serving
Calories: 187
% Calories from fat: 16
Protein (g): 18.8
Carbohydrates (g): 21.1
Fat (g): 3.3
Saturated fat (g): 1.1
Cholesterol (mg): 35.4
Sodium (mg): 153
Exchanges
Milk: 0.0
Veg.: 2.0
Fruit: 0.0
Bread: 0.5
Meat: 2.0
Fat: 0.0

1. Spray large Dutch oven with cooking spray; heat over medium heat until hot. Cook beef over medium heat until browned, 8 to 10 minutes. Add onion, celery, carrots, and garlic; cook 5 minutes more. Stir in flour; cook 1 minute longer.

2. Add water, beef broth, and herbs to Dutch oven; heat to boiling. Reduce heat and simmer, covered, until beef is very tender, 1 to 1¹/₂ hours.

3. Add tomatoes and liquid, green beans, and parsnips; simmer, covered, until vegetables are tender, about 10 minutes. Add peas and barley and heat to boiling; reduce heat and simmer, covered, until barley is tender, about 10 minutes. Discard bay leaf; season to taste with salt and pepper.

BEEF WITH RED WINE SOUP

This soup is reminiscent of classic Beef Burgundy—but with much less fuss.

6 servings

Per Serving
Calories: 336
% Calories from fat: 17
Protein (g): 28.1
Carbohydrates (g): 32.5
Fat (g): 6.2
Saturated fat (g): 1.8
Cholesterol (mg): 51.8
Sodium (mg): 280
Exchanges
Milk: 0.0
Veg.: 1.0
Fruit: 0.0
Bread: 1.5
Meat: 4.0
Fat: 0.0

- 16 ounces lean stew beef, fat trimmed, cut into 3/4-inch pieces
- 1 tablespoon flour
- 1 large onion, chopped
- 2 garlic cloves, minced
- 6 ounces mushrooms, sliced
- 2 ounces Canadian bacon, fat trimmed, diced
- 2 teaspoons olive oil
- 1 quart Beef Stock (see p. 6)
- 1 1/2 cups dry red wine
- 1 can (8 ounces) reduced-sodium tomato sauce
- 2 medium carrots, sliced
- 2 large ribs celery, sliced
- 2 tablespoons pearl barley
- 1 1/2 teaspoon dried thyme leaves
- 2 large bay leaves
- 4 cups cubed red potatoes (1/2-inch)
  Salt and pepper, to taste

1. Coat beef cubes lightly with flour. Cook beef, onion, garlic, mushrooms, and bacon in oil in Dutch oven until beef is browned and onion is tender, 8 to 10 minutes; drain fat.

2. Add remaining ingredients, except potatoes, salt, and pepper, and heat to boiling. Reduce heat and simmer, covered, until beef and barley are tender, 50 to 60 minutes, adding potatoes during last 15 minutes. Discard bay leaves; season to taste with salt and pepper.

SOUTHERN-STYLE SOUP WITH GREENS

A country soup—savory, substantial, and good.

4-5 servings

2 medium onions, coarsely chopped
2 teaspoons canola oil
1 quart reduced-sodium chicken broth
2¹/₂ cups water
2 small ham hocks
10 ounces collard greens, washed, torn into pieces
4 medium carrots, cut into ¹/₄-inch slices
1 large bay leaf
¹/₄ teaspoon dried thyme leaves
¹/₄ teaspoon pepper
4¹/₂ cups cubed thin-skinned potatoes
¹/₂ cup diced very lean cooked ham
Salt, to taste

Per Serving
Calories: 313
% Calories from fat: 15
Protein (g): 11.6
Carbohydrates (g): 56.5
Fat (g): 5.6
Saturated fat (g): 1.3
Cholesterol (mg): 19.8
Sodium (mg): 651
Exchanges
Milk: 0.0
Veg.: 2.0
Fruit: 0.0
Bread: 3.0
Meat: 1.0
Fat: 0.0

1. Saute onions in oil in large saucepan until soft, about 5 minutes. Add broth, water, and ham hocks and heat to boiling. Add collards, carrots, bay leaf, thyme, and pepper; simmer, covered, 10 minutes. Add potatoes and ham and simmer, covered, 30 minutes. Discard bay leaf and ham hocks; skim fat from soup. Season to taste with salt.

SAUSAGE AND SUCCOTASH SOUP

Try this soup with hominy in place of the lima beans for something a little bit different.

4 servings

  1   cup sliced celery
$^2/_3$ cup chopped onion
$^1/_2$ cup chopped red bell pepper
  1   tablespoon margarine
$^1/_4$ cup all-purpose flour
  2   cups fat-free milk
  2   cups reduced-sodium fat-free chicken broth
12   ounces reduced-sodium reduced-fat smoked sausage, sliced, browned, drained
  1   can (15 ounces) reduced-sodium creamed corn
  1   package (10 ounces) frozen baby lima beans
    Hot pepper sauce, to taste
    Salt and pepper, to taste
$^1/_2$-1   cup (2-4 ounces) shredded Cheddar cheese

Per Serving
Calories: 407
% Calories from fat: 25
Protein (gm): 32.4
Carbohydrate (gm): 45.4
Fat (gm): 11.6
Saturated fat (gm): 4.9
Cholesterol (mg): 56.8
Sodium (mg): 867
Exchanges
Milk: 0.0
Veg.: 3.0
Fruit: 0.0
Bread: 2.0
Meat: 3.0
Fat: 0.5

1. Saute celery, onion, and bell pepper in margarine in large saucepan until tender, about 10 minutes; sprinkle with flour and cook 1 to 2 minutes longer. Stir in milk and chicken broth; heat to boiling. Boil, stirring, until thickened.

2. Stir in sausage, creamed corn, and lima beans; heat to boiling. Reduce heat and simmer, covered, until beans are tender, about 10 minutes. Season to taste with hot pepper sauce, salt, and pepper. Stir in cheese until melted.

CHEESY MEXICAN CORN SOUP

Monterey Jack cheese gives this chicken-based soup a rich flavor; use pepper-Jack cheese for a spicier soup.

8 servings

16 ounces boneless, skinless chicken breasts, cubed (¹/₂-inch)

1¹/₂ cups chopped onion

1 cup chopped red, *or* green, bell pepper

1 small jalapeño chili, chopped

1 clove garlic, chopped

1 teaspoon ground cumin

1 tablespoon vegetable oil

1 tablespoon flour

1 quart Rich Chicken Stock (see p. 4)

2 cups frozen whole-kernel corn

Salt and pepper, to taste

1-1¹/₂ cups (4-6 ounces) shredded reduced-fat Monterey Jack cheese

Per Serving
Calories: 194
% Calories from fat: 30
Protein (gm): 21.4
Carbohydrate (gm): 12.3
Fat (gm): 6.4
Saturated fat (gm): 2.6
Cholesterol (mg): 45.1
Sodium (mg): 163
Exchanges
Milk: 0.0
Veg.: 0.0
Fruit: 0.0
Bread: 1.0
Meat: 2.0
Fat: 0.0

1. Saute chicken, onion, bell pepper, jalapeño, garlic, and cumin in oil in large saucepan until lightly browned, about 10 minutes; sprinkle with flour and cook 1 to 2 minutes longer.

2. Stir in Rich Chicken Broth and corn. Heat to boiling; reduce heat and simmer, covered, until chicken is done and vegetables are tender, about 15 minutes. Season to taste with salt and pepper. Add cheese, stirring until melted.

Variation:
El Paso Pork and Hominy Soup—Make recipe as above, substituting lean pork for the chicken, rinsed, drained, canned hominy for the corn, and 1 poblano chili for the bell pepper. Omit Monterey Jack cheese; sprinkle each serving of soup with 1 tablespoon crumbled Mexican white cheese or feta cheese.

SOUTH-OF-THE-BORDER POTATO, BEAN, AND CHEESE SOUP

Salsa and other spicy ingredients intensify the flavor of reduced-fat Cheddar.

6-7 servings

1	cup chopped onion
1	garlic clove, minced
2	teaspoons olive oil
1	quart reduced-sodium fat-free chicken broth
1½	cups 1% reduced-fat milk
5	cups cubed, peeled boiling potatoes (½-inch)
¼	teaspoon pepper
1	teaspoon chili powder
1¼	cups (5 ounces) shredded reduced-fat Cheddar cheese
4	cups cooked kidney beans, *or* 2 cans (16 ounces each) kidney beans, drained
1½	cups reduced-sodium mild salsa

Per Serving
Calories: 394
% Calories from fat: 15
Protein (g): 21
Carbohydrates (g): 64
Fat (g): 6.8
Saturated fat (g): 3.4
Cholesterol (mg): 23
Sodium (mg): 793
Exchanges
Milk: 0.0
Veg.: 1.0
Fruit: 0.0
Bread: 3.5
Meat: 2.0
Fat: 0.5

1. Saute onion and garlic in oil in large saucepan until onion is soft. Add broth, milk, potatoes, and pepper; heat to boiling. Reduce heat and simmer, covered, until potatoes are tender, about 15 minutes, stirring occasionally.

2. Process soup in blender or food processor until smooth. Return to saucepan. Add chili powder and cheese, stirring until cheese is melted. Add beans and salsa; simmer 3 to 4 minutes.

POTATO-KALE SOUP

Fresh kale adds a subtle and pleasing flavor to this creamy soup, which is based on a traditional Irish recipe.

5-6 servings

2 medium onions, finely chopped
1 large garlic clove, minced
2 teaspoons margarine
1 quart Beef Stock (see p. 6)
4¹/₂ cups cubed, peeled potatoes (³/₄-inch)
¹/₂ teaspoon dried thyme leaves
¹/₄ teaspoon dry mustard
¹/₈ teaspoon finely crushed celery seeds
2 cups whole milk
6 cups coarsely chopped kale leaves, midribs removed
¹/₄ teaspoon pepper
Salt, to taste

Per Serving
Calories: 267
% Calories from fat: 15
Protein (g): 10.9
Carbohydrates (g): 47.2
Fat (g): 4.6
Saturated fat (g): 2
Cholesterol (mg): 11
Sodium (mg): 130
Exchanges
Milk: 0.0
Veg.: 2.0
Fruit: 0.0
Bread: 2.0
Meat: 1.0
Fat: 0.5

1. Saute onions, and garlic in margarine in large saucepan until onion is tender, about 5 minutes. Add Beef Stock, potatoes, thyme, dry mustard, and celery seeds; heat to boiling. Reduce heat and simmer, covered, until potatoes are very tender, about 15 minutes.

2. Process half the soup in blender or food processor until smooth. Return to pan; add milk, kale, and pepper; heat to boiling. Reduce heat and simmer, covered, until kale is just tender, about 5 minutes. Season to taste with salt

ONION AND LEEK SOUP WITH PASTA

An Italian-style soup, which combines onions, leeks, and pasta. Soup pasta, small shells, or bow ties can be alternate pasta choices.

6 servings (about 1¼ cups each)

Vegetable cooking spray
4 cups sliced onions
2 cups sliced leeks, white parts only
6 cloves garlic, minced
1 teaspoon sugar
7 cups reduced-sodium fat-free chicken broth
5 ounces uncooked small pasta rings
Salt and white pepper, to taste
6 teaspoons grated fat-free Parmesan cheese

Per Serving
Calories: 211
% Calories from fat: 3
Protein (g): 12.9
Carbohydrates (g): 37.1
Fat (g): 0.8
Saturated fat (g): 0.1
Cholesterol (mg): 0
Sodium (mg): 234
Exchanges
Milk: 0.0
Veg.: 2.0
Fruit: 0.0
Bread: 2.0
Meat: 0.0
Fat: 0.0

1. Spray large saucepan with cooking spray; heat over medium heat until hot. Add onions, leeks, and garlic and cook, covered, over medium heat until onions are wilted, 5 to 8 minutes. Stir in sugar; cook, uncovered, over medium-low heat until onion mixture is very soft and browned, 15 to 20 minutes.

2. Add broth to saucepan and heat to boiling; add pasta, reduce heat, and simmer, uncovered, until pasta is al dente, 6 to 8 minutes. Season to taste with salt and white pepper. Pour soup into bowls; sprinkle 1 teaspoon Parmesan cheese over each.

KALE AND RAVIOLI SOUP

Make this soup 2 to 3 days in advance, enhancing flavors. Add pasta to the soup when reheating for serving so that the pasta is fresh and perfectly cooked.

6 servings (about 1 cup each)

Vegetable cooking spray
1 cup sliced carrots
1 cup chopped plum tomates
1/4 cup chopped onion
4 cups thinly sliced celery
2 cloves garlic, minced
1 teaspoon dried basil leaves
1/2 teaspoon dried rosemary leaves
2 cans (15 ounces each) reduced-sodium chicken broth
1 1/2 cups water
1 package (9 ounces) fresh low-fat, herb ravioli
3 cups torn kale
2-3 teaspoons lemon juice
1/8 teaspoon pepper

Per Serving
Calories: 171
% Calories from fat: 15
Protein (g): 11.1
Carbohydrates (g): 25
Fat (g): 2.8
Saturated fat (g): 1.5
Cholesterol (mg): 25.8
Sodium (mg): 285
Exchanges
Milk: 0.0
Veg.: 2.0
Fruit: 0.0
Bread: 1.0
Meat: 1.0
Fat: 0.0

1. Spray bottom of large saucepan with cooking spray; heat over medium heat until hot. Saute carrots, tomatoes, onion, celery, garlic, basil, and rosemary until onions are tender, about 5 minutes.

2. Add chicken broth and water to saucepan; heat to boiling. Reduce heat and simmer, covered, 10 minutes.

3. Heat broth mixture to boiling; stir in ravioli and kale. Reduce heat and simmer, uncovered, until ravioli are al dente, about 5 minutes. Stir in lemon juice and pepper.

BORSCHT

For convenience, Step 1 of the recipe can be completed 1 to 2 days in advance; cool strained broth and beef and refrigerate, covered.

6 servings

4 pounds beef shank
1 large marrow bone
2 quarts water
1 can (16 ounces) diced tomatoes, undrained
1 medium onion, peeled, quartered
1 rib celery, chopped
3 parsley sprigs
10 peppercorns
2 bay leaves
3 cups coarsely shredded cabbage
1¹/₂ cups sliced carrot
1 cup chopped onion
2 tablespoons fresh, *or* 3 teaspoons dried, dill weed
¹/₃ cup cider vinegar
1 can (16 ounces) shredded beets, undrained
Salt and pepper, to taste
Sour cream, as garnish
Snipped fresh dill weed, as garnish

Per Serving
Calories: 333
% Calories from fat: 25
Protein (gm): 48.6
Carbohydrate (gm): 12.6
Fat (gm): 9.1
Saturated fat (gm): 3.2
Cholesterol (mg): 108.5
Sodium (mg): 278
Exchanges
Milk: 0.0
Veg.: 2.0
Fruit: 0.0
Bread: 0.0
Meat: 5.0
Fat: 0.0

1. Heat beef shank, marrow bone, and water to boiling in Dutch oven; reduce heat and simmer, covered, 1 hour. Add tomatoes and liquid, onion, celery, parsley, peppercorns, and bay leaves; simmer, covered, 2 hours. Strain soup and reserve broth. Discard marrow bone and vegetables. Remove beef from shanks and return with broth to Dutch oven. Discard shank bones.

2. Add remaining ingredients, except salt, pepper, sour cream, and dill weed; heat to boiling. Reduce heat and simmer, covered, 30 minutes or until beef and vegetables are tender. Season to taste with salt and pepper. Cool and refrigerate overnight; skim fat from top of soup.

3. Serve in bowls, garnished with dollops of sour cream and sprinkled with fresh dill.

RUSSIAN BORSCHT

This hearty Russian soup is traditionally made with beef shanks or beef brisket; our version uses lean stew meat, which cooks more quickly.

12 servings

3 cans (14½ ounces each) reduced-sodium fat-free beef broth

1 pound lean beef stew meat, fat trimmed, cubed (½-inch)

2 bay leaves

1 teaspoon dried thyme leaves

4 cups thinly sliced cabbage

2 cups shredded beets

2 cups shredded carrots

1 cup chopped onion

1 cup shredded turnip

1 can (14½ ounces) diced tomatoes with roasted garlic, undrained

1 tablespoon sugar

3-4 tablespoons red wine vinegar

Salt and pepper, to taste

Dill Sour Cream (recipe follows)

Per Serving
Calories: 137
% Calories from fat: 21
Protein (gm): 14.4
Carbohydrate (gm): 12.8
Fat (gm): 3.2
Saturated fat (gm): 1.7
Cholesterol (mg): 28.7
Sodium (mg): 289
Exchanges
Milk: 0.0
Veg.: 3.0
Fruit: 0.0
Bread: 0.0
Meat: 1.0
Fat: 0.0

1. Combine broth, stew meat, bay leaves, and thyme in large saucepan and heat to boiling; reduce heat and simmer, covered, until meat is tender, about 1 hour.

2. Stir in vegetables, tomatoes and liquid, and sugar and heat to boiling; reduce heat and simmer, covered, until vegetables are tender, about 20 minutes. Season to taste with vinegar, salt, and pepper; discard bay leaves. Serve in bowls; drizzle with Dill Sour Cream.

Dill Sour Cream

makes about ³/₄ cup

> ³/₄ cup reduced-fat sour cream
> 1 tablespoon dried dill weed
> 2-3 tablespoons fat-free milk

1. Mix all ingredients, using enough milk to make a thick, pourable consistency.

Variation:
Ukrainian Borscht—Make soup as in Step 1 above, substituting lean cubed pork for the beef. Add 1 can Great Northern beans, rinsed, drained, and 8 ounces smoked turkey sausage, sliced, browned, and drained, with vegetables in Step 2. Complete soup as above.

EASTERN EUROPEAN BORSCHT WITH MEAT

Be sure to start the soup at least one day ahead of serving time, as the beets need to stand overnight.

8 servings

> 1¹/₂ pounds beets, boiled, peeled, grated (about 3¹/₂ cups), divided
> 2 tablespoons red wine vinegar
> 1 teaspoon sugar
> 1 pound lean beef stew meat
> 2 quarts water
> 2 teaspoons dried marjoram leaves
> 2 teaspoons dill seeds
> 4 cups shredded cabbage
> 2 cups shredded, peeled potatoes
> 1 cup shredded carrots
> 1 cup sliced onion
> 2 pounds reduced-sodium, reduced-fat smoked sausage, cut into 12 pieces
> ¹/₄ cup chopped parsley
>   Salt and pepper, to taste
> 1 cup fat-free sour cream
> ¹/₄ cup chopped fresh dill weed

Per Serving
Calories: 380
% Calories from fat: 18
Protein (gm): 37.6
Carbohydrate (gm): 41.5
Fat (gm): 7.7
Saturated fat (gm): 2.6
Cholesterol (mg): 88.4
Sodium (mg): 851
Exchanges
Milk: 0.0
Veg.: 3.0
Fruit: 0.0
Bread: 2.0
Meat: 3.0
Fat: 0.0

1. Combine $1/2$ cup beets, vinegar, and sugar in small bowl; refrigerate, covered, overnight. Reserve and refrigerate remaining beets.

2. Place beef, water, marjoram, and dill seeds in large saucepan; heat to boiling. Reduce heat and simmer, covered, until beef is tender, about $1^1/2$ hours.

3. Stir in reserved beets, cabbage, potatoes, carrots, onion, smoked sausage, and parsley; simmer, covered, 30 minutes. Stir in remaining beets; simmer 5 minutes. Season to taste with salt and pepper. Serve in bowls with generous dollops of sour cream; sprinkle with dill weed.

HEARTY CABBAGE AND VEGETABLE SOUP

This soup is a delicious way to use leftovers in an unsuspecting manner!

8 servings (about $1^1/2$ cups each)

1 quart Fragrant Beef Stock (see p. 6)
2 cups reduced-sodium tomato juice
3 cups shredded green, *or* red, cabbage
1 cup thinly sliced onion
1 cup thinly sliced carrots
1 cup thinly sliced mushrooms
1 cup cubed, unpeeled potatoes ($1/2$-inch)
4 cups cubed, cooked lean beef
2 tablespoons raisins
1 tablespoon sugar
1 teaspoon caraway seeds
1 teaspoon paprika
2-3 teaspoons vinegar
     Salt and pepper, to taste
     Dilled Sour Cream (recipe follows)

Per Serving
Calories: 214
% Calories from fat: 28
Protein (gm): 20.2
Carbohydrate (gm): 18.7
Fat (gm): 6.9
Saturated fat (gm): 3
Cholesterol (mg): 51.1
Sodium (mg): 83
Exchanges
Milk: 0.0
Veg.: 2.0
Fruit: 0.0
Bread: 0.5
Meat: 2.0
Fat: 0.0

1. Combine all ingredients, except salt, pepper, and Dilled Sour Cream, in large saucepan. Heat to boiling; reduce heat and simmer, covered, until vegetables are tender, about 20 minutes. Season to taste with salt and pepper. Ladle into bowls; top with dollops of Dilled Sour Cream.

Dilled Sour Cream

makes about ¹/₂ cup

- ¹/₂ cup reduced-fat sour cream
- ¹/₂ teaspoon dried dill weed
- 1-2 teaspoons lemon juice

1. Mix all ingredients.

Variation:

Vegetarian Cabbage and Vegetable Soup—Make recipe as above, substituting Vegetable Stock (see p. 11) for the Beef Stock; omit beef. Add 1 can (15 ounces each) rinsed and drained navy and kidney beans. Serve with Garlic Croutons (see p. 785).

CORNED BEEF AND CABBAGE SOUP

This unusual soup duplicates the zesty taste of a New England boiled dinner.

7 servings

- 1 large onion, chopped
- 2 large garlic cloves, minced
- ¹/₂ tablespoon olive oil
- 1³/₄ quarts reduced-sodium fat-free chicken broth
- 8 ounces deli corned beef, fat trimmed, cut into small pieces
- 4 cups thinly sliced cabbage
- 14 baby carrots, halved
- 2 large bay leaves
- 1 tablespoon apple cider vinegar
- 2 teaspoons Dijon-style mustard
- 2 teaspoons caraway seeds
- ¹/₈ teaspoon pepper
- 4 cups cubed red potatoes (¹/₂-inch)
  Salt, to taste

Per Serving
Calories: 220
% Calories from fat: 8
Protein (g): 15.4
Carbohydrates (g): 37.1
Fat (g): 2
Saturated fat (g): 0.4
Cholesterol (mg): 31.7
Sodium (mg): 743
Exchanges
Milk: 0.0
Veg.: 1.0
Fruit: 0.0
Bread: 2.0
Meat: 1.0
Fat: 0.0

1. Saute onion and garlic in oil in large saucepan until onion is tender, about 5 minutes. Add remaining ingredients, except potatoes and salt; heat to boiling. Reduce heat and simmer, covered, 30 minutes. Add potatoes and simmer, covered, until potatoes are tender, about 15 minutes. Discard bay leaves; season to taste with salt.

BAKED VEGETABLE SOUP WITH CABBAGE ROLLS

Stuffed cabbage leaves are baked in this vegetable soup to make a hearty dinner treat!

4 servings

1¼ quarts Chicken Stock (see p. 2)
4 ribs celery, sliced
1 large potato, peeled, cubed
1 carrot, sliced
1 onion, chopped
   Salt and pepper, to taste
   Cabbage Rolls (recipe follows)
1 large tomato, peeled, seeded, chopped
1 cup frozen whole-kernel corn
¼-½ cup (2 ounces) shredded Gruyère, *or* Swiss, cheese

Per Serving
Calories: 373
% Calories from fat: 22
Protein (gm): 35.4
Carbohydrate (gm): 37.3
Fat (gm): 9.6
Saturated fat (gm): 3.4
Cholesterol (mg): 200.2
Sodium (mg): 765
Exchanges
Milk: 0.0
Veg: 2.0
Fruit: 0.0
Bread: 2.0
Meat: 3.0
Fat: 0.0

1. Combine Chicken Stock, celery, potato, carrot, and onion in large saucepan; heat to boiling. Reduce heat and simmer, covered, until vegetables are tender. Season to taste with salt and pepper.

2. Place Cabbage Rolls, seam sides down, in 2½-quart casserole; add soup, tomato, and corn. Bake, covered, at 350 degrees for 30 minutes.

3. To serve, arrange cabbage rolls in bottoms of ovenproof bowls; ladle soup over and sprinkle with cheese. Broil, 4 inches from heat source, until cheese is golden, about 3 minutes.

Cabbage Rolls

makes 8

>   12 medium cabbage leaves
>   3 slices firm white bread, coarsely crumbled
>   1/4 cup water
>   12 ounces lean ground veal
>   2 eggs
>   3/4 teaspoon salt
> 3/4-1 teaspoon dried marjoram leaves
> 3/4-1 teaspoon dried thyme leaves

1. Cook cabbage leaves in boiling, salted water until limp, about 5 minutes; rinse in cold water and pat dry on paper toweling.

2. Combine bread and water in medium bowl; let stand until bread is soft, about 5 minutes. Mix in veal, egg, salt, and herbs.

3. Place cabbage leaves, vein sides down, on cutting board. Place about 2 tablespoons veal mixture on stem end of each leaf; fold end over veal mixture, fold sides in and roll to form packets. Secure with toothpicks.

SLOW-COOKER GOULASH SOUP

This soup is delicious with Dill Sour Cream and Hearty Vegetable-Rye Bread (see pp. 48, 796).

6-8 servings

>   1 large onion, finely chopped
>   1 large carrot, thinly sliced
>   1 large rib celery, diced
>   2 large garlic cloves, minced
>   2 cups diced, peeled potatoes
>   1 cup cut green beans (3/4-inch)
>   2 tablespoons pearl barley
>   16 ounces beef round, fat trimmed, cut
>   into 3/4-inch cubes
>   1 1/4 quarts hot water
>   4 beef bouillon cubes
>   1 bay leaf
>   2 teaspoons sugar

Per Serving
Calories: 175
% Calories from fat: 13
Protein (g): 13.9
Carbohydrates (g): 25.3
Fat (g): 2.5
Saturated fat (g): 0.7
Cholesterol (mg): 27.4
Sodium (mg): 547
Exchanges
Milk: 0.0
Veg.: 0.0
Fruit: 0.0
Bread: 1.5
Meat: 1.0
Fat: 0.0

1¹/₂ teaspoons paprika
¹/₂ teaspoon dry mustard
¹/₂ teaspoon dried thyme leaves
¹/₄ teaspoon black pepper
1 can (15 ounces) reduced-sodium
   tomato sauce
2 tablespoons tomato paste
   Salt, to taste

1. Combine all ingredients, except tomato sauce, tomato paste, and salt, in slow cooker; cover and cook on High 1 hour. Change setting to Low and cook 7 to 8 hours.

2. Combine tomato sauce and tomato paste in bowl; stir into soup. Cover and cook 1 to 1¹/₂ hours longer on Low. Season to taste with salt.

BASQUE VEGETABLE SOUP

A marvelous chickpea soup with a Spanish accent!

8 servings

1¹/₂ cups dried chickpeas, soaked overnight,
   drained
2 large onions, chopped
5 large garlic cloves, chopped
1 medium turnip, cubed (¹/₂-inch)
4 carrots, chopped
4 medium potatoes, unpeeled, cubed
   (¹/₂-inch)
2 leeks, white parts only, chopped
1 red bell pepper, julienned
1 green bell pepper, julienned
1¹/₄ pounds boneless, skinless chicken
   breast, cut into ³/₄-inch pieces
2 teaspoons dried thyme leaves
¹/₂ small cabbage head, shredded
1 cup dry red wine
   Salt and pepper, to taste
1¹/₂ cups Sourdough Croutons (¹/₂ recipe)
   (see p. 784)

Per Serving
Calories: 407
% Calories from fat: 10
Protein (gm): 29
Carbohydrate (gm): 59.1
Fat (gm): 4.6
Saturated fat (gm): 1.3
Cholesterol (mg): 46
Sodium (mg): 117
Exchanges
Milk: 0.0
Veg.: 3.0
Fruit: 0.0
Bread: 3.0
Meat: 2.0
Fat: 0.0

1. Place all ingredients, except cabbage, wine, salt, pepper, and croutons, in large saucepan and add water to cover; heat to boiling. Reduce heat and simmer, covered, until vegetables are tender, about 20 minutes. Add cabbage and wine and simmer, covered, 15 to 20 minutes. Season to taste with salt and pepper.

2. Serve soup in bowls; sprinkle each with Sourdough Croutons.

MINESTRONE PRIMAVERA

A chunky soup chock-full of vegetables often opens an Italian meal—or it can be the meal.

8 servings

1   cup chopped onion
2   small leeks, white parts only, thinly sliced
2   tablespoons olive oil
3   cups coarsely shredded cabbage
4   cups quartered, seeded, peeled tomatoes
12   small new potatoes, quartered
1¹/₄   quarts reduced-sodium fat-free chicken broth, divided
2   cups sliced carrots (¹/₂-inch)
³/₄   cup chopped fennel bulb
1   cup cooked garbanzo beans, drained
1   cup cut green beans (1-inch)
2   cups small cauliflower florets
2   cups cooked small shell pasta, *or* macaroni
2   cups fresh, *or* frozen, peas
     Salt and pepper, to taste
2   tablespoons chopped fresh, *or* 2 teaspoons dried, basil leaves
1   tablespoon chopped fresh, *or* 1 teaspoon dried, oregano leaves
¹/₂   cup finely chopped Italian parsley
     Grated Parmesan cheese, as garnish

Per Serving
Calories: 338
% Calories from fat: 17
Protein (g): 11.5
Carbohydrates (g): 61.4
Fat (g): 6.8
Saturated fat (g): 1.2
Cholesterol (mg): 1.5
Sodium (mg): 189
Exchanges
Milk: 0.0
Veg.: 4.0
Fruit: 0.0
Bread: 2.5
Meat: 0.0
Fat: 1.0

1. Saute onion and leeks in oil in large saucepan until onion is tender, about 5 minutes. Add cabbage and saute 1 minute longer. Add tomatoes, potatoes, and broth; heat to boiling. Simmer, covered, 10 minutes.

2. Add carrots, fennel, garbanzo beans, green beans, cauliflower, and pasta; simmer, covered, 10 minutes. Add peas; simmer until peas and pasta are tender, about 5 minutes. Season to taste with salt and pepper; stir in herbs. Sprinkle each serving with Parmesan cheese.

CHICKPEA AND PASTA MINESTRONE

Try this interesting minestrone variation. Substantial and wonderfully flavorful, it's a snap to make. If you don't have leftover ham, you can use Canadian bacon.

7 servings

- 1 large onion, chopped
- 2 large carrots, peeled, thinly sliced
- 2 large ribs celery, thinly sliced
- 2 cups chopped cabbage
- 2 garlic cloves, minced
- 1¹/₂ quarts reduced-sodium fat-free chicken broth
- 1 can (15 ounces) chickpeas, rinsed, drained
- 1 can (14¹/₂ ounces) reduced-sodium Italian-style tomatoes, coarsely chopped
- 1 medium pork hock
- 4-5 ounces reduced-sodium ham, diced
- 1 tablespoon Italian seasoning
- ¹/₈ teaspoon pepper
- ¹/₂ cup cooked orzo
  Salt, to taste

Per Serving
Calories: 191
% Calories from fat: 13
Protein (g): 11.5
Carbohydrates (g): 31
Fat (g): 2.9
Saturated fat (g): 0.5
Cholesterol (mg): 3.7
Sodium (mg): 684
Exchanges
Milk: 0.0
Veg.: 2.0
Fruit: 0.0
Bread: 1.5
Meat: 0.5
Fat: 0.0

1. Combine all ingredients, except orzo and salt, in large saucepan. Reduce heat and simmer, covered, 30 to 35 minutes, stirring occasionally. Add pasta to the soup, and simmer until al dente, 8 to 10 minutes. Discard pork hock; skim fat from soup. Season to taste with salt.

BEEFY MINESTRONE

Make this chunky soup the centerpiece of an Italian family-style supper. Serve it with a tossed salad and crusty bread.

8 servings

16 ounces beef round, fat trimmed, cut into ³/₄-inch pieces
   Flour for coating
1 large onion, chopped
2 garlic cloves, minced
1 teaspoon olive oil
1 can (6 ounces) tomato paste
2 quarts Beef Stock (see p. 6)
2 cups chopped green cabbage
2 medium carrots, thinly sliced
2 bay leaves
1 tablespoon Italian seasoning
¹/₄ teaspoon pepper
1 can (19 ounces) cannellini beans, rinsed, drained
2 cups coarsely diced zucchini
3 cups cooked elbow macaroni
   Salt, to taste

Per Serving
Calories: 220
% Calories from fat: **13**
Protein (g): 22.1
Carbohydrates (g): 31.2
Fat (g): 3.4
Saturated fat (g): 0.8
Cholesterol (mg): 27.4
Sodium (mg): 388
Exchanges
Milk: 0.0
Veg.: 2.0
Fruit: 0.0
Bread: 1.0
Meat: 2.0
Fat: 0.0

1. Coat beef cubes lightly with flour. Cook beef, onion, and garlic in oil in Dutch oven over medium heat until beef is browned and onion is tender, 8 to 10 minutes. Add tomato paste, Beef Stock, cabbage, carrots, and seasonings; heat to boiling. Reduce heat and simmer, covered, until beef is tender, about 40 minutes. Add beans and zucchini; simmer, covered, 20 minutes. Discard bay leaves. Add pasta and simmer 2 to 3 minutes; season to taste with salt.

MEATY MINESTRONE

Beef and Italian sausage make this easy vegetable soup extra-hearty.

8 servings

1¼ pounds lean beef stew meat, cubed (½-inch)
1 large onion, chopped
2 carrots, sliced
1 rib celery, sliced
2 cloves garlic, minced
1-2 teaspoons olive oil
1½ quarts Beef Stock (see p. 6)
2 teaspoons dried basil leaves
1 teaspoon dried oregano leaves
1 bay leaf
1 can (15 ounces) Great Northern beans, rinsed, drained
1 can (14½ ounces) reduced-sodium diced tomatoes, undrained
4 ounces Italian-style turkey sausage, cooked, drained, sliced
1 package (10 ounces) frozen Italian green beans
2 ounces uncooked rotini, *or* shell pasta
Salt and pepper, to taste
Shredded Parmesan cheese, as garnish

Per Serving
Calories: 235
% Calories from fat: 30
Protein (gm): 24
Carbohydrate (gm): 19
Fat (gm): 8.5
Saturated fat (gm): 2.6
Cholesterol (mg): 52
Sodium (mg): 280
Exchanges
Milk: 0.0
Veg.: 1.0
Fruit: 0.0
Bread: 1.0
Meat: 2.0
Fat: 0.5

1. Saute beef, onion, carrots, celery, and garlic in oil in large saucepan until lightly browned, about 15 minutes. Stir in Beef Stock and herbs; heat to boiling. Reduce heat and simmer, covered, until meat is tender, about 1 hour.

2. Stir in remaining ingredients, except salt, pepper, and Parmesan cheese. Heat to boiling; reduce heat and simmer, covered, until pasta is al dente, about 15 minutes. Discard bay leaf; season to taste with salt and pepper. Serve soup in bowls; sprinkle with Parmesan cheese.

Variation:
Vegetarian Minestrone Gratin—Make recipe as above, adding 1 can (15 ounces) rinsed, drained kidney beans and 1 large cubed zucchini; omit beef, Beef Stock, and Italian-style turkey sausage. Toast 8 slices (1/2-inch) French bread under broiler; sprinkle each with 2 tablespoons shredded reduced-fat mozzarella cheese and broil until melted, 1 to 2 minutes. Top each bowl of soup with a bread slice and sprinkle with chopped parsley.

HEARTY MINESTRONE WITH PEPPERONI

Pepperoni adds great flavor to this full-bodied soup. Serve with crusty bread and a salad for an easy, satisfying supper.

5 servings

1	large onion, chopped
1	large rib celery, coarsely diced
2	medium carrots, coarsely chopped
3/4	cup coarsely chopped red bell pepper
2	large garlic cloves, minced
1	tablespoon olive oil
1/4	cup finely diced pepperoni, *or* hard salami
1	quart reduced-sodium fat-free chicken broth
2	cups water
2 1/2	teaspoons dried basil leaves
1	teaspoon dried marjoram leaves
1/2	teaspoon dried oregano leaves
1/4	teaspoon pepper, to taste
	Pinch crushed red pepper
1/2	cup uncooked elbow macaroni
2	medium zucchini, diced
1	can (28 ounces) reduced-sodium Italian-style tomatoes, undrained
1	can (19 ounces) cannellini beans, *or* Great Northern beans, rinsed, drained
	Salt, to taste

Per Serving
Calories: 265
% Calories from fat: 20
Protein (g): 17
Carbohydrates (g): 45.1
Fat (g): 6.9
Saturated fat (g): 1.4
Cholesterol (mg): 0
Sodium (mg): 603
Exchanges
Milk: 0.0
Veg.: 3.0
Fruit: 0.0
Bread: 2.0
Meat: 0.5
Fat: 0.5

1. Saute onion, celery, carrots, bell pepper, and garlic in oil in large saucepan. Add pepperoni; cook 4 to 5 minutes or until onion is browned. Add broth, water, and herbs; heat to boiling. Reduce heat and simmer, covered, 15 minutes.

2. Heat soup to boiling; add macaroni and zucchini. Reduce heat and simmer, uncovered, until macaroni is almost al dente, 8 to 10 minutes. Stir in tomatoes and liquid and beans and simmer 5 minutes longer; season to taste with salt.

ITALIAN MEATBALL SOUP

Flavorful meatballs for this soup are made with low-fat ground turkey rather than ground beef. Substitute other pastas for the spaghetti, if you like, such as orrechiette (little ears) or conchiglie (shells).

8 servings (about 2 cups each)

1¹/₂ pounds ground turkey

2 egg whites

¹/₄ cup seasoned dry bread crumbs

4 cloves garlic, minced, divided

3 tablespoons Italian seasoning, divided
Olive oil cooking spray

4 cans (15 ounces each) reduced-sodium chicken broth

3 cups water

2 cups green beans, diagonally cut into ¹/₂-inch pieces

4 medium carrots, sliced

2 medium onions, coarsely chopped

8 ounces uncooked thin spaghetti, broken into 2- to 3-inch pieces

2 medium plum tomatoes, coarsely chopped
Salt and pepper, to taste

Per Serving
Calories: 270
% Calories from fat: 28
Protein (g): 19
Carbohydrates (g): 30.2
Fat (g): 8.7
Saturated fat (g): ?
Cholesterol (mg): 31.7
Sodium (mg): 174
Exchanges
Milk: 0.0
Veg.: 1.0
Fruit: 0.0
Bread: 1.5
Meat: 2.0
Fat: 0.5

1. Mix ground turkey, egg whites, bread crumbs, half the garlic, and 2 tablespoons Italian seasoning until well blended; shape mixture into 32 meatballs. Spray large saucepan with cooking spray; heat over medium heat until hot. Cook meatballs until browned on all sides, 5 to 7 minutes.

2. Add chicken broth, water, green beans, carrots, onions, remaining garlic, and remaining 1 tablespoon Italian seasoning to saucepan; heat to boiling. Reduce heat and simmer, covered, until vegetables are almost tender, about 8 minutes.

3. Heat soup to boiling; add pasta and tomatoes. Reduce heat and simmer, uncovered, until pasta is al dente, about 10 minutes. Season to taste with salt and pepper.

VEGETABLE SOUP WITH CHILI MEATBALLS

Lightly spiced meatballs add the perfect touch to this simple vegetable soup.

8 servings (about 1³/₄ cups each)

1 cup thinly sliced onion
³/₄ cup thinly sliced carrots
2 teaspoons olive oil
2 quarts Chicken Stock (see p. 2)
1 cup frozen Mexican-style whole-kernel corn
1 package (10 ounces) frozen chopped spinach
¹/₄ cup dry sherry, optional
   Chili Meatballs (recipe follows)
   Salt and pepper, to taste

Per Serving
Calories: 192
% Calories from fat: 28
Protein (gm): 20.6
Carbohydrate (gm): 14.8
Fat (gm): 6
Saturated fat (gm): 1.6
Cholesterol (mg): 71.2
Sodium (mg): 279
Exchanges
Milk: 0.0
Veg.: 0.0
Fruit: 0.0
Bread: 1.0
Meat: 2.0
Fat: 0.0

1. Saute onion and carrots in oil in large saucepan until tender, about 5 minutes. Stir in Chicken Stock, corn, and spinach. Heat to boiling; reduce heat and simmer, covered, 5 minutes. Stir in sherry and Chili Meatballs; season to taste with salt and pepper.

Chili Meatballs

makes 32 meatballs

1 ¹/₂ pounds ground beef round
¹/₃ cup finely chopped onion
1 teaspoon minced garlic
¹/₃ cup unseasoned dry bread crumbs
1 tablespoon chili powder
2 teaspoons ground cumin
¹/₂ teaspoon salt
1 egg

1. Combine all ingredients. Shape into 32 balls and place on jelly roll pan. Bake at 325 degrees until no longer pink in center, about 10 minutes.

MEATBALL SOUP

A great favorite in Mexico, this soup is traditionally seasoned with mint; we've offered oregano as an addition or alternative, if you like.

4 servings

Vegetable cooking spray
1/4 cup chopped onion
2 cloves garlic, minced
1 small jalapeño chili, seeds and veins discarded, minced
1 tablespoon flour
2 cups reduced-sodium tomato juice
2 cups water
2 cans (14 1/2 ounces each) reduced-sodium fat-free chicken broth
3 medium carrots, sliced
2 medium zucchini, sliced
1/2 teaspoon dried mint leaves, *and/or* 1 1/2-2 teaspoons dried oregano leaves
Meatballs (recipe follows)
Salt and pepper, to taste

Per Serving
Calories: 227
% Calories from fat: 16
Protein (g): 28
Carbohydrates (g): 20.2
Fat (g): 4.1
Saturated fat (g): 1.4
Cholesterol (mg): 54.7
Sodium (mg): 426
Exchanges
Milk: 0.0
Veg.: 3.0
Fruit: 0.0
Bread: 0.0
Meat: 3.0
Fat: 0.0

1. Spray large saucepan with cooking spray; heat over medium heat until hot. Saute onion, garlic, and jalapeño chili until tender, about 5 minutes. Stir in flour; cook over medium heat 1 to 2 minutes.

2. Add tomato juice, water, chicken broth, carrots, zucchini, and mint to saucepan; heat to boiling. Add Meatballs; reduce heat and simmer, covered, until vegetables are tender and Meatballs are cooked, 10 to 15 minutes. Season to taste with salt and pepper. Serve in bowls.

Meatballs

makes 24

> 1 pound ground beef eye of round
> 1/4 cup cooked rice
> 1/3 cup finely chopped onion
> 1 clove garlic, minced
> 1/2 teaspoon dried mint leaves
> 1/4 teaspoon dried oregano leaves
> 1/4 teaspoon ground cumin
> 1/2 teaspoon salt
> 1/4 teaspoon pepper

1. Mix all ingredients; form into 24 small meatballs. Refrigerate, covered, until ready to cook (no longer than 8 hours).

CURRY SOUP WITH MEATBALLS

This lightly thickened soup is delicately flavored with curry powder.

4 servings

> 1/2 cup chopped onion
> 2 teaspoons minced garlic
> 2 teaspoons curry powder
> 1 teaspoon margarine
> 2 tablespoons flour
> 1¼ quarts Beef Stock (see p. 6)
> Curry Meatballs (recipe follows)
> 2 ounces uncooked vermicelli, broken into 2-inch lengths
> Salt and pepper, to taste
> 1 tablespoon chopped mint
> 2 tablespoons chopped parsley

Per Serving
Calories: 216
% Calories from fat: 37
Protein (gm): 13.8
Carbohydrate (gm): 19.9
Fat (gm): 8.8
Saturated fat (gm): 3
Cholesterol (mg): 35.6
Sodium (mg): 49
Exchanges
Milk: 0.0
Veg.: 0.0
Fruit: 0.0
Bread: 1.0
Meat: 2.0
Fat: 0.5

1. Saute onion, garlic, and curry powder in margarine in large skillet until tender, about 5 minutes; sprinkle with flour and cook 1 to 2 minutes longer. Stir in Beef Stock and heat to boiling, stirring until thickened.

2. Stir in Curry Meatballs and vermicelli; simmer, uncovered, until meatballs float, about 10 minutes. Season to taste with salt and pepper. Stir in mint and parsley.

Curry Meatballs

    8 ounces lean ground beef
    $^1/_3$ cup minced onion
  1$^1/_2$ teaspoons curry powder

1. Combine all ingredients; shape into 12 $^1/_2$-inch meatballs.

LAMB AND WHITE BEAN SOUP

If you like bean soup, try this version with lamb shanks.

7-8 servings

  1$^1/_2$ cups dried Great Northern, *or* navy,
      beans, sorted, rinsed
    2 lamb shanks (about 1$^3/_4$ pounds total)
    2 quarts Beef Stock (see p. 6)
    2 large carrots, sliced
    2 large ribs celery, sliced
    1 large onion, finely chopped
    2 large garlic cloves, minced
    3 bay leaves
  1$^1/_2$ teaspoons dried thyme leaves
  1$^1/_4$ teaspoons dried marjoram leaves
   $^1/_2$ teaspoon celery seeds, crushed
   $^1/_2$ teaspoon dry mustard
   $^1/_4$ teaspoon pepper
    3 cups thinly sliced cabbage
      Salt, to taste

Per Serving
Calories: 215
% Calories from fat: 18
Protein (g): 24.7
Carbohydrates (g): 20.1
Fat (g): 4.2
Saturated fat (g): 1.4
Cholesterol (mg): 42.4
Sodium (mg): 124
Exchanges
Milk: 0.0
Veg.: 1.0
Fruit: 0.0
Bread: 1.0
Meat: 2.0
Fat: 0.0

1. Place beans in large saucepan, cover with 2 inches of water, and heat to boiling. Reduce heat and simmer, covered, 2 minutes. Remove pan from heat and let stand, covered, 1 hour. Drain.

2. Combine beans and remaining ingredients, except cabbage and salt, in large saucepan; heat to boiling. Reduce heat and simmer, covered, until beans are tender, about 1 hour, adding cabbage during last 20 minutes.

3. Skim fat from soup. Remove lamb shanks; cut meat into bite-sized pieces, and return to saucepan. Discard meat bones and bay leaves; season to taste with salt.

LAMB SOUP WITH BARLEY

This vegetable soup can also be made with lean pork or beef.

8 servings (about 1¹/₂ cups each)

1¹/₂ pounds lean lamb stew meat, fat trimmed, cubed

1 quart water

1 bay leaf

1¹/₂ cups sliced onions

1¹/₂ cups sliced carrots

1¹/₂ cups cubed turnips

1 cup sliced celery

1 tablespoon minced garlic

1 tablespoon olive oil

1¹/₂ quarts Low-Salt Chicken Stock (see p. 3)

1 cup dry white wine, *or* Low-Salt Chicken Stock

1 cup pearl barley

2 teaspoons dried oregano leaves

1 teaspoon dried rosemary leaves
Salt and pepper, to taste

Per Serving
Calories: 241
% Calories from fat: 20
Protein (gm): 16.1
Carbohydrate (gm): 27.9
Fat (gm): 5.5
Saturated fat (gm): 1.5
Cholesterol (mg): 38.9
Sodium (mg): 70
Exchanges
Milk: 0.0
Veg.: 2.0
Fruit: 0.0
Bread: 1.0
Meat: 2.0
Fat: 0.0

1. Place lamb, water, and bay leaf in large saucepan; heat to boiling. Reduce heat and simmer, covered, until lamb is tender, about 1¹/₂ hours, skimming occasionally to remove fat and foam. Remove bay leaf.

2. Saute onions, carrots, turnips, celery, and garlic in oil in large saucepan until lightly browned, about 10 minutes. Stir in lamb and liquid, Low-Salt Chicken Stock, wine, barley, oregano, and rosemary; heat to boiling. Reduce heat and simmer, covered, until barley is tender, about 45 minutes. Season to taste with salt and pepper.

LAMB, SPLIT-PEA, BEAN, AND BARLEY SOUP

If you like split-pea soup made with a ham bone, try this slightly milder variation, using lamb.

8-9 servings

2³/4 quarts water
3 pounds lamb shanks
2 cups dry green split peas, sorted, rinsed
¹/4 cup pearl barley
³/4 cup dry navy, *or* Great Northern, beans, sorted, rinsed
3 bay leaves
2-5 beef bouillon cubes
2 large onions, coarsely chopped
2 large carrots, thinly sliced
2 ribs celery, including leaves, thinly sliced
2 garlic cloves, minced
1¹/2 teaspoons dried thyme leaves
1 teaspoon dried basil leaves
¹/2 teaspoon finely crushed celery seeds
1-2 teaspoons salt, optional
¹/2 teaspoon black pepper

Per Serving
Calories: 331
% Calories from fat: 11
Protein (g): 29
Carbohydrates (g): 46
Fat (g): 4.1
Saturated fat (g): 1.3
Cholesterol (mg): 41
Sodium (mg): 253
Exchanges
Milk: 0.0
Veg.: 1.0
Fruit: 0.0
Bread: 2.5
Meat: 2.5
Fat: 0.0

1. Combine water, lamb, split peas, barley, and beans in large saucepan and heat to boiling. Add remaining ingredients, except salt and pepper. Reduce heat and simmer, covered, 2 to 2¹/2 hours or until beans are tender and soup is thickened. Discard bay leaves; skim fat from surface. Add salt, if desired, and pepper. Remove lamb shanks. Cut lean meat off shanks in bite-sized pieces and return to soup. Discard bones.

SLOW-COOKER CREOLE-STYLE LAMB SOUP

Let this luscious soup cook all day while you're away.

6-7 servings

1	large onion, finely chopped
2	large garlic cloves, minced
1	large green bell pepper, diced
1	large rib celery, sliced
1	cup diced zucchini
2	cans (15 ounces each) reduced-sodium tomato sauce
1	cup water
3	cups fat-free beef broth
16	ounces lean lamb for stew, fat trimmed, cut into 1/2-inch cubes
1/3	cup chopped parsley
1/3	cup uncooked white rice
2	teaspoons sugar
1	bay leaf
1	teaspoon dried marjoram leaves
1/2	teaspoon dried thyme leaves
1/2	teaspoon dried basil leaves
1/4	teaspoon dry mustard
1/4	teaspoon black pepper
	Dash cayenne pepper
	Salt, to taste
	Hot pepper sauce, to taste

Per Serving
Calories: 217
% Calories from fat: 10
Protein (g): 16.1
Carbohydrates (g): 34.6
Fat (g): 2.5
Saturated fat (g): 0.7
Cholesterol (mg): 27.4
Sodium (mg): 383
Exchanges
Milk: 0.0
Veg.: 0.0
Fruit: 0.0
Bread: 2.5
Meat: 1.0
Fat: 0.0

1. Combine all ingredients, except salt and hot pepper sauce, in slow cooker. Cover and cook on High for 1 hour. Change setting to Low and cook 7 to 9 hours or until meat and vegetables are tender. Skim fat from surface. Discard bay leaf; season to taste with salt. Serve with hot pepper sauce.

FOUR-BEAN SOUP WITH SAUSAGE

This hearty soup has a Mexican accent and spicy flavor, and it can be made very quickly.

8 servings (about 1½ cups each)

8 ounces reduced-sodium, reduced-fat smoked sausage, sliced

1 cup chopped onion

½ cup chopped green bell pepper

½ cup chopped celery

1 teaspoon minced garlic

1 small jalapeño chili, chopped

2 teaspoons vegetable oil

1 can (15 ounces) garbanzo beans, rinsed, drained

1 can (15 ounces) pinto beans, rinsed, drained

1 can (15 ounces) black beans, rinsed, drained

1 package (10 ounces) frozen cut green beans

1 can (14½ ounces) reduced-sodium stewed tomatoes, undrained

1 can (14½ ounces) reduced-sodium fat-free chicken broth

1 jar (8 ounces) mild salsa

1 can (6 ounces) spicy vegetable juice cocktail

2-3 teaspoons chili powder

1 teaspoon dried oregano leaves

Salt, to taste

Hot pepper sauce, to taste

Per Serving
Calories: 245
% Calories from fat: **13**
Protein (gm): 15.3
Carbohydrate (gm): **42.6**
Fat (gm): 4.1
Saturated fat (gm): **0.7**
Cholesterol (mg): **13.2**
Sodium (mg): 911
Exchanges
Milk: 0.0
Veg.: 2.0
Fruit: 0.0
Bread: 2.0
Meat: 1.0
Fat: 0.0

1. Saute sausage, onion, green pepper, celery, garlic, and jalapeño chili in oil in large saucepan until lightly browned, about 8 minutes. Add remaining ingredients, except salt and hot pepper sauce, and heat to boiling. Reduce heat and simmer, covered, 10 minutes. Season to taste with salt and hot pepper sauce.

SMOKY SEVEN-BEAN SOUP

*Beans are slowly simmered with smoked pork in this richly flavored soup.
Use any bean combination your family enjoys.*

12 servings

2 pounds smoked pork shoulder, cut into
  ³/₄-inch cubes
4 quarts Fragrant Beef Stock (see p. 6), *or*
  reduced-sodium fat-free beef broth
³/₄ cup dried red kidney beans
³/₄ cup dried navy beans
¹/₂ cup dried pinto beans
¹/₂ cup dried baby lima beans
¹/₂ cup black beans
¹/₂ cup garbanzo beans
¹/₂ cup dried lentils
¹/₂ cup chopped onion
¹/₃ cup very-low-sodium Worcestershire
  sauce
2 bay leaves
2 teaspoons dried Italian seasoning
1 cup chopped carrots
2 ribs celery, sliced
  Salt and pepper, to taste
  Hot pepper sauce, to taste

Per Serving
Calories: 397
% Calories from fat: 22
Protein (gm): 34
Carbohydrate (gm): 43.7
Fat (gm): 10
Saturated fat (gm): 3.5
Cholesterol (mg): 58.4
Sodium (mg): 146
Exchanges
Milk: 0.0
Veg.: 0.0
Fruit: 0.0
Bread: 3.0
Meat: 3.0
Fat: 0.0

1.   Combine pork, Fragrant Beef Stock, beans, onion, Worcestershire sauce, bay leaves, and Italian seasoning in Dutch oven.
Heat to boiling; reduce heat and simmer, covered, until beans
are almost tender, 1 to 1¹/₂ hours.

2.   Stir in carrots and celery; heat to boiling. Reduce heat and simmer, covered, 45 minutes or until beans and vegetables are very
tender. Season to taste with salt, pepper, and hot pepper sauce.

Variations:
Barley-Bean Soup—Make soup as above, substituting 1 cup
pearl barley for the garbanzo beans and lentils, and ³/₄ teaspoon
each dried rosemary and sage leaves for the Italian seasoning.
Add 2 cups whole-kernel corn during last 10 minutes cooking
time.

Smoky Red and Black Bean Soup—Make soup as above, using 2 cups each dried red and black beans for all the beans, and substituting 1 to 1¹/₂ pounds sliced reduced-sodium, reduced-fat smoked sausage for the pork shoulder. Reduce Italian seasoning to 1 teaspoon and add ¹/₂ teaspoon ground cumin. Stir in 1 to 2 cups cooked rice during last 10 minutes of cooking time.

YANKEE BEAN SOUP

Make this soup the old-fashioned way, with trimmings from a holiday ham, and 1 cup dried beans soaked in water overnight with the ham bone. Or do it the quick and easy way—our way! Delicious, no matter what.

6 servings (about 1¹/₂ cups each)

8-12 ounces reduced-sodium lean ham, fat trimmed, cubed (¹/₂-inch)
  1 large onion, chopped
  2 carrots, chopped
  1 rib celery, chopped
  2 cloves garlic, minced
  1 tablespoon olive oil
  1 quart Chicken Stock (see p. 2)
  2 cans (15 ounces each) navy beans, rinsed, drained
  1 can (14¹/₂ ounces) reduced-sodium diced tomatoes, undrained
  1 teaspoon dried rosemary leaves
  1 teaspoon dried oregano leaves
  1 teaspoon dried basil leaves
  Salt and pepper, to taste

Per Serving
Calories: 284
% Calories from fat: 17
Protein (gm): 20.9
Carbohydrate (gm): 39.2
Fat (gm): 5.7
Saturated fat (gm): 1.3
Cholesterol (mg): 22.4
Sodium (mg): 836
Exchanges
Milk: 0.0
Veg.: 2.0
Fruit: 0.0
Bread: 2.0
Meat: 2.0
Fat: 0.0

1. Saute ham, onion, carrots, celery, and garlic in oil in large saucepan until lightly browned, about 12 minutes. Add remaining ingredients, except salt and pepper. Heat to boiling; reduce heat and simmer, covered, until vegetables are tender, about 20 minutes. Season to taste with salt and pepper.

BEEFY BEAN SOUP

Meaty beef shanks flavor this bean soup. Double or triple the recipe, and freeze some for comfort food on cold winter nights.

8 servings

1   pound meaty beef shanks
2   quarts water
1   rib celery, cut into 2-inch pieces
1   onion, halved
1   teaspoon dried oregano leaves
1   teaspoon dried thyme leaves
1   bay leaf
2   cans (15 ounces each) kidney beans, rinsed, drained
1   can (14½ ounces) stewed tomatoes, undrained
1   cup sliced carrots
1   cup sliced onion
1   cup diced turnips
1   cup cut fresh, *or* frozen, green beans
    Salt and pepper, to taste

Per Serving
Calories: 158
% Calories from fat: 10
Protein (gm): 10.2
Carbohydrate (gm): 26.8
Fat (gm): 2
Saturated fat (gm): 0.6
Cholesterol (mg): 8.7
Sodium (mg): 510
Exchanges
Milk: 0.0
Veg.: 1.0
Fruit: 0.0
Bread: 2.0
Meat: 0.0
Fat: 0.0

1. Combine beef shanks, water, celery, halved onion, and herbs in large saucepan; heat to boiling. Reduce heat and simmer, covered, until meat is tender, about 2 hours. Strain soup and reserve broth; skim off fat. Cut meat from bones and reserve. Discard bones, celery, onion, and bay leaf. Return broth and meat to saucepan.

2. Stir in remaining ingredients, except salt and pepper; heat to boiling. Reduce heat and simmer, covered, until vegetables are tender, about 20 minutes. Season to taste with salt and pepper.

BEAN AND SPINACH SOUP PRONTO

Beans and spinach are a classic Italian combination, which we've used together in this hearty soup.

7 servings

1¹/₂ quarts chicken broth
¹/₂ cup uncooked orzo
6 ounces Canadian bacon, julienned
1 tablespoon Italian seasoning
1 garlic clove, minced
¹/₈ teaspoon pepper
1 can (15 ounces) reduced-sodium tomato sauce
1 can (19 ounces) cannellini beans, undrained
1 package (10 ounce) frozen chopped spinach, thawed
Salt, to taste

Per Serving
Calories: 211
% Calories from fat: 10
Protein (g): 18.8
Carbohydrates (g): 33.8
Fat (g): 6.7
Saturated fat (g): 1.3
Cholesterol (mg): 8.5
Sodium (mg): 511
Exchanges
Milk: 0.0
Veg.: 2.0
Fruit: 0.0
Bread: 2.0
Meat: 1.0
Fat: 0.5

1. Heat broth to boiling in large saucepan; add orzo, Canadian bacon, Italian seasoning, garlic, and pepper. Cook, uncovered, until orzo is tender, about 10 minutes. Add remaining ingredients, except salt; heat to boiling. Reduce heat and simmer, 15 minutes. Season to taste with salt.

NAVY BEAN SOUP WITH HAM

A quick-soak method is used for the beans. If you prefer soaking the beans overnight, delete Step 1 and proceed with Step 2 in the recipe.

6 servings (about 1¼ cups each)

8 ounces dried navy, *or* Great Northern, beans, washed, sorted

1½ cups cubed lean smoked ham (8 ounces), fat trimmed

⅔ cup chopped onion

⅔ cup chopped carrots

1 rib celery, thinly sliced

2 cloves garlic, minced

1 tablespoon vegetable oil

1 tablespoon flour

1 quart reduced-sodium chicken broth

1 cup water

¼ teaspoon dried thyme leaves

1 bay leaf

Salt and pepper, to taste

Per Serving
Calories: 223
% Calories from fat: 16
Protein (g): 20.1
Carbohydrates (g): 29.5
Fat (g): 4
Saturated fat (g): 0.9
Cholesterol (mg): 21.6
Sodium (mg): 639
Exchanges
Milk: 0.0
Veg.: 0.0
Fruit: 0.0
Bread: 2.0
Meat: 2.0
Fat: 0.0

1. Cover beans with 2 inches of water in large saucepan; heat to boiling and boil, uncovered, 2 minutes. Remove from heat and let stand, covered, 1 hour; drain.

2. Saute ham, onion, carrots, celery, and garlic in oil in large saucepan until vegetables are tender, 5 to 8 minutes. Stir in flour; cook over medium heat 1 minute.

3. Add beans, broth, water, and herbs to the saucepan; heat to boiling. Reduce heat and simmer, covered, until beans are tender, 1¼ to 1½ hours. Discard bay leaf; season to taste with salt and pepper.

BEAN AND BARLEY SOUP WITH KALE

Serve this nutritious soup with Tomato-Basil Focaccia (see p. 789).

8 servings (about 1¹/₂ cups each)

1¹/₂ cups chopped onions
  1 cup chopped carrots
  1 pound mushrooms, sliced
  1 teaspoon minced garlic
  2 teaspoons dried thyme leaves
 ¹/₂ teaspoon crushed red pepper
  2 teaspoons olive oil
  7 cups Fragrant Beef Stock (¹/₂ recipe) (see p. 6)
 ¹/₂ cup quick-cooking barley
  2 cans (15 ounces each) Great Northern beans, rinsed, drained
  1 pound kale, sliced
  1 tablespoon lemon juice
    Salt and pepper, to taste

Per Serving
Calories: 183
% Calories from fat: 10
Protein (gm): 11.7
Carbohydrate (gm): 35.6
Fat (gm): 2.3
Saturated fat (gm): 0.5
Cholesterol (mg): 2.6
Sodium (mg): 350
Exchanges
Milk: 0.0
Veg.: 1.0
Fruit: 0.0
Bread: 2.0
Meat: 0.0
Fat: 0.5

1. Saute onions, carrots, mushrooms, garlic, thyme, and red pepper in olive oil in large saucepan until tender, about 10 minutes. Stir in remaining ingredients, except lemon juice, salt, and pepper. Heat to boiling; reduce heat and simmer, covered, until barley is tender, about 10 minutes. Stir in lemon juice; season to taste with salt and pepper.

SLOW-COOKER WORKDAY BEAN SOUP

This easy, economical slow-cooker soup is designed to fit into a work schedule. The beans are placed in the slow cooker at night; the remaining ingredients are added in the morning. Ten or twelve hours later, when the cook returns home from work, a savory soup is waiting.

5-6 servings

1¹/4 cups dried pinto, *or* cranberry, beans, sorted, rinsed

1 cup dried Great Northern beans, sorted, rinsed

1 medium smoked pork hock

1 large onion, chopped

2 medium ribs celery, coarsely chopped

1 medium carrot, chopped

¹/2 cup finely diced red, *or* green, bell pepper

1 quart fat-free beef broth

1 cup water

1 bay leaf

3 tablespoons catsup

2 tablespoons sugar

1 tablespoon apple cider vinegar

1¹/4 teaspoons chili powder

¹/4 teaspoon dried thyme leaves

¹/4 teaspoon dry mustard

¹/4 teaspoon ground allspice

¹/4 teaspoon pepper

1 can (8 ounces) reduced-sodium tomato paste

Salt, to taste

Per Serving
Calories: 288
% Calories from fat: 4
Protein (g): 18.5
Carbohydrates (g): 53.5
Fat (g): 1.3
Saturated fat (g): 0.3
Cholesterol (mg): 1.8
Sodium (mg): 186
Exchanges
Milk: 0.0
Veg.: 1.0
Fruit: 0.0
Bread: 3.0
Meat: 1.0
Fat: 0.0

1. Cover beans with 3 inches hot water in slow cooker. Cover and cook on Low 8 to 10 hours; drain. Return beans to slow cooker.

2. Add remaining ingredients, except tomato sauce and salt, to slow cooker. Cover and cook on Low 10 to 12 hours. Discard bay leaf and pork hock; skim fat from surface. Stir in tomato sauce. Cover and cook on High until hot, about 30 minutes.

CORN AND BEAN SOUP WITH BEAN BISCUITS

Smoky chipotle chilies give this soup a unique flavor; biscuits made with pureed beans provide extra protein, fiber, and vitamins.

6 servings (about 1¹/₂ cups each)

1	cup chopped onion
1	cup chopped red bell pepper
1	teaspoon chopped garlic
1	teaspoon vegetable oil
2	cans (15 ounces each) Great Northern beans, rinsed, drained, coarsely mashed
1¹/₂	quarts Rich Chicken Stock (see p. 4)
2	cups frozen whole-kernel corn
¹/₂	small chipotle chili in adobo, chopped
1	teaspoon dried thyme leaves
	Salt and pepper, to taste
¹/₂	cup fat-free sour cream
	Bean Biscuits (recipe follows)

Per Serving
Calories: 361
% Calories from fat: 23
Protein (gm): 18.3
Carbohydrate (gm): 55.2
Fat (gm): 10
Saturated fat (gm): 2.4
Cholesterol (mg): 1.1
Sodium (mg): 789
Exchanges
Milk: 0.0
Veg.: 1.0
Fruit: 0.0
Bread: 3.0
Meat: 1.0
Fat: 1.5

1. Saute onion, bell pepper, and garlic in oil in large saucepan until tender, about 5 minutes. Stir in beans, Rich Chicken Stock, corn, chipotle chili, and thyme. Heat to boiling; reduce heat and simmer, uncovered, 10 minutes. Season to taste with salt and pepper. Garnish servings with dollops of sour cream and serve with Bean Biscuits.

Bean Biscuits

makes 6

³/₄	cup all-purpose flour
2	teaspoons baking powder
1¹/₂	teaspoons sugar
¹/₄	teaspoon salt
¹/₄	cup vegetable shortening
¹/₂	can (15-ounce size) Great Northern beans, rinsed drained
3	tablespoons fat-free milk

1. Combine flour, baking powder, sugar, and salt in medium bowl; cut in shortening until mixture resembles coarse crumbs.

2. Process beans with milk in food processor or blender until almost smooth; add bean mixture to flour mixture and mix just until dough comes together.

3. Drop dough by spoonfuls onto ungreased baking sheet. Bake at 375 degrees until light brown, about 12 minutes.

RED BEANS, RICE, AND SAUSAGE SOUP

Low-fat sausage gives this easy but satisfying soup its zip. The sausage retains its flavor best when it is added near the end of the cooking time.

6-8 servings

1 large onion, finely chopped
1 large garlic clove, minced
1 teaspoon olive oil
1 1/4 quarts chicken broth
1 large carrot, diced
1 large rib celery, diced
1/2 red bell pepper, diced
1 can (15 ounces) reduced-sodium tomato sauce
2 cans (16 ounces each) reduced-sodium dark red kidney beans, drained
1/4 teaspoon dried thyme leaves
1 bay leaf
1/4 teaspoon pepper
1/3 cup long-grain rice
6 ounces smoked reduced-fat sausage, cut into 1/4-inch slices
Salt, to taste

Per Serving
Calories: 221
% Calories from fat: 11
Protein (g): 15.4
Carbohydrates (g): 34.7
Fat (g): 2.7
Saturated fat (g): 0.5
Cholesterol (mg): 13.5
Sodium (mg): 417
Exchanges
Milk: 0.0
Veg.: 1.0
Fruit: 0.0
Bread: 2.0
Meat: 1.0
Fat: 0.0

1. Saute onion and garlic in oil in large saucepan until onion begins to brown. Add remaining ingredients, except sausage and salt; heat to boiling. Reduce heat and simmer, covered, 20 minutes, stirring occasionally. Add sausage and simmer, uncovered, 10 minutes or until soup has thickened slightly; discard bay leaf and season to taste with salt.

PINTO SOUP WITH CHILI CRISPS

The flavor of this vegetable soup is enhanced by a garnish of fresh toma-toes and chili-flavored tortilla strips. Chicken or beef broth can be substi-tuted for the Roasted Vegetable Stock.

8 servings (about 1½ cups each)

2 quarts Roasted Vegetable Stock (see p. 14)
2 cups sliced onions
2 cups sliced carrots
2 cups sliced mushrooms
2 cups cubed, unpeeled red potatoes
1 tablespoon minced garlic
2 teaspoons dried oregano leaves
1 teaspoon ground cumin
1 teaspoon dried thyme leaves
½ teaspoon crushed red pepper
2 cans (15 ounces each) pinto beans, rinsed, drained
Salt and pepper, to taste
Chili Crisps (recipe follows)
2 cups chopped, peeled, seeded tomatoes
¼ cup chopped cilantro, *or* parsley

Per Serving
Calories: 206
% Calories from fat: 7
Protein (gm): 8.1
Carbohydrate (gm): 38.2
Fat (gm): 1.6
Saturated fat (gm): 0.3
Cholesterol (mg): 0
Sodium (mg): 277
Exchanges
Milk: 0.0
Veg.: 2.0
Fruit: 0.0
Bread: 2.0
Meat: 0.0
Fat: 0.0

1. Heat Roasted Vegetable Stock, onions, carrots, mushrooms, potatoes, garlic, herbs, and red pepper to boiling in Dutch oven; reduce heat and simmer, covered, until vegetables are tender, about 20 minutes. Stir in pinto beans; heat until hot and season to taste with salt and pepper.

2. Ladle soup into bowls; sprinkle with Chili Crisps, tomatoes, and cilantro.

Chili Crisps

makes about 3 cups

>   3 corn tortillas (6-inch)
>   Olive oil cooking spray
>   1/2 teaspoon garlic powder
>   1/2 teaspoon chili powder

1. Spray both sides of tortillas with cooking spray; sprinkle tops with garlic and chili powder. Cut tortillas in half; cut halves into thin strips. Arrange on cookie sheet and bake at 425 degrees until crisp, about 10 minutes.

SAUSAGE AND BLACK BEAN SOUP

Smoked sausage flavors this hearty black bean soup.

6 servings

Per Serving
Calories: 370
% Calories from fat: 16
Protein (gm): 24.9
Carbohydrate (gm): 55.7
Fat (gm): 6.7
Saturated fat (gm): 1.7
Cholesterol (mg): 28.2
Sodium (mg): 403
Exchanges
Milk: 0.0
Veg.: 1.0
Fruit: 0.0
Bread: 3.0
Meat: 2.0
Fat: 0.0

>   1 pound dried black beans
>   1 cup sliced carrots
>   1 cup chopped onion
>   1/2 cup chopped celery
>   1 tablespoon margarine
>   2 quarts Low-Salt Chicken Stock (see p. 3)
>   2 tablespoons very-low-sodium Worcestershire sauce
>   2 teaspoons dried marjoram leaves
>   1 bay leaf
>   8 ounces smoked turkey sausage, sliced
>   Salt and pepper, to taste
>   Lemon slices, as garnish

1. Place beans in large saucepan with water to cover by 2 inches. Heat to boiling; boil 2 minutes. Let stand, covered, 1 hour; drain.

2. Saute carrots, onion, and celery in margarine in large saucepan until lightly browned, about 8 minutes. Stir in beans, Low-Salt Chicken Stock, Worcestershire sauce, marjoram, and bay leaf. Heat to boiling; reduce heat and simmer, covered, until beans are tender, about 1 to 1 1/2 hours, adding sausage 1/2 hour before end of cooking time. Discard bay leaf; season to taste with salt and pepper. Serve in bowls, garnished with lemon slices.

Variation:

Sherried Black Bean Soup—Make recipe as above, substituting crushed cumin seeds for the marjoram and adding 1 teaspoon dried oregano leaves and 1 to 2 teaspoons brown sugar. Before serving, season to taste with 1 to 2 tablespoons dry sherry.

GOULASH BEAN SOUP

Caraway seeds and paprika give a Hungarian twist to this vegetable and bean soup. Excellent with Hearty Vegetable-Rye Bread (see p. 796).

8 servings (about 1¹/₂ cups each)

Vegetable cooking spray

1¹/₂ pounds beef round steak, fat trimmed, cubed (¹/₂-inch)

2 cups chopped onions

1 cup chopped carrots

1 cup chopped red bell pepper

1 tablespoon minced garlic

2 tablespoons flour

1 tablespoon paprika

2 teaspoons caraway seeds, crushed

1 teaspoon dried thyme leaves

1 quart Beef Stock (see p. 6)

1 can (16 ounces) whole tomatoes, undrained, chopped

3 cups sliced cabbage

2 cans (15 ounces each) light red kidney beans

Salt and pepper, to taste

¹/₂ cup fat-free sour cream

Per Serving
Calories: 253
% Calories from fat: 13
Protein (gm): 24.1
Carbohydrate (gm): 31.6
Fat (gm): 3.7
Saturated fat (gm): 1.1
Cholesterol (mg): 41.4
Sodium (mg): 512
Exchanges
Milk: 0.0
Veg.: 0.0
Fruit: 0.0
Bread: 2.0
Meat: 2.0
Fat: 0.0

1. Spray large saucepan with cooking spray; heat over medium heat until hot. Cook beef until browned, about 5 minutes; remove and reserve.

2. Add onions, carrots, bell pepper, and garlic to saucepan; saute until lightly browned, about 5 minutes. Return reserved beef to pan; sprinkle with flour, paprika, caraway seeds, and thyme. Cook 1 to 2 minutes.

3. Stir in Beef Stock and tomatoes and liquid. Heat to boiling; reduce heat and simmer, covered, until beef is tender, 45 to 60 minutes, adding cabbage and beans during last 20 minutes. Season to taste with salt and pepper. Serve with dollops of sour cream.

TUSCAN BEAN SOUP

The Tuscans love beans. This wonderful, robust soup is just one of the reasons why!

6 servings

2 cups dried cannellini, *or* Great Northern, beans, soaked overnight
1 large onion, chopped
3 medium carrots, diced
2 large garlic cloves, minced
2 tablespoons olive oil
8 ounces reduced-sodium reduced-fat ham, chopped
3 cups reduced-sodium fat-free chicken broth, divided
1/2 teaspoon dried thyme leaves
1/2 teaspoon dried marjoram leaves
1/2 teaspoon dried rosemary leaves
1/8 teaspoon black pepper
1/8 teaspoon crushed red pepper
1 cup diced reduced-sodium Italian-style tomatoes, undrained
Salt, to taste

Per Serving
Calories: 265
% Calories from fat: 22
Protein (g): 19.3
Carbohydrates (g): 33.8
Fat (g): 6.7
Saturated fat (g): 1.3
Cholesterol (mg): 8.5
Sodium (mg): 511
Exchanges
Milk: 0.0
Veg.: 2.0
Fruit: 0.0
Bread: 2.0
Meat: 1.0
Fat: 0.5

1. Heat beans and 2 quarts water to boiling in large saucepan; reduce heat and simmer, covered, until beans are tender, 45 to 60 minutes. Drain.

2. Saute onion, carrots, and garlic in oil in large saucepan until onions are lightly browned, 5 to 8 minutes. Add ham and saute 2 minutes longer. Add 2 cups broth, herbs, and peppers.

3. Process 1¹/₂ cups beans and remaining 1 cup broth in blender or food processor until smooth; add to soup and heat to boiling. Reduce heat and simmer, covered, 35 to 45 minutes, stirring frequently. Add remaining beans and tomatoes and liquid; simmer 10 minutes more. Season to taste with salt.

NAVY BEAN AND SPINACH SOUP

A delicious, hearty entrèe with the meaty taste of smoked pork, this soup is a meal in a bowl.

6-8 servings

1¹/₂ cups dried navy beans
1 large onion, chopped
2 garlic cloves, minced
2 teaspoons olive oil
2 quarts Low-Salt Chicken Stock (see p. 3)
¹/₄ cup pearl barley
1 pork hock
2 large carrots, sliced
2 large ribs celery, including leaves, sliced
2 large bay leaves
³/₄ teaspoon dried marjoram leaves
³/₄ teaspoon dried basil leaves
¹/₂ teaspoon dried thyme leaves
¹/₄ teaspoon black pepper
   Dash cayenne pepper
1 can (14¹/₂ ounces) reduced-sodium stewed tomatoes, undrained
1 package (10 ounces) frozen chopped spinach, thawed, drained
   Salt, to taste

Per Serving
Calories: 225
% Calories from fat: 8
Protein (g): 16
Carbohydrates (g): 37.6
Fat (g): 2.2
Saturated fat (g): 0.4
Cholesterol (mg): 1.3
Sodium (mg): 385
Exchanges
Milk: 0.0
Veg.: 1.0
Fruit: 0.0
Bread: 2.0
Meat: 1.0
Fat: 0.0

1. Cover beans with 2 inches of water in large saucepan and heat to boiling. Reduce heat and boil 2 minutes. Remove from heat; let stand, covered, 1 hour. Drain.

2. Saute onion and garlic in olive oil in large saucepan until onion is tender, about 5 minutes. Add beans and remaining ingredients, except tomatoes, spinach, and salt; heat to boiling. Reduce heat and simmer, covered, until beans are tender, about 1 hour. Discard pork hock and bay leaves; skim fat from soup. Add tomatoes and liquid and spinach; simmer, stirring occasionally, 5 minutes. Season to taste with salt.

GARBANZO AND COUSCOUS SOUP

Couscous, a quick-cooking, mild-flavored wheat product used in Middle Eastern cuisine, is available in most large grocery stores. In this soup it combines very pleasantly with garbanzo beans.

6 servings

1 medium onion, chopped
1 clove garlic, minced
2 teaspoons olive oil
1¼ quarts reduced-sodium fat-free chicken broth
1 rib celery, finely chopped
1 large carrot, finely chopped
1 cup diced zucchini
1 cup small cauliflower florets
½ medium green bell pepper, diced
1 can (14½ ounces) whole tomatoes, undrained, chopped
2 cups cooked garbanzo beans, *or* 1 can (15 ounces) garbanzo beans, rinsed, drained
1 bay leaf
1 teaspoon sugar
¾ teaspoon ground cumin
¾ teaspoon dried thyme leaves
Dash ground cloves
⅓ cup couscous
Salt and pepper, to taste

Per Serving
Calories: 202
% Calories from fat: 15
Protein (g): 11.8
Carbohydrates (g): 33
Fat (g): 3.4
Saturated fat (g): 0.4
Cholesterol (mg): 0
Sodium (mg): 413
Exchanges
Milk: 0.0
Veg.: 1.0
Fruit: 0.0
Bread: 2.0
Meat: 0.0
Fat: 0.5

1. Saute onion and garlic in oil in Dutch oven until tender, about 5 minutes. Add remaining ingredients, except couscous salt, and pepper; heat to boiling. Reduce heat and simmer, covered, 15 to 20 minutes or until vegetables are tender.

2. Heat soup to boiling; add couscous and boil 2 minutes. Remove from heat and let stand, covered, 5 minutes before serving. Discard bay leaf; season to taste with salt and pepper.

GARBANZO BEAN SOUP

Garbanzo beans are commonly found in the cuisines of central and southern Mexico.

4 servings (about 1¹/₄ cups each)

Vegetable cooking spray
2 medium onions, chopped
2 cloves garlic, minced
2 cans (15¹/₄ ounces each) garbanzo beans, rinsed, drained
2 cans (14¹/₂ ounces each) reduced-sodium fat-free chicken broth, divided
1 teaspoon ground cumin
¹/₂-³/₄ teaspoon dried thyme leaves
Salt and pepper, to taste
¹/₄ cup fat-free sour cream
Paprika, *or* chili powder, as garnish

Per Serving
Calories: 264
% Calories from fat: 14
Protein (g): 16
Carbohydrates (g): 42.9
Fat (g): 4.1
Saturated fat (g): 0.6
Cholesterol (mg): 0
Sodium (mg): 333
Exchanges
Milk: 0.0
Veg.: 0.0
Fruit: 0.0
Bread: 3.0
Meat: 1.0
Fat: 0.0

1. Spray large saucepan with cooking spray; heat over medium heat until hot. Saute onions and garlic until tender, about 5 minutes. Process onion mixture, garbanzo beans, and 1 can chicken broth in food processor or blender until smooth.

2. Return mixture to saucepan; add remaining broth, cumin, and thyme and heat to boiling. Reduce heat and simmer, covered, 5 minutes. Season to taste with salt and pepper.

3. Serve soup in bowls; top with dollops of sour cream and sprinkle with paprika.

LENTIL SOUP WITH ORZO

For a hearty vegetarian dinner, make this soup with Roasted Vegetable Stock (see p.14), and serve with Parmesan Garlic Bread (see p. 795).

6 servings (about 1¹/₂ cups each)

1¹/₂ cups chopped onions

³/₄ cup chopped carrot

¹/₂ cup chopped celery

1 tablespoon minced garlic

1 teaspoon crushed red pepper

1 teaspoon dried oregano leaves

2 teaspoons olive oil

2 cups Quick-Spiced Beef Stock (see p. 7)

2 cans (14¹/₂ ounces each) Italian-style stewed tomatoes, undrained

1 cup water

8 ounces dried lentils

4 ounces uncooked orzo, *or* other small soup pasta

2 cups packed spinach leaves, sliced
    Salt and pepper, to taste

¹/₃ cup chopped parsley

Per Serving
Calories: 252
% Calories from fat: 9
Protein (gm): 12.3
Carbohydrate (gm): 45.7
Fat (gm): 2.4
Saturated fat (gm): 0.3
Cholesterol (mg): 0
Sodium (mg): 293
Exchanges
Milk: 0.0
Veg.: 2.0
Fruit: 0.0
Bread: 2.0
Meat: 1.0
Fat: 0.0

1. Saute onions, carrot, celery, garlic, red pepper, and oregano in oil in large saucepan until tender, about 8 minutes. Stir in Quick-Spiced Beef Stock, tomatoes and liquid, water, and lentils. Heat to boiling; reduce heat and simmer, covered, until lentils are almost tender, about 20 minutes.

2. Stir in orzo and simmer until tender, about 10 minutes. Stir in spinach; season to taste with salt and pepper and stir in parsley.

SAUSAGE AND LENTIL SOUP

Thick, hearty, and accented with the robust flavor of Italian sausage.

10 servings (about 1¹/₂ cups each)

8-12 ounces reduced-sodium reduced-fat Italian-style turkey sausage, casing removed

1¹/₂ cups chopped onions

³/₄ cup chopped carrots

16 ounces dried lentils

3 quarts Beef Stock (see p. 6)

1 can (28 ounces) reduced-sodium diced tomatoes, undrained, chopped

¹/₂ teaspoon dried marjoram leaves

¹/₂ teaspoon dried thyme leaves

1 bay leaf

2-3 teaspoons lemon juice

Salt and pepper, to taste

Per Serving
Calories: 192
% Calories from fat: **15**
Protein (gm): 14.3
Carbohydrate (gm): 28.8
Fat (gm): 3.4
Saturated fat (gm): 0.8
Cholesterol (mg): 12.5
Sodium (mg): 202
Exchanges
Milk: 0.0
Veg.: 0.0
Fruit: 0.0
Bread: 2.0
Meat: 1.0
Fat: 0.0

1. Cook sausage in large saucepan over medium heat until browned; drain and crumble with a fork. Remove sausage and reserve. Add onions and carrots to saucepan; saute until tender, 8 to 10 minutes.

2. Return reserved sausage to saucepan; add lentils, Beef Stock, tomatoes and liquid, and herbs and heat to boiling. Reduce heat and simmer, covered, until lentils are tender, about 45 minutes. Discard bay leaf; season to taste with lemon juice, salt, and pepper.

Variation:
Lentil Soup with Fennel—Make recipe as above, omitting Italian sausage. Saute ¹/₂ cup sliced fennel bulb with the onions and carrots. Substitute 1 teaspoon lightly crushed fennel seeds for the marjoram and thyme. After Step 2, process soup in food processor or blender until smooth. Garnish soup with finely chopped fennel tops.

LENTIL-BARLEY SOUP WITH BEEF

Very hearty, healthful, and economical, this soup features a savory blend of lentils, rice, barley, corn, and beef.

5-7 servings

3 pounds meaty beef neck bones
1 cup water
1¹/₂ quarts Beef Stock (see p. 6)
3 medium onions, finely chopped
3 large ribs celery, finely chopped
¹/₃ cup chopped parsley
¹/₄ cup dried lentils, sorted, washed
¹/₄ cup pearl barley
2 tablespoons uncooked brown rice
1 teaspoon dried thyme leaves
¹/₈ teaspoon ground allspice
¹/₄ teaspoon pepper
2 large carrots, diced
1 medium turnip, diced
1 cup frozen whole-kernel corn
   Salt, to taste

Per Serving
Calories: 273
% Calories from fat: 22
Protein (g): 24.3
Carbohydrates (g): 30.1
Fat (g): 6.8
Saturated fat (g): 2.6
Cholesterol (mg): 39.2
Sodium (mg): 132
Exchanges
Milk: 0.0
Veg.: 0.0
Fruit: 0.0
Bread: 1.5
Meat: 3.0
Fat: 0.0

1. Rinse and drain bones; pat dry with paper toweling. Roast bones in large roasting pan at 400 degrees 30 minutes, turning occasionally. Drain fat. Roast 30 to 40 minutes longer, stirring occasionally; drain well.

2. Transfer bones to Dutch oven. Add water to roasting pan and scrape up browned bits sticking to pan; add to Dutch oven. Add Beef Stock, onions, celery, and parsley; heat to boiling. Reduce heat and simmer, covered, 45 minutes. Add remaining ingredients, except corn and salt, and simmer 1 hour. Skim fat from surface. Remove bones; cut meat into pieces and return meat to Dutch oven. Add corn and simmer, uncovered, 5 minutes; season to taste with salt.

SPLIT-PEA SOUP JARDINIÈRE

This "gardener's-style" split-pea soup is flavored the old-fashioned way with a ham bone and leeks, turnips, and carrots from the fall garden.

8 servings

1 pound dried split green peas
2¹/₂ quarts water
1 meaty ham bone
1 small onion, quartered
4 whole cloves
2 teaspoons dried thyme leaves
1 bay leaf
2 leeks, white parts only, sliced
3 carrots, sliced
2 ribs celery, sliced
1 turnip, peeled, cubed (¹/₂-inch)
2 large tomatoes, chopped
2 cloves garlic, minced
Salt and pepper, to taste

Per Serving
Calories: 175
% Calories from fat: 6
Protein (gm): 11.6
Carbohydrate (gm): 31.5
Fat (gm): 1.2
Saturated fat (gm): 0.3
Cholesterol (mg): 4.8
Sodium (mg): 156
Exchanges
Milk: 0.0
Veg.: 2.0
Fruit: 0.0
Bread: 1.0
Meat: 1.0
Fat: 0.0

1. Combine peas, water, ham bone, onion, cloves, thyme, and bay leaf in large saucepan. Heat to boiling; reduce heat and simmer, covered, 2 hours. Remove ham bone; cut off, chop, and reserve meat. Discard bone. Strain broth and discard solids. Return broth and ham to pan.

2. Add vegetables to soup; heat to boiling. Reduce heat and simmer until vegetables are tender and soup is thick, about 30 minutes. Season to taste with salt and pepper.

Variations:

Canadian Pea Soup—Make soup as above, substituting yellow split peas for the green split peas, 2 to 4 ounces diced lean salt pork for the ham bone and ham, and 2 parsnips, diced, for the turnip. Omit celery.

Dutch Split-Pea Soup—Make soup as above, omitting ham bone and ham, onion, and cloves and substituting ¹/₂ cup diced celery root for the parsnips. When vegetables are tender, puree soup in food processor or blender; season to taste with salt and pepper and stir in 8 ounces reduced-sodium, reduced-fat smoked sausage, sliced.

SPLIT-PEA SOUP WITH HAM

A perfect main-dish soup for hearty appetites on a crisp autumn or winter day. Serve with thick slices of Garlic Bread (see p. 795).

8 servings (about 1 cup each)

1¹/2 cups chopped onions
1 cup chopped carrots
¹/2 cup sliced celery
1¹/2 cups cubed lean smoked ham (8 ounces), fat trimmed
1 tablespoon vegetable oil
1¹/2 quarts water
1 can (14¹/2 ounces) reduced-sodium chicken broth
1 pound dried split peas, sorted, washed
1-2 teaspoons beef bouillon crystals
1 teaspoon dried marjoram leaves
Salt and pepper, to taste

Per Serving
Calories: 264
% Calories from fat: 11
Protein (g): 21.6
Carbohydrates (g): 39.9
Fat (g): 3.4
Saturated fat (g): 0.6
Cholesterol (mg): 16.2
Sodium (mg): 513
Exchanges
Milk: 0.0
Veg.: 1.0
Fruit: 0.0
Bread: 2.0
Meat: 2.0
Fat: 0.0

1. Saute onions, carrots, celery, and ham in oil in large saucepan until tender, 8 to 10 minutes. Add water, chicken broth, split peas, bouillon crystals, and marjoram; heat to boiling. Reduce heat and simmer, covered, until peas are tender, 1 to 1¹/4 hours. Season to taste with salt and pepper.

Variations:
Savory Pea Soup with Smoked Sausage—Make soup as above, substituting 8 ounces smoked turkey sausage, halved lengthwise and sliced, for the ham, and adding 2 cups diced potato, 1 teaspoon dried thyme leaves, and 1 bay leaf. Remove bay leaf before serving, and season with hot pepper sauce.

Split-Pea Soup with Barley—Make soup as above, omitting ham. Increase water to 8 cups, and add ¹/2 cup barley with the split peas. Cook until tender.

SEVEN

Seafood Soups

CLAM BISQUE

This soup can be made in less than 10 minutes. Substitute canned lobster, crab meat, or shrimp for the clams to create a different bisque.

4 servings (about 1 cup each)

1 tablespoon grated onion
2 teaspoons margarine
1 tablespoon flour
1/2 teaspoon celery salt
2 cups fat-free milk
1 cup reduced-sodium fat-free chicken broth, *or* water
1 can (6¹/2 ounces) minced clams, undrained
Salt and pepper, to taste
1 tablespoon chopped parsley

Per Serving
Calories: 76
% Calories from fat: 26
Protein (gm): 6.1
Carbohydrate (gm): 7.8
Fat (gm): 2.2
Saturated fat (gm): 0.5
Cholesterol (mg): 3.6
Sodium (mg): 347
Exchanges
Milk: 0.0
Veg.: 0.0
Fruit: 0.0
Bread: 0.5
Meat: 0.5
Fat: 0.0

1. Saute onion in margarine in medium saucepan 1 minute; stir in flour and celery salt and cook 1 minute. Stir in milk and broth; heat to boiling. Boil, stirring, 1 minute. Stir in clams and liquor; cook over medium heat 2 to 3 minutes. Season to taste with salt and pepper. Stir in parsley.

LINGUINE CLAM SOUP

Remember to buy only the freshest clams available. Buy only clams that are tightly closed, and after cooking discard any that have not opened.

6 servings

32 little neck, *or* cherrystone, clams, scrubbed
6 cloves garlic, minced
1 cup dry white wine
1 quart bottled clam juice
1/4 teaspoon crushed red pepper
Salt and black pepper, to taste
1/2 pound linguine, broken into pieces, cooked
1/4 cup minced parsley

Per Serving
Calories: 210
% Calories from fat: 8
Protein (gm): 17.1
Carbohydrate (gm): 25.2
Fat (gm): 1.8
Saturated fat (gm): 0.1
Cholesterol (mg): 34
Sodium (mg): 501
Exchanges
Milk: 0.0
Veg.: 0.0
Fruit: 0.0
Bread: 1.5
Meat: 2.0
Fat: 0.0

1. Heat clams, garlic, and wine to boiling in large saucepan. Reduce heat and simmer 4 to 5 minutes or until clams have opened. Remove clams from shells and reserve; discard unopened clams.

2. Add clam juice and red pepper to saucepan and heat to boiling; reduce heat and simmer, covered, 4 to 5 minutes. Stir in reserved clams; simmer 1 to 2 minutes. Season to taste with salt and pepper. Ladle over linguine in bowls and sprinkle with parsley.

MUSSEL SOUP WITH SAFFRON

Brightly colored bits of vegetables and a savory broth bring out the flavor of the mussels in this tempting, eye-catching soup. It should be served immediately, as the colors and flavors begin to fade if the soup is allowed to stand.

4-5 servings

1¹/₄ cups bottled clam juice
³/₄ cup water
²/₃ cup dry white wine
2¹/₄ pounds mussels, scrubbed
¹/₃ cup julienned carrot
¹/₃ cup julienned celery
1 large garlic clove, minced
4 green onions and tops, julienned
2 teaspoons margarine
1 bay leaf
10 saffron threads, finely crumbled
¹/₄ cup peeled, seeded, finely chopped tomatoes
Salt and cayenne, to taste
Chives, *or* parsley, finely chopped, as garnish

Per Serving
Calories: 146
% Calories from fat: 25
Protein (g): 16
Carbohydrates (g): 5.8
Fat (g): 3.9
Saturated fat (g): 0.3
Cholesterol (mg): 50.5
Sodium (mg): 402
Exchanges
Milk: 0.0
Veg.: 0.0
Fruit: 0.0
Bread: 0.5
Meat: 2.0
Fat: 0.0

1. Combine clam juice, water, and wine in large saucepan; heat to boiling. Add mussels, reduce heat, and simmer, covered, 5 minutes or until shells open. Drain and reserve cooking liquid. Remove mussels from shells and reserve; discard unopened mussels.

2. Saute carrot, celery, garlic, and green onions in margarine in large saucepan 5 minutes. Stir in reserved mussel liquid, bay leaf, and saffron and heat to boiling. Reduce heat and simmer, covered, 10 minutes.

3. Add tomatoes and reserved mussels and simmer 2 minutes. Discard bay leaf; season to taste with salt and cayenne pepper. Garnish each serving with chopped chives.

GREEN LIP MUSSEL AND SAFFRON SOUP

Green lip mussels are from New Zealand. Larger in size, they are about 2 inches long and are very tasty.

4 servings

1 onion, sliced
1 carrot, chopped
1/2 cup dry white wine
1/2 teaspoon dried thyme leaves
2 bay leaves
Pinch saffron
2 pounds green lip mussels, scrubbed
2 cups bottled clam juice, divided
2 tablespoons cornstarch
2 cups 2% reduced-fat milk
Salt and pepper, to taste

Per Serving
Calories: 218
% Calories from fat: 21
Protein (gm): 18.3
Carbohydrate (gm): 19.5
Fat (gm): 5
Saturated fat (gm): 2
Cholesterol (mg): 40.9
Sodium (mg): 675
Exchanges
Milk: 0.0
Veg.: 1.0
Fruit: 0.0
Bread: 0.5
Meat: 2.0
Fat: 1.0

1. Heat onion, carrot, wine, thyme, bay leaves, and saffron to boiling in large saucepan; reduce heat and add mussels. Cover and simmer 3 to 5 minutes or until mussels open. Remove mussels and reserve; discard unopened mussels. Discard bay leaf.

2. Process mixture with 1 1/2 cups clam juice in food processor or blender until smooth; return to saucepan and heat to boiling. Stir in combined remaining 1/2 cup clam juice and cornstarch; boil, stirring, until thickened, 1 to 2 minutes. Add mussels and milk; reduce heat and simmer, covered, 5 minutes. Season to taste with salt and pepper.

POTATO-MUSSEL SAFFRON SOUP

Saffron gives a beautiful color and flavor to this soup.

8 servings

Olive oil cooking spray
6 shallots, minced
3 cloves garlic
3 large potatoes, peeled, diced
3 large carrots, thinly sliced
2 leeks, white parts only, chopped
1 quart water
4 ripe tomatoes, peeled, seeded, chopped
1 can (16 ounces) crushed tomatoes, undrained
1/2 cup chopped parsley
2 bay leaves
1 teaspoon fennel seeds
1/4 teaspoon saffron
1/4 teaspoon white pepper
32 mussels, scrubbed
Salt, to taste

Per Serving
Calories: 222
% Calories from fat: **30**
Protein (gm): 8.3
Carbohydrate (gm): **31.4**
Fat (gm): 7.6
Saturated fat (gm): **1.9**
Cholesterol (mg): **45.9**
Sodium (mg): **401**
Exchanges
Milk: 0.0
Veg.: 3.0
Fruit: 0.0
Bread: 1.0
Meat: 0.0
Fat: 1.5

1. Spray large saucepan with cooking spray; heat over medium heat until hot. Saute shallots, garlic, potatoes, carrots, and leeks 5 minutes. Add 1 quart water and heat to boiling. Add remaining ingredients, except mussels and salt. Reduce heat and simmer, covered, until vegetables are tender, about 15 minutes.

2. Add mussels, cover, and cook until mussels are opened, 3 to 5 minutes; discard any unopened mussels. Season to taste with salt; discard bay leaves.

OYSTER SOUP

A classic first course for Christmas dinner, or any month with an "r"! You can buy shucked oysters at most large supermarkets during the holiday season.

4 servings (about 1¹/₃ cups each)

2/3 cup chopped celery

2/3 cup chopped onion

2/3 cup chopped carrots

  2 teaspoons margarine

  3 tablespoons flour

  1 pint shucked oysters, undrained

  3 cups fat-free milk

  1 cup fat-free half-and-half, *or* fat-free milk

    Salt and pepper, to taste

  3 tablespoons chopped parsley

  2 tablespoons chopped chives

    Oyster crackers, not included in nutritional data

Per Serving
Calories: 190
% Calories from fat: 16
Protein (gm): 12.4
Carbohydrate (gm): 25.6
Fat (gm): 3.2
Saturated fat (gm): 0.9
Cholesterol (mg): 17.5
Sodium (mg): 300
Exchanges
Milk: 1.0
Veg.: 0.0
Fruit: 0.0
Bread: 0.5
Meat: 1.0
Fat: 0.0

1. Saute celery, onion, and carrots in margarine in medium saucepan until softened, about 5 minutes. Sprinkle with flour and cook 2 minutes. Drain oysters and add liquor to pan, stirring well. Stir in milk; heat to boiling. Reduce heat and simmer, covered, until vegetables are tender, about 10 minutes.

2. Stir in oysters and simmer until edges of oysters curl, about 2 minutes; do not boil. Stir in half-and-half and simmer 2 to 3 minutes longer. Season to taste with salt and pepper; stir in parsley and chives. Serve with oyster crackers.

OYSTER AND MUSHROOM BISQUE

A creamy mushroom soup is enhanced with oysters and sherry to make this elegant soup.

4 servings (about 1 cup each)

8 ounces mushrooms, sliced
1 teaspoon margarine
1 tablespoon flour
1 cup reduced-sodium fat-free chicken broth
1 egg yolk
1 cup fat-free half-and-half, *or* fat-free milk
1 pint oysters, undrained
3 tablespoons dry sherry
Salt and white pepper, to taste
Oyster crackers, as garnish

Per Serving
Calories: 140
% Calories from fat: 23
Protein (gm): 8.6
Carbohydrate (gm): 14.2
Fat (gm): 3.4
Saturated fat (gm): 0.9
Cholesterol (mg): 67.4
Sodium (mg): 219
Exchanges
Milk: 0.0
Veg.: 0.0
Fruit: 0.0
Bread: 1.0
Meat: 0.5
Fat: 1.0

1. Saute mushrooms in margarine in medium saucepan until tender, about 5 minutes; stir in flour and cook 1 minute longer. Process mushrooms, chicken broth, and egg yolk in food processor or blender until smooth; return mixture to saucepan and stir in half-and-half. Cook, stirring constantly, over medium heat until lightly thickened; do not boil.

2. Heat oysters and liquor in small saucepan and cook over low heat, stirring, until edges curl, 1 to 2 minutes; stir into mushroom mixture. Stir in sherry; season to taste with salt and white pepper. Serve with oyster crackers.

MARDI GRAS OYSTER SOUP

Oysters, a New Orleans favorite, are combined with clam juice and wine in this special celebration soup.

6 servings (about 1 cup each)

1 1/2 pounds fresh, *or* canned, oysters, undrained

2/3 cup chopped onion

1-2 teaspoons margarine

1/4 cup all-purpose flour

1 quart bottled clam juice

2 egg yolks, lightly beaten

1/2 cup dry white wine, *or* water

Salt and cayenne pepper, to taste

Hot pepper sauce, to taste

Chopped chives, as garnish

Per Serving
Calories: 132
% Calories from fat: 29
Protein (gm): 7.6
Carbohydrate (gm): 12
Fat (gm): 4.2
Saturated fat (gm): 1.2
Cholesterol (mg): 99.4
Sodium (mg): 586
Exchanges
Milk: 0.0
Veg.: 0.0
Fruit: 0.0
Bread: 0.5
Meat: 1.0
Fat: 1.0

1. Drain oysters, reserving liquor; coarsely chop about 1 cup oysters. Cut remaining oysters in half.

2. Saute onion in margarine in large saucepan until tender, about 5 minutes. Stir in flour; cook over medium heat 2 minutes. Stir in reserved oyster liquor and clam juice; heat to simmering. Whisk about 1 cup clam juice mixture into egg yolks; whisk egg yolk mixture into saucepan and simmer, whisking until thickened, 1 to 2 minutes.

3. Stir in wine and oysters and simmer until hot, 2 to 3 minutes; do not boil. Season to taste with salt, cayenne pepper, and hot pepper sauce. Serve soup in bowls; sprinkle with chives.

CHINESE OYSTER SOUP

Another very quick soup, with an oriental accent of Chinese cabbage and vegetables.

4 servings (about 1¹/₃ cups each)

2¹/₂ cups Oriental Vegetable Stock (see p. 16), *or* reduced-sodium fat-free chicken broth

2 tablespoons reduced-sodium soy sauce

¹/₂ tablespoon grated gingerroot

1 pint oysters, undrained

2 cups sliced Napa cabbage

8 ounces mushrooms, sliced

¹/₂ cup bean sprouts

4 green onions and tops, sliced

Salt and pepper, to taste

Per Serving
Calories: 72
% Calories from fat: 15
Protein (gm): 6.2
Carbohydrate (gm): 10.2
Fat (gm): 1.3
Saturated fat (gm): 0.3
Cholesterol (mg): 14.2
Sodium (mg): 444
Exchanges
Milk: 0.0
Veg.: 0.0
Fruit: 0.0
Bread: 0.5
Meat: 1.0
Fat: 0.0

1. Heat Oriental Vegetable Stock, soy sauce, and gingerroot to boiling in large saucepan; add oysters and liquor, cabbage, and mushrooms. Heat to boiling; reduce heat and simmer until cabbage is tender, about 3 minutes. Stir in bean sprouts and green onions; season to taste with salt and pepper.

SQUASH AND SCALLOP SOUP

Frozen cubed winter squash can be used in this recipe. Simply thaw and add with the scallops in Step 2.

6 servings

   1 cup chopped celery
 1/2 cup chopped onion
   1 tablespoon margarine
 1/4 cup all-purpose flour
   2 cups fat-free milk
   1 cup reduced sodium fat-free chicken broth
   2 cups cubed, peeled butternut, *or* Hubbard, squash (1/2-inch)
 1/4 teaspoon ground ginger
 16 ounces bay scallops
1-2 teaspoons very-low sodium Worcestershire sauce
    Salt and white pepper, to taste

Per Serving
Calories: 161
% Calories from fat: **17**
Protein (gm): 19.3
Carbohydrate (gm): 14.5
Fat (gm): 3.1
Saturated fat (gm): 0.5
Cholesterol (mg): 33.6
Sodium (mg): 276
Exchanges
Milk: 0.0
Veg.: 0.0
Fruit: 0.0
Bread: 1.0
Meat: 2.0
Fat: 0.0

1. Saute celery and onion in margarine in large saucepan until tender, about 5 minutes; sprinkle with flour and cook 1 to 2 minutes. Stir in milk, broth, squash, and ginger. Heat to boiling; reduce heat and simmer, covered, until squash is tender, about 20 minutes.

2. Stir in scallops; simmer until scallops are tender, about 5 minutes. Stir in Worcestershire sauce; season to taste with salt and white pepper.

SHERRIED CRAB MEAT SOUP

This delicately seasoned soup is easily made with canned crab meat.

4 servings (about 1¹/₂ cups each)

1¹/₂ cups Easy Fish Stock (see p. 9)
  1 cup sliced celery
  2 cans (6¹/₂ ounces each) crab meat, drained, divided
  1 cup 2% reduced-fat milk
¹/₄ teaspoon ground mace
  1 tablespoon cornstarch
  3 tablespoons dry sherry, *or* water
    Salt and cayenne pepper, to taste
    Thinly sliced celery, as garnish

Per Serving
Calories: 168
% Calories from fat: **20**
Protein (gm): 19.9
Carbohydrate (gm): **7.8**
Fat (gm): 3.5
Saturated fat (gm): **1.2**
Cholesterol (mg): 100.**4**
Sodium (mg): 524
Exchanges
Milk: 0.0
Veg.: 0.0
Fruit: 0.0
Bread: 0.5
Meat: 2.0
Fat: 0.0

1. Combine Easy Fish Stock, celery, and 1 can crab meat in large saucepan. Heat to boiling; reduce heat and simmer, covered, until celery is tender, about 10 minutes. Process mixture in food processor or blender until smooth; return to saucepan.

2. Stir in milk and mace and heat to boiling; stir in combined cornstarch and sherry and stir until thickened. Stir in remaining 1 can crab meat; reduce heat and simmer 2 to 3 minutes. Season to taste with salt and cayenne pepper. Serve soup in bowls; garnish with sliced celery.

MARYLAND CRAB SOUP

Old Bay is a popular herb and spice blend used with crab and other sea-food in the Chesapeake region. If not available, its flavor can be approximated by substituting ¹/₂ teaspoon each celery salt, paprika, dry mustard; ¹/₄ teaspoon each black and crushed red pepper; ¹/₈ teaspoon ground cloves; and a pinch each ground mace and ground ginger.

7-8 servings

2 slices bacon, finely diced
1 teaspoon margarine
2 large onions, finely chopped
2 large carrots, finely chopped
2 large ribs celery, finely chopped
¹/₂ cup finely chopped parsley
1 quart fat-free beef broth
2¹/₂ cups bottled clam juice
2 cups water
1 small smoked pork hock
2 bay leaves
¹/₂ teaspoon dry mustard
1-2 tablespoons Old Bay seasoning
3 cups diced, peeled red potatoes
2¹/₂ cups coarsely chopped, canned un-drained plum tomatoes
1 cup whole-kernel corn
12 ounces fresh backfin crab meat, carti-lage and shell discarded, cut into ¹/₂-inch pieces
Salt and pepper, to taste

Per Serving
Calories: 209
% Calories from fat: 12
Protein (g): 15.3
Carbohydrates (g): 31.3
Fat (g): 2.9
Saturated fat (g): 0.7
Cholesterol (mg): 43.4
Sodium (mg): 460
Exchanges
Milk: 0.0
Veg.: 0.0
Fruit: 0.0
Bread: 2.0
Meat: 1.0
Fat: 0.0

1. Cook bacon in large saucepan until almost crisp; drain fat. Add margarine, onions, carrots, celery, and parsley; saute until onions are tender, 8 to 10 minutes. Add remaining ingredients, except potatoes, tomatoes, corn, crab, salt, and pepper; heat to boiling. Reduce heat and simmer, covered, 10 minutes.

2. Add potatoes, tomatoes, and corn and simmer, covered, until tender, 10 to 15 minutes. Stir in crab meat and simmer 5 minutes; discard pork hock and bay leaves. Season to taste with salt and pepper.

EGG DROP CRAB SOUP

This delicious soup can be made in less than 10 minutes.

4 servings

4 green onions and tops, sliced
2 teaspoons minced garlic
1 teaspoon minced gingerroot
1-2 teaspoons dark sesame oil
1 quart Rich Chicken Stock (see p. 4), *or* chicken broth
1 can (15 ounces) reduced-sodium cream-style corn
1 can (6 ounces) crabmeat, drained
Salt and pepper, to taste
1 egg
3 egg whites
1 tablespoon chopped cilantro

Per Serving
Calories: 160
% Calories from fat: **25**
Protein (gm): 18.8
Carbohydrate (gm): **9.4**
Fat (gm): 4.3
Saturated fat (gm): 1
Cholesterol (mg): **96.5**
Sodium (mg): **313**
Exchanges
Milk: 0.0
Veg.: 0.0
Fruit: 0.0
Bread: 0.5
Meat: 2.0
Fat: 0.0

1. Saute green onions, garlic, and gingerroot in oil in large saucepan 2 minutes. Stir in Rich Chicken Stock, corn, and crabmeat. Heat to boiling; reduce heat and simmer 5 minutes. Season to taste with salt and pepper. Beat egg and egg whites in small bowl until combined; slowly stir into soup. Stir in cilantro.

SHRIMP BISQUE

The shrimp are finely chopped for this recipe, so use any size you like. Also, Fish Stock (see p. 9) may be substituted for the chicken broth for extra-good flavor.

4 servings (about 1 cup each)

3/4 cup chopped onion
2 teaspoons margarine
12 ounces uncooked shrimp, peeled, deveined
3 tablespoons flour
3 tablespoons tomato paste
2 teaspoons curry powder
1/4 teaspoon paprika
3 cups reduced-sodium fat-free chicken broth
1/2 cup fat-free half-and-half, *or* fat-free milk
Salt and cayenne pepper, to taste
3/4 cup chopped tomato
1 cup Garlic Croutons (1/3 recipe) (see p. 785)

Per Serving
Calories: 199
% Calories from fat: 15
Protein (gm): 22
Carbohydrate (gm): 18.5
Fat (gm): 3.3
Saturated fat (gm): 0.7
Cholesterol (mg): 130
Sodium (mg): 470
Exchanges
Milk: 0.0
Veg.: 0.0
Fruit: 0.0
Bread: 1.0
Meat: 2.0
Fat: 0.0

1. Saute onion in margarine in large saucepan until tender, about 5 minutes; stir in shrimp and saute until pink and curled, 5 to 8 minutes. Sprinkle with flour and cook 1 to 2 minutes longer. Stir in tomato paste, curry powder, and paprika and cook 1 minute. Stir in broth and heat to boiling, stirring until thickened, 1 to 2 minutes longer.

2. Process soup in blender or food processor until almost smooth. Return soup to saucepan; stir in half-and-half and simmer 2 to 3 minutes. Season to taste with salt and cayenne pepper. Sprinkle each serving with tomato and Garlic Croutons.

LIGHT SALMON BISQUE WITH DILL

Dill weed complements the flavor of fresh salmon nicely in this light, tempting bisque.

4-5 servings

2¹/₂ cups Fish Stock (see p. 9), *or* bottled clam juice, divided
8 ounces North Atlantic, *or* king, salmon fillets
1 cup chopped onion
¹/₄ cup chopped celery and leaves
2 tablespoons chopped carrot
2 teaspoons margarine
1 tablespoon flour
¹/₄ teaspoon dry mustard
¹/₈ teaspoon white pepper
1¹/₂ cups chopped, peeled potatoes
1 tablespoon tomato paste
1¹/₄ cups whole milk
2¹/₂ teaspoons lemon juice
¹/₂ teaspoon salt
1 tablespoon finely chopped fresh, *or* 1¹/₂ teaspoons dried, dill weed
Dill weed sprigs, as garnish

Per Serving
Calories: 213
% Calories from fat: 28
Protein (g): 20.3
Carbohydrates (g): 22.5
Fat (g): 6.7
Saturated fat (g): 2
Cholesterol (mg): 38.7
Sodium (mg): 508
Exchanges
Milk: 0.0
Veg.: 0.0
Fruit: 0.0
Bread: 1.5
Meat: 2.0
Fat: 0.0

1. Heat ¹/₂ cup Fish Stock to simmering in medium skillet; add salmon fillets, skin side down. Simmer, covered, until salmon is tender and flakes with a fork, 5 to 7 minutes. Remove fish, lay skin side up on a plate, and cool; remove and discard skin. Flake fish into small pieces. Strain fish stock through a fine sieve over the fish and reserve.

2. Saute onion, celery, and carrot in margarine in large saucepan until onion is tender, about 5 minutes. Stir in flour and cook 1 minute. Stir in remaining 2 cups Fish Stock, dry mustard, white pepper, and potatoes; heat to boiling. Reduce heat and simmer until potatoes are tender, about 10 minutes.

3. Process stock mixture and tomato paste in blender or food processor until smooth; return to saucepan and heat to boiling. Add reserved salmon and remaining ingredients, except sprigs of dill weed; reduce heat and simmer, uncovered, just until hot, 3 to 4 minutes. Garnish each serving with a sprig of dill weed.

SALMON WILD RICE SOUP

A very special soup—the rich flavor of salmon is amplified by the wild rice.

6 servings

2 slices bacon
1¹/₂ cups sliced mushrooms
³/₄ cup chopped onion
¹/₂ cup sliced celery
1 teaspoon minced garlic
2 tablespoons flour
¹/₂ teaspoon dry mustard
¹/₂ teaspoon dried rosemary leaves
3 cups Easy Fish Stock (see p. 9), *or* fat-free chicken broth
16 ounces salmon, skin and bones removed, cubed
1 cup cooked wild rice
1 cup fat-free half-and-half, *or* fat-free milk
Salt and cayenne pepper, to taste

Per Serving
Calories: 200
% Calories from fat: 20
Protein (gm): 20.3
Carbohydrate (gm): **15.5**
Fat (gm): 3.9
Saturated fat (gm): 0.8
Cholesterol (mg): **44.7**
Sodium (mg): 142
Exchanges
Milk: 0.0
Veg.: 0.0
Fruit: 0.0
Bread: 1.0
Meat: 2.0
Fat: 0.0

1. Cook bacon in large saucepan until crisp. Drain on paper toweling; crumble and reserve. Drain all but 2 teaspoons fat from saucepan; add mushrooms, onion, celery, and garlic and saute until tender, about 8 minutes. Stir in flour, mustard, and rosemary and cook 1 to 2 minutes longer.

2. Add Easy Fish Stock and heat to boiling; reduce heat and simmer, covered, 5 minutes. Stir in salmon and wild rice; simmer, covered, until salmon flakes with a fork, about 5 minutes. Stir in half-and-half; simmer 3 to 4 minutes longer. Season to taste with salt and cayenne pepper. Sprinkle each serving with reserved bacon.

Variation:
Tuna-Rice Soup—Make soup as above, substituting tarragon for the rosemary, tuna steaks for the salmon, and white rice for the wild rice. Add lemon juice to taste.

ZUCCHINI AND TUNA SOUP

This soup is made easy and delicious with canned tuna. Canned salmon would also work well.

4 servings

Vegetable cooking spray
3/4 cup chopped onion
1/2 cup chopped celery
2 teaspoons minced garlic
2 tablespoons flour
1 can (6 1/2 ounces) tuna in water, drained
2 1/2 cups Low-Salt Chicken Stock (see p. 3), *or* chicken broth
1 cup fat-free milk
1/2-1 cup (2-4 ounces) shredded Cheddar cheese
1 cup shredded zucchini
1 teaspoon lemon juice
Salt and pepper, to taste
Hot pepper sauce, to taste

Per Serving
Calories: 174
% Calories from fat: 28
Protein (gm): 19.6
Carbohydrate (gm): 11.5
Fat (gm): 5.4
Saturated fat (gm): 3.2
Cholesterol (mg): 32
Sodium (mg): 292
Exchanges
Milk: 0.0
Veg.: 0.0
Fruit: 0.0
Bread: 1.0
Meat: 2.0
Fat: 0.0

1. Spray large saucepan with vegetable cooking spray; heat over medium heat until hot. Saute onion, celery, and garlic until tender, about 5 minutes. Sprinkle with flour and cook 1 to 2 minutes longer. Stir in tuna, Low-Salt Chicken Stock, and milk. Heat to boiling; reduce heat and simmer 5 minutes. Stir in cheese until melted.

2. Process soup in food processor or blender until smooth; return to saucepan. Stir in zucchini and lemon juice and stir over medium heat until hot. Season to taste with salt, pepper, and hot pepper sauce.

SEAFOOD WONTON SOUP

Won ton wrappers may be purchased at most supermarkets and oriental food stores.

4 servings

Seafood Filling (recipe follows)
16 wonton wrappers
1 egg white, lightly beaten
1¹/₂ quarts Fish Stock, *or* Low-Salt Chicken Stock (see pp. 9, 3)
1 cup sliced spinach leaves
¹/₄ teaspoon white pepper
¹/₄ cup minced parsley

Per Serving
Calories: 178
% Calories from fat: 6
Protein (gm): 13.2
Carbohydrate (gm): 21.5
Fat (gm): 0.9
Saturated fat (gm): 0.1
Cholesterol (mg): 18.2
Sodium (mg): 283
Exchanges
Milk: 0.0
Veg.: 1.0
Fruit: 0.0
Bread: 1.0
Meat: 1.5
Fat: 0.0

1. Put 1 teaspoon Seafood Filling in the center of each wonton wrapper. Moisten edges with egg white; fold opposite corners together and seal.

2. Heat Fish Stock to boiling in large saucepan. Reduce heat and add won tons and remaining ingredients; simmer, uncovered, until wontons float to the surface, 5 to 7 minutes.

Seafood Filling

4 ounces orange roughy fillets, finely chopped
2 green onions and tops, minced
¹/₄ cup finely chopped cooked broccoli
1 egg white, slightly beaten
¹/₂ teaspoon light soy sauce
¹/₂ teaspoon ground ginger

1. Mix ingredients.

CANTONESE FISH SOUP

This light, delicate fish soup is very easy to make and can be prepared with frozen fish.

4 servings

1-1¹/₄ quarts Fish Stock (see p. 9)
   16 ounces haddock fillets, cut into 1-inch strips
  1-2 tablespoons dry white wine
    2 teaspoons minced fresh gingerroot
    3 green onions and tops, minced
  ¹/₂ teaspoon oriental sesame oil
  ¹/₄ teaspoon pepper
    1 cup sliced spinach leaves
     Salt, to taste

Per Serving
Calories: 138
% Calories from fat: 8
Protein (gm): 24.1
Carbohydrate (gm): 1.8
Fat (gm): 1
Saturated fat (gm): 0.2
Cholesterol (mg): 71.7
Sodium (mg): 100
Exchanges
Milk: 0.0
Veg.: 0.0
Fruit: 0.0
Bread: 0.0
Meat: 3.0
Fat: 0.0

1. Heat Fish Stock to boiling in a large saucepan; add remaining ingredients, except salt. Reduce heat and simmer, uncovered, until fish is tender and flakes with a fork, about 10 minutes. Season to taste with salt.

THAI FISH SOUP

Oriental vegetables and fish "meatballs" swim in a delicious clear broth.

4 servings

1¹/₂ quarts Fish Stock (see p. 9)
  2 teaspoons reduced-sodium soy sauce
  1 teaspoon minced garlic
  1 teaspoon minced gingerroot
   Pinch ground Szechuan peppercorns, optional
¹/₂ pound flounder fillets, ground
¹/₂ teaspoon salt
¹/₂ teaspoon pepper
¹/₂ cup sliced mushrooms
¹/₂ cup sliced snow peas
  2 tablespoons chopped cilantro
   Salt and pepper, to taste

Per Serving
Calories: 114
% Calories from fat: 10
Protein (gm): 15.1
Carbohydrate (gm): 3.5
Fat (gm): 0.9
Saturated fat (gm): 0.2
Cholesterol (mg): 39.8
Sodium (mg): 444
Exchanges
Milk: 0.0
Veg.: 0.0
Fruit: 0.0
Bread: 0.0
Meat: 2.0
Fat: 0.0

1. Combine Fish Stock, soy sauce, garlic, gingerroot, and peppercorns in large saucepan; heat to boiling. Reduce heat and simmer, covered, 5 minutes.

2. Mix ground fish, salt, and pepper and shape into 1-inch balls. Heat soup to boiling; drop fish balls into soup. Simmer until fish balls float to the surface, about 5 minutes. Stir in mushrooms, snow peas, and cilantro; simmer until snow peas are crisp-tender, 2 to 3 minutes. Season to taste with salt and pepper.

GINGER FISH SOUP

Ginger and soy sauce give an oriental accent to this very quick fish soup.

4 servings

1 quart Low-Salt Chicken Stock (see p. 3), *or* chicken broth
1 cup water
1 tablespoon reduced-sodium soy sauce
1 tablespoon minced gingerroot
1 teaspoon minced garlic
2 ounces vermicelli, broken
8 ounces skinless fish fillets (flounder, whitefish, *or* perch), cut into ¹/₂-inch slices
4 ounces small shrimp, peeled, deveined
1 small cucumber, peeled, seeded, thinly sliced
1 cup sliced mushrooms
4 cups packed spinach leaves, sliced
Salt and cayenne pepper, to taste
¹/₄ cup sliced green onions and tops

Per Serving
Calories: 171
% Calories from fat: 9
Protein (gm): 21.5
Carbohydrate (gm): 17.6
Fat (gm): 1.7
Saturated fat (gm): 0.3
Cholesterol (mg): 76.8
Sodium (mg): 278
Exchanges
Milk: 0.0
Veg.: 0.0
Fruit: 0.0
Bread: 1.0
Meat: 2.0
Fat: 0.0

1. Heat Low-Salt Chicken Stock, water, soy sauce, gingerroot, and garlic to boiling in large saucepan; stir in vermicelli. Reduce heat and simmer, uncovered, until pasta is al dente, about 4 minutes.

2. Stir in fish, shrimp, cucumber, and mushrooms and simmer, uncovered, until fish flakes with a fork, about 2 minutes. Stir in spinach. Season to taste with salt and cayenne pepper. Sprinkle each serving with green onions.

FISH SOUP WITH LETTUCE

Marinated fish combines with lettuce in this delicately flavored soup.

4 servings

8 ounces skinless walleye fillets, *or* other white fish, sliced into $1/2$-inch slices

2 teaspoons vegetable oil

1 teaspoon cornstarch

1 teaspoon reduced-sodium soy sauce

$1/4$ teaspoon toasted sesame oil

Dash white pepper

1 quart Easy Fish Stock (see p. 9), *or* chicken broth

4 cups thinly sliced romaine lettuce leaves

Salt and cayenne pepper, to taste

1 green onion and top, thinly sliced

Per Serving
Calories: 136
% Calories from fat: 30
Protein (gm): 15.2
Carbohydrate (gm): 3.2
Fat (gm): 3.5
Saturated fat (gm): 0.5
Cholesterol (mg): 58.6
Sodium (mg): 95
Exchanges
Milk: 0.0
Veg.: 1.0
Fruit: 0.0
Bread: 0.0
Meat: 2.0
Fat: 0.0

1. Toss fish with vegetable oil, cornstarch, soy sauce, sesame oil, and white pepper in medium bowl until well coated. Refrigerate, covered, 30 minutes.

2. Heat Easy Fish Stock to boiling in medium saucepan; stir in lettuce and heat to boiling. Stir in fish; reduce heat and simmer, uncovered, until tender, 2 to 3 minutes. Remove from heat; season to taste with salt and cayenne pepper. Stir in green onion.

SEAFOOD MONGOLIAN HOT POT

This one-pot meal is cooked at the table by none other than the guests themselves. The original hot pot had a coal-burning brazier, but we've had success with an electric wok or fry pan. Offer a side dish of rice and sauces such as Hoisin or lemon.

6 servings

1¹/₂-2 quarts Fish Stock, *or* Low-Salt Chicken Stock (see pp. 9, 3)
16 ounces fish fillets, such as haddock, grouper, or snapper, cut into thin strips
¹/₂ pound fresh spinach, trimmed
¹/₂ pound medium shrimp, peeled, deveined, butterflied
2 cups shredded lettuce
¹/₂ cup cubed firm tofu (¹/₂-inch)
¹/₂ cup minced onions
1 can (6¹/₂ ounces) water chestnuts, sliced
¹/₂ cup thinly sliced tomatoes
¹/₂ cup diced green, *or* red, bell peppers
¹/₃ cup chili sauce, optional

Per Serving
Calories: 198
% Calories from fat: 15
Protein (gm): 28.2
Carbohydrate (gm): 10.4
Fat (gm): 3.1
Saturated fat (gm): 0.5
Cholesterol (mg): 107.8
Sodium (mg): 168
Exchanges
Milk: 0.0
Veg.: 2.0
Fruit: 0.0
Bread: 0.0
Meat: 3.0
Fat: 0.0

1. Heat Fish Stock and transfer to electric wok set in center of table. Arrange remaining ingredients on platters.

2. Add desired foods to wok and cook, covered, on High about 10 minutes. Ladle food and some of the broth into shallow bowls; add chili sauce to taste. Repeat with remaining foods.

GUMBO

This classic Southern soup is updated to a lighter version here.

6 servings

Vegetable cooking spray
1 cup sliced onion
2 cups sliced okra
3 cups peeled, seeded, chopped tomatoes
1 quart Fish Stock, *or* Low-Salt Chicken Stock (see pp. 9, 3)
1 green bell pepper, sliced
1 bay leaf
1/4 teaspoon crushed red pepper
12 ounces red snapper fillets
12 ounces extra-large shrimp, peeled, deveined
1 teaspoon gumbo file powder
Salt and pepper, to taste
2 cups cooked rice, warm

Per Serving
Calories: 239
% Calories from fat: 8
Protein (gm): 25.9
Carbohydrate (gm): 26
Fat (gm): 2
Saturated fat (gm): 0.4
Cholesterol (mg): 111.8
Sodium (mg): 146
Exchanges
Milk: 0.0
Veg.: 2.0
Fruit: 0.0
Bread: 1.0
Meat: 2.0
Fat: 0.0

1. Spray large saucepan with cooking spray; saute onions and okra until onions are tender, about 5 minutes. Add tomatoes and Fish Stock and heat to boiling; reduce heat and simmer, covered, 5 minutes.

2. Add remaining ingredients, except file powder, salt, pepper, and rice; simmer, uncovered, until fish is tender and flakes with a fork, about 10 minutes. Discard bay leaf; stir in gumbo file and season to taste with salt and pepper. Serve over rice.

GEORGIA FISH SOUP

Okra, green peppers, tomatoes, and peanut butter combine in this unusual fish soup. We've used cod, but other firm-fleshed fish can be substituted.

6 servings

Vegetable cooking spray
1 cup thinly sliced onion
1/2 cup chopped green bell pepper
2 teaspoons minced garlic
2 teaspoons chili powder
1/2 teaspoon dried thyme leaves
1 can (28 ounces) reduced-sodium tomatoes, undrained, chopped
1/3-1/2 cup reduced-fat peanut butter
1 package (10 ounces) frozen sliced okra
16 ounces cod fillets, cut into 1/2-inch slices
Salt and pepper, to taste
Hot pepper sauce, to taste

Per Serving
Calories: 210
% Calories from fat: 28
Protein (gm): 19.9
Carbohydrate (gm): 19.2
Fat (gm): 6.7
Saturated fat (gm): 1.3
Cholesterol (mg): 32.4
Sodium (mg): 166
Exchanges
Milk: 0.0
Veg.: 3.0
Fruit: 0.0
Bread: 0.0
Meat: 2.0
Fat: 0.5

1. Spray large saucepan with cooking spray; heat over medium heat until hot. Saute onion, green pepper, garlic, chili powder, and thyme until onion is tender, about 5 minutes. Stir in tomatoes and liquid and peanut butter; heat to boiling. Reduce heat and simmer, uncovered, 5 minutes

2. Stir in okra and cod; simmer, covered, until okra is tender, about 10 minutes. Season to taste with salt, pepper, and hot pepper sauce.

CARIBBEAN-STYLE FLOUNDER

Here's our version of an island fisherman's feast—a flavorful dish of flounder, sweet potatoes, and tomatoes that's cooked to perfection in less than 30 minutes.

4 servings

2 teaspoons peanut oil

1 tablespoon annatto seeds

1 medium onion, thinly sliced

2 cups reduced-sodium fat-free chicken broth

1 sweet potato, peeled, cut into 1/2-inch cubes

1 can (14 ounces) reduced-sodium whole tomatoes, undrained, cut up

1 teaspoon dried thyme leaves

1 cup frozen peas

1 pound flounder fillets, cut into 3/4-inch cubes

4 teaspoons lemon juice

Salt and pepper, to taste

Per Serving
Calories: 240
% Calories from fat: 16
Protein (g): 28.5
Carbohydrates (g): 21.4
Fat (g): 4.2
Saturated fat (g): 0.8
Cholesterol (mg): 60.1
Sodium (mg): 227
Exchanges
Milk: 0.0
Veg.: 0.0
Fruit: 0.0
Bread: 1.0
Meat: 3.0
Fat: 0.0

1. Heat oil in large saucepan over medium-high heat; add annatto seeds and saute for 3 minutes. Remove seeds with slotted spoon and discard. Add onion to saucepan; saute 2 minutes.

2. Add broth, potato, tomatoes and liquid, and thyme. Heat to boiling; reduce heat and simmer, covered, until potato is tender, about 10 minutes.

3. Add peas and flounder; simmer until fish is tender and flakes with a fork, about 10 minutes. Stir in lemon juice; season to taste with salt and pepper.

SOPA AZTECA

This soup is reminiscent of the fare you'll find in a Mexican café.

4 servings

   2 corn tortillas, cut into thin strips
     Olive oil cooking spray
   1 cup sliced red onion
   4 cloves garlic, minced
 1¹/₂ quarts Fish Stock (see p. 9)
  12 ounces red snapper fillets, cut into
     1-inch pieces
 ¹/₂ teaspoon cumin seeds
 ¹/₂ teaspoon crushed red pepper
 ¹/₄ cup minced cilantro
 ¹/₄ cup chopped avocado
     Lime juice, to taste
     Salt, to taste
   6 tablespoons (1¹/₂ ounces) shredded
     reduced-fat Cheddar cheese

Per Serving
Calories: 237
% Calories from fat: 26
Protein (gm): 26
Carbohydrate (gm): 12.7
Fat (gm): 5.9
Saturated fat (gm): 2
Cholesterol (mg): 48.6
Sodium (mg): 163
Exchanges
Milk: 0.0
Veg.: 0.0
Fruit: 0.0
Bread: 1.0
Meat: 3.0
Fat: 0.0

1. Spray tortillas with cooking spray and cook over medium heat in large saucepan until crisp. Remove from saucepan and reserve.

2. Spray large saucepan with cooking spray; heat over medium heat until hot. Saute onion and garlic until tender, about 5 minutes. Add Fish Stock, red snapper, cumin seeds, and red pepper; heat to boiling. Reduce heat and simmer, uncovered, until fish is tender and flakes with a fork, 5 to 10 minutes.

3. Stir in cilantro and avocado; season to taste with lime juice and salt. Sprinkle each serving with cheese and reserved tortilla strips.

LIGHT FISH CHOWDER

Use any kind of fish you like in this nutritious fish chowder.

4 servings

1 large onion, chopped
3 medium carrots, sliced
2 ribs celery, sliced
2 teaspoons margarine
3 tablespoons flour
2 cups water
1 large potato, peeled, cubed
1/2 teaspoon dried thyme leaves
1 bay leaf
16 ounces lean whitefish fillets, skin
removed, cubed
2 cups fat-free milk
1/4 cup chopped parsley
Salt and white pepper, to taste

Per Serving
Calories: 258
% Calories from fat: **13**
Protein (gm): 28.1
Carbohydrate (gm): **27.3**
Fat (gm): 3.8
Saturated fat (gm): 0.9
Cholesterol (mg): 62.3
Sodium (mg): **219**
Exchanges
Milk: 0.5
Veg.: 1.0
Fruit: 0.0
Bread: 1.0
Meat: 2.0
Fat: 0.0

1. Saute onion, carrots, and celery in margarine in large saucepan until tender, about 10 minutes. Sprinkle with flour and cook 1 to 2 minutes longer. Add water and heat to boiling; stir in potato, thyme, and bay leaf. Reduce heat and simmer, covered, until potato is tender, about 15 minutes.

2. Stir in fish and milk; simmer, uncovered, until fish flakes with a fork, about 5 minutes. Stir in parsley; season to taste with salt and pepper.

SCANDINAVIAN FISH CHOWDER

This fish soup features cod, with accents of dill, cucumber, and hard-cooked egg.

8 servings

1 cup chopped celery
1/2 cup chopped onion
1 tablespoon margarine
1/4 cup all-purpose flour
2 cups water
2 cups diced, peeled potatoes
1/4 teaspoon ground allspice
2 cups fat-free milk
16 ounces cod fillets, cut into 1/2-inch pieces
1 teaspoon dried dill weed
1 cup chopped, seeded cucumber
2 tablespoons lemon juice
1/2 teaspoon paprika
Salt and pepper, to taste
Hard-cooked egg slices, as garnish

Per Serving
Calories: 159
% Calories from fat: 11
Protein (gm): 14.2
Carbohydrate (gm): 21
Fat (gm): 2.1
Saturated fat (gm): 0.5
Cholesterol (mg): 25.4
Sodium (mg): 99
Exchanges
Milk: 0.0
Veg.: 1.0
Fruit: 0.0
Bread: 1.0
Meat: 1.0
Fat: 0.0

1. Saute celery and onion in margarine in large saucepan until tender, about 5 minutes; sprinkle with flour and cook 1 to 2 minutes longer. Stir in water, potatoes, and allspice. Heat to boiling; reduce heat and simmer, covered, until potatoes are tender, about 15 minutes.

2. Stir in milk, cod, and dill weed; simmer until fish flakes with a fork, about 8 minutes. Stir in cucumber, lemon juice, and paprika; simmer 2 to 3 minutes longer. Season to taste with salt and pepper. Ladle soup into bowls; garnish with egg slices.

MAGYAR FISH SOUP

Hungarian paprika and caraway seeds flavor this interesting soup.

8 servings

2 quarts Easy Fish Stock (double recipe) (see p. 9)
1 teaspoon caraway seeds
1 tablespoon Hungarian paprika
2 pounds bass fillets, cut into 1-inch pieces
8 ounces halibut steaks, cut into 8 pieces
1 tomato, chopped
1 red bell pepper, chopped
Salt and pepper, to taste

Per Serving
Calories: 198
% Calories from fat: 18
Protein (gm): 30.6
Carbohydrate (gm): 2.9
Fat (gm): 3.3
Saturated fat (gm): 0.7
Cholesterol (mg): 65.8
Sodium (mg): 112
Exchanges
Milk: 0.0
Veg.: 0.0
Fruit: 0.0
Bread: 0.0
Meat: 4.0
Fat: 0.0

1. Heat Easy Fish Stock to boiling in large saucepan; add caraway seeds and Hungarian paprika. Reduce heat and simmer, covered, 10 minutes.

2. Add fish and simmer, uncovered, until fish is tender and flakes with a fork, 10 to 15 minutes. Stir in tomato and bell pepper; season to taste with salt and pepper.

FISH SOUP WITH VEGETABLES

This soup is delicious served with Roasted Red Pepper Bread (see p. 797).

8 servings

1 onion, chopped
4 cloves garlic, minced
2 ribs celery, chopped
2 carrots, sliced
1 green bell pepper, chopped
1 cup sliced mushrooms
2 tablespoons olive oil
2 cans (28 ounces each) crushed tomatoes, undrained
1 can (16 ounces) low-sodium tomato juice

Per Serving
Calories: 245
% Calories from fat: 19
Protein (g): 20.3
Carbohydrates (g): 25.1
Fat (g): 5.2
Saturated fat (g): 0.8
Cholesterol (mg): 32.8
Sodium (mg): 275
Exchanges
Milk: 0.0
Veg.: 2.5
Fruit: 0.0
Bread: 1.0
Meat: 2.0
Fat: 0.0

   1 bottle (6 ounces) clam juice
   3 medium potatoes, peeled, diced
 1/2 teaspoon black pepper
   1 teaspoon dried oregano leaves
   6 fresh basil leaves, chopped
   8 ounces halibut, cut into bite-sized
      pieces
   8 ounces sole, cut into bite-sized pieces
   8 ounces snapper, cut into bite-sized
      pieces
   1 cup dry white wine, *or* water
      Salt, to taste
3-4 tablespoons chopped parsley
   6 fresh basil sprigs, as garnish

1. Saute onion, garlic, celery, carrots, bell pepper, and mushrooms in oil in large saucepan until onion is tender, about 5 minutes. Add tomatoes and liquid, tomato juice, clam juice, potatoes, pepper, oregano, and chopped basil; heat to boiling. Reduce heat and simmer, covered, until potatoes are tender, about 15 minutes.

2. Add fish and wine; simmer, covered, until fish is tender and flakes with a fork, about 10 minutes. Season to taste with salt and stir in parsley. Garnish each serving with basil.

HEARTY FISH SOUP

This soup makes a hearty meal when served with salad and a crusty bread; a fruit dessert completes the meal.

6 servings

Vegetable cooking spray
1/4 cup finely chopped onion
2 ribs celery, sliced
2 carrots, sliced
1 green bell pepper, chopped
3 cans (16 ounces each) low-sodium whole tomatoes, undrained, chopped
1 bottle (6 ounces) clam juice
3 medium potatoes, peeled, diced
1 teaspoon dried oregano leaves
1/2 teaspoon pepper
8 ounces fillet of sole, cut into bite-sized pieces
8 ounces flounder, cut into bite-sized pieces
8 ounces orange roughy, cut into bite-sized pieces
1 cup dry white wine, *or* water
Salt and pepper, to taste
6 tablespoons chopped parsley
2 tablespoons finely chopped basil

Per Serving
Calories: 242
% Calories from fat: 6
Protein (gm): 23.3
Carbohydrate (gm): 28.6
Fat (gm): 1.7
Saturated fat (gm): 0.3
Cholesterol (mg): 46.7
Sodium (mg): 204
Exchanges
Milk: 0.0
Veg.: 2.0
Fruit: 0.0
Bread: 1.0
Meat: 2.0
Fat: 0.0

1. Spray large saucepan with cooking spray; heat over medium heat until hot. Saute onion, celery, carrots, and bell pepper until tender, about 5 minutes. Add tomatoes and liquid, clam juice, potatoes, oregano, and pepper and heat to boiling; reduce heat and simmer, covered, 20 minutes.

2. Add fish and wine; simmer, uncovered, until fish is tender and flakes with a fork, about 10 minutes. Season to taste with salt; stir in parsley and basil.

FISHERMAN'S CATCH

Use your favorite varieties of fish in this delicious soup, or cook up the catch of the day!

6 servings (about 1¹/₂ cups each)

¹/₂ cup chopped onion
¹/₂ cup chopped celery
¹/₂ cup chopped carrot
¹/₃ cup chopped parsley
 1 teaspoon dried rosemary leaves
 1 tablespoon margarine
 3 tablespoons flour
 1 can (15 ounces) diced tomatoes, undrained
 2 cups dry white wine, *or* vegetable broth
 1 bottle (8 ounces) clam juice
 8 ounces flounder, *or* ocean perch fillets, cut into 1-inch pieces
 8 ounces pike, *or* trout fillets, cut into 1-inch pieces
 8 ounces grouper, haddock, *or* halibut fillets, cut into 1-inch pieces
¹/₃ cup fat-free half-and-half, *or* fat-free milk
   Salt and pepper, to taste
 6 slices Italian bread, toasted

Per Serving
Calories: 302
% Calories from fat: 13
Protein (gm): 26.4
Carbohydrate (gm): 25.1
Fat (gm): 4.2
Saturated fat (gm): 0.9
Cholesterol (mg): 48.7
Sodium (mg): 662
Exchanges
Milk: 0.0
Veg.: 2.0
Fruit: 0.0
Bread: 1.0
Meat: 3.0
Fat: 0.0

1. Saute onion, celery, carrot, parsley, and rosemary in margarine in large saucepan until onion is tender, about 10 minutes. Sprinkle with flour and cook 1 to 2 minutes longer. Stir in tomatoes and liquid, wine, and clam juice; heat to boiling. Reduce heat and simmer, covered, 10 minutes.

2. Stir in fish; simmer until fish flakes with a fork, about 10 minutes. Stir in half-and-half; simmer 2 to 3 minutes. Season to taste with salt and pepper. Place bread in soup bowls; ladle soup over.

Variation:

Pesto Fish Soup—Make soup as above, adding 1 cup cooked cannellini, *or* Great Northern, beans, and omitting half-and-half. Stir ¹/₂ cup Fennel Pesto (see p. 814) into soup before serving.

FISH-OF-THE-DAY SOUP

The great fish stews, such as cioppino, are made with the fish catch of the day. Fish of similar types can be interchanged easily with good taste results.

6 servings

Olive oil cooking spray
1 cup chopped onion
4 cloves garlic, minced
4 large tomatoes, chopped
1/4 cup minced parsley
1/2 teaspoon dried oregano leaves
1/2 teaspoon dried basil leaves
3 bay leaves
1/2 teaspoon pepper
1/2 cup dry white wine
1 cup tomato juice
16 ounces cod, *or* halibut fillets, cut into 1 inch pieces
8 ounces red snapper fillets, cut into 1-inch pieces
8 little-neck clams, *or* cherrystone clams, scrubbed
8 ounces jumbo shrimp, peeled, deveined
1 1/4 quarts Fish Stock (see p. 9)
Salt, to taste
1 1/2 cups Garlic Croutons (1/2 recipe) (see p. 785)

Per Serving
Calories: 258
% Calories from fat: 13
Protein (gm): 35.3
Carbohydrate (gm): 13.4
Fat (gm): 3.3
Saturated fat (gm): 0.6
Cholesterol (mg): 105.2
Sodium (mg): 333
Exchanges
Milk: 0.0
Veg.: 0.0
Fruit: 0.0
Bread: 0.5
Meat: 4.0
Fat: 0.0

1. Spray large saucepan with cooking spray; heat over medium heat until hot. Saute onion and garlic until tender, about 5 minutes. Add tomatoes, herbs, pepper, wine, and tomato juice and heat to boiling; reduce heat and simmer, covered, 5 minutes. Add seafood and Fish Stock; simmer, uncovered, until fish is tender and flakes with a fork. Discard any unopened clams. Discard bay leaves; season to taste with salt. Serve with Garlic Croutons.

NIÇOISE FISH SOUP

Every fisherman has his own version of fish soup. For the most authentic flavor, use several different varieties of fish.

8 servings

1 cup chopped onion
1 tablespoon minced garlic
1 tablespoon olive oil
3 cups water
1 cup bottled clam juice
2 cups chopped tomatoes
1/2 teaspoon dried thyme leaves
1/2 teaspoon crushed fennel seeds
1/2 teaspoon ground turmeric
1 bay leaf
2 pounds assorted firm, lean fish (halibut, haddock, red snapper, cod, etc.), cut into 1-inch chunks
Salt and cayenne pepper, to taste
Bruschetta (see p. 785)

Per Serving
Calories: 240
% Calories from fat: 20
Protein (gm): 27
Carbohydrate (gm): 19.9
Fat (gm): 5.4
Saturated fat (gm): 0.8
Cholesterol (mg): 36.1
Sodium (mg): 309
Exchanges
Milk: 0.0
Veg.: 1.0
Fruit: 0.0
Bread: 1.0
Meat: 2.5
Fat: 0.0

1. Saute onion and garlic in oil in large saucepan until tender, about 5 minutes. Stir in water, clam juice, tomatoes, and herbs. Heat to boiling; reduce heat and simmer, covered, 10 minutes. Discard bay leaf.

2. Add fish and heat to boiling; reduce heat and simmer until fish flakes with a fork, about 5 minutes. Season to taste with salt and cayenne pepper. Place Bruschetta in soup bowls; ladle soup over.

FISH SOUP MARSEILLES

Fresh fennel gives this soup its authentic South-of-France flavor; substitute 2 teaspoons fennel seeds if you prefer.

6 servings (about 1¹/₂ cups each)

1 medium onion, chopped

1 small fennel bulb, sliced

1 tablespoon minced garlic

2 teaspoons olive oil

1 can (14¹/₂ ounces) Italian-style stewed tomatoes, undrained

3-4 cups Mediterranean Vegetable Stock (see p. 15), *or* reduced-sodium fat-free chicken broth

1 cup uncooked orzo, *or* other small soup pasta

8 ounces firm, white-fleshed fish, cut into 1-inch pieces

6 ounces small shrimp, peeled, deveined

Salt and pepper, to taste

Per Serving
Calories: 231
% Calories from fat: 14
Protein (gm): 16.5
Carbohydrate (gm): 29.9
Fat (gm): 3.4
Saturated fat (gm): 0.5
Cholesterol (mg): 63.4
Sodium (mg): 227
Exchanges
Milk: 0.0
Veg.: 0.0
Fruit: 0.0
Bread: 2.0
Meat: 2.0
Fat: 0.0

1. Saute onion, fennel, and garlic in oil in large saucepan until tender, about 8 minutes. Stir in stewed tomatoes and liquid and Mediterranean Vegetable Stock. Heat to boiling; stir in orzo and reduce heat. Simmer, covered, until orzo is almost tender, about 8 minutes.

2. Add fish and shrimp; simmer, uncovered, until fish is tender and flakes with a fork and shrimp are pink, 5 to 10 minutes. Season to taste with salt and pepper.

SHORTCUT FISH SOUP

This soup is made easy with a base of prepared spaghetti sauce.

6 servings (about 1¹/₃ cups each)

1 medium onion, thinly sliced
2 cloves garlic, minced
1 teaspoon crushed red pepper
1 teaspoon olive oil
1 jar (20 ounces) spaghetti sauce
1 bottle (8 ounces) clam juice
1 cup water
¹/₂ cup dry white wine
1¹/₂ pounds assorted skinless lean fish fillets (whitefish, cod, snapper, *or* flounder)
1 can (6 ounces) whole clams, undrained
Salt and pepper, to taste
¹/₄ cup chopped parsley

Per Serving
Calories: 227
% Calories from fat: 24
Protein (gm): 22.4
Carbohydrate (gm): 17.6
Fat (gm): 6.1
Saturated fat (gm): 0.9
Cholesterol (mg): 49.4
Sodium (mg): 695
Exchanges
Milk: 0.0
Veg.: 3.0
Fruit: 0.0
Bread: 0.0
Meat: 3.0
Fat: 0.0

1. Saute onion, garlic, and red pepper in oil in large saucepan until tender, about 5 minutes. Stir in spaghetti sauce, clam juice, water, and wine; heat to boiling. Reduce heat and simmer, covered, 10 minutes.

2. Stir in fish and clams with liquor; heat to boiling. Reduce heat and simmer, covered, until fish is tender and flakes with a fork, about 10 minutes. Season to taste with salt and pepper. Stir in parsley.

FISH SOUP

Along the Tuscan coast, each town boasts its own incomparable fish soup. The pride of Livorno is known as cacciucco. Although many versions can be found, each usually holds a touch of hot red chili and five different kinds of fish, one for each of the c's in the dish's name. If you prefer, you can use just two kinds of fish.

6 servings

- 3 cloves garlic, minced
- 2 medium onions, chopped
  Olive oil
- 3/4 teaspoon crushed red pepper
- 2 tablespoons chopped Italian parsley
- 1 cup dry red wine
- 3 pounds tomatoes, peeled, seeded, chopped
- 1 quart chicken broth
- 1 1/2 pounds mixed skinless fish fillets, such as sole, flounder, rockfish, snapper, tuna, and halibut, cut into 3/4-inch chunks
- 4 ounces medium shrimp, peeled, deveined
- 2 tablespoons fresh Italian parsley
- 2 tablespoons fresh, *or* 1 teaspoon dried, oregano leaves
- 2 tablespoons fresh, *or* 1 teaspoon dried, sage leaves
- 2 tablespoons fresh, *or* 1 teaspoon dried, rosemary leaves
  Salt and pepper, to taste
- 6 slices crusty Italian bread, toasted
- 2 cloves garlic, halved

Per Serving
Calories: 337
% Calories from fat: 19
Protein (g): 28.6
Carbohydrates (g): 33.7
Fat (g): 7.1
Saturated fat (g): 1.1
Cholesterol (mg): 82.2
Sodium (mg): 337
Exchanges
Milk: 0.0
Veg.: 2.5
Fruit: 0.0
Bread: 1.5
Meat: 3.0
Fat: 0.0

1. Saute garlic and onions in olive oil in large saucepan until onions are tender, about 5 minutes. Stir in crushed red pepper and parsley and saute 1 to 2 minutes; add wine and cook 2 minutes longer.

2. Add tomatoes and broth and heat to boiling. Reduce heat and simmer, covered, 20 minutes; add fish and shrimp and cook, uncovered, until fish is tender and flakes with a fork, about 10 minute. Stir in herbs; season to taste with salt and pepper.

3. Rub warm toasted bread with halved garlic cloves. Place a slice in each serving bowl and ladle soup over.

CIOPPINO

Our version of this classic Italian soup is made with shellfish. Clams in their shells are traditionally used, but canned whole clams may be substituted, if you prefer.

6 servings

1 large onion, thinly sliced
1 green bell pepper, diced
1 cup sliced green onions and tops
3 cloves garlic, minced
1 tablespoon olive oil
1 can (14^1/$_2$ ounces) reduced-sodium diced tomatoes, undrained
1 cup dry white wine, *or* clam juice
1 cup water
1 teaspoon dried tarragon leaves
1 teaspoon dried thyme leaves
^{1}/$_4$ teaspoon dried rosemary leaves, crumbled
1 bay leaf
1 cup diced fresh tomato
1 pound crabmeat, flaked, *or* firm whitefish, cubed
8-12 ounces shrimp, peeled, deveined
16 clams in shells, scrubbed
Salt and pepper, to taste

Per Serving
Calories: 201
% Calories from fat: 19
Protein (g): 24.1
Carbohydrates (g): 10.2
Fat (g): 4.3
Saturated fat (g): 0.6
Cholesterol (mg): 130.6
Sodium (mg): 276
Exchanges
Milk: 0.0
Veg.: 2.0
Fruit: 0.0
Bread: 0.0
Meat: 3.0
Fat: 0.0

1. Saute onion, bell pepper, green onions, and garlic in oil in large saucepan until tender, about 8 minutes. Add canned tomatoes and liquid, wine, water, and herbs. Heat to boiling; reduce heat and simmer, covered, 20 minutes.

2. Add diced tomato, crabmeat, shrimp, and clams; heat to boiling. Reduce heat and simmer until shrimp are cooked and clams have opened, about 8 minutes. Discard bay leaf and any clams that have not opened. Season to taste with salt and pepper.

CIOPPINO MEDITERRANEAN

This popular California fish soup is given an Italian accent.

6 servings

 ¹/₄ cup chopped green bell pepper
 2 tablespoons finely chopped onion
 1 clove garlic, minced
 1 tablespoon olive oil
 2 cans (16 ounces each) whole tomatoes, undrained, chopped
 1 can (6 ounces) low-sodium tomato paste
 1 cup water
 ¹/₂ cup dry red wine
 3 tablespoons chopped parsley
 ¹/₂ teaspoon Spike
 1 teaspoon dried oregano leaves
 1 teaspoon dried basil leaves
 16 ounces fillet of sole, cut into bite-sized pieces
 16 ounces shrimp, peeled, deveined
 1 can (7¹/₂ ounce) minced clams, undrained
 Salt and pepper, to taste

Per Serving
Calories: 224
% Calories from fat: 18
Protein (gm): 29.4
Carbohydrate (gm): 14.4
Fat (gm): 4.5
Saturated fat (gm): 0.8
Cholesterol (mg): 156.7
Sodium (mg): 312
Exchanges
Milk: 0.0
Veg.: 2.0
Fruit: 0.0
Bread: 0.0
Meat: 3.0
Fat: 0.0

1. Saute bell pepper, onion, and garlic in oil in large saucepan until tender, about 5 minutes. Add remaining ingredients, except seafood, salt, and pepper, and heat to boiling. Reduce heat and simmer, covered, 20 minutes.

2. Add sole, shrimp, and clams and liquor and simmer until sole is tender and flakes with a fork, about 5 minutes. Season to taste with salt and pepper.

MEDITERRANEAN-STYLE SHRIMP VEGETABLE SOUP

A fragrant soup with a citrus accent.

6 servings (about 1½ cups each)

Olive oil cooking spray
2 cups sliced mushrooms
1 medium onion, chopped
½ medium green bell pepper, chopped
3 cloves garlic, minced
1 can (16 ounces) reduced-sodium whole tomatoes, undrained, coarsely chopped
1 can (8 ounces) reduced-sodium tomato sauce
1 pound peeled, deveined shrimp
1-2 cups vegetable broth
½ cup dry white wine, *or* orange juice
½-1 cup clam juice
2 strips orange rind (3 x ½ inch)
2 bay leaves
1 teaspoon dried marjoram leaves
½-¾ teaspoon dried savory leaves
¼ teaspoon fennel seeds, crushed
Salt and pepper, to taste

Per Serving
Calories: 121
% Calories from fat: 8
Protein (g): 14.8
Carbohydrates (g): 10.7
Fat (g): 1.1
Saturated fat (g): 0.2
Cholesterol (mg): 115.6
Sodium (mg): 211
Exchanges
Milk: 0.0
Veg.: 2.0
Fruit: 0.0
Bread: 0.0
Meat: 1.0
Fat: 0.0

1. Spray large saucepan with cooking spray; heat over medium heat until hot. Add mushrooms, onion, bell pepper, and garlic; saute, covered, until vegetables are tender, 8 to 10 minutes. Add remaining ingredients, except salt and pepper; heat to boiling. Reduce heat and simmer, covered, 10 to 15 minutes. Season to taste with salt and pepper.

KAKAVIA

What the French call bouillabaisse the Greeks call kakavia. This is a favorite entertaining recipe because it feeds a crowd and can be made in advance. Add baby lobster tails for a special occasion.

12 servings

Vegetable cooking spray
4 cups chopped onions
2 ribs celery, chopped
1 tablespoon minced garlic
2 leeks, white parts only, sliced
3 large carrots, peeled, chopped
1 can (16 ounces) plum tomatoes, undrained, coarsely chopped
1 quart water
1 cup dry white wine
1 tablespoon Spike
1 teaspoon pepper
3 tablespoons lemon juice
4-6 pounds fish fillets (striped bass, sea bass, *or* red snapper), cut into bite-sized pieces
12 clams, scrubbed
12 shrimp, peeled, deveined
12 mussels, scrubbed
3 bay leaves
1/2 teaspoon dried thyme leaves
1/4 cup minced parsley
Salt, to taste

Per Serving
Calories: 241
% Calories from fat: 15
Protein (gm): 34.2
Carbohydrate (gm): 13.4
Fat (gm): 3.9
Saturated fat (gm): 0.9
Cholesterol (mg): 81.7
Sodium (mg): 249
Exchanges
Milk: 0.0
Veg.: 2.0
Fruit: 0.0
Bread: 0.0
Meat: 4.0
Fat: 0.0

1. Spray large saucepan with cooking spray; heat over medium heat until hot. Saute onions, celery, garlic, leeks, and carrots until onions are tender, about 10 minutes.

2. Add tomatoes and liquid, water, wine, Spike, pepper, and lemon juice; heat to boiling. Add remaining ingredients, except parsley and salt; reduce heat and simmer, covered, until fish is tender and clams and mussels open, about 10 minutes. Discard any unopened clams and mussels; discard bay leaves. Stir in parsley; season to taste with salt.

CALDO DE PESCADO

This South American fish soup includes a medley of vegetables, with a flavor accent of orange.

10 servings

2 cups chopped onions

3 cloves garlic, minced

1 large red bell pepper, chopped

1 tablespoon olive oil

2 cups peeled, sliced potatoes

3 cups Fish Stock (see p. 9)

1 can (28 ounce) crushed red tomatoes, undrained

2 large ears corn, husked, cut into 1-inch pieces

1/4 teaspoon grated orange rind

1/4 teaspoon cayenne pepper

1/4 teaspoon turmeric

16 ounces Pacific rockfish fillets, cut into 1-inch strips

12 ounces red snapper fillets, cut into 1-inch strips

12 ounces large shrimp, peeled, deveined, cut into 1-inch pieces

Salt, to taste

Per Serving
Calories: 223
% Calories from fat: **13**
Protein (gm): 24.9
Carbohydrate (gm): 22.1
Fat (gm): 3.1
Saturated fat (gm): 0.6
Cholesterol (mg): 82
Sodium (mg): 305
Exchanges
Milk: 0.0
Veg.: 2.0
Fruit: 0.0
Bread: 1.0
Meat: 2.0
Fat: 0.0

1. Saute onions, garlic, and bell pepper in olive oil in large saucepan until onion is soft. Add remaining ingredients, except fish, shrimp, and salt, and heat to boiling. Reduce heat and simmer, covered, 15 to 20 minutes. Add fish and shrimp and cook until fish is tender and flakes with a fork, 5 to 10 minutes; season to taste with salt.

SPANISH FISH SOUP

This unique soup is flavored with ground almonds and thickened with bread.

8 servings (about 1¼ cups each)

Olive oil cooking spray
1 cup chopped onion
½ teaspoon crushed red pepper
½ teaspoon paprika
¼ teaspoon cumin seeds
3 cups water
3 cups bottled clam juice
2 cups dry white wine, *or* clam juice
⅓ cup ground almonds
2 slices firm white bread, crusts removed, cubed
1 cup fat-free milk
2 pounds halibut, *or* other firm whitefish, cubed (1-inch)
2 hard-cooked egg yolks, finely chopped
1 cup fat-free half-and-half, *or* fat-free milk
Salt and pepper, to taste
8 thin slices lemon
Chopped parsley, as garnish

Per Serving
Calories: 275
% Calories from fat: **23**
Protein (gm): 28.1
Carbohydrate (gm): **11.5**
Fat (gm): 6.5
Saturated fat (gm): **1**
Cholesterol (mg): **90**
Sodium (mg): **356**
Exchanges
Milk: 0.0
Veg.: 0.0
Fruit: 0.0
Bread: 1.0
Meat: 3.0
Fat: 1.0

1. Spray large saucepan with cooking spray; heat over medium heat until hot. Saute onion, crushed red pepper, paprika, and cumin until tender, about 5 minutes. Stir in water, clam juice, wine, and almonds. Heat to boiling; reduce heat and simmer, uncovered, 20 minutes.

2. Soak bread in milk; mash until smooth. Stir bread mixture into soup; simmer, uncovered, 10 minutes.

3. Stir halibut and egg yolk into soup; simmer until fish is tender and flakes with a fork, about 5 minutes. Stir in half-and-half; simmer 2 to 3 minutes longer. Season to taste with salt and pepper. Serve soup in bowls; float lemon slices on top and sprinkle with parsley.

PORTUGUESE-STYLE FISHERMAN'S POT

This is an attractive, robustly seasoned soup offering.

5-6 servings

2	large onions, finely chopped
1	large carrot, finely chopped
1	small rib celery, finely chopped
1/2	cup diced red bell pepper
1/4	cup parsley, finely chopped
1	large garlic clove, minced
1	tablespoon olive oil
1 1/2	cups fat-free chicken broth
3-4	medium red potatoes, peeled, cut into 1/2-inch cubes
2	cans (16 ounces each) tomatoes, undrained, coarsely chopped
3/4	cup dry white wine
1	teaspoon sugar
1	bay leaf
1 3/4	teaspoons chili powder
1 3/4	teaspoons paprika
1/4	teaspoon celery seeds
1/4	teaspoon dried thyme leaves
	Pinch of saffron threads, crumbled, optional
1/4	teaspoon black pepper
	Pinch crushed red pepper
20-24	fresh mussels, scrubbed
1 1/2	pounds skinless cod, haddock, *or* lean whitefish fillets, cut into bite-sized pieces
8	ounces medium shrimp, peeled, deveined
	Salt, to taste

Per Serving
Calories: 363
% Calories from fat: 15
Protein (g): 40.3
Carbohydrates (g): 32.8
Fat (g): 5.9
Saturated fat (g): 0.7
Cholesterol (mg): 144.5
Sodium (mg): 723
Exchanges
Milk: 0.0
Veg.: 0.0
Fruit: 0.0
Bread: 2.0
Meat: 4.0
Fat: 0.0

1. Saute onions, carrot, celery, bell pepper, parsley, and garlic in oil in large saucepan until onions are tender, about 10 minutes. Add broth and potatoes and heat to boiling. Reduce heat and simmer, covered, 10 to 15 minutes or until potatoes are tender.

2. Add tomatoes and liquid, wine, sugar, herbs, and pepper; simmer, uncovered, until slightly thickened, about 20 minutes. Add mussels and fish and simmer, covered, 5 minutes. Stir in shrimp and simmer, covered, until mussels open and fish and shrimp are tender, about 5 minutes. Discard bay leaf and any mussels that do not open; season to taste with salt.

EIGHT

Vegetarian Soups

GAZPACHO

The perfect mid-summer treat with garden-ripe tomatoes.

4 servings (about 1¼ cups each)

3 cups chopped, peeled, seeded tomatoes
1½ cups no-salt-added tomato juice
¾ cup chopped, peeled, seeded cucumber
⅓ cup chopped onion
⅓ cup plus 4 teaspoons chopped green
    bell pepper, divided
1 clove garlic, minced
2 tablespoons balsamic vinegar
¼ teaspoon hot pepper sauce
4 cucumber slices

Per Serving
Calories: 77
% Calories from fat: **7**
Protein (gm): 2.7
Carbohydrate (gm): **17.5**
Fat (gm): 0.7
Saturated fat (gm): **0.1**
Cholesterol (mg): 0
Sodium (mg): 29
Exchanges
Milk: 0.0
Veg.: 3.0
Fruit: 0.0
Bread: 0.0
Meat: 0.0
Fat: 0.0

1. Process tomatoes, tomato juice, cucumber, onion, ⅓ cup bell pepper, and garlic in food processor or blender until almost smooth. Pour into large bowl; stir in vinegar and hot pepper sauce. Cover and chill at least 2 hours.

2. Serve in bowls; garnish with cucumber slices and remaining 4 teaspoons bell pepper.

WHITE GAZPACHO

Something different that is sure to please!

4 servings (about 1 cup each)

Vegetable cooking spray
1 large onion, sliced
4 cloves garlic, minced
1-2 cups fat-free milk
1/2-1 vegetable bouillon cube
1 cup fat-free plain yogurt
2 teaspoons lemon juice
2 dashes hot pepper sauce
Salt and white pepper, to taste
1/3 cup chopped, seeded cucumber
1/3 cup chopped, seeded yellow tomato
1/3 cup cubed avocado
Finely chopped cilantro, *or* parsley, as garnish

Per Serving
Calories: 109
% Calories from fat: 27
Protein (g): 6.7
Carbohydrates (g): 14.3
Fat (g): 3.4
Saturated fat (g): 0.6
Cholesterol (mg): 2
Sodium (mg): 196
Exchanges
Milk: 0.5
Veg.: 2.0
Fruit: 0.0
Bread: 0.0
Meat: 0.0
Fat: 0.5

1. Spray large saucepan with cooking spray; heat over medium heat until hot. Cook onion and garlic over medium-low heat until very tender, about 15 minutes. Add milk and bouillon cube; cook over medium-high heat, stirring frequently, until mixture is hot and bouillon cube is dissolved.

2. Process soup, yogurt, lemon juice, and hot pepper sauce in food processor or blender until smooth. Season to taste with salt and white pepper. Cool; refrigerate until chilled, 3 to 4 hours.

3. Stir cucumber, tomato, and avocado into soup; pour into bowls and sprinkle with cilantro.

BEAN GAZPACHO

Pureed beans contribute a creamy texture and subtle flavor to this unusual gazpacho. Canned pinto beans, rinsed and drained, can be substituted for the dried.

8 servings (about 1¹/₃ cups each)

4 cups cooked dried pinto beans, divided
1 quart reduced-sodium tomato juice
3-4 tablespoons lime juice
2 teaspoons reduced-sodium Worcestershire sauce
1 jar (16 ounces) thick and chunky mild, *or* medium, salsa
1 cup chopped, peeled, seeded cucumber
1 cup thinly sliced celery
¹/₂ cup chopped onion
¹/₂ cup chopped green bell pepper
2 teaspoons minced roasted garlic
¹/₂ small avocado, peeled, chopped
1¹/₂ cups Herb Croutons (¹/₂ recipe) (see p. 784)

Per Serving
Calories: 422
% Calories from fat: **7**
Protein (gm): 23.3
Carbohydrate (gm): 78.4
Fat (gm): 3.4
Saturated fat (gm): 0.7
Cholesterol (mg): 0.1
Sodium (mg): 512
Exchanges
Milk: 0.0
Veg.: 2.0
Fruit: 0.0
Bread: 5.0
Meat: 0.0
Fat: 0.5

1. Process 2 cups beans, tomato juice, lime juice, and Worcestershire sauce in food processor or blender until smooth; pour into large bowl. Mix in remaining 2 cups beans and remaining ingredients, except avocado and Herb Croutons. Refrigerate until chilled, 3 to 4 hours.

2. Mix avocado into soup and pour into bowls; sprinkle with Herb Croutons.

BEET SOUP WITH MASHED POTATOES AND YOGURT

The concept of cold soup served with hot potatoes is interesting and surprising; the flavors meld unusually well.

8 servings

1¹/₂ pounds beets, washed, trimmed
1 quart water
2 teaspoons sugar
1 tablespoon red wine vinegar
  Salt and pepper, to taste
4 large Idaho potatoes
2 cups fat-free plain yogurt

Per Serving
Calories: 126
% Calories from fat: 2
Protein (gm): 5.6
Carbohydrate (gm): 26.1
Fat (gm): 0.3
Saturated fat (gm): 0.1
Cholesterol (mg): 1
Sodium (mg): 103
Exchanges
Milk: 0.0
Veg.: 2.0
Fruit: 0.0
Bread: 1.0
Meat: 0.0
Fat: 0.0

1. Place beets in large saucepan and cover with water. Heat to boiling; reduce heat and simmer, covered, until tender, about 35 minutes. Drain and cool beets; peel and slice. Process beets in food processor until smooth.

2. Return beets to saucepan. Mix in 1 quart water, sugar, and vinegar. Heat mixture to boiling; reduce heat and simmer, covered, 20 minutes, stirring occasionally. Season to taste with salt and pepper. Cool; refrigerate several hours until chilled.

3. Bake potatoes at 425 degrees 45 minutes or until tender. Peel and mash potatoes; season to taste with salt and pepper.

4. Ladle chilled soup into bowls; spoon hot mashed potatoes into center of each bowl and spoon in yogurt to the side.

SPINACH SOUP WITH ONION FLOWERS

An attractive appetizer offering! Roasted Chicken, Roasted Vegetable, or Oriental Vegetable Stocks (see pp. 4, 14, 16) can also be used to make this soup.

8 servings (about 1 cup each)

8 small onions, peeled
2¹/₄ quarts Canned Vegetable Stock (1¹/₂ recipes) (see p. 11), divided
1 package (10 ounces) frozen spinach
Salt and white pepper, to taste
Green onions and tops, thinly sliced, as garnish

Per Serving
Calories: 107
% Calories from fat: 9
Protein (g): 2.6
Carbohydrates (g): 15.7
Fat (g): 1.1
Saturated fat (g): 0.1
Cholesterol (mg): 0
Sodium (mg): 85
Exchanges
Milk: 0.0
Veg.: 2.0
Fruit: 0.0
Bread: 0.5
Meat: 0.0
Fat: 0.0

1. Cut onions into ¹/₄-inch slices from top to bottom, cutting to, but not through, the bottoms. Turn onions a quarter turn; cut into ¹/₄-inch slices, intersecting previous slices and cutting to, but not through, the bottoms.

2. Heat 6 cups Canned Vegetable Stock to boiling in large saucepan; add onions. Reduce heat and simmer, covered, until onions are tender, about 20 minutes. Remove onions from stock with slotted spoon. Reserve stock.

3. Heat spinach and remaining 3 cups Canned Vegetable Stock to boiling in medium saucepan; reduce heat and simmer, covered, 10 minutes. Strain, pressing lightly on spinach to extract all juice. Discard spinach, or reserve for other use.

4. Combine stock from onions and spinach; heat until hot. Season to taste with salt and white pepper. Arrange onions in serving bowls; pour soup around onions and sprinkle with green onions. Serve with knives, forks, and spoons.

WONTON SOUP

Wontons can be assembled up to 1 day in advance; dust lightly with flour and refrigerate in a single layer on a plate, covered tightly with plastic wrap.

6 servings

24 Five-Spice Wontons (recipe follows)
6 cups Oriental Vegetable Stock (see p. 16), *or* vegetable broth
1 cup sliced spinach
Reduced-sodium tamari soy sauce
Pepper, to taste
1 medium green onion, sliced

Per Serving
Calories: 109
% Calories from fat: 7
Protein (g): 6.4
Carbohydrates (g): 18.7
Fat (g): 0.9
Saturated fat (g): 0.1
Cholesterol (mg): 3.3
Sodium (mg): 363
Exchanges
Milk: 0.0
Veg.: 1.0
Fruit: 0.0
Bread: 1.0
Meat: 0.0
Fat: 0.0

1. Make Five-Spice Wontons.

2. Heat Oriental Stock to boiling in large saucepan. Add wontons and simmer, uncovered, until wontons rise to the surface, 2 to 3 minutes. Stir in spinach; simmer 2 to 3 minutes longer. Season to taste with soy sauce and pepper.

3. Pour soup into bowls; sprinkle with green onion.

Five-Spice Wontons

makes 24

Vegetable cooking spray
1 cup sliced Chinese cabbage
1/4 cup shredded carrot
2 tablespoons thinly sliced green onions and tops
2 tablespoons thinly sliced celery
1/2-1 teaspoon minced gingerroot
1 small clove garlic, minced
1/2 tablespoon wheat germ
1/2 tablespoon reduced-sodium tamari soy sauce
1/4 teaspoon hot chili paste
1/4 teaspoon five-spice powder

>   1 ounce light tofu, cut into small cubes or
>   coarsely crumbled
>   24 won ton, *or gyoza*, wrappers
>   1 egg white, beaten

1. Spray wok or large skillet with cooking spray; heat over medium heat until hot. Stir-fry cabbage, carrot, green onions, celery, gingerroot, and garlic over medium-high heat until cabbage is wilted, 2 to 3 minutes. Remove from heat; stir in wheat germ, tamari soy sauce, chili paste, and five-spice powder. Add tofu, toss lightly, and cool.

2. Spoon 1/2 tablespoon filling on won ton wrapper; brush edges of wrapper with egg white. Fold wrapper in half and press edges to seal. Repeat with remaining filling, wrappers, and egg white.

CREAMED CORN SOUP

Garnish this colorful soup with a sprinkling of finely chopped cilantro or parsley.

6 servings

    Vegetable cooking spray
1/2 cup chopped onion
  1 medium Idaho potato, peeled, cubed
  2 cloves garlic, minced
  1 can (15 1/2 ounces) whole-kernel corn, drained
  3 tablespoons flour
1/2 teaspoon ground coriander
1/8 teaspoon cayenne pepper
  2 cans (14 1/2 ounces each) vegetable broth
  1 cup fat-free milk
  2 medium tomatoes, chopped
    Salt and pepper, to taste
    Paprika, as garnish

Per Serving
Calories: 144
% Calories from fat: 6
Protein (g): 5.2
Carbohydrates (g): 31.2
Fat (g): 1
Saturated fat (g): 0.2
Cholesterol (mg): 0.7
Sodium (mg): 313
Exchanges
Milk: 0.0
Veg.: 0.0
Fruit: 0.0
Bread: 2.0
Meat: 0.0
Fat: 0.0

1. Spray large saucepan with cooking spray; heat over medium heat until hot. Saute onion, potato, and garlic until onion is tender, 3 to 5 minutes. Stir in corn, flour, coriander, and cayenne pepper; cook 1 to 2 minutes. Stir in broth and heat to boiling; reduce heat and simmer, covered, until potato is tender, about 10 minutes.

2. Process mixture in food processor or blender until almost smooth; return to saucepan. Stir in milk and tomatoes; simmer, uncovered, 5 minutes. Season to taste with salt and pepper. Serve soup in bowls; sprinkle with paprika.

Variation:

Latin-American Corn and Avocado Soup—Make soup as above, omitting tomatoes and adding 1/2 teaspoon crushed saffron in Step 1. Beat 2 eggs with 4 ounces fat-free cream cheese and 2 tablespoons prepared chili sauce. Gradually whisk into pureed soup in Step 2. Garnish soup with avocado slices.

CORN SOUP WITH EPAZOTE

Epazote is a popular Mexican herb, which can be purchased in Mexican groceries. It's easy to grow but must be planted annually in northern climates. One-half to one teaspoon of dried epazote or dried thyme leaves can be substituted.

4 servings (about 1 1/2 cups each)

3/4 cup chopped onion
1 medium jalapeño chili, finely chopped
1 clove garlic, minced
1 tablespoon vegetable oil
3 1/2 cups Roasted Vegetable Stock (see p. 14), *or* vegetable broth
5 cups frozen whole-kernel corn
2 tablespoons finely chopped fresh, *or* 1/2 teaspoon dried, epazote, *or* dried thyme leaves
Salt, cayenne, and white pepper, to taste
3/4 cup Roasted Red Pepper Sauce (1/2 recipe) (see p. 213)

Per Serving
Calories: 162
% Calories from fat: 28
Protein (g): 3.2
Carbohydrates (g): 20.6
Fat (g): 5
Saturated fat (g): 0.7
Cholesterol (mg): 0
Sodium (mg): 202
Exchanges
Milk: 0.0
Veg.: 1.0
Fruit: 0.0
Bread: 1.5
Meat: 0.0
Fat: 0.5

1. Saute onion, jalapeño chili, and garlic in oil in large saucepan until tender, about 5 minutes. Add Roasted Vegetable Stock and corn; heat to boiling. Reduce heat and simmer, covered, 10 minutes.

2. Process soup in food processor or blender until almost smooth; stir in epazote and season to taste with salt and cayenne and white pepper.

3. Serve soup warm, or refrigerate until chilled and serve cold. Pour soup into bowls; swirl about 3 tablespoons Roasted Red Pepper Sauce into each bowl.

EASY MEXICAN CORN AND BEAN SOUP

This spicy soup is quick and easy to prepare.

4-5 servings

1 large onion, finely chopped
1 large garlic clove, minced
1 tablespoon canola oil
2¹/₂ cups reduced-sodium tomato juice
1 medium green bell pepper, diced
1 can (14¹/₂ ounces) reduced-sodium tomatoes, undrained, pureed
2 cups cooked kidney beans, *or* 1 can (16 ounces) kidney beans, rinsed, drained
2 cups whole-kernel corn
1 tablespoon chili powder
1 teaspoon ground cumin
1 teaspoon sugar
¹/₄ teaspoon black pepper
Salt, to taste

Per Serving
Calories: 232
% Calories from fat: **14**
Protein (g): 10.6
Carbohydrates (g): **44.2**
Fat (g): 3.8
Saturated fat (g): 0.3
Cholesterol (mg): 0
Sodium (mg): 45
Exchanges
Milk: 0.0
Veg.: 2.0
Fruit: 0.0
Bread: 2.0
Meat: 0.0
Fat: 0.5

1. Saute onion and garlic in oil in large saucepan until onion is soft. Add remaining ingredients, except salt, and heat to boiling. Reduce heat and simmer, covered, 20 to 25 minutes or until flavors are well blended. Add salt to taste.

SOUTHWEST-STYLE POTATO-CORN CHOWDER CON QUESO

Add jalapeño chilies to this satisfying soup, if you like a fiery tang.

5 servings

2/3 cup chopped onion
2 teaspoons margarine
1 tablespoon flour
3 cups Vegetable Stock (see p. 11)
3 1/2 cups cubed, peeled, boiling potatoes
1 bay leaf
1/2 teaspoon dry mustard
1/4 teaspoon dried marjoram leaves
1/4 teaspoon white pepper
1 package (10 ounces) whole-kernel corn
3 ounces reduced-fat sharp Cheddar cheese, cut into chunks
2 1/2 cups 2% reduced-fat milk
1 can (4 ounces) chopped mild green chilies, drained
Finely chopped fresh chives, as garnish

Per Serving
Calories: 324
% Calories from fat: 18
Protein (g): 12.8
Carbohydrates (g): 55.3
Fat (g): 6.8
Saturated fat (g): 3
Cholesterol (mg): 18.1
Sodium (mg): 648
Exchanges
Milk: 0.5
Veg.: 0.0
Fruit: 0.0
Bread: 3.0
Meat: 0.0
Fat: 1.0

1. Saute onion in margarine in large saucepan until soft. Stir in flour and cook 30 seconds. Add Vegetable Stock, potatoes, bay leaf, mustard, marjoram, and pepper; heat to boiling. Reduce heat and simmer, covered, 15 minutes. Add corn and simmer 5 minutes longer or until vegetables are tender. Discard bay leaf.

2. Process 1 cup of mixture with cheese in blender or food processor until smooth. Return to saucepan with milk and chilies. Cook, stirring, until hot; do not boil. Garnish with chives.

GARLIC SOUP

Serve this soup with a colorful tossed vegetable salad and small wedges of reduced-fat Swiss cheese.

4 servings

1¹/₂ quarts water
  3 tablespoons tomato paste
 18 cloves garlic, crushed
  1 cup finely chopped Italian parsley
  1 tablespoon Italian seasoning
  1 bay leaf
    Salt and pepper, to taste
  4 slices hard-crusted Italian bread, toasted
 ¹/₂ cup grated Parmesan cheese

Per Serving
Calories: 166
% Calories from fat: 23
Protein (gm): 8.7
Carbohydrate (gm): 23.9
Fat (gm): 4.4
Saturated fat (gm): 2.2
Cholesterol (mg): 7.9
Sodium (mg): 469
Exchanges
Milk: 0.0
Veg.: 0.0
Fruit: 0.0
Bread: 1.5
Meat: 0.0
Fat: 1.0

1. Heat water, tomato paste, garlic, parsley, Italian seasoning, and bay leaf to boiling in large saucepan. Reduce heat and simmer 15 minutes. Discard bay leaf; season to taste with salt and pepper.

2. To serve, place toasted bread in bottom of soup bowl and sprinkle with cheese; ladle soup over.

GOULASH SOUP

Caraway seeds and paprika flavor this easy vegetable soup.

4 servings

1¹/₂ cups chopped onions
  2 green bell peppers, seeded, thinly sliced
  3 carrots, thinly sliced
  1 large parsnip, sliced
  1 cup chopped celery
  1 tablespoon margarine
1¹/₂ quarts water
  2 cups tomato juice
  2 large red potatoes, peeled, chopped
 ¹/₄ teaspoon paprika

Per Serving
Calories: 216
% Calories from fat: 15
Protein (gm): 6
Carbohydrate (gm): 41
Fat (gm): 3.9
Saturated fat (gm): 0.9
Cholesterol (mg): 1.7
Sodium (mg): 507
Exchanges
Milk: 0.0
Veg.: 2.0
Fruit: 0.0
Bread: 2.0
Meat: 0.0
Fat: 0.5

1 teaspoon caraway seeds
^{1}/4 teaspoon pepper
Salt, to taste
^{1}/2 cup low-fat plain yogurt

1. Saute onions, bell peppers, carrots, parsnip, and celery in margarine in large saucepan 10 minutes. Stir in remaining ingredients, except salt and yogurt. Heat to boiling; reduce heat and simmer, covered, until vegetables are very tender, about 40 minutes. Season to taste with salt. Ladle soup into bowls; garnish with dollops of yogurt.

CABBAGE SOUP

Easy to make, and satisfying to eat. Serve with Peasant Bread (see p. 800) for a pleasing contrast of flavors and textures.

6 servings (about 1 ^{1}/3 cups each)

1 medium head cabbage, shredded
2 large onions, thinly sliced
2 carrots, sliced
1 large potato, peeled, sliced
1 bay leaf
^{1}/2 teaspoon dried dill weed
^{1}/2 teaspoon dried rosemary leaves
^{1}/2 cup water
3 cups fat-free milk
2 tablespoons low-fat plain yogurt
Salt and pepper, to taste

Per Serving
Calories: 134
% Calories from fat: 5
Protein (gm): 8.7
Carbohydrate (gm): 25.0
Fat (gm): 0.8
Saturated fat (gm): 0.2
Cholesterol (mg): 2.5
Sodium (mg): 112
Exchanges
Milk: 0.5
Veg.: 1.0
Fruit: 0.0
Bread: 1.0
Meat: 0.0
Fat: 0.0

1. Place vegetables, herbs, and water in large saucepan; heat to boiling. Reduce heat and simmer, covered, until very tender, about 25 minutes. Add milk and yogurt; heat until hot. Discard bay leaf; season to taste with salt and pepper.

SHERRIED WINTER SQUASH SOUP

Any type of winter squash can be used in this Italian-accented soup.

4 servings

1/2 cup chopped onion

2 cloves garlic, minced

2 teaspoons olive oil

1 can (28 ounces) reduced-sodium whole tomatoes, undrained, chopped

5 cups Roasted Vegetable Stock (see p. 14), *or* vegetable broth

1 large butternut squash, peeled, seeded, cubed (1/2-inch)

4 medium potatoes, cubed (1/2-inch)

1 bay leaf

1 teaspoon dried basil leaves

1/2 teaspoon dried thyme leaves

1/2 cup chopped parsley

1/3 cup dry sherry, optional

Salt and pepper, to taste

Per Serving
Calories: 260
% Calories from fat: 10
Protein (gm): 5.9
Carbohydrate (gm): 51.4
Fat (gm): 2.9
Saturated fat (gm): 0.4
Cholesterol (mg): 0
Sodium (mg): 51
Exchanges
Milk: 0.0
Veg.: 1.0
Fruit: 0.0
Bread: 3.0
Meat: 0.0
Fat: 0.5

1. Saute onion and garlic in oil in large saucepan until tender, about 5 minutes.

2. Stir in remaining ingredients, except sherry, salt, and pepper. Heat to boiling; reduce heat and simmer, covered, until squash is tender, about 25 minutes. Stir in sherry. Discard bay leaf; season to taste with salt and pepper.

CINNAMON-SPICED PUMPKIN SOUP

Any yellow winter squash, such as butternut, Hubbard, or acorn, can be substituted for the pumpkin. Or, for convenience, canned pumpkin can be used; simply omit cooking the pumpkin in Step 1.

4 servings (about 1¹/₄ cups each)

4	cups cubed, peeled, seeded pumpkin
2	cups fat-free half-and-half, *or* fat-free milk
1-2	tablespoons light brown sugar
¹/₂	teaspoon ground cinnamon
¹/₄-¹/₂	teaspoon ground nutmeg
	Salt and white pepper, to taste
	Snipped chives, as garnish

Per Serving
Calories: 125
% Calories from fat: 1
Protein (g): 5.2
Carbohydrates (g): 23.2
Fat (g): 0.2
Saturated fat (g): 0.1
Cholesterol (mg): 0
Sodium (mg): 122
Exchanges
Milk: 1.0
Veg.: 0.0
Fruit: 0.0
Bread: 0.5
Meat: 0.0
Fat: 0.0

1. Cook pumpkin in medium saucepan, covered, in 1 inch simmering water until tender, about 15 minutes. Drain well. Process pumpkin and half-and-half in food processor or blender until smooth; return to saucepan.

2. Stir in brown sugar and spices and heat just to boiling; reduce heat and simmer, uncovered, 5 minutes. Season to taste with salt and white pepper. Pour soup into bowls; sprinkle with chives.

ORANGE-SCENTED SQUASH SOUP

Subtly seasoned with orange and spices, this delicious soup can be served warm or cold.

6 servings (about 1 1/3 cups each)

Vegetable cooking spray
3/4 cup chopped onion
1 teaspoon ground cinnamon
1/4 teaspoon ground nutmeg
1/4 teaspoon ground cloves
1 1/2 cups water
3 pounds winter yellow squash (Hubbard, butternut, or acorn), peeled, cubed
1 large tart cooking apple, peeled, cubed
1 strip orange rind (3 x 1/2 inch)
1/4-1/2 cup orange juice
1 1/2-2 cups fat-free half-and-half, *or* fat-free milk
Salt and white pepper, to taste
6 thin orange slices
Finely chopped chives, as garnish

Per Serving
Calories: 114
% Calories from fat: 8
Protein (g): 4.1
Carbohydrates (g): 30.2
Fat (g): 1.4
Saturated fat (g): 0.3
Cholesterol (mg): 0
Sodium (mg): 64
Exchanges
Milk: 0.0
Veg.: 0.0
Fruit: 0.0
Bread: 2.0
Meat: 0.0
Fat: 0.0

1. Spray large saucepan with cooking spray; heat over medium heat until hot. Saute onion until tender, about 5 minutes. Stir in spices; cook 1 to 2 minutes longer.

2. Add water, squash, apple, and orange rind to saucepan; heat to boiling. Reduce heat and simmer, covered, until squash is tender, 10 to 15 minutes.

3. Process soup in food processor or blender until smooth; add orange juice and half-and-half. Season to taste with salt and white pepper. Serve soup warm, or refrigerate and serve chilled.

4. Pour soup into bowls; garnish each with an orange slice and sprinkle with chives.

WINTER SQUASH SOUP

An autumn or winter favorite, with apple cider, cinnamon, and spices for sweetness.

6 servings (about 1 cup each)

Per Serving
Calories: 139
% Calories from fat: 13
Protein (g): 2.5
Carbohydrates (g): 29.5
Fat (g): 2.2
Saturated fat (g): 0.4
Cholesterol (mg): 0
Sodium (mg): 49
Exchanges
Milk: 0.0
Veg.: 0.0
Fruit: 0.5
Bread: 1.5
Meat: 0.0
Fat: 0.0

- $1/2$ cup chopped onion
- 1 tablespoon margarine
- 1 pound butternut, *or* other yellow winter squash, peeled, seeded, cubed
- 1 cup cubed, peeled Idaho potato
- 1 cup cubed, peeled, cored tart cooking apple
- $1^1/2$ cups water
- $1/2$ teaspoon ground cinnamon
- $1/4$ teaspoon ground ginger
- $1/8$ teaspoon ground nutmeg
- $1/8$-$1/4$ teaspoon ground cumin
- 1 cup apple cider, *or* apple juice
- $1/2$ 1 cup fat-free half-and-half, *or* fat-free milk
  Salt and white pepper, to taste
  Ground nutmeg, as garnish

1. Saute onion in margarine until tender, 3 to 4 minutes. Add squash, potato, and apple; cook over medium heat 5 minutes. Add water and spices and heat to boiling; reduce heat and simmer, covered, until squash and potato are tender, 10 to 15 minutes.

2. Process mixture in food processor or blender until smooth; return to saucepan. Stir in apple cider and half-and-half; cook over medium heat until hot through. Season to taste with salt and white pepper.

3. Pour soup into bowls; sprinkle lightly with nutmeg.

PUREED ROASTED VEGETABLE SOUP

We've served this soup over rice, but it is also delicious served without rice and topped with Garlic Croutons (see p. 785).

6 servings (about 1½ cups each)

    Olive oil cooking spray
1 medium eggplant, peeled
2 pattypan squash, *or* zucchini
1 medium red bell pepper
1 medium red onion
1 small poblano chili, *or* green bell pepper
3 cloves garlic, peeled
1½ tablespoons herbs de Provence
1 teaspoon pepper
1 quart reduced-sodium vegetable broth, divided
1-2 tablespoons lemon juice
1 teaspoon grated lemon rind
    Salt, to taste
3 cups cooked rice, warm
¾-1¼ cups fat-free plain yogurt

Per Serving
Calories: 219
% Calories from fat: 4
Protein (g): 6.7
Carbohydrates (g): 47.4
Fat (g): 1.1
Saturated fat (g): 0.2
Cholesterol (mg): 0.5
Sodium (mg): 87
Exchanges
Milk: 0.0
Veg.: 3.0
Fruit: 0.0
Bread: 2.0
Meat: 0.0
Fat: 0.0

1. Spray aluminum-foil-lined jelly roll pan with cooking spray. Cut vegetables, except garlic, into 1-inch pieces; arrange vegetables in single layer on pan. Spray vegetables with cooking spray; sprinkle with herbs and pepper.

2. Roast vegetables at 425 degrees until browned and tender, about 40 minutes, removing garlic when soft, after about 20 minutes. Process vegetables and 1 cup broth in food processor or blender until smooth. Heat vegetable mixture, remaining 3 cups broth, lemon juice, and rind in large saucepan to boiling; reduce heat and simmer, uncovered, 5 minutes. Season to taste with salt.

3. Serve soup over rice in bowls; stir 2 to 3 tablespoons yogurt into each bowl.

EVERYTHING-BUT-CABBAGE SOUP

Load your shopping cart with healthful vegetables to make this tasty soup—go ahead and add cabbage, if you insist!

6 servings

- ³/₄ cup minced onion
- 2 tablespoons margarine
- 1¹/₂ quarts low-sodium vegetable broth
- 3 cups diced, peeled baking potatoes
- 3 ears corn, each cut into 3 pieces
- ³/₄ cup cut green beans
- ³/₄ cup diced carrots
- ³/₄ cup diced celery
- ³/₄ cup diced sweet potatoes
- ³/₄ cup diced butternut squash
- ³/₄ cup diced zucchini
- ¹/₄ cup diced parsnip
- 1 can (16 ounces) unsalted tomatoes, undrained, coarsely chopped
- 1 tablespoon tomato paste
- 1 teaspoon white wine vinegar
- 1 teaspoon sugar
- 1 bay leaf
- ¹/₂ teaspoon pepper
- ¹/₂ teaspoon dried thyme leaves
  Pinch dried marjoram leaves
- ³/₄ cup frozen peas
  Salt, to taste
- ¹/₄ cup chopped parsley

Per Serving
Calories: 324
% Calories from fat: 10
Protein (g): 9.9
Carbohydrates (g): 70
Fat (g): 4
Saturated fat (g): 0.6
Cholesterol (mg): 0
Sodium (mg): 567
Exchanges
Milk: 0.0
Veg.: 5.0
Fruit: 0.0
Bread: 2.5
Meat: 0.0
Fat: 0.0

1. Saute onion in margarine in large saucepan until soft. Add vegetable broth and heat to boiling; add remaining ingredients, except peas, salt, and parsley. Simmer 30 minutes, uncovered, or until vegetables are tender. Add peas and simmer until heated. Season to taste with salt; stir in parsley.

SPRING SOUP

This soup is best in spring, when peas and asparagus are in season, but it can also be made with frozen vegetables at other times.

6 servings (about 1½ cups each)

1/2 cup finely chopped onion
1 tablespoon olive oil
1 tablespoon safflower oil
1 cup chopped tomatoes
1 tablespoon finely chopped Italian
parsley
1 quart water
1 cup diced potatoes
1/4 cup rice, uncooked
1½ cups asparagus, cut into 1-inch pieces
1 cup fresh, *or* frozen, peas
1 cup coarsely chopped scallions
Spike, to taste
Salt and pepper, to taste

Per Serving
Calories: 151
% Calories from fat: 29
Protein (g): 4.6
Carbohydrates (g): 23.6
Fat (g): 5
Saturated fat (g): 0.6
Cholesterol (mg): 0
Sodium (mg): 32
Exchanges
Milk: 0.0
Veg.: 1.5
Fruit: 0.0
Bread: 1.0
Meat: 0.0
Fat: 1.0

1. Saute onion in both oils in large saucepan until lightly browned, about 8 minutes. Add tomatoes; cook over medium heat 5 minutes. Add parsley, water, and potatoes; heat to boiling. Stir in rice, reduce heat, and simmer until rice is tender, about 20 to 25 minutes, adding asparagus, peas, and scallions during last 5 to 7 minutes of cooking time. Season to taste with Spike, salt, and pepper.

MOTHER HUBBARD'S SOUP

Even when you don't feel like going to the grocery, you can still make a nutritious, delicious vegetable soup. Use this opportunity to clean out the refrigerator and pantry!

8 servings (about 1³/₄ cups each)

4 small potatoes, cubed

1 sweet potato, peeled, cubed

2 ribs celery, sliced

1 cup julienned, *or* sliced, carrots

2 cups sliced cabbage

8 ounces frozen snap peas

8 ounces frozen broccoli

1 cup frozen peas

1 cup frozen whole-kernel corn

1 can (14¹/₂ ounces) diced tomatoes with roasted garlic, undrained

4 cans (14¹/₂ ounces each) reduced-sodium vegetable broth, *or* chicken broth, *or* beef broth

1 teaspoon dried rosemary leaves

¹/₂ teaspoon dried thyme leaves

¹/₂ teaspoon dried oregano leaves

Salt and pepper, to taste

Per Serving
Calories: 172
% Calories from fat: 2
Protein (gm): 6.4
Carbohydrate (gm): 37.9
Fat (gm): 0.5
Saturated fat (gm): 0.1
Cholesterol (mg): 0
Sodium (mg): 337
Exchanges
Milk: 0.0
Veg.: 1.0
Fruit: 0.0
Bread: 2.0
Meat: 0.0
Fat: 0.0

1. Combine all ingredients, except salt and pepper, in large saucepan; heat to boiling. Reduce heat and simmer, covered, until vegetables are tender, about 25 minutes. Season to taste with salt and pepper.

POTATO PISTOU

A rich and flavorful soup with a velvety texture.

6 servings

2 quarts water
2 cups chopped onions
4 red potatoes, peeled, diced
5 tomatoes, peeled, seeded, chopped
3/4 cup cut green beans (1 1/2-inch)
2 medium zucchini, sliced
1/4 teaspoon dried marjoram leaves
1/4 teaspoon pepper
1/4 teaspoon saffron threads
1 1/2 cups packed basil leaves
5 cloves garlic, minced
1/4 cup grated Parmesan cheese
    Salt, to taste

Per Serving
Calories: 136
% Calories from fat: 10
Protein (gm): 5.1
Carbohydrate (gm): 28.4
Fat (gm): 1.6
Saturated fat (gm): 0.7
Cholesterol (mg): 2.6
Sodium (mg): 106
Exchanges
Milk: 0.0
Veg.: 2.0
Fruit: 0.0
Bread: 1.0
Meat: 0.0
Fat: 0.0

1. Heat water, onions, and potatoes to boiling in large Dutch oven; reduce heat and simmer, covered, 35 minutes. Add tomatoes, green beans, zucchini, marjoram, pepper, and saffron; simmer 20 minutes longer.

2. Process soup in food processor or blender until smooth; return to Dutch oven and simmer, uncovered, 5 minutes.

4. Process basil, garlic, and Parmesan cheese in food processor until smooth; stir into soup. Season to taste with salt.

SPINACH AND TORTELLINI SOUP

Pasta soups can be made 2 to 3 days in advance, enhancing flavors. Add pasta to the soup at the time of re-heating for serving so that the pasta is fresh and perfectly cooked.

4 servings (about 1½ cups each)

Vegetable cooking spray

2 cups sliced carrots

¼ cup sliced green onions and tops

2 cloves garlic, minced

1 teaspoon dried basil leaves

5 cups Canned Vegetable Stock (see p. 11), *or* vegetable broth

1 package (9 ounces) fresh low-fat tomato-and-cheese tortellini

3 cups torn spinach leaves

2-3 teaspoons lemon juice

⅛-¼ teaspoon ground nutmeg

⅛ teaspoon pepper

Per Serving
Calories: 290
% Calories from fat: **9**
Protein (g): 12.1
Carbohydrates (g): 48
Fat (g): 2.8
Saturated fat (g): 1
Cholesterol (mg): 3.8
Sodium (mg): 395
Exchanges
Milk: 0.0
Veg.: 2.0
Fruit: 0.0
Bread: 2.5
Meat: 1.0
Fat: 0.0

1. Spray large saucepan with cooking spray; heat over medium heat until hot. Saute carrots, green onions, garlic, and basil until onions are tender, about 5 minutes. Add Canned Vegetable Stock; heat to boiling. Reduce heat and simmer, covered, 10 minutes.

2. Heat soup to boiling; stir in tortellini and spinach. Reduce heat and simmer, uncovered, until tortellini are al dente, about 5 minutes. Season to taste with lemon juice, nutmeg, and pepper.

TORTELLINI SOUP WITH KALE

Fast and easy to make when there's no time to cook!

8 servings (about 1½ cups each)

1 cup sliced leek, white part only, *or* green onions and tops

3 cloves garlic, minced

1 tablespoon olive oil

3 quarts Roasted Vegetable, *or* Rich Mushroom, Stock (see pp. 14, 17)

2 cups packed kale, coarsely chopped

1 cup sliced mushrooms

½ package (9-ounce size) mushroom, *or* herb, tortellini

Salt and white pepper, to taste

Per Serving
Calories: 105
% Calories from fat: 24
Protein (g): 3
Carbohydrates (g): 11.6
Fat (g): 3.1
Saturated fat (g): 0.8
Cholesterol (mg): 8.4
Sodium (mg): 69
Exchanges
Milk: 0.0
Veg.: 2.0
Fruit: 0.0
Bread: 0.0
Meat: 0.0
Fat: 1.0

1. Saute leek and garlic in oil in Dutch oven until leek is tender, 5 to 8 minutes. Add Roasted Vegetable Stock and heat to boiling; stir in kale and mushrooms. Reduce heat and simmer, covered, 5 minutes.

2. Add tortellini to pan; simmer, uncovered, until tortellini are al dente, about 7 minutes. Season to taste with salt and white pepper.

TOMATO SOUP WITH SOUR CREAM AND FOUR ACCOMPANIMENTS

This flavorful tomato soup turns into a hearty meal with the addition of cubed potatoes, winter squash, peas, and croutons.

6 servings

 1 large onion, thinly sliced
 2 tablespoons margarine
1¼ quarts water
 1 cup dry white wine, optional
 5 low-sodium vegetable bouillon cubes
½ cup coarsely chopped carrots
½ cup coarsely chopped potato
 8 large tomatoes, peeled, seeded, quartered
 1 bay leaf
½ teaspoon sugar
¼ teaspoon white pepper
¼ teaspoon dried basil leaves
1¾ cup fat-free sour cream, divided
   Salt, to taste
 6 teaspoons chopped fresh dill
1½ cups cubed, peeled potatoes, cooked, warm
1½ cups cubed, peeled butternut squash, *or* sweet potatoes, cooked, warm
1½ cups peas, cooked, warm
1½ cups plain croutons

Per Serving
Calories: 302
% Calories from fat: 10
Protein (g): 12.2
Carbohydrates (g): 54.3
Fat (g): 3.8
Saturated fat (g): 0.6
Cholesterol (mg): 0.1
Sodium (mg): 684
Exchanges
Milk: 0.0
Veg.: 2.0
Fruit: 0.0
Bread: 3.0
Meat: 2.0
Fat: 0.5

1. Saute onion in margarine in large saucepan until soft; stir in water, wine, bouillon cubes, carrots, chopped potato, tomatoes, bay leaf, sugar, white pepper, and basil. Heat to boiling; reduce heat and simmer 20 minutes or until carrots and potatoes are soft.

2. Process soup in blender or food processor until smooth. Return soup to saucepan and whisk in 1 cup sour cream; cook until hot. Season to taste with salt. Ladle soup into bowls. Garnish with remaining ½ cup sour cream and dill. Pass cubed potatoes, squash, peas, and croutons to add to soup.

GARLICKY LIMA BEAN SOUP

For those who love garlic! The garlic, of course, can be reduced in amount if you prefer a more subtle dish.

6 servings (about 1 cup each)

Garlic-flavored vegetable cooking spray
2 cups coarsely chopped onions
10 large cloves garlic, peeled, quartered
1 teaspoon crushed red pepper
2 cans (17 ounces each) lima beans, rinsed, drained
3 cups Basic Vegetable Stock (see p. 10), *or* reduced-sodium vegetable broth
1 teaspoon dried thyme leaves
1/2 cup fat-free half-and-half
Salt and white pepper, to taste
Cayenne pepper, *or* paprika, as garnish
Parsley, finely chopped, as garnish

Per Serving
Calories: 169
% Calories from fat: 5
Protein (g): 9.2
Carbohydrates (g): 31.8
Fat (g): 0.9
Saturated fat (g): 0.2
Cholesterol (mg): 0
Sodium (mg): 429
Exchanges
Milk: 0.0
Veg.: 1.0
Fruit: 0.0
Bread: 2.0
Meat: 0.0
Fat: 0.0

1. Spray large saucepan with cooking spray; heat over medium heat until hot. Cook onions, garlic, and crushed red pepper, covered, over medium to medium-low heat until onions are tender, 8 to 10 minutes. Add beans, Basic Vegetable Stock, and thyme; heat to boiling. Reduce heat and simmer, covered, 5 to 10 minutes longer.

2. Process soup in food processor or blender until smooth; return to saucepan. Stir in half-and-half; cook over medium heat 5 minutes, stirring occasionally. Season to taste with salt and white pepper.

3. Serve soup in bowls; sprinkle lightly with cayenne pepper and parsley.

DITALINI WITH WHITE BEANS AND COLLARDS

Create a stir with this knockout entrée that's full of beans, pasta, and healthful greens. If you'd like some crunch, top each serving with crispy croutons. Kale or cabbage can be substituted for the collards, if desired.

4 servings

1 onion, chopped
1 teaspoon olive oil
1 can (16 ounces) diced tomatoes, undrained
1 can (14 ounces) reduced-sodium vegetable broth
1 can (15 ounces) small white beans, rinsed, drained
2/3 cup uncooked ditalini
1 teaspoon dried oregano leaves
2 cups packed torn collard greens
2 teaspoons hot pepper sauce
2 teaspoons grated lemon rind
2 tablespoons shredded provolone cheese
   Salt and pepper, to taste

Per Serving
Calories: 234
% Calories from fat: 14
Protein (gm): 12.8
Carbohydrate (gm): 44.1
Fat (gm): 4
Saturated fat (gm): 1.4
Cholesterol (mg): 4.9
Sodium (mg): 826
Exchanges
Milk: 0.0
Veg.: 3.0
Fruit: 0.0
Bread: 2.0
Meat: 0.0
Fat: 0.5

1. Saute onion in oil in large saucepan until soft. Add tomatoes, broth, beans, ditalini, and oregano. Cover and heat to boiling. Reduce heat and simmer until ditalini are al dente, 10 to 12 minutes. Stir in collard greens; simmer until tender, about 5 minutes. Stir in hot pepper sauce, lemon rind, and provolone; season to taste with salt and pepper.

GARLIC VEGETABLE SOUP

A real garlic lover's soup—add more garlic, if you like!

8 servings

1	cup chopped leeks, white parts only
6	large garlic cloves, minced
1-2	tablespoons olive oil
2¹/₂	quarts water
1	can (15 ounces) navy, *or* Great Northern, beans, rinsed, drained
1	pound tomatoes, peeled, seeded, coarsely chopped
1	cup new potatoes, diced
1	cup carrots, coarsely chopped
¹/₂	cup chopped celery
1	cup cut green beans (¹/₂-inch)
2-4	tablespoons dried basil leaves
1	tablespoon dried tarragon leaves
2	tablespoons tomato paste
	Salt and pepper, to taste

Per Serving
Calories: 148
% Calories from fat: 14
Protein (gm): 6.4
Carbohydrate (gm): 27.5
Fat (gm): 2.4
Saturated fat (gm): 0.4
Cholesterol (mg): 0
Sodium (mg): 222
Exchanges
Milk: 0.0
Veg.: 2.0
Fruit: 0.0
Bread: 2.0
Meat: 0.0
Fat: 0.5

1. Cook leeks and garlic in oil in large saucepan over medium to medium-low heat until very soft, about 10 minutes. Add remaining ingredients, except salt and pepper, and heat to boiling. Reduce heat and simmer, covered, 30 minutes, stirring occasionally. Season to taste with salt and pepper.

ALSATIAN PEASANT SOUP

Root vegetables, cabbage, and beans combine for a robust soup that is almost a stew. Serve with a crusty rye bread and a good beer.

6 servings (about 1¹/₂ cups each)

¹/₂ cup chopped onion
¹/₂ cup sliced celery
1 tablespoon olive oil
1 large potato, unpeeled, cubed
1 cup cubed, peeled parsnip, *or* turnip
³/₄ cup sliced carrots
1 teaspoon dried thyme leaves
¹/₂ teaspoon crushed caraway seeds
1 bay leaf
3 cups Mediterranean Vegetable Stock (see p. 15), *or* vegetable broth
2 cups thinly sliced cabbage
2 cans (15 ounces each) Great Northern beans, rinsed, drained
Salt and pepper, to taste
³/₄ cup (3 ounces) shredded reduced-fat Swiss cheese
1¹/₂ cups Rye Croutons (½ recipe) (see p. 784)

Per Serving
Calories: 331
% Calories from fat: **17**
Protein (g): 18
Carbohydrates (g): 50.1
Fat (g): 6.5
Saturated fat (g): 2.2
Cholesterol (mg): 10.1
Sodium (mg): 119
Exchanges
Milk: 0.0
Veg.: 2.0
Fruit: 0.0
Bread: 2.5
Meat: 1.0
Fat: 1.0

1. Saute onion and celery in oil in large saucepan until tender, about 5 minutes. Add potato, parsnip, carrots, thyme, caraway, and bay leaf; cook over medium heat 5 minutes.

2. Add Mediterranean Vegetable Stock, cabbage, and beans to saucepan; heat to boiling. Reduce heat and simmer, covered, until vegetables are tender, 10 to 15 minutes. Discard bay leaf; season to taste with salt and pepper.

3. Ladle soup into bowls; sprinkle each with 2 tablespoons shredded cheese and ¹/₄ cup Rye Croutons.

VEGETARIAN MINESTRONE

The combination of vegetables and herbs is particularly appealing in this meatless version of a traditional Italian favorite.

5-6 servings

1 medium onion, finely chopped
1 garlic clove, minced
2 teaspoons olive oil
1 quart Vegetable Stock (see p. 11)
1 can (15 ounces) reduced-sodium tomato sauce
2 cups cooked garbanzo beans, *or* 1 can (15 ounces) garbanzo beans, drained
1 large rib celery, diced
1 medium carrot, thinly sliced
1 large potato, cut into 3/4-inch cubes
1 medium zucchini, diced
1/4 cup chopped fresh parsley
1 teaspoon dried basil leaves
1/2 teaspoon dried marjoram leaves
1/4 teaspoon dried thyme leaves
1/4 teaspoon black pepper
1/8 teaspoon ground celery seeds
Dash cayenne pepper
1/2 cup uncooked small shell pasta
Salt, to taste

Per Serving
Calories: 211
% Calories from fat: 15
Protein (g): 8.6
Carbohydrates (g): 37.5
Fat (g): 3.5
Saturated fat (g): 0.4
Cholesterol (mg): 0
Sodium (mg): 310
Exchanges
Milk: 0.0
Veg.: 2.0
Fruit: 0.0
Bread: 2.0
Meat: 0.0
Fat: 0.5

1. Saute onion and garlic in olive oil in Dutch oven until onion is tender. Add remaining ingredients, except pasta and salt, and heat to boiling. Reduce heat and simmer, covered, 15 minutes.

2. Heat to boiling and add pasta. Reduce heat and simmer, 15 to 20 minutes or until vegetables and pasta are tender. Season to taste with salt.

PASTA E FAGIOLI

Perhaps the only soup that's better than a good pasta e fagioli is a pasta e fagioli the second day. If you make it a day ahead, wait to add the pasta until just before you serve it.

12 servings

1 cup chopped onion
1/2 cup diced celery
1/2 cup diced carrot
1 1/2 tablespoons minced garlic
2 tablespoons olive oil
2 cups dried Great Northern beans, *or* cannellini beans, soaked overnight, drained
2 1/4 quarts water
4 1/2 cups diced, peeled, seeded tomatoes
5 ounces elbow macaroni, *or* other pasta, cooked
Spike and pepper, to taste
Grated Parmesan cheese, as garnish

Per Serving
Calories: 124
% Calories from fat: 21
Protein (g): 5
Carbohydrates (g): 20.4
Fat (g): 3.1
Saturated fat (g): 1.1
Cholesterol (mg): 10.2
Sodium (mg): 18
Exchanges
Milk: 0.0
Veg.: 1.0
Fruit: 0.0
Bread: 1.0
Meat: 0.0
Fat: 0.5

1. Saute onion, celery, carrot, and garlic in oil in Dutch oven until soft, about 5 minutes. Add beans and water; heat to boiling. Reduce heat and simmer, covered, until beans are tender, 45 to 60 minutes.

2. Add tomatoes and simmer, covered, 10 minutes; add pasta and simmer, covered, 5 minutes. Season to taste with Spike and pepper. Sprinkle each serving with Parmesan cheese.

ROASTED VEGETABLE MINESTRONE

Oven roasting enhances the natural flavors of vegetables, making this soup a favorite in our repertory.

8 servings (about 1³/₄ cups each)

Olive oil cooking spray
1 medium eggplant, unpeeled
1 large Idaho potato, unpeeled
2 medium zucchini
2 medium tomatoes
¹/₂ small butternut squash, peeled
1 large green bell pepper
1 large red bell pepper
1 teaspoon dried rosemary leaves
³/₄ teaspoon dried oregano leaves
¹/₂ teaspoon dried sage leaves
¹/₄-¹/₂ teaspoon dried thyme leaves
1 cup coarsely chopped onion
4 cloves garlic, minced
1 can (15¹/₂ ounces) cannellini, *or* Great Northern, beans, rinsed, drained
1³/₄ quarts vegetable broth
2-3 tablespoons white balsamic vinegar
Salt and pepper, to taste

Per Serving
Calories: 200
% Calories from fat: **5**
Protein (g): 11.6
Carbohydrates (g): 45.3
Fat (g): 1.3
Saturated fat (g): 0.1
Cholesterol (mg): 0
Sodium (mg): 292
Exchanges
Milk: 0.0
Veg.: 3.0
Fruit: 0.0
Bread: 2.0
Meat: 0.0
Fat: 0.0

1. Line large jelly roll pan with aluminum foil and spray with cooking spray. Cut eggplant, potato, zucchini, tomatoes, squash, and bell peppers into ³/₄-inch pieces. Arrange vegetables on jelly roll pan; spray generously with cooking spray and sprinkle with combined herbs. Bake at 425 degrees until vegetables are browned and tender, 30 to 40 minutes.

2. Spray large saucepan with cooking spray; heat over medium heat until hot. Saute onion and garlic until tender, about 5 minutes. Add roasted vegetables, beans, and vegetable broth; heat to boiling. Simmer, covered, 10 minutes. Season to taste with vinegar, salt, and pepper.

GARDEN MINESTRONE

This green soup is wonderful in spring, when fresh asparagus and peas are in season, but make it whenever you're in the mood for delicious soup!

6 servings

1¹/₂ quarts Basic Vegetable Stock (see p. 10)
1 cup thinly sliced onion
1 cup uncooked broken spinach fettuccine
2 cans (15 ounces each) Great Northern beans, rinsed, drained
2 cups sliced zucchini
1¹/₂ cups small broccoli florets
1¹/₂ cups cut asparagus (1-inch pieces)
1 cup cut green beans
1 cup fresh, *or* frozen, peas
¹/₄ cup lightly packed parsley
¹/₄ cup lightly packed fresh, *or* 2 teaspoons dried, basil leaves
1 tablespoon fresh, *or* 1 teaspoon dried, rosemary leaves
2 large cloves garlic
Salt and pepper, to taste
Shredded Parmesan cheese, as garnish

Per Serving
Calories: 186
% Calories from fat: 6
Protein (gm): 13.1
Carbohydrate (gm): 38.8
Fat (gm): 1.4
Saturated fat (gm): 0.3
Cholesterol (mg): 14
Sodium (mg): 478
Exchanges
Milk: 0.0
Veg.: 2.0
Fruit: 0.0
Bread: 2.0
Meat: 0.0
Fat: 0.0

1. Heat Basic Vegetable Stock and onion to boiling in large saucepan; stir in fettuccine. Reduce heat and simmer 5 minutes. Stir in Great Northern beans, zucchini, broccoli, asparagus, and green beans; simmer, covered, until broccoli is tender, about 5 minutes. Stir in peas.

2. Finely chop combined parsley, basil, rosemary, and garlic; stir into soup. Season to taste with salt and pepper. Ladle soup into bowls and sprinkle with cheese.

SUMMER MINESTRONE

Thick and savory, this traditional Italian soup is always a favorite.

6 servings (about 1¹/₃ cups each)

Vegetable cooking spray

2 medium potatoes, cubed

2 medium carrots, thinly sliced

1 small zucchini, cubed

1 cup halved green beans

1 cup thinly sliced cabbage

¹/₂ cup thinly sliced celery

1 medium onion, coarsely chopped

3-4 cloves garlic, minced

2 teaspoons Italian seasoning

1-2 teaspoons dried oregano leaves

4 cups Mediterranean Vegetable Stock (see p. 15), *or* vegetable broth

1 can (15 ounces) no-salt-added stewed tomatoes, undrained

1 can (15 ounces) kidney beans, rinsed, drained

2 cups water

1¹/₂ cups (4 ounces) uncooked mostaccioli (penne)

¹/₂ teaspoon pepper

2 tablespoons grated Parmesan, *or* Romano, cheese

Per Serving
Calories: 264
% Calories from fat: 9
Protein (g): 12.3
Carbohydrates (g): 50.5
Fat (g): 2.7
Saturated fat (g): 0.6
Cholesterol (mg): 1.6
Sodium (mg): 216
Exchanges
Milk: 0.0
Veg.: 3.0
Fruit: 0.0
Bread: 2.0
Meat: 1.0
Fat: 0.0

1. Spray large saucepan with cooking spray; heat over medium heat until hot. Saute fresh vegetables until crisp-tender, 10 to 12 minutes. Stir in herbs; cook 1 minute longer.

2. Add Mediterranean Vegetable Stock, tomatoes and liquid, beans, and water; heat to boiling. Reduce heat and simmer, covered, 10 minutes. Heat soup to boiling; add pasta. Reduce heat and simmer, uncovered, until pasta is al dente, 10 to 12 minutes. Stir in pepper. Spoon soup into bowls; sprinkle with cheese.

TWO-BEAN MINESTRONE

Cannellini beans and chickpeas enrich this soup with protein, fiber, and vitamins.

8-10 servings

Per Serving
Calories: 267
% Calories from fat: 17
Protein (gm): 9
Carbohydrate (gm): 43.1
Fat (gm): 5.3
Saturated fat (gm): 0.9
Cholesterol (mg): 1.3
Sodium (mg): 331
Exchanges
Milk: 0.0
Veg.: 2.0
Fruit: 0.0
Bread: 2.0
Meat: 0.0
Fat: 1.5

- 2 cloves garlic, minced
- 1/2 cup chopped onion
- 2 tablespoons olive oil
- 3 large carrots, sliced
- 2 medium potatoes, diced
- 1 medium leek, white part only, thinly sliced
- 3 ribs celery, sliced
- 1 cup chopped parsley, divided
- 1 1/2 quarts water
- 1 can (14 ounces) plum tomatoes, undrained, chopped
- 1 cup dry red wine
- 1 tablespoon dried oregano leaves
- 1 tablespoon dried basil leaves
- 1/2 cup uncooked small elbow macaroni
- 1 can (15 ounces) cannellini, *or* Great Northern, beans, rinsed, drained
- 1 can (15 ounces) chickpeas, rinsed, drained
- 2 zucchini, sliced
- 2 cups shredded cabbage
  Salt and pepper, to taste
- 8 teaspoons grated Parmesan cheese

1. Saute garlic and onion in olive oil in large saucepan until onion is tender. Add carrots, potatoes, leek, celery, 1/2 of the parsley, water, plum tomatoes with liquid, red wine, and herbs; heat to boiling. Reduce heat and simmer, covered, until vegetables are almost tender, about 15 minutes.

2. Heat to boiling; stir in macaroni. Reduce heat and simmer uncovered 7 minutes. Add remaining ingredients, except salt, pepper, and Parmesan cheese, and simmer until pasta is al dente, about 5 minutes. Season to taste with salt and pepper. Ladle soup into bowls and top with 1 teaspoon Parmesan and remaining parsley.

ITALIAN BEAN SOUP

For a creamy textured soup, puree ¹/₂ the cooked bean mixture before adding the macaroni and garbanzo beans.

4 servings

  1 cup dried cannellini beans
  2 quarts water
  1 cup chopped onion
  1 cup chopped green bell pepper
  1 cup chopped carrots
¹/₂ cup chopped celery
  1 teaspoon dried basil leaves
  1 teaspoon dried oregano leaves
  1 teaspoon low-sodium vegetable
    bouillon crystals
¹/₄ teaspoon dry mustard
  2 cloves garlic, minced
  3 cans (8 ounces) salt-free tomato sauce
¹/₂ cup uncooked whole-wheat elbow
    macaroni
  1 can (15 ounces) garbanzo beans,
    rinsed, drained
    Salt and pepper, to taste

Per Serving
Calories: 436
% Calories from fat: 5
Protein (gm): 24.1
Carbohydrate (gm): 84
Fat (gm): 2.7
Saturated fat (gm): 0.3
Cholesterol (mg): 0
Sodium (mg): 291
Exchanges
Milk: 0.0
Veg.: 2.0
Fruit: 0.0
Bread: 5.0
Meat: 0.0
Fat: 0.5

1. Cover beans with 2 inches of water in Dutch oven; heat to boiling and boil 2 minutes. Remove from heat, cover, and let stand 1 hour.

2. Drain beans; return to Dutch oven with 2 quarts water and remaining ingredients, except tomato sauce, macaroni, garbanzo beans, salt, and pepper. Heat to boiling; reduce heat and simmer, covered, until beans are tender, 45 to 60 minutes, stirring occasionally.

3. Add tomato sauce, macaroni, and garbanzo beans and cook until macaroni is tender, 10 to 12 minutes; season to taste with salt and pepper.

FOUR-BEAN AND VEGETABLE SOUP

Any kind of dried beans can be used in the soup, or use prepackaged mixed dried beans.

12 servings (about 1½ cups each)

8 ounces dried black beans
8 ounces dried navy beans
8 ounces dried pinto beans
8 ounces dried garbanzo beans
2 cups chopped green bell pepper
1 cup chopped onion
6-8 cloves garlic, minced
2 tablespoons olive oil
6 cups Roasted Vegetable Stock (see p. 14), *or* vegetable broth
2-3 teaspoons dried thyme leaves
3 bay leaves
2 cans (16 ounces each) reduced-sodium diced tomatoes, undrained
2 cups sliced carrots
2 cups green beans, cut into 2-inch pieces
Salt, cayenne, and black pepper, to taste

Per Serving
Calories: 342
% Calories from fat: 11
Protein (g): 18.1
Carbohydrates (g): 58.5
Fat (g): 4.3
Saturated fat (g): 0.5
Cholesterol (mg): 0
Sodium (mg): 35
Exchanges
Milk: 0.0
Veg.: 3.0
Fruit: 0.0
Bread: 3.0
Meat: 1.0
Fat: 0.0

1. Cover beans with 2 inches water in large saucepan; heat to boiling. Remove pan from heat; let stand 1 hour. Drain.

2. Saute bell pepper, onion, and garlic in oil in Dutch oven until tender, 4 to 5 minutes. Add beans, Roasted Vegetable Stock, and herbs; heat to boiling. Reduce heat and simmer, covered, until beans are tender (add water if necessary), 1 to 1½ hours, adding tomatoes with liquid, carrots, and green beans during last 15 to 20 minutes of cooking time. Discard bay leaves; season to taste with salt, cayenne, and black pepper.

TUSCAN BEAN SOUP

A hearty bean soup, savory with sage, rosemary, and thyme.

8 servings (about 1½ cups each)

1 cup chopped onion
½ cup sliced celery
½ cup chopped green bell pepper
2 teaspoons minced roasted garlic
2 tablespoons olive oil
1 tablespoon flour
¾-1 teaspoon dried rosemary leaves
½ teaspoon dried sage leaves
¼ teaspoon dried thyme leaves
2 bay leaves
7 cups Mediterranean Vegetable Stock (see p. 15), *or* vegetable broth
2 cans (15 ounces each) cannellini, *or* Great Northern, beans, rinsed, drained
2 tablespoons reduced-sodium tomato paste
½ cup quick-cooking barley
1 large Idaho potato, unpeeled, cut into ½-inch pieces
1 cup sliced carrots
1 cup packed sliced spinach leaves
Salt and pepper, to taste

Per Serving
Calories: 233
% Calories from fat: 18
Protein (g): 10.7
Carbohydrates (g): 40.8
Fat (g): 5.6
Saturated fat (g): 0.7
Cholesterol (mg): 0
Sodium (mg): 245
Exchanges
Milk: 0.0
Veg.: 2.0
Fruit: 0.0
Bread: 2.0
Meat: 0.0
Fat: 1.0

1. Saute onion, celery, bell pepper, and garlic in oil in Dutch oven until tender, about 5 minutes. Add flour and herbs; cook 1 to 2 minutes longer.

2. Add Mediterranean Vegetable Stock, beans, and tomato paste to Dutch oven; heat to boiling. Reduce heat and simmer, uncovered, 20 to 25 minutes, adding barley, potato, carrots, and spinach during last 10 minutes of cooking time. Discard bay leaves. Season to taste with salt and pepper.

BEAN-THICKENED SOUP

This soup is very quick and easy to make. The pureed beans contribute a hearty texture and subtle flavor.

4 servings (about 1¹/₃ cups each)

Vegetable cooking spray
2 carrots, sliced
1 small onion, chopped
2 large cloves garlic, minced
1³/₄ cups vegetable broth
1 can (16 ounces) whole tomatoes, undrained, coarsely chopped
1 can (15 ounces) Great Northern beans, rinsed, drained, pureed
¹/₄-¹/₂ teaspoon dried thyme leaves
¹/₂-³/₄ teaspoon dried sage leaves
Salt and pepper, to taste
Minced parsley, as garnish

Per Serving
Calories: 176
% Calories from fat: **5**
Protein (g): 9.8
Carbohydrates (g): **34**
Fat (g): 1
Saturated fat (g): 0.2
Cholesterol (mg): 0
Sodium (mg): 208
Exchanges
Milk: 0.0
Veg.: 2.0
Fruit: 0.0
Bread: 1.5
Meat: 0.5
Fat: 0.0

1. Spray large saucepan with cooking spray; heat over medium heat until hot. Saute carrots, onion, and garlic until onion is tender, about 5 minutes. Stir in broth, tomatoes and liquid, pureed beans, and herbs. Heat to boiling; reduce heat and simmer, covered, until carrots are tender, about 10 minutes. Season to taste with salt and pepper.

2. Pour soup into bowls; sprinkle with parsley.

CHICKPEA AND PASTA SOUP

Many fresh garden vegetables can be substituted for the zucchini and celery in this soup: carrots, cauliflower, broccoli florets, mushrooms, peas, and green beans are possible choices.

4 servings (about 1³/₄ cups each)

Olive oil cooking spray
1 small zucchini, cubed
2 ribs celery, thinly sliced
1 medium onion, chopped
3-4 cloves garlic, minced
1 teaspoon dried rosemary leaves
1 teaspoon dried thyme leaves
¹/₈ teaspoon crushed red pepper
1 quart Canned Vegetable Stock (see p. 11), *or* vegetable broth
1 can (15 ounces) no-salt-added stewed tomatoes, undrained
1 can (15 ounces) chickpeas, rinsed, drained
1 cup (4 ounces) uncooked farfalle (bow ties)
2 tablespoons finely chopped parsley
2-3 teaspoons lemon juice
Salt and pepper, to taste

Per Serving
Calories: 322
% Calories from fat: 10
Protein (g): 11.5
Carbohydrates (g): 56.4
Fat (g): 3.7
Saturated fat (g): 0.5
Cholesterol (mg): 0
Sodium (mg): 514
Exchanges
Milk: 0.0
Veg.: 3.0
Fruit: 0.0
Bread: 3.0
Meat: 0.0
Fat: 0.5

1. Spray large saucepan with cooking spray; heat over medium heat until hot. Saute zucchini, celery, onion, and garlic until zucchini is crisp-tender, about 8 minutes. Stir in herbs and red pepper; cook 1 to 2 minutes.

2. Add Canned Vegetable Stock, tomatoes and liquid, and chickpeas; heat to boiling. Reduce heat and simmer, covered, 10 minutes.

3. Heat soup to boiling; add pasta. Reduce heat and simmer, uncovered, until pasta is al dente, about 8 minutes. Stir in parsley; season to taste with lemon juice, salt, and pepper.

TWO-BEAN AND PASTA SOUP

This substantial soup thickens upon standing; thin with additional stock or water, if necessary.

6 servings (about 2 cups each)

Vegetable cooking spray
1¹/2 cups cubed carrots
1 medium green bell pepper, chopped
¹/2 cup sliced green onions and tops
3 cloves garlic, minced
2 teaspoons dried basil leaves
2 teaspoons dried oregano leaves
4 cups Basic Vegetable Stock (see p. 10)
1 cup water
1 can (15 ounces) no-salt-added stewed tomatoes
1 can (15 ounces) cannellini, *or* Great Northern, beans, rinsed, drained
1 can (15 ounces) fava, *or* pinto, beans, rinsed, drained
1¹/2 cups (4 ounces) uncooked rigatoni
2-3 teaspoons lemon juice
¹/4 teaspoon salt
¹/2 teaspoon pepper

Per Serving
Calories: 225
% Calories from fat: 7
Protein (g): 13.6
Carbohydrates (g): 45.7
Fat (g): 2
Saturated fat (g): 0
Cholesterol (mg): 0
Sodium (mg): 522
Exchanges
Milk: 0.0
Veg.: 2.0
Fruit: 0.0
Bread: 2.5
Meat: 0.0
Fat: 0.0

1. Spray large saucepan with cooking spray; saute carrots, bell pepper, green onions, and garlic until vegetables are tender, about 7 minutes. Stir in herbs; cook 1 to 2 minutes longer.

2. Add Basic Vegetable Stock, water, tomatoes, and beans to saucepan; heat to boiling. Reduce heat and simmer, covered, 10 minutes.

3. Heat soup to boiling; add pasta. Reduce heat and simmer, uncovered, until pasta is al dente, 12 to 15 minutes. Season with lemon juice, salt, and pepper.

MEDITERRANEAN VEGETABLE SOUP

A fragrant vegetable soup with a citrus accent.

6 servings (about 1¹/₂ cups each)

Olive oil cooking spray
2 cups sliced mushrooms
1 medium onion, chopped
¹/₂ medium green bell pepper, chopped
3 cloves garlic, minced
3¹/₂ cups Mediterranean Vegetable Stock (see p. 15)
1 can (16 ounces) reduced-sodium whole tomatoes, undrained, coarsely chopped
1 can (8 ounces) reduced-sodium tomato sauce
16 ounces light firm tofu, drained, cut into ¾-inch pieces
¹/₂ cup dry white wine, optional
2 strips orange rind (3 x ½ inch)
2 bay leaves
1 teaspoon dried marjoram leaves
¹/₂-³/₄ teaspoon dried savory leaves
¹/₄ teaspoon crushed fennel seeds
Salt and pepper, to taste

Per Serving
Calories: 109
% Calories from fat: 15
Protein (g): 8.1
Carbohydrates (g): 13.8
Fat (g): 2
Saturated fat (g): 0.1
Cholesterol (mg): 0
Sodium (mg): 104
Exchanges
Milk: 0.0
Veg.: 2.5
Fruit: 0.0
Bread: 0.0
Meat: 0.5
Fat: 0.0

1. Spray large saucepan with cooking spray; heat over medium heat until hot. Add mushrooms, onion, bell pepper, and garlic; saute, covered, until vegetables are tender, 8 to 10 minutes.

2. Add remaining ingredients, except salt and pepper; heat to boiling. Reduce heat and simmer, covered, 10 to 15 minutes. Season to taste with salt and pepper. Remove bay leaves and serve in bowls.

WHITE BEAN AND SWEET POTATO SOUP WITH CRANBERRY COULIS

An unusual but most pleasing combination of colors and flavors!

6 servings (about 1¹/₄ cups each)

Vegetable cooking spray
1 cup chopped onion
1 pound sweet potatoes, peeled, cubed
1 large tart cooking apple, peeled, cored, chopped
1¹/₂ teaspoons minced gingerroot
2 cans (15 ounces each) navy, *or* Great Northern, beans, rinsed, drained
3 cups Basic Vegetable Stock (see p. 10)
¹/₂ teaspoon dried marjoram leaves
Salt, cayenne, and white pepper, to taste
Cranberry Coulis (recipe follows)

Per Serving
Calories: 310
% Calories from fat: 3
Protein (g): 12.6
Carbohydrates (g): 64.6
Fat (g): 1.2
Saturated fat (g): 0.3
Cholesterol (mg): 0
Sodium (mg): 650
Exchanges
Milk: 0.0
Veg.: 1.0
Fruit: 1.0
Bread: 3.0
Meat: 0.0
Fat: 0.0

1. Spray large saucepan with cooking spray; heat over medium heat until hot. Saute onion, sweet potatoes, apple, and gingerroot 5 minutes. Add beans, Basic Vegetable Stock, and marjoram and heat to boiling. Reduce heat and simmer, covered, until vegetables are tender, about 15 minutes.

2. Process soup in blender or food processor until smooth; season to taste with salt, cayenne, and white pepper. Pour soup into bowls; swirl 2 tablespoons Cranberry Coulis into each bowl.

Cranberry Coulis

makes about 1 cup

1¹/₂ cups fresh, *or* frozen, cranberries
1 cup orange juice
2-3 tablespoons sugar
1-2 tablespoons honey

1. Heat cranberries and orange juice to boiling in small saucepan; reduce heat and simmer, covered, until cranberries are tender, 5 to 8 minutes. Add sugar and honey and process mixture in food processor or blender until almost smooth.

CREAM OF FAVA BEAN SOUP

This very unusual soup is based on fava beans, which are available canned or dried in markets with a Middle Eastern section. The chives are a necessary flavor ingredient and should not be omitted.

4 servings

2 medium onions, coarsely chopped, divided

2 ribs celery, cut into 1-inch pieces

1 large tart apple, peeled, coarsely chopped

2 tablespoons margarine

2 teaspoons curry powder

1 low-sodium vegetable bouillon cube

1^1/$_2$ quarts water

1 can (16 ounces) fava beans, rinsed, drained

^{1}/$_2$ cup coarsely chopped potatoes

2 teaspoons Worcestershire sauce

^{1}/$_2$ teaspoon pepper

1^1/$_2$ cups fat-free sour cream, divided

^{1}/$_2$ teaspoon salt, optional

8 teaspoons chopped fresh chives, divided

Per Serving
Calories: 244
% Calories from fat: 15
Protein (g): 14.6
Carbohydrates (g): 41.7
Fat (g): 4.3
Saturated fat (g): 0.6
Cholesterol (mg): 0
Sodium (mg): 732
Exchanges
Milk: 0.0
Veg.: 1.0
Fruit: 0.0
Bread: 3.0
Meat: 0.0
Fat: 0.5

1. Saute onions, celery, and apple in margarine in large saucepan until tender; add curry powder and cook 1 minute. Stir in bouillon cube and water; heat to boiling. Add fava beans and potatoes; simmer 15 to 20 minutes or until potatoes are tender.

2. Process soup in blender or food processor until smooth. Return soup to saucepan. Add Worcestershire sauce, pepper, and 1 cup sour cream and heat until hot. Season to taste with salt.

3. Ladle soup into bowls; garnish each serving with 2 tablespoons remaining sour cream and 2 teaspoons chives.

TANGY THREE-BEAN SOUP

The spicy barbecue flavor of this dish is a nice change of pace from the usual "tamer" bean soups.

5-6 servings

1/2 cup dried black-eyed peas
1/2 cup dried baby lima beans
1/2 cup dried Great Northern beans
2 1/2 quarts water
1 large garlic clove, minced
1 large onion, finely chopped
1 large carrot, thinly sliced
1 large rib celery, thinly sliced
1/8 teaspoon ground cloves
1 bay leaf
1 can (15 ounces) tomato sauce
1-2 tablespoons brown sugar
1 tablespoon apple cider vinegar
1 tablespoon light molasses
1/2 teaspoon dry mustard
1/2 teaspoon chili powder
1/4 teaspoon ground celery seeds
1/4 teaspoon dried thyme leaves
1/4 teaspoon paprika
1/4 teaspoon black pepper
1/8 teaspoon cayenne pepper, or to taste
Salt, to taste

Per Serving
Calories: 167
% Calories from fat: 5
Protein (g): 9.2
Carbohydrates (g): 33
Fat (g): 0.9
Saturated fat (g): 0.2
Cholesterol (mg): 0
Sodium (mg): 447
Exchanges
Milk: 0.0
Veg.: 1.0
Fruit: 0.0
Bread: 2.0
Meat: 0.0
Fat: 0.0

1. Cover beans with 2 inches water in Dutch oven and heat to boiling. Boil 2 minutes. Remove from heat and let stand, covered, 1 hour. Drain beans, discarding soaking liquid.

2. Return beans to Dutch oven; add 2 1/2 quarts water, garlic, onion, carrot, celery, cloves, and bay leaf; heat to boiling. Reduce heat and simmer, covered, 1 1/4 to 1 1/2 hours or until beans are very tender and have thickened soup. Add remaining ingredients, except salt, and simmer 25 to 30 minutes or until flavors are well blended. Add salt to taste. Discard bay leaf.

DOWN EAST BEAN CHOWDER

This soup combines the flavors of Boston baked beans with old-fashioned New England potato chowder.

8 servings

2 cups chopped onions
1 cup sliced celery
1 cup sliced carrots
1 tablespoon margarine
2 cups diced peeled potatoes
1¹/₂ quarts Basic Vegetable Stock (see p. 10)
1 teaspoon dried thyme leaves
1 can (15 ounces) navy beans, rinsed, drained, coarsely mashed
1 can (14 ounces) vegetarian baked beans in molasses sauce
1 can (15 ounces) reduced-sodium tomato sauce
Liquid smoke, to taste
Salt and pepper, to taste

Per Serving
Calories: 221
% Calories from fat: 11
Protein (gm): 8.9
Carbohydrate (gm): 41.7
Fat (gm): 3
Saturated fat (gm): 0.8
Cholesterol (mg): 0
Sodium (mg): 397
Exchanges
Milk: 0.0
Veg.: 2.0
Fruit: 0.0
Bread: 2.0
Meat: 0.0
Fat: 0.5

1. Saute onions, celery, and carrots in margarine in large saucepan until tender, about 10 minutes. Add potatoes, Basic Vegetable Stock, and thyme. Heat to boiling; reduce heat and simmer, covered, until potatoes are tender, about 15 minutes.

2. Stir in navy beans, baked beans, and tomato sauce; simmer until slightly thickened, about 10 minutes. Season to taste with liquid smoke, salt, and pepper.

BLACK BEAN SOUP

Dried beans can also be "quick soaked" rather than soaked overnight before cooking. Place beans in a large saucepan and cover with 2 inches water; heat to boiling and boil 2 minutes. Remove from heat and let stand l hour; drain and continue with Step 2 in recipe below. Or, substitute three cans (15 ounces each) rinsed, drained canned black beans for the dried.

4 servings (about 1¹/₄ cups each)

1¹/₂ cups dried black beans
Vegetable cooking spray
1 large onion, chopped
4 cloves garlic, minced
1 teaspoon dried oregano leaves
¹/₂ teaspoon dried thyme leaves
1 tomato, chopped
Salt and pepper, to taste
6 tablespoons fat-free sour cream
Finely chopped oregano, *or* parsley, as garnish

Per Serving
Calories: 200
% Calories from fat: **4**
Protein (g): 13.8
Carbohydrates (g): 39
Fat (g): 0.9
Saturated fat (g): 0.2
Cholesterol (mg): 0
Sodium (mg): 20
Exchanges
Milk: 0.0
Veg.: 1.0
Fruit: 0.0
Bread: 2.0
Meat: 0.5
Fat: 0.0

1. Cover beans with 4 inches water in large saucepan; soak overnight and drain.

2. Spray large saucepan with cooking spray; heat over medium heat until hot. Saute onion and garlic 2 to 3 minutes; add herbs and cook 2 to 3 minutes longer. Add beans to saucepan; cover with 2 inches water and heat to boiling. Reduce heat and simmer, covered, until beans are very tender, 45 to 60 minutes, adding tomatoes during last 10 minutes; add additional water to cover beans if necessary. Drain mixture, reserving liquid.

3. Process bean mixture in food processor or blender until smooth, adding enough reserved cooking liquid to make desired consistency. Return soup to saucepan; heat over medium heat until hot, 3 to 4 minutes. Season to taste with salt and pepper.

4. Serve soup in bowls; top each with dollop of sour cream and sprinkle with oregano.

BLACK BEAN SOUP WITH SUN-DRIED TOMATOES AND CILANTRO CREAM

Cilantro Cream adds a fresh accent to this South-of-the-Border favorite.

4 servings (about 1¹/₂ cups each)

3/4   cup sun-dried tomatoes (not in oil)
1¹/4   cups boiling water
   Vegetable cooking spray
   1   cup chopped onion
   2   cloves garlic, minced
   1   jalapeño chili, minced
   3   cups Basic Vegetable Stock (see p. 10)
   3   cups cooked dried black beans, *or* 2
       cans (15 ounces each) black beans,
       rinsed, drained
3/4   teaspoon ground cumin
1/2   teaspoon dried oregano leaves
1/4-1/2   teaspoon hot pepper sauce
   Salt and pepper, to taste
1/4   cup finely chopped cilantro
   Cilantro Cream (recipe follows)

Per Serving
Calories: 239
% Calories from fat: 5
Protein (g): 15.2
Carbohydrates (g): 44
Fat (g): 1.5
Saturated fat (g): 0.3
Cholesterol (mg): 0
Sodium (mg): 256
Exchanges
Milk: 0.0
Veg.: 1.0
Fruit: 0.0
Bread: 3.0
Meat: 0.0
Fat: 0.0

1.   Combine sun-dried tomatoes and boiling water in bowl; let stand until softened, about 10 minutes.

2.   Spray large saucepan with cooking spray; heat over medium heat until hot. Saute onion, garlic, and jalapeño chili until tender, 5 to 8 minutes. Add Basic Vegetable Stock, beans, cumin, oregano, and sun-dried tomatoes with liquid to saucepan; heat to boiling. Reduce heat and simmer, covered, 10 minutes. Season to taste with hot pepper sauce, salt, and pepper; stir in cilantro.

3.   Process soup in food processor or blender until smooth. Pour into bowls; garnish with dollops of Cilantro Cream.

Cilantro Cream

makes about ¹/₃ cup

- ¹/₃ cup fat-free sour cream
- 2 tablespoons minced cilantro
- 1 teaspoon lemon, *or* lime, juice
- ³/₄ teaspoon ground coriander
- 2-3 dashes white pepper

1. Mix all ingredients; refrigerate until serving time.

Variation:

Ancho Black Bean and Pumpkin Soup—Make soup as above, omitting sun-dried tomatoes, boiling water, and Cilantro Cream. Heat 1 ancho chili in dry skillet over medium heat until softened; remove chili and discard veins and seeds. Add chili and 1 can (15 ounces) pumpkin with beans in Step 2.

CUBAN BLACK BEAN SOUP

Although a number of steps are required to make this soup, the spicy, authentic Caribbean flavor is ample reward. Black beans can vary in cooking time, so check them for doneness after the first hour.

9 servings

- 2 cups dried black beans
- 1³/₄ quarts water
- 3 large onions, finely chopped
- 3 large garlic cloves, minced
- ¹/₂ teaspoon black pepper
- 4-5 drops hot pepper sauce
- 2 large green bell peppers, finely chopped
- 1 tablespoon olive oil
- 2 teaspoons ground cumin
- 2 teaspoons dried oregano leaves
  Salt, to taste
  Cuban Rice, warm (recipe follows)

Per Serving
Calories: 274
% Calories from fat: 11
Protein (g): 11.8
Carbohydrates (g): 50.1
Fat (g): 3.5
Saturated fat (g): 0.5
Cholesterol (mg): 0
Sodium (mg): 480
Exchanges
Milk: 0.0
Veg.: 1.0
Fruit: 0.0
Bread: 3.0
Meat: 0.0
Fat: 0.5

1. Cover beans with 2 inches of water in Dutch oven and heat to boiling. Boil for 2 minutes; remove from heat and let stand, covered, 1 hour. Drain beans, discarding liquid.

2. Return beans to Dutch oven; add 1³/4 quarts water, onions, garlic, black pepper, and hot pepper sauce and heat to boiling. Reduce heat and simmer, covered, until beans have softened and thickened the soup, about 1¹/2 hours.

3. Saute bell peppers in oil in medium skillet until softened, about 3 minutes. Stir in cumin and oregano and cook 2 minutes. Stir peppers into soup; simmer 10 minutes. Season to taste with salt. Ladle soup into large bowls; spoon Cuban Rice into soup.

Cuban Rice

   1 cup uncooked long-grain white rice
   1 tablespoon chopped onion
   2 cups water
   2 teaspoons olive oil
1¹/2 tablespoons apple cider vinegar

1. Combine rice, onion, and water in saucepan; heat to boiling. Reduce heat and simmer, covered, 20 minutes or until rice is tender. Stir in oil and vinegar.

SPLIT-PEA SOUP WITH THREE ACCOMPANIMENTS

This thick and beautiful green soup is served with cubed sweet potatoes, fresh peas, and croutons.

6 servings

$^1/_2$ cup minced onion

1 rib celery, chopped

2 tablespoons margarine

1$^1/_2$ quarts water

1 cup dry white wine

1 pound dry split peas

2 vegetable bouillon cubes

2 sprigs parsley

$^1/_2$ teaspoon dried thyme leaves

1 bay leaf

$^1/_2$ teaspoon pepper

Salt, to taste

1 cup cooked green peas, warm

1 cup cubed, cooked, peeled sweet potatoes, warm

1 cup plain croutons

Per Serving
Calories: 374
% Calories from fat: 8
Protein (g): 21.5
Carbohydrates (g): 60.7
Fat (g): 3.4
Saturated fat (g): 0.5
Cholesterol (mg): 0.1
Sodium (mg): 441
Exchanges
Milk: 0.0
Veg.: 0.0
Fruit: 0.0
Bread: 4.0
Meat: 1.0
Fat: 0.5

1. Saute onion and celery in margarine in large saucepan until tender, about 5 minutes. Stir in remaining ingredients, except salt, green peas, sweet potatoes, and croutons. Heat to boiling; reduce heat and simmer, covered, about 45 minutes or until split peas are just soft.

2. Process soup in blender or food processor until smooth; season to taste with salt. Ladle soup into bowls. Pass green peas, sweet potatoes, and croutons to sprinkle on soup.

EASIEST BLACK-EYED PEA AND LENTIL SOUP

This soup will thicken if refrigerated, so stir in additional broth when re-heating. The soup freezes well, too.

6 servings (about 1²/₃ cups each)

3 medium carrots, chopped
2 medium ribs celery, sliced
1 medium onion, chopped
1 teaspoon minced garlic
2 tablespoons olive oil
6-8 cups reduced-sodium vegetable broth
¾ cup dried black-eyed peas
1 teaspoon dried thyme leaves
¹/₂ teaspoon dried marjoram leaves
¹/₂ teaspoon dried oregano leaves
1 bay leaf
3 medium tomatoes, chopped
1¹/₂ cups dried lentils
    Salt and pepper, to taste

Per Serving
Calories: 356
% Calories from fat: 14
Protein (g): 20.7
Carbohydrates (g): 58.3
Fat (g): 5.9
Saturated fat (g): 0.9
Cholesterol (mg): 0
Sodium (mg): 119
Exchanges
Milk: 0.0
Veg.: 2.0
Fruit: 0.0
Bread: 3.0
Meat: 1.0
Fat: 1.0

1. Saute carrots, celery, onion, and garlic in oil in large sauce-pan 5 minutes. Add 6 cups broth, black-eyed peas, and herbs to saucepan; heat to boiling. Reduce heat and simmer, covered, 30 minutes.

2. Stir tomatoes and lentils into soup. Simmer, covered, until peas and lentils are tender, about 30 minutes, adding additional broth if necessary. Discard bay leaf; season to taste with salt and pepper.

COUNTRY LENTIL SOUP

A light soup, wholesome in flavor and texture. This soup freezes well, so make extra.

4 servings (about 1³/4 cups each)

1¹/2 cups chopped onions
1 cup sliced celery
1 cup sliced carrots
2 teaspoons minced garlic
1 tablespoon olive oil
3 cups Roasted Vegetable Stock (see p. 14), or vegetable broth
2 cups water
1 cup dried lentils, washed, sorted
1 can (14¹/2 ounces) reduced-sodium whole tomatoes, undrained, crushed
2 tablespoons finely chopped parsley
1 teaspoon dried marjoram leaves
¹/2 teaspoon dried oregano leaves
¹/4 teaspoon dried thyme leaves
Salt and pepper, to taste
4 tablespoons grated fat-free Parmesan cheese

Per Serving
Calories: 275
% Calories from fat: 14
Protein (g): 15.8
Carbohydrates (g): 42.8
Fat (g): 4.4
Saturated fat (g): 0.6
Cholesterol (mg): 0
Sodium (mg): 109
Exchanges
Milk: 0.0
Veg.: 3.0
Fruit: 0.0
Bread: 2.0
Meat: 0.5
Fat: 0.5

1. Saute onions, celery, carrots, and garlic in oil in Dutch oven 5 to 8 minutes. Add Roasted Vegetable Stock, water, lentils, tomatoes and liquid, and herbs; heat to boiling. Reduce heat and simmer, covered, until lentils are tender, about 30 minutes. Season to taste with salt and pepper.

2. Pour soup into bowls; sprinkle each with 1 tablespoon Parmesan cheese.

EASY INDIAN LENTIL SOUP

This hearty but very easy main-dish soup tastes best made with tiny beige Indian lentils available in Indian specialty food stores. However, regular brown lentils can also be used.

4 servings

1 large onion, finely chopped
1 garlic clove, minced
2 teaspoons canola oil
2¹/₂ quarts water
2 cups dried Indian lentils, sorted, rinsed
2 large ribs celery with leaves, thinly sliced
1 large carrot, thinly sliced
2-3 teaspoons mild curry powder, *or* to taste
1 teaspoon sugar
¹/₄ teaspoon pepper
Salt, to taste

Per Serving
Calories: 306
% Calories from fat: 18
Protein (g): 20.8
Carbohydrates (g): 51.2
Fat (g): 3
Saturated fat (g): 2
Cholesterol (mg): 0
Sodium (mg): 28
Exchanges
Milk: 0.0
Veg.: 0.0
Fruit: 0.0
Bread: 4.0
Meat: 0.0
Fat: 0.0

1. Saute onion and garlic in oil in Dutch oven until onion is soft. Add remaining ingredients, except salt, and heat to boiling. Reduce heat and simmer, covered, until lentils soften and thicken the soup, about 1 hour. Season to taste with salt.

CURRIED LENTIL-SPINACH SOUP

Lentils and spinach blend nicely to lend flavor and texture to this very low-fat soup.

6-7 servings

2	cups chopped onions
2	large garlic cloves, minced
2	teaspoons olive oil
1¼	quarts reduced-sodium vegetable broth
2	cups water
1	rib celery, thinly sliced
1	large carrot, peeled, thinly sliced
1	cup dried brown lentils, rinsed, drained
2-2½	teaspoons mild curry powder, *or* to taste
½	teaspoon chili powder
¼	teaspoon black pepper
1	package (10 ounces) frozen chopped spinach, thawed, well-drained
1	can (14½ ounces) reduced-sodium tomatoes, undrained, chopped
	Salt, to taste

Per Serving
Calories: 181
% Calories from fat: **10**
Protein (g): 10.5
Carbohydrates (g): 32.6
Fat (g): 2
Saturated fat (g): **0.3**
Cholesterol (mg): 0
Sodium (mg): 104
Exchanges
Milk: 0.0
Veg.: 2.0
Fruit: 0.0
Bread: 1.5
Meat: 0.5
Fat: 0.0

1. Saute onions and garlic in oil in large saucepan until onion is soft. Add remaining ingredients, except spinach, tomatoes, and salt; heat to boiling. Reduce heat and simmer, covered, 45 minutes. Add spinach and tomatoes and liquid; simmer 10 minutes. Season to taste with salt.

INDIAN LENTIL SOUP

This soup (Dal Shorba) from India is flavored with curry powder and sweet coriander. Red, green, or brown lentils can be used.

6 servings (about 1¹/₃ cups each)

Per Serving
Calories: 280
% Calories from fat: 11
Protein (g): 19.4
Carbohydrates (g): 44.7
Fat (g): 3.6
Saturated fat (g): 0.5
Cholesterol (mg): 0.3
Sodium (mg): 26
Exchanges
Milk: 0.0
Veg.: 1.0
Fruit: 0.0
Bread: 2.5
Meat: 1.5
Fat: 0.0

¹/₂ cup chopped onion
1 clove garlic
2 teaspoons curry powder
1 teaspoon crushed coriander seeds
1 teaspoon crushed cumin seeds
¹/₂ teaspoon ground turmeric
¼ teaspoon crushed red pepper
1 tablespoon olive oil
5 cups Basic Vegetable Stock (see p. 10)
4 cups water
2 cups dried red, *or* brown, lentils, sorted, rinsed
Salt and pepper, to taste
6 tablespoons fat-free plain yogurt

1. Saute onion, garlic, herbs, and red pepper in oil in large saucepan until onion is tender, about 5 minutes, stirring frequently. Add Basic Vegetable Stock, water, and lentils; heat to boiling. Reduce heat and simmer, covered, until lentils are tender, about 30 minutes. Season to taste with salt and pepper.

2. Pour soup into bowls; garnish each with a tablespoon of yogurt.

BEAN AND BARLEY SOUP

This soup can be easily increased to serve a crowd; make it a day ahead of time for best flavor.

6 servings

1 cup chopped onion

3/4 cup chopped red, *or* green, bell pepper

2 teaspoons minced roasted garlic

2 tablespoons olive oil

1 tablespoon flour

1 1/2 teaspoons Italian seasoning

7 cups salt-free vegetable broth

2 cans (15 ounces each) cannellini, *or* Great Northern, beans, rinsed, drained

2 tablespoons reduced-sodium tomato paste

1/2 cup quick-cooking barley

1 large Idaho potato, unpeeled, cut into 1/2-inch pieces

1 cup sliced carrots

1 cup packed baby spinach leaves

Salt and pepper, to taste

Per Serving
Calories: 297
% Calories from fat: 17
Protein (g): 10
Carbohydrates (g): 52.1
Fat (g): 5.6
Saturated fat (g): 0.7
Cholesterol (mg): 0
Sodium (mg): 325
Exchanges
Milk: 0.0
Veg.: 1.0
Fruit: 0.0
Bread: 3.0
Meat: 0.0
Fat: 1.0

1. Saute onion, bell pepper, and garlic in oil in Dutch oven 5 minutes. Add flour and Italian seasoning; cook 1 to 2 minutes longer.

2. Add remaining ingredients, except spinach, salt, and pepper, to Dutch oven; heat to boiling. Reduce heat and simmer, uncovered, 20 to 25 minutes, adding spinach during last 5 minutes of cooking time. Season to taste with salt and pepper.

POTATO BARLEY SOUP

You can vary the flavor of this homey soup by using different stocks, as well as different vegetables.

8 servings

Olive oil cooking spray
1 cup chopped onion
3 cloves garlic, minced
3 cups chopped, peeled potatoes
2 large carrots, sliced
3 ribs celery, sliced
1 parsnip, sliced
2 bay leaves
1 cup tomato juice
3/4 cup quick-cooking barley
1 quart Low-Salt Vegetable Stock (see p. 12)
1/2 teaspoon dried thyme leaves
1/2 teaspoon dried marjoram leaves
1/2 teaspoon salt
1/2 teaspoon pepper

Per Serving
Calories: 186
% Calories from fat: **3**
Protein (gm): 5.1
Carbohydrate (gm): 41.8
Fat (gm): 0.7
Saturated fat (gm): 0.1
Cholesterol (mg): 0
Sodium (mg): 285
Exchanges
Milk: 0.0
Veg.: 0.0
Fruit: 0.0
Bread: 2.5
Meat: 0.0
Fat: 0.0

1. Spray Dutch oven with cooking spray; heat over medium heat until hot. Saute onion, garlic, and potatoes 5 minutes. Add remaining ingredients and heat to boiling. Reduce heat and simmer, covered, until vegetables are tender, about 20 minutes. Discard bay leaves.

SAVORY MUSHROOM AND BARLEY SOUP

Fast and easy to make with quick-cooking barley. Other grains, such as wild rice or oat groats, can be substituted for the barley; cook them before adding to the soup.

4 servings (about 1¹/₂ cups each)

Vegetable cooking spray
1 cup chopped onion
1 cup sliced celery
²/₃ cup sliced carrots
1 teaspoon dried savory leaves
³/₄ teaspoon fennel seeds, crushed
1 quart water
1 can (16 ounces) reduced-sodium whole tomatoes, undrained, coarsely chopped
¹/₂ cup quick-cooking barley
2 cups sliced cremini, *or* white, mushrooms
Salt and pepper, to taste
Finely chopped parsley, as garnish

Per Serving
Calories: 151
% Calories from fat: 8
Protein (g): 5.6
Fat (g): 1.4
Saturated fat (g): 0.1
Cholesterol (mg): 0
Sodium (mg): 53
Exchanges
Milk: 0.0
Veg.: 2.0
Fruit: 0.0
Bread: 1.5
Meat: 0.0
Fat: 0.0

1. Spray large saucepan with cooking spray; heat over medium heat until hot. Saute onion, celery, and carrots until onion is tender, about 5 minutes. Stir in herbs; cook 1 to 2 minutes longer.

2. Add water, tomatoes and liquid, barley, and mushrooms to saucepan; heat to boiling. Cook, covered, until barley is tender, 10 to 15 minutes. Season to taste with salt and pepper.

3. Pour soup into bowls; sprinkle with parsley.

POLISH-STYLE MUSHROOM-BARLEY SOUP

Use dried Polish mushrooms, or any favorite type for this woodsy-flavored soup.

4 servings

1/4 ounce dried mushrooms

2¼ quarts water, divided

5 low-sodium vegetable bouillon cubes

1/2 cup pearl barley

3 medium baking potatoes, peeled, diced

1 small onion, coarsely chopped

1 rib celery with leaves, sliced

1/2 cup quartered baby carrots

1 cup dry white wine, optional

2 sprigs parsley

1/2 teaspoon white pepper

1 cup frozen peas
   Salt, to taste

1/2 cup fat-free sour cream

4 teaspoons chopped fresh dill weed

Per Serving
Calories: 293
% Calories from fat: 4
Protein (g): 9.9
Carbohydrates (g): 54.7
Fat (g): 1.5
Saturated fat (g): 0.1
Cholesterol (mg): 0
Sodium (mg): 777
Exchanges
Milk: 0.0
Veg.: 3.0
Fruit: 0.0
Bread: 3.0
Meat: 0.0
Fat: 0.0

1. Heat mushrooms and 2 cups water to boiling in small saucepan. Remove from heat and let stand 1 hour; drain, reserving liquid. Chop mushrooms coarsely.

2. Heat remaining 1³/4 quarts water, bouillon, and barley to boiling in large saucepan; reduce heat and simmer, covered, 40 minutes. Stir in reserved mushroom liquid, chopped mushrooms, and remaining ingredients, except peas, salt, sour cream and dill. Simmer 20 minutes or until vegetables and barley are tender. Add peas and simmer 3 minutes; season to taste with salt. Garnish individual servings with sour cream and dill.

SPICY BARLEY SOUP

Herbs and dry mustard give this barley soup its savor.

6-7 servings

2 large onions, finely chopped
1 large garlic clove, minced
1/4 pound mushrooms, sliced
1 tablespoon canola oil
2 quarts vegetable broth
1 large carrot, thinly sliced
2 ribs celery, thinly sliced
3 tablespoons reduced-sodium tomato paste
1/2 cup diced turnip
1/4 cup pearl barley
1/4 cup chopped parsley
2 bay leaves
1 teaspoon dried marjoram leaves
1/2 teaspoon dried thyme leaves
1/2 teaspoon dry mustard
1/4 teaspoon celery seeds
1/4 teaspoon black pepper
Dash cayenne pepper

Per Serving
Calories: 95
% Calories from fat: 25
Protein (g): 2.6
Carbohydrates (g): 16.5
Fat (g): 2.8
Saturated fat (g): 0.2
Cholesterol (mg): 0
Sodium (mg): 492
Exchanges
Milk: 0.0
Veg.: 0.0
Fruit: 0.0
Bread: 1.0
Meat: 0.0
Fat: 0.5

1. Saute onions, garlic, and mushrooms in oil in large saucepan until onion is soft. Add remaining ingredients and heat to boiling. Reduce heat and simmer, covered, until barley is tender and has thickened the soup, about 1 1/4 hours.

NINE

Quick-and-Easy Soups

TROPICAL MELON SOUP

Enjoy this refreshing soup as a first course, a light dessert, or a midday snack.

4 servings

- 1/2 small cantaloupe, peeled, seeded, cubed
- 1 1/2 cups cubed honeydew melon
- 1/4 cup fresh lemon juice
- 1/4 cup dry white wine
- 1 tablespoon sugar
  Shredded coconut, as garnish
  Grated lime rind, as garnish

Per Serving
Calories: 97
% Calories from fat: 2
Protein (gm): 1.7
Carbohydrate (gm): 22.7
Fat (gm): 0.2
Saturated fat (gm): 0
Cholesterol (mg): 0
Sodium (mg): 38
Exchanges
Milk: 0.0
Veg.: 0.0
Fruit: 1.5
Bread: 0.0
Meat: 0.0
Fat: 0.0

1. Process melon chunks in blender or food processor until smooth; pour into bowl. Stir in lemon juice, wine, and sugar. Refrigerate until chilled.

2. Serve soup in bowl; sprinkle with coconut and lime rind.

FRAGRANT MELON SOUP

The flavor of the soup is determined by the ripeness and flavor of the melon.

4 servings (about 1 cup each)

- 1 quart cubed, peeled, seeded ripe cantaloupe
- 1/2 cup orange juice
- 3-4 tablespoons lemon, *or* lime, juice
- 2 tablespoons honey
- 1/4-1/2 cup fat-free half-and-half, *or* fat-free milk
- 4 thin lemon, *or* lime, slices
  Mint, *or* lemon, balm sprigs, as garnish

Per Serving
Calories: 116
% Calories from fat: 4
Protein (g): 2.2
Carbohydrates (g): 28
Fat (g): 0.5
Saturated fat (g): 0
Cholesterol (mg): 0
Sodium (mg): 30
Exchanges
Milk: 0.0
Veg.: 0.0
Fruit: 2.0
Bread: 0.0
Meat: 0.0
Fat: 0.0

1. Process cantaloupe, orange and lemon juice, and honey in food processor or blender until smooth; stir in half-and-half. Refrigerate until chilled, 3 to 4 hours.

2. Pour soup into bowls; float lemon slice in each and garnish with herb sprigs.

ICED VEGETABLE GAZPACHO

This refreshing soup is the easiest gazpacho ever.

4 servings (about ³/₄ cup each)

1 medium zucchini
1 large cucumber, peeled, seeded
¹/₂ green bell pepper
1 clove garlic
¹/₄ jalapeño chili, seeded
2 tablespoons chopped chives
1¹/₂ cups reduced-sodium tomato juice
¹/₄ cup reduced-sodium fat-free beef broth
1 tablespoon sugar
Salt and pepper, to taste

Per Serving
Calories: 48
% Calories from fat: 4
Protein (gm): 2.1
Carbohydrate (gm): 11
Fat (gm): 0.2
Saturated fat (gm): 0
Cholesterol (mg): 0
Sodium (mg): 22
Exchanges
Milk: 0.0
Veg.: 2.0
Fruit: 0.0
Bread: 0.0
Meat: 0.0
Fat: 0.0

1. Cut vegetables into 1-inch pieces. Process all ingredients, except salt and pepper, in blender or food processor until finely chopped; add additional beef broth if needed to achieve desired consistency. Season to taste with salt and pepper; refrigerate until chilled. Serve in chilled bowls.

EASY GAZPACHO

If the yen for gazpacho strikes and fresh tomatoes are unavailable, try this version, which uses canned tomatoes.

4-6 servings

2 cans (14½ ounces) plum tomatoes, undrained
1 small garlic clove, minced
1-2 tablespoons chopped scallions, *or* chives
1 medium cucumber, peeled, seeded, diced
1 rib celery, diced
½ large green bell pepper, diced
2-3 drops hot pepper sauce
¼ teaspoon black pepper
Salt, to taste
4-6 sprigs parsley, as garnish

Per Serving
Calories: 38
% Calories from fat: **9**
Protein (g): 1.8
Carbohydrates (g): 8.2
Fat (g): 0.4
Saturated fat (g): 0.1
Cholesterol (mg): 0
Sodium (mg): 230
Exchanges
Milk: 0.0
Veg.: 2.0
Fruit: 0.0
Bread: 0.0
Meat: 0.0
Fat: 0.0

1. Process tomatoes and liquid with garlic in blender or food processor until smooth. Transfer to mixing bowl and add remaining ingredients except salt and parsley. Chill, covered, several hours. Season to taste with salt; garnish with fresh parsley sprigs.

CITRUS-TOMATO SOUP

Orange and lemon juices add a refreshing tang to this easy tomato soup.

4-5 servings

2 tablespoons finely chopped onion
1 cup reduced-sodium fat-free chicken broth
2 tablespoons light brown sugar
1 quart reduced-sodium tomato juice
⅓ cup frozen orange juice concentrate
2 tablespoons lemon juice
1-2 drops hot pepper sauce
Salt, to taste
Thin orange slices, as garnish

Per Serving
Calories: 92
% Calories from fat: **1**
Protein (g): 2.9
Carbohydrates (g): 21.9
Fat (g): 0.2
Saturated fat (g): 0
Cholesterol (mg): 0
Sodium (mg): 90
Exchanges
Milk: 0.0
Veg.: 2.0
Fruit: 0.5
Bread: 0.0
Meat: 0.0
Fat: 0.0

1. Simmer onion in broth in small saucepan until tender.

2. Combine remaining ingredients, except salt and orange slices, in mixing bowl. Add onion mixture; season to taste with salt. Refrigerate several hours; garnish with orange slices.

HERBED CUCUMBER SOUP

This soup is very delicate in flavor. Use a serrated grapefruit spoon to seed cucumbers quickly and easily.

6 servings (about 1¹/₃ cups each)

Vegetable cooking spray

¹/₂ cup chopped onion

6 medium cucumbers (about 3 pounds), peeled, seeded, chopped

3 tablespoons flour

1 quart reduced-sodium fat-free chicken broth

1 teaspoon dried mint, *or* dill weed

¹/₂ cup fat-free half-and-half, *or* fat-free milk

Salt and white pepper, to taste

Paprika, as garnish

6 thin slices cucumber

Per Serving
Calories: 83
% Calories from fat: 4
Protein (g): 6.8
Carbohydrates (g): 12.5
Fat (g): 0.4
Saturated fat (g): 0.1
Cholesterol (mg): 0
Sodium (mg): 139
Exchanges
Milk: 0.0
Veg.: 2.0
Fruit: 0.0
Bread: 0.0
Meat: 0.5
Fat: 0.0

1. Spray large saucepan with cooking spray; heat over medium heat until hot. Saute onion until tender, 3 to 5 minutes. Add cucumbers and cook over medium heat 5 minutes; stir in flour and cook 1 to 2 minutes longer.

2. Add broth to saucepan; heat to boiling. Reduce heat and simmer, covered, 10 minutes. Process soup in food processor or blender until smooth; stir in mint and half-and-half; season to taste with salt and pepper. Cool; refrigerate until chilled, 3 to 4 hours.

3. Pour soup into bowls; sprinkle lightly with paprika and top each with a cucumber slice.

CUCUMBER-YOGURT SOUP

The Greeks love yogurt, which is the basis for this delicious and refreshing no-cook soup.

4 servings

   3 cups low-fat plain yogurt
1¹/2 cups grated, peeled, seeded cucumber
   1 teaspoon Spike
  ³/4 cup cold water
   3 tablespoons minced chives
   1 tablespoon minced dill weed
   1 tablespoon minced garlic
   1 teaspoon white pepper
   4 thin slices cucumber

Per Serving
Calories: 119
% Calories from fat: 20
Protein (gm): 9.5
Carbohydrate (gm): 14.4
Fat (gm): 2.7
Saturated fat (gm):
Cholesterol (mg): 1.7
Sodium (mg): 121
Exchanges
Milk: 1.0
Veg.: 1.0
Fruit: 0.0
Bread: 0.0
Meat: 0.0
Fat: 0.5

1. Combine all ingredients, except cucumber slices, in mixing bowl; chill. Top each serving with cucumber slice.

ZUCCHINI SOUP

Try this soup when your garden is overflowing with zucchini.

4 servings

   2 cups reduced-sodium fat-free chicken broth
   2 cups sliced zucchini
   1 cup chopped onion
   3 cloves garlic, minced
   1 tablespoon tarragon vinegar
   1 teaspoon curry powder
  ¹/2 teaspoon dried marjoram leaves
  ¹/8 teaspoon cayenne pepper
  ¹/8 teaspoon celery seeds
   2 tablespoons fat-free dry milk
   1 cup fat-free yogurt
     Salt and pepper, to taste
   2 tablespoons diced pimiento, as garnish

Per Serving
Calories: 84
% Calories from fat: 4
Protein (gm): 8.5
Carbohydrate (gm): 11.9
Fat (gm): 0.4
Saturated fat (gm): 0.1
Cholesterol (mg): 1.4
Sodium (mg): 144
Exchanges
Milk: 0.5
Veg.: 2.0
Fruit: 0.0
Bread: 0.0
Meat: 0.0
Fat: 0.0

1. Heat all ingredients, except dry milk, yogurt, salt, pepper, and pimiento, to boiling in medium saucepan; reduce heat and simmer until vegetables are tender, about 8 minutes.

2. Process soup in blender or food processor with dry milk and yogurt until smooth; season to taste with salt and pepper. Chill before serving; garnish with pimiento.

SUMMER POTATO-BUTTERMILK SOUP

This refreshing cold soup is perfect for lunch on a hot summer day.

4 servings

3 medium red potatoes, cooked, peeled, cubed (1/2-inch)

2 cups chopped, peeled, seeded cucumber

1/4 cup chopped fresh, *or* 2 to 3 teaspoons dried, dill weed

1 teaspoon dry mustard

1/2 teaspoon sugar

1/2 teaspoon ground cumin

1 quart low-fat buttermilk

Salt and pepper, to taste

Per Serving
Calories: 199
% Calories from fat: 11
Protein (gm): 10.4
Carbohydrate (gm): 34.1
Fat (gm): 2.6
Saturated fat (gm): 1.4
Cholesterol (mg): 8.6
Sodium (mg): 264
Exchanges
Milk: 1.0
Veg.: 0.0
Fruit: 0.0
Bread: 1.5
Meat: 0.0
Fat: 0.5

1. Combine all ingredients, except salt and pepper, in large bowl; season to taste with salt and pepper. Refrigerate at least 30 minutes before serving.

VELVET VICHYSSOISE

Although typically served chilled, this soup is also delicious served warm.

6 servings

- ½ cup chopped onion
- ½ cup chopped leek, white part only
- 2 tablespoons margarine
- 3 tablespoons flour
- 2 cups reduced-sodium fat-free chicken broth
- 3½ cups cubed, peeled Idaho potatoes
- 2 cups fat-free milk

  Salt and pepper, to taste

  Minced chives, as garnish

Per Serving
Calories: 227
% Calories from fat: 16
Protein (gm): 8.3
Carbohydrate (gm): 39.4
Fat (gm): 4.2
Saturated fat (gm): 0.9
Cholesterol (mg): 1.5
Sodium (mg): 151
Exchanges
Milk: 0.0
Veg.: 2.0
Fruit: 0.0
Bread: 2.0
Meat: 0.0
Fat: 1.0

1. Saute onion and leek in margarine in large saucepan until tender, 5 to 8 minutes. Stir in flour; cook over medium-low heat, stirring constantly, 1 minute.

2. Add broth and potatoes to saucepan; heat to boiling. Reduce heat and simmer, covered, until potatoes are tender, 10 to 15 minutes. Stir in milk; simmer until hot, 3 to 4 minutes. Season to taste with salt and pepper.

3. Cool; process soup in food processor or blender until smooth. Refrigerate until chilled. Sprinkle each serving with chives.

QUICK VICHYSSOISE

The vegetables are pureed in the food processor for this ultra-fast potato soup. It can also be made with sweet potatoes.

4 servings

1 cup reduced-sodium fat-free chicken broth
1 cup cubed, peeled potatoes
1¹/2 cups chopped leeks, white parts only
Pinch celery seeds
2 cups fat-free milk
1 tablespoon part-skim ricotta cheese
Salt and white pepper, to taste
Cayenne pepper, to taste

Per Serving
Calories: 150
% Calories from fat: **4**
Protein (gm): 8.3
Carbohydrate (gm): **27.9**
Fat (gm): 0.8
Saturated fat (gm): 0.4
Cholesterol (mg): 3.4
Sodium (mg): 126
Exchanges
Milk: 0.5
Veg.: 0.0
Fruit: 0.0
Bread: 1.5
Meat: 0.0
Fat: 0.0

1. Process broth, potatoes, and leeks in blender or food processor until smooth. Transfer to medium saucepan; heat to boiling. Reduce heat and simmer 5 minutes.

2. Process milk and ricotta in blender or food processor until smooth; stir into soup. Season to taste with salt, white pepper, and cayenne pepper. Chill before serving.

BRUSSELS SPROUTS SOUP

A perfect fall soup, when tiny fresh Brussels sprouts are available; Roasted Red Pepper Bread (see p. 797) would be a colorful accompaniment.

4 servings (about 1 cup each)

¹/2 cup chopped onion
2 teaspoons minced garlic
1 tablespoon margarine
2 tablespoons flour
1²/3 cups fat-free milk
1 pound Brussels sprouts, cleaned, halved
1 teaspoon dried rosemary leaves
Salt and white pepper, to taste
Ground nutmeg, as garnish

Per Serving
Calories: 136
% Calories from fat: **23**
Protein (gm): 7.6
Carbohydrate (gm): **21.3**
Fat (gm): 3.8
Saturated fat (gm): 0.9
Cholesterol (mg): 1.9
Sodium (mg): 115
Exchanges
Milk: 0.0
Veg.: 4.0
Fruit: 0.0
Bread: 0.0
Meat: 0.0
Fat: 0.5

1. Saute onion and garlic in margarine in large saucepan until tender, about 5 minutes; sprinkle with flour and cook over medium heat, whisking constantly, 2 minutes. Whisk in milk and heat to boiling; whisk until smooth. Stir in Brussels sprouts and rosemary. Heat to boiling; reduce heat and simmer until sprouts are tender, about 15 minutes.

2. Process soup in food processor or blender until smooth. Return to saucepan. Heat to boiling; season to taste with salt and white pepper. Sprinkle lightly with nutmeg.

HOT-AND-SOUR CABBAGE SOUP

Reminiscent of classic Chinese hot-and-sour soup, this version cooks in under 15 minutes!

5 servings

1 large carrot, shredded

1/4 cup julienned red bell pepper

1 1/2 teaspoons peanut oil

4-5 green onions and tops, thinly sliced, divided

3 cups shredded green cabbage

1 large garlic clove, minced

1 tablespoon minced gingerroot

2 quarts reduced-sodium fat-free chicken broth

1 1/2 tablespoons apple cider vinegar

1 tablespoon plus 1 teaspoon light brown sugar

3 tablespoons reduced-sodium soy sauce

1/2 teaspoon oriental hot chili oil

2 tablespoons cornstarch

Per Serving
Calories: 81
% Calories from fat: 21
Protein (g): 6.2
Carbohydrates (g): 10.8
Fat (g): 2
Saturated fat (g): 0.3
Cholesterol (mg): 0
Sodium (mg): 635
Exchanges
Milk: 0.0
Veg.: 2.0
Fruit: 0.0
Bread: 0.0
Meat: 0.0
Fat: 0.5

1. Saute carrot and bell pepper in oil in large saucepan 2 minutes. Add half the green onions, cabbage, garlic, and gingerroot and cook 2 minutes. Add broth; heat to boiling. Reduce heat and simmer 5 minutes.

2. Combine vinegar, brown sugar, soy sauce, chili oil, and cornstarch in small bowl. Stir into soup; simmer 2 minutes or until soup thickens. Garnish with remaining green onions.

CREAMY CARROT SOUP

Orange and ginger flavor this quick soup. The soup is also excellent served chilled.

4 servings

2 cups sliced carrots
1/2 teaspoon chopped gingerroot
2 teaspoons canola oil
1 teaspoon flour
2 cups reduced-sodium fat-free chicken broth
1 cup fat-free milk
1/4 cup fat-free dry milk
2 teaspoons frozen orange juice concentrate
1/4 teaspoon dried tarragon leaves
1/4 teaspoon dried thyme leaves
1 bay leaf
Salt and pepper, to taste
Sprigs of mint *or* parsley, as garnish

Per Serving
Calories: 104
% Calories from fat: 22
Protein (gm): 7.3
Carbohydrate (gm): 12.7
Fat (gm): 2.6
Saturated fat (gm): 0.3
Cholesterol (mg): 1.9
Sodium (mg): 159
Exchanges
Milk: 0.5
Veg.: 1.0
Fruit: 0.0
Bread: 0.0
Meat: 0.0
Fat: 0.5

1. Saute carrots and gingerroot in oil in large saucepan until lightly browned, about 8 minutes; sprinkle with flour and cook 1 minute longer. Stir in remaining ingredients, except salt, pepper, and mint. Heat to boiling; reduce heat and simmer, covered, until carrots are tender, about 10 minutes. Discard bay leaf.

2. Process mixture in blender or food processor until smooth. Season to taste with salt and pepper. Garnish with mint sprigs.

CAULIFLOWER SOUP

This velvety soup can be ready to serve in less than 15 minutes—even sooner if you don't puree it!

4 servings

1 pound cauliflower florets
1 medium carrot, diced
1 rib celery with leaves, sliced
1/2 onion, sliced
2 1/2 cups water
1/4 cup fat-free dry milk
1 teaspoon chicken bouillon granules
1 teaspoon curry powder
1 teaspoon caraway seeds
1/2 teaspoon crushed red pepper
   Juice of 1/2 lemon
   Salt and pepper, to taste
   Chopped parsley, as garnish
   Paprika, as garnish

Per Serving
Calories: 67
% Calories from fat: 10
Protein (gm): 4.3
Carbohydrate (gm): 12.4
Fat (gm): 0.8
Saturated fat (gm): 0.1
Cholesterol (mg): 0.8
Sodium (mg): 316
Exchanges
Milk: 0.0
Veg.: 2.0
Fruit: 0.0
Bread: 0.0
Meat: 0.0
Fat: 0.0

1. Combine all ingredients, except lemon juice, salt, pepper, parsley, and paprika, in large saucepan; heat to boiling. Reduce heat and simmer, covered, until cauliflower is tender, about 10 minutes.

2. Process soup in blender or food processor until smooth. Add lemon juice; season to taste with salt and pepper. Garnish with parsley and paprika.

CURRIED CORN SOUP

A variety of spices, coconut milk, and corn make this soup an exotic treat.

6 servings (about 1¹/₄ cups each)

1¹/₂ cup chopped onions
2 jalapeño chilies, finely chopped
1 tablespoon minced garlic
2 teaspoons chopped gingerroot
2 teaspoons margarine
2 tablespoons flour
1 teaspoon ground cumin
¹/₂ teaspoon ground coriander
¹/₂ teaspoon ground cinnamon
  Generous pinch ground cloves
2 cups reduced-sodium fat-free chicken broth
2 cups frozen whole-kernel corn
1 can (14 ounces) light coconut milk
1 cup fat-free half-and-half, *or* fat-free milk
  Salt and pepper, to taste
  Chopped cilantro, as garnish

Per Serving
Calories: 161
% Calories from fat: 27
Protein (gm): 6.2
Carbohydrate (gm): 23.5
Fat (gm): 4.9
Saturated fat (gm): 0.3
Cholesterol (mg): 0
Sodium (mg): 117
Exchanges
Milk: 0.0
Veg.: 1.0
Fruit: 0.0
Bread: 1.0
Meat: 0.0
Fat: 1.0

1. Saute onions, jalapeño chilies, garlic, and gingerroot in margarine until tender, about 5 minutes. Stir in flour and spices and cook 1 minute. Stir in chicken broth and corn and heat to boiling. Reduce heat and simmer, covered, 10 minutes.

2. Stir in coconut milk and half-and-half and heat until hot; season to taste with salt and pepper. Serve in bowls and sprinkle with cilantro.

MEXICAN CORN SOUP

No need to puree this soup, if you prefer a chunky texture.

4 servings

- 1 carrot, shredded
- 1 medium green bell pepper, chopped
- 1/4 cup chopped shallots
- 1 teaspoon vegetable oil
- 1 cup whole-kernel corn
- 2 cups reduced-sodium fat-free chicken broth
- 1/2 cup fat-free dry milk mixed with enough water to make 1 cup
- 1/8 teaspoon crushed red pepper
- 1/4 teaspoon celery seeds
  Salt and pepper, to taste

Per Serving
Calories: 103
% Calories from fat: 13
Protein (gm): 7.6
Carbohydrate (gm): 15.8
Fat (gm): 1.5
Saturated fat (gm): 0.2
Cholesterol (mg): 1.6
Sodium (mg): 141
Exchanges
Milk: 0.0
Veg.: 0.0
Fruit: 0.0
Bread: 1.0
Meat: 0.0
Fat: 0.5

1. Saute carrot, green pepper, and shallots in oil in large saucepan until tender, about 8 minutes. Add remaining ingredients, except salt and pepper; heat to boiling. Reduce heat and simmer, covered, 5 minutes.

2. Process soup in blender or food processor until smooth; season to taste with salt and pepper.

CRUNCHY VEGETABLE SOUP

Any combination of vegetables may be used for this potage—broccoli, cauliflower, cucumbers, radishes—just as long as they're crunchable.

4 servings

- 1 1/2 cups cut asparagus (1-inch)
- 1 medium carrot, finely chopped
- 1 rib celery, finely chopped
- 2 tablespoons chopped onion
- 2 medium mushrooms, sliced
- 1 cup reduced-sodium fat-free chicken broth
- 1 cup fat-free plain yogurt
  Pinch dried tarragon leaves

Per Serving
Calories: 63
% Calories from fat: 4
Protein (gm): 6.3
Carbohydrate (gm): 9.3
Fat (gm): 0.3
Saturated fat (gm): 0.1
Cholesterol (mg): 1
Sodium (mg): 102
Exchanges
Milk: 0.0
Veg.: 2.0
Fruit: 0.0
Bread: 0.0
Meat: 0.0
Fat: 0.0

Dash cayenne pepper
Black pepper, to taste
Diced pimientos, as garnish

1. Process vegetables and chicken broth in blender or food processor until finely chopped. Pour into medium saucepan. Heat to boiling; reduce heat and simmer 6 to 8 minutes or until vegetables are crisp-tender. Stir in yogurt, tarragon, cayenne, and black pepper; garnish each serving with pimientos.

CONFETTI SOUP

This colorful soup can be made in minutes using frozen broccoli and cauliflower.

8 servings

Vegetable cooking spray
2 carrots, sliced
1 cup sliced leeks, white parts only, *or* green onions and tops
1 package (10 ounces) frozen chopped broccoli
1 package (10 ounces) frozen cauliflower
1¹/₂ cups reduced-sodium fat-free chicken broth
3 cups fat-free milk, divided
1 tablespoon cornstarch
1 teaspoon Spike
Pepper, to taste

Per Serving
Calories: 75
% Calories from fat: 4
Protein (gm): 6.3
Carbohydrate (gm): 12.6
Fat (gm): 0.4
Saturated fat (gm): 0.1
Cholesterol (mg): 1.7
Sodium (mg): 104
Exchanges
Milk: 0.0
Veg.: 3.0
Fruit: 0.0
Bread: 0.0
Meat: 0.0
Fat: 0.0

1. Spray large saucepan with cooking spray; heat over medium heat until hot. Saute carrots and leeks until lightly browned, about 8 minutes. Add broccoli, cauliflower, and chicken broth; heat to boiling. Reduce heat and simmer, covered, until vegetables are tender, about 5 minutes.

2. Process half the vegetable mixture in blender or food processor until smooth; return to saucepan and heat to boiling. Stir in combined ¹/₂ cup milk and cornstarch; boil, stirring, until thickened, about 1 minute. Stir in remaining 2¹/₂ cups milk; simmer, covered, 5 minutes longer. Stir in Spike; season to taste with pepper.

GARLIC SOUP WITH TOASTED BREAD

Traditionally, a whole beaten egg is slowly stirred into the simmering soup before serving, similar to Chinese egg drop soup. Try this for a change of pace!

4 servings (about 1 cup each)

1 tablespoon vegetable oil
6-8 cloves garlic, finely chopped
1/2 teaspoon ground cumin
1/4 teaspoon dried oregano leaves
1/4 teaspoon cayenne pepper
2 cans (14 1/2 ounces each) reduced-sodium fat-free chicken broth
Salt, to taste
4 slices firm bread (French *or* sourdough)
Vegetable cooking spray
Finely chopped cilantro, as garnish

Per Serving
Calories: 124
% Calories from fat: 30
Protein (g): 6.8
Carbohydrates (g): 14.7
Fat (g): 4.3
Saturated fat (g): 0.6
Cholesterol (mg): 0
Sodium (mg): 216
Exchanges
Milk: 0.0
Veg.: 0.0
Fruit: 0.0
Bread: 1.0
Meat: 0.0
Fat: 1.0

1. Heat oil in medium saucepan until hot; add garlic and cook over low heat until garlic is very soft and very lightly browned, 5 to 8 minutes. Stir in cumin, oregano, and cayenne pepper; cook 1 to 2 minutes. Add broth to saucepan; heat to boiling. Reduce heat and simmer, covered, 5 minutes. Season to taste with salt.

2. Spray both sides of bread slices generously with cooking spray; cook in large skillet, over medium heat, until golden on both sides. Place slices of bread in bottoms of 4 shallow bowls; ladle soup over. Sprinkle with cilantro.

GARLIC AND SWEET PEPPER SOUP

Two heart-healthy foods combine in this flavorful soup.

6 servings (about ³/₄ cup each)

1/2 cup chopped onion

6 cloves garlic, chopped

2 teaspoons olive oil

1 cup cubed, peeled, uncooked potato

1 cup chopped red bell pepper

3¹/₂ cups reduced-sodium fat-free chicken broth

Salt and pepper, to taste

6 tablespoons reduced-fat sour cream

Chopped parsley, as garnish

Per Serving

Calories: 107

% Calories from fat: **25**

Protein (gm): 6

Carbohydrate (gm): **14.1**

Fat (gm): 2.9

Saturated fat (gm): **1.2**

Cholesterol (mg): 5

Sodium (mg): 113

Exchanges

Milk: 0.0

Veg.: 0.0

Fruit: 0.0

Bread: 1.0

Meat: 0.0

Fat: 0.5

1. Saute onion and garlic in oil in medium saucepan until tender, about 3 minutes. Add potato, bell pepper, and broth. Heat to boiling; reduce heat and simmer, covered, until potato is tender, about 15 minutes.

2. Process soup in food processor or blender until smooth; season to taste with salt and pepper. Refrigerate until cold; top each serving with a dollop of sour cream and sprinkle with parsley.

SWEET RED PEPPER SOUP

Use jarred roasted peppers for this soup, or roast 2 medium red bell peppers yourself. To roast peppers: cut in half and discard seeds. Place, skin sides up, on foil-lined pan. Broil 4 inches from heat source until skins are blackened. Place peppers in plastic bag 5 minutes to loosen skins, then peel and discard skins.

4 servings

Vegetable cooking spray

1 medium onion, chopped

1/2 small jalapeño chili, seeded, veins discarded, minced

1 clove garlic, minced

1 jar (5 ounces) roasted red bell peppers, drained

1 cup reduced-sodium tomato juice

1 can (14¹/₂ ounces) vegetable broth

1/4 teaspoon dried marjoram leaves

Salt and pepper, to taste

1/4 cup fat-free sour cream

1 small green onion and top, thinly sliced

Per Serving
Calories: 60
% Calories from fat: **3**
Protein (g): 2.8
Carbohydrates (g): 13.3
Fat (g): 0.2
Saturated fat (g): 0
Cholesterol (mg): 0
Sodium (mg): 62
Exchanges
Milk: 0.0
Veg.: 2.0
Fruit: 0.0
Bread: 0.0
Meat: 0.0
Fat: 0.0

1. Spray medium saucepan with cooking spray; heat over medium heat until hot. Saute onion, jalapeño chili, and garlic until tender.

2. Process onion mixture, roasted peppers, and tomato juice in blender or food processor until smooth. Return mixture to saucepan and add vegetable broth and marjoram; heat to boiling. Reduce heat and simmer, covered, 15 minutes. Season to taste with salt and pepper.

3. Serve soup warm, or refrigerate and serve cold. Top each serving with a dollop of sour cream and sprinkle with green onion.

GREEN VEGETABLE SOUP

Fresh herbs make this soup especially flavorful. Purchased pesto can be substituted for the No-Fat Pesto, but nutritional information will change.

6 servings

₁/2 cup chopped green cabbage
1 medium onion, chopped
1 medium potato, diced
₁/2 cup chopped celery
₁/2 cup chopped broccoli
₁/2 cup cut green beans
₁/2 cup diced zucchini
2 tablespoons chopped Italian parsley
2 tablespoons chopped fresh basil
1 quart water
1 tablespoon safflower oil
₁/2 cup uncooked ditalini
Salt and pepper, to taste
2 tablespoons No-Fat Pesto (see p. 235)

Per Serving
Calories: 96
% Calories from fat: 26
Protein (g): 2.9
Carbohydrates (g): 15.6
Fat (g): 2.8
Saturated fat (g): 0.4
Cholesterol (mg): 0.7
Sodium (mg): 29
Exchanges
Milk: 0.0
Veg.: 1.5
Fruit: 0.0
Bread: 0.5
Meat: 0.0
Fat: 0.5

1. Combine all ingredients, except ditalini, salt, pepper, and No-Fat Pesto, in large saucepan and heat to boiling. Stir in ditalini; reduce heat and simmer, covered, until vegetables and pasta are tender, about 15 minutes. Season to taste with salt and pepper. Stir in No-Fat Pesto.

GARDEN GREEN SOUP

Use the freshest greens your garden, or grocer, can provide. This soup can be served hot or cold.

4 servings

- 4 shallots, sliced
- 3 cloves garlic, minced
- 1 teaspoon canola oil
- 4 cups mixed greens, rinsed, shredded (romaine, red leaf, *or* Boston lettuce, spinach, escarole, *or* sorrel)
- 2 cups fat-free milk
- 1 cup reduced-sodium fat-free chicken broth
- 1 tablespoon oat bran
- 1/4 cup chopped fresh, *or* 1 tablespoon dried, basil leaves
  Grated rind of 1 lemon
  Salt and pepper, to taste

Per Serving
Calories: 81
% Calories from fat: 17
Protein (gm): 7.3
Carbohydrate (gm): 10.4
Fat (gm): 1.7
Saturated fat (gm): 0.3
Cholesterol (mg): 2.2
Sodium (mg): 123
Exchanges
Milk: 0.5
Veg.: 1.0
Fruit: 0.0
Bread: 0.0
Meat: 0.0
Fat: 0.5

1. Saute shallots and garlic in oil in large saucepan until tender, about 3 minutes. Add greens and stir until wilted. Add remaining ingredients, except lemon rind, salt, and pepper, and heat to boiling; reduce heat and simmer 5 minutes. Process in blender or food processor until smooth. Stir in lemon rind; season to taste with salt and pepper.

CHINESE SNOW PEA SOUP

This fresh-tasting soup has oriental accents of soy, gingerroot, and tofu.

4 servings

1 quart reduced-sodium fat-free chicken broth
¹/₄ cup minced scallions
¹/₄ cup finely chopped carrots
1 clove garlic, minced
1 teaspoon grated gingerroot
1 teaspoon light soy sauce
¹/₄ cup sliced mushrooms
1 cup sliced snow peas
4 ounces firm tofu, cut into ¹/₂-inch cubes
Scallions, sliced, as garnish

Per Serving
Calories: 94
% Calories from fat: 25
Protein (gm): 11.9
Carbohydrate (gm): 5.5
Fat (gm): 2.6
Saturated fat (gm): 0.4
Cholesterol (mg): 0
Sodium (mg): 223
Exchanges
Milk: 0.0
Veg.: 1.0
Fruit: 0.0
Bread: 0.0
Meat: 1.0
Fat: 0.0

1. Combine broth, scallions, carrots, garlic, gingerroot, and soy sauce in medium saucepan; heat to boiling. Reduce heat and simmer, covered, 5 minutes longer. Add mushrooms and simmer 5 minutes longer. Add snow peas and tofu and simmer 1 minute. Garnish with scallions.

SUMMER SNOW PEA SOUP

Make this soup a day in advance so that flavors can blend.

6 servings (about 1¹/₄ cups each)

¹/₂ cup sliced green onions and tops
¹/₂ cup chopped onion
1 tablespoon margarine
1 pound snow peas, trimmed
1 quart coarsely chopped romaine lettuce
1 quart reduced-sodium fat-free chicken broth
¹/₂ teaspoon dried tarragon leaves
¹/₂ teaspoon dried mint leaves
Salt and white pepper, to taste
6 tablespoons fat-free plain yogurt
Fresh mint, *or* tarragon sprigs, as garnish

Per Serving
Calories: 87
% Calories from fat: 23
Protein (g): 7.7
Carbohydrates (g): 8.7
Fat (g): 2.2
Saturated fat (g): 0.4
Cholesterol (mg): 0.3
Sodium (mg): 153
Exchanges
Milk: 0.0
Veg.: 2.0
Fruit: 0.0
Bread: 0.0
Meat: 0.0
Fat: 0.5

1. Saute onions in margarine in large saucepan until tender, about 5 minutes. Add snow peas and lettuce; saute 3 to 4 minutes longer. Add broth, tarragon, and mint; heat to boiling. Reduce heat and simmer, covered, 15 minutes or until snow peas are very tender.

2. Process soup in food processor or blender until smooth; strain. Season to taste with salt and white pepper. Heat and serve warm, or refrigerate and serve cold.

3. Pour soup into bowls; garnish each with a tablespoon of yogurt and fresh herb sprigs.

CREAM OF MUSHROOM SOUP

Creamy and rich, this soup resembles the favorite-brand canned soup we remember. For a richer tasting soup, use fat-free half-and-half instead of fat-free milk.

4 servings (about 1¼ cups each)

1 pound mushrooms
2 tablespoons margarine, divided
1 cup chopped onion
2½ cups reduced-sodium chicken broth
2½ cups fat-free milk, divided
2 tablespoons plus 2 teaspoons cornstarch
Salt and pepper, to taste
Minced parsley leaves, as garnish

Per Serving
Calories: 183
% Calories from fat: 31
Protein (g): 11
Carbohydrates (g): 21.8
Fat (g): 6.5
Saturated fat (g): 1.4
Cholesterol (mg): 2.5
Sodium (mg): 361
Exchanges
Milk: 0.5
Veg.: 3.0
Fruit: 0.0
Bread: 0.0
Meat: 0.0
Fat: 1.5

1. Slice enough mushroom caps to make 2 cups; finely chop stems and remaining mushrooms. Saute sliced mushrooms in 1 tablespoon margarine in large saucepan until browned, about 5 minutes; remove and reserve. Saute onion and chopped mushrooms in remaining 1 tablespoon margarine until onion is tender, about 5 minutes.

2. Add broth and 2 cups milk to saucepan; heat to boiling. Mix remaining ½ cup milk and cornstarch; whisk into boiling mixture. Boil, whisking constantly, until thickened, about 1 minute. Stir in reserved sliced mushrooms. Season to taste with salt and pepper. Serve in bowls; sprinkle with parsley.

CREAMY MUSHROOM-BASIL SOUP

This wonderful creamy soup takes only minutes to make because it's thickened with instant mashed potatoes. In summer I love to make it with fresh basil, but dried works well, too.

4 servings

8 ounces fresh mushrooms, sliced
1 teaspoon chopped garlic
1 tablespoon margarine
1 quart reduced-sodium fat-free chicken broth
1/2 cup whole milk
2 tablespoons dry sherry
1 1/4 cups instant mashed potatoes
1/4 cup chopped fresh, *or* 2 tablespoons dried, basil leaves
    Salt and white pepper, to taste

Per Serving
Calories: 166
% Calories from fat: 22
Protein (gm): 10.2
Carbohydrate (gm): 21
Fat (gm): 4.1
Saturated fat (gm): 1.2
Cholesterol (mg): 4.2
Sodium (mg): 230
Exchanges
Milk: 0.0
Veg.: 1.0
Fruit: 0.0
Bread: 1.0
Meat: 0.0
Fat: 1.0

1. Saute mushrooms and garlic in margarine in large saucepan until mushrooms are tender, about 8 minutes. Stir in broth, milk, sherry, mashed potatoes, and basil; heat to boiling. Reduce heat and simmer 10 minutes; season to taste with salt and white pepper.

CREAM OF ARTICHOKE AND MUSHROOM SOUP

Shiitake or cremini mushrooms can be substituted for the portobello mushrooms. Serve with Sourdough Croutons (see p. 784), if desired.

4 servings (about 1 cup each)

3/4 cup chopped portobello mushrooms
2 tablespoons finely chopped onion
1 tablespoon margarine
1 tablespoon flour
3 cups fat-free milk
1 vegetable bouillon cube
1 package (9 ounces) frozen artichoke hearts, cooked, finely chopped
    Salt and white pepper, to taste
    Paprika, as garnish

Per Serving
Calories: 135
% Calories from fat: 22
Protein (g): 9.2
Carbohydrates (g): 18.9
Fat (g): 3.6
Saturated fat (g): 0.8
Cholesterol (mg): 3
Sodium (mg): 422
Exchanges
Milk: 1.0
Veg.: 1.0
Fruit: 0.0
Bread: 0.0
Meat: 0.0
Fat: 0.5

1. Saute mushrooms and onion in margarine in medium saucepan until tender, about 5 minutes. Stir in flour; cook 1 minute. Stir in milk and bouillon cube; heat to boiling, stirring constantly.

2. Stir in artichoke hearts; reduce heat and simmer, uncovered, 5 minutes. Season to taste with salt and white pepper. Pour soup into bowls; sprinkle with paprika.

ITALIAN MUSHROOM SOUP

This is a very sophisticated soup that is ideal for entertaining.

4 servings

Vegetable cooking spray

2 medium onions, chopped

1 pound mushrooms (white, cremini, *or* chanterelles), thinly sliced

1 quart Rich Chicken Stock (see p. 4), *or* fat-free chicken broth

6 tablespoons tomato puree

6 tablespoons sweet vermouth

Spike, to taste

1 tablespoon minced fresh, *or* 1 teaspoon dried, basil leaves

¹/4 cup minced chives

Parmesan cheese, grated, as garnish

Per Serving
Calories: 139
% Calories from fat: 19
Protein (gm): 9.8
Carbohydrate (gm): 13.3
Fat (gm): 3
Saturated fat (gm): 0.5
Cholesterol (mg): 1
Sodium (mg): 138
Exchanges
Milk: 0.0
Veg.: 3.0
Fruit: 0.0
Bread: 0.0
Meat: 0.0
Fat: 1.0

1. Spray large saucepan with cooking spray; heat over medium heat until hot. Saute onions and mushrooms until tender, about 10 minutes. Add Rich Chicken Stock, tomato puree, vermouth, and Spike; heat to boiling. Reduce heat and simmer, covered, 5 minutes. Stir in basil and chives; sprinkle with Parmesan.

MUSHROOM SOUP

Use your favorite mushroom—portobello or shiitake are flavorful choices.

4-6 servings

   1 pound mushrooms, finely chopped
   4 teaspoons margarine
   2 tablespoons flour
   2 cups reduced-sodium fat-free chicken broth
   1 can (13 ounces) evaporated fat-free milk
     Salt and pepper, to taste

Per Serving
Calories: 175
% Calories from fat: **29**
Protein (gm): 15
Carbohydrate (gm): **17.9**
Fat (gm): 6.1
Cholesterol (mg): **1.2**
Sodium (mg): 254
Exchanges
Milk: 1.0
Veg.: 1.0
Fruit: 0.0
Bread: 0.0
Meat: 0.0
Fat: 1.5

1. Saute mushrooms in margarine in large saucepan until tender, about 5 minutes. Sprinkle with flour and cook 1 minute longer. Add chicken broth; heat to boiling. Reduce heat and simmer 5 minutes. Stir in evaporated milk; simmer until hot, 3 to 4 minutes. Season to taste with salt and pepper.

MUSHROOM SOUP DANIELLE

You'll love this delicately flavored mushroom soup.

4 servings

    1 pound mushrooms
    2 teaspoons margarine
 1 1/2 tablespoons flour
    1 quart Fragrant Beef Stock (see p. 6), *or* reduced-sodium beef broth
    4 teaspoons light soy sauce
    2 tablespoons dry sherry
  1/2 teaspoon lemon juice
     Salt and pepper, to taste
    3 tablespoons chopped chives

Per Serving
Calories: 86
% Calories from fat: **28**
Protein (gm): 6
Carbohydrate (gm): **9.2**
Fat (gm): 2.9
Saturated fat (gm): **0.7**
Cholesterol (mg): 3
Sodium (mg): 245
Exchanges
Milk: 0.0
Veg.: 2.0
Fruit: 0.0
Bread: 0.0
Meat: 0.0
Fat: 0.5

1. Slice 4 large mushroom caps and reserve. Chop remaining mushrooms and stems. Saute chopped mushrooms in margarine in large saucepan until mushrooms are tender and juices almost evaporated, about 8 minutes. Sprinkle with flour and cook 1 minute longer. Add Fragrant Beef Stock and soy sauce; heat to boiling. Reduce heat and simmer 5 minutes.

2. Process in blender or food processor until smooth. Return to saucepan and heat to simmering. Add sliced mushroom caps to soup; simmer 5 minutes. Stir in sherry and lemon juice. Season to taste with salt and pepper; sprinkle with chives.

ITALIAN MUSHROOM-BARLEY SOUP

This is a wonderful low-fat soup that you can serve again and again. It freezes well, too.

10 servings

1¹/₂ cups quick-cooking barley
3 tomatoes, chopped
2 carrots, chopped
1 medium onion, chopped
2 cloves garlic, minced
1¹/₂ quarts chicken broth
2 cups tomato juice
4 fresh basil leaves, chopped
1 tablespoon chopped fresh, *or* 1 teaspoon dried, oregano leaves
1 cup thinly sliced mushrooms
Salt and pepper, to taste
Low-fat yogurt, as garnish

Per Serving
Calories: 135
% Calories from fat: 7
Protein (g): 5.3
Carbohydrates (g): 27.7
Fat (g): 1.1
Saturated fat (g): 0.2
Cholesterol (mg): 0
Sodium (mg): 208
Exchanges
Milk: 0.0
Veg.: 1.5
Fruit: 0.0
Bread: 1.5
Meat: 0.0
Fat: 0.0

1. Combine all ingredients, except mushrooms, salt, pepper, and yogurt, in large saucepan and heat to boiling. Reduce heat and simmer, covered, 10 minutes more. Stir in mushrooms and simmer 10 minutes. Season to taste with salt and pepper. Ladle into soup bowls and top each with spoonful of yogurt.

CREAM OF TOMATO SOUP

This tastes just like the favorite-brand canned tomato soup we all remember! Canned tomatoes are necessary for the flavor, so don't substitute fresh.

4 servings

2 cans (14¹/₂ ounces each) no-salt-added whole tomatoes, undrained
2-3 teaspoons beef bouillon crystals
2 cups fat-free milk
3 tablespoons cornstarch
¹/₈ teaspoon baking soda
2 teaspoons sugar
1-2 tablespoons margarine
Salt and pepper, to taste

Per Serving
Calories: 143
% Calories from fat: 23
Protein (g): 6.5
Carbohydrates (g): 22.9
Fat (g): 3.9
Saturated fat (g): 0.8
Cholesterol (mg): 2
Sodium (mg): 628
Exchanges
Milk: 0.5
Veg.: 2.0
Fruit: 0.0
Bread: 0.5
Meat: 0.0
Fat: 0.5

1. Process tomatoes and liquid in food processor or blender until smooth; heat tomatoes and bouillon crystals in large saucepan to boiling. Mix milk and cornstarch; whisk into boiling mixture. Boil, whisking constantly, until thickened, about 1 minute.

2. Add baking soda, sugar, and margarine to soup, stirring until margarine is melted. Season to taste with salt and pepper.

SICILIAN SUMMER TOMATO SOUP

Perfect for a summer day, when tomatoes are at their best. Orange rind adds a pleasant accent.

10 servings

2 red onions, finely chopped
2 yellow onions, finely chopped
2 tablespoons olive oil
1 bunch green onions and tops, chopped
¹/₂ cup chopped carrot
¹/₂ cup chopped celery
1 cup sliced mushrooms
¹/₄ cup chopped garlic
1 quart Chicken Stock (see p. 2), *or* fat-free chicken broth

Per Serving
Calories: 146
% Calories from fat: 22
Protein (g): 5.8
Carbohydrates (g): 22.2
Fat (g): 4.1
Saturated fat (g): 0.6
Cholesterol (mg): 0
Sodium (mg): 103
Exchanges
Milk: 0.0
Veg.: 4.0
Fruit: 0.0
Bread: 0.0
Meat: 0.0
Fat: 1.0

 1 cup dry white wine, *or* Chicken Stock
 1/4 cup orange juice
 2 tablespoons tomato paste
 18 plum tomatoes, peeled, seeded,
    chopped
 1 1/2 pounds spinach, coarsely chopped
 1 cup chopped parsley
 1/2 cup chopped fresh, *or* 2 tablespoons
    dried, basil leaves
 1 teaspoon sugar
    Grated rind of 1 orange
    Spike and pepper, to taste

1. Saute red and yellow onions in olive oil in large saucepan until tender, about 5 minutes. Add green onions, carrot, celery, mushrooms, and garlic; saute 2 to 3 minutes. Add remaining ingredients, except Spike and pepper; heat to boiling; reduce heat and simmer, covered, 10 minutes.

2. Process soup in blender or food processor until smooth; season to taste with Spike and pepper.

ASPARAGUS-TOMATO SOUP WITH CHEESE

Although this soup is elegant enough to serve at a luncheon or elaborate dinner, it is also good as a family lunch or supper entrée.

6 servings

 1 medium onion, chopped
 2 tablespoons chopped carrot
 1/2 tablespoon butter
 1/2 cup instant rice
 3 cups reduced-sodium fat-free chicken
    broth, divided
 1/2 teaspoon dried marjoram leaves
 1/4 teaspoon dry mustard
 1/4 teaspoon white pepper
 1 cup (4 ounces) shredded reduced-fat
    Cheddar cheese
 1 1/4 pounds asparagus spears, cut into
    1/2-inch pieces

Per Serving
Calories: 141
% Calories from fat: 26
Protein (g): 10.2
Carbohydrates (g): 17.3
Fat (g): 4.2
Saturated fat (g): 2
Cholesterol (mg): 12.7
Sodium (mg): 558
Exchanges
Milk: 0.0
Veg.: 2.0
Fruit: 0.0
Bread: 0.5
Meat: 1.0
Fat: 0.0

1 can (14^1/$_2$ ounces) tomatoes, undrained, chopped
Salt, to taste

1. Saute onion and carrot in butter in large saucepan until onion begins to brown, about 5 minutes. Add rice, 2 cups broth,
marjoram, dry mustard, and white pepper; heat to boiling. Reduce heat and simmer 10 minutes.

2. Process broth mixture and cheese in blender or food processor until smooth; reserve.

3. Combine asparagus and remaining 1 cup broth in large
saucepan and simmer, covered, until asparagus is tender, about
5 minutes. Stir in reserved broth and cheese mixture, tomatoes
and liquid, and simmer 5 minutes. Add salt to taste.

CELERY-TOMATO SOUP

*This quick and easy recipe showcases the delicate flavor and crisp texture
of a vegetable that is usually assigned a supporting rather than primary
role in soup cookery. The soup is also good served cold.*

0 servings

4 cups thinly sliced celery
2 medium onions, finely chopped
1 tablespoon margarine
3 cups fat-free chicken broth
^{1}/$_4$ cup finely chopped parsley
^{1}/$_2$ cup dry white wine
1 teaspoon dried marjoram leaves
^{1}/$_4$ teaspoon dried thyme leaves
^{1}/$_4$ teaspoon dried tarragon leaves
^{1}/$_8$ teaspoon black pepper
2 cans (14^1/$_2$ ounces each) tomatoes,
undrained, pureed
1 teaspoon sugar
Salt, to taste

Per Serving
Calories: 76
% Calories from fat: 20
Protein (g): 3.6
Carbohydrates (g): 10.5
Fat (g): 1.8
Saturated fat (g): 0.3
Cholesterol (mg): 0
Sodium (mg): 365
Exchanges
Milk: 0.0
Veg.: 2.0
Fruit: 0.0
Bread: 0.0
Meat: 0.0
Fat: 0.5

1. Saute celery and onion in margarine in large saucepan until
onion is tender, about 8 minutes. Add remaining ingredients,
except tomatoes, sugar, and salt, and heat to boiling. Reduce
heat and simmer, covered, about 10 minutes or until celery is
tender. Add tomatoes and sugar and simmer 5 minutes. Season
to taste with salt.

TOMATO WARM-UP

Delicious and rich in vitamins—especially nice on a cold winter day.

2 servings

2 cups tomato juice
2 teaspoons minced parsley
1 tablespoon sugar
1 teaspoon powdered vegetable concentrate, optional
Dash pepper
Dash ground mace
Salt and pepper, to taste

Per Serving
Calories: 75
% Calories from fat: 0
Protein (gm): 2
Carbohydrate (gm): 15.3
Fat (gm): 0
Saturated fat (gm): 0
Cholesterol (mg): 0
Sodium (mg): 861
Exchanges
Milk: 0.0
Veg.: 3.0
Fruit: 0.0
Bread: 0.0
Meat: 0.0
Fat: 0.0

1. Combine all ingredients, except salt and pepper, in small saucepan and heat to boiling; reduce heat and simmer, covered, 5 minutes. Season to taste with salt and pepper.

TOMATO VEGETABLE SOUP

Pureed tomatoes provide the base for this tasty soup.

4 servings

3 cups canned Italian tomatoes, undrained, pureed
1 tablespoon frozen apple juice concentrate
1 tablespoon minced scallions
2 whole cloves
1 bay leaf
1/2 cup frozen, thawed, peas
1/2 cup frozen, thawed, whole-kernel corn
Salt and pepper, to taste

Per Serving
Calories: 78
% Calories from fat: 2
Protein (gm): 3.1
Carbohydrate (gm): 14.9
Fat (gm): 0.2
Saturated fat (gm): 0
Cholesterol (mg): 0
Sodium (mg): 350
Exchanges
Milk: 0.0
Veg.: 3.0
Fruit: 0.0
Bread: 0.0
Meat: 0.0
Fat: 0.0

1. Heat tomatoes, apple juice, scallions, cloves, and bay leaf to boiling in medium saucepan; reduce heat and simmer, covered, 5 minutes. Add peas and corn and simmer 3 to 4 minutes or until heated through. Discard bay leaf and cloves. Season to taste with salt and pepper.

RIPE TOMATO AND LEEK SOUP

Use the summer's ripest tomatoes for this soup, cooking only briefly to maintain their sweetness. Peel the tomatoes, or not, as you prefer.

6 servings (about 1¼ cups each)

2 cups sliced leeks, white parts only
3 cloves garlic, minced
1 tablespoon margarine, *or* olive oil
6 large tomatoes (about 2½ pounds)
1 quart reduced-sodium fat-free chicken broth
½-1 teaspoon dried basil leaves
Salt and white pepper, to taste
6 tablespoons fat-free sour cream, *or* fat-free plain yogurt
Basil sprigs, as garnish

Per Serving
Calories: 120
% Calories from fat: **19**
Protein (g): 7.3
Carbohydrates (g): **17.7**
Fat (g): 2.6
Saturated fat (g): 0.5
Cholesterol (mg): 0
Sodium (mg): 173
Exchanges
Milk: 0.0
Veg.: 3.0
Fruit: 0.0
Bread: 0.0
Meat: 0.5
Fat: 0.5

1. Saute leeks and garlic in margarine in large saucepan until tender, about 8 minutes. Add tomatoes, broth, and basil to saucepan; heat to boiling. Reduce heat and simmer, covered, 10 minutes longer.

2. Process soup in food processor or blender until smooth; season to taste with salt and white pepper. Heat and serve soup warm, or refrigerate and serve chilled.

3. Pour soup into bowls; garnish each with a tablespoon of sour cream and a basil sprig.

CREOLE TOMATO SOUP

Tomatoes, green pepper, and spices combine to give this soup a Creole flavor.

4 servings

1	medium green bell pepper, diced
1	medium onion, finely chopped
1	medium garlic clove, minced
2	teaspoons margarine
2	cups reduced-sodium fat-free chicken broth, *or* vegetable broth
2	cans (14$^1/_2$ ounces each) tomatoes, undrained, pureed
2	teaspoons sugar
1	teaspoon dried marjoram leaves
$^1/_2$	teaspoon dried basil leaves
$^1/_4$	teaspoon dried thyme leaves
2	bay leaves
$^1/_4$	teaspoon black pepper
	Dash cayenne pepper
	Salt, to taste

Per Serving
Calories: 98
% Calories from fat: 21
Protein (g): 4.9
Carbohydrates (g): 16.1
Fat (g): 2.5
Saturated fat (g): 0.5
Cholesterol (mg): 0
Sodium (mg): 526
Exchanges
Milk: 0.0
Veg.: 3.0
Fruit: 0.0
Bread: 0.0
Meat: 0.0
Fat: 0.5

1. Saute bell pepper, onion, and garlic in margarine in large saucepan 5 minutes. Add remaining ingredients except salt; heat to boiling. Reduce heat and simmer, covered, until green pepper is very tender, about 10 minutes. Add salt to taste.

SPRING PARSLEY SOUP

Serve this delicately flavored soup with Wild Rice Muffins (see p. 810).

4 servings

2 Idaho potatoes, peeled, diced
2 medium onions, chopped
1 tablespoon margarine
3/4 cup water
1 can (10³/4 ounces) reduced-sodium fat-free chicken broth
1 cup packed parsley sprigs
1/2 teaspoon Spike
   Dash Worcestershire sauce
2 cans (12 ounces each) evaporated fat-free milk
   Salt and white pepper, to taste

Per Serving
Calories: 271
% Calories from fat: **11**
Protein (gm): 18.7
Carbohydrate (gm): 41.4
Fat (gm): 3.5
Saturated fat (gm): 0.8
Cholesterol (mg): 6.9
Sodium (mg): 321
Exchanges
Milk: 1.0
Veg.: 0.0
Fruit: 0.0
Bread: 2.0
Meat: 0.0
Fat: 1.0

1. Combine potatoes, onions, margarine, and 3/4 cup water in large saucepan and heat to boiling; reduce heat and simmer, covered, until potatoes are tender, about 15 minutes. Add chicken broth, parsley, Spike, and Worcestershire sauce and heat to boiling; reduce heat and simmer, uncovered, until parsley is wilted, 2 to 3 minutes.

2. Process soup in blender or food processor until smooth. Return to saucepan, add milk, and cook over medium heat until hot, about 5 minutes. Season to taste with salt and white pepper.

GREEN ONION-POTATO SOUP WITH DILL

Very simple, and very good. Use fresh dill for best results.

6-7 servings

2¹/₂ cups chopped green onions and tops
1 tablespoon margarine
2 tablespoons flour
1¹/₂ quarts fat-free chicken broth, divided
1³/₄ cups cubed, peeled potatoes
¹/₄ teaspoon white pepper
2 tablespoons finely chopped fresh, *or* 1 tablespoon dried dill weed
¹/₄ cup low-fat plain yogurt
Salt, to taste

Per Serving
Calories: 105
% Calories from fat: 16
Protein (g): 6.2
Carbohydrates (g): 16.6
Fat (g): 1.9
Saturated fat (g): 0.4
Cholesterol (mg): 0.5
Sodium (mg): 316
Exchanges
Milk: 0.0
Veg.: 0.0
Fruit: 0.0
Bread: 1.0
Meat: 0.0
Fat: 0.5

1. Saute onions in margarine in large saucepan until tender, about 5 minutes. Stir in flour and cook 30 seconds longer. Stir in 3 cups broth, potatoes, white pepper, and dill; heat to boiling. Reduce heat and simmer, covered, about 12 minutes or until potatoes are tender.

2. Process ¹/₂ cup soup in blender or food processor until smooth. Add 1 cup broth and yogurt and process until smooth; return to saucepan. Thin soup to desired consistency with remaining 2 cups broth and heat to simmering; do not boil. Add salt to taste.

EASY CURRIED POTATO SOUP

This good, hearty soup can be made when the cupboard is nearly bare.

5 servings

1 large onion, chopped

2 teaspoons peeled, minced gingerroot

1/2 teaspoon caraway seeds

2 teaspoons butter

2 large garlic cloves, minced

4 1/2 cups cubed, peeled baking potatoes

1 medium golden Delicious, *or* other sweet, apple, peeled, cored, diced

1 1/4 quarts reduced-sodium, fat-free chicken broth

2-3 teaspoons curry powder

1/2 teaspoon ground allspice

1 can (14 1/2 ounces) stewed tomatoes, undrained, chopped

Salt, to taste

Per Serving
Calories: 271
% Calories from fat: 7
Protein (g): 9.7
Carbohydrates (g): 56.2
Fat (g): 2.1
Saturated fat (g): 1
Cholesterol (mg): 4.1
Sodium (mg): 572
Exchanges
Milk: 0.0
Veg.: 1.0
Fruit: 0.0
Bread: 3.0
Meat: 0.0
Fat: 0.5

1. Saute onion, gingerroot, and caraway seeds in butter in large saucepan until onion is tender; add garlic and saute 1 minute longer. Add potatoes, apple, broth, curry powder, and allspice; heat to boiling. Reduce heat and simmer until potatoes are tender, about 10 minutes.

2. Process 2 cups potato mixture in blender or food processor until smooth. Return puree to saucepan with tomatoes and liquid; simmer 5 minutes. Add salt to taste.

VEGETABLE-CHEESE SOUP

Frozen mashed potatoes are a great addition to cheese soups since they're low in fat and add instant creaminess.

6 servings

1 quart reduced-sodium fat-free chicken broth

1 package (16 ounces) frozen stir-fry vegetables

1 cup 1% low-fat milk

3 cups frozen mashed potatoes

5-6 drops hot pepper sauce

1 1/2 cups (6 ounces) shredded reduced-fat sharp Cheddar cheese

Per Serving
Calories: 197
% Calories from fat: 30
Protein (g): 11.8
Carbohydrates (g): 22
Fat (g): 6.5
Saturated fat (g): 3
Cholesterol (mg): 19.4
Sodium (mg): 730
Exchanges
Milk: 0.0
Veg.: 0.0
Fruit: 0.0
Bread: 1.5
Meat: 1.0
Fat: 0.5

1. Combine broth and vegetables in large saucepan and heat to boiling. Reduce heat and simmer, covered, 8 to 9 minutes or until vegetables are tender. Add milk, potatoes, and hot pepper sauce and simmer 2 minutes. Add cheese, stirring until melted.

POTATO AND CABBAGE SOUP

Purchased prepared ingredients make this soup extra-easy to make.

6 servings (about 1 cup each)

4 ounces reduced-fat, reduced-sodium smoked sausage, thinly sliced

1 medium onion, chopped

1 rib celery, sliced

2 cups coleslaw mix

1-2 tablespoons vegetable oil

16 ounces frozen hash brown potatoes

2 cans (14 1/2 ounces each) reduced-sodium fat-free chicken broth

2 cups water

1/3 cup reduced-fat sour cream

1 tablespoons flour

1/4 cup fat-free milk

Salt and pepper, to taste

Per Serving
Calories: 353
% Calories from fat: 9
Protein (gm): 15.7
Carbohydrate (gm): 68.5
Fat (gm): 4
Saturated fat (gm): 1.4
Cholesterol (mg): 13.1
Sodium (mg): 536
Exchanges
Milk: 0.0
Veg.: 2.0
Fruit: 0.0
Bread: 4.0
Meat: 0.0
Fat: 0.5

1. Cook sausage, onion, celery, and coleslaw mix in oil in large saucepan over medium heat until sausage is browned and onion is tender, about 5 minutes; drain.

2. Add potatoes, broth, and water; heat to boiling. Reduce heat and simmer, covered, 10 minutes. Stir in combined sour cream, flour, and milk; simmer, stirring, 2 minutes longer. Season to taste with salt and pepper.

POTATO-VEGETABLE CHEDDAR SOUP

Instant mashed potatoes are the secret ingredient in this quick and creamy soup. If you like, frozen peas or peas and carrots can be substituted for the cauliflower.

4 servings

1 quart reduced-sodium fat-free chicken broth

5 cups small cauliflower, *or* broccoli, florets

1 medium onion, chopped

2 garlic cloves, minced

1/4 teaspoon dry mustard

1/8 teaspoon white pepper

1 1/2 cups 1% low-fat milk

1 1/2 cups instant mashed potatoes

1 cup (4 ounces) reduced-fat Cheddar cheese

Per Serving
Calories: 226
% Calories from fat: **25**
Protein (g): 19.6
Carbohydrates (g): 24.4
Fat (g): 6.4
Saturated fat (g): 3.6
Cholesterol (mg): 23.7
Sodium (mg): 573
Exchanges
Milk: 0.0
Veg.: 2.0
Fruit: 0.0
Bread: 1.0
Meat: 1.0
Fat: 0.5

1. Combine all ingredients, except milk, mashed potatoes, and cheese in saucepan; heat to boiling. Reduce heat and simmer, covered, 5 to 6 minutes or until cauliflower is tender. Add milk and mashed potatoes; simmer 2 to 3 minutes longer. Stir in cheese until melted.

SPEEDY SQUASH SOUP

For quickest preparation, cook halved squash in microwave on High power 10 to 12 minutes or until tender.

6 servings

  2 acorn squash, halved, seeded, cooked
  1/2 cup chopped onion
  2 cups reduced-sodium fat-free chicken broth
  1/2 teaspoon ground cinnamon
  1/4 teaspoon ground coriander
  1/4 teaspoon ground cumin
  1/8 teaspoon ground turmeric
  1 cup buttermilk
  1/4 cup fat-free dry milk crystals
  1 tablespoon apple cider vinegar
  1 tablespoon light soy sauce
    Salt and pepper, to taste
  1 tablespoon chopped parsley

Per Serving
Calories: 84
% Calories from fat: 6
Protein (gm): 5.6
Carbohydrate (gm): 15.2
Fat (gm): 0.5
Saturated fat (gm): 0.3
Cholesterol (mg): 1.9
Sodium (mg): 207
Exchanges
Milk: 0.0
Veg.: 0.0
Fruit: 0.0
Bread: 1.0
Meat: 0.0
Fat: 0.0

1. Scrape cooked squash from shells, discarding shells. Process in blender or food processor with onion and chicken broth until smooth. Transfer to medium saucepan and add remaining ingredients, except salt, pepper, and parsley. Stir over medium heat until soup simmers; do not boil. Season to taste with salt and pepper; sprinkle with parsley.

ORIENTAL WATERCRESS SOUP

Spinach can be substituted for the watercress in this fragrant Cantonese offering.

6 servings (about 1 cup each)

1¹/₂ quarts reduced-sodium fat-free chicken broth

3 slices gingerroot (scant ¹/₄-inch)

2 large bunches watercress (about 2 cups packed), stems trimmed

Salt and white pepper, to taste

2 green onions and tops, sliced

2 tablespoons shredded carrot

Per Serving
Calories: 35
% Calories from fat: 1
Protein (g): 6.4
Carbohydrates (g): 1
Fat (g): 0
Saturated fat (g): 0
Cholesterol (mg): 0
Sodium (mg): 176
Exchanges
Milk: 0.0
Veg.: 1.0
Fruit: 0.0
Bread: 0.0
Meat: 0.0
Fat: 0.0

1. Heat broth and gingerroot to boiling in large saucepan; reduce heat and simmer, covered, 5 minutes. Remove gingerroot with slotted spoon and discard.

2. Cut watercress into 2-inch lengths. Add to soup and simmer, uncovered, 10 to 15 minutes. Season to taste with salt and white pepper. Pour soup into bowls; sprinkle with green onions and carrot.

EGG DROP SOUP

The easiest egg drop soup ever! Use the most flavorful broth you can find.

4 servings

1 quart reduced-sodium fat-free chicken broth

1¹/₂ tablespoons cornstarch

2 tablespoons cold water

2 scallions, chopped

2 egg whites, beaten

Salt and white pepper, to taste

Per Serving
Calories: 51
% Calories from fat: 0
Protein (gm): 7.8
Carbohydrate (gm): 3.1
Fat (gm): 0
Saturated fat (gm): 0
Cholesterol (mg): 0
Sodium (mg): 198
Exchanges
Milk: 0.0
Veg.: 0.0
Fruit: 0.0
Bread: 0.0
Meat: 1.0
Fat: 0.0

1. Heat broth to boiling in medium saucepan. Mix cornstarch and water; stir into broth. Stir in scallions. Remove from heat and stir in egg whites with a fork. Add salt and white pepper to taste.

GREEK LEMON-RICE SOUP

Nicely tart; use fresh lemon juice for the best flavor. If making this soup in advance, do not add egg until reheating for serving.

4 servings (about 1 cup each)

3¹/₂ cups reduced-sodium fat-free chicken broth
¹/₄ cup uncooked long-grain rice
2 large cloves garlic, minced
¹/₄-¹/₃ cup fresh lemon juice
1 egg, lightly beaten
2 tablespoons finely chopped parsley
Salt and white pepper, to taste

Per Serving
Calories: 64
% Calories from fat: 19
Protein (g): 7.3
Carbohydrates (g): 4.9
Fat (g): 1.3
Saturated fat (g): 0.4
Cholesterol (mg): 53
Sodium (mg): 166
Exchanges
Milk: 0.0
Veg.: 0.0
Fruit: 0.0
Bread: 0.5
Meat: 0.5
Fat: 0.0

1. Heat broth to boiling in medium saucepan; stir in rice and garlic. Reduce heat and simmer, covered, until rice is tender, about 20 minutes.

2. Mix lemon juice and egg; slowly stir into soup. Stir in parsley; season to taste with salt and white pepper.

QUICK CHICKEN AND CORN SOUP

This quick soup makes an easy workday meal.

6 servings

2 cups diced, peeled potatoes
³/₄ cup chopped onion
1¹/₂ cups cubed cooked chicken breast
1 can (16 ounces) cream-style corn
3 cups fat-free milk
Salt and pepper, to taste

Per Serving
Calories: 244
% Calories from fat: 9
Protein (gm): 18
Carbohydrate (gm): 38.9
Fat (gm): 2.5
Saturated fat (gm): 0.6
Cholesterol (mg): 32
Sodium (mg): 295
Exchanges
Milk: 0.5
Veg.: 0.0
Fruit: 0.0
Bread: 2.0
Meat: 1.0
Fat: 0.0

1. Place potatoes and onion in large saucepan and add 2 inches water; heat to boiling. Reduce heat and simmer, covered, until potatoes are tender, 15 to 20 minutes; drain. Add chicken, corn, and milk; heat to simmering. Season to taste with salt and pepper.

HAMBURGER GOULASH SOUP

This is a good, easy, meal-in-a-bowl soup. Be sure to use extra-lean ground beef.

5 servings

Vegetable cooking spray
12 ounces extra-lean ground beef
 1 medium onion, chopped
 1 large red, *or* green, bell pepper, coarsely chopped
³/₄ teaspoon caraway seeds
³/₄ teaspoon dried thyme leaves
 3 tablespoons paprika
³/₄ teaspoon chili powder
³/₄ teaspoon garlic powder
 1 quart reduced-sodium fat-free beef broth
 1 tablespoon Worcestershire sauce
 3 cups diced boiling potatoes
 1 cup no-salt-added stewed tomatoes, undrained
¹/₄ cup catsup
1-2 teaspoons sugar, optional
Salt and pepper, to taste

Per Serving
Calories: 336
% Calories from fat: 24
Protein (g): 21.9
Carbohydrates (g): 44.3
Fat (g): 9.3
Saturated fat (g): 3.4
Cholesterol (mg): 42.1
Sodium (mg): 302
Exchanges
Milk: 0.0
Veg.: 0.0
Fruit: 0.0
Bread: 3.0
Meat: 2.0
Fat: 0.0

1. Spray large saucepan with cooking spray; heat over medium heat until hot. Saute beef, onion, bell pepper, caraway seeds, and thyme 5 minutes. Add paprika, chili powder, and garlic powder and cook 2 minutes. Add broth, Worcestershire sauce, and potatoes; heat to boiling. Reduce heat and simmer, covered, until potatoes are tender, about 15 minutes. Add tomatoes and liquid and catsup; simmer 5 minutes. Add sugar, if desired. Season to taste with salt and pepper.

HAM, SPINACH, AND PASTA SOUP

Leaf spinach and angel hair pasta are excellent ingredients for fast soups since they both cook so quickly.

4-5 servings

Vegetable cooking spray

1 medium onion, chopped

1¹/₄ quarts reduced-sodium fat-free chicken broth

1 can (15 ounces) reduced-sodium tomato sauce

6 ounces lean reduced-sodium deli ham, cut into bite-sized pieces

2 teaspoons Italian seasoning

1 cup uncooked angel hair pasta, broken into 2-inch pieces

3 cups loosely packed sliced spinach leaves

Salt and pepper, to taste

Per Serving
Calories: 188
% Calories from fat: 10
Protein (g): 14.7
Carbohydrates (g): 29.5
Fat (g): 2.3
Saturated fat (g): 0.3
Cholesterol (mg): 19.1
Sodium (mg): 653
Exchanges
Milk: 0.0
Veg.: 2.0
Fruit: 0.0
Bread: 1.0
Meat: 1.0
Fat: 0.0

1. Spray large saucepan with cooking spray; heat over medium heat until hot. Saute onion 5 minutes; stir in broth, tomato sauce, ham, and Italian seasoning and heat to boiling. Add pasta, reduce heat and simmer, uncovered, 2 to 3 minutes or until pasta is al dente. Stir in spinach; season to taste with salt and pepper.

CHUNKY CHICKEN AND PASTA SOUP

This colorful soup always gets an enthusiastic reception, yet it's very quick and easy to make.

5-6 servings

8 ounces boneless, skinless chicken breast, cut into 1/2-inch cubes

1 tablespoon olive oil

1 large onion, finely chopped

1 garlic clove, minced

1/2 large green bell pepper, diced

1/2 large red bell pepper, diced

3 1/2 cups fat-free chicken broth

1 can (14 1/2 ounces) tomatoes, un-drained, coarsely chopped

1/4 cup chopped parsley

3/4 teaspoon dried basil leaves

1/2 teaspoon dried oregano leaves

1 bay leaf

1/4 teaspoon black pepper

1 cup uncooked vermicelli, broken into 2-inch lengths

Salt, to taste

Per Serving
Calories: 155
% Calories from fat: 22
Protein (g): 14
Carbohydrates (g): 16.8
Fat (g): 3.7
Saturated fat (g): 0.6
Cholesterol (mg): 23
Sodium (mg): 330
Exchanges
Milk: 0.0
Veg.: 1.0
Fruit: 0.0
Bread: 1.0
Meat: 1.0
Fat: 0.0

1. Saute chicken in oil in large saucepan until it begins to brown. Remove chicken and reserve.

2. Saute onion and garlic in same saucepan 5 minutes; add bell peppers and saute 5 minutes more. Add broth, tomatoes and liquid, reserved chicken, herbs and pepper; heat to boiling. Add vermicelli and simmer, uncovered, until vermicelli is al dente, about 8 minutes. Discard bay leaf; season to taste with salt.

TORTELLINI SOUP

We rely on prepared tortellini from the dairy case for this flavorful and speedy soup, which makes a nice luncheon or light supper entrée.

4 servings

1	large onion, chopped
1	garlic clove, minced
2	teaspoons olive oil
1	cup finely chopped parsley
1¹/₄	quarts Chicken Stock (see p. 2), *or* reduced-sodium fat-free chicken broth
3	tablespoons dry sherry, *or* white wine, optional
1	package (9 ounces) reduced-fat cheese-and-garlic tortellini
2	teaspoons Italian seasoning
¹/₈	teaspoon pepper
1	can (15 ounces) reduced-sodium tomato sauce
1	teaspoon sugar
	Salt, to taste

Per Serving
Calories: 298
% Calories from fat: 16
Protein (g): 17.3
Carbohydrates (g): 46.2
Fat (g): 5.5
Saturated fat (g): 1.9
Cholesterol (mg): 33.7
Sodium (mg): 659
Exchanges
Milk: 0.0
Veg.: 3.0
Fruit: 0.0
Bread: 2.0
Meat: 1.0
Fat: 0.5

1. Saute onion and garlic in oil in large saucepan until onions are tender, about 5 minutes; stir in parsley. Add Chicken Stock, sherry, tortellini, Italian seasoning, and pepper; heat to boiling. Reduce heat and simmer, uncovered, until tortellini float to the top and are al dente, 5 to 8 minutes. Stir in tomato sauce and simmer 5 minutes. Stir in sugar and season to taste with salt.

TORTELLINI AND BEAN SOUP

Using purchased pasta sauce, refrigerated tortellini, and canned beans, you can whip up a flavorful soup in minutes.

7-8 servings

1¹/₂ quarts reduced-sodium fat-free chicken broth

2 cups reduced-fat garlic-and-herb spaghetti sauce

2 cans (16 ounces each) reduced-sodium red kidney beans, rinsed, drained

1 package (9 ounces) light cheese tortellini

Per Serving
Calories: 171
% Calories from fat: 7
Protein (g): 12.3
Carbohydrates (g): 28.5
Fat (g): 1.4
Saturated fat (g): 0.3
Cholesterol (mg): 1.7
Sodium (mg): 503
Exchanges
Milk: 0.0
Veg.: 0.0
Fruit: 0.0
Bread: 2.0
Meat: 0.0
Fat: 0.5

1. Combine broth, spaghetti sauce, and beans in large saucepan and heat to boiling; stir in tortellini. Reduce heat and simmer 8 minutes or until tortellini are al dente.

EASY SPINACH-PASTA SOUP WITH BASIL

Serve this fragrant soup with Garlic Bread or Spinach Mushroom Flatbread (see pp. 795, 791).

4-5 servings

1 small onion, finely chopped

1 small garlic clove, minced

2 teaspoons olive oil

1¹/₂ quarts Chicken Stock (see p. 2), *or* fat-free chicken broth

1 cup water

³/₄ cup uncooked broken vermicelli (2-inch pieces)

1 package (10 ounces) frozen chopped spinach, thawed

¹/₄ cup chopped fresh, *or* 1¹/₂ tablespoons dried, basil leaves

¹/₄ teaspoon pepper

1 cup chopped plum tomatoes

Per Serving
Calories: 193
% Calories from fat: 18
Protein (g): 13.3
Carbohydrates (g): 27.6
Fat (g): 3.9
Saturated fat (g): 0.9
Cholesterol (mg): 2
Sodium (mg): 563
Exchanges
Milk: 0.0
Veg.: 0.0
Fruit: 0.0
Bread: 2.0
Meat: 1.0
Fat: 0.0

1 cup cooked dried, *or* canned, drained
  and rinsed, garbanzo beans
  Salt, to taste
2 tablespoons grated Parmesan cheese, as
  garnish

1. Saute onion and garlic in oil in large saucepan until tender, about 5 minutes. Add Chicken Stock and water; heat to boiling. Add vermicelli; reduce heat, and simmer, uncovered, until tender, 7 to 10 minutes.

2. Add remaining ingredients, except salt and Parmesan cheese; simmer 5 minutes. Season to taste with salt. Sprinkle each serving with Parmesan cheese.

ASIAN SHIITAKE AND NOODLE SOUP

Shiitake mushrooms and Japanese udon noodles give this soup its distinctive Asian flavor.

6 servings (about 1¹/₂ cups each)

2 cups thinly sliced shiitake, *or* other wild, mushrooms, tough stem discarded
1 cup diced red bell pepper
1 cup julienned carrots
2 green onions and tops, sliced
¹/₂ teaspoon minced gingerroot
¹/₂ teaspoon minced garlic
1-2 teaspoons dark sesame oil
1 quart reduced-sodium fat-free beef broth
1 teaspoon reduced-sodium tamari soy sauce
1 cup packed fresh spinach, sliced
1 package (8¹/₂ ounces) Japanese udon noodles, cooked, warm

Per Serving
Calories: 208
% Calories from fat: 10
Protein (gm): 10.7
Carbohydrate (gm): 38
Fat (gm): 2.4
Saturated fat (gm): 0.1
Cholesterol (mg): 0
Sodium (mg): 215
Exchanges
Milk: 0.0
Veg.: 1.0
Fruit: 0.0
Bread: 2.0
Meat: 0.0
Fat: 0.5

1. Saute mushrooms, bell pepper, carrots, green onions, gingerroot, and garlic in sesame oil in large saucepan until tender, about 8 minutes. Stir in beef broth and soy sauce and heat to boiling; reduce heat and simmer 5 minutes.

2. Stir in spinach and simmer until hot. Place noodles in soup bowls and ladle soup over.

CHINESE BEEF AND NOODLE SOUP

We've used Chinese lo mein noodles in this easy and flavorful soup.

6 servings

2 tablespoons light soy sauce

2 tablespoons dry sherry

1/2 teaspoon ground ginger

1 garlic clove, minced

3-4 drops oriental hot chili oil, *or* hot pepper sauce, optional

1 1/2 tablespoons cornstarch

12 ounces round steak, fat trimmed, very thinly sliced

1/4 cup chopped scallions

1 tablespoon oriental sesame oil

1 1/4 quarts reduced-sodium fat-free chicken broth, divided

1 can (8 ounces) sliced water chestnuts, drained

2/3 package (10-ounce size) Chinese lo mein noodles

Per Serving
Calories: 268
% Calories from fat: **19**
Protein (g): **20.4**
Carbohydrates (g): **32.1**
Fat (g): 5.5
Saturated fat (g): 1.2
Cholesterol (mg): 28
Sodium (mg): 498
Exchanges
Milk: 0.0
Veg.: 0.0
Fruit: 0.0
Bread: 2.0
Meat: 2.0
Fat: 0.0

1. Combine soy sauce, sherry, ginger, garlic, hot chili oil if desired, and cornstarch in small bowl. Stir in beef and scallions until well coated.

2. Saute beef mixture in sesame oil in large saucepan until browned. Add 1 cup broth and stir well. Heat, stirring, until mixture has boiled and thickened.

3. Stir in remaining 1 quart broth and heat to boiling; add water chestnuts and noodles. Reduce heat, and simmer 3 to 4 minutes or until noodles are tender.

RICE AND ADZUKI BEANS WITH VEGETABLES

In this easy khichuri, a classic Indian grain-and-bean stew, slightly sweet adzuki beans replace the usual dal, or legume.

6 servings

1 can (15 ounces) adzuki beans, rinsed, drained
1/2 cup uncooked rice
2 cans (14 1/2 ounces each) reduced-sodium fat-free chicken broth
1 teaspoon ground cumin
1 teaspoon minced gingerroot
1/4 teaspoon ground turmeric
1 small jalapeño chili, seeded, minced
3 carrots, thinly sliced
2 cups cut wax beans
4 plum tomatoes, coarsely chopped
Salt and pepper, to taste
1/4 cup toasted sunflower seeds

Per Serving
Calories: 323
% Calories from fat: 10
Protein (gm): 10.3
Carbohydrate (gm): 62.4
Fat (gm): 3.5
Saturated fat (gm): 0.4
Cholesterol (mg): 0
Sodium (mg): 209
Exchanges
Milk: 0.0
Veg.: 3.0
Fruit: 0.0
Bread: 3.0
Meat: 0.0
Fat: 0.5

1. Combine all ingredients, except tomatoes, salt, pepper, and sunflower seeds, in medium saucepan; heat to boiling. Reduce heat and simmer, covered, until vegetables and rice are tender, about 20 minutes. Add tomatoes and cook 2 minutes longer; season to taste with salt and pepper. Sprinkle each serving with sunflower seeds.

RED AND WHITE BEAN AND BACON SOUP WITH PASTA

With canned beans and Canadian bacon, you can have a hearty bean and bacon soup on the table in minutes.

7 servings

6 ounces Canadian bacon, cut into thin strips

1 large onion, chopped

2 large ribs celery, minced

2 teaspoons olive oil

1¹/₂ quarts reduced-sodium fat-free chicken broth

1 can (18 ounces) cannellini beans, rinsed, drained

1 can (15 ounces) reduced-sodium red kidney beans, rinsed, drained

1 can (15 ounces) reduced-sodium tomato sauce

2 teaspoons Italian seasoning

¹/₂ cup uncooked orzo

Per Serving
Calories: 257
% Calories from fat: **13**
Protein (g): 20.6
Carbohydrates (g): **40.3**
Fat (g): 4
Saturated fat (g): 0.8
Cholesterol (mg): 11.6
Sodium (mg): 771
Exchanges
Milk: 0.0
Veg.: 2.0
Fruit: 0.0
Bread: 2.0
Meat: 1.0
Fat: 0.0

1. Saute bacon, onion, and celery in oil in large saucepan until onion is tender, about 5 minutes. Add broth, beans, tomato sauce, and Italian seasoning; heat to boiling and add orzo. Reduce heat and simmer until pasta is al dente, about 10 minutes.

TURKEY CON SALSA SOUP

We've used the trick of adding a small amount of instant mashed potatoes to thicken the broth. While they give the soup body, they're otherwise undetectable.

7 servings

Vegetable cooking spray
12 ounces ground turkey breast
1 large onion, chopped
2 garlic cloves, minced
2 teaspoons chili powder
1 teaspoon ground cumin
1¹/₄ quarts reduced-sodium fat-free beef broth
2 cups reduced-sodium mild salsa
1 can (15¹/₂ ounces) reduced-sodium kidney beans, rinsed, drained
2 cups whole-kernel corn
¹/₂ cup instant mashed potatoes
Salt and pepper, to taste

Per Serving
Calories: 181
% Calories from fat: 8
Protein (g): 17.2
Carbohydrates (g): 25.5
Fat (g): 1.6
Saturated fat (g): 0.3
Cholesterol (mg): 18.9
Sodium (mg): 384
Exchanges
Milk: 0.0
Veg.: 0.0
Fruit: 0.0
Bread: 1.5
Meat: 2.0
Fat: 0.0

1. Spray large saucepan with cooking spray; heat over medium heat until hot. Saute turkey, onion, garlic, chili powder, and cumin until turkey is browned, about 5 minutes. Add broth, salsa, beans, and corn; heat to boiling. Reduce heat and simmer, covered, 10 minutes. Stir in instant mashed potatoes and simmer 2 minutes longer or until soup has thickened slightly. Season to taste with salt and pepper.

PEPPERS, CORN, AND BLACK BEAN SOUP, PRONTO

Bottled roasted red peppers and canned black beans are great time-savers in this hearty, colorful soup. For a delicious vegetarian version, simply omit the ham and substitute vegetable broth for the chicken broth.

4 servings

2 cups chopped onions

1 tablespoon olive oil

$2/3$ cup instant rice

1 quart reduced-sodium fat-free chicken broth, divided

$3/4$ teaspoon dried thyme leaves

Pinch crushed red pepper

Pinch ground allspice

1 jar (12 ounces) roasted, peeled red bell peppers, drained, diced, divided

2 cups frozen whole-kernel corn

1 can (15 ounces) black beans, rinsed, drained

$1/2$ cup diced lean ham, optional

Chopped fresh chives, *or* fresh cilantro, as garnish

Per Serving
Calories: 313
% Calories from fat: 12
Protein (g): 18.4
Carbohydrates (g): 60.5
Fat (g): 4.8
Saturated fat (g): 0.5
Cholesterol (mg): 0
Sodium (mg): 677
Exchanges
Milk: 0.0
Veg.: 2.0
Fruit: 0.0
Bread: 3.0
Meat: 0.0
Fat: 1.0

1. Saute onions in oil in large saucepan until browned, about 8 minutes. Add rice, $2^1/2$ cups broth, thyme, crushed red pepper, and allspice; heat to boiling. Reduce heat and simmer, covered, until rice is tender, about 5 minutes.

2. Process mixture in blender or food processor with 8 ounces roasted peppers until smooth. Return to saucepan; add remaining $1^1/2$ cups broth and 4 ounces roasted red peppers, corn, black beans, and ham. Simmer until hot, about 5 minutes. Garnish with chives.

QUICK ITALIAN BREAD SOUP

The name comes from the fact that the soup is ladled over a generous portion of croutons just before serving.

5 servings

3/4 cup diced, trimmed, Canadian bacon
1/3 cup diced red bell pepper
   2 teaspoons olive oil
   2 garlic cloves, minced
   1 quart reduced-sodium fat-free chicken broth
   1 cup uncooked small elbow macaroni
1/2 teaspoon dried marjoram leaves
1/2 teaspoon dried sage leaves
1/4 teaspoon black pepper
   1 can (19 ounces) cannellini beans, rinsed, drained, divided
2/3 cup herbed croutons
      Parmesan cheese, grated, as garnish

Per Serving
Calories: 235
% Calories from fat: 14
Protein (g): 18.2
Carbohydrates (g): 39.4
Fat (g): 4.2
Saturated fat (g): 0.7
Cholesterol (mg): 8.1
Sodium (mg): 731
Exchanges
Milk: 0.0
Veg.: 0.0
Fruit: 0.0
Bread: 2.5
Meat: 1.0
Fat: 0.0

1.   Saute bacon and bell pepper in oil in large saucepan until bacon begins to brown, about 5 minutes. Add garlic and saute 1 minute longer. Add broth and heat to boiling. Stir in macaroni, marjoram, sage, and black pepper; simmer 7 to 9 minutes or until macaroni is almost tender.

2.   Process 1 1/2 cups beans and 3/4 cup water in food processor or blender until smooth. Add to saucepan with remaining 1/2 cup beans; simmer until hot, about 5 minutes. Place croutons in soup bowls; ladle soup over. Sprinkle with Parmesan cheese.

CANNELLINI AND CABBAGE SOUP

Tuscany is known for its dishes with white cannellini beans; canned Great Northern beans may be substituted.

4 servings (about 2 cups each)

Vegetable cooking spray

3 cups thinly sliced, *or* chopped, cabbage

1 small onion, coarsely chopped

3 cloves garlic, minced

1 teaspoon crushed caraway seeds

2 cans (15 ounces each) reduced-sodium chicken broth

1 cup water

1 can (15 ounces) cannellini, *or* Great Northern, beans, rinsed, drained

1/2 cup (4 ounces) uncooked mostaccioli (penne)

Salt and pepper, to taste

Per Serving
Calories: 213
% Calories from fat: 7
Protein (g): 13.8
Carbohydrates (g): 43.7
Fat (g): 1.9
Saturated fat (g): 0.1
Cholesterol (mg): 0
Sodium (mg): 350
Exchanges
Milk: 0.0
Veg.: 2.0
Fruit: 0.0
Bread: 2.0
Meat: 0.5
Fat: 0.0

1. Spray large saucepan with cooking spray; heat over medium heat until hot. Saute cabbage, onion, garlic, and caraway seeds until cabbage begins to wilt, 8 to 10 minutes.

2. Add chicken broth, water, and beans to saucepan; heat to boiling. Stir in pasta; reduce heat and simmer, uncovered, until pasta is al dente, about 15 minutes. Season to taste with salt and pepper.

GARBANZO AND PASTA SOUP

Quick, easy, and good, this soup makes a nice luncheon entrée.

4-5 servings

1 medium onion, chopped
1 clove garlic, minced
2 teaspoons olive oil
1 quart Chicken Stock (see p. 2), *or* fat-free chicken broth
1 rib celery, finely chopped
1 large carrot, finely chopped
$1/2$ cup diced zucchini
1 bay leaf
$1/2$ teaspoon dried thyme leaves
$1/2$ teaspoon dried basil leaves
    Dash pepper
$1/3$ cup uncooked small soup pasta
1 can (8 ounces) reduced-sodium tomato sauce
2 cups cooked dried garbanzo beans, *or* 1 can (15 ounces) garbanzo beans, rinsed, drained
    Salt, to taste

Per Serving
Calories: 209
% Calories from fat: 16
Protein (g): 12.4
Carbohydrates (g): 32.5
Fat (g): 3.8
Saturated fat (g): 0.4
Cholesterol (mg): 0
Sodium (mg): 333
Exchanges
Milk: 0.0
Veg.: 0.0
Fruit: 0.0
Bread: 2.0
Meat: 1.0
Fat: 0.0

1. Saute onion and garlic in oil in large saucepan until onion is tender, about 5 minutes. Add Chicken Stock, celery, carrot, zucchini, herbs, and pepper; heat to boiling. Reduce heat and simmer, covered, 7 to 8 minutes or until celery is almost tender.

2. Heat soup to boiling; add pasta. Reduce heat and simmer, uncovered, until pasta is al dente, 4 to 5 minutes. Stir in tomato sauce and garbanzo beans; simmer 5 minutes longer. Discard bay leaf; season to taste with salt.

CURRIED BEAN SOUP

Use any white bean, such as cannellini, navy, soy, lima, or garbanzo, in this rich, aromatic soup.

4 servings (about 1¹/₂ cups each)

1 cup chopped onion
1 cup sliced leeks, white parts only
1 tablespoon minced garlic
1 tablespoon curry powder
2 tablespoons margarine
2 cans (15¹/₂ ounces each) Great Northern beans, rinsed, drained
3¹/₂ cups reduced-sodium chicken broth
¹/₂ cup 2% reduced-fat milk
Salt and pepper, to taste
6 tablespoons reduced-fat sour cream, *or* plain yogurt
3 tablespoons finely chopped cilantro
2 tablespoons finely chopped red, *or* green, bell pepper

Per Serving
Calories: 288
% Calories from fat: **29**
Protein (g): 16.1
Carbohydrates (g): **42.3**
Fat (g): 10.7
Saturated fat (g): **3.9**
Cholesterol (mg): **9.8**
Sodium (mg): **735**
Exchanges
Milk: 0.0
Veg.: 0.0
Fruit: 0.0
Bread: 3.0
Meat: 0.0
Fat: 1.5

1. Saute onion, leeks, garlic, and curry powder in margarine in large saucepan 5 minutes. Add beans and broth to saucepan; heat to boiling. Reduce heat and simmer, covered, 5 minutes.

2. Process bean mixture in food processor or blender until smooth; return to saucepan. Stir in milk; cook over medium heat until hot, 2 to 3 minutes. Season to taste with salt and pepper.

3. Serve soup in bowls; top each with a dollop of sour cream. Sprinkle with cilantro and bell pepper.

CLAM SOUP

You can make this dish with mussels as well. Or, make the soup with 1 pound peeled, deveined shrimp, simmering just until shrimp are cooked and tender, about 5 minutes.

4 servings

3 large garlic cloves

2 tablespoons olive oil

4 dozen clams (littlenecks *or* cherrystones), scrubbed

1 cup tomato sauce

1 cup dry white wine

1/4 cup minced parsley

1 teaspoon crushed red pepper, *or* hot pepper sauce

1 1/2 teaspoons dried oregano leaves

1 teaspoon dried thyme leaves

Spike and pepper, to taste

4-8 slices Italian bread, toasted

Per Serving
Calories: 275
% Calories from fat: 26
Protein (g): 15.2
Carbohydrates (g): 25.9
Fat (g): 7.9
Saturated fat (g): 1.1
Cholesterol (mg): 28.9
Sodium (mg): 575
Exchanges
Milk: 0.0
Veg.: 0.0
Fruit: 0.0
Bread: 2.0
Meat: 2.0
Fat: 0.5

1. Saute garlic in oil in large saucepan until browned; discard garlic. Add remaining ingredients, except Spike, pepper, and bread, and heat to boiling; reduce heat and simmer, covered, 5 minutes or until clams have opened. Discard any clams that have not opened; season to taste with Spike and pepper.

2. Serve clams in broth with toasted Italian bread on the side.

FIFTEEN-MINUTE CLAM SOUP

Serve this delicious soup with crusty bread and dry white wine.

6 servings

Vegetable cooking spray
1/2 medium onion, finely chopped
2 cloves garlic, chopped
4 thin slices day-old bread, cubed
2 medium tomatoes, peeled, seeded, finely chopped
3 cups clam juice, *or* Fish Stock (see p. 9)
3 cups water
1/2 cup dry sherry
1 teaspoon paprika
24 clams, *or* mussels, scrubbed
Salt and pepper, to taste
2 tablespoons chopped parsley, as garnish

Per Serving
Calories: 101
% Calories from fat: 8
Protein (gm): 6.6
Carbohydrate (gm): 12.8
Fat (gm): 0.9
Saturated fat (gm): 0.1
Cholesterol (mg): 12.1
Sodium (mg): 374
Exchanges
Milk: 0.0
Veg.: 1.0
Fruit: 0.0
Bread: 0.5
Meat: 0.0
Fat: 0.5

1. Spray large saucepan with cooking spray; heat over medium heat until hot. Saute onion, garlic, and bread until onion is soft, about 5 minutes. Add remaining ingredients, except salt, pepper, and parsley, and simmer, covered, until clams or mussels open, about 10 minutes. Discard shellfish that do not open. Season broth to taste with salt and pepper. Sprinkle servings with parsley.

SEAFOOD PASTA SOUP

Small bay scallops or other seafood can be used in this colorful soup.

6 servings

1/2 cup chopped onion
1/2 cup diced green bell pepper
1/2 cup diced red, *or* yellow, bell pepper
1/2 teaspoon minced garlic
  8 ounces mushrooms, sliced
  2 tablespoons olive oil
  1 can (14 ounces) Italian plum tomatoes, undrained, chopped
  2 cups reduced-sodium fat-free chicken broth
1/2 cup dry white wine, *or* chicken broth
  1 pound sea scallops, halved
1/4 cup finely chopped parsley
1/2 pound uncooked small pasta, cooked
1/4-1/2 cup grated Parmesan cheese
      Salt and pepper, to taste

Per Serving
Calories: 323
% Calories from fat: 20
Protein (gm): 24.1
Carbohydrate (gm): 37.4
Fat (gm): 7.4
Saturated fat (gm): 1.3
Cholesterol (mg): 34.8
Sodium (mg): 382
Exchanges
Milk: 0.0
Veg.: 1.0
Fruit: 0.0
Bread: 2.0
Meat: 2.5
Fat: 0.0

1. Saute onion, bell peppers, garlic, and mushrooms in oil in large saucepan until mushrooms are tender, about 10 minutes. Add remaining ingredients, except Parmesan cheese, salt, and pepper; heat to boiling. Remove from heat and let stand, covered, 5 minutes. Stir in Parmesan cheese; season to taste with salt and pepper.

SHRIMP CREOLE SOUP

Canned ingredients makes this shrimp soup easy.

4 servings

1 can (8 ounces) stewed tomatoes, undrained

1 can (10³/₄ ounces) condensed chicken gumbo soup

1 cup water

1 cup chopped onion

1 small red bell pepper, chopped

¹/₄ cup uncooked rice

2 cloves garlic, minced

1 teaspoon dried basil leaves

1 teaspoon dried thyme leaves

1 bay leaf

16 ounces peeled, deveined shrimp

Salt, to taste

Hot pepper sauce, to taste

Per Serving
Calories: 209
% Calories from fat: 9
Protein (gm): 22.1
Carbohydrate (gm): 24.5
Fat (gm): 2.2
Saturated fat (gm): 0.6
Cholesterol (mg): 179.7
Sodium (mg): 956
Exchanges
Milk: 0.0
Veg.: 1.0
Fruit: 0.0
Bread: 1.0
Meat: 2.0
Fat: 0.0

1. Combine all ingredients, except shrimp, salt, and hot pepper sauce, in large saucepan; heat to boiling. Reduce heat and simmer, covered, until rice is tender, about 20 minutes.

2. Stir in shrimp; simmer until shrimp are cooked and pink, about 5 minutes. Season to taste with salt and hot pepper sauce.

SHRIMP-CORN CHOWDER

Canned and frozen ingredients make this soup "souper"-easy.

6 servings

2 slices reduced-sodium bacon

1/3 cup chopped onion

1/4 cup chopped celery

1 can (10 1/2 ounces) cream of shrimp soup

1 1/2 cups fat-free milk

2 cups cubed frozen potatoes

1 1/2 cups frozen whole-kernel corn

12 ounces small shrimp, peeled, deveined

Salt and cayenne pepper, to taste

Per Serving
Calories: 176
% Calories from fat: 18
Protein (gm): 14.9
Carbohydrate (gm): 22.4
Fat (gm): 3.6
Saturated fat (gm): 1.8
Cholesterol (mg): 96
Sodium (mg): 577
Exchanges
Milk: 0.0
Veg.: 0.0
Fruit: 0.0
Bread: 1.5
Meat: 1.0
Fat: 0.0

1. Fry bacon in medium saucepan until crisp; drain on paper toweling, crumble, and reserve. Drain all but 2 teaspoons fat from saucepan; saute onion and celery until tender, about 5 minutes.

2. Stir in cream of shrimp soup and milk; heat to boiling, stirring until smooth. Stir in potatoes, corn, and shrimp; heat to boiling. Reduce heat and simmer 5 minutes or until vegetables are tender. Season to taste with salt and cayenne pepper.

CURRIED SHRIMP AND BROCCOLI SOUP

Here's another rich-tasting, creamy-textured soup that takes advantage of the quick-thickening ability of instant mashed potatoes. It can be on the table in about 15 minutes.

4-5 servings

4 cups small broccoli florets and chopped stems

1 quart reduced-sodium fat-free chicken broth

2 1/2 teaspoons mild curry powder

1 garlic clove, minced

1/4 teaspoon ground allspice

1/8 teaspoon black pepper

1 cup 2% reduced-fat milk

Per Serving
Calories: 145
% Calories from fat: 12
Protein (g): 19.4
Carbohydrates (g): 13.3
Fat (g): 1.9
Saturated fat (g): 0.8
Cholesterol (mg): 108.6
Sodium (mg): 440
Exchanges
Milk: 0.0
Veg.: 0.0
Fruit: 0.0
Bread: 1.0
Meat: 2.0
Fat: 0.0

1¹/₄ cups instant mashed potatoes
12 ounces cooked shrimp
Salt, to taste

1. Combine all ingredients, except milk, potatoes, shrimp, and salt in large saucepan; heat to boiling. Reduce heat and simmer, covered, 5 to 7 minutes or until broccoli is tender. Stir in milk and potatoes; cook until hot. Add shrimp and simmer until hot, about 2 minutes; season to taste with salt.

RED SNAPPER SOUP

This "snappy" soup couldn't be easier.

6 servings

5 cups water
2 onions, finely chopped
3 potatoes, peeled, chopped
1 can (15 ounces) diced tomatoes, undrained
2 pounds red snapper fillets, cut into 1-inch pieces
Salt and cayenne pepper, to taste

Per Serving
Calories: 241
% Calories from fat: 8
Protein (gm): 33.4
Carbohydrate (gm): 20.5
Fat (gm): 2.2
Saturated fat (gm): 0.5
Cholesterol (mg): 55.4
Sodium (mg): 352
Exchanges
Milk: 0.0
Veg.: 0.0
Fruit: 0.0
Bread: 1.0
Meat: 3.0
Fat: 0.0

1. Combine all ingredients, except fish, salt, and cayenne pepper, in large saucepan; heat to boiling. Reduce heat and simmer, covered, until potatoes are tender, about 20 minutes, adding fish during last 5 to 8 minutes cooking time. Season to taste with salt and cayenne pepper.

TEN

Meat Stews

COUNTRY BEEF STEW

Simmer this stew for a long time for old-fashioned goodness. Use your family's favorite vegetables, and serve the thick stew over cooked noodles in shallow bowls.

4 servings (about 1 cup each)

Vegetable cooking spray
1 pound lean beef stew meat, fat trimmed, cubed
1/2 cup chopped onion
1/2 cup chopped celery
2 cloves garlic, minced
1 cup reduced-sodium beef broth
1/2 cup dry red wine, *or* reduced-sodium beef broth
1 tablespoon tomato paste
1/2 teaspoon dried thyme leaves
1/2 teaspoon dried rosemary leaves
1 bay leaf
1 cup cubed, unpeeled potato
1 cup sliced carrots (1-inch)
1/2 cup cubed, peeled parsnip, *or* turnip
1/2 cup frozen peas
2 tablespoons flour
1/4 cup cold water
Salt and pepper, to taste

Per Serving
Calories: 326
% Calories from fat: 16
Protein (g): 33.5
Carbohydrates (g): 29.6
Fat (g): 5.8
Saturated fat (g): 2
Cholesterol (mg): 70.9
Sodium (mg): 171
Exchanges
Milk: 0.0
Veg.: 2.0
Fruit: 0.0
Bread: 1.5
Meat: 3.0
Fat: 0.0

1. Spray large saucepan with cooking spray; heat over medium heat until hot. Add beef and cook until browned, 5 to 8 minutes. Add onion, celery, and garlic; cook until tender, about 5 minutes.

2. Add broth, wine, tomato paste, and herbs to saucepan; heat to boiling. Reduce heat and simmer, covered, until beef is tender, 1 1/2 to 2 hours. Add remaining vegetables during last 30 minutes of cooking time.

3. Heat stew to boiling. Mix flour and water and stir into stew; boil, stirring constantly, until thickened, 1 to 2 minutes. Discard bay leaf; season to taste with salt and pepper.

TRADITIONAL BEEF STEW

Here's a simple, fast version of a family favorite with all the great familiar flavors.

4 servings

16 ounces beef round steak, fat trimmed, cut into thin, short strips
2 onions, cut into wedges
1 teaspoon olive oil
1¹/₂ cups fat-free beef broth
¹/₂ cup dry red wine, *or* beef broth
1 teaspoon cocoa
2 medium potatoes, cut into ¹/₂-inch cubes
3 carrots, cut into ¹/₂-inch slices
2 cups cut wax beans
¹/₂ teaspoon black pepper
   Salt, to taste

Per Serving
Calories: 292
% Calories from fat: **16**
Protein (gm): 26
Carbohydrate (gm): 29.7
Fat (gm): 5.1
Saturated fat (gm): **1.5**
Cholesterol (mg): 55
Sodium (mg): 140
Exchanges
Milk: 0.0
Veg.: 0.0
Fruit: 0.0
Bread: 2.0
Meat: 3.0
Fat: 0.0

1. Saute beef and onions in oil in Dutch oven until beef is lightly browned, 8 to 10 minutes. Add broth, wine, and cocoa; heat to boiling. Reduce heat and simmer, covered, until meat is tender, 45 to 60 minutes, adding vegetables and pepper during last 20 minutes. Season to taste with salt.

VERY SPECIAL BEEF STEW

This beef stew boasts an ample assortment of vegetables to make a well-rounded meal.

6 servings

   Vegetable cooking spray
1¹/₂ pounds boneless beef round steak, fat trimmed, cut into 1-inch cubes
1¹/₂ cups water
¹/₂ cup red wine, *or* water
1 teaspoon Worcestershire sauce
2 bay leaves
1 clove garlic, minced
¹/₄ teaspoon pepper

Per Serving
Calories: 289
% Calories from fat: **13**
Protein (gm): 24.5
Carbohydrate (gm): 35.9
Fat (gm): 4.1
Saturated fat (gm): 1.4
Cholesterol (mg): 55
Sodium (mg): 96
Exchanges
Milk: 0.0
Veg.: 1.0
Fruit: 0.0
Bread: 1.5
Meat: 3.0
Fat: 0.0

8 medium carrots, quartered
4 small potatoes, peeled, quartered
2 small zucchini, sliced
4 small onions, quartered
1/2 cup small mushrooms
1 tablespoon cornstarch
1/4 cup cold water
Salt, to taste

1. Spray Dutch oven with cooking spray; heat over medium heat until hot. Cook beef until well-browned, about 10 minutes. Add water, wine, Worcestershire sauce, bay leaves, garlic, and pepper; heat to boiling. Reduce heat and simmer, covered, until beef is tender, 1 to 1 1/2 hours, adding vegetables during last 30 minutes.

2. Heat stew to boiling; stir in combined cornstarch and water. Boil, stirring, until stew is thickened, 1 to 2 minutes. Discard bay leaves; season to taste with salt.

BEEF STEW

This Italian-seasoned beef stew would be delicious served over noodles, rice, or Polenta (see p. 811).

6 servings

Vegetable cooking spray
2 pounds lean beef, fat trimmed, cut into 1-inch cubes
2 onions, chopped
2 cloves garlic, minced
1/2 cup beef broth
1/2 cup dry red wine, *or* beef broth
1/4 teaspoon black pepper
1 teaspoon dried oregano leaves
1 teaspoon dried thyme leaves
1 can (14 ounces) Italian tomatoes, undrained, chopped
Salt, to taste

Per Serving
Calories: 290
% Calories from fat: 34
Protein (g): 35.4
Carbohydrates (g): 8.6
Fat (g): 10.7
Saturated fat (g): 3.8
Cholesterol (mg): 103
Sodium (mg): 246
Exchanges
Milk: 0.0
Veg.: 1.5
Fruit: 0.0
Bread: 0.0
Meat: 5.0
Fat: 0.0

1. Spray Dutch oven with cooking spray; heat over medium heat until hot. Cook beef until browned, 10 to 12 minutes. Add onions and garlic, and cook until lightly browned, 3 to 4 minutes. Add remaining ingredients, except salt, and simmer, covered, 45 to 60 minutes or until beef is tender. Season to taste with salt.

FAMILY FAVORITE BEEF STEW

Add your family's favorite vegetables to this stew. A great recipe for using leftover vegetables too!

8 servings

1 1/2 cups chopped onions
   4 cloves garlic, minced
   1 teaspoon dried basil leaves
 1/2 teaspoon dried marjoram leaves
 1/2 teaspoon dried thyme leaves
   1 bay leaf
1-2 tablespoons vegetable oil
   2 pounds lean beef stew meat, fat trimmed, cut into 1-inch pieces
   3 tablespoons flour
   1 can (15 ounces) reduced-sodium diced tomatoes, undrained
   1 can (14 1/2 ounces) reduced-sodium fat-free beef broth
   4 medium potatoes, unpeeled, cubed (1/2-inch)
   4 large carrots, cut into 1/2-inch pieces
   2 cups cubed, peeled rutabaga, *or* turnips
   2 large ribs celery, sliced
2-3 teaspoons very-low-sodium Worcestershire sauce
      Salt and pepper, to taste

Per Serving
Calories: 314
% Calories from fat: 22
Protein (gm): 32.8
Carbohydrate (gm): 28.5
Fat (gm): 7.5
Saturated fat (gm): 2.3
Cholesterol (mg): 70.9
Sodium (mg): 134
Exchanges
Milk: 0.0
Veg.: 0.0
Fruit: 0.0
Bread: 2.0
Meat: 3.0
Fat: 0.0

1. Saute onions, garlic, and herbs in oil in large saucepan 5 minutes; add beef and saute until browned, about 5 minutes. Stir in flour; cook 1 minute longer.

2. Add tomatoes and liquid and beef broth; heat to boiling. Reduce heat and simmer, covered, until beef is tender, 50 to 60 minutes, adding vegetables during last 15 minutes of cooking time. Discard bay leaf; season to taste with Worcestershire sauce, salt, and pepper.

BEEF RAGOUT

Any favorite vegetable can be added to this easy stew. If you prefer a thicker gravy, add 1-2 tablespoons of flour mixed with 1/4 cup cold water after meat is tender.

8 servings

Vegetable cooking spray
2 pounds lean beef, fat trimmed, cut into 1-inch cubes
3 cups beef broth
1 clove garlic, chopped
1/2 teaspoon pepper
1 teaspoon dried oregano leaves
1 teaspoon dried thyme leaves
2 cups sliced carrots
2 cups sliced celery
1/2 pound small white onions
Salt, to taste

Per Serving
Calories: 215
% Calories from fat: 35
Protein (g): 27.1
Carbohydrates (g): 7.2
Fat (g): 8.4
Saturated fat (g): 2.9
Cholesterol (mg): 77.2
Sodium (mg): 386
Exchanges
Milk: 0.0
Veg.: 1.0
Fruit: 0.0
Bread: 0.0
Meat: 3.5
Fat: 0.0

1. Spray Dutch oven with cooking spray; heat over medium heat until hot. Cook beef until browned, 10 to 12 minutes. Add broth, garlic, pepper, and herbs and heat to boiling; reduce heat and simmer, covered, until beef is tender, 1 to 1 1/2 hours, adding carrots, celery, and onions during last 30 minutes of cooking time. Season to taste with salt.

SLOW-COOKER STEW

A robust beef stew that includes both potatoes and rice. The potatoes add chunky texture and the rice helps thicken the flavorful sauce.

5-6 servings

1 large onion, finely chopped

2 garlic cloves, minced

1 pound boiling potatoes, cut into $^3/_4$-inch cubes

1$^1/_2$ cups coarsely shredded cabbage

1 large carrot, sliced

$^1/_4$ cup long-grain rice

16 ounces beef round, fat trimmed, cut into bite-sized pieces

1$^1/_2$ cups fat-free beef broth

$^3/_4$ cup dry red wine, *or* beef broth

$^1/_4$ cup catsup

2 teaspoons brown sugar

$^1/_2$ tablespoon cider vinegar

1$^1/_2$ teaspoons dried thyme leaves

1 teaspoon chili powder

$^1/_2$ teaspoon dry mustard

$^1/_4$ teaspoon black pepper

Salt, to taste

Per Serving
Calories: 289
% Calories from fat: 18
Protein (g): 21
Carbohydrates (g): 34
Fat (g): 6.0
Saturated fat (g): 1.9
Cholesterol (mg): 51
Sodium (mg): 287
Exchanges
Milk: 0.0
Veg.: 1.5
Fruit: 0.0
Bread: 1.5
Meat: 2.5
Fat: 0.0

1. Combine all ingredients, except salt, in slow cooker and stir well. Cover and cook on High 1 hour. Stir and cook on Low until meat is tender, 6$^1/_2$ to 8 hours. Season to taste with salt.

HARVEST STEW

Summer's harvest yields sun-ripened tomatoes and squash for this sumptuous stew, served over creamy polenta.

8 servings

2 pounds boneless lean beef, fat trimmed, cut into scant 1-inch cubes
1-2 tablespoons vegetable oil
1/2 cup chopped onion
2 tablespoons flour
1 cup reduced-sodium fat-free beef broth
4 medium tomatoes, chopped
3/4 teaspoon dried marjoram leaves
3/4 teaspoon dried savory leaves
1/4 teaspoon dried thyme leaves
3 cups cubed butternut, *or* Hubbard, squash
3 medium zucchini, cubed
Salt and pepper, to taste
6 cups Polenta (double recipe) (see p. 811)

Per Serving
Calories: 284
% Calories from fat: 20
Protein (gm): 25.2
Carbohydrate (gm): 32.4
Fat (gm): 6.6
Saturated fat (gm): 1.7
Cholesterol (mg): 55
Sodium (mg): 84
Exchanges
Milk: 0.0
Veg.: 1.0
Fruit: 0.0
Bread: 1.5
Meat: 3.0
Fat: 0.0

1. Cook beef in oil in Dutch oven over medium heat until browned, about 5 minutes; add onion and cook until tender, about 5 minutes. Add flour and cook 1 minute longer.

2. Add beef broth, tomatoes, and herbs; heat to boiling. Reduce heat and simmer, covered, until beef is tender, about 1 hour, adding squash and zucchini during last 15 minutes of cooking time. Season to taste with salt and pepper. Serve over Polenta.

ORANGE-SCENTED BEEF STEW

Orange and tomato juices combine to give this stew a unique flavor accent.

6 servings

1¹/₂ pounds extra-lean beef cubes, fat trimmed

1¹/₂ tablespoons canola oil

³/₄ cup reduced-sodium fat-free beef broth, divided

1 cup low-sodium tomato juice

1 cup orange juice

Grated rind of 1 orange

2 teaspoons cornstarch

Salt and pepper, to taste

1¹/₂ cups cooked spinach noodles, warm

Per Serving
Calories: 239
% Calories from fat: 30
Protein (gm): 23.9
Carbohydrate (gm): 17.5
Fat (gm): 7.8
Saturated fat (gm): 1.7
Cholesterol (mg): 68.2
Sodium (mg): 74
Exchanges
Milk: 0.0
Veg.: 0.0
Fruit: 0.0
Bread: 1.0
Meat: 3.0
Fat: 0.0

1. Brown beef in oil in Dutch oven. Add ¹/₂ cup beef broth, tomato juice, and orange juice; heat to boiling. Reduce heat and simmer, covered, until beef is tender, about 1 hour.

2. Heat stew to boiling and stir in orange rind; stir in combined cornstarch and remaining ¹/₄ cup beef broth. Boil, stirring, until thickened, 1 to 2 minutes. Season to taste with salt and pepper. Serve over spinach noodles.

BEEF BOURGUIGNON

Try this French-style stew for special occasions, when ordinary beef stew is not quite fancy enough!

6 servings

1¹/₂ pounds beef eye of round steak, fat trimmed, cut into scant 1¹/₂-inch cubes

¹/₄ cup all-purpose flour

1 tablespoon olive, *or* vegetable, oil

1 cup Burgundy wine, *or* reduced-sodium beef broth

1 cup water

1¹/₂ cups peeled pearl onions

3 cups cubed, *or* julienned, carrots

Per Serving
Calories: 507
% Calories from fat: 16
Protein (g): 34.9
Carbohydrates (g): 65
Fat (g): 8.8
Saturated fat (g): 2.1
Cholesterol (mg): 120.2
Sodium (mg): 288
Exchanges
Milk: 0.0
Veg.: 2.0
Fruit: 0.0
Bread: 4.0
Meat: 3.0
Fat: 0.0

8 ounces small whole mushrooms
1 teaspoon dried marjoram leaves
1 teaspoon dried thyme leaves
2 bay leaves
$^1/_2$ teaspoon salt
$^1/_4$ teaspoon pepper
16 ounces egg noodles, cooked, warm

1. Coat beef cubes with flour; saute in oil in Dutch oven until browned on all sides, about 10 minutes. Add wine and water; heat to boiling.

2. Transfer Dutch oven to oven and bake, covered, at 350 degrees until beef is very tender, about 2 hours. Add vegetables, herbs, salt, and pepper during last 30 minutes of baking time. Discard bay leaves. Serve over noodles.

BOEUF À LA BOURGUIGNON

Serve this delicious stew over noodles or rice, with a crisp green salad on the side.

8 servings

Vegetable cooking spray
2 pounds lean beef stew meat
1$^1/_2$ cups chopped onions
12 medium mushrooms, sliced
3 tablespoons flour
1 cup Burgundy, *or* other red wine
1 cup fat-free beef broth
2 tablespoons dry sherry, optional
1 tablespoon tomato paste
1 teaspoon meat glaze
   Herb bouquet (sprig parsley, 1 teaspoon thyme, 1 teaspoon rosemary, 1 teaspoon tarragon in a cheesecloth bag)
$^1/_2$ cup chopped fresh parsley
   Salt and pepper, to taste

Per Serving
Calories: 230
% Calories from fat: 23
Protein (gm): 30.4
Carbohydrate (gm): 7.4
Fat (gm): 5.6
Saturated fat (gm): 2
Cholesterol (mg): 70.9
Sodium (mg): 98
Exchanges
Milk: 0.0
Veg.: 1.0
Fruit: 0.0
Bread: 0.0
Meat: 4.0
Fat: 0.0

1. Spray Dutch oven with cooking spray; heat over medium heat until hot. Saute beef until browned, 8 to 10 minutes. Remove and reserve.

2. Saute onions and mushrooms in Dutch oven until tender, about 5 minutes. Sprinkle with flour and cook 2 minutes longer. Stir in reserved beef and remaining ingredients, except parsley, salt, and pepper. Heat to boiling; reduce heat and simmer, covered, until beef is tender, about 1¹/₄ hours. Discard herb bouquet; stir in parsley and season to taste with salt and pepper.

WINE-BRAISED BEEF STEW

The slow simmering gives this dish a rich flavor. A good-quality Chianti works well in this traditional Italian recipe.

6 servings

- 1¹/₂ pounds boneless beef round steak, fat trimmed, cubed
- 2 tablespoons flour
- 1-2 tablespoons olive oil
- 1 large onion, chopped
- 1 teaspoon minced garlic
- 2 cups sliced mushrooms
- 1 cup reduced-sodium fat-free beef broth
- 1 can (15 ounces) reduced-sodium tomato sauce
- 1 cup dry red wine, *or* beef broth
- ¹/₂ teaspoon dry mustard
- 1 teaspoon dried thyme leaves
- 2 large bay leaves
- ¹/₈ teaspoon celery seeds
- 2 large ribs celery, sliced
- 10 baby carrots
- 5 medium potatoes, halved
  Salt and pepper, to taste

Per Serving
Calories: 366
% Calories from fat: 18
Protein (g): 31.2
Carbohydrates (g): 36.9
Fat (g): 7.4
Saturated fat (g): 2.2
Cholesterol (mg): 55.9
Sodium (mg): 115
Exchanges
Milk: 0.0
Veg.: 2.0
Fruit: 0.0
Bread: 2.0
Meat: 3.0
Fat: 0.0

1. Toss beef with flour in large shallow baking pan; cook in oil in Dutch oven over medium heat until browned, 8 to 10 minutes. Add onion, garlic, and mushrooms; cook until onion is tender, about 5 minutes.

2. Add broth, tomato sauce, wine, dry mustard, and herbs and heat to boiling; transfer Dutch oven to oven and bake at 350 degrees, covered, until beef is tender, 1 to 1½ hours, adding celery, carrots, and potatoes during last 30 minutes. Discard bay leaves; season to taste with salt and pepper.

BEEF STEW DA VINCI

A bounty of Italian flavors, served over linguine!

4 servings

Vegetable cooking spray
1¼ pounds lean, boneless beef round steak, fat trimmed, cut into 1-inch cubes
1 cup chopped onion
1 cup chopped green bell peppers
1 clove garlic, minced
¼ cup dried shallots
1 can (14½ ounces) whole tomatoes, undrained, chopped
1 teaspoon beef bouillon crystals
1 teaspoon dried oregano leaves
½ teaspoon dried basil leaves
1 teaspoon garlic powder
½ cup sliced mushrooms
Salt, to taste
2 cups cooked linguine, warm
¼ cup chopped Italian parsley
¼ cup grated Parmesan cheese

Per Serving
Calories: 393
% Calories from fat: 17
Protein (gm): 36.1
Carbohydrate (gm): 46.2
Fat (gm): 7.7
Saturated fat (gm): 2.6
Cholesterol (mg): 72.6
Sodium (mg): 596
Exchanges
Milk: 0.0
Veg.: 1.0
Fruit: 0.0
Bread: 2.0
Meat: 4.0
Fat: 0.0

1. Spray large skillet with cooking spray; heat over medium heat until hot. Saute beef, onion, bell peppers, garlic, and shallots until meat is browned, about 10 minutes.

2. Add remaining ingredients, except salt, linguine, parsley, and Parmesan cheese, and simmer, covered, until meat is tender, about 1 hour. Simmer, uncovered, 15 minutes longer. Season to taste with salt. Serve over linguine; sprinkle with parsley and Parmesan cheese.

HOME-STYLE STEAK STEW

Here's round steak in an easy tomato sauce. To complete the meal, add a green vegetable such as broccoli florets or sliced zucchini.

4 servings

- 12 ounces round steak, fat trimmed, cut into thin strips
- Salt and pepper, to taste
- Vegetable cooking spray
- 1 large onion, chopped
- 2 garlic cloves, minced
- 2 teaspoons olive oil
- 1 can (14^1/$_2$ ounces) reduced-sodium tomatoes, undrained, coarsely chopped
- 1 can (8 ounces) reduced-sodium tomato sauce
- ^{1}/$_4$ cup reduced-sodium fat-free beef broth
- 1 teaspoon dried basil leaves
- ^{1}/$_4$ teaspoon dried thyme leaves
- 8 ounces spaghetti, cooked, warm

Per Serving
Calories: 396
% Calories from fat: 15
Protein (g): 26.1
Carbohydrates (g): 57.6
Fat (g): 6.4
Saturated fat (g): 1.5
Cholesterol (mg): 41
Sodium (mg): 94
Exchanges
Milk: 0.0
Veg.: 3.0
Fruit: 0.0
Bread: 3.0
Meat: 2.0
Fat: 0.0

1. Sprinkle round steak lightly with salt and pepper. Spray large skillet with cooking spray; heat over medium heat until hot. Cook meat until browned, about 8 minutes; remove from skillet and reserve.

2. Saute onion and garlic in oil until tender, about 5 minutes. Add reserved meat and remaining ingredients, except spaghetti, and heat to boiling. Reduce heat and simmer, covered, until meat is tender, 45 to 60 minutes. Simmer, uncovered, until sauce is thickened, about 5 minutes; season to taste with salt and pepper. Serve over spaghetti.

BEEF STEW WITH ROSEMARY

For a tasty variation on a popular theme, try this stew, flavored with a kiss of rosemary, thyme, and bay.

5-6 servings

1	cup finely chopped onion
1	large garlic clove, minced
2	teaspoons olive oil
16	ounces lean stew beef, fat trimmed, cut into bite-sized pieces
1¹/2	tablespoons flour
1³/4	cups fat-free chicken broth
¹/2	cup dry sherry, *or* fat-free chicken broth
1	can (15 ounces) tomato sauce
1	teaspoon dried rosemary leaves
¹/4	teaspoon dried thyme leaves
1	bay leaf
1	teaspoon sugar
2	large carrots, sliced
2	ribs celery, sliced
3	cups cut green beans
	Salt and pepper, to taste
1¹/2	cups white rice, cooked, warm

Per Serving
Calories: 395
% Calories from fat: 13
Protein (g): 25.6
Carbohydrates (g): 54.9
Fat (g): 5.8
Saturated fat (g): 1.7
Cholesterol (mg): 47.3
Sodium (mg): 534
Exchanges
Milk: 0.0
Veg.: 3.0
Fruit: 0.0
Bread: 3.0
Meat: 2.0
Fat: 0.0

1. Saute onion and garlic in oil in Dutch oven until onion is tender, about 5 minutes; stir in meat and cook until lightly browned, about 5 minutes. Sprinkle with flour and cook 2 minutes longer.

2. Add broth, sherry, tomato sauce, herbs, and sugar; heat to boiling. Reduce heat and simmer, covered, until meat is tender, 1 to 1¹/2 hours, adding carrots, celery, and green beans during last 30 minutes. Simmer, uncovered, until sauce thickens, about 15 minutes. Discard bay leaf; season to taste with salt and pepper; serve over rice.

STEAK AND SWEET POTATO STEW

Apples give this hearty stew a touch of sweetness. Enjoy it in fall when apples are at their peak.

4 servings

1 pound boneless beef round steak, fat trimmed, cut into ³/₄-inch cubes

¹/₄ cup all-purpose flour

1 large onion, cut into thin wedges

1 teaspoon olive oil

1³/₄ cups reduced-sodium fat-free beef broth

1¹/₄ pounds sweet potatoes, peeled, cut into ¹/₂-inch cubes

1 teaspoon dried savory leaves

¹/₄ teaspoon lemon pepper ·

1 pound McIntosh apples, unpeeled, cut into 1-inch cubes

1¹/₂ cups frozen peas

Salt and pepper, to taste

Per Serving
Calories: 442
% Calories from fat: 13
Protein (g): 34.2
Carbohydrates (g): 62.3
Fat (g): 6.7
Saturated fat (g): 2.1
Cholesterol (mg): 55.9
Sodium (mg): 197
Exchanges
Milk: 0.0
Veg.: 0.0
Fruit: 1.0
Bread: 3.0
Meat: 3.0
Fat: 0.0

1. Toss beef with flour to coat well; cook beef and onion in olive oil in large saucepan until beef is browned, about 8 minutes. Add broth and heat to boiling; reduce heat and simmer, covered, until meat is tender, 45 to 60 minutes, adding sweet potatoes, savory, and lemon pepper during last 20 minutes of cooking.

2. Stir in apples and peas; simmer until apples are crisp-tender, about 5 minutes. Season to taste with salt and pepper.

BEEF STROGANOFF

A favorite for buffet entertaining, this dish enjoys well-deserved popularity.

4 servings

1 pound beef eye of round, *or* sirloin steak, fat trimmed, cut into 1¹/2 x ¹/2-inch strips
1 tablespoon margarine
3 cups sliced mushrooms
¹/2 cup sliced onion
2 cloves garlic, minced
2 tablespoons flour
1¹/2 cups reduced-sodium beef broth
1 teaspoon Dijon-style mustard
¹/4 teaspoon dried thyme leaves
¹/2 cup fat-free sour cream
   Salt and pepper, to taste
3 cups cooked no-yolk noodles, warm
   Finely chopped parsley leaves, as garnish

Per Serving
Calories: 423
% Calories from fat: 21
Protein (g): 39
Carbohydrates (g): 45.1
Fat (g): 10
Saturated fat (g): 2.2
Cholesterol (mg): 64
Sodium (mg): 167
Exchanges
Milk: 0.0
Veg.: 1.0
Fruit: 0.0
Bread: 2.5
Meat: 4.0
Fat: 0.0

1. Saute beef in margarine in large skillet until browned on all sides, about 5 minutes; remove from pan. Add mushrooms, onion, and garlic; saute until tender, 5 to 8 minutes. Stir in flour and cook, stirring, 1 to 2 minutes longer.

2. Add beef, beef broth, mustard, and thyme. Heat to boiling; reduce heat and simmer, covered, until beef is tender, 45 to 60 minutes. Reduce heat to low; stir in sour cream and cook 2 to 3 minutes. Season to taste with salt and pepper. Serve over warm noodles; sprinkle with parsley.

CREAMY BEEF STROGANOFF WITH RICE

Fat-free sour cream imparts an incredibly rich and creamy taste and texture to this version.

5-7 servings

Vegetable cooking spray
1 pound beef top round, fat trimmed, cut into 2-inch strips
1 large onion, finely chopped
8 ounces fresh mushrooms, sliced
2 large garlic cloves, minced
2 teaspoons margarine
1 tablespoon flour
2 cups fat-free beef broth
1/4 cup red Burgundy wine, optional
3 tablespoons tomato paste
2 teaspoons sugar
1 teaspoon dried thyme leaves
1 teaspoon prepared horseradish
1 bay leaf
3/4 cup fat-free sour cream
Salt and pepper, to taste
1 1/2 cups uncooked long-grain white rice, cooked, warm
Parsley sprigs, as garnish

Per Serving
Calories: 336
% Calories from fat: 16
Protein (g): 24
Carbohydrates (g): 44
Fat (g): 6
Saturated fat (g): 2
Cholesterol (mg): 55
Sodium (mg): 242
Exchanges
Milk: 0.0
Veg.: 1.0
Fruit: 0.0
Bread: 2.5
Meat: 2.5
Fat: 0.0

1. Spray large skillet with cooking spray; heat over medium heat until hot. Cook meat until browned, about 10 minutes; remove meat and reserve.

2. Saute onion, mushrooms, and garlic in margarine in large skillet until tender, about 8 minutes; sprinkle with flour and cook 1 minute longer. Add reserved meat and remaining ingredients, except sour cream, salt, pepper, rice, and parsley; heat to boiling. Reduce heat and simmer, covered, until meat is tender, about 45 minutes; stir in sour cream and cook 3 to 4 minutes longer. Discard bay leaf; season to taste with salt and pepper. Serve over rice; garnish with parsley sprigs.

HUNGARIAN-STYLE BEEF STEW

Serve this rich-tasting stew with noodles to soak up the delicious sauce.

5-6 servings

Vegetable cooking spray

16 ounces beef top round steak, fat trimmed, cut into small strips

1 cup finely chopped onion

1 large garlic clove, minced

1 1/2 cups reduced-sodium fat-free beef broth

1/2 cup dry red wine, *or* reduced-sodium fat-free beef broth

1 can (15 ounces) tomato sauce

1 teaspoon dried thyme leaves

1 teaspoon paprika

1 bay leaf

1/4 teaspoon dry mustard

2 large carrots, sliced

2 ribs celery, sliced

1 pound boiling potatoes, cut into 3/4-inch cubes

1/4 teaspoon black pepper

1/2 cup fat-free sour cream

Salt, to taste

Per Serving
Calories: 217
% Calories from fat: 12
Protein (g): 19.1
Carbohydrates (g): 26.9
Fat (g): 2.9
Saturated fat (g): 0.9
Cholesterol (mg): 36.5
Sodium (mg): 525
Exchanges
Milk: 0.0
Veg.: 1.0
Fruit: 0.0
Bread: 1.0
Meat: 2.0
Fat: 0.0

1. Spray Dutch oven with cooking spray; heat over medium heat until hot. Saute beef, onion, and garlic until beef is browned, about 10 minutes.

2. Stir in broth, wine, tomato sauce, herbs, and dry mustard and heat to boiling; reduce heat and simmer, covered, until meat and vegetables are tender, about 45 to 60 minutes, adding vegetables during last 20 minutes. Stir in pepper and sour cream and cook 3 to 4 minutes. Discard bay leaf; season to taste with salt.

HUNGARIAN GOULASH

All the traditional flavors of goulash combine in an easy-to-assemble baked stew.

6 servings

2 pounds beef round steak, fat trimmed, cut into 1/2-inch cubes
1 medium onion, finely chopped
1 teaspoon minced garlic
2 tablespoons flour
1 1/2 teaspoons paprika
1/4 teaspoon dried thyme leaves
1 bay leaf
1 can (14 1/2 ounces) diced tomatoes, undrained
1 container (8 ounces) fat-free sour cream
Salt and pepper, to taste
12 ounces egg, *or* no yolk, wide noodles, cooked, warm

Per Serving
Calories: 471
% Calories from fat: 17
Protein (g): 44.6
Carbohydrates (g): 50.5
Fat (g): 8.7
Saturated fat (g): 2.9
Cholesterol (mg): 123.5
Sodium (mg): 367
Exchanges
Milk: 0.0
Veg.: 1.0
Fruit: 0.0
Bread: 3.0
Meat: 4.0
Fat: 0.0

1. Combine beef, onion, and garlic in small Dutch oven; sprinkle with flour, paprika, and thyme and toss to coat. Stir in bay leaf and tomatoes and liquid; heat to boiling.

2. Transfer to oven and bake, covered, at 325 degrees until beef is tender, about 1 1/2 hours. Stir in sour cream and bake, uncovered, until hot through, about 10 minutes. Discard bay leaf; season to taste with salt and pepper. Serve over noodles.

Variation:
Triple Threat Goulash—Make recipe as above, using 3/4 pound each: cubed lean beef, pork, and veal in place of the beef round steak. Add 1 teaspoon caraway seeds and 1/2 teaspoon dried dill weed in Step 1. Add 8 ounces sliced mushrooms with the sour cream in Step 2.

MIDDLE EASTERN BEEF AND BEAN HOT POT

If you think of beans and rice as primarily a Latin American combination, think again. Here's another delicious, and very different, interpretation.

6 servings

1 cup dry Great Northern beans
16 ounces lean stew beef, fat trimmed, cut into bite-sized pieces
2 cups chopped onions
2 large garlic cloves, minced
2 teaspoons olive oil
1¼ quarts fat-free beef broth
1 teaspoon dried thyme leaves
¼ teaspoon ground cinnamon
2 bay leaves
¼ teaspoon black pepper
1¼ cups long-grain white rice
1½ cups peeled, diced fresh tomatoes
Salt and pepper, to taste
Parsley sprigs, as garnish

Per Serving
Calories: 427
% Calories from fat: 17
Protein (g): 35
Carbohydrates (g): 52
Fat (g): 8.1
Saturated fat (g): 4.4
Cholesterol (mg): 71
Sodium (mg): 595
Exchanges
Milk: 0.0
Veg.: 2.0
Fruit: 0.0
Bread: 3.0
Meat: 3.0
Fat: 0.0

1. Cover beans with 2 inches water in Dutch oven and heat to boiling. Boil 2 minutes; remove from heat and let stand, covered, 1 hour. Drain.

2. Cook beef, onions, and garlic in oil in Dutch oven over medium heat until beef is browned, about 10 minutes; add beans and remaining ingredients, except rice, tomatoes, salt, pepper, and parsley; heat to boiling. Reduce heat and simmer, covered, until meat is almost tender, about 1 hour.

3. Add rice and tomatoes; heat to boiling. Reduce heat and simmer, covered, until rice is tender, about 20 minutes. Discard bay leaves; season to taste with salt and pepper. Garnish with parsley sprigs.

CURRIED BEEF STEW WITH CHIVE DUMPLINGS

Part of the beef in this aromatic stew is coarsely chopped, giving the stew an extra-rich texture.

8 servings

2 pounds boneless lean beef, fat trimmed
1-2 tablespoons vegetable oil
1¹/₂ cups chopped onions
3 tablespoons flour
1¹/₂ teaspoons curry powder
2 cups reduced-sodium beef broth
1 large tomato, coarsely chopped
1 bay leaf
1 package (10 ounces) frozen peas
Salt and pepper, to taste
Chive Dumplings (recipe follows)

Per Serving
Calories: 297
% Calories from fat: 22
Protein (gm): 27.1
Carbohydrate (gm): 29.4
Fat (gm): 7.3
Saturated fat (gm): 1.9
Cholesterol (mg): 55.3
Sodium (mg): 416
Exchanges
Milk: 0.0
Veg.: 0.0
Fruit: 0.0
Bread: 2.0
Meat: 3.0
Fat: 0.0

1. Cut 1 pound beef into scant 1-inch cubes; coarsely chop remaining 1 pound beef. Cook beef in oil in Dutch oven over medium heat until browned, about 5 minutes; add onions and cook until tender, 5 to 8 minutes. Stir in flour and curry and cook 1 minute longer.

2. Add beef broth, tomato, and bay leaf and heat to boiling; reduce heat and simmer, covered, until beef is tender, about 1 hour, adding peas during last 10 minutes of cooking time. Discard bay leaf; season to taste with salt and pepper.

3. Heat stew to boiling; drop Chive Dumpling dough onto top of stew. Cook, uncovered, 10 minutes; cook, covered, 10 minutes longer or until dumplings are dry.

Chive Dumplings

1²/₃ cups reduced-fat all-purpose baking mix
2 tablespoons finely chopped chives
¹/₄-¹/₂ teaspoon curry powder
²/₃ cup fat-free milk

1. Combine baking mix, chives, and curry powder in bowl; mix in milk, forming a soft dough.

BEEF AND ANCHO CHILI STEW

This stew has lots of delicious sauce, so serve with crusty warm rolls, warm tortillas, or over rice. Vary the number of ancho chilies according to your taste.

8 servings

4-6   ancho chilies, stems, seeds, and veins discarded
2   cups boiling water
4   medium tomatoes, cut into wedges
    Vegetable cooking spray
2   pounds boneless beef eye of round, fat trimmed, cut into ³/₄-inch cubes
1   large onion, chopped
2   cloves garlic, minced
1   teaspoon minced serrano, *or* jalapeño, chili
1   teaspoon dried oregano leaves
1   teaspoon crushed cumin seeds
2   tablespoons flour
    Salt and pepper, to taste

Per Serving
Calories: 159
% Calories from fat: 23
Protein (g): 22.1
Carbohydrates (g): 8.3
Fat (g): 4
Saturated fat (g): 1.3
Cholesterol (mg): 54.7
Sodium (mg): 56
Exchanges
Milk: 0.0
Veg.: 1.0
Fruit: 0.0
Bread: 0.0
Meat: 2.5
Fat: 0.0

1. Place ancho chilies in bowl; pour boiling water over. Let stand until chilies are softened, about 10 minutes. Process chilies with water and tomatoes in food processor or blender until smooth.

2. Spray large saucepan with cooking spray; heat over medium heat until hot. Cook beef until browned on all sides, about 5 minutes. Add onion, garlic, serrano chili, and herbs and cook until onion is tender, about 5 minutes. Stir in flour; cook over medium heat 1 to 2 minutes.

3. Add ancho chili mixture to saucepan; heat to boiling. Reduce heat and simmer, covered, until beef is tender, about 45 minutes. Season to taste with salt and pepper. Serve in shallow bowls.

SLOW-COOKER BARBECUED BEEF AND BEAN STEW

If you love a meal that's both easy and spicy, this barbecued beef and bean dinner is for you.

6-7 servings

1¹/₂ cups finely chopped onion

1 can (8 ounces) tomato sauce

¹/₂ cup mild, *or* medium, salsa

2 tablespoons cider vinegar

1¹/₂ tablespoons brown sugar

1 tablespoon chili powder

2 teaspoons Worcestershire sauce

¹/₄ teaspoon black pepper

16 ounces beef round, fat trimmed, cut into narrow strips

2 garlic cloves, minced

6 cups cooked kidney beans, *or* 3 cans (16 ounces each) kidney beans, drained
Salt, to taste

Per Serving
Calories: 363
% Calories from fat: 14
Protein (g): 35
Carbohydrates (g): 44
Fat (g): 5.8
Saturated fat (g): 1.8
Cholesterol (mg): 63
Sodium (mg): 398
Exchanges
Milk: 0.0
Veg.: 1.0
Fruit: 0.0
Bread: 2.5
Meat: 3.0
Fat: 0.0

1. Combine all ingredients, except salt, in slow cooker; cover, and cook on High 1 hour. Reduce heat to Low and cook 5 to 6 hours or until beef is tender. Season to taste with salt.

FIVE-SPICE BEEF STEW

A simple-to-make stew with lots of Asian-style zing—thanks to five-spice powder and Chinese chili sauce. Bean thread noodles, sometimes known as cellophane or glass noodles, can be found in the ethnic foods section of most supermarkets.

4 servings

1 pound boneless beef round steak, fat trimmed, cut into 1-inch strips
1 cup orange juice
1 cup reduced-sodium fat-free beef broth
1 tablespoon low-sodium teriyaki sauce
1¼ teaspoons five-spice powder
1 onion, cut into thin wedges
4 ounces bean thread noodles
1 red bell pepper, thinly sliced
1 teaspoon Chinese chili sauce with garlic
2 cups coarsely sliced Napa cabbage

Per Serving
Calories: 321
% Calories from fat: 14
Protein (g): 28.8
Carbohydrates (g): 39.3
Fat (g): 5
Saturated fat (g): 1.8
Cholesterol (mg): 55.9
Sodium (mg): 208
Exchanges
Milk: 0.0
Veg.: 1.0
Fruit: 0.0
Bread: 2.0
Meat: 3.0
Fat: 0.0

1. Heat beef, orange juice, broth, teriyaki sauce, five-spice powder, and onion to boiling in large saucepan. Reduce heat and simmer, covered, until beef is tender, about 30 minutes.

2. Soak bean threads in hot water to cover in large bowl for 15 minutes; drain.

3. Stir bell pepper, chili sauce, and cabbage into beef mixture; cook for 3 minutes. Stir noodles into beef mixture; cook 2 minutes longer.

ASIAN BEEF STEW WITH SESAME NOODLES

This ginger-spiked stew can be prepared in a large, covered wok, if you prefer.

8 servings

2 pounds boneless lean beef, cut into 1-inch cubes

1-2 tablespoons peanut, *or* vegetable, oil

1¹/₂ cups water

2 thin slices gingerroot

2 cloves garlic, halved

2 green onions and tops, cut into 1-inch pieces

2-4 tablespoons reduced-sodium soy sauce

1 tablespoon sugar

1 tablespoon cornstarch

2 tablespoons dry sherry, *or* water

Salt and pepper, to taste

Sesame Noodles (recipe follows)

1 tablespoon sesame seeds, toasted

Finely chopped cilantro, as garnish

Per Serving
Calories: 295
% Calories from fat: 23
Protein (gm): 26.8
Carbohydrate (gm): 27.6
Fat (gm): 7.3
Saturated fat (gm): 1.7
Cholesterol (mg): 57.1
Sodium (mg): 518
Exchanges
Milk: 0.0
Veg.: 0.0
Fruit: 0.0
Bread: 2.0
Meat: 3.0
Fat: 0.0

1. Cook beef in peanut oil in large saucepan over medium heat until browned. Add water, gingerroot, garlic, green onions, soy sauce, and sugar; heat to boiling. Reduce heat and simmer, covered, until beef is tender, about 45 minutes.

2. Heat stew to boiling; stir in combined cornstarch and sherry. Boil, stirring, until thickened, about 1 minute. Season to taste with salt and pepper. Serve over Sesame Noodles; sprinkle with sesame seeds and cilantro.

Sesame Noodles

makes 8 servings

1-2 packages (12 ounces each) Asian noodles, *or* any thin noodles, cooked, warm

2-4 teaspoons reduced-sodium soy sauce

2 teaspoons oriental sesame oil

2 green onions and tops, thinly sliced

1. Toss warm noodles with remaining ingredients.

CHUCK WAGON STEW WITH DILL DUMPLINGS

One of the heartiest stews you can rustle up!

6 servings

1 1/2 pounds lean boneless beef round steak, fat trimmed, cut into 3/4-inch cubes
Flour

1/2 cup chopped onion

1 tablespoon vegetable oil

1 can (16 ounces) reduced-sodium whole tomatoes, undrained, coarsely chopped

3/4 cup reduced-sodium fat-free beef broth

3 small potatoes, unpeeled, cut into 1-inch pieces

3 large carrots, cut into 1-inch pieces

1 can (15 ounces) red kidney beans, rinsed, drained

2-3 teaspoons very-low-sodium Worcestershire sauce
Salt and pepper, to taste

1/4 cup all-purpose flour

1/2 cup cold water
Dill Dumplings (recipe follows)

Per Serving
Calories: 437
% Calories from fat: 17
Protein (gm): 30.8
Carbohydrate (gm): 59
Fat (gm): 8.4
Saturated fat (gm): 2.1
Cholesterol (mg): 55.3
Sodium (mg): 693
Exchanges
Milk: 0.0
Veg.: 2.0
Fruit: 0.0
Bread: 3.0
Meat: 3.0
Fat: 0.0

1. Coat beef lightly with flour. Saute beef and onion in oil in large saucepan until beef is browned, 5 to 8 minutes. Add tomatoes and liquid and broth; heat to boiling. Reduce heat and simmer, covered, until beef is tender, about 45 minutes.

2. Add potatoes, carrots, and beans; simmer, covered, until tender, 10 to 15 minutes. Season to taste with Worcestershire sauce, salt, and pepper.

3. Heat stew to boiling; stir in combined 1/4 cup flour and water. Boil, stirring, until thickened, about 1 minute.

4. Drop Dill Dumpling dough by spoonfuls onto top of stew. Simmer, uncovered, 10 minutes; simmer, covered, until dumplings are dry, about 10 minutes longer.

Dill Dumplings

   1¹/₂ cups reduced-fat all-purpose baking mix
    2 teaspoons dried dill weed
  ¹/₂ cup fat-free milk

1. Mix baking mix, dill weed, and milk to form soft dough.

MEATBALL AND PASTA STEW

Onion-and-cheese-seasoned meatballs combine with vegetables and tricolor pasta for a delectable one-dish dinner on the double.

4 servings

    8 ounces ground beef eye of round
    1 egg white, lightly beaten
  ¹/₂ cup quick oats
    3 tablespoons dried minced onions, divided
    2 teaspoons Italian seasoning, divided
  ¹/₂ cup grated Romano cheese
    1 can (15 ounces) plum tomatoes, undrained, chopped
    3 cans (14 ounces each) fat-free beef broth
    4 ounces tri-color corkscrew pasta
    2 cups small broccoli florets
      Salt and pepper, to taste

Per Serving
Calories: 335
% Calories from fat: 19
Protein (gm): 29.9
Carbohydrate (gm): 39.1
Fat (gm): 7.1
Saturated fat (gm): 3.3
Cholesterol (mg): 42.2
Sodium (mg): 577
Exchanges
Milk: 0.0
Veg.: 2.0
Fruit: 0.0
Bread: 2.0
Meat: 3.0
Fat: 0.0

1. Combine beef, egg white, oats, 1 tablespoon onions, ¹/₂ teaspoon Italian seasoning, and Romano cheese in a bowl. Shape mixture into 16 meatballs. Cook meatballs in Dutch oven until brown on all sides, about 10 minutes.

2. Stir in tomatoes and liquid, broth, and remaining 2 tablespoons onions and 1¹/₂ teaspoons Italian seasoning and heat to boiling. Add pasta and broccoli; reduce heat and simmer, uncovered, 10 minutes or until pasta is al dente. Season to taste with salt and pepper.

HEARTY MEATBALL 'N VEGGIE STEW

For flavor variation in the Hearty Meatballs, substitute 8 ounces low-fat Italian sausage for 8 ounces of the ground beef.

6 servings

Vegetable cooking spray
Hearty Meatballs (recipe follows)
1¹/2 cups water, *or* reduced-sodium beef broth
1 can (28 ounces) reduced-sodium tomatoes, undrained, coarsely chopped
1 teaspoon Italian seasoning
¹/2 teaspoon dried rosemary leaves
3 medium zucchini, cubed
3 medium carrots, cut into ¹/2-inch slices
¹/2 cup frozen peas
2 tablespoons cornstarch
¹/4 cup cold water
Salt and pepper, to taste
12 ounces yolk-free noodles, *or* fettuccine, cooked, warm

Per Serving
Calories: 554
% Calories from fat: 26
Protein (gm): 35.8
Carbohydrate (gm): 65.3
Fat (gm): 16
Saturated fat (gm): 5.8
Cholesterol (mg): 105.8
Sodium (mg): 536
Exchanges
Milk: 0.0
Veg.: 2.0
Fruit: 0.0
Bread: 4.0
Meat: 3.0
Fat: 1.0

1. Spray Dutch oven with cooking spray; heat over medium heat until hot. Add Hearty Meatballs and cook over medium-low to medium heat until browned, 5 to 8 minutes.

2. Add water, tomatoes and liquid, and herbs; heat to boiling. Reduce heat and simmer, covered, 30 minutes, adding zucchini, carrots, and peas during last 15 minutes of cooking time.

3. Heat stew to boiling; stir in combined cornstarch and cold water. Boil, stirring, until stew is thickened, about 1 minute. Season to taste with salt and pepper. Serve stew over noodles.

Hearty Meatballs

makes 18

1¹/2 pounds lean ground beef
¹/3 cup finely chopped onion
1 egg
¹/2 cup dry unseasoned bread crumbs
2 cloves garlic, minced

1-2 teaspoons beef-flavor bouillon crystals
$^1/_2$ teaspoon salt
$^1/_4$ teaspoon pepper

1. Mix all ingredients; shape mixture into 18 meatballs.

PORK TENDERLOIN STEW WITH GREMOLATA

Gremolata is a refreshing blend of garlic, lemon peel, and parsley that is often used to flavor Italian dishes. Here it enlivens a stew of pork, potatoes, and tomatoes.

4 servings

1 pound pork tenderloin, fat trimmed, cut into 1-inch pieces
1 teaspoon olive oil
4 shallots, thinly sliced
1 cup reduced-sodium fat-free beef broth
2 medium potatoes, cut into $^1/_2$-inch cubes
1 can (15 ounces) diced tomatoes, undrained
Salt and pepper, to taste
Gremolata (recipe follows)

Per Serving
Calories: 289
% Calories from fat: 17
Protein (g): 28.6
Carbohydrates (g): 31.2
Fat (g): 5.5
Saturated fat (g): 1.6
Cholesterol (mg): 65.7
Sodium (mg): 523
Exchanges
Milk: 0.0
Veg.: 0.0
Fruit: 0.0
Bread: 2.0
Meat: 3.0
Fat: 0.0

1. Cook pork in oil in large saucepan over medium heat until lightly browned, 5 to 8 minutes. Add shallots and saute until shallots are tender, 2 to 3 minutes. Stir in broth and heat to boiling; reduce heat and simmer, covered, 10 minutes.

2. Add potatoes and tomatoes and liquid; simmer, covered, until potatoes are tender, about 15 minutes. Season to taste with salt and pepper. Spoon stew into bowls; sprinkle with Gremolata.

Gremolata

makes about $^1/_2$ cup

1 cup packed parsley sprigs
1-2 tablespoons grated lemon rind
4 large cloves garlic, minced

1. Process all ingredients in food processor until finely minced. Refrigerate until ready to use.

CANTONESE PORK STEW

Strips of pork are stewed in an oriental-flavored sauce.

6 servings

- 1¹/2   pounds pork steak, ¹/2 inch thick, fat trimmed, cut into strips
- 2   tablespoons vegetable oil
- 1   large onion, sliced
- 1   red bell pepper, cut into strips
- 1   cup sliced mushrooms
- 1   can (8 ounces) tomato sauce
- 3   tablespoons brown sugar
- 1¹/2   tablespoons cider vinegar
- 2   teaspoons Worcestershire sauce
- 1   tablespoon dry sherry, optional
- 3   cups cooked rice, warm

Per Serving
Calories: 384
% Calories from fat: 29
Protein (gm): 30.9
Carbohydrate (gm): 36
Fat (gm): 12.1
Saturated fat (gm): 3.1
Cholesterol (mg): 64.4
Sodium (mg): 321
Exchanges
Milk: 0.0
Veg.: 1.0
Fruit: 0.0
Bread: 2.0
Meat: 4.0
Fat: 0.0

1. Cook pork in oil in large skillet until browned, 5 to 8 minutes; stir in onion, bell pepper, and mushrooms and saute 5 minutes. Add remaining ingredients, except rice, and heat to boiling; reduce heat and simmer, covered, until meat is tender, about 20 minutes. Serve over rice.

PORK AND PEPPER STEW

For variation, chicken breast strips can be substituted for the pork in this recipe.

4 servings

- 1   pound pork tenderloin, fat trimmed, cut into strips
- 1   tablespoon olive oil
- 1   can (15 ounces) reduced-sodium tomato sauce
- 1   package (16 ounces) frozen stir-fry pepper blend
- 2   tablespoons dry sherry, optional
- 1   teaspoon minced garlic

Per Serving
Calories: 464
% Calories from fat: 17
Protein (g): 33.9
Carbohydrates (g): 58.6
Fat (g): 8.4
Saturated fat (g): 2
Cholesterol (mg): 65.7
Sodium (mg): 99
Exchanges
Milk: 0.0
Veg.: 3.0
Fruit: 0.0
Bread: 3.0
Meat: 3.0
Fat: 0.0

1 teaspoon dried basil leaves
1 teaspoon dried thyme leaves
    Salt and pepper, to taste
8 ounces fusilli, cooked, warm

1. Cook pork in olive oil in large skillet over medium heat until browned, 5 to 8 minutes; add tomato sauce, pepper blend, sherry, garlic, and herbs. Heat to boiling; reduce heat and simmer, covered, until pork is tender, about 15 minutes. Simmer, uncovered, until sauce is slightly thickened, 2 to 3 minutes longer. Season to taste with salt and pepper. Serve over fusilli.

MEDITERRANEAN CURRIED STEW

Taste buds will be tantalized by the melding of cinnamon-spice and curry flavors this stew offers. Brightly colored rice completes the dish perfectly.

6 servings (about 1½ cups each)

1 pound pork tenderloin, *or* beef eye of round, fat trimmed, cut into ³/₄-inch cubes
2 tablespoons extra-virgin olive oil, divided
1 small eggplant (about 12 ounces), unpeeled, cut into 1-inch pieces
3 small onions, quartered
½ cup chopped green bell pepper
½ cup sliced celery
2 cloves garlic, minced
1 tablespoon flour
½ teaspoon ground cinnamon
½ teaspoon ground nutmeg
½ teaspoon ground cumin
¼ teaspoon curry powder
⅛ teaspoon cayenne pepper
2 cans (14½ ounces each) reduced-sodium whole tomatoes, undrained, coarsely chopped
1 medium zucchini, cubed

Per Serving
Calories: 446
% Calories from fat: 22
Protein (g): 35.7
Carbohydrates (g): 61.3
Fat (g): 11.1
Saturated fat (g): 2
Cholesterol (mg): 43.8
Sodium (mg): 427
Exchanges
Milk: 0.0
Veg.: 3.0
Fruit: 0.0
Bread: 3.0
Meat: 2.0
Fat: 1.0

1 cup cubed, seeded, peeled butternut squash

1 can (15 ounces) garbanzo beans, rinsed, drained

1/2 cup vegetable broth
   Salt and pepper, to taste

1 cup long-grain rice

1/4-1/2 teaspoon ground turmeric

3 tablespoons raisins

3 tablespoons slivered almonds, toasted

1. Cook pork in 1 tablespoon oil in large saucepan over medium heat until browned, about 5 minutes. Add eggplant, onions, bell pepper, celery, garlic, and remaining 1 tablespoon oil and cook 10 minutes or until eggplant is beginning to brown. Stir in flour and spices; cook 1 to 2 minutes longer.

2. Add tomatoes and liquid, zucchini, squash, beans, and broth to saucepan; heat to boiling. Reduce heat and simmer, covered, until vegetables and meat are tender, about 15 minutes. Season to taste with salt and pepper.

3. Cook rice according to package directions, adding turmeric to cooking water. Serve stew over rice; sprinkle with raisins and almonds.

CARIBBEAN GINGER, BEAN, AND PORK STEW

Fresh gingerroot accents the flavor contrasts in this tasty stew.

6 servings (about 1 cup each)

12 ounces boneless pork loin, fat trimmed, cut into 3/4-inch pieces

1 tablespoon olive oil

1 cup chopped onion

1 cup chopped red bell pepper

1 jalapeño chili, minced

2 teaspoons minced garlic

1 tablespoon minced gingerroot

1/2 teaspoon dried thyme leaves

1/2 teaspoon ground allspice

Per Serving
Calories: 369
% Calories from fat: 15
Protein (g): 18.9
Carbohydrates (g): 66.3
Fat (g): 6.8
Saturated fat (g): 1.6
Cholesterol (mg): 24.6
Sodium (mg): 704
Exchanges
Milk: 0.0
Veg.: 0.0
Fruit: 1.0
Bread: 3.0
Meat: 2.0
Fat: 0.0

1 can (15 ounces) black beans, rinsed, drained

1 can (15 ounces) black-eyed peas, rinsed, drained

³/₄ cup fresh, *or* frozen, cut okra

¹/₃ cup orange juice

¹/₃ cup jalapeño chili jelly, *or* orange marmalade

1 can (11 ounces) Mandarin orange segments, drained

Salt and pepper, to taste

3 cups cooked brown, *or* white, rice, warm

1. Cook pork in oil in large skillet over medium heat until browned, 5 to 8 minutes. Add onion, bell pepper, jalapeño chili, and garlic and cook until onion is tender, about 5 minutes. Stir in gingerroot, thyme, and allspice; cook 1 to 2 minutes longer, stirring frequently.

2. Add beans, black-eyed peas, okra, orange juice, and chili jelly to mixture; heat to boiling. Reduce heat and simmer, covered, until okra is tender, 5 to 10 minutes. Stir in orange segments; cook 1 to 2 minutes longer. Season to taste with salt and pepper. Serve over rice.

SAVORY STEWED PORK AND CHORIZO

A versatile dish, this shredded pork and chorizo "stew" can be served rolled in a tortilla or used as a topping for tostadas.

6 servings

12 ounces pork tenderloin, fat trimmed, cut into 1-inch cubes

Vegetable cooking spray

Chorizo (see p. 180)

1 small onion, sliced

1 clove garlic, minced

2 large tomatoes, chopped

¹/₄ teaspoon dried oregano leaves

¹/₄ teaspoon dried thyme leaves

Per Serving
Calories: 298
% Calories from fat: 15
Protein (g): 27.2
Carbohydrates (g): 35
Fat (g): 4.7
Saturated fat (g): 1.5
Cholesterol (mg): 65.7
Sodium (mg): 313
Exchanges
Milk: 0.0
Veg.: 0.0
Fruit: 0.0
Bread: 2.0
Meat: 3.0
Fat: 0.0

1 bay leaf
2-3 pickled jalapeño chilies, finely chopped
1 tablespoon pickled jalapeño chili juice
Salt and pepper, to taste
4 cups cooked rice, warm

1. Cover pork with water in medium saucepan; heat to boiling. Reduce heat and simmer, covered, until tender, 20 to 30 minutes. Cool; drain, reserving ¹/₂ cup broth. Finely shred pork; reserve.

2. Spray large skillet with cooking spray; heat over medium heat until hot. Cook Chorizo over medium heat until browned, crumbling with a fork; remove from skillet and reserve.

3. Add onion and garlic to skillet; saute 2 to 3 minutes. Add tomatoes and herbs and cook over medium heat 5 minutes, stirring occasionally. Add reserved pork, Chorizo, and ¹/₂ cup broth, jalapeño chilies, and jalapeño juice to skillet. Cook, uncovered, over medium heat about 10 minutes, stirring occasionally (mixture should be moist, not dry). Discard bay leaf; season to taste with salt and pepper. Serve over rice.

TOMATILLO PORK STEW

Tomatillos (Mexican green tomatoes) add a special flavor to this South-of-the-Border version of pork stew.

8 servings

1¹/₂ cups chopped onions
1 small poblano chili, *or* green bell pepper, chopped
4 cloves garlic, minced
1-2 tablespoons vegetable oil
2 pounds boneless lean pork, cut into ³/₄-inch cubes
2 tablespoons flour
³/₄ teaspoon dried oregano leaves
¹/₂ teaspoon ground cumin
¹/₄ teaspoon dried thyme leaves
¹/₂ cup reduced-sodium fat-free chicken broth

Per Serving
Calories: 374
% Calories from fat: 24
Protein (gm): 32.1
Carbohydrate (gm): 37.6
Fat (gm): 9.9
Saturated fat (gm): 2.9
Cholesterol (mg): 64.4
Sodium (mg): 118
Exchanges
Milk: 0.0
Veg.: 2.0
Fruit: 0.0
Bread: 2.0
Meat: 3.0
Fat: 0.0

   2 large tomatoes, chopped

  12 ounces Mexican green tomatoes (toma-
       tillos), husked, chopped

   1 can (4 ounces) mild, *or* hot chopped
       green chilies

 1-2 teaspoons lime juice
       Salt and pepper, to taste

   5 cups cooked rice
       Minced cilantro, *or* parsley, as garnish
       Toasted pine nuts, *or* almonds, as
       garnish

1. Saute onions, poblano chili, and garlic in oil in large saucepan 2 to 3 minutes; add pork and saute until browned, about 5
minutes. Stir in flour and herbs and cook 2 minutes longer.

2. Add chicken broth, tomatoes, green tomatoes, and green
chilies and heat to boiling; reduce heat and simmer, covered,
until pork is tender, 40 to 50 minutes. Season to taste with lime
juice, salt, and pepper.

3. Serve stew over rice, sprinkle with cilantro and pine nuts.

PORK LOIN, POTATO, AND CABBAGE STEW

Grated potatoes thicken the sauce in this robust pork stew.

4-5 servings

Per Serving
Calories: 328
% Calories from fat: 18
Protein (gm): 23.4
Carbohydrate (gm): 45.4
Fat (gm): 6.8
Saturated fat (gm): 2.2
Cholesterol (mg): 49.3
Sodium (mg): 101
Exchanges
Milk: 0.0
Veg.: 3.0
Fruit: 0.0
Bread: 2.0
Meat: 2.0
Fat: 0.0

  16 ounces boneless pork loin, fat trimmed,
       cut into strips

   1 pound red potatoes, peeled, grated

   1 can (14^1/$_2$ ounces) reduced-sodium
       stewed tomatoes, undrained

   1 can (15 ounces) reduced-sodium
       tomato sauce

   3 cups thinly sliced cabbage

   1 large onion, finely chopped

   2 garlic cloves, minced

   1 tablespoon brown sugar

   2 teaspoons balsamic vinegar

   2 teaspoons dried thyme leaves

   1 bay leaf
       Salt and pepper, to taste

1. Combine all ingredients, except salt and pepper, in large saucepan; heat to boiling. Reduce heat and simmer, covered, until meat is tender, about 30 minutes. Discard bay leaf; season to taste with salt and pepper.

PORK AND SAUERKRAUT STEW

A wonderful stew of pork and sauerkraut, flavored with caraway; serve in shallow bowls with crusty rye rolls.

4-5 servings

16	ounces lean pork loin, fat trimmed, cut into ³/₄-inch pieces
2	teaspoons olive oil
1	pound red potatoes, peeled, cut into thin slices
1	large onion, finely chopped
1	can (16 ounces) reduced-sodium tomatoes, undrained, coarsely chopped
1	teaspoon caraway seeds
¹/₄	teaspoon black pepper
1	package (16 ounces) fresh sauerkraut, drained
¹/₄	cup fat-free sour cream
	Salt and pepper, to taste

Per Serving
Calories: 245
% Calories from fat: 25
Protein (g): 18.2
Carbohydrates (g): 28.5
Fat (g): 7
Saturated fat (g): 2
Cholesterol (mg): 39.7
Sodium (mg): 650
Exchanges
Milk: 0.0
Veg.: 2.0
Fruit: 0.0
Bread: 1.0
Meat: 2.0
Fat: 0.0

1. Cook pork in oil in large skillet over medium heat until browned, 5 to 8 minutes. Add remaining ingredients, except sour cream, salt, and pepper; heat to boiling. Reduce heat and simmer, covered, until meat and potatoes are tender, about 25 minutes. Stir in sour cream; season to taste with salt and pepper.

FINNISH PORK STEW WITH BEETS AND NOODLES

This Scandinavian dish is tasty and colorful.

4-5 servings

Vegetable cooking spray

16 ounces boneless pork loin, fat trimmed, sliced into 2-inch strips

1 cup chopped onion

1 can (16 ounces) julienned beets, undrained

3 tablespoons cider vinegar

1/2 cup fat-free beef broth

1 1/2 teaspoons prepared horseradish

1/2 teaspoon dried thyme leaves

2 teaspoons cornstarch

1/4 cup cold water

Salt and pepper, to taste

8-9 ounces reduced-fat egg noodles, cooked, warm

Per Serving
Calories: 291
% Calories from fat: 21
Protein (g): 20
Carbohydrates (g): 38
Fat (g): 6.9
Saturated fat (g): 2.2
Cholesterol (mg): 78
Sodium (mg): 345
Exchanges
Milk: 0.0
Veg.: 1.5
Fruit: 0.0
Bread: 2.0
Meat: 2.0
Fat: 0.0

1. Spray large skillet with cooking spray; heat over medium heat until hot. Add pork and onion, and cook until pork is browned, about 8 minutes.

2. Drain and reserve beets; stir 1/2 cup beet juice into skillet with vinegar, broth, horseradish, and thyme. Heat to boiling; reduce heat and simmer, covered, until meat is tender, about 20 minutes.

3. Heat stew to boiling; stir in combined cornstarch and water. Boil, stirring, until thickened, about 1 minute. Add reserved beets and simmer, uncovered, 5 minutes. Season to taste with salt and pepper. Serve over noodles.

IRISH LAMB STEW

A comfort food from Ireland, this simply seasoned stew is always welcome on cold winter evenings. Dumplings are served with the stew in some parts of Ireland; see the recipe variation below.

6 servings

1¹/₂ pounds boneless lean leg of lamb, fat trimmed, cut into ³/₄-inch cubes

2 medium onions, sliced

1-2 tablespoons vegetable oil

3 tablespoons flour

2 cups reduced-sodium fat-free chicken broth, *or* water

¹/₄-¹/₂ teaspoon dried thyme leaves

1 bay leaf

6 medium potatoes, unpeeled, quartered

6 medium carrots, cut into ¹/₂-inch slices

1-1¹/₂ teaspoons very-low-sodium Worcestershire sauce

Salt and pepper, to taste

Per Serving
Calories: 312
% Calories from fat: 20
Protein (gm): 21.4
Carbohydrate (gm): 41
Fat (gm): 6.9
Saturated fat (gm): 1.9
Cholesterol (mg): 48.5
Sodium (mg): 130
Exchanges
Milk: 0.0
Veg.: 2.0
Fruit: 0.0
Bread: 2.0
Meat: 2.0
Fat: 0.0

1. Cook lamb and onions in oil in Dutch oven over medium heat until lamb is browned, about 8 minutes; sprinkle with flour and cook 1 minute longer.

2. Add chicken broth and herbs and heat to boiling. Reduce heat and simmer, covered, until lamb is tender, 45 to 60 minutes, adding potatoes and carrots during last 20 minutes of cooking time. Discard bay leaf; season to taste with Worcestershire sauce, salt, and pepper.

Variations:
Irish Lamb Stew with Parsley Dumplings—Make lamb stew as above. Make Dill Dumplings (see p. 553), substituting 2 tablespoons finely chopped parsley for the dill weed; spoon dumpling mixture onto stew. Simmer, uncovered, 10 minutes; simmer, covered, 10 minutes or until dumplings are dry.

Easy Shepherd's Pie—Make stew as above, substituting 3 to 4 medium parsnips for the potatoes; pour into 1¹/₂-quart casserole. Mash 1 pound peeled, cooked, Idaho potatoes; mix in ¹/₄ cup fat-free sour cream, 2 to 3 tablespoons fat-free milk, and 1 tablespoon margarine; season to taste with salt and pepper. Spoon potatoes over top of stew. Bake at 400 degrees until potatoes are browned, about 10 minutes.

HEARTY ROSEMARY LAMB WITH SWEET POTATOES

The pairing of rosemary and lamb is classic, distinctive, and delightful. Here, we offer the two in a robust stew with sweet potatoes and cut green beans.

4 servings

1 pound boneless lamb shoulder, fat trimmed, cut into 3/4-inch cubes

2 tablespoons chopped fresh, *or* 2 teaspoons dried, rosemary leaves

2 tablespoons chopped fresh, *or* 2 teaspoons dried, thyme leaves

1 teaspoon olive oil

1 large onion, cut into thin wedges

3 cups reduced-sodium fat-free beef broth

2 bay leaves

1¹/₄ pounds sweet potatoes, peeled, cut into ³/₄-inch cubes

1¹/₂ cups cut green beans
Salt and pepper, to taste

Per Serving
Calories: 285
% Calories from fat: 23
Protein (g): 20.6
Carbohydrates (g): 34.7
Fat (g): 7.4
Saturated fat (g): 2.5
Cholesterol (mg): 47.2
Sodium (mg): 171
Exchanges
Milk: 0.0
Veg.: 1.0
Fruit: 0.0
Bread: 2.0
Meat: 2.0
Fat: 0.0

1. Toss lamb with herbs; saute in oil in large saucepan until lightly browned, about 10 minutes. Add onion, broth, and bay leaves. Heat to boiling; reduce heat and simmer, covered, 30 minutes.

2. Stir sweet potatoes and beans into stew; simmer, covered, until vegetables are tender, about 15 minutes. Discard bay leaves; season to taste with salt and pepper.

LAMB RATATOUILLE

In this main-dish version of ratatouille, the vegetables are roasted and combined with stewed lamb.

8 servings

Savory Tomato Sauce (recipe follows)
2 pounds boneless lean lamb, fat trimmed, cut into 1-inch cubes
1/4 cup dry vermouth *or* chicken broth
2 tablespoons lemon juice
Salt and pepper, to taste
Vegetable cooking spray
1 medium eggplant, unpeeled, cut into 1-inch cubes
2 large zucchini, cut into 1/2-inch slices
2 green bell peppers, cut into 1-inch cubes
2 medium onions, cut into 1/4-inch slices
3/4 teaspoon dried rosemary leaves
1/2 teaspoon dried thyme leaves
1-2 tablespoons olive oil
Rosemary, *or* parsley, sprigs, as garnish

Per Serving
Calories: 193
% Calories from fat: 30
Protein (gm): 18
Carbohydrate (gm): 15.4
Fat (gm): 6.6
Saturated fat (gm): 1.8
Cholesterol (mg): 48.5
Sodium (mg): 60
Exchanges
Milk: 0.0
Veg.: 3.0
Fruit: 0.0
Bread: 0.0
Meat: 2.0
Fat: 0.0

1. Combine Savory Tomato Sauce, lamb, vermouth, and lemon juice in large Dutch oven; heat to boiling. Reduce heat and simmer, covered, until lamb is very tender, 45 to 60 minutes. Season to taste with salt and pepper.

2. Spray aluminum-foil-lined jelly roll pan with cooking spray. Arrange eggplant, zucchini, bell peppers, and onions on pan; spray with cooking spray. Sprinkle vegetables with herbs. Roast at 400 degrees until lightly browned and tender, 30 to 40 minutes. Drizzle vegetables with oil and sprinkle lightly with salt and pepper.

3. Arrange vegetables on large serving platter; spoon lamb and tomato mixture over vegetables. Garnish with rosemary sprigs.

Savory Tomato Sauce

makes about 1 quart

- 5 large tomatoes, peeled, coarsely chopped
- 2/3 cup finely chopped celery
- 2/3 cup finely chopped green onions and tops
- 1 large green pepper, finely chopped
- 3/4 cup reduced-sodium tomato juice
- 1/2 teaspoon ground cumin
- 1/2 teaspoon garlic powder
- 1/8 teaspoon ground cloves
  Salt and pepper, to taste

1. Heat all ingredients, except salt and pepper, to boiling in large saucepan. Reduce heat and simmer, uncovered, until sauce is a medium-thick consistency, about 30 minutes. Season to taste with salt and pepper.

EASIEST LAMB STEW

The easiest stew ever—just stir it all together, place in the oven, and put your feet up with a good book while it cooks.

6 servings

- 2 pounds boneless lean lamb, cut into 1-inch cubes
- 1/4 teaspoon salt
- 1/4 teaspoon pepper
- 1 bay leaf
- 4 medium potatoes, peeled and quartered
- 3 medium carrots, cut into 1/2-inch slices
- 2 small onions, thinly sliced
- 1/4 cup quick-cooking tapioca
- 1 package (10 ounces) frozen peas
- 2 cups water

Per Serving
Calories: 395
% Calories from fat: 26
Protein (g): 34.7
Carbohydrates (g): 37.5
Fat (g): 11.4
Saturated fat (g): 4.3
Cholesterol (mg): 98.2
Sodium (mg): 230
Exchanges
Milk: 0.0
Veg.: 1.0
Fruit: 0.0
Bread: 2.0
Meat: 4.0
Fat: 0.0

1. Combine all ingredients in 2 1/2-quart casserole; stir well. Bake, covered, at 325 degrees until lamb is tender, 1 1/2 to 2 hours, stirring halfway through cooking time. Discard bay leaf.

SLOW-COOKER IRISH STEW

For a no-fuss dinner, try this lamb stew. Crisp-tender green beans, broccoli, or Brussels sprouts make the perfect accompaniment.

6 servings

1¹/₂ pounds shoulder of lamb, fat trimmed, cut into 1-inch cubes
6 white potatoes, thinly sliced
6 small white onions, quartered
6 carrots, sliced
2¹/₂ teaspoons Spike
2 teaspoons dried rosemary leaves
¹/₂ teaspoon dried thyme leaves
1 bay leaf
2 cups water
Pepper, to taste

Per Serving
Calories: 320
% Calories from fat: 17
Protein (gm): 18.5
Carbohydrate (gm): 48.5
Fat (gm): 6.5
Saturated fat (gm): 2.3
Cholesterol (mg): 47.2
Sodium (mg): 74
Exchanges
Milk: 0.0
Veg.: 3.0
Fruit: 0.0
Bread: 2.0
Meat: 2.0
Fat: 0.0

1. Combine ingredients in slow-cooker and cook, covered, on High 1 hour. Reduce heat to Low and cook until lamb and vegetables are very tender, 10 to 12 hours. Season to taste with pepper.

SAVORY LAMB STEW

Enjoy this rich and flavorful combination of lamb shanks, lentils, vegetables, and spices.

6-7 servings

2 pounds lamb shanks, fat trimmed
1 tablespoon flour
2 teaspoons olive oil
2 cups chopped onions
2 garlic cloves, minced
2 cups fat-free chicken broth
1 can (14¹/₂ ounces) tomatoes, undrained, coarsely chopped
2 large carrots, sliced
¹/₂ cup brown lentils
1 medium green bell pepper, seeded, diced

Per Serving
Calories: 325
% Calories from fat: 26
Protein (g): 25
Carbohydrates (g): 40
Fat (g): 7.8
Saturated fat (g): 2.2
Cholesterol (mg): 56
Sodium (mg): 246
Exchanges
Milk: 0.0
Veg.: 1.5
Fruit: 0.0
Bread: 2.0
Meat: 2.0
Fat: 0.0

$^1/_4$ cup chopped fresh parsley

2 bay leaves

2 teaspoons dried thyme leaves

$^1/_4$ teaspoon ground cinnamon

$^1/_4$ teaspoon ground cloves

$^1/_4$ teaspoon black pepper

Salt, to taste

$1^1/_4$ cups uncooked brown rice, cooked, warm

Parsley sprigs, as garnish

1. Coat lamb shanks with flour; brown in oil in Dutch oven. Stir in onions and garlic and cook until lightly browned, about 5 minutes. Stir in remaining ingredients, except salt, rice, and parsley sprigs, and heat to boiling. Reduce heat and simmer, covered, $1^1/_2$ to 2 hours or until lamb shanks are tender. Discard bay leaves.

2. Remove lamb shanks; remove lean meat and cut into bite-sized pieces. Return meat to stew; season to taste with salt.

3. Arrange rice on serving platter and spoon lamb stew over. Garnish with parsley sprigs.

CHILI LAMB STEW

A delicious blending of flavors! Serve in bowls with tortillas or crusty bread. Beef eye of round steak and beef broth can be substituted for the lamb and chicken broth.

4 servings

Vegetable cooking spray

1 large onion, halved, sliced

4 cloves garlic, minced

1 small jalapeño chili, minced

16 ounces boneless lean lamb, fat trimmed, cubed ($^3/_4$-inch)

1 teaspoon dried rosemary leaves

$^1/_2$ teaspoon dried oregano leaves

$^1/_4$ teaspoon dried thyme leaves

2 tablespoons flour

Per Serving
Calories: 293
% Calories from fat: **15**
Protein (gm): 22.8
Carbohydrate (gm): 41.6
Fat (gm): 5.3
Saturated fat (gm): 1.7
Cholesterol (mg): 48.5
Sodium (mg): 270
Exchanges
Milk: 0.0
Veg.: 2.0
Fruit: 0.0
Bread: 2.0
Meat: 2.0
Fat: 0.0

  1 cup reduced-sodium fat-free chicken
    broth
  2 cans (15 ounces each) reduced-sodium
    diced tomatoes, undrained
2-3 cans (4 ounces each) chopped mild
    green chilies
  2 medium potatoes, cubed (1/2-inch)
  2 large yellow summer squash, cubed
    (1/2-inch)
1/2 cup frozen whole-kernel corn
    Salt and pepper, to taste

1. Spray large saucepan with cooking spray; heat over medium heat until hot. Saute onion, garlic, and jalapeño chili 2 minutes. Add lamb and cook until browned, about 5 minutes. Stir in herbs and flour and cook 1 minute longer.

2. Add chicken broth, tomatoes and liquid, and chilies and heat to boiling; reduce heat and simmer, covered, until lamb is tender, about 45 minutes, adding potatoes, squash, and corn during the last 10 minutes of cooking time. Season to taste with salt and pepper.

LAMB AND TURNIP STEW WITH CILANTRO

This homespun lamb dish has been updated with fresh sage and cilantro. Serve it with crusty bread to sop up the delicious broth.

4 servings

  1 pound boneless lamb shoulder, fat
    trimmed, cut into 1-inch pieces
  1 medium onion, chopped
  1 teaspoon olive oil
  1 tablespoon minced garlic
1/2 cup dry red wine, *or* beef broth
2 1/2 cups reduced-sodium tomato juice,
    divided
  2 medium potatoes, cut into 3/4-inch
    cubes
  1 large turnip, cut into 3/4-inch cubes

Per Serving
Calories: 269
% Calories from fat: 24
Protein (g): 17.4
Carbohydrates (g): 30
Fat (g): 7.3
Saturated fat (g): 2.4
Cholesterol (mg): 47.2
Sodium (mg): 81
Exchanges
Milk: 0.0
Veg.: 0.0
Fruit: 0.0
Bread: 2.0
Meat: 2.0
Fat: 0.0

1 tablespoon chopped fresh, *or* 1 teaspoon dried, sage leaves
Salt and pepper, to taste
1/2 cup chopped cilantro

1. Saute lamb and onion in oil in 4-quart saucepan until lightly browned; add garlic, wine, and 1 1/2 cups tomato juice and heat to boiling; reduce heat and simmer, covered, until lamb is tender, about 1 hour, adding potatoes, turnip, and remaining 1 cup tomato juice during last 20 minutes.

2. Stir in sage; season to taste with salt and pepper. Spoon stew into bowls; sprinkle with cilantro.

MOROCCAN LAMB STEW

Sweet spices season this stew and raisins, almonds, and hard-cooked eggs provide colorful garnish.

8 servings

Vegetable cooking spray
2 pounds boneless lean lamb, fat trimmed, cut into 3/4-inch cubes
1 1/2 cups chopped onions
2 large cloves garlic, minced
2 teaspoons minced gingerroot
1 1/2 cups reduced-sodium fat-free chicken broth
1 cup reduced-sodium tomato puree
1/2 teaspoon ground cinnamon
1/4 teaspoon ground turmeric
Generous pinch ground cloves
1 bay leaf
Salt and pepper, to taste
1/3 cup raisins
2-4 tablespoons whole almonds, toasted
2 hard-cooked eggs, chopped
Finely chopped cilantro, *or* parsley, as garnish
5 cups cooked couscous, *or* rice, warm

Per Serving
Calories: 308
% Calories from fat: 20
Protein (gm): 23.8
Carbohydrate (gm): 37.4
Fat (gm): 6.6
Saturated fat (gm): 2
Cholesterol (mg): 101.5
Sodium (mg): 103
Exchanges
Milk: 0.0
Veg.: 1.0
Fruit: 0.0
Bread: 2.0
Meat: 2.5
Fat: 0.0

1. Spray Dutch oven with cooking spray; heat over medium heat until hot. Add lamb and saute until browned, 5 to 8 minutes; remove from pan. Add onions, garlic, and gingerroot; saute until onions are tender, about 5 minutes. Return meat to Dutch oven.

2. Add chicken broth, tomato puree, and spices; heat to boiling. Reduce heat and simmer, covered, until lamb is tender, 45 to 60 minutes. Simmer, uncovered, until thickened to desired consistency, about 10 minutes longer. Discard bay leaf; season to taste with salt and pepper. Stir in raisins.

3. Spoon stew onto rimmed serving platter; sprinkle with almonds, eggs, and cilantro. Serve with couscous.

LAMB AND VEGETABLE TAJINE

From the Moroccan cuisine, tajines are traditionally cooked in earthenware pots. Serve with couscous and a crusty bread.

6 servings (about 1½ cups each)

Vegetable cooking spray
1 medium onion, chopped
1 rib celery, sliced
1-2 teaspoons minced gingerroot
1 teaspoon minced garlic
1 cinnamon stick
2 teaspoons paprika
2 teaspoons ground cumin
2 teaspoons ground coriander
1½ teaspoons black pepper
12-16 ounces cooked lean lamb, _or_ beef, fat trimmed, cubed
2 cans (14½ ounces each) reduced-sodium diced tomatoes, undrained
1 can (16 ounces) garbanzo beans, rinsed, drained
1 cup cubed yellow winter squash (butternut _or_ acorn)
1 cup cubed turnip, _or_ rutabaga
1 large carrot, sliced
1½ cups whole green beans, ends trimmed

Per Serving
Calories: 466
% Calories from fat: 15
Protein (g): 24.8
Carbohydrates (g): 76.9
Fat (g): 8.4
Saturated fat (g): 2
Cholesterol (mg): 38.9
Sodium (mg): 580
Exchanges
Milk: 0.0
Veg.: 3.0
Fruit: 0.0
Bread: 4.0
Meat: 2.0
Fat: 0.0

      1 cup pitted prunes
  1/4 cup pitted small black olives
  1/2 cup reduced-sodium fat-free beef broth
      Salt and pepper, to taste
  4¹/2 cups cooked couscous, warm
      Minced parsley, as garnish

1. Spray Dutch oven with cooking spray; heat over medium heat until hot. Saute onion, celery, gingerroot, and garlic until onion is tender, 5 to 8 minutes. Stir in spices; cook 1 minute longer.

2. Add remaining ingredients, except salt and pepper, couscous, and parsley, to Dutch oven. Bake, covered, at 350 degrees until vegetables are tender, 20 to 30 minutes. Season to taste with salt and pepper. Serve over couscous in bowls; sprinkle with parsley.

MARRAKESH LAMB STEW

For a simplified version of this flavorful stew, substitute 3 cans (15 ounces each) navy or Great Northern beans for the dry beans. Delete Step 1 of the recipe; make recipe as directed in Steps 2 and 3, except do not add beans until the last 30 minutes of cooking time.

8 servings

      8 ounces dried navy, *or* Great Northern, beans
      2 pounds boneless lean lamb, fat trimmed, cut into scant 1-inch cubes
  1-2 tablespoons olive oil
      4 ounces portobello, *or* cremini, mushrooms, coarsely chopped
      2 medium carrots, sliced
      1 medium onion, sliced
      3 large cloves garlic, minced
  1/4 cup all-purpose flour
      1 teaspoon ground cumin
  1/2 teaspoon dried thyme leaves
  1/2 teaspoon dried savory leaves

Per Serving
Calories: 409
% Calories from fat: 15
Protein (gm): 31.2
Carbohydrate (gm): 52.6
Fat (gm): 6.8
Saturated fat (gm): 1.9
Cholesterol (mg): 48.5
Sodium (mg): 164
Exchanges
Milk: 0.0
Veg.: 1.0
Fruit: 0.0
Bread: 3.0
Meat: 3.0
Fat: 0.0

2 bay leaves
1 quart reduced-sodium fat-free chicken broth
1/2 cup dry white wine, *or* reduced-sodium fat-free chicken broth
1-2 tablespoons tomato paste
3/4 cup sliced roasted red peppers
8 ounces spinach, sliced
Salt and pepper, to taste
5 cups cooked couscous, *or* rice, warm

1. Cover beans with water in large saucepan; heat to boiling. Remove from heat and let stand, covered, 1 hour. Drain.

2. Saute lamb in oil in Dutch oven until browned, about 5 minutes; add vegetables and saute 5 minutes. Add flour and herbs; cook 1 minute longer.

3. Add chicken broth, wine, and beans; heat to boiling. Reduce heat and simmer, covered, until lamb and beans are tender, 45 to 60 minutes. Stir in tomato paste, roasted red peppers, and spinach; cook until spinach is wilted, about 2 minutes. Discard bay leaves; season to taste with salt and pepper. Serve over couscous.

CURRIED LAMB STEW

Known in India as Rogan Josh, this flavorful stew is best prepared 1 to 2 days in advance for flavors to meld; cool stew and refrigerate. Serve with a variety of condiments for flavor and color contrast.

12 servings

3 pounds boneless lean leg of lamb, fat trimmed, cut into 1-inch cubes
1 1/4 cups low-fat plain yogurt
1/4 teaspoon crushed red pepper
2 cups chopped onions
1 tablespoon minced gingerroot
2 cloves garlic, minced
2 teaspoons coriander seeds, lightly crushed

Per Serving
Calories: 257
% Calories from fat: 21
Protein (gm): 19.8
Carbohydrate (gm): 29.4
Fat (gm): 5.9
Saturated fat (gm): 2
Cholesterol (mg): 49.9
Sodium (mg): 82
Exchanges
Milk: 0.0
Veg.: 0.0
Fruit: 0.0
Bread: 2.0
Meat: 2.0
Fat: 0.0

    1 teaspoon cumin seeds, lightly crushed
  1/2 teaspoon cardamom seeds, lightly crushed
    1 teaspoon ground turmeric
  1/2 teaspoon ground cinnamon
      Generous pinch ground cloves
  1/2 teaspoon pepper
 1-2 tablespoons margarine, *or* vegetable oil
    1 cup reduced-sodium fat-free chicken broth
      Salt and pepper, to taste
      Turmeric Rice (recipe follows)
      Condiments: raisins, toasted slivered almonds, chopped onion and cucumber, finely chopped cilantro *or* parsley (not included in nutritional data)

1. Combine lamb, yogurt, and red pepper in bowl; refrigerate several hours or overnight, stirring occasionally.

2. Saute onions, gingerroot, garlic, and spices in margarine in Dutch oven until onions are tender, 5 to 8 minutes. Stir in lamb mixture and chicken broth; heat to boiling. Reduce heat and simmer, covered, until lamb is tender, 50 to 60 minutes. Season to taste with salt and pepper. Serve stew over Turmeric Rice; pass condiments.

Turmeric Rice

makes 12 servings (about 2/3 cup each)

  41/2 cups water
  3/4 teaspoon turmeric
  1/4 teaspoon salt, optional
    2 cups uncooked long-grain rice

1. Heat water to boiling in large saucepan; stir in turmeric and salt. Stir in rice; reduce heat and simmer, covered, until rice is tender, 20 to 25 minutes.

LAMB BIRIANI

Biriani is a traditional Indian meat-and-rice dish that can be made with lamb, chicken, or beef. Although the meat can be served over any white rice, it's worth using basmati rice, which is available in specialty markets.

4-5 servings

16 ounces boneless lean leg of lamb, fat trimmed, cubed
   Vegetable cooking spray
2 cups chopped onions
1 garlic clove, minced
2 teaspoons margarine
1 cup fat-free chicken broth
1 teaspoon ground coriander
1 teaspoon ground ginger
1/2 teaspoon chili powder
1/4 teaspoon ground cinnamon
1/4 teaspoon ground cloves
3/4 cup fat-free plain yogurt
   Salt and pepper, to taste
   Basmati Rice Pilaf (recipe follows)
   Parsley sprigs, as garnish

Per Serving
Calories: 280
% Calories from fat: 26
Protein (g): 22
Carbohydrates (g): 30
Fat (g): 8.2
Saturated fat (g): 2.1
Cholesterol (mg): 46
Sodium (mg): 332
Exchanges
Milk: 0.0
Veg.: 1.5
Fruit: 0.0
Bread: 1.5
Meat: 2.0
Fat: 0.5

1. Spray Dutch oven with cooking spray; heat over medium heat until hot. Cook lamb until browned on all sides. Remove and reserve.

2. Saute onions and garlic in margarine in Dutch oven until tender. Add reserved lamb, broth, and spices and heat to boiling. Reduce heat and simmer, covered, until meat is tender, about 30 minutes. Stir in yogurt; season to taste with salt and pepper.

3. Spoon Basmati Rice Pilaf onto serving platter; spoon stew over. Garnish with parsley.

Basmati Rice Pilaf

makes 3 cups

- 1 cup chopped onion
- 2 teaspoons margarine
- 1 cup uncooked basmati rice
- 2¼ cups fat-free chicken broth
- Pinch saffron
- ¼ teaspoon white pepper
- 1 medium carrot, grated

1. Saute onion in margarine in large saucepan until onion is tender, about 5 minutes; stir in basmati rice and cook until lightly browned, about 3 minutes. Add remaining ingredients and heat to boiling. Reduce heat and simmer, covered, 20 minutes or until rice is tender.

SAVORY VEAL STEW

The veal in this recipe is extremely tender. Caraway and anise seeds provide an unexpected flavor nuance.

8 servings

- 2 pounds veal stew cubes, fat trimmed
- 3 cloves garlic, minced
- 1 teaspoon caraway seeds, crushed
- ¾ teaspoon anise seeds, crushed
- 2 bay leaves
- 1 cup reduced-sodium fat-free chicken broth
- ½ cup dry white wine, *or* reduced-sodium fat-free chicken broth
- 1 small head cabbage, cut into 8 wedges
- 3 leeks, white parts only, cut into 1-inch pieces
- Salt and pepper, to taste
- 8 ounces mushrooms, sliced
- 1-2 tablespoons margarine
- 1 tablespoon cornstarch
- 3 tablespoons water
- ½ cup reduced-fat, *or* fat-free, sour cream
- Finely chopped parsley, as garnish

Per Serving
Calories: 284
% Calories from fat: 28
Protein (gm): 32.4
Carbohydrate (gm): 16.5
Fat (gm): 8.8
Saturated fat (gm): 2.9
Cholesterol (mg): 104.5
Sodium (mg): 161
Exchanges
Milk: 0.0
Veg.: 3.0
Fruit: 0.0
Bread: 0.0
Meat: 4.0
Fat: 0.0

1. Combine veal, garlic, herbs, chicken broth, and wine in large Dutch oven; heat to boiling. Reduce heat and simmer, covered, until veal is very tender, 1 to 1¹/₂ hours, adding cabbage and leeks during last 20 minutes of cooking time. Remove veal and vegetables to a shallow serving dish and sprinkle lightly with salt and pepper; keep warm. Reserve chicken broth mixture; discard bay leaves.

2. Saute mushrooms in margarine in Dutch oven until tender, about 5 minutes. Add reserved chicken broth mixture and heat to boiling; stir in combined cornstarch and water. Boil, stirring, until thickened, about 1 minute. Stir in sour cream; season to taste with salt and pepper. Pour mixture over veal and vegetables; sprinkle with parsley.

VEAL SAUVIGNON AND SWISS CHARD RAGOUT

Delight your taste buds with this elegantly flavored stew.

4 servings

1	pound boneless veal cutlets, fat trimmed, cut into thin 2-inch-long strips
2	teaspoons olive oil
1	medium onion, thinly sliced
1	teaspoon minced garlic
1¹/₂	cups Sauvignon blanc, *or* other dry white wine
1	tablespoon tomato paste
1	teaspoon dried marjoram leaves
3	cups small cauliflower florets
2	cups torn Swiss chard leaves
	Salt and pepper, to taste
8	ounces ziti, *or* other pasta, cooked, warm

Per Serving
Calories: 455
% Calories from fat: 16
Protein (g): 30
Carbohydrates (g): 51
Fat (g): 8
Saturated fat (g): 1.7
Cholesterol (mg): 74.6
Sodium (mg): 148
Exchanges
Milk: 0.0
Veg.: 1.0
Fruit: 0.0
Bread: 3.0
Meat: 2.0
Fat: 2.0

1. Saute veal in oil in large saucepan until lightly browned, about 8 minutes; add onion and garlic and saute until tender, about 5 minutes longer.

2. Add wine, tomato paste, and marjoram and heat to boiling; reduce heat and simmer, covered, until veal is tender, 20 to 30 minutes, adding cauliflower and Swiss chard during last 5 minutes. Season to taste with salt and pepper. Serve over ziti.

VEAL STEW WITH PASTA

Veal shanks can be hard to find and may have to be ordered, but their flavor makes the search worthwhile.

6 servings

6 veal shanks, fat trimmed
2 tablespoons canola oil
1 onion, coarsely chopped
2 carrots, coarsely chopped
1 rib celery, coarsely chopped
1 tablespoon fresh, *or* 1 teaspoon dried, thyme leaves
1 bay leaf
1 1/2 cups fat-free chicken stock
    Salt and pepper, to taste
    Tomato, Caper, and Black Olive Sauce (recipe follows)
6 cups cooked pasta, warm

Per Serving
Calories: 458
% Calories from fat: 28
Protein (gm): 39
Carbohydrate (gm): 43.2
Fat (gm): 14.3
Saturated fat (gm): 2.6
Cholesterol (mg): 114.4
Sodium (mg): 651
Exchanges
Milk: 0.0
Veg.: 2.0
Fruit: 0.0
Bread: 2.0
Meat: 4.0
Fat: 0.0

1. Cook veal shanks in oil in Dutch oven over medium heat until well browned, about 10 minutes; add remaining ingredients, except salt and pepper, Tomato, Caper, and Black Olive Sauce, and pasta.

2. Heat to boiling; transfer to oven and bake, covered, at 350 degrees until veal is tender, about 2 hours. Season to taste with salt and pepper.

3. Serve with Tomato, Caper, and Black Olive Sauce over pasta.

Tomato, Caper, and Black Olive Sauce

makes 2 cups

- 1 large garlic clove
- 2 teaspoons olive oil
- 1 can (10 ounces) reduced-sodium tomatoes, undrained, chopped
- 2 tablespoons low-sodium tomato paste
- 1/3 cup drained capers
- 1/3 cup sliced black olives
- 1 tablespoon chopped fresh, *or* 1 teaspoon dried, basil leaves
- 1 tablespoon sugar
  Salt and pepper, to taste

1. Saute garlic in oil in medium saucepan. Add tomatoes and liquid and tomato paste; heat to boiling. Reduce heat and simmer, covered, 15 minutes. Add capers, olives, basil, and sugar; simmer 5 minutes. Season to taste with salt and pepper.

OSSO BUCCO

Gremolata, a pungent mixture of finely chopped parsley, lemon rind, and garlic, is traditionally added to this classic northern Italian stew.

6 servings

- 6 medium veal shanks (about 4 pounds), fat trimmed
  Flour
- 1-2 tablespoons olive oil
- 3 medium carrots, finely chopped
- 2 ribs celery, thinly sliced
- 1 medium onion, chopped
- 3 cloves garlic, minced
- 2 cans (16 ounces each) reduced-sodium diced tomatoes, undrained
- 1/2 cup dry white wine, *or* chicken broth
- 3/4 teaspoon dried basil leaves
- 3/4 teaspoon dried thyme leaves
- 2 bay leaves
  Gremolata (see p. 555), divided
  Salt and pepper, to taste
- 4 cups cooked rice, warm

Per Serving
Calories: 364
% Calories from fat: 15
Protein (gm): 28.8
Carbohydrate (gm): 44.5
Fat (gm): 6.2
Saturated fat (gm): 1.7
Cholesterol (mg): 85.8
Sodium (mg): 91
Exchanges
Milk: 0.0
Veg.: 2.0
Fruit: 0.0
Bread: 2.0
Meat: 3.0
Fat: 0.0

1. Coat veal shanks lightly with flour; cook in oil in Dutch oven over medium heat until browned on all sides, about 10 minutes. Add carrots, celery, onion, and garlic and saute until tender, 3 to 5 minutes.

2. Add tomatoes and liquid, wine, and herbs; heat to boiling. Reduce heat and simmer, covered, until veal is tender, about 1¹/₂ hours. Stir in ¹/₄ cup Gremolata. Discard bay leaves; season to taste with salt and pepper. Serve over rice; pass remaining Gremolata.

TWO-MEAT GOULASH

Caraway and fennel seeds add new flavor interest to this distinctive goulash.

8 servings

16 ounces boneless beef eye of round steak, fat trimmed, cubed (³/₄-inch)

16 ounces boneless lean pork, fat trimmed, cubed (³/₄-inch)

1-2 tablespoons vegetable oil

1¹/₂ cups chopped onions

2 cloves garlic, minced

2 tablespoons paprika

2 tablespoons flour

¹/₂ teaspoon caraway seeds, crushed

¹/₂ teaspoon fennel seeds, crushed

2 bay leaves

1 cup reduced-sodium fat-free beef broth

1 can (16 ounces) reduced-sodium diced tomatoes, undrained

2 tablespoons reduced-sodium tomato paste

4 ounces small mushrooms, cut into halves

¹/₂ cup fat-free, *or* reduced-fat, sour cream
Salt and pepper, to taste

16 ounces no-yolk noodles, cooked, warm

Per Serving
Calories: 443
% Calories from fat: 16
Protein (gm): 36.7
Carbohydrate (gm): 53.9
Fat (gm): 8.1
Saturated fat (gm): 2.2
Cholesterol (mg): 59.7
Sodium (mg): 133
Exchanges
Milk: 0.0
Veg.: 1.0
Fruit: 0.0
Bread: 3.0
Meat: 4.0
Fat: 0.0

1. Saute meats in oil in Dutch oven until browned, 5 to 8 minutes; add onions and garlic and saute until onions are tender, about 5 minutes. Stir in paprika, flour, and herbs and cook 1 minute longer.

2. Add beef broth, tomatoes and liquid, and tomato paste; heat to boiling. Reduce heat and simmer, covered, until meats are tender, about 45 minutes, adding mushrooms during last 10 minutes of cooking time. Stir in sour cream and simmer 2 to 3 minutes; discard bay leaves and season to taste with salt and pepper. Serve over noodles.

LAMB AND BEEF STEW WITH COGNAC

The flavors of the 2 meats, wine, and cognac blend uniquely in this elegant oven stew.

6 servings

- ³/₄ cup dry white wine, *or* apple juice
- 3 tablespoons cognac, *or* apple juice
- ¹/₂ teaspoon ground cinnamon
- ¹/₄ teaspoon ground mace
- 16 ounces boneless beef eye of round steak, fat trimmed, cubed (³/₄-inch)
- 16 ounces boneless lean lamb, fat trimmed, cubed (³/₄-inch)
- 1-2 tablespoons vegetable oil
- 2 tablespoons flour
- 3 ribs celery, finely chopped
- 3 large carrots, finely chopped
- 1 medium onion, finely chopped
  Salt and pepper, to taste
- 8 ounces baby carrots
- 8 ounces small broccoli florets
- 8 ounces tiny white onions

Per Serving
Calories: 314
% Calories from fat: 25
Protein (gm): 30.7
Carbohydrate (gm): 19
Fat (gm): 8.6
Saturated fat (gm): 2.5
Cholesterol (mg): 74
Sodium (mg): 123
Exchanges
Milk: 0.0
Veg.: 4.0
Fruit: 0.0
Bread: 0.0
Meat: 3.0
Fat: 0.0

1. Pour combined wine, cognac, cinnamon, and mace over meats in glass bowl; refrigerate, covered, 6 hours or overnight, stirring occasionally. Drain, reserving marinade.

2. Saute meats in oil in Dutch oven until browned; sprinkle with flour and cook 1 to 2 minutes longer. Remove meat from Dutch oven.

3. Mix chopped vegetables and spoon into Dutch oven; add reserved marinade and heat to boiling. Reduce heat and simmer, uncovered, 5 minutes. Stir in meat.

4. Bake, covered, at 350 degrees until meats are tender, about 45 minutes; season to taste with salt and pepper.

5. Cook carrots, broccoli, and onions in 1-inch simmering water in large saucepan, covered, until crisp-tender, 8 to 10 minutes. Season to taste with salt and pepper. Spoon meats into shallow serving dishes; arrange carrots, broccoli, and onions around meat.

TWO MEAT-TWO MUSHROOM STEW

Substitute any favorite dried and fresh mushrooms for the shiitake mushrooms in this richly flavored stew.

6 servings

1/2 cup boiling water
3 medium dried shiitake mushrooms
1 cup chopped onion
1/2 teaspoon fennel seeds, lightly crushed
1 tablespoon margarine
12 ounces boneless lean pork, cubed (3/4-inch)
12 ounces boneless lean veal, cubed (3/4-inch)
2 tablespoons flour
1/2 cup dry white wine, *or* reduced-sodium fat-free chicken broth
1-2 teaspoons beef-flavor instant bouillon
4 ounces small cremini, *or* white button, mushrooms, halved
Salt and pepper, to taste
4 cups cooked brown, *or* white, rice
Finely chopped parsley, as garnish

Per Serving
Calories: 384
% Calories from fat: 22
Protein (gm): 33.9
Carbohydrate (gm): 36.8
Fat (gm): 9
Saturated fat (gm): 2.7
Cholesterol (mg): 89.4
Sodium (mg): 221
Exchanges
Milk: 0.0
Veg.: 1.0
Fruit: 0.0
Bread: 2.0
Meat: 4.0
Fat: 0.0

1. Pour boiling water over dried mushrooms in small bowl; let stand until mushrooms are softened, 5 to 10 minutes. Drain, reserving liquid; strain liquid. Slice mushrooms into thin strips, discarding hard centers.

2. Saute onion and fennel seeds in margarine in large saucepan 2 to 3 minutes; add meats and saute until lightly browned, 5 to 8 minutes. Sprinkle with flour and cook 1 minute longer.

3. Add wine, bouillon, and reserved mushroom liquid to saucepan; heat to boiling. Reduce heat and simmer, covered, until meats are tender, about 30 minutes, adding mushrooms during last 10 minutes of cooking time. Season to taste with salt and pepper. Serve over rice; sprinkle with parsley.

KARELIAN RAGOUT

Allspice gently seasons beef, pork, and lamb in this Finnish stew. Serve over cooked rice or noodles, if you wish, with warm crusty bread or rolls.

12 servings

16 ounces boneless lean beef, fat trimmed
16 ounces boneless lean lamb, fat trimmed
16 ounces boneless lean pork, fat trimmed
   Flour
 1 teaspoon ground allspice
   Salt and pepper, to taste
 5 medium onions, thinly sliced
 1 quart reduced-sodium fat-free beef broth
 6 whole allspice berries
 4 whole peppercorns
 2 bay leaves
 1/4 cup finely chopped parsley

Per Serving
Calories: 163
% Calories from fat: 29
Protein (gm): 23.5
Carbohydrate (gm): 4.6
Fat (gm): 5.1
Saturated fat (gm): 1.8
Cholesterol (mg): 55.9
Sodium (mg): 107
Exchanges
Milk: 0.0
Veg.: 0.0
Fruit: 0.0
Bread: 0.0
Meat: 3.0
Fat: 0.0

1. Cut meats into scant 1-inch cubes and coat lightly with flour. Sprinkle meats with ground allspice; sprinkle lightly with salt and pepper.

2. Layer meats and onions in Dutch oven; add remaining ingredients, except parsley, and heat to boiling. Reduce heat and simmer, covered, until meats are tender, about 1 hour. Discard bay leaves; stir in parsley.

STEW WITH THREE MEATS

The combined flavors of beef, veal, and pork make this stew especially good. Serve with crusty bread.

6 servings

Vegetable cooking spray
1 large onion, minced
16 ounces lean beef, fat trimmed, cut into 1-inch cubes
8 ounces lean pork, fat trimmed, cut into 1-inch cubes
8 ounces lean veal, fat trimmed, cut into 1-inch cubes
1 cup water
1 cup reduced-sodium fat-free beef broth
1 teaspoon paprika
1 teaspoon Spike
¹/₄ teaspoon pepper
1 can (8 ounces) Italian tomatoes, undrained, chopped

Per Serving
Calories: 225
% Calories from fat: 26
Protein (g): 34.7
Carbohydrates (g): 4.8
Fat (g): 6.4
Saturated fat (g): 2.2
Cholesterol (mg): 96.2
Sodium (mg): 172
Exchanges
Milk: 0.0
Veg.: 0.0
Fruit: 0.0
Bread: 0.0
Meat: 4.0
Fat: 0.0

1. Spray Dutch oven with cooking spray; heat over medium heat until hot. Saute onion, beef, pork, and veal until browned, about 10 minutes. Add remaining ingredients, except tomatoes, and heat to boiling; reduce heat and simmer, covered, 1 hour. Add tomatoes and liquid and simmer, covered, 45 minutes or until meats are tender.

MEAT AND VEGETABLE STEW MADRID

This traditional Spanish stew includes beef, chicken, ham, and sausage to make a truly hearty dish.

12 servings

2 pounds lean beef stew meat, fat trimmed, cubed

4 quarts water

1 pound skinless chicken breast, cut into 1-inch pieces

1 pound skinless chicken thighs, cut into 1-inch pieces

8 ounces lean ham, fat trimmed, cubed

2 carrots, sliced

2 leeks, white parts only, sliced

2 medium tomatoes, chopped

12 ounces Chorizo (1/2 recipe) (see p. 180), shaped into small patties, browned

1 pound spinach

Salt and pepper, to taste

1 cup chopped onion

2 teaspoons olive oil

2 cups uncooked rice

2 teaspoons paprika

1/2 teaspoon ground cumin

1 tablespoon tomato paste

Per Serving
Calories: 417
% Calories from fat: 21
Protein (gm): 46.5
Carbohydrate (gm): 33.4
Fat (gm): 9.8
Saturated fat (gm): 3
Cholesterol (mg): 112.6
Sodium (mg): 437
Exchanges
Milk: 0.0
Veg.: 2.0
Fruit: 0.0
Bread: 2.0
Meat: 4.0
Fat: 0.0

1. Combine beef and water in large Dutch oven; heat to boiling. Reduce heat and simmer, 1 hour, skimming foam from surface.

2. Stir in chicken, ham, carrots, leeks, and tomatoes and simmer, covered, until chicken and beef are tender, 45 to 60 minutes, stirring Chorizo and spinach into soup during last 15 minutes. Season to taste with salt and pepper.

3. Remove meats and vegetables to large serving bowl; keep warm. Strain broth. Measure broth, adding water if necessary to make 9 cups; keep warm and reserve.

4. Saute onion in oil in large saucepan until tender, about 5 minutes. Stir in rice and cook, stirring, until rice is lightly browned, about 8 minutes. Stir in paprika, cumin, tomato paste, and 4 cups reserved broth. Heat to boiling; reduce heat and simmer, covered, until rice is tender, about 20 minutes.

5. Spoon rice into soup bowls; spoon meats and vegetables over rice, and ladle remaining 5 cups broth over.

THREE-MEAT GOULASH

The mingled juices of 3 kinds of meat yield unsurpassed flavor.

12 servings

- 8 ounces mushrooms, sliced
- 1 cup chopped onion
- 1/2 cup thinly sliced green onions and tops
- 1-2 tablespoons vegetable oil
- 1 tablespoon paprika
- 1 teaspoon caraway seeds, crushed
- 1/2 teaspoon dried dill weed
- 1 pound boneless beef eye of round steak, fat trimmed, cubed (3/4-inch)
- 1 pound boneless lean pork, fat trimmed, cubed (3/4-inch)
- 1 pound boneless lean veal, fat trimmed, cubed (3/4-inch)
- 1 cup reduced-sodium fat-free beef broth
- 4 large tomatoes, coarsely chopped
- 4-6 tablespoons reduced-sodium tomato paste
- 3/4 cup reduced-fat, *or* fat-free, sour cream
- 3 tablespoons flour
  Salt and pepper, to taste
- 24 ounces no-yolk noodles, cooked, warm

Per Serving
Calories: 446
% Calories from fat: 18
Protein (gm): 40.3
Carbohydrate (gm): 49.5
Fat (gm): 8.6
Saturated fat (gm): 3.1
Cholesterol (mg): 85.4
Sodium (mg): 125
Exchanges
Milk: 0.0
Veg.: 1.0
Fruit: 0.0
Bread: 3.0
Meat: 4.0
Fat: 0.0

1. Saute mushrooms, onion, and green onions in oil in large Dutch oven 5 minutes; stir in paprika, caraway seeds, and dill weed and cook 1 minute longer. Remove and reserve.

2. Add meats to Dutch oven; cook over medium heat until browned, 8 to 10 minutes. Return vegetable mixture to Dutch oven. Stir in beef broth, tomatoes, and tomato paste; heat to boiling. Reduce heat and simmer, covered, until meats are tender, about 40 minutes.

3. Mix sour cream and flour and stir into stew; simmer, stirring, until thickened, 2 to 3 minutes. Season to taste with salt and pepper. Serve over noodles.

SAUSAGE AND BEAN STEW

Serve this hearty winter stew over Polenta (see p. 811) with warm, crusty Garlic Bread (see p. 795)

8 servings

1¹/2 cups chopped onions
¹/2 cup chopped green bell pepper
2 cloves garlic, minced
1-2 tablespoons olive oil
1 pound low-fat smoked sausage, cut into scant ¹/2-inch slices
¹/2 teaspoon dried thyme leaves
¹/2 teaspoon dried savory leaves
1 bay leaf
2 tablespoons flour
1 quart water
2 cans (16 ounces each) reduced-sodium diced tomatoes, undrained
2 cans (15¹/2 ounces each) light red kidney beans, rinsed, drained
1 can (15¹/2 ounces) Great Northern beans, rinsed, drained
Salt and pepper, to taste

Per Serving
Calories: 255
% Calories from fat: 15
Protein (gm): 19.2
Carbohydrate (gm): 39.4
Fat (gm): 4.6
Saturated fat (gm): 1.1
Cholesterol (mg): 26.5
Sodium (mg): 791
Exchanges
Milk: 0.0
Veg.: 1.0
Fruit: 0.0
Bread: 2.0
Meat: 2.0
Fat: 0.0

1. Saute onions, bell pepper, and garlic in olive oil in large saucepan 3 to 4 minutes; add sausage, thyme, savory, and bay leaf and saute until sausage is browned, about 5 minutes. Stir in flour and cook 1 minute longer.

2. Add remaining ingredients, except salt and pepper, and heat to boiling. Reduce heat and simmer, covered, 30 minutes. Discard bay leaf; season to taste with salt and pepper.

ACORN SQUASH STEW WITH SMOKED SAUSAGE

We love the way smoked sausage perks up this chunky, vegetable-rich stew.

4 servings

8 ounces reduced-sodium smoked sausage, halved lengthwise, thinly sliced
1 teaspoon olive oil
2 teaspoons flour
1 can (14 ounces) fat-free beef broth
2 pounds acorn squash, peeled, seeded, cut into 1-inch cubes
1 medium onion, cut into thin wedges
1 can (15 ounces) stewed tomatoes, undrained
1 cup frozen peas
Salt and pepper, to taste

Per Serving
Calories: 298
% Calories from fat: 11
Protein (gm): 17.2
Carbohydrate (gm): 54.9
Fat (gm): 4
Saturated fat (gm): 1
Cholesterol (mg): 26.5
Sodium (mg): 709
Exchanges
Milk: 0.0
Veg.: 0.0
Fruit: 0.0
Bread: 3.0
Meat: 2.0
Fat: 0.0

1. Saute sausage in oil in Dutch oven until lightly browned, about 5 minutes; sprinkle with flour and cook 1 minute longer. Add broth, squash, onion, and tomatoes and liquid. Simmer, covered, until squash is tender, about 10 minutes. Add peas and simmer until heated through, about 3 minutes. Season to taste with salt and pepper.

ELEVEN

Poultry Stews

CHICKEN-IN-THE-POT

If you can find a nice stewing hen for this recipe, you will be rewarded with a wealth of old-fashioned flavor.

8 servings

1 large stewing chicken (about 5 pounds)
Water to cover
3¹/₂ quarts water
1 large onion, quartered
8 medium carrots, sliced, divided
6 leeks, white parts only, sliced, divided
8 ribs celery, sliced, divided
8 sprigs parsley, divided
1 whole clove
¹/₂ cup sliced mushrooms
¹/₂ pound small white onions
Salt and pepper, to taste
4 cups cooked rice, warm

Per Serving
Calories: 496
% Calories from fat: 27
Protein (gm): 40.6
Carbohydrate (gm): 48.7
Fat (gm): 15
Saturated fat (gm): 4.1
Cholesterol (mg): 105.5
Sodium (mg): 147
Exchanges
Milk: 0.0
Veg.: 2.0
Fruit: 0.0
Bread: 3.0
Meat: 4.0
Fat: 0.0

1. Clean chicken and truss legs and wings; place in stockpot, add water to cover, and heat to boiling. Reduce heat and simmer, covered, 5 minutes; remove chicken and discard water.

2. Return chicken to pot with 3¹/₂ quarts water and heat to boiling; reduce heat and simmer, covered, 1 hour, occasionally skimming foam that rises to the surface.

3. Add quartered onion, 1 carrot, 2 leeks, 2 ribs celery and 4 sprigs parsley; simmer, covered, 1 hour. Remove chicken and cut into serving pieces. Strain stew, discarding vegetables. Combine broth, chicken, garlic, remaining vegetables and parsley to pot and simmer, covered, until vegetables are tender, about 20 minutes; season to taste with salt and pepper. Serve over rice in bowls.

CHICKEN STEW WITH PARSLEY DUMPLINGS

For variation, omit the dumplings and serve this savory stew over noodles or mashed potatoes.

6 servings

Vegetable cooking spray
1 cup chopped onion
3 carrots, cut into 3/4-inch pieces
1/2 cup sliced celery
3 cups reduced-sodium chicken broth, divided
1 1/2 cups cubed boneless, skinless chicken breast
1/2-3/4 teaspoon dried sage leaves
1/2 cup frozen peas
2 tablespoons finely chopped parsley leaves
5 tablespoons flour
Salt and pepper, to taste
Parsley Dumplings (recipe follows)

Per Serving
Calories: 233
% Calories from fat: 20
Protein (g): 19.2
Carbohydrates (g): 26.7
Fat (g): 5.1
Saturated fat (g): 1.4
Cholesterol (mg): 35.5
Sodium (mg): 383
Exchanges
Milk: 0.0
Veg.: 2.0
Fruit: 0.0
Bread: 1.0
Meat: 1.5
Fat: 0.5

1. Spray large saucepan with cooking spray; heat over medium heat until hot. Saute onion, carrots, and celery 5 minutes. Add 2 1/2 cups chicken broth, chicken, and sage; heat to boiling. Reduce heat and simmer, covered, until chicken is cooked and vegetables are tender, 10 to 15 minutes.

2. Stir peas and parsley into stew; heat to boiling. Mix flour and remaining 1/2 cup chicken broth; stir into stew. Boil, stirring constantly, until thickened, 1 to 2 minutes. Season to taste with salt and pepper.

3. Spoon dumpling dough into 6 mounds on top of boiling chicken and vegetables (do not drop directly into liquid). Reduce heat and simmer, covered, 10 minutes. Simmer, uncovered, 10 minutes longer.

Parsley Dumplings

3/4 cup all-purpose flour
1 teaspoon baking powder
1/4 teaspoon salt
1 1/2 tablespoons vegetable shortening
1/3 cup 2% reduced-fat milk
1 tablespoon finely chopped parsley

1. Combine flour, baking powder, and salt in small bowl. Cut in shortening with pastry blender until mixture resembles coarse crumbs. Stir in milk to make a soft dough; stir in parsley.

CHICKEN FRICASSEE

Cloves and bay leaf add a flavor update to this dish; more traditional seasonings of rosemary and thyme can be substituted, if desired.

6 servings

Vegetable cooking spray
6 skinless chicken breast halves
(6 ounces each)
1 medium onion, cut into wedges
4 medium carrots, cut into 1-inch pieces
4 ribs celery, cut into l-inch pieces
2 cloves garlic, minced
3 tablespoons flour
2 cans (14 1/2 ounces each) reduced-
sodium fat-free chicken broth
16 whole cloves
2 bay leaves
1 teaspoon lemon juice
1/2 teaspoon sugar
1/2 teaspoon salt
1/4 teaspoon pepper
12 ounces fettuccine, *or* no-yolk noodles,
cooked, warm
Minced parsley leaves, as garnish

Per Serving
Calories: 361
% Calories from fat: 13
Protein (g): 35.9
Carbohydrates (g): 41.5
Fat (g): 5.1
Saturated fat (g): 0.9
Cholesterol (mg): 78.6
Sodium (mg): 401
Exchanges
Milk: 0.0
Veg.: 2.0
Fruit: 0.0
Bread: 2.0
Meat: 3.0
Fat: 0.0

1. Spray large skillet or Dutch oven with cooking spray; heat over medium heat until hot. Cook chicken until browned, about 8 minutes. Remove from skillet. Add vegetables to skillet; saute until tender, about 5 minutes. Stir in flour and cook 1 minute, stirring constantly.

2. Return chicken to skillet. Add chicken broth, cloves, and bay leaves tied in cheesecloth, lemon juice, and sugar. Heat to boiling; reduce heat and simmer, covered, until chicken is tender, about 20 minutes. Simmer, uncovered, until sauce is thickened to medium consistency, about 10 minutes longer. Discard spice packet; stir in salt and pepper. Serve over pasta, topping each serving with a chicken breast; sprinkle with parsley.

CHICKEN STEW WITH SUNFLOWER SEED DUMPLINGS

A recipe from the heartland, with old-fashioned flavor and unique Sunflower Seed Dumplings.

8 servings

Vegetable cooking spray
1 large onion, thinly sliced
2 ribs celery, cut into 1-inch pieces
3 pounds skinless chicken breasts and thighs
1/2 cup dry vermouth, *or* water
3/4 cup reduced-sodium fat-free chicken broth
1 teaspoon minced garlic
1/2 teaspoon dried thyme leaves
4 new potatoes, cut into 1/2-inch cubes
4 large carrots, quartered
Salt and pepper, to taste
Sunflower Seed Dumplings (recipe follows)

Per Serving
Calories: 397
% Calories from fat: 19
Protein (gm): 42.7
Carbohydrate (gm): 32.7
Fat (gm): 8.1
Saturated fat (gm): 1.9
Cholesterol (mg): 103.8
Sodium (mg): 368
Exchanges
Milk: 0.0
Veg.: 0.0
Fruit: 0.0
Bread: 2.0
Meat: 5.0
Fat: 0.0

1. Spray Dutch oven with cooking spray; heat over medium heat until hot. Saute onion and celery until onion is tender, about 5 minutes. Add chicken, vermouth, broth, garlic, and thyme; heat to boiling. Reduce heat and simmer, covered, until chicken is tender, 30 to 40 minutes, adding potatoes and carrots last 15 minutes. Season to taste with salt and pepper.

2. Spoon Sunflower Seed Dumpling dough into 8 mounds on top of boiling stew. Reduce heat and simmer, uncovered, 10 minutes; cover and simmer until dumplings are dry on top, about 10 minutes.

Sunflower Seed Dumplings

makes 8 dumplings

> 1 cup unbleached flour
> 2 teaspoons baking powder
> 1/4 teaspoon salt
> 2 tablespoons margarine
> 1 tablespoon toasted sunflower seeds
> 1/2 cup fat-free milk

1. Combine flour, baking powder, and salt in medium bowl. Cut in margarine with pastry blender until mixture resembles coarse crumbs. Stir in sunflower seeds. Mix in milk, forming a soft dough.

SPRING STEW WITH HERBED CHICKEN AND VEGETABLES

Serve this fresh-flavored stew with crisp-tender asparagus or green beans to celebrate the spring season.

4 servings

> 1 chicken (about 2 pounds), cut into pieces
> 2 quarts water
> Vegetable cooking spray
> 1 medium onion, finely chopped
> 3 garlic cloves, minced
> 1 pound new potatoes, peeled, diced
> 3 medium carrots, cut into 1-inch pieces
> 2 ribs celery, cut into 1-inch pieces
> 8 ounces mushrooms, halved

Per Serving
Calories: 381
% Calories from fat: 28
Protein (gm): 32.8
Carbohydrate (gm): 35.4
Fat (gm): 12
Saturated fat (gm): 3.3
Cholesterol (mg): 84.4
Sodium (mg): 94
Exchanges
Milk: 0.0
Veg.: 1.0
Fruit: 0.0
Bread: 2.0
Meat: 3.0
Fat: 1.0

2 tablespoons fresh, *or* 2 teaspoons dried, dill weed

2 sprigs fresh thyme, *or* 1/2 teaspoon dried thyme leaves

1 teaspoon fresh, *or* 1/2 teaspoon dried, marjoram leaves

1/2 teaspoon fresh, *or* pinch dried, sage leaves

Salt and pepper, to taste

1. Place chicken and water in large saucepan; heat to boiling. Reduce heat and simmer until very tender, about 30 minutes. Remove chicken and reserve 2 cups stock. Remove meat from chicken, cut into bite-sized pieces, and reserve; discard bones.

2. Spray large saucepan with cooking spray; heat over medium heat until hot. Saute onion and garlic until onion is tender, about 5 minutes. Add potatoes, carrots, celery, mushrooms, and 2 cups reserved stock; simmer 10 minutes. Add reserved chicken and herbs; simmer until vegetables are tender, about 10 minutes longer. Season to taste with salt and pepper.

BRUNSWICK STEW

Serve with warm Vinegar Biscuits (see p. 809) for a real down-home taste.

4 servings

1 pound boneless, skinless chicken breast, cut into 1-inch cubes

1/2 cup chopped onion

1/2 cup chopped green bell pepper

1/2 teaspoon crushed red pepper

2 tablespoons margarine

3 tablespoons flour

2 cups reduced-sodium fat-free chicken broth

1 can (15 ounces) butter beans, rinsed drained

1 can (16 ounces) tomatoes, undrained, chopped

1 cup frozen whole-kernel corn

1/2 cup sliced fresh, *or* frozen, okra

Salt and pepper, to taste

Per Serving
Calories: 348
% Calories from fat: 27
Protein (gm): 30.6
Carbohydrate (gm): 37.5
Fat (gm): 11.3
Saturated fat (gm): 2.6
Cholesterol (mg): 51.7
Sodium (mg): 630
Exchanges
Milk: 0.0
Veg.: 1.0
Fruit: 0.0
Bread: 2.0
Meat: 3.0
Fat: 0.5

1. Saute chicken, onion, bell pepper, and crushed red pepper in margarine in large saucepan until lightly browned, about 10 minutes. Sprinkle with flour; cook 2 minutes longer. Stir in broth, beans, and tomatoes and juice; heat to boiling. Reduce heat and simmer, covered, 15 minutes.

2. Stir in corn and okra; simmer, uncovered, until chicken is tender, about 10 minutes. Season to taste with salt and pepper.

ROYAL PALACE CHICKEN AND POTATO STEW

Duchess Potatoes add the royal touch to this lovely stew.

4 servings

4 boneless, skinless chicken breast halves (4 ounces each)
¼ cup all-purpose flour
½ teaspoon paprika
1 tablespoon canola oil
½ cup dry white wine, *or* fat-free chicken broth
¼ cup water
4 ounces pearl onions, peeled
2 medium carrots, julienned
¼ teaspoon dried thyme leaves
Salt and pepper, to taste
Duchess Potatoes (recipe follows)

Per Serving
Calories: 378
% Calories from fat: 26
Protein (gm): 29.9
Carbohydrate (gm): 35.1
Fat (gm): 10.7
Saturated fat (gm): 2.1
Cholesterol (mg): 122.4
Sodium (mg): 420
Exchanges
Milk: 0.0
Veg.: 1.0
Fruit: 0.0
Bread: 2.0
Meat: 3.0
Fat: 1.0

1. Coat chicken with combined flour and paprika. Saute chicken in oil in large skillet until browned on both sides, 5 to 8 minutes. Remove and reserve.

2. Add wine, water, onions, carrots, and thyme to skillet; heat to boiling. Reduce heat and simmer, covered, 10 minutes. Add chicken and simmer, covered, until chicken is tender, 20 to 30 minutes. Season to taste with salt and pepper. Serve in bowls and top with Duchess Potatoes.

Duchess Potatoes

- 1 pound potatoes, peeled, cubed, cooked
- 2 tablespoons fat-free milk
- 2 tablespoons fat-free sour cream
- 1/2 teaspoon salt
  - Dash white pepper
- 1 egg yolk, beaten
- 1 tablespoon margarine, melted

1. Mash potatoes until smooth, gradually adding milk. Mix in sour cream, salt, white pepper, and egg yolk. Drop mixture by spoonfuls onto ungreased cookie sheet and refrigerate until cold.

2. Brush potatoes with margarine; bake at 425 degrees until golden brown, about 15 minutes.

STEWED PLUM CHICKEN

Plum jam and Dijon-style mustard flavor the wine sauce for this chicken. Try apricot jam for variation another time.

6 servings

- 1 1/2 pounds boneless, skinless chicken breast halves
- 1/3 cup all-purpose flour
- 1 teaspoon paprika
- 2 tablespoons margarine
- 1/2 cup red plum jam
- 1/4 cup dry white wine, *or* water
- 2 tablespoons Dijon-style mustard
- 1 teaspoon dried rosemary leaves, crushed
  - Salt and pepper, to taste
- 4 cups cooked rice, warm

Per Serving
Calories: 409
% Calories from fat: 17
Protein (gm): 29.4
Carbohydrate (gm): 53.1
Fat (gm): 7.5
Saturated fat (gm): 1.7
Cholesterol (mg): 69.1
Sodium (mg): 145
Exchanges
Milk: 0.0
Veg.: 0.0
Fruit: 0.0
Bread: 2.5
Meat: 3.0
Fat: 0.0

1. Coat chicken with combined flour and paprika; saute in margarine in large skillet until browned on all sides, about 10 minutes. Stir in combined jam, wine, mustard, and rosemary; heat to boiling. Reduce heat and simmer, covered, until chicken is cooked, about 30 minutes. Season to taste with salt and pepper; serve over rice in bowls.

CHICKEN STEW PAPRIKASH

Lean veal or pork can be substituted for the chicken.

4 servings

1 pound boneless, skinless chicken breast, cut into scant 1-inch cubes
1 tablespoon margarine
1 cup chopped onion
4 cloves garlic, minced
1/2 cup reduced-sodium chicken broth
1/4 cup dry white wine, *or* reduced-sodium chicken broth
1 cup chopped tomato
1 teaspoon paprika
2 tablespoons flour
1/4 cup cold water
1/2 cup fat-free sour cream
Salt and white pepper, to taste
3 cups cooked no-yolk noodles, *or* rice, warm
Finely chopped parsley leaves, as garnish

Per Serving
Calories: 416
% Calories from fat: 18
Protein (g): 35.9
Carbohydrates (g): 47.9
Fat (g): 8.4
Saturated fat (g): 1.4
Cholesterol (mg): 69
Sodium (mg): 139
Exchanges
Milk: 0.0
Veg.: 1.0
Fruit: 0.0
Bread: 3.0
Meat: 3.0
Fat: 0.0

1. Saute chicken in margarine in large saucepan until browned. Add onion and garlic and saute until tender, about 5 minutes. Add chicken broth, wine, tomato, and paprika and heat to boiling; reduce heat and simmer, covered, until chicken is tender, 15 to 20 minutes.

2. Heat mixture to boiling. Mix flour and water; stir into boiling stew. Boil, stirring constantly, until thickened, about 1 minute. Reduce heat to low; stir in sour cream and cook 2 to 3 minutes. Season to taste with salt and white pepper. Serve over noodles; sprinkle with parsley.

NAPA VALLEY BRAISED CHICKEN STEW

Grapes, white wine, and sherry flavor the chicken breast in this recipe. Try it with Spinach Rice (see p. 612).

4 servings

1 pound boneless, skinless chicken breast, cut into strips
1 clove garlic, minced
2 tablespoons chopped onion
1 tablespoon canola oil
2 tablespoons flour
1 cup dry white wine, *or* fat-free chicken broth
1 cup dry sherry, *or* fat-free chicken broth
2 tablespoons chopped parsley
1 bay leaf
1 cup halved white seedless grapes
Salt and pepper, to taste

Per Serving
Calories: 385
% Calories from fat: 28
Protein (gm): 31.1
Carbohydrate (gm): 12.8
Fat (gm): 11.7
Saturated fat (gm): 2.6
Cholesterol (mg): 82.5
Sodium (mg): 75
Exchanges
Milk: 0.0
Veg.: 0.0
Fruit: 1.0
Bread: 0.0
Meat: 4.0
Fat: 2.0

1. Saute chicken, garlic, and onion in oil in large skillet until chicken is browned, about 5 minutes; sprinkle with flour and cook 1 minute longer. Add remaining ingredients, except grapes, salt, and pepper, and heat to boiling. Reduce heat and simmer, covered, 5 minutes. Add grapes and simmer until chicken is tender, 5 to 10 minutes; season to taste with salt and pepper.

SLOW-COOKER CREOLE CHICKEN STEW

Use large bone-in chicken breasts for this New Orleans-inspired recipe, as small breasts will cook too quickly.

4 servings

1 cup fat-free chicken broth
1 can (6 ounces) tomato paste
1 large onion, chopped
2 cups chopped cabbage
1 large green bell pepper, seeded, diced
2 large garlic cloves, minced
1 bay leaf
1 tablespoon lemon juice
1 tablespoon Worcestershire sauce
1 tablespoon sugar
2 teaspoons dried basil leaves
2 teaspoons Dijon mustard
1/4 teaspoon black pepper
3-4 drops hot pepper sauce
2 1/2-3 pounds chicken breast halves, skinned, fat trimmed
Salt, to taste
1 1/4 cups rice, cooked, warm

Per Serving
Calories: 423
% Calories from fat: 11
Protein (g): 40
Carbohydrates (g): 53
Fat (g): 5.0
Saturated fat (g): 1.3
Cholesterol (mg): 91
Sodium (mg): 235
Exchanges
Milk: 0.0
Veg.: 2.5
Fruit: 0.0
Bread: 2.5
Meat: 3.5
Fat: 0.0

1. Combine chicken broth and tomato paste in slow cooker; add remaining ingredients, except salt and rice, and mix well; cover and cook on High 1 hour. Cook on Low 5 to 6 hours.

2. Remove chicken and cut meat into strips, discarding bones; stir back into slow cooker. Discard bay leaf; season to taste with salt. Serve over rice in bowls.

SLOW-COOKER COQ AU VIN

Just add a salad or green vegetable to make a well-rounded meal.

6 servings

1   chicken (about 2¹/₂ pounds), cut up
²/₃ cup chopped green onions and tops
18 pearl onions, peeled
¹/₂ pound whole mushrooms
1   clove garlic, crushed
1   teaspoon Spike
¹/₄ teaspoon pepper
¹/₂ teaspoon dried thyme leaves
6   small new potatoes, unpeeled, scrubbed
1   cup reduced-sodium fat-free chicken broth
1   cup Burgundy wine, *or* reduced-sodium fat-free chicken broth

Per Serving
Calories: 292
% Calories from fat: 16
Protein (gm): 24.2
Carbohydrate (gm): 30.5
Fat (gm): 5.2
Saturated fat (gm): 1.4
Cholesterol (mg): 60.2
Sodium (mg): 91
Exchanges
Milk: 0.0
Veg.: 0.0
Fruit: 0.0
Bread: 2.0
Meat: 3.0
Fat: 0.0

1. Saute chicken and green onions in large skillet until chicken is browned on all sides, about 10 minutes. Place in slow cooker with remaining ingredients, except wine; cover and cook on Low 8 to 10 hours, adding wine during last hour.

SLOW-COOKER STEWED CHICKEN WITH MUSHROOMS AND WINE

One nice feature of the slow cooker is that mushrooms develop a rich, hearty flavor without sauteing. Be sure to use large, bone-in chicken breasts, as small ones will cook too quickly.

5 servings

1¹/₄ cups Burgundy wine, *or* fat-free chicken broth
1   can (6 ounces) tomato paste
1   tablespoon Worcestershire sauce
1   large onion, finely chopped
2   garlic cloves, minced
2   large carrots, grated
8   ounces mushrooms, sliced
1   bay leaf

Per Serving
Calories: 511
% Calories from fat: 11
Protein (g): 48.7
Carbohydrates (g): 55.4
Fat (g): 5.9
Saturated fat (g): 1.5
Cholesterol (mg): 106.7
Sodium (mg): 239
Exchanges
Milk: 0.0
Veg.: 2.0
Fruit: 0.0
Bread: 3.0
Meat: 4.5
Fat: 0.0

4 large chicken breast halves, skinned, fat trimmed
2 teaspoons Italian seasoning
1/4 teaspoon dry mustard
1/4 teaspoon black pepper
Salt, to taste
10 ounces spaghetti, cooked, warm

1. Combine wine, tomato paste, and Worcestershire sauce in slow cooker; stir in remaining ingredients, except salt and spaghetti. Cover and cook on High 1 hour. Cook on Low 5 to 6 hours.

2. Remove chicken and cut into strips, discarding bones; stir back into slow cooker. Discard bay leaf; season to taste with salt. Serve over spaghetti in bowls.

COQ AU VIN

This easy version of the French classic can be assembled in advance and refrigerated if you like; just increase cooking time by 10 minutes.

6 servings

6 boneless, skinless chicken breast halves (4 ounces each), cut into halves
5 slices reduced-sodium bacon, diced
3 green onions and tops, sliced
5 pearl onions, peeled, halved
8 ounces whole small mushrooms
8 small new potatoes, halved
1 teaspoon minced garlic
1/2 teaspoon dried thyme leaves
1/2 teaspoon salt
1/4 teaspoon pepper
1/2 cup water
1/2 cup Burgundy, *or* other dry red, wine, *or* reduced-sodium chicken broth

Per Serving
Calories: 343
% Calories from fat: 13
Protein (g): 31.2
Carbohydrates (g): 39.3
Fat (g): 4.9
Saturated fat (g): 1.5
Cholesterol (mg): 73.2
Sodium (mg): 357
Exchanges
Milk: 0.0
Veg.: 1.0
Fruit: 0.0
Bread: 2.0
Meat: 3.0
Fat: 0.0

1. Place chicken and bacon in 2¹/₂-quart casserole; sprinkle with green onions. Add pearl onions, mushrooms, and potatoes. Sprinkle with combined garlic, thyme, salt, and pepper. Pour water and wine over.

2. Bake, covered, at 325 degrees until chicken and potatoes are tender, about 1¹/₂ hours.

CHICKEN STEW VERONIQUE

Breast of chicken is cooked in a broth with mushrooms, capers, grapes, and wine.

4 servings

1 cup sliced mushrooms

3 tablespoons sliced green onions and tops

2 tablespoons vegetable oil

1 pound boneless, skinless chicken breast, cubed

1 tablespoon flour

1 cup reduced-sodium fat-free chicken broth

¹/₄ cup dry white wine, *or* reduced-sodium chicken broth

1 cup halved seedless green grapes

1 tablespoon drained capers

Salt and pepper, to taste

2 cups cooked rice, warm

Per Serving
Calories: 341
% Calories from fat: 27
Protein (g): 29.6
Carbohydrates (g): 28.8
Fat (g): 10.1
Saturated fat (g): 1.8
Cholesterol (mg): 69
Sodium (mg): 184
Exchanges
Milk: 0.0
Veg.: 0.0
Fruit: 0.5
Bread: 1.5
Meat: 3.0
Fat: 0.5

1. Saute mushrooms and green onions in oil in large skillet until tender; add chicken and saute 5 minutes or until browned. Sprinkle with flour and cook, stirring, 2 to 3 minutes. Stir in broth and white wine. Heat to boiling; reduce heat and simmer, covered, until chicken is cooked, 5 to 8 minutes.

2. Stir in grapes and capers; season to taste with salt and pepper. Serve over rice.

TARRAGON-MUSTARD CHICKEN STEW

Tarragon and mustard team up to give this chicken its tangy flavor.

5 servings

1 pound boneless, skinless chicken breast, cut into bite-sized pieces

1 cup chopped onion

2 large ribs celery, chopped

2 teaspoons olive oil

1¹/₂ cups fat-free chicken broth

2 tablespoons Dijon-style mustard

2 teaspoons brown sugar

1 teaspoon lemon juice

2¹/₂ teaspoons dried tarragon leaves

¹/₄ teaspoon white pepper

2 teaspoons cornstarch

¹/₄ cup water

Salt, to taste

1¹/₄ cups rice, cooked, warm

Per Serving
Calories: 247
% Calories from fat: 14
Protein (g): 16
Carbohydrates (g): 37
Fat (g): 3.8
Saturated fat (g): 0.8
Cholesterol (mg): 30
Sodium (mg): 193
Exchanges
Milk: 0.0
Veg.: 0.5
Fruit: 0.0
Bread: 2.0
Meat: 1.5
Fat: 0.0

1. Saute chicken, onion, and celery in oil in large saucepan until lightly browned, about 10 minutes. Add remaining ingredients, except cornstarch, water, salt, and rice; heat to boiling. Reduce heat and simmer, covered, until chicken is tender, about 20 minutes.

2. Heat to boiling; stir in combined cornstarch and water. Boil, stirring, until thickened, 1 to 2 minutes. Season to taste with salt; serve over rice.

HONEY-MUSTARD CHICKEN STEW

The honey-mustard flavor of this delicious chicken recipe is enhanced by the addition of a little curry powder.

5 servings

1 pound boneless, skinless chicken breast, cut into bite-sized pieces
1 cup chopped onion
2 teaspoons olive oil
1³/₄ cups reduced-sodium fat-free chicken broth
2 tablespoons honey
1 tablespoon Dijon mustard
1-2 teaspoons curry powder
2 cups small cauliflower florets
1 large carrot, thinly sliced
Salt and pepper, to taste
1¹/₄ cups rice, cooked, warm

Per Serving
Calories: 299
% Calories from fat: 12
Protein (g): 22.2
Carbohydrates (g): 42.5
Fat (g): 4
Saturated fat (g): 0.9
Cholesterol (mg): 46
Sodium (mg): 188
Exchanges
Milk: 0.0
Veg.: 1.0
Fruit: 0.0
Bread: 2.5
Meat: 2.0
Fat: 0.0

1. Saute chicken and onion in oil in large saucepan until lightly browned, about 8 minutes. Add remaining ingredients, except salt, pepper, and rice, and heat to boiling. Reduce heat and simmer, covered, until chicken is tender, 15 to 20 minutes. Simmer, uncovered, until stew has thickened to desired consistency, 5 to 10 minutes longer. Season to taste with salt and pepper; serve over rice.

ORANGE CHICKEN AND VEGETABLE STEW

Both orange juice and rind are used to accent this flavorful stew.

6 servings

Vegetable cooking spray
6 boneless, skinless chicken breast halves (4 ounces each)
1 large onion, sliced
2 cloves garlic, chopped
1 tablespoon flour
3 medium tomatoes, chopped
1/2 teaspoon dried marjoram leaves
1/4 teaspoon dried thyme leaves
1 piece cinnamon stick (1-inch)
1 1/2 cups orange juice
2 teaspoons grated orange rind
3 large carrots, cut into 1-inch pieces
3 medium potatoes, unpeeled, cubed
Salt and pepper, to taste

Per Serving
Calories: 318
% Calories from fat: 10
Protein (g): 29.4
Carbohydrates (g): 42.4
Fat (g): 3.5
Saturated fat (g): 0.9
Cholesterol (mg): 69
Sodium (mg): 87
Exchanges
Milk: 0.0
Veg.: 2.0
Fruit: 0.5
Bread: 1.5
Meat: 2.5
Fat: 0.0

1. Spray large skillet with cooking spray; heat over medium heat until hot. Cook chicken over medium heat until browned, about 5 minutes on each side. Arrange chicken in glass baking dish, 12 x 9 inches.

2. Spray skillet with cooking spray; add onion and garlic and saute until tender, 5 to 8 minutes. Stir in flour; cook over medium heat 1 to 2 minutes. Add tomatoes, marjoram, thyme, and cinnamon stick; saute 1 to 2 minutes. Add orange juice and rind to skillet; heat to boiling. Reduce heat and simmer, uncovered, 5 minutes.

3. Arrange carrots and potatoes around chicken; pour orange juice mixture over. Bake, covered, at 350 degrees until chicken is tender, about 30 minutes. Season to taste with salt and pepper.

ROSEMARY CHICKEN STEW

Simple yet elegant, this healthful entrée is excellent served with Microwave Risotto (see p. 661) and a simple vegetable or salad.

4 servings

1½ teaspoons olive oil

1 teaspoon balsamic vinegar

2 large garlic cloves, minced

Grated rind of 1 lemon

¼ teaspoon pepper

4 boneless, skinless chicken breast halves, cut into 2-inch pieces

Vegetable cooking spray

⅓ cup dry white wine, *or* reduced-sodium fat-free chicken broth

¼ teaspoon finely chopped fresh, *or* ½ teaspoon crumbled dried, rosemary leaves

½ cup diced, peeled tomato

Salt, to taste

Per Serving
Calories: 173
% Calories from fat: **25**
Protein (g): 25.6
Carbohydrates (g): **2.4**
Fat (g): 4.7
Saturated fat (g): **1.1**
Cholesterol (mg): **69**
Sodium (mg): 64

Exchanges
Milk: 0.0
Veg.: 0.0
Fruit: 0.0
Bread: 0.0
Meat: 3.0
Fat: 0.0

1. Combine oil, vinegar, garlic, lemon rind, and pepper in medium bowl. Add chicken, toss to coat, and let stand 10 minutes.

2. Spray large skillet with cooking spray; heat over medium heat until hot. Cook chicken until browned on both sides, about 10 minutes. Add remaining ingredients, except salt; heat to boiling. Reduce heat and simmer, covered, until chicken is tender, about 15 minutes. Season to taste with salt.

CHICKEN AND PASTA STEW MARENGO

The orange-scented tomato sauce, subtly seasoned with herbs and wine, benefits from day-ahead preparation, giving flavors an opportunity to meld.

6 servings

6 small boneless, skinless chicken breast halves (3 to 4 ounces each)
  Flour
1 tablespoon olive oil
1 small onion, chopped
3 cloves garlic, minced
1 can (14^1/$_2$ ounces) reduced-sodium chicken broth
^{1}/$_2$ cup dry white wine, *or* reduced-sodium chicken broth
3 tablespoons tomato paste
2 tablespoons grated orange rind
1 teaspoon dried tarragon leaves
1 teaspoon dried thyme leaves
2 cups sliced mushrooms
^{1}/$_4$ teaspoon salt, optional
^{1}/$_4$ teaspoon pepper
12 ounces pappardelle, *or* other wide, flat pasta, cooked, warm

Per Serving
Calories: 343
% Calories from fat: 16
Protein (g): 25.4
Carbohydrates (g): 42.7
Fat (g): 6.1
Saturated fat (g): 1.1
Cholesterol (mg): 43.5
Sodium (mg): 133
Exchanges
Milk: 0.0
Veg.: 1.0
Fruit: 0.0
Bread: 2.5
Meat: 2.5
Fat: 0.0

1. Coat chicken breasts lightly with flour. Saute in oil in Dutch oven until browned, about 5 minutes each side. Remove chicken. Add onion and garlic to Dutch oven; saute until tender, 3 to 4 minutes.

2. Add chicken broth, wine, tomato paste, orange rind, and herbs to Dutch oven; heat to boiling. Add chicken and bake, loosely covered, at 350 degrees until chicken is tender, 45 to 60 minutes, adding mushrooms during last 15 to 20 minutes of cooking time. Stir in salt and pepper. Serve over pasta in bowls, toping each serving with a chicken breast.

CHICKEN STEW PROVENÇAL

Spinach Rice is a flavorful accompaniment to this French-style stew.

5 servings

1 chicken (about 2 pounds), cut up
1 tablespoon olive oil
1 medium onion, chopped
1 clove garlic, chopped
1 cup sliced mushrooms
1/4 cup pitted black olives
8 medium tomatoes, peeled, seeded, coarsely chopped
1 can (6 ounces) reduced-sodium tomato paste
2 teaspoons sugar
1/2 teaspoon dried basil leaves
1/2 teaspoon dried tarragon leaves
1/2 teaspoon dried oregano leaves
Pinch ground nutmeg
2 medium zucchini, sliced
1 medium red bell pepper, sliced
Salt and pepper, to taste
Spinach Rice (recipe follows)

Per Serving
Calories: 491
% Calories from fat: 29
Protein (g): 33.3
Carbohydrates (g): 54.7
Fat (g): 16.4
Saturated fat (g): 3.6
Cholesterol (mg): 67.5
Sodium (mg): 417
Exchanges
Milk: 0.0
Veg.: 2.0
Fruit: 0.0
Bread: 2.5
Meat: 4.0
Fat: 1.0

1. Cook chicken in oil in large skillet over medium heat until browned on all sides, about 10 minutes. Stir in onion and garlic and cook 3 minutes. Stir in mushrooms, olives, tomatoes, tomato paste, sugar, and herbs; heat to boiling. Reduce heat and simmer, covered, until chicken is almost tender, about 25 minutes.

2. Stir in zucchini and bell pepper; simmer until vegetables and chicken are tender, about 8 minutes. Season to taste with salt and pepper. Serve with Spinach Rice.

Spinach Rice

makes 3 cups

   $1/4$ cup chopped onion
   1 teaspoon margarine
   1 cup rice
   $2^1/4$ cups reduced-sodium fat-free chicken
       broth
   2 cups packed spinach leaves, sliced

1. Saute onion in margarine in medium saucepan until tender; stir in rice and broth and heat to boiling. Reduce heat and simmer, covered, until rice is tender, about 25 minutes, stirring in spinach during last 10 minutes of cooking time.

MEDITERRANEAN CHICKEN STEW

Wine, balsamic vinegar, black olives, and rosemary blend to create a Mediterranean flavor.

6 servings

   Vegetable cooking spray
   1 chicken (4 pounds), cut into pieces
   3 cloves garlic, minced
   $1/2$ cup dry white wine, *or* water
   $1/4$ cup balsamic vinegar
   5 plum tomatoes, seeded, chopped
   2 tablespoons sliced black olives
   1 tablespoon dried rosemary leaves
   2 tablespoons fresh, *or* 1 tablespoon
       dried, oregano leaves
   Salt and pepper, to taste

Per Serving
Calories: 220
% Calories from fat: 39
Protein (g): 21.2
Carbohydrates (g): 8.9
Fat (g): 9.6
Saturated fat (g): 2.4
Cholesterol (mg): 59.7
Sodium (mg): 139
Exchanges
Milk: 0.0
Veg.: 1.5
Fruit: 0.0
Bread: 0.0
Meat: 3.0
Fat: 0.5

1. Spray large skillet with cooking spray; heat over medium heat until hot. Cook chicken until browned on all sides, about 10 minutes. Remove chicken and reserve.

2. Saute garlic in skillet until tender, about 3 minutes. Add wine; heat to boiling. Boil until reduced by half, about 3 minutes. Add reserved chicken and remaining ingredients, except salt and pepper; heat to boiling. Reduce heat and simmer, covered, until chicken is cooked, about 20 minutes. Season to taste with salt and pepper.

HUNTER'S STEW

Any game brought back from the hunt was used in this stew of Italian origin.

5 servings

1^1/$_3$ pounds boneless, skinless chicken breast, cut into 1-inch cubes
^{1}/$_4$ cup all-purpose flour
1^1/$_2$ tablespoons olive oil
2 medium onions, chopped
1 medium carrot, coarsely diced
1 cup diced red bell pepper
1 cup diced green bell pepper
2 large garlic cloves, minced
1 can (14^1/$_2$ ounces) reduced-sodium Italian-style chopped tomatoes, un-drained
1^1/$_2$-2 cups reduced-sodium fat-free chicken broth
^{3}/$_4$ teaspoon dried thyme leaves
^{3}/$_4$ teaspoon dried marjoram leaves
^{1}/$_4$ cup tomato paste
^{1}/$_4$ cup water
Salt and pepper, to taste

Per Serving
Calories: 291
% Calories from fat: **24**
Protein (g): 32.1
Carbohydrates (g): 23.8
Fat (g): 7.9
Saturated fat (g): 1.5
Cholesterol (mg): 73.6
Sodium (mg): 393
Exchanges
Milk: 0.0
Veg.: 3.0
Fruit: 0.0
Bread: 0.5
Meat: 3.5
Fat: 0.0

1. Coat chicken with flour; saute in oil in Dutch oven until browned, about 8 minutes. Stir in onions, carrot, bell peppers, and garlic; saute until vegetables begin to brown, about 5 minutes.

2. Add remaining ingredients, except tomato paste, water, salt, and pepper; heat to boiling. Reduce heat and simmer, covered, until chicken is tender, about 25 minutes. Add tomato paste and water and simmer 5 minutes longer; season to taste with salt and pepper.

TUSCAN CHICKEN STEW

This chicken dish is rich with the hearty flavors of country Tuscan cooking.

6 servings

1 cup reduced-sodium fat-free chicken broth, hot

1 package (1 ounce) dried porcini, *or* shiitake mushrooms

6 boneless, skinless chicken breast halves (1¹/₂ pounds)

2 tablespoons flour

2 tablespoons olive oil

¹/₂ cup dry white wine, *or* reduced-sodium fat-free chicken broth

1 can (14 ounces) Italian-seasoned tomato sauce
   Salt and pepper, to taste

Per Serving
Calories: 233
% Calories from fat: 29
Protein (gm): 28.3
Carbohydrate (gm): 9.2
Fat (gm): 7.5
Saturated fat (gm): 1.4
Cholesterol (mg): 69
Sodium (mg): 439
Exchanges
Milk: 0.0
Veg.: 2.0
Fruit: 0.0
Bread: 0.0
Meat: 3.0
Fat: 0.0

1. Pour broth over mushrooms in small bowl; let stand until softened, about 10 minutes. Drain mushrooms, reserving broth. Slice mushrooms, discarding any tough pieces.

2. Coat chicken pieces with flour; saute in oil in large skillet until browned, about 5 minutes on each side. Stir in wine, tomato sauce, reserved broth, and mushrooms; heat to boiling. Reduce heat and simmer, covered, until chicken is tender, about 20 minutes. Remove lid and cook over medium-high heat for 5 minutes to thicken sauce; season to taste with salt and pepper. Serve in shallow bowls.

CHICKEN STEW PEPERONATA

Serve this Italian dish over rice or your favorite pasta.

4 servings

1 pound boneless, skinless chicken breast, cut into 1-inch cubes

1/2 teaspoon minced garlic

1 tablespoon olive oil

2 cups frozen stir-fry pepper blend

1 can (15 ounces) chunky Italian-seasoned tomato sauce

Salt and pepper, to taste

2 tablespoons grated Parmesan cheese

Per Serving
Calories: 215
% Calories from fat: 29
Protein (g): 28.5
Carbohydrates (g): 9.7
Fat (g): 7
Saturated fat (g): 1.8
Cholesterol (mg): 71
Sodium (mg): 674
Exchanges
Milk: 0.0
Veg.: 2.0
Fruit: 0.0
Bread: 0.0
Meat: 3.0
Fat: 0.0

1. Saute chicken and garlic in oil in large skillet until lightly browned. Push chicken to side of pan; add stir-fry pepper blend and cook until softened, 3 to 4 minutes. Stir in tomato sauce. Heat to boiling; reduce heat and simmer, covered, until chicken is cooked through, about 10 minutes. Season to taste with salt and pepper; sprinkle with Parmesan cheese.

CHICKEN AND PASTA SKILLET STEW

Sun-dried tomatoes and black olives lend a rich, earthy flavor to this colorful one-dish meal.

4 servings

1/2 cup chopped onion

1/2 cup chopped green bell pepper

1 tablespoon olive oil

1 pound boneless, skinless chicken breast, cut into 1-inch cubes

4 ounces rigatoni, cooked

1 large zucchini, cubed

1 can (15 1/2 ounces) Italian-seasoned diced tomatoes, undrained

1 teaspoon dried marjoram leaves

Per Serving
Calories: 330
% Calories from fat: 25
Protein (g): 30.9
Carbohydrates (g): 30.7
Fat (g): 9.1
Saturated fat (g): 1.6
Cholesterol (mg): 69
Sodium (mg): 761
Exchanges
Milk: 0.0
Veg.: 1.0
Fruit: 0.0
Bread: 2.0
Meat: 3.0
Fat: 0.0

 3 tablespoons chopped sun-dried
   tomatoes
 2 tablespoons chopped, pitted, oil-cured
   black, *or* Greek, olives
   Salt and pepper, to taste

1. Saute onion and bell pepper in olive oil in large skillet until tender; add chicken and cook, stirring, about 5 minutes. Stir in remaining ingredients, except salt and pepper. Heat to boiling; reduce heat and simmer, uncovered, until thickened, about 10 minutes. Season to taste with salt and pepper.

TOMATO-CHICKEN STEW

This recipe is great served over rice or Herbed Polenta (see p. 812).

6 servings

 1¹/2 pounds boneless, skinless chicken
       breast, cubed
    1 cup sliced onion
    2 cloves garlic, minced
    1 tablespoon canola oil
    1 can (14¹/2 ounces) diced tomatoes,
      undrained
 1¹/2 cups reduced-sodium fat-free chicken
       broth
  ¹/4 cup low-sodium tomato paste
  ¹/2 cup dry white wine, *or* water
    2 teaspoons lemon juice
    1 bay leaf
  ¹/2 teaspoon dried oregano leaves
  ¹/4 teaspoon dried thyme leaves
    2 cups sliced mushrooms
    1 can (15 ounces) Great Northern beans,
      rinsed, drained
      Salt and pepper, to taste

Per Serving
Calories: 253
% Calories from fat: 19
Protein (gm): 32
Carbohydrate (gm): 18.1
Fat (gm): 5.5
Saturated fat (gm): 1
Cholesterol (mg): 69
Sodium (mg): 659
Exchanges
Milk: 0.0
Veg.: 1.0
Fruit: 0.0
Bread: 1.0
Meat: 3.0
Fat: 0.0

1. Saute chicken, onion, and garlic in oil in Dutch oven until browned, about 10 minutes. Add remaining ingredients, except mushrooms, beans, salt, and pepper; heat to boiling. Reduce heat and simmer, covered, 10 minutes. Add mushrooms and beans; simmer, uncovered, until chicken is tender and sauce has thickened, about 10 minutes. Discard bay leaf; season to taste with salt and pepper.

STEWED CHICKEN MARINARA

Team this stew with Focaccia (see p. 788) and a salad, for an easy Italian meal.

4 servings

Vegetable cooking spray
2 cups chopped onions
1¹/₂ cups chopped celery
1 clove garlic, minced
1 pound boneless, skinless chicken breast, cubed
³/₄ teaspoon crushed dried basil leaves
¹/₈ teaspoon crushed dried rosemary leaves
¹/₄ teaspoon crushed dried thyme leaves
1 can (16 ounces) crushed tomatoes, undrained
2 cups chopped zucchini
Salt and pepper, to taste
8 ounces linguine, cooked, warm

Per Serving
Calories: 356
% Calories from fat: 16
Protein (gm): 28.1
Carbohydrate (gm): 48.6
Fat (gm): 6.8
Saturated fat (gm): 1.5
Cholesterol (mg): 51.7
Sodium (mg): 544
Exchanges
Milk: 0.0
Veg.: 2.0
Fruit: 0.0
Bread: 2.0
Meat: 3.0
Fat: 0.0

1. Spray large saucepan with cooking spray; heat over medium heat until hot. Saute onions, celery, garlic, and chicken until lightly browned. Add herbs, tomatoes and liquid, and zucchini; heat to boiling. Reduce heat and simmer, covered, 10 minutes. Simmer, uncovered, until chicken is tender and sauce is thickened, about 10 minutes longer. Season to taste with salt and pepper; serve over linguine.

CHICKEN, MUSHROOM, AND TOMATO STEW WITH POLENTA

Polenta originated as Italian peasant fare but has become a well-known and trendy dish. Easy to make, too, particularly with this easy microwave method.

4 servings

1	medium onion, chopped
2	garlic cloves, minced
2	teaspoons olive oil
8	ounces mushrooms, sliced
1	large carrot, grated
2	cans (14¹/₂ ounces each) Italian tomatoes, undrained, coarsely chopped
1	can (8 ounces) tomato sauce
2	tablespoons tomato paste
1	teaspoon sugar
1	teaspoon dried basil leaves
1	teaspoon dried thyme leaves
2¹/₄	pounds skinned chicken breast, fat trimmed
	Salt and pepper, to taste
	Microwave Polenta (recipe follows)

Per Serving
Calories: 403
% Calories from fat: 17
Protein (g): 38
Carbohydrates (g): 46
Fat (g): 7.8
Saturated fat (g): 1.9
Cholesterol (mg): 85
Sodium (mg): 691
Exchanges
Milk: 0.0
Veg.: 3.0
Fruit: 0.0
Bread: 1.5
Meat: 4.0
Fat: 0.0

1. Saute onion and garlic in oil in Dutch oven until onion is tender, about 5 minutes. Add remaining ingredients, except salt, pepper, and Microwave Polenta; heat to boiling. Reduce heat and simmer, covered, until chicken is tender, about 35 minutes. Remove chicken and cut meat into ¹/₂-inch strips, discarding bones. Return chicken to Dutch oven; season to taste with salt and pepper. Serve over Microwave Polenta.

Microwave Polenta

makes about 3 cups

1¹/₃	cups yellow cornmeal
1	tablespoon sugar
¹/₂	teaspoon salt, optional
3	cups water
1	cup 1% low-fat milk
1	medium onion, diced

1. Combine all ingredients in 2¹/₂-quart microwave-safe casserole. Cook, uncovered, on High power 8 to 9 minutes, stirring occasionally. Remove and stir with wire whisk until smooth. Cover and cook on High 6 to 7 minutes. Remove from microwave and let stand, covered, 3 to 4 minutes.

CHICKEN CACCIATORE WITH ZITI

A stew packed with tender chicken, pungent shallots, mild zucchini, and served over a hearty pasta.

4 servings

1 pound boneless, skinless chicken breast, cut into ³/₄-inch cubes

2 teaspoons olive oil

¹/₂ cup chopped shallots

2 cups cut up canned plum tomatoes

¹/₄ cup dry red wine, *or* reduced-sodium fat-free chicken broth

1 small zucchini, sliced

1 teaspoon Italian seasoning

Salt and pepper, to taste

4 ounces ziti, cooked, warm

Per Serving
Calories: 299
% Calories from fat: 18
Protein (gm): 30.2
Carbohydrate (gm): 27.9
Fat (gm): 6.1
Saturated fat (gm): 1.3
Cholesterol (mg): 69
Sodium (mg): 73
Exchanges
Milk: 0.0
Veg.: 2.0
Fruit: 0.0
Bread: 1.0
Meat: 3.0
Fat: 0.0

1. Saute chicken in oil in large saucepan until lightly browned, about 5 minutes. Add shallots; saute until tender, about 3 minutes. Add tomatoes, wine, zucchini, and Italian seasoning; heat to boiling. Reduce heat and simmer, covered, until chicken is tender, about 15 minutes; season to taste with salt and pepper. Serve over pasta.

CHICKEN STEW WITH RED WINE

Serve this stew with rice or noodles to soak up the delicious broth.

4 servings

4 boneless, skinless chicken breast halves
2 teaspoons olive oil
1 medium onion, chopped
2 large garlic cloves, minced
1 tablespoon flour
3/4 cup reduced-sodium fat-free chicken broth
3/4 cup dry red wine, *or* reduced-sodium fat-free chicken broth
1 bay leaf
1 1/2 teaspoons dried oregano leaves
1/2 teaspoon dried thyme leaves
1/4 teaspoon black pepper
Salt, to taste

Per Serving
Calories: 207
% Calories from fat: 24
Protein (g): 26.8
Carbohydrates (g): 4.7
Fat (g): 5.3
Saturated fat (g): 1.2
Cholesterol (mg): 69
Sodium (mg): 152
Exchanges
Milk: 0.0
Veg.: 1.0
Fruit: 0.0
Bread: 0.0
Meat: 3.0
Fat: 0.0

1. Cook chicken in oil in large skillet until browned on both sides, about 8 minutes. Stir in onion and garlic and saute until tender, about 5 minutes; sprinkle with flour and cook 1 to 2 minutes longer.

2. Add remaining ingredients, except salt; heat to boiling. Reduce heat and simmer, uncovered, until chicken is tender, about 15 minutes; simmer, uncovered, until thickened to desired consistency, 5 to 10 minutes. Discard bay leaf; season to taste with salt.

CHICKEN STEW, ROMAN-STYLE

Serve this delicious stew with Easy Herb Lavosh (see p. 793).

6 servings

Vegetable cooking spray
1 large red bell pepper, thinly sliced
1 large yellow bell pepper, thinly sliced
1 large clove garlic, minced
1 chicken (3¹/₂ pounds), cut up
¹/₄ cup dry white wine, *or* water
2 cans (28 ounces each) plum tomatoes, drained, chopped
2 tablespoons fresh, *or* 1 tablespoon dried, oregano leaves
Spike and pepper, to taste

Per Serving
Calories: 208
% Calories from fat: **33**
Protein (g): 20.4
Carbohydrates (g): 13.6
Fat (g): 7.8
Saturated fat (g): 2.1
Cholesterol (mg): 52.3
Sodium (mg): 462
Exchanges
Milk: 0.0
Veg.: 2.5
Fruit: 0.0
Bread: 0.0
Meat: 2.5
Fat: 0.0

1. Spray Dutch oven with cooking spray; heat over medium heat until hot. Saute bell peppers, garlic, and chicken until chicken is browned, about 10 minutes. Add wine, tomatoes, and oregano; heat to boiling. Reduce heat and simmer, covered, until chicken is tender, about 25 minutes. Season to taste with Spike and pepper.

MED-RIM CHICKEN STEW

Serve this excellent Mediterranean-style stew over Polenta (see p. 811).

4 servings

1 pound boneless, skinless chicken breasts, cubed
¹/₃ cup all-purpose flour
1 clove garlic, crushed
3 tablespoons chopped onion
1 cup sliced mushrooms
1-2 tablespoons olive oil
4 tomatoes, quartered
1 cup dry white wine
1 tablespoon chopped parsley

Per Serving
Calories: 32.8
% Calories from fat: **27**
Protein (gm): 29
Carbohydrate (gm): 20.9
Fat (gm): 10
Saturated fat (gm): 1.7
Cholesterol (mg): 69
Sodium (mg): 376
Exchanges
Milk: 0.0
Veg.: 2.0
Fruit: 0.0
Bread: 0.5
Meat: 3.0
Fat: 1.5

1 teaspoon dried thyme leaves
1 teaspoon dried rosemary leaves
1 teaspoon dried tarragon leaves
¹/₄ cup sliced black olives
2 tablespoons cornstarch
¹/₂ cup reduced-sodium fat-free chicken broth
Salt and pepper, to taste

1. Coat chicken with flour. Saute chicken, garlic, onion, and mushrooms in oil in large skillet until chicken is browned. Add tomatoes, wine, herbs, and olives; simmer, covered, until chicken is tender, about 30 minutes. Remove chicken from skillet and reserve.

2. Heat stew to boiling; stir in combined cornstarch and chicken broth, stirring until thickened, 1 to 2 minutes. Add reserved chicken; season to taste with salt and pepper.

HEARTY CHICKEN AND LENTIL STEW

Lentils thicken this hearty stew, and bacon and white wine add flavor accents.

7 servings

4 slices bacon, cut into 2-inch pieces
1 chicken (about 2¹/₂ pounds), skinned, cut into serving pieces
1 cup dried lentils
1 large rib celery, cut into 1-inch pieces
1 medium onion, chopped
1 large clove garlic, minced
1-1¹/₂ cups water, *or* fat-free chicken broth
¹/₂ cup dry white wine, *or* water
1 can (16 ounces) chopped tomatoes, undrained
¹/₂ teaspoon dried thyme leaves
Salt and pepper, to taste
1 tablespoon chopped parsley

Per Serving
Calories: 257
% Calories from fat: **27**
Protein (gm): 25.7
Carbohydrate (gm): 18.5
Fat (gm): 7.8
Saturated fat (gm): 2
Cholesterol (mg): 54.7
Sodium (mg): 246
Exchanges
Milk: 0.0
Veg.: 1.0
Fruit: 0.0
Bread: 1.0
Meat: 3.0
Fat: 0.0

1. Saute bacon in large saucepan until crisp; remove bacon and reserve. Drain all but 2 teaspoons bacon fat from saucepan; add chicken to saucepan and saute until browned on all sides, about 10 minutes.

2. Add reserved bacon, lentils, celery, onion, garlic, 1 cup water, wine, tomatoes, and thyme; heat to boiling. Reduce heat and simmer, covered, until chicken is tender, about 40 minutes, adding remaining 1/2 cup water if needed for desired consistency. Season to taste with salt and pepper; sprinkle with parsley.

MEXICAN CHICKEN, PORK, AND PINEAPPLE STEW

A luscious stew with flavor accents of tropical fruit, sweet cinnamon, and piquant ancho chili.

6 servings

Vegetable cooking spray
12 ounces boneless, skinless chicken breast, cut into 1 1/2-inch cubes
12 ounces pork tenderloin, cut into 1 1/2-inch cubes
2 tablespoons slivered almonds
1 tablespoon sesame seeds
1 piece cinnamon stick (1-inch)
3 ancho chilies, stems, seeds, and veins discarded
2 medium tomatoes, cut into 1-inch pieces
1 can (14 1/2 ounces) reduced-sodium fat-free chicken broth, divided
1 cup cubed jicama
1 cup cubed pineapple, *or* 1 can (8 ounces) pineapple chunks, drained
1 small ripe plantain, cut into 1/2-inch pieces
Salt and pepper, to taste
4 cups cooked rice, warm, optional

Per Serving
Calories: 239
% Calories from fat: 22
Protein (g): 28.1
Carbohydrates (g): 19.6
Fat (g): 5.9
Saturated fat (g): 1.4
Cholesterol (mg): 67.2
Sodium (mg): 81
Exchanges
Milk: 0.0
Veg.: 1.0
Fruit: 1.0
Bread: 0.0
Meat: 3.0
Fat: 0.0

1. Spray large skillet with cooking spray; heat over medium heat until hot. Cook chicken and pork over medium heat until browned, about 5 minutes. Remove from skillet.

2. Add almonds, sesame seeds, and cinnamon stick to skillet. Cook over medium heat until almonds and sesame seeds are toasted, 3 to 4 minutes; transfer mixture to blender container. Add chilies and tomatoes to skillet and cook over medium heat until tomatoes are soft, 1 to 2 minutes; transfer to blender. Add 1 cup broth to blender and process until mixture is smooth.

3. Spray medium saucepan with cooking spray; heat over medium heat until hot. Cook chili mixture over medium heat until slightly thickened, 4 to 5 minutes. Add meat mixture, remaining broth, jicama, and fruit; heat to boiling. Reduce heat and simmer, covered, until meats are tender, about 30 minutes. Season to taste with salt and pepper. Serve over rice, if desired.

GREEN SALSA CHICKEN STEW

The homemade Refried Black Beans are especially good, but canned can be substituted for convenience.

6 servings

6 boneless, skinless chicken breast halves
1 tablespoon vegetable oil
1/3 cup chopped onion
1 clove garlic, chopped
2 cups mild, *or* hot, green salsa
3 cups packed sliced romaine lettuce leaves
1/2 cup reduced-sodium fat-free chicken broth
1/4 cup fat-free sour cream
1 teaspoon flour
2 tablespoons chopped cilantro
Salt and pepper, to taste
Refried Black Beans (recipe follows)
3 cups cooked rice, warm

Per Serving
Calories: 459
% Calories from fat: 13
Protein (gm): 39.5
Carbohydrate (gm): 57.9
Fat (gm): 6.2
Saturated fat (gm): 1.4
Cholesterol (mg): 73
Sodium (mg): 386
Exchanges
Milk: 0.0
Veg.: 0.0
Fruit: 0.0
Bread: 4.0
Meat: 3.0
Fat: 0.0

1. Cook chicken in oil in large skillet over medium heat until browned on both sides, about 8 minutes. Stir in onion and garlic; cook 2 minutes longer.

2. Process salsa, lettuce, and broth in food processor or blender until almost smooth. Add to skillet; heat to boiling. Reduce heat and simmer, covered, until chicken is tender and juices run clear, about 35 minutes.

3. Stir in combined sour cream and flour; simmer 1 minute. Stir in cilantro; season to taste with salt and pepper. Serve with Refried Black Beans and rice.

Refried Black Beans

makes 3 cups

1¹/₄ cups dried black beans
     Vegetable cooking spray
¹/₂ cup chopped onion
     Salt and pepper, to taste

1. Cover beans with 2 inches water in large saucepan; heat to boiling and boil, uncovered, 2 minutes. Let stand, covered, 1 hour. Drain beans; cover with 2 inches water and heat to boiling; reduce heat and simmer until tender, about 1 hour. Drain, reserving 2 cups liquid.

2. Spray large skillet with cooking spray; heat over medium heat until hot. Saute onion until tender, about 5 minutes. Add 1 cup beans and 1 cup reserved liquid to skillet. Cook over high heat, mashing beans until almost smooth with potato masher or meat mallet. Add half the remaining beans and liquid; continue cooking and mashing beans. Repeat with remaining beans and liquid. Season to taste with salt and pepper.

CARIBBEAN CHICKEN STEW

Chicken stew lightly flavored with curry, dried apricots, and raisins and served with peanut and banana garnishes.

6 servings

1½ pounds boneless, skinless chicken breast, cubed
½ medium onion, finely chopped
2 tablespoons margarine, divided
1 bay leaf
1 tablespoon curry powder
¼ teaspoon crushed red pepper
1½ cups reduced-sodium fat-free chicken broth
1 cup dried apples
½ cup chopped dried apricots
½ cup raisins
2 tablespoons sugar
2 teaspoons lemon juice
Salt and pepper, to taste
1 banana, sliced
4 cups cooked rice, warm
¼ cup chopped unsalted peanuts

Per Serving
Calories: 485
% Calories from fat: 23
Protein (gm): 26.2
Carbohydrate (gm): 68.7
Fat (gm): 12.6
Saturated fat (gm): 2.8
Cholesterol (mg): 51.7
Sodium (mg): 147
Exchanges
Milk: 0.0
Veg.: 0.0
Fruit: 2.0
Bread: 2.5
Meat: 3.0
Fat: 0.5

1. Saute chicken and onion in 1 tablespoon margarine in large saucepan until chicken is browned, about 8 minutes. Add remaining ingredients, except salt, pepper, banana, peanuts, and rice; heat to boiling. Reduce heat and simmer, covered, until chicken is tender, about 20 minutes. Season to taste with salt and pepper.

2. Saute bananas in small skillet in remaining 1 tablespoon margarine. Serve stew over rice; top with sauteed bananas and peanuts.

CARIBBEAN STEWED CHICKEN WITH BLACK BEANS

The flavors of the islands come alive in this chicken-and-black bean skillet dinner.

4 servings

1 pound boneless, skinless chicken breast, cut into strips
1 medium onion, chopped
2 garlic cloves, minced
2 teaspoons margarine
1 cup fat-free chicken broth
1 can (8 ounces) tomato sauce
1/4 cup light rum, *or* fat-free chicken broth
1 green bell pepper, diced
1/2 teaspoon ground cinnamon
1/4 teaspoon ground cloves
2 cups cooked black beans, *or* 1 can (16 ounces) black beans, drained
Salt and cayenne pepper, to taste
1 1/4 cups rice, cooked, warm

Per Serving
Calories: 336
% Calories from fat: 9
Protein (g): 20
Carbohydrates (g): 50
Fat (g): 3.4
Saturated fat (g): 1.0
Cholesterol (mg): 32
Sodium (mg): 390
Exchanges
Milk: 0.0
Veg.: 0.5
Fruit: 0.0
Bread: 3.0
Meat: 2.0
Fat: 0.0

1. Saute chicken, onion, and garlic in margarine in large skillet until browned, about 10 minutes. Add remaining ingredients, except black beans, salt, cayenne pepper, and rice, and heat to boiling. Reduce heat and simmer 15 minutes or until chicken is tender. Add beans and simmer 2 to 3 minutes. Season to taste with salt and cayenne pepper; serve over rice.

CHICKEN STEW MADRID

This simple stew of chicken, artichokes, and tomatoes would be lovely served over Orange Cilantro Rice (see p. 205).

4 servings

4 boneless, skinless chicken breast halves
1 small onion, sliced
1 tablespoon canola oil
1 can (14¹/2 ounces) reduced-sodium stewed tomatoes, undrained
¹/2 can (15-ounce size) artichoke hearts, drained
Salt and pepper, to taste

Per Serving
Calories: 228
% Calories from fat: 27
Protein (gm): 29.3
Carbohydrate (gm): 11.3
Fat (gm): 6.8
Saturated fat (gm): 1.1
Cholesterol (mg): 73
Sodium (mg): 223
Exchanges
Milk: 0.0
Veg.: 2.0
Fruit: 0.0
Bread: 0.0
Meat: 3.0
Fat: 0.0

1. Saute chicken and onion in oil in large saucepan until chicken is lightly browned. Add tomatoes and liquid and artichoke hearts and simmer, covered, until chicken is tender, about 25 minutes.

SPANISH CHICKEN AND RICE STEW

The Spanish name of this dish, Arroz con Pollo, translates as "rice with chicken." A simple name for a classic and flavorful stew.

6 servings

1 pound boneless, skinless chicken breast, cut into bite-sized pieces
2 teaspoons olive oil
1 large onion, chopped
2 garlic cloves, minced
2¹/2 cups fat-free chicken broth
¹/2 cup dry sherry, *or* fat-free chicken broth
1 large green bell pepper, diced
1 large red bell pepper, diced
¹/4 teaspoon crushed saffron threads
¹/4 teaspoon black pepper
Dash cayenne pepper
1¹/4 cups uncooked rice
1¹/2 cups frozen green peas
Salt, to taste

Per Serving
Calories: 246
% Calories from fat: 12
Protein (g): 15
Carbohydrates (g): 35
Fat (g): 3.1
Saturated fat (g): 1.0
Cholesterol (mg): 30
Sodium (mg): 255
Exchanges
Milk: 0.0
Veg.: 1.0
Fruit: 0.0
Bread: 2.0
Meat: 1.5
Fat: 0.0

1. Saute chicken in oil in Dutch oven until lightly browned, 8 to 10 minutes. Stir in onion and garlic and saute until onion is tender, about 5 minutes.

2. Add remaining ingredients, except green peas and salt, and heat to boiling. Reduce heat and simmer, covered, until rice is tender, 20 to 25 minutes, stirring in peas during last 5 minutes of cooking time. Season to taste with salt.

PAELLA

Paella, a staple of Spanish cookery, was traditionally prepared with whatever the cook had on hand, so it can be made with a variety of ingredients.

4 servings

8 ounces boneless, skinless chicken breast, cut into bite-sized pieces

3 ounces Canadian bacon, fat trimmed, cut into thin strips

1 large onion, chopped

2 garlic cloves, minced

2 teaspoons olive oil

2³/₄ cups reduced-sodium fat-free chicken broth

¹/₄ teaspoon crushed saffron threads

1 can (14¹/₂ ounces) Italian-style tomatoes, undrained, coarsely chopped

1 can (14³/₄ ounces) artichoke hearts, drained

1 large red bell pepper, diced

1 large green bell pepper, diced

1 teaspoon dried thyme leaves

¹/₂ teaspoon dried basil leaves

¹/₄ teaspoon cayenne pepper

¹/₄ teaspoon pepper

1¹/₄ cups uncooked rice

8 ounces medium shrimp, peeled, deveined

Salt, to taste

Per Serving
Calories: 371
% Calories from fat: 11
Protein (g): 28
Carbohydrates (g): 56
Fat (g): 4.6
Saturated fat (g): 1.2
Cholesterol (mg): 101
Sodium (mg): 678
Exchanges
Milk: 0.0
Veg.: 2.0
Fruit: 0.0
Bread: 3.0
Meat: 2.0
Fat: 0.0

1. Saute chicken, Canadian bacon, onion, and garlic in oil in Dutch oven until lightly browned, about 10 minutes. Add remaining ingredients, except shrimp and salt; heat to boiling. Reduce heat and simmer, covered, until rice is almost tender, about 20 minutes. Add shrimp and simmer 5 to 6 minutes or until rice is tender and shrimp are cooked and pink. Season to taste with salt.

CHICKEN STEW, CATALAN STYLE

Lightly sauteed eggplant, zucchini, and bell peppers are added to this stew near the end of cooking time.

4 servings

Vegetable cooking spray
1 chicken (about 3 pounds), cut into serving pieces
2 onions, finely chopped
1 clove garlic, minced
2 tomatoes, peeled, seeded, chopped
1 bay leaf
1/2 cup dry white wine, *or* fat-free chicken broth
1 small eggplant, cubed
2 zucchini, sliced
2 green, *or* red, bell peppers, seeded, chopped
1/2 cup tomato sauce
1 teaspoon Spike
1 teaspoon dried basil leaves
2 tablespoons chopped cilantro
2 tablespoons chopped parsley

Per Serving
Calories: 357
% Calories from fat: 24
Protein (gm): 39.8
Carbohydrate (gm): 24.2
Fat (gm): 9.6
Saturated fat (gm): 2.6
Cholesterol (mg): 108.4
Sodium (mg): 294
Exchanges
Milk: 0.0
Veg.: 5.0
Fruit: 0.0
Bread: 0.0
Meat: 4.0
Fat: 0.0

1. Spray Dutch oven with cooking spray; heat over medium heat until hot. Cook chicken until browned on all sides, about 10 minutes; remove chicken and reserve.

2. Saute onions and garlic in Dutch oven until tender, about 5 minutes. Add reserved chicken, tomatoes, bay leaf, and white wine; heat to boiling. Reduce heat and simmer, covered, 30 minutes.

3. Spray large skillet with cooking spray; heat over medium heat until hot. Saute eggplant, zucchini, and peppers until lightly browned. Add to Dutch oven with remaining ingredients, except cilantro and parsley, and simmer, uncovered, until chicken is tender, 10 to 20 minutes. Discard bay leaf. Stir in cilantro and parsley.

CHICKEN STEW ATHENOS

Cinnamon and lemon give this tomato-based stew the signature flavors of Greek cooking. Crumbly feta cheese tops the dish off with an unexpected salty tang.

4 servings

1 pound boneless, skinless chicken breast, cut into 3/4-inch pieces

1 teaspoon olive oil

1 can (14 ounces) reduced-sodium stewed tomatoes, undrained

1 tablespoon lemon juice

2 teaspoons minced garlic

1 cinnamon stick

1 bay leaf

1/4 cup dry sherry, *or* reduced-sodium chicken broth

Salt and pepper, to taste

8 ounces medium egg noodles, cooked, warm

1/4 cup crumbled feta cheese

Per Serving
Calories: 412
% Calories from fat: 17
Protein (g): 34.4
Carbohydrates (g): 46
Fat (g): 7.9
Saturated fat (g): 2.5
Cholesterol (mg): 124.2
Sodium (mg): 370
Exchanges
Milk: 0.0
Veg.: 2.0
Fruit: 0.0
Bread: 2.0
Meat: 4.0
Fat: 0.0

1. Saute chicken in oil in large saucepan until lightly browned, 5 to 8 minutes. Add tomatoes and liquid, lemon juice, garlic, cinnamon stick, bay leaf, and sherry. Heat to boiling; reduce heat and simmer, covered, until chicken is cooked through, about 15 minutes. Season to taste with salt and pepper; discard bay leaf and cinnamon stick. Serve over noodles; sprinkle with cheese.

MIDDLE EASTERN-STYLE CHICKEN STEW

Couscous cooks quickly and lends a uniquely pleasing texture to one-pot meals like this one.

5 servings

1	pound boneless, skinless chicken breast, cut into 1-inch cubes
1	large onion, chopped
2	garlic cloves, minced
2	teaspoons olive oil
1³/₄	cups fat-free chicken broth
1	green bell pepper, diced
2	cups chopped fresh tomato
2	cups cooked garbanzo beans, *or* 1 can (15 ounces) garbanzo beans, rinsed, drained
¹/₂	cup raisins
1	bay leaf
1¹/₂	teaspoons dried thyme leaves
1	teaspoon ground cumin
¹/₄	teaspoon ground allspice
¹/₈	teaspoon ground cloves
¹/₈	teaspoon black pepper
1	cup couscous
	Salt, to taste
	Chopped parsley, as garnish

Per Serving
Calories: 389
% Calories from fat: 12
Protein (g): 24
Carbohydrates (g): 63
Fat (g): 5.4
Saturated fat (g): 1
Cholesterol (mg): 34
Sodium (mg): 235
Exchanges
Milk: 0.0
Veg.: 1.0
Fruit: 1.0
Bread: 3.0
Meat: 1.5
Fat: 0.0

1. Saute chicken, onion, and garlic in oil in Dutch oven until lightly browned, about 10 minutes. Add remaining ingredients, except couscous, salt, and parsley; heat to boiling. Reduce heat and simmer, covered, 20 to 25 minutes or until chicken is tender. Discard bay leaf.

2. Add couscous and heat to boiling; boil for 2 minutes. Let stand, covered, 10 to 15 minutes. Add salt to taste; sprinkle with parsley.

MOROCCAN CHICKEN STEW WITH COUSCOUS

Tantalize your taste buds with this extra-easy version of an exotic Middle-Eastern stew.

4 servings

    1/4 teaspoon cinnamon
    1/2 teaspoon ground coriander
      1 pound boneless, skinless chicken breast, cut into 3/4-inch cubes
      1 teaspoon olive oil
      2 teaspoons minced garlic
    1/2 teaspoon cumin seeds
      1 dried cayenne pepper, minced
      3 cups stewed tomatoes
    3/4 cup dried apricots
    1/2 cup dried currants
      1 cup couscous, cooked, warm

Per Serving
Calories: 499
% Calories from fat: 8
Protein (gm): 34.5
Carbohydrate (gm): 80.1
Fat (gm): 4.8
Saturated fat (gm): 1.1
Cholesterol (mg): 69
Sodium (mg): 498
Exchanges
Milk: 0.0
Veg.: 2.0
Fruit: 0.0
Bread: 2.5
Meat: 3.0
Fat: 0.0

1. Combine cinnamon and coriander, and sprinkle over chicken. Saute chicken in oil in Dutch oven until lightly browned. Add remaining ingredients, except couscous, and heat to boiling. Reduce heat and simmer, covered, until chicken is cooked and apricots are tender, about 15 minutes. Serve over couscous.

MOROCCAN CHICKEN AND CHICKPEA STEW

This dish is great for entertaining because it serves eight and can be doubled easily.

8 servings

      2 cloves garlic, crushed
      1 teaspoon ground ginger
  3 1/2 teaspoons Spike, divided
    1/4 teaspoon black pepper
      1 tablespoon water
      4 pounds skinless chicken pieces
    1/2 cup chopped onion
      1 teaspoon ground turmeric

Per Serving
Calories: 357
% Calories from fat: 23
Protein (gm): 42.9
Carbohydrate (gm): 24.3
Fat (gm): 9
Saturated fat (gm): 2.4
Cholesterol (mg): 115.7
Sodium (mg): 254
Exchanges
Milk: 0.0
Veg.: 0.0
Fruit: 0.0
Bread: 2.0
Meat: 4.0
Fat: 0.0

2 tablespoons chopped parsley

1 cinnamon stick

1 can (14^1/$_2$ ounces) reduced-sodium fat-free chicken broth

1 can (15 ounces) chickpeas, rinsed, drained

1 cup sliced onion

^{1}/$_2$ cup raisins

Salt, to taste

1.   Combine garlic, ginger, ^{1}/$_2$ teaspoon Spike, pepper, and 1 tablespoon water in small bowl and mix well. Brush mixture over chicken and chill 1 hour.

2.   Combine chopped onion, turmeric, parsley, cinnamon stick, and chicken broth in large stock pot; heat to boiling. Reduce heat, add chicken and marinade; simmer 1 hour or until chicken is tender, adding chickpeas, onions, and raisins 10 minutes before end of cooking time. Discard cinnamon stick; season to taste with salt.

GARDEN STEW WITH CHICKEN AND COUSCOUS

Take advantage of your garden's bounty with this quick and easy stew, substituting vegetables you have in abundance.

6 servings (about 1^1/$_2$ cups each)

Garlic-flavored vegetable cooking spray

6 boneless, skinless chicken breast halves (4 ounces each)

Salt and pepper, to taste

2 medium onions, cut into 1-inch pieces

8 ounces shiitake, *or* white, mushrooms, sliced

1 small jalapeño chili, finely chopped

1 tablespoon flour

2 cups reduced-sodium fat-free chicken broth

2 medium zucchini, sliced

1 medium turnip, cut into ^{1}/$_4$-inch cubes

Per Serving
Calories: 397
% Calories from fat: 6
Protein (g): 29
Carbohydrates (g): **63**
Fat (g): 2.7
Saturated fat (g): 0.7
Cholesterol (mg): 46
Sodium (mg): 141
Exchanges
Milk: 0.0
Veg.: 3.0
Fruit: 0.0
Bread: 3.0
Meat: 2.0
Fat: 0.0

8 ounces baby carrots, halved

4 medium tomatoes, coarsely chopped

$^1/_2$ cup loosely packed cilantro leaves

2 packages (5.9 ounces each) couscous, spice packets discarded, cooked, warm

1. Spray large skillet with cooking spray; heat over medium heat until hot. Cook chicken over medium heat until no longer pink in the center, 15 to 20 minutes, turning to brown both sides. Season to taste with salt and pepper. Remove from skillet; keep warm.

2. Add onions, mushrooms, and jalapeño chili to skillet; saute 5 minutes. Stir in flour; cook 1 minute longer.

3. Add broth, zucchini, turnip, and carrots to skillet; heat to boiling. Reduce heat and simmer, covered, until vegetables are tender, 10 to 12 minutes. Add tomatoes and cilantro to stew; season to taste with salt and pepper. Serve over couscous in bowls, topping each serving with a chicken breast.

GINGER-ORANGE CHICKEN AND SQUASH STEW

Any winter squash, such as acorn, butternut, or Hubbard, is appropriate for this orange-and-ginger-accented stew; sweet potatoes can be substituted too.

6 servings (about 1$^1/_2$ cups each)

1 pound boneless, skinless chicken breast, cubed

2 medium onions, chopped

2 medium green bell peppers, coarsely chopped

2 cloves garlic, minced

1 tablespoon basil-flavored, *or* regular, olive oil

3 cups cubed, peeled, seeded winter yellow squash (about 2 pounds) ($^1/_2$-inch cubes)

3 medium Idaho potatoes, peeled, cut into $^1/_2$-inch cubes

1 can (14$^1/_2$ ounces) reduced-sodium diced tomatoes, undrained

Per Serving
Calories: 425
% Calories from fat: 13
Protein (g): 30
Carbohydrates (g): 60.4
Fat (g): 6.1
Saturated fat (g): 1.2
Cholesterol (mg): 81.2
Sodium (mg): 162
Exchanges
Milk: 0.0
Veg.: 3.0
Fruit: 0.0
Bread: 3.0
Meat: 2.0
Fat: 0.0

> 2 cups reduced-sodium fat-free chicken broth
> 1/2 cup orange juice
> 1/4 teaspoon ground ginger
> 1 cup fat-free sour cream
> 2 tablespoons minced parsley
> 1 tablespoon grated orange rind
> Salt and pepper, to taste
> 4 cups cooked noodles, *or* brown basmati rice, warm

1. Saute chicken, onions, peppers, and garlic in oil in large saucepan until chicken is browned and vegetables are tender, 8 to 10 minutes. Add squash, potatoes, tomatoes and liquid, broth, orange juice, and ginger; heat to boiling. Reduce heat and simmer, uncovered, 30 minutes.

2. Reduce heat to low; stir in sour cream, parsley, and orange rind; season to taste with salt and pepper. Serve over noodles.

CHICKEN STEW WITH DRIED FRUIT

Prunes and dried apricots make a wonderfully sweet broth for chicken.

4 servings

> 1 pound boneless, skinless chicken breast, cut into bite-sized pieces
> 1 large onion, chopped
> 1 garlic clove, minced
> 2 teaspoons olive oil
> 1 cup fat-free chicken broth
> 1/4 cup light rum, *or* fat-free chicken broth
> 1 1/2 cups mixed pitted prunes and dried apricots
> 1/2 red bell pepper, diced
> 1/2 teaspoon ground ginger
> 1 bay leaf
> Salt and pepper, to taste
> 1 1/4 cups rice, cooked, warm

Per Serving
Calories: 406
% Calories from fat: 9
Protein (g): 19
Carbohydrates (g): 68
Fat (g): 4.2
Saturated fat (g): 0.8
Cholesterol (mg): 36
Sodium (mg): 105
Exchanges
Milk: 0.0
Veg.: 1.0
Fruit: 2.0
Bread: 2.5
Meat: 1.5
Fat: 0.0

1. Saute chicken, onion, and garlic in oil in large saucepan until onion is tender. Add remaining ingredients, except salt, pepper, and rice; heat to boiling. Reduce heat and simmer, covered, until chicken is cooked, about 20 minutes. Simmer, uncovered, until sauce has thickened slightly and chicken is tender, about 5 minutes longer. Discard bay leaf; season to taste with salt and pepper; serve over rice.

CURRY-GINGER CHICKEN STEW

This stew is seasoned with a unique Ginger Spice Blend.

10 servings

2 cups chopped onions

2 cloves garlic, finely chopped

2 tablespoons corn oil

Curry-Ginger Spice Blend (recipe follows)

2 chickens (about 2¹/₂ pounds each), cut up, skinned

1 cup chopped, peeled, seeded tomatoes

¹/₂ cup low-fat plain yogurt

1¹/₂ cups frozen peas

¹/₄ cup chopped cilantro

Salt and pepper, to taste

5 cups cooked rice, warm

Per Serving
Calories: 334
% Calories from fat: 27
Protein (gm): 28.8
Carbohydrate (gm): 31.3
Fat (gm): 9.8
Saturated fat (gm): 2.2
Cholesterol (mg): 73
Sodium (mg): 328
Exchanges
Milk: 0.0
Veg.: 0.0
Fruit: 0.0
Bread: 2.0
Meat: 3.0
Fat: 0.5

1. Saute onions and garlic in oil in Dutch oven until tender, about 8 minutes; stir in Curry-Ginger Spice Blend and saute 2 minutes. Stir in chicken and cook over medium heat 5 minutes.

2. Stir in tomatoes and yogurt; heat to boiling. Reduce heat and simmer, covered, until chicken is tender, about 40 minutes. Stir in peas and simmer until hot; stir in cilantro and season to taste with salt and pepper. Serve over rice.

Curry-Ginger Spice Blend

makes about 1/4 cup

2 tablespoons finely chopped gingerroot
1 tablespoon sesame seeds
1 teaspoon salt
2 teaspoons coriander seeds
1 teaspoon cumin seeds
1 teaspoon ground turmeric
1/2 teaspoon peppercorns
1/4 teaspoon crushed red pepper
1/4 teaspoon fennel seeds

1. Process all ingredients in blender until powdered.

CURRIED CHICKEN AND APPLE STEW

*The flavors of apple and ginger make this stew a special treat. Serve with
Basmati Rice Pilaf (see p. 577).*

6 servings

3 pounds boneless, skinless chicken
    breast halves
2 tablespoons margarine
1 cup chopped onion
1 cup coarsely chopped, peeled cooking
    apples
1 cup sliced carrots
1 teaspoon minced garlic
1 1/2 tablespoons curry powder
1 teaspoon ground ginger
2 tablespoons flour
2 cups reduced-sodium fat-free chicken
    broth
    Salt and pepper, to taste
1 cup fat-free plain yogurt

Per Serving
Calories: 384
% Calories from fat: 24
Protein (gm): 55.6
Carbohydrate (gm): 14.8
Fat (gm): 10
Saturated fat (gm): 2.5
Cholesterol (mg): 138.7
Sodium (mg): 258
Exchanges
Milk: 0.0
Veg.: 1.0
Fruit: 0.5
Bread: 0.0
Meat: 6.0
Fat: 0.0

1. Cook chicken in margarine in Dutch oven over medium heat
until browned on all sides, about 10 minutes. Remove chicken
and reserve. Add onion, apples, carrots, and garlic and saute 5
minutes; stir in curry powder, ginger, and flour and cook 2 minutes longer.

2. Stir in broth and reserved chicken; heat to boiling. Reduce heat and simmer, covered, until chicken is cooked, about 40 minutes. Season to taste with salt and pepper; stir in yogurt.

INDIAN CURRY CHICKEN AND VEGETABLE STEW

The mixture of spices gives this stew a unique flavor; however, 3 tablespoons of curry powder can be substituted for the Curry Seasoning.

4 servings

- 1 large onion, finely chopped
- 1 cup evaporated fat-free milk
- 2 tablespoons white wine vinegar
- 1 can (15 ounces) crushed tomatoes, undrained
- 1 can (6 ounces) tomato paste
- 2 tablespoons brown sugar
- 1 can ($13^3/4$ ounces) reduced-sodium vegetable broth
- 1-2 tablespoons Curry Seasoning (recipe follows)
- 1 boneless, skinless chicken breast, cut into 1-inch pieces
- 8 ounces mushrooms, roughly chopped
- 1 cup chopped carrots
- 1 cup sliced okra
- 1 cup small cauliflower florets
- 1 cup cut green beans
- 1 large potato, peeled, cut into 1-inch cubes
- 2 cups cooked brown rice, warm

Per Serving
Calories: 478
% Calories from fat: 12
Protein (gm): 30.5
Carbohydrate (gm): 77.7
Fat (gm): 6.5
Saturated fat (gm): 1.6
Cholesterol (mg): 43.6
Sodium (mg): 770
Exchanges
Milk: 0.5
Veg.: 2.0
Fruit: 0.0
Bread: 4.0
Meat: 2.0
Fat: 0.0

1. Combine onion, evaporated milk, vinegar, tomatoes and liquid, tomato paste, brown sugar, broth, and Curry Seasoning in large saucepan; heat to boiling; reduce heat and simmer 5 minutes.

2. Stir in remaining ingredients, except brown rice; heat to boiling. Reduce heat and simmer, covered, until chicken is tender, about 25 minutes. Serve over brown rice.

Curry Seasoning

makes about 2 tablespoons

    2 teaspoons ground coriander
    1 teaspoon ground turmeric
  1/2 teaspoon ground cumin
  1/2 teaspoon dry mustard
  1/2 teaspoon ground ginger
  1/2 teaspoon black pepper
  1/4 teaspoon chili powder

1. Combine all ingredients in small bowl.

CURRIED CHICKEN AND VEGETABLE STEW

A variety of spices and herbs are combined to make the fragrant curry that seasons this dish.

4 servings

        Vegetable cooking spray
 12-16 ounces boneless, skinless chicken
        breast, cubed
  1/2 cup chopped onion
    2 cloves garlic
    1 medium head cauliflower, cut into
        florets
    2 medium potatoes, peeled, cut into
        1/2-inch cubes
    2 large carrots, cut into 1/2-inch slices
 11/2 cups reduced-sodium fat-free chicken
        broth
  3/4 teaspoon ground turmeric
  1/4 teaspoon dry mustard
  1/4 teaspoon ground cumin
  1/4 teaspoon ground coriander
    1 tablespoon flour
    2 tablespoons cold water
    1 large tomato, chopped
    2 tablespoons finely chopped parsley
  1-2 tablespoons lemon juice
        Salt, cayenne, and black pepper, to taste

Per Serving
Calories: 250
% Calories from fat: 11
Protein (g): 28.4
Carbohydrates (g): 29
Fat (g): 3.1
Saturated fat (g): 0.7
Cholesterol (mg): 51.7
Sodium (mg): 203
Exchanges
Milk: 0.0
Veg.: 2.0
Fruit: 0.0
Bread: 1.0
Meat: 2.0
Fat: 0.0

1. Spray large saucepan with cooking spray; heat over medium heat until hot. Saute chicken, onion, and garlic until chicken is browned, 5 to 6 minutes. Add cauliflower, potatoes, carrots, broth, spices, and herbs to saucepan; heat to boiling. Reduce heat and simmer, covered, until chicken and vegetables are tender, 10 to 15 minutes.

2. Heat mixture to boiling. Mix flour and water; stir into boiling mixture. Cook, stirring constantly, until thickened. Stir in tomato, parsley, and lemon juice; simmer 2 to 3 minutes longer. Season to taste with salt, cayenne, and black pepper.

THAI-SPICED CHICKEN AND CARROT STEW

Peanut sauce, gingerroot, and sesame oil add plenty of Asian-style flavor to this dish!

4 servings

1 pound boneless, skinless chicken breast, cut into $1/2$-inch cubes

4 carrots, diagonally sliced

1 tablespoon minced gingerroot

1 tablespoon minced garlic

1 can ($14^1/2$ ounces) reduced-sodium fat-free chicken broth

1 tablespoon reduced-sodium soy sauce

$3/4$ cup sliced scallions

1 tablespoon Thai peanut sauce, *or* **1** tablespoon peanut butter and $1/2$ teaspoon crushed red pepper

1 teaspoon sugar

$1/2$ teaspoon dark sesame oil

3 cups cooked rice, warm

Per Serving
Calories: 358
% Calories from fat: **11**
Protein (g): 32.8
Carbohydrates (g): **44.4**
Fat (g): 4.3
Saturated fat (g): 1.3
Cholesterol (mg): 69
Sodium (mg): 371
Exchanges
Milk: 0.0
Veg.: 2.0
Fruit: 0.0
Bread: 2.0
Meat: 3.0
Fat: 0.0

1. Combine chicken, carrots, gingerroot, garlic, broth, and soy sauce in large saucepan. Heat to boiling; reduce heat and simmer, covered, until chicken is cooked and carrots are tender, about 15 minutes.

2. Add scallions, peanut sauce, sugar, and sesame oil; simmer 5 minutes longer. Serve over rice.

SHERRY-STEWED CHICKEN

Chicken is simmered in a ginger, sherry, and soy accented broth.

4 servings

1 pound boneless, skinless chicken breast, cubed

1 teaspoon dark sesame oil

1 cup chopped onion

1 cup sliced snow peas

1/2 cup chopped red bell pepper

1 teaspoon minced garlic

1 teaspoon minced gingerroot

1 cup reduced-sodium fat-free chicken broth

1/4 cup dry sherry, *or* water

1 1/2 tablespoons cornstarch

3-4 tablespoons low-sodium soy sauce

12 ounces Chinese egg noodles, *or* vermicelli, cooked, warm

1/4 cup sliced green onions and tops

Per Serving
Calories: 491
% Calories from fat: 18
Protein (gm): 33.7
Carbohydrate (gm): 63.8
Fat (gm): 9.7
Saturated fat (gm): 2.3
Cholesterol (mg): 125.1
Sodium (mg): 501
Exchanges
Milk: 0.0
Veg.: 2.0
Fruit: 0.0
Bread: 4.0
Meat: 3.0
Fat: 0.0

1. Saute chicken in oil in large skillet until browned, about 5 minutes; stir in onion, snow peas, bell pepper, garlic, and gingerroot. Saute 5 minutes; stir in broth and sherry. Heat to boiling. Simmer, covered, until chicken is tender, about 15 minutes. Stir in combined cornstarch and soy sauce; simmer until thickened. Serve over noodles; sprinkle with green onions.

SWEET-SOUR CHICKEN AND VEGETABLE STEW

Chicken and vegetables are simmered in cider and seasoned with honey and vinegar for a refreshing sweet-sour flavor.

6 servings (about 1 1/2 cups each)

Butter-flavored vegetable cooking spray
- 1 pound boneless, skinless chicken breast, cubed
- 1/2 cup chopped shallots
- 1 medium red bell pepper, chopped
- 2 cloves garlic, minced
- 1 can (14 1/2 ounces) reduced-sodium diced tomatoes, undrained
- 1 cup apple cider, *or* apple juice
- 1 1/2 tablespoons honey
- 1 1/2 tablespoons cider vinegar
- 1 bay leaf
- 1/4 teaspoon ground nutmeg
- 3 1/2 cups cubed, peeled yellow winter squash (butternut *or* acorn)
- 4 medium Idaho potatoes, peeled, cut into 3/4-inch cubes
- 2 medium sweet potatoes, peeled, cut into 3/4-inch cubes
- 2 medium tart green apples, unpeeled, cut into 3/4-inch pieces
- 1 1/2 cups fresh, *or* frozen, whole-kernel corn
  Salt and pepper, to taste
- 4 cups cooked basmati, *or* other aromatic, rice, warm

Per Serving
Calories: 530
% Calories from fat: 4
Protein (g): 24.9
Carbohydrates (g): 103.3
Fat (g): 2.7
Saturated fat (g): 0.7
Cholesterol (mg): 46
Sodium (mg): 64
Exchanges
Milk: 0.0
Veg.: 2.0
Fruit: 1.0
Bread: 4.5
Meat: 2.0
Fat: 0.0

1. Spray large saucepan with cooking spray; heat over medium heat until hot. Saute chicken, shallots, bell pepper, and garlic until chicken is browned, 6 to 8 minutes.

2. Add tomatoes and liquid, cider, honey, vinegar, bay leaf, nutmeg, squash, Idaho and sweet potatoes to saucepan. Heat to boiling; reduce heat and simmer, covered, 15 minutes or until potatoes are tender. Add apples and corn and simmer until apples are tender, about 5 minutes.

3. Discard bay leaf; season stew to taste with salt and pepper. Serve over rice.

COUNTRY TURKEY RAGOUT WITH WHITE WINE

Turkey simmers with white wine and herbs to make a flavorful stew; delicious over rice or Polenta (see p. 811).

5 servings

1¹/₂ pounds skinless turkey breast, cut into 1-inch cubes
¹/₃ cup all-purpose flour
2 tablespoons plus ¹/₂ teaspoon olive oil
2 large garlic cloves, minced
1 large onion, chopped
2 large carrots, coarsely diced
1 large rib celery, cut into ¹/₄-inch slices
2¹/₂ cups sliced mushrooms
1 can (15 ounces) reduced-sodium Italian tomatoes, undrained
¹/₂ cup dry white wine
¹/₄ cup reduced-sodium fat-free chicken broth
¹/₄ teaspoon dried rosemary leaves
¹/₄ teaspoon sage
Salt and pepper, to taste

Per Serving
Calories: 278
% Calories from fat: 30
Protein (g): 26.7
Carbohydrates (g): 18.3
Fat (g): 9.3
Saturated fat (g): 1.8
Cholesterol (mg): 52.8
Sodium (mg): 95
Exchanges
Milk: 0.0
Veg.: 2.0
Fruit: 0.0
Bread: 0.5
Meat: 3.0
Fat: 0.0

1. Coat turkey with flour; cook turkey in oil in large skillet over medium heat until browned, 8 to 10 minutes. Stir in vegetables and saute until they begin to brown, about 5 minutes.

2. Stir in remaining ingredients, except salt and pepper; heat to boiling. Reduce heat and simmer, covered, until turkey is tender, about 30 minutes. Season to taste with salt and pepper.

TURKEY-WILD RICE STEW

Get ready to dine on the wild side—the wild side of rice, that is! In this recipe, we've combined wild rice with another native American food, turkey, to create a super stick-to-your-ribs supper.

4 servings

1 pound boneless, skinless turkey breast, cut into ¹/₂-inch cubes

1 teaspoon olive oil

1 onion, chopped

3 cups reduced-sodium fat-free chicken broth

¹/₂ cup wild rice

2 carrots, thinly sliced

2 cups chopped broccoli florets

1 tablespoon chopped fresh, *or* 1 teaspoon dried, sage leaves

Salt and pepper, to taste

Per Serving
Calories: 250
% Calories from fat: 13
Protein (g): 29
Carbohydrates (g): 24.6
Fat (g): 3.8
Saturated fat (g): 0.9
Cholesterol (mg): 44.7
Sodium (mg): 196
Exchanges
Milk: 0.0
Veg.: 1.0
Fruit: 0.0
Bread: 1.0
Meat: 3.0
Fat: 0.0

1. Saute turkey in oil in large saucepan until lightly browned. Add onion and cook until tender. Stir in broth, wild rice, and carrots. Heat to boiling; reduce heat and simmer, covered, until rice is tender, about 45 minutes.

2. Stir in broccoli and sage; simmer until broccoli is tender, about 5 minutes. Season to taste with salt and pepper.

TURKEY STEW, MILAN STYLE

This recipe recalls the tangy flavor of osso bucco, the Italian classic dish featuring veal shanks braised in wine.

5 servings

1¼ pounds skinless turkey breast, cut into bite-sized pieces
3 tablespoons flour
2 teaspoons olive oil
1 large onion, chopped
2 garlic cloves, minced
1¼ cups dry white wine
1 cup reduced-sodium fat-free beef broth
1 can (8 ounces) reduced-sodium tomato paste
8 baby carrots, halved
2 ribs celery, thinly sliced
¼ cup chopped fresh parsley
1½ dried thyme leaves
2 bay leaves
3 strips lemon zest
Salt and pepper, to taste
1½ cups rice, cooked

Per Serving
Calories: 434
% Calories from fat: 10
Protein (g): 26.7
Carbohydrates (g): 59.5
Fat (g): 4.9
Saturated fat (g): 1.2
Cholesterol (mg): 44
Sodium (mg): 99
Exchanges
Milk: 0.0
Veg.: 2.0
Fruit: 0.0
Bread: 3.0
Meat: 3.0
Fat: 0.0

1. Coat turkey with flour; cook in oil in Dutch oven until browned, about 5 minutes. Stir in onion and garlic; cook until tender, about 5 minutes.

2. Stir in remaining ingredients, except salt, pepper, and rice, and heat to boiling. Reduce heat and simmer, covered, until turkey is tender, about 40 minutes. Discard bay leaves; season to taste with salt and pepper. Serve over rice.

TURKEY SANCOCHE

Sancoche is a hearty stew of meats, fish, vegetables, and seasonings that hails from Latin America. Our one-pot version features turkey, winter vegetables, and black beans, topped with toasted cashews.

4 servings

- 1 pound boneless, skinless turkey breast, cut into 3/4-inch cubes
- 1 sweet potato, peeled, cut into 3/4-inch cubes
- 1 white potato, peeled, cut into 3/4-inch cubes
- 1 small butternut squash, peeled, cut into 3/4-inch cubes
- 1 onion, chopped
- 1 can (15 ounces) black beans, rinsed, drained
- 1 can (14 1/2 ounces) reduced-sodium fat-free chicken broth
- 1 jalapeño chili, minced
- 1 teaspoon annatto seeds, optional
- 1 teaspoon cumin seeds, toasted
  Salt and pepper, to taste
- 1/4 cup coarsely chopped cashews, toasted

Per Serving
Calories: 324
% Calories from fat: 18
Protein (g): 29.6
Carbohydrates (g): 43.7
Fat (g): 7.2
Saturated fat (g): 1.5
Cholesterol (mg): 44.7
Sodium (mg): 652
Exchanges
Milk: 0.0
Veg.: 0.0
Fruit: 0.0
Bread: 2.5
Meat: 2.0
Fat: 0.0

1. Combine all ingredients, except salt, pepper, and cashews, in 4-quart saucepan. Heat to boiling; reduce heat and simmer, covered, until turkey and vegetables are tender, about 20 minutes. Season to taste with salt and pepper. Spoon into serving bowls and sprinkle with cashews.

SOUTHWEST TURKEY STEW WITH CHILI-CHEESE DUMPLINGS

Turkey tenderloin and Southwest seasonings, topped with savory Chili-Cheese Dumplings, make an outstanding meal.

6 servings

1¹/2 pounds turkey tenderloins, cut into 1-inch pieces
1 tablespoon vegetable oil
1 green bell pepper, chopped
1 red bell pepper, chopped
1 medium onion, chopped
1 jalapeño chili, minced
2 cloves garlic, minced
1 tablespoon chili powder
1 teaspoon ground cumin
1 can (15 ounces) chili beans in spicy sauce, undrained
1 can (14¹/2 ounces) reduced-sodium stewed tomatoes, undrained
1 cup reduced-sodium fat-free chicken broth
Salt and pepper, to taste
Chili Cheese Dumplings (recipe follows)

Per Serving
Calories: 352
% Calories from fat: 25
Protein (gm): 30
Carbohydrate (gm): 37.7
Fat (gm): 10.2
Saturated fat (gm): 2.7
Cholesterol (mg): 48.5
Sodium (mg): 786
Exchanges
Milk: 0.0
Veg.: 2.0
Fruit: 0.0
Bread: 2.0
Meat: 3.0
Fat: 0.0

1. Saute turkey in oil in large saucepan until browned, about 10 minutes; stir in bell peppers, onion, jalapeño chili, garlic, chili powder, and cumin. Saute until onion is tender, about 5 minutes.

2. Stir in beans and liquid, tomatoes and liquid, and broth. Heat to boiling; reduce heat and simmer, covered, 10 minutes. Season to taste with salt and pepper. Drop Chili-Cheese Dumpling dough onto stew; cook, uncovered, 10 minutes. Cook covered until dumplings are done, about 10 minutes longer.

Chili-Cheese Dumplings

makes 6 dumplings

2/3 cup all-purpose flour
1/3 cup yellow cornmeal
1 1/2 teaspoons baking powder
1 teaspoon chili powder
1/2 teaspoon salt
2 tablespoons vegetable shortening
1/4 cup (1 ounce) shredded reduced-fat
Monterey Jack cheese
1 tablespoon finely chopped cilantro
1/2 cup fat-free milk

1. Combine flour, cornmeal, baking powder, chili powder, and salt in medium bowl; cut in shortening with pastry blender until mixture resembles coarse crumbs. Mix in cheese and cilantro; stir in milk, forming a soft dough.

TURKEY STEW WITH APRICOTS AND CHILIES

This quick and easy recipe proves that leftover turkey doesn't have to be boring. The tangy combination of chilies and apricots is reminiscent of Indian flavors.

4 servings

1 cup chopped onion
2 garlic cloves, minced
2 teaspoons margarine
1 1/4 cups fat-free chicken broth
1 teaspoon ground cumin
1/4 teaspoon ground coriander
1/4 teaspoon ground allspice
10 dried apricots, quartered
1 tablespoon chopped canned green chilies
1 cup chopped fresh tomato
1 pound cooked turkey breast, cut into bite-sized pieces
Salt and pepper, to taste
1 1/4 cups rice, cooked, warm

Per Serving
Calories: 319
% Calories from fat: 7
Protein (g): 27
Carbohydrates (g): 46
Fat (g): 2.6
Saturated fat (g): 0.7
Cholesterol (mg): 65
Sodium (mg): 260
Exchanges
Milk: 0.0
Veg.: 0.0
Fruit: 0.5
Bread: 2.0
Meat: 3.0
Fat: 0.0

1. Saute onion and garlic in margarine in large saucepan until onion is tender, about 5 minutes. Add remaining ingredients, except salt, pepper, and rice; heat to boiling. Reduce heat and simmer, covered, until turkey is tender, about 20 minutes. Season to taste with salt and pepper; serve over rice.

ITALIAN-STYLE TURKEY SAUSAGE AND FENNEL STEW

Sweet Italian sausage seasons this stew of squash, parsnips, and Brussels sprouts. For spicier flavor, replace the sweet sausage with the hot variety.

4 servings

Vegetable cooking spray
12-16 ounces mild Italian-style turkey sausage
1 medium onion, cut into thin wedges
1 can (15 ounces) reduced-sodium diced tomatoes, undrained
1 cup reduced-sodium fat-free chicken broth
1 pound butternut squash, peeled, cut into $3/4$-inch cubes
2 parsnips, peeled, sliced
1 fennel bulb, trimmed, cut into $1/2$-inch slices
12 Brussels sprouts, halved
$1/2$ teaspoon crushed red pepper
1 teaspoon Italian seasoning
Salt and pepper, to taste

Per Serving
Calories: 310
% Calories from fat: 26
Protein (g): 21.8
Carbohydrates (g): 39.4
Fat (g): 9.7
Saturated fat (g): 2.6
Cholesterol (mg): 45.6
Sodium (mg): 780
Exchanges
Milk: 0.0
Veg.: 2.0
Fruit: 0.0
Bread: 2.0
Meat: 2.0
Fat: 0.0

1. Spray large saucepan with cooking spray; heat over medium heat until hot. Add sausage and cook until browned, about 10 minutes; remove sausage and slice. Add onion to saucepan; saute until tender, about 5 minutes.

2. Stir in tomatoes and liquid, broth, squash, parsnips, fennel, and sliced sausage. Heat to boiling; reduce heat and simmer, covered, 10 minutes. Stir in Brussels sprouts, crushed red pepper, and Italian seasoning. Simmer until Brussels sprouts are tender, 10 to 15 minutes. Season to taste with salt and pepper.

TWELVE

Seafood Stews

SAVORY FISH STEW

Serve with generous squares of warm Roasted Chili Cornbread (see p. 804).

8 servings

Per Serving
Calories: 175
% Calories from fat: 20
Protein (gm): 21.5
Carbohydrate (gm): 10.2
Fat (gm): 4
Saturated fat (gm): 0.7
Cholesterol (mg): 79.7
Sodium (mg): 539
Exchanges
Milk: 0.0
Veg.: 2.0
Fruit: 0.0
Bread: 0.0
Meat: 2.0
Fat: 0.0

    1   cup chopped onion
    4   cloves garlic, minced
    2   tablespoons margarine
    2   teaspoons dried basil leaves
 1¹/₂   teaspoons dried oregano leaves
  ¹/₂   teaspoon ground turmeric
  ¹/₄   teaspoon crushed red pepper
    2   bay leaves
    1   can (28 ounces) stewed tomatoes,
        undrained
    2   cups clam juice, *or* water
  ³/₄   cup white wine, *or* water
    1   pound cod, *or* other whitefish fillets,
        cut into 1-inch pieces
 8-12   ounces peeled, deveined shrimp
 8-12   ounces bay scallops
        Salt and pepper, to taste

1.   Saute onion and garlic in margarine in large saucepan until tender, about 5 minutes. Stir in basil, oregano, turmeric, crushed red pepper, and bay leaves; cook 1 to 2 minutes longer.

2.   Add tomatoes and liquid, clam juice, and wine; heat to boiling. Reduce heat and simmer, covered, 20 minutes.

3.   Add seafood and simmer, covered, until cod is tender and flakes with a fork, 5 to 8 minutes. Discard bay leaves; season to taste with salt and pepper.

Variation:
Creamy Scallop Stew—Make recipe through Step 2, omitting oregano, crushed red pepper, tomatoes, and white wine. Heat stew to boiling; stir in combined ¹/₄ cup all-purpose flour and 1 cup fat-free half-and-half, *or* fat-free milk. Boil, stirring, until thickened, 1 to 2 minutes. Add 1 to 1¹/₂ pounds bay scallops, omitting cod and shrimp; reduce heat and simmer, uncovered, until scallops are tender, 5 to 8 minutes. Season to taste with salt and pepper.

FRUITS OF THE SEA STEW

Fennel seed, orange rind, and white wine add subtle flavor to this aromatic stew.

8 servings

3	carrots, chopped
1	large onion, thinly sliced
3	cloves garlic. minced
1-2	tablespoons margarine
1	tablespoon flour
1	teaspoon fennel seeds, lightly crushed
1	tablespoon minced orange rind
1	quart Fish Stock (see p. 9), *or* clam juice
1/2-1	cup dry white wine, *or* water
5	medium tomatoes, peeled, chopped
2	rounds firm fish fillets (cod, red snapper, salmon, orange roughy, halibut, etc.), cut into 1 1/2-inch pieces
1/4	cup chopped parsley
	Salt and pepper, to taste

Per Serving
Calories: 174
% Calories from fat: 14
Protein (gm): 22.8
Carbohydrate (gm): 10.1
Fat (gm): 2.6
Saturated fat (gm): 0.5
Cholesterol (mg): 51.9
Sodium (mg): 110
Exchanges
Milk: 0.0
Veg.: 2.0
Fruit: 0.0
Bread: 0.0
Meat: 2.0
Fat: 0.0

1. Saute carrots, onion, and garlic in margarine in large saucepan until onion is tender, about 8 minutes; add flour, fennel seeds, and orange rind and cook 1 to 2 minutes longer.

2. Add Fish Stock, wine, and tomatoes; heat to boiling. Reduce heat and simmer, covered, 30 minutes. Add fish and simmer, uncovered, until fish is tender and flakes with a fork, about 10 minutes. Stir in parsley; season to taste with salt and pepper.

Variation:

Fish Stew Salsa Verde—Make recipe as above, sauteing 1 chopped small jalapeño chili with the carrots, onion, and garlic. Decrease tomatoes to 3 and add 1 pound chopped, husked tomatillos, 1/2 teaspoon crushed cumin seeds, and 1/2 teaspoon dried oregano leaves; omit fennel seeds and orange rind. Sprinkle each serving generously with finely chopped cilantro.

FISH STEW WITH VEGETABLES AND GARLIC

This dish is a garlic lover's dream. Serve with crusty bread and salad for a wonderful meal any time of year.

6 servings

1	large red onion, peeled, sliced
2	tablespoons olive oil
2-3	pounds small potatoes, peeled, cut into 1/2-inch slices
2	large carrots, cut into 1-inch slices
1-2	ribs celery, cut into 1/2-inch pieces
	Black pepper, to taste
1	teaspoon dried basil leaves
4-6	garlic cloves, chopped
	Spike, to taste
2 1/2	pounds whitefish fillets, cut into 2-inch pieces
1/4	cup lemon juice
	Pepper, to taste

Per Serving
Calories: 358
% Calories from fat: **17**
Protein (gm): 38.8
Carbohydrate (gm): **34.2**
Fat (gm): **7**
Saturated fat (gm): **1.2**
Cholesterol (mg): 100.**2**
Sodium (mg): 177
Exchanges
Milk: 0.0
Veg.: 1.0
Fruit: 0.0
Bread: 2.0
Meat: 4.0
Fat: 0.0

1. Saute onion in oil in Dutch oven until tender, about 5 minutes. Add potatoes, carrots, celery, and pepper; saute 3 to 4 minutes. Add basil, garlic, Spike, and enough water to cover vegetables; heat to boiling. Reduce heat and simmer, covered, 10 to 15 minutes. Add fish and simmer, uncovered, until fish is tender and flakes with a fork, about 10 minutes. Add lemon juice; season to taste with pepper.

CIOPPINO WITH PASTA

A California favorite! Feel free to substitute other kinds of fresh fish, according to season, availability, and price.

6 servings (about 1 cup each)

1 cup chopped green bell pepper
1 cup chopped onion
1 cup sliced mushrooms
4 cloves garlic, minced
1 tablespoon olive oil
3 cups chopped tomatoes
1/2 cup dry white wine, *or* clam juice
1 tablespoon tomato paste
2 tablespoons finely chopped parsley
2 teaspoons dried oregano leaves
2 teaspoons dried basil leaves
1 teaspoon ground turmeric
8 ounces sea scallops
8 ounces crabmeat, cut into 1/2-inch pieces
1 halibut, *or* haddock, steak (4 ounces), cut into 1-inch pieces
12 mussels, scrubbed
1/2 teaspoon salt
1/4 teaspoon pepper
12 ounces fettuccine, cooked, warm

Per Serving
Calories: 516
% Calories from fat: **24**
Protein (g): 32.6
Carbohydrates (g): 63
Fat (g): 13.6
Saturated fat (g): 2.8
Cholesterol (mg): 107.8
Sodium (mg): 685
Exchanges
Milk: 0.0
Veg.: 3.0
Fruit: 0.0
Bread: 3.0
Meat: 3.0
Fat: 1.0

1. Saute bell pepper, onion, mushrooms, and garlic in oil in large saucepan until onion is tender, about 5 minutes.

2. Stir in tomatoes, wine, tomato paste, and herbs; heat to boiling. Reduce heat and simmer, covered, 5 minutes. Simmer, uncovered, 20 minutes or until thickened to desired consistency.

3. Add seafood; simmer, covered, until halibut is tender and flakes with a fork, about 10 minutes. Discard any mussels that have not opened; season to taste with salt and pepper. Serve over fettuccine in bowls.

PINE BARK FISH STEW

I happened upon this wonderfully satisfying fish stew at a restaurant on River Street in Savannah. In this reduced-fat version, some of the ingredients are different, but I've recreated the rich and creamy taste and texture of the original stew.

8 servings

2 cups chopped onions
1 large garlic clove, minced
2 teaspoons margarine
2¹/₂ cups fat-free chicken broth
1 bottle (8 ounces) clam juice
3¹/₂ cups cubed, peeled potato (³/₄-inch)
2 cups coarsely chopped cauliflower
¹/₃ cup dry sherry, *or* fat-free chicken broth
1 bay leaf
2 teaspoons lemon juice
1¹/₂ teaspoons dried thyme leaves
1 teaspoon dried basil leaves
¹/₄ teaspoon dry mustard
¹/₄ teaspoon white pepper
³/₄ cup 1% reduced-fat milk
8 ounces lean whitefish such as flounder, turbot, *or* haddock, cut into bite-sized pieces
8 ounces medium shrimp, peeled, deveined
8 ounces bay scallops
¹/₄ teaspoon salt

Per Serving
Calories: 163
% Calories from fat: 13
Protein (g): 18
Carbohydrates (g): 18
Fat (g): 2.4
Saturated fat (g): 0.8
Cholesterol (mg): 68
Sodium (mg): 363
Exchanges
Milk: 0.0
Veg.: 0.5
Fruit: 0.0
Bread: 1.0
Meat: 1.5
Fat: 0.0

1. Saute onions and garlic in margarine in Dutch oven until onion is tender, about 5 minutes. Add broth, clam juice, potatoes, cauliflower, sherry, bay leaf, lemon juice, thyme, basil, dry mustard, and white pepper; heat to boiling. Reduce heat and simmer, covered, 12 to 15 minutes or until vegetables are tender. Discard bay leaf.

2. Process 3 cups mixture in blender or food processor until smooth. Return to Dutch oven and stir in milk. Add seafood and simmer, uncovered, until fish is tender and flakes with a fork, 5 to 8 minutes. Stir in salt.

BAYOU SNAPPER STEW

Serve this Southern-style favorite with Green Chili Cornbread (see p. 803).
Flounder, sole, or whitefish fillets can be substituted for the red snapper.

4-6 servings

1	medium onion, chopped
1	medium green bell pepper, chopped
1	medium carrot, chopped
2	cloves garlic, minced
1-2	tablespoons olive oil
1	can (16 ounces) reduced-sodium stewed tomatoes, undrained
1/2	cup frozen cut okra
1/2	cup bottled clam juice, *or* water
1-1 1/2	pounds red snapper fillets
2-3	teaspoons Worcestershire sauce
1/8	teaspoon cayenne pepper
	Hot pepper sauce, to taste
	Salt and pepper, to taste
4-6	cups cooked rice, warm

Per Serving
Calories: 414
% Calories from fat: **13**
Protein (gm): 29.8
Carbohydrate (gm): **59.2**
Fat (gm): 5.9
Saturated fat (gm): 0.9
Cholesterol (mg): 41.6
Sodium (mg): 184
Exchanges
Milk: 0.0
Veg.: 2.0
Fruit: 0.0
Bread: 3.0
Meat: 3.0
Fat: 0.0

1. Saute onion, bell pepper, carrot, and garlic in oil in large saucepan until onion is tender, about 5 minutes. Add tomatoes and liquid, okra, and clam juice; heat to boiling. Reduce heat and simmer, covered, 10 minutes.

2. Add fish, Worcestershire sauce, and cayenne pepper; simmer, uncovered, until fish is tender and flakes with a fork, about 10 minutes. Season to taste with hot pepper sauce, salt, and pepper. Serve over rice in bowls.

GULF COAST SNAPPER STEW

This Gulf Coast favorite has a robust sauce with just a hint of cayenne heat. The red snapper is marinated, then cooked and added to the Creole sauce. Red Pepper Rice is the perfect accompaniment.

6 servings

1¹/₂ pounds red snapper fillets
   4 cloves garlic, minced
 ¹/₂ teaspoon paprika
 ¹/₄ teaspoon cayenne pepper
   1 medium onion, chopped
   1 medium green bell pepper, chopped
   4 green onions and tops, sliced
   1 rib celery, thinly sliced
 1-2 tablespoons margarine
   1 can (28 ounces) reduced-sodium whole
       tomatoes, undrained, chopped
 2-3 tablespoons tomato paste
   1 teaspoon sugar
 ²/₃ teaspoon dried oregano leaves
   1 bay leaf
       Red pepper sauce, to taste
       Salt and pepper, to taste
       Red Pepper Rice (recipe follows)

Per Serving
Calories: 445
% Calories from fat: 18
Protein (gm): 21.4
Carbohydrate (gm): 70.4
Fat (gm): 9.1
Saturated fat (gm): 2.5
Cholesterol (mg): 25.2
Sodium (mg): 303
Exchanges
Milk: 0.0
Veg.: 2.0
Fruit: 0.0
Bread: 4.0
Meat: 2.0
Fat: 0.0

1. Rub fish fillets with combined garlic, paprika, and cayenne pepper; refrigerate, covered, 1 hour; cut fillets into 1-inch pieces.

2. Saute onion, bell pepper, green onions, and celery in margarine in large saucepan until tender, about 5 minutes. Add tomatoes and liquid, tomato paste, sugar, oregano, and bay leaf and heat to boiling; reduce heat and simmer, covered, 10 minutes.

3. Add fish; simmer, uncovered, until fish is tender and flakes with a fork, about 10 minutes. Discard bay leaf; season to taste with red pepper sauce, salt, and pepper. Serve over Red Pepper Rice in bowls.

Red Pepper Rice

makes 6 cups

 2 cups uncooked long-grain rice
 1/4 teaspoon ground turmeric
 1/2 teaspoon paprika
 1 roasted red pepper, coarsely chopped

1. Cook rice according to package directions, stirring turmeric into water. Stir paprika and roasted red pepper into cooked rice.

Variation:
Catfish Creole—Make recipe as above, substituting catfish fillets for the red snapper, and 1/2 teaspoon each dried marjoram and thyme leaves, celery seeds, and ground cumin for the oregano and bay leaf. Serve over plain cooked rice.

CARIBBEAN SWEET-SOUR SALMON STEW

Sweet and sour flavors team with salmon, pineapple, and beans in this island-inspired stew.

6 servings

 Vegetable cooking spray
 2 medium onions, cut into 1-inch pieces
 1 large red bell pepper, cut into strips
 1 large green bell pepper, cut into strips
 4 cloves garlic, minced
 2 teaspoons minced gingerroot
 1-2 jalapeño chilies, finely chopped
 1 can (20 ounces) pineapple chunks in juice, undrained
 2 tablespoons light brown sugar
 2-3 teaspoons curry powder
 2-3 tablespoons apple cider vinegar
 1 1/2 tablespoons cornstarch
 1/4 cup cold water
 12-16 ounces salmon steaks, cut into 1 1/2-inch cubes
 1 can (15 ounces) black beans, rinsed, drained
 4 cups cooked rice, warm
 3 small green onions and tops, sliced

Per Serving
Calories: 350
% Calories from fat: 6
Protein (g): 17.9
Carbohydrates (g): 67.1
Fat (g): 2.5
Saturated fat (g): 0.4
Cholesterol (mg): 28.6
Sodium (mg): 334
Exchanges
Milk: 0.0
Veg.: 0.0
Fruit: 1.0
Bread: 3.0
Meat: 1.5
Fat: 0.0

1. Spray large skillet with cooking spray; heat over medium heat until hot. Saute onions, bell peppers, garlic, gingerroot, and jalapeño chilies until onions are tender, about 5 minutes.

2. Drain pineapple, adding enough water to juice to make 1^1/$_2$ cups. Add pineapple and juice, brown sugar, curry powder, and vinegar to skillet; heat to boiling. Stir in combined cornstarch and water; boil, stirring mixture until thickened, about 1 minute.

3. Stir in salmon and beans; simmer, uncovered, until salmon is tender and flakes with a fork, about 5 minutes. Serve stew over rice in bowls; sprinkle with green onions.

SEAFOOD STEW WITH RISOTTO, MILANESE STYLE

A combination of microwave and range-top cooking speeds preparation of this unusual stew.

4-6 servings

1 medium onion, chopped
1 garlic clove, minced
^{1}/$_4$ teaspoon crushed saffron threads
2 teaspoons margarine
1-1^1/$_2$ cups reduced-sodium fat-free chicken broth, divided
1 can (16 ounces) reduced-sodium tomatoes, undrained, chopped
1 cup diced zucchini
8 ounces bay scallops
8 ounces medium shrimp, peeled, deveined
Microwave Risotto (recipe follows)
^{1}/$_4$ cup grated Parmesan cheese
Salt, to taste

Per Serving
Calories: 353
% Calories from fat: 17
Protein (gm): 31.8
Carbohydrate (gm): 39.7
Fat (gm): 6.9
Saturated fat (gm): 1.9
Cholesterol (mg): 114.7
Sodium (mg): 527
Exchanges
Milk: 0.0
Veg.: 2.0
Fruit: 0.0
Bread: 2.0
Meat: 3.0
Fat: 0.0

1. Saute onion, garlic, and saffron in margarine in large saucepan until onion is tender, about 5 minutes. Add 1 cup broth, tomatoes and liquid, and zucchini; heat to boiling. Reduce heat and simmer, covered, 10 minutes.

2. Stir in scallops and shrimp and simmer, uncovered, until shrimp and scallops are cooked, about 5 minutes. Stir in Microwave Risotto and Parmesan cheese; simmer, uncovered, 5 minutes, adding remaining $1/2$ cup broth, if desired. Season to taste with salt.

Microwave Risotto

$3/4$ cup uncooked arborio rice
2 teaspoons margarine
$2^2/3$ cups reduced-sodium fat-free chicken broth
$1/2$ teaspoon dried thyme leaves
$1/4$ teaspoon white pepper

1. Combine rice and margarine in $2^1/2$-quart microwave-safe casserole; microwave, uncovered, on High power 1 minute. Stir in remaining ingredients; microwave, covered, on High, 7 to 8 minutes, turning casserole $1/2$ turn after 4 minutes. Stir well and microwave, uncovered, on High, 11 to 13 minutes longer or until broth is absorbed. Let stand, covered, 2 to 3 minutes.

CALDO DE PEIXE

This generously flavored stew is traditionally served over rice.

8 servings

1 teaspoon Spike
2-3 green bananas, sliced
1 yellow onion, sliced
2 tablespoons olive oil
2 cloves garlic, minced
1 bay leaf
1 small jalapeño chili, *or* $1/2$ teaspoon cayenne pepper
$1/2$ cup finely chopped parsley
2 large tomatoes, chopped
1 quart water, divided
$1/4$ cup all-purpose flour
$1/4$ cup dry unseasoned bread crumbs
$1/2$ small cabbage, chopped

Per Serving
Calories: 352
% Calories from fat: 14
Protein (gm): 26.6
Carbohydrate (gm): 49.3
Fat (gm): 5.6
Saturated fat (gm): 0.9
Cholesterol (mg): 60.1
Sodium (mg): 150
Exchanges
Milk: 0.0
Veg.: 0.0
Fruit: 0.5
Bread: 3.0
Meat: 2.0
Fat: 0.0

4-6 large Idaho potatoes, peeled, cubed
4-6 sweet potatoes, peeled, cubed
2 pounds fish fillets (flounder, salmon, orange roughy, *or* halibut)
Salt and pepper, to taste

1. Sprinkle Spike over bananas; cover with water in small bowl and let stand 10 to 15 minutes. Drain and reserve.

2. Saute onion in oil in large saucepan until browned, about 5 minutes. Add garlic, bay leaf, jalapeño chili, parsley, and tomatoes; saute 3 to 4 minutes.

3. Add 3¹/2 cups water and heat to boiling; stir in combined flour and remaining ¹/2 cup water. Boil, stirring, until thickened, 1 to 2 minutes. Stir in reserved bananas, bread crumbs, cabbage, and potatoes; reduce heat and simmer, covered, 20 minutes. Add fish and simmer, uncovered, until fish is tender and flakes with a fork, about 10 minutes. Discard bay leaf; season to taste with salt and pepper.

FISH AND SUN-DRIED TOMATO STEW

The combination of tomato sauce and sun-dried tomatoes lends rich color and flavor. Red snapper or other firm-fleshed whitefish can be substituted for the halibut.

4 servings

1 large onion, chopped
1 teaspoon minced garlic
1 tablespoon olive oil
1 cup clam juice, *or* reduced-fat chicken broth
3 tablespoons chopped sun-dried tomatoes (not in oil)
1 teaspoon dried marjoram leaves
¹/2 teaspoon dried oregano leaves
4 halibut steaks (about 4 ounces each), cut into 1-inch pieces
1 can (8 ounces) reduced-sodium tomato sauce
Salt and pepper, to taste

Per Serving
Calories: 204
% Calories from fat: 30
Protein (g): 25.4
Carbohydrates (g): 9.6
Fat (g): 6.8
Saturated fat (g): 0.9
Cholesterol (mg): 36.1
Sodium (mg): 232
Exchanges
Milk: 0.0
Veg.: 2.0
Fruit: 0.0
Bread: 0.0
Meat: 3.0
Fat: 0.0

1. Saute onion and garlic in oil in large skillet until tender and well-browned, about 8 minutes. Stir in clam juice, sun-dried tomatoes, and herbs; heat to boiling. Reduce heat and simmer, covered, 5 minutes.

2. Add fish and tomato sauce; simmer gently until fish is tender and flakes with a fork, about 5 minutes. Season to taste with salt and pepper.

FISH STEW MARSALA

Marsala wine adds a distinctive, appealing note to this simple Italian fish stew. Substitute any lean whitefish you prefer.

4 servings

1 large onion, chopped
1 cup chopped mixed red and green bell peppers
1/2 cup chopped celery
1 teaspoon minced garlic
1 1/2 tablespoons olive oil
2 1/4 cups reduced-sodium fat-free chicken broth
1/3 cup dry Marsala wine, *or* fat-free chicken broth
1 teaspoon dried thyme leaves
1/4 cup reduced-sodium tomato paste
2 tablespoons lemon juice
2 cups medium pasta shells, cooked, warm
1 pound haddock steaks, cut into 1 1/2-inch pieces
Salt and pepper, to taste
Chopped parsley, as garnish

Per Serving
Calories: 409
% Calories from fat: 15
Protein (g): 33
Carbohydrates (g): 49
Fat (g): 7
Saturated fat (g): 1
Cholesterol (mg): 65.2
Sodium (mg): 206
Exchanges
Milk: 0.0
Veg.: 1.0
Fruit: 0.0
Bread: 3.0
Meat: 3.0
Fat: 0.0

1. Saute onion, bell peppers, celery, and garlic in oil in large skillet until tender and lightly browned, about 5 minutes. Add broth, Marsala, and thyme. Heat to boiling; reduce heat and simmer, uncovered, 10 minutes.

2. Stir in tomato paste, lemon juice, pasta, and fish; simmer, covered, until fish is tender and flakes with a fork, about 5 minutes. Season to taste with salt and pepper. Serve in large soup plates or bowls; sprinkle with parsley.

EASY BOUILLABAISSE

This easy version of a bouillabaisse can be made in less than 30 minutes!

8-10 servings

1 cup chopped onion
$^1/_2$ cup chopped celery
1 clove garlic, minced
1-2 tablespoons olive oil
1 cup water
1 cup dry white wine, *or* clam juice
2 cans (14$^1/_2$ ounces each) reduced-sodium whole tomatoes, undrained, chopped
3 leeks, white parts only, julienned
1 bay leaf
1 teaspoon dried thyme leaves
1 teaspoon grated orange rind
3 pounds salmon steaks, skinned, cut into 1$^1/_2$-inch pieces
8 ounces crabmeat
8 ounces bay scallops
12 mussels, scrubbed
$^1/_4$ cup chopped parsley
Salt and pepper, to taste

Per Serving
Calories: 362
% Calories from fat: 26
Protein (gm): 46.1
Carbohydrate (gm): 15.8
Fat (gm): 10.2
Saturated fat (gm): 1.7
Cholesterol (mg): 133.5
Sodium (mg): 326
Exchanges
Milk: 0.0
Veg.: 3.0
Fruit: 0.0
Bread: 0.0
Meat: 5.0
Fat: 0.0

1. Saute onion, celery, and garlic in oil in Dutch oven until onion is tender, about 5 minutes. Add remaining ingredients, except seafood, parsley, salt, and pepper; heat to boiling. Reduce heat and simmer, covered, 10 minutes. Add seafood and simmer, covered, until salmon is tender and flakes with a fork, about 10 minutes. Discard any unopened mussels. Stir in parsley; season to taste with salt and pepper.

BOUILLABAISSE ST. TROPEZ

The love for bouillabaisse is universal; Aioli sauce adds the finishing touch.

8 servings

8 ounces haddock, *or* halibut, fillets
8 ounces cod, sole, *or* flounder fillets
8 ounces crabmeat
8 ounces lobster
8 ounces shucked oysters
1 quart water
$^1/_2$ cup chopped onion
2 cloves garlic, minced
1-2 tablespoons olive oil
1 can (16 ounces) reduced-sodium tomatoes, undrained, chopped
$^1/_8$ teaspoon crushed saffron threads
1 teaspoon dried basil leaves
$^1/_2$ teaspoon dried thyme leaves
$^1/_8$ teaspoon crushed fennel seeds
1 bay leaf
$^1/_2$ teaspoon crushed red pepper
$^1/_4$ cup all-purpose flour
$^1/_2$ cup water
    Salt and pepper, to taste
8 lemon slices
8 slices French bread
    Aioli (recipe follows)

Per Serving
Calories: 290
% Calories from fat: 18
Protein (gm): 30.2
Carbohydrate (gm): **27.7**
Fat (gm): 5.7
Saturated fat (gm): 1.2
Cholesterol (mg): 116.3
Sodium (mg): 701
Exchanges
Milk: 0.0
Veg.: 1.0
Fruit: 0.0
Bread: 1.5
Meat: 3.0
Fat: 0.0

1. Arrange all seafood in large Dutch oven; add water and heat just to boiling; reduce heat and simmer, covered, until haddock and cod are tender and flake with a fork, 5 to 8 minutes. Remove seafood and arrange on serving platter; keep warm. Measure cooking liquid, adding enough water to make 5 cups; reserve.

2. Saute onion and garlic in oil in large Dutch oven until tender, about 5 minutes. Add reserved cooking liquid, tomatoes and liquid, saffron, herbs, and red pepper; heat to boiling. Reduce heat and simmer, covered, 15 minutes.

3. Heat stew to boiling; stir in combined flour and $1/2$ cup water. Boil, stirring, until thickened, 1 to 2 minutes. Discard bay leaf; season to taste with salt and pepper. Stir in lemon slices.

4. Spread bread slices with Aioli and place in bottoms of 8 soup bowls; ladle stew over bread. Let each person add desired seafood to stew. Serve with remaining Aioli.

Aioli

makes about $3/4$ cup

> $3/4$ cup fat-free mayonnaise
> 1 teaspoon tarragon vinegar
> 1 teaspoon lemon juice
> $1/2$-1 teaspoon Dijon-style mustard
> 3 cloves garlic, minced
> Salt and white pepper, to taste

1. Mix all ingredients, except salt and white pepper; season to taste with salt and white pepper.

MEDITERRANEAN FISHERMEN'S STEW

Bottled clam juice makes a quick and easy alternative to homemade fish stock in this recipe.

4 servings

> 1 large onion, chopped
> 4 teaspoons minced garlic
> 1 teaspoon olive oil
> 1 can (28 ounces) plum tomatoes, undrained, chopped
> 2 medium zucchini, sliced
> 2 carrots, thinly sliced
> 1 bottle (10 ounces) clam juice
> $1/2$-1 teaspoon lemon pepper
> 1 pound cod, cut into 1-inch cubes
> 1 tablespoon finely chopped basil
> $1/2$ cup chopped flat-leaf parsley
> Salt and pepper, to taste

Per Serving
Calories: 192
% Calories from fat: 12
Protein (gm): 23.9
Carbohydrate (gm): 19.9
Fat (gm): 2.9
Saturated fat (gm): 0.4
Cholesterol (mg): 48.6
Sodium (mg): 282
Exchanges
Milk: 0.0
Veg.: 2.0
Fruit: 0.0
Bread: 0.0
Meat: 3.0
Fat: 0.0

1. Saute onion and garlic in oil in Dutch oven until tender, about 5 minutes. Add tomatoes and liquid, zucchini, carrots, clam juice, and lemon pepper; heat to boiling. Reduce heat and simmer, covered, 20 to 25 minutes.

2. Add cod and basil; simmer, uncovered, until cod is tender and flakes with a fork, 5 to 10 minutes. Stir in parsley; season to taste with salt and pepper.

SCALLOP STEW, ITALIAN STYLE

Scallops make a quick and easy skillet stew, which is also wonderfully low in fat.

4 servings

1 medium onion, chopped
1 garlic clove, minced
1 medium green bell pepper, chopped
2 teaspoons olive oil
1 can (14^1/$_2$ ounces) Italian-style toma-
　toes, undrained, coarsely chopped
^{1}/$_4$ cup fat-free chicken broth
^{1}/$_2$ cup dry sherry, *or* chicken broth
1 bay leaf
1 teaspoon dried basil leaves
^{1}/$_4$ teaspoon black pepper
2 cups small broccoli florets
2 teaspoons cornstarch
^{1}/$_4$ cup cold water
12 ounces bay, *or* sea, scallops
　Salt, to taste
1^1/$_4$ cups long-grain white rice, cooked,
　warm

Per Serving
Calories: 339
% Calories from fat: 9
Protein (g): 22
Carbohydrates (g): 50
Fat (g): 3.5
Saturated fat (g): 0.4
Cholesterol (mg): 37
Sodium (mg): 352
Exchanges
Milk: 0.0
Veg.: 2.0
Fruit: 0.0
Bread: 2.5
Meat: 2.0
Fat: 0.0

1. Saute onion, garlic, and green pepper in oil in large saucepan until onion is tender, about 5 minutes. Add tomatoes and liquid, broth, sherry, bay leaf, basil, pepper, and broccoli; heat to boiling. Reduce heat and simmer, covered, until broccoli is crisp-tender, about 5 minutes.

2. Heat stew to boiling; add combined cornstarch and water, stirring until thickened, 1 to 2 minutes. Add scallops, reduce heat, and simmer, covered, until cooked and opaque, about 5 minutes. Season to taste with salt. Serve over rice.

SCALLOP, SHRIMP, AND PEPPER STEW WITH PASTA

A light, colorful medley that's simple to make.

4 servings

2 cups cubed mixed red, yellow, and green bell peppers (1-inch)
1 large onion, coarsely chopped
2 large garlic cloves, minced
2 tablespoons olive oil
1¹/₂ cups bottled clam juice, *or* reduced-sodium fat-free chicken broth
¹/₃ cup chopped fresh parsley
1¹/₂ tablespoons lemon juice
1 teaspoon grated lemon rind
¹/₂ teaspoon dried thyme leaves
Pinch crushed red pepper
1 large ripe tomato, peeled, coarsely chopped
8 ounces medium shrimp, peeled, deveined
8 ounces bay scallops
¹/₄ teaspoon salt
12 ounces uncooked vermicelli, cooked, warm

Per Serving
Calories: 544
% Calories from fat: 16
Protein (g): 33.9
Carbohydrates (g): 80.3
Fat (g): 9.9
Saturated fat (g): 1.3
Cholesterol (mg): 111.6
Sodium (mg): 342
Exchanges
Milk: 0.0
Veg.: 5.0
Fruit: 0.0
Bread: 4.0
Meat: 2.0
Fat: 0.5

1. Saute bell peppers, onion, and garlic in oil in large saucepan until onion begins to brown, 8 to 10 minutes. Remove and reserve.

2. Add clam juice, parsley, lemon juice and rind, thyme, red pepper, and tomato to saucepan; heat to boiling. Reduce heat and simmer, covered, 5 minutes.

3. Add shrimp, scallops, and reserved vegetables. Simmer until shellfish is cooked and shrimp are pink, 5 to 8 minutes. Season to taste with salt. Serve over vermicelli.

SHRIMP AND SAUSAGE GUMBO

Okra plays a dual role in this fast-to-make version of the bayou favorite, gumbo. It thickens the stew while giving it a characteristic Creole flavor.

4 servings

4 ounces smoked turkey sausage, halved, thinly sliced

1 teaspoon margarine

2 cloves garlic, minced

1 red bell pepper, chopped

8 ounces fresh, *or* frozen, thawed, okra, cut into 1/2-inch slices

2 cans (14 ounces each) reduced-sodium stewed tomatoes, undrained

1 dried cayenne chili, minced, *or* 1/2 teaspoon crushed red pepper

8 ounces medium shrimp, peeled, deveined

Salt, to taste

3 cups cooked rice, warm

Per Serving
Calories: 316
% Calories from fat: 14
Protein (g): 19.9
Carbohydrates (g): 48.9
Fat (g): 5
Saturated fat (g): 1.2
Cholesterol (mg): 104.4
Sodium (mg): 395
Exchanges
Milk: 0.0
Veg.: 3.0
Fruit: 0.0
Bread: 2.0
Meat: 2.0
Fat: 0.0

1. Saute sausage in margarine in large saucepan until browned, about 5 minutes; add garlic and saute 1 minute longer. Stir in bell pepper, okra, tomatoes and liquid, and cayenne chili; heat to boiling. Reduce heat and simmer, covered, until vegetables are tender, about 10 minutes. Add shrimp and simmer, uncovered, until shrimp are cooked and pink, about 5 minutes. Season to taste with salt; serve over rice.

SHRIMP, ARTICHOKE, AND PEPPER STEW

This skillet stew is quick, easy, and brimming with flavor.

4 servings

2 cups frozen stir-fry pepper blend

1 teaspoon minced garlic

1 tablespoon olive oil

1 can (15 ounces) reduced-sodium chunky tomato sauce

1 can (14 ounces) artichoke hearts, drained, quartered

3 tablespoons dry sherry, *or* chicken broth

2 teaspoons Italian seasoning

12 ounces medium shrimp, peeled, deveined

Salt and pepper, to taste

8 ounces penne, cooked, warm

Chopped parsley, as garnish

Per Serving
Calories: 415
% Calories from fat: 11
Protein (g): 26.1
Carbohydrates (g): 60.8
Fat (g): 5.1
Saturated fat (g): 0.8
Cholesterol (mg): 130
Sodium (mg): 438
Exchanges
Milk: 0.0
Veg.: 3.0
Fruit: 0.0
Bread: 3.0
Meat: 2.0
Fat: 0.0

1. Saute pepper blend and garlic in oil in large skillet until tender; add tomato sauce, artichoke hearts, and sherry. Heat to boiling; reduce heat and simmer, covered, 5 minutes.

2. Stir in Italian seasoning and shrimp and simmer, uncovered, until shrimp are cooked and pink, about 5 minutes. Season to taste with salt and pepper. Spoon over penne in bowls; sprinkle with parsley.

Variations:
Shrimp and Okra Stew—Make recipe as above, substituting 1 cup chopped onions for the stir-fry pepper blend and 2 cups fresh *or* frozen cut okra for the artichoke hearts; omit dry sherry and penne. Serve over Polenta (see p. 811) and sprinkle with parsley.

Shrimp and Artichoke Stew au Vin—Make recipe as above, substituting 1/2 cup dry white wine for the sherry; omit penne. Stir 1/2 to 1 cup fat-free half-and-half *or* fat-free milk into stew and simmer until hot, about 5 minutes. Stir in 2 to 4 tablespoons grated Parmesan cheese; serve in shallow bowls with Garlic Bread (see p. 795).

ITALIAN-STYLE FISH STEW

Enjoy the flavors of Italy in this well-seasoned fish stew.

4 servings

3 large garlic cloves, minced
1 tablespoon olive oil
1 1/2 pounds tomatoes, peeled, chopped
1 tablespoon dried oregano leaves
1 teaspoon dried thyme leaves
1 small bunch parsley, chopped
1/4 teaspoon crushed red pepper
1/2 cup dry white wine
1/2 cup sliced mushrooms
4 thinly cut grouper, *or* other firm-fleshed fish, steaks (4 ounces each)
Spike, to taste
Black pepper, to taste

Per Serving
Calories: 201
% Calories from fat: 23
Protein (gm): 24.1
Carbohydrate (gm): 10.5
Fat (gm): 5.3
Saturated fat (gm): 0.9
Cholesterol (mg): 41.6
Sodium (mg): 67
Exchanges
Milk: 0.0
Veg.: 2.0
Fruit: 0.0
Bread: 0.0
Meat: 3.0
Fat: 0.0

1. Saute garlic in oil in Dutch oven until golden, 1 to 2 minutes. Add remaining ingredients, except fish, Spike, and black pepper; heat to boiling. Reduce heat and simmer, covered, 10 minutes. Add fish and simmer, uncovered, until fish is tender and flakes with a fork, about 10 minutes. Season to taste with Spike and pepper.

HERBED SHRIMP STEW WITH RICE

Enjoy an easy-to-make, herb-seasoned stew with a bounty of perfectly cooked shrimp.

5 servings

1 medium onion, chopped
1 rib celery, diced
2 garlic cloves, minced
1 tablespoon olive oil
1 can (15 ounces) reduced-sodium tomato sauce
1/2 cup chopped parsley
1 teaspoon dried thyme leaves

Per Serving
Calories: 366
% Calories from fat: 10
Protein (gm): 24.8
Carbohydrate (gm): 54.9
Fat (gm): 4.2
Saturated fat (gm): 0.8
Cholesterol (mg): 173.3
Sodium (mg): 238
Exchanges
Milk: 0.0
Veg.: 2.0
Fruit: 0.0
Bread: 3.0
Meat: 2.0
Fat: 0.0

1 teaspoon dried basil leaves
1 teaspoon dried oregano leaves
1/4 teaspoon salt, optional
1/4 teaspoon black pepper
1 1/4 pounds medium shrimp, peeled, deveined
1 1/2 cups white rice, cooked, warm

1. Saute onion, celery, and garlic in oil in large saucepan until tender, about 5 minutes. Add remaining ingredients, except rice, and heat to boiling. Reduce heat and simmer, covered, until shrimp are cooked and pink, about 5 minutes. Stir in rice and cook 2 to 3 minutes longer.

Variation:
Shrimp and Garlic Stew—Make Caramelized Garlic: Cook 25 peeled cloves garlic in 2 to 4 tablespoons olive oil in small skillet over medium to medium-low heat until garlic is golden, 20 to 25 minutes. Coarsely mash garlic with 1 to 2 tablespoons dry white wine. Make recipe as above, omitting garlic and rice. Serve stew in bowls; pass Caramelized Garlic to stir into stew.

SPICY SHRIMP AND RICE STEW

This full-bodied shrimp and rice stew is seasoned with a creative combination of spices.

6 servings

1 large onion, chopped
2 large garlic cloves, minced
2 teaspoons olive oil
3 cups reduced-sodium fat-free chicken broth
2 ribs celery, diced
1 large carrot, peeled, diced
1 large green bell pepper, seeded, chopped
1 can (14 1/2 ounces) reduced-sodium diced tomatoes, undrained
1 large bay leaf

Per Serving
Calories: 217
% Calories from fat: 9
Protein (g): 14.2
Carbohydrates (g): 34.6
Fat (g): 2.1
Saturated fat (g): 0.4
Cholesterol (mg): 87.5
Sodium (mg): 217
Exchanges
Milk: 0.0
Veg.: 1.0
Fruit: 0.0
Bread: 2.0
Meat: 1.0
Fat: 0.0

1¹/₂ teaspoons dried thyme leaves

³/₄ teaspoon paprika

1 cup uncooked long-grain white rice

1 pound medium shrimp, peeled, deveined

Salt, cayenne, and black pepper, to taste

1. Saute onion and garlic in oil in large saucepan until onion is tender, about 5 minutes. Add remaining ingredients, except rice, shrimp, salt, cayenne, and black pepper, and heat to boiling. Reduce heat and simmer, covered, 15 minutes.

2. Heat to boiling and add rice; reduce heat and simmer, covered, until rice is tender, about 20 minutes. Add shrimp; simmer, covered, until shrimp are cooked and pink. Discard bay leaf; season to taste with salt, cayenne, and black pepper.

CREOLE STEW WITH SHRIMP AND HAM

Crisply cooked strips of ham and dry sherry add complementary flavors to this stew.

6 servings

4 ounces lean ham, thinly sliced, cut into thin strips

1-2 tablespoons vegetable oil

¹/₂ cup chopped onion

¹/₂ cup chopped celery

¹/₂ cup chopped red, *or* green, bell pepper

3 cloves garlic, minced

1 can (28 ounces) stewed tomatoes, undrained

2-3 tablespoons tomato paste

¹/₂ cup bottled clam juice, *or* water

2-4 tablespoons dry sherry, optional

¹/₄-¹/₂ teaspoon hot pepper sauce

¹/₂ teaspoon pepper

1-1¹/₂ pounds peeled, deveined shrimp

Salt, to taste

4 cups cooked rice, warm

Per Serving
Calories: 301
% Calories from fat: 14
Protein (gm): 22
Carbohydrate (gm): 43
Fat (gm): 4.5
Saturated fat (gm): 0.9
Cholesterol (mg): 126
Sodium (mg): 778
Exchanges
Milk: 0.0
Veg.: 2.0
Fruit: 0.0
Bread: 2.0
Meat: 2.0
Fat: 0.0

1. Cook ham in oil in large saucepan over medium-high heat until browned and crisp, 3 to 4 minutes; remove and reserve. Add onion, celery, bell pepper, and garlic to pan and saute until vegetables are tender, 5 to 8 minutes.

2. Add tomatoes and liquid, tomato paste, clam juice, sherry, hot pepper sauce, and pepper; heat to boiling. Reduce heat and simmer, covered, 30 minutes.

3. Add reserved ham and shrimp and simmer, covered, until shrimp are cooked and pink, about 5 minutes. Season to taste with salt; serve over rice in bowls.

LOBSTER AND SHRIMP STEW

This luxurious stew can, of course, be made entirely with lobster or with shrimp.

6 servings

1 medium onion, chopped
1 leek, white part only, chopped
2 cloves garlic, minced
1-2 tablespoons margarine
$1/2$ teaspoon dried oregano leaves
$1/4$ teaspoon dried thyme leaves
$1/4$ teaspoon dried marjoram leaves
$1/4$ teaspoon fennel seeds, lightly crushed
$1/4$ teaspoon ground turmeric
1 cup clam juice
3 large tomatoes, chopped
12-16 ounces peeled, deveined shrimp
12-16 ounces lobster tail, shell removed, cut into $3/4$-inch pieces
Salt and pepper, to taste
Turmeric Rice (see p. 575)

Per Serving
Calories: 375
% Calories from fat: 8
Protein (gm): 25.7
Carbohydrate (gm): 58.3
Fat (gm): 3.5
Saturated fat (gm): 0.7
Cholesterol (mg): 124.5
Sodium (mg): 429
Exchanges
Milk: 0.0
Veg.: 2.0
Fruit: 0.0
Bread: 3.0
Meat: 2.0
Fat: 0.0

1. Saute onion, leek, and garlic in margarine in large saucepan until tender, 5 to 8 minutes; stir in herbs and cook 1 to 2 minutes longer.

2. Add clam juice and tomatoes; heat to boiling. Reduce heat and simmer, covered, 30 minutes. Add shrimp and lobster; simmer, covered, until shrimp are cooked and pink and lobster is opaque, 5 to 8 minutes. Season to taste with salt and pepper. Serve over Turmeric Rice.

Variations:

Shrimp, Chicken, and Sausage Stew—Make recipe as above, substituting fat-free chicken broth for the clam juice, and cubed chicken breast for the lobster. Saute 4 ounces sliced reduced-sodium, reduced-fat sausage with the onion, leek, and garlic. Season to taste with hot pepper sauce.

Lobster Stew Cantonese—Make recipe as above, substituting 6 sliced green onions and tops for the leek, pineapple juice for the clam juice, and lobster for the shrimp; omit herbs. Add 1 cup pineapple chunks and 2 ounces trimmed snow peas to stew with the lobster, simmering until lobster is cooked and snow peas are crisp-tender, about 5 minutes. Season to taste with 1 to 2 teaspoons each cider vinegar and soy sauce. Serve over plain rice.

THIRTEEN

Vegetarian Stews

HASTY STEW

Many vegetable stews are long-simmered to attain their goodness. This stew is easily made in less than 30 minutes and boasts fresh flavors and textures.

4 servings (about 1 cup each)

Vegetable cooking spray
2 medium onions, cut into wedges
8 ounces mushrooms, sliced
2 cloves garlic, minced
1/4 cup finely chopped parsley leaves
1 teaspoon dried savory leaves
1 bay leaf
2 medium zucchini, sliced
3/4 pound potatoes, unpeeled, cubed
8 ounces cauliflower florets
1 large tomato, cut into wedges
2 cans (14¹/2 ounces each) vegetable broth
Salt and pepper, to taste
3 cups cooked millet, *or* couscous, warm

Per Serving
Calories: 404
% Calories from fat: 6
Protein (g): 13.4
Carbohydrates (g): 84.6
Fat (g): 2.6
Saturated fat (g): 0.4
Cholesterol (mg): 0
Sodium (mg): 116
Exchanges
Milk: 0.0
Veg.: 3.0
Fruit: 0.0
Bread: 4.5
Meat: 0.0
Fat: 0.0

1. Spray large saucepan with vegetable cooking spray; heat over medium heat until hot. Saute onions, mushrooms, garlic, and herbs until onions are tender, about 5 minutes.

2. Add vegetables, except tomato, and broth to saucepan; heat to boiling. Reduce heat and simmer, covered, until cauliflower is tender, about 10 minutes. Add tomato during last 5 minutes of cooking time. Season to taste with salt and pepper; discard bay leaf. Serve with millet.

VEGGIE STEW WITH DUMPLINGS

Dumplings, soft, fluffy, and seasoned with herbs, top this colorful stew.

6 servings (about 1¹/₂ cups each)

1 cup coarsely chopped onion
1 large red bell pepper, sliced
1 rib celery, sliced
1 tablespoon vegetable oil
3²/₃ cups Basic Vegetable Stock (see p. 10),
   or vegetable broth, divided
¹/₃ cup all-purpose flour
3 medium potatoes, unpeeled, cut into
   1-inch pieces
2 cups cubed yellow winter squash
   (butternut *or* acorn)
1 medium zucchini, sliced
4 ounces cremini, *or* white, mushrooms,
   halved
³/₄ cup frozen peas
1 teaspoon dried basil leaves
¹/₂ teaspoon dried oregano leaves
¹/₄ teaspoon dried thyme leaves
   Salt and pepper, to taste
   Herb Dumplings (recipe follows)

Per Serving
Calories: 328
% Calories from fat: 13
Protein (g): 9.8
Carbohydrates (g): 63.6
Fat (g): 5
Saturated fat (g): 0.4
Cholesterol (mg): 0.4
Sodium (mg): 697
Exchanges
Milk: 0.0
Veg.: 3.0
Fruit: 0.0
Bread: 3.0
Meat: 0.0
Fat: 1.0

1. Saute onion, bell pepper, and celery in oil in large saucepan until onion is tender, about 5 minutes. Stir in 3 cups Basic Vegetable Stock; heat to boiling. Mix remaining ²/₃ cup stock and flour; stir into boiling mixture. Boil, stirring constantly, until thickened, about 1 minute.

2. Stir potatoes, squash, zucchini, mushrooms, peas, and herbs into stew. Simmer, covered, until vegetables are tender, 10 to 15 minutes. Season to taste with salt and pepper.

3. Spoon Herb Dumplings on top of stew in 6 large spoonfuls; cook over low heat, uncovered, 10 minutes. Cook, covered, 10 minutes longer or until dumplings are tender and toothpick inserted in center comes out clean. Serve in bowls.

Herb Dumplings

makes 6

   2   cups reduced-fat biscuit mix
   1/2 teaspoon dried basil leaves
   1/4 teaspoon dried oregano leaves
   1/8 teaspoon dried thyme leaves
   2/3 cup fat-free milk

1. Combine biscuit mix and herbs in small bowl; stir in milk to form soft dough. Cook as directed in recipe.

VEGGIE STEW WITH BULGUR

Bulgur is a nutritious addition, and it also thickens this stew. Serve with warm, crusty Italian bread.

4 servings (about 1 2/3 cups each)

   3/4 cup boiling water
   1/2 cup uncooked bulgur
       Vegetable cooking spray
   2   medium onions, coarsely chopped
   2   cups cut-up carrots (1-inch pieces)
   1   cup cut-up Idaho potatoes, unpeeled
       (1-inch pieces)
   1   red bell pepper, cut into 1-inch pieces
   1   green bell pepper, cut into 1-inch pieces
2-3   cloves garlic, minced
   1   can (14 1/2 ounces) reduced-sodium
       tomato wedges, undrained
2-3   cups spicy tomato juice
   2   medium zucchini, cubed
   1   medium yellow summer squash, cubed
   2   cups halved cremini, *or* white, mush-
       rooms
1 1/2 teaspoons dried thyme leaves
   1   teaspoon dried oregano leaves
       Salt and pepper, to taste

Per Serving
Calories: 259
% Calories from fat: 5
Protein (g): 9.9
Carbohydrates (g): 57.4
Fat (g): 1.4
Saturated fat (g): 0.2
Cholesterol (mg): 0
Sodium (mg): 694
Exchanges
Milk: 0.0
Veg.: 5.0
Fruit: 0.0
Bread: 2.0
Meat: 0.0
Fat: 0.0

1. Stir boiling water into bulgur in bowl; let stand until bulgur is softened, about 20 minutes.

2. Spray Dutch oven or large saucepan with cooking spray; heat over medium heat until hot. Saute onions, carrots, potatoes, bell peppers, and garlic until onions are tender, 8 to 10 minutes.

3. Add bulgur and remaining ingredients, except salt and pepper, to Dutch oven; heat to boiling. Reduce heat and simmer, uncovered, until vegetables are tender and stew is thickened, 10 to 15 minutes. Season to taste with salt and pepper. Serve in bowls.

CABBAGE RAGOUT WITH REAL MASHED POTATOES

Fresh fennel, gingerroot, and apple lend aromatic flavor highlights to this cabbage stew. If fresh fennel is not available, substitute celery and increase the amount of fennel seeds to 1¹/₂ teaspoons.

6 servings (about 1¹/₃ cups each)

1 medium eggplant (about 1¹/₄ pounds), unpeeled, cut into ¹/₂-inch cubes
1 cup chopped onion
¹/₂ cup thinly sliced fennel bulb
2 teaspoons minced garlic
4 teaspoons minced gingerroot
1 teaspoon fennel seeds, crushed
1-2 tablespoons vegetable oil
8 cups thinly sliced cabbage
2 cups reduced-sodium vegetable broth
2 medium unpeeled apples, cored, cubed
1 cup fat-free sour cream
Salt and pepper, to taste
Real Mashed Potatoes (recipe follows)

Per Serving
Calories: 333
% Calories from fat: 16
Protein (gm): 9.8
Carbohydrate (gm): 66.8
Fat (gm): 6.9
Saturated fat (gm): 1.2
Cholesterol (mg): 0.2
Sodium (mg): 159
Exchanges
Milk: 0.0
Veg.: 1.0
Fruit: 0.0
Bread: 4.0
Meat: 0.0
Fat: 1.0

1. Saute eggplant, onion, fennel, garlic, gingerroot, and fennel seeds in oil in large saucepan until vegetables are tender and beginning to brown, about 10 minutes, stirring occasionally.

2. Add cabbage and broth; heat to boiling. Reduce heat and simmer, covered, until cabbage is wilted and crisp-tender, about 5 minutes. Stir apples into cabbage mixture; cook, covered, until apples are tender, about 5 minutes. Stir in sour cream; cook over medium heat until hot through, 3 to 4 minutes. Season to taste with salt and pepper. Serve over Real Mashed Potatoes.

Real Mashed Potatoes

makes about 4 cups

>   2 pounds Idaho potatoes, unpeeled,
>   quartered, cooked
> 1/2 cup fat-free sour cream
> 1/4 cup fat-free milk, hot
>   2 tablespoons margarine
>   Salt and pepper, to taste

1. Mash potatoes, or beat until smooth, in medium bowl, adding sour cream, milk, and margarine. Season to taste with salt and pepper.

RAGOUT OF WINTER VEGETABLES

On a chilly day, there's something soul-warming about a flavorful one-dish meal like this.

4 servings

>   8 ounces mushrooms, quartered
>   1 large onion, chopped
>   3 cloves garlic, minced
>   2 teaspoons olive oil
>   2 cans (14 1/2 ounces each) reduced-
>   sodium vegetable broth
> 1/2 cup uncooked mixed wild and long-
>   grain rice
>   3 small sweet potatoes, peeled, cubed
>   2 carrots, sliced
>   1 teaspoon dried thyme leaves
>   Salt and pepper, to taste

Per Serving
Calories: 270
% Calories from fat: 11
Protein (gm): 6.9
Carbohydrate (gm): 55.4
Fat (gm): 3.6
Saturated fat (gm): 0.4
Cholesterol (mg): 0
Sodium (mg): 408
Exchanges
Milk: 0.0
Veg.: 1.0
Fruit: 0.0
Bread: 3.0
Meat: 0.0
Fat: 0.5

1. Saute mushrooms, onion, and garlic in oil in large saucepan until lightly browned, about 8 minutes. Add broth and rice and heat to boiling; reduce heat and simmer, covered, 35 minutes.

2. Add sweet potatoes, carrots, and thyme; simmer, covered, until vegetables are tender, about 20 minutes. Season to taste with salt and pepper.

SQUASH AND POTATO GOULASH

This goulash would also be delicious with Caraway Dumplings (see p. 691), rather than noodles.

6 servings

1 clove garlic, minced
2 medium onions, coarsely chopped
1¹/₂ cups diced red bell pepper
1¹/₂ cups diced green bell pepper
2 tablespoons margarine
3 cups cubed, peeled butternut squash
3 cups cubed, peeled baking potatoes
1 can (16 ounces) whole tomatoes, undrained, coarsely chopped
1 cup dry white wine
2 cups water
2 vegetable bouillon cubes
3 tablespoons paprika
1 cup fat-free sour cream
  Salt and pepper, to taste
4¹/₂ cups cooked wide noodles, warm
¹/₄ cup chopped fresh parsley
  Caraway seeds, as garnish

Per Serving
Calories: 491
% Calories from fat: 9
Protein (g): 15.3
Carbohydrates (g): 95.8
Fat (g): 5
Saturated fat (g): 0.9
Cholesterol (mg): 39.8
Sodium (mg): 533
Exchanges
Milk: 0.0
Veg.: 3.0
Fruit: 0.0
Bread: 5.0
Meat: 0.0
Fat: 1.0

1. Saute garlic, onion, and peppers in margarine in large saucepan until onion is tender. Add remaining vegetables, wine, water, and bouillon cubes; heat to boiling. Reduce heat and simmer, uncovered, until vegetables are tender and broth is thickened, about 30 minutes. Stir in paprika and sour cream; season to taste with salt and pepper. Serve over noodles; sprinkle with parsley and caraway seeds.

SWEET-SOUR SQUASH AND POTATO STEW

The vegetables are simmered in cider and seasoned with honey and vinegar for a refreshing sweet-sour flavor.

6 servings (about 1 1/2 cups each)

Butter-flavored vegetable cooking spray
1/2 cup chopped shallots
1 medium red bell pepper, chopped
2 cloves garlic, minced
1 can (14 1/2 ounces) reduced-sodium diced tomatoes, undrained
1 cup apple cider, *or* apple juice
1 1/2 tablespoons honey
1 1/2 tablespoons cider vinegar
1 bay leaf
1/4 teaspoon ground nutmeg
3 1/2 cups cubed, peeled yellow winter squash (butternut *or* acorn)
4 medium Idaho potatoes, peeled, cut into 3/4-inch cubes
2 medium sweet potatoes, peeled, cut into 3/4-inch cubes
2 medium tart green apples, unpeeled, cored, cut into 3/4-inch pieces
1 1/2 cups fresh, *or* frozen, whole-kernel corn
Salt and pepper, to taste
4 cups cooked basmati, *or* other aromatic, rice, warm

Per Serving
Calories: 411
% Calories from fat: 4
Protein (g): 9.7
Carbohydrates (g): 95.9
Fat (g): 1.8
Saturated fat (g): 0.2
Cholesterol (mg): 0
Sodium (mg): 52
Exchanges
Milk: 0.0
Veg.: 3.0
Fruit: 1.0
Bread: 3.5
Meat: 0.0
Fat: 0.0

1. Spray large saucepan with cooking spray; heat over medium heat until hot. Saute shallots, bell pepper, and garlic until softened, about 4 minutes.

2. Add tomatoes and liquid, cider, honey, vinegar, bay leaf, nutmeg, squash, Idaho and sweet potatoes to saucepan. Heat to boiling; reduce heat and simmer, covered, 15 minutes or until potatoes are tender. Add apples and corn and simmer until apples are tender, about 5 minutes.

3. Discard bay leaf; season stew to taste with salt and pepper. Serve over rice.

VEGGIE STEW WITH CHILI-CHEESE DUMPLINGS

With only 30 minutes cooking time, this is a stew you'll prepare often. One green bell pepper and one jalapeño chili can be substituted for the poblano chili.

6 servings (about 1¹/₂ cups each)

2 cups chopped onions

1 medium red bell pepper, coarsely chopped

1 medium yellow bell pepper, coarsely chopped

1 large poblano chili, coarsely chopped

3 cloves garlic, minced

2-3 tablespoons chili powder

1¹/₂-2 teaspoons ground cumin

1 teaspoon dried oregano leaves

¹/₂ teaspoon dried marjoram leaves

2 tablespoons olive oil

2 cans (15 ounces each) reduced-sodium whole tomatoes, undrained, coarsely chopped

1 can (15 ounces) black-eyed peas, rinsed, drained

1 can (15 ounces) red beans, rinsed, drained

1¹/₂ cups cubed, peeled butternut, *or* acorn, squash

1 cup fresh, *or* frozen, thawed, okra

Salt and pepper, to taste

Chili-Cheese Dumplings (recipe follows)

Per Serving
Calories: 433
% Calories from fat: 29
Protein (g): 17.4
Carbohydrates (g): 65.9
Fat (g): 14.9
Saturated fat (g): 2.7
Cholesterol (mg): 3.7
Sodium (mg): 713
Exchanges
Milk: 0.0
Veg.: 3.0
Fruit: 0.0
Bread: 3.0
Meat: 1.0
Fat: 2.0

1. Saute onions, bell peppers, poblano chili, garlic, chili powder, and herbs in oil in large saucepan until tender, about 10 minutes. Stir in remaining ingredients, except salt, pepper, and Chili-Cheese Dumplings; heat to boiling. Reduce heat and simmer, covered, until okra and squash are tender, 8 to 10 minutes. Season to taste with salt and pepper.

2. Spoon dumpling dough into 6 mounds on top of stew. Cook, uncovered, 5 minutes. Cook, covered, until dumplings are dry, 5 to 10 minutes longer.

Chili-Cheese Dumplings

makes 6 dumplings

> 2/3 cup all-purpose flour
> 1/3 cup yellow cornmeal
> 1 1/2 teaspoons baking powder
> 1 teaspoon chili powder
> 1/2 teaspoon salt
> 2 tablespoons vegetable shortening
> 1/4 cup (1 ounce) shredded reduced-fat Monterey Jack cheese
> 1 tablespoon finely chopped cilantro
> 1/2 cup fat-free milk

1. Combine flour, cornmeal, baking powder, chili powder, and salt in medium bowl; cut in shortening with pastry blender until mixture resembles coarse crumbs. Mix in cheese and cilantro; stir in milk, forming a soft dough.

WINTER STEW STROGANOFF

A warming stew for cold winter evenings. Substitute turnips, parsnips, or rutabagas for one of the potatoes, if you like.

6 servings

> 1 pound Idaho potatoes, peeled, cubed
> 1 pound sweet potatoes, peeled, cubed
> 3 medium onions, thinly sliced
> 8 ounces mushrooms, halved
> 3 tablespoons margarine
> 1 cup frozen peas
> 1 1/3 cups boiling water
> 2 vegetable bouillon cubes
> 1 tablespoon dry mustard
> 1 tablespoon sugar
> 1 cup fat-free sour cream
> 1/4 cup coarsely chopped parsley
>   Salt and pepper, to taste
> 4 1/2 cups cooked wide noodles, warm

Per Serving
Calories: 414
% Calories from fat: 13
Protein (g): 14.4
Carbohydrates (g): 78.9
Fat (g): 6.1
Saturated fat (g): 1
Cholesterol (mg): 39.8
Sodium (mg): 653
Exchanges
Milk: 0.0
Veg.: 2.0
Fruit: 0.0
Bread: 4.5
Meat: 0.0
Fat: 1.0

1. Simmer Idaho and sweet potatoes in 2 inches water in large saucepan until tender, 8 to 10 minutes; drain and reserve.

2. Saute onions and mushrooms in margarine in large saucepan until onions are tender. Stir in reserved potatoes, peas, water, and bouillon cubes; heat to boiling. Reduce heat and simmer 5 minutes.

3. Stir in combined dry mustard, sugar, and sour cream; simmer until hot, 3 to 4 minutes. Stir in parsley; season to taste with salt and pepper. Serve over noodles.

FIRESIDE STEW

Chock-full of vegetables and pasta and melty with cheese, this stew is sure to please!

8 servings

1 can (15 ounces) navy beans, rinsed, drained

1 can (15 ounces) red kidney beans, rinsed, drained

1 can (14^1/$_2$ ounces) tomatoes with roasted garlic, undrained

2 cans (14^1/$_2$ ounces each) reduced-sodium vegetable broth

1 cup sliced carrots

1 cup cubed zucchini

^{1}/$_2$ cup chopped onion

2 cloves garlic, minced

1 teaspoon Italian seasoning

6 ounces small shell pasta

Salt and pepper, to taste

1 cup (4 ounces) shredded reduced-fat Monterey Jack cheese

Per Serving
Calories: 263
% Calories from fat: 11
Protein (gm): 15.4
Carbohydrate (gm): 43.6
Fat (gm): 3.4
Saturated fat (gm): 1.9
Cholesterol (mg): 10.1
Sodium (mg): 665
Exchanges
Milk: 0.0
Veg.: 2.0
Fruit: 0.0
Bread: 2.0
Meat: 1.0
Fat: 0.0

1. Combine all ingredients, except pasta, salt, pepper, and cheese in large saucepan; heat to boiling. Stir in pasta, reduce heat and simmer, covered, until pasta is al dente, about 10 minutes; season to taste with salt and pepper.

2. Serve in bowls; stir 2 tablespoons cheese into each.

WILD MUSHROOM STEW

This stew can include any mushrooms you like; we've included several fla-vorful varieties. Dried mushrooms, softened in warm water, can substi-tute for some of the fresh mushrooms and give an even richer taste.

6 servings

2 cups chopped portobello mushrooms
2 cups sliced shiitake mushrooms
2 cups sliced cremini, *or* white, mush-
    rooms
1 cup sliced leeks, white parts only
1 cup chopped red bell pepper
1/2 cup chopped onion
1 tablespoon minced garlic
1/2 teaspoon crushed red pepper
2 tablespoons olive oil
3 tablespoons flour
1 cup reduced-sodium vegetable broth
1 cup dry white wine
3 cans (15 ounces each) Great Northern
    beans, rinsed, drained
4 cups sliced Swiss chard, *or* kale, leaves
1/2 teaspoon dried rosemary leaves
1/2 teaspoon dried thyme leaves
    Salt and pepper, to taste
    Creamy Polenta (see p. 713)

Per Serving
Calories: 341
% Calories from fat: **13**
Protein (gm): 16.3
Carbohydrate (gm): 63
Fat (gm): 5.5
Saturated fat (gm): 0.8
Cholesterol (mg): 0
Sodium (mg): 758
Exchanges
Milk: 0.0
Veg.: 3.0
Fruit: 0.0
Bread: 3.0
Meat: 0.0
Fat: 1.0

1.   Saute mushrooms, leeks, bell pepper, onion, garlic, and red pepper in oil in large saucepan until tender, about 10 minutes. Stir in flour; cook 1 to 2 minutes. Stir in remaining ingredients, except salt, pepper, and polenta; heat to boiling. Reduce heat and simmer, covered, 10 minutes. Season to taste with salt and pepper; serve over Creamy Polenta.

WINTER BEAN AND VEGETABLE STEW

Root vegetables and beans combine in this satisfying stew, perfect for cold-weather meals. Serve with crusty Italian bread.

6 servings (about 1¹/₃ cups each)

1	cup chopped onion
1	medium Idaho potato, unpeeled, cut into 1-inch cubes
1	large sweet potato, peeled, cut into 1-inch cubes
³/₄	cup chopped green bell pepper
1	teaspoon minced garlic
2	tablespoons olive oil
1	tablespoon flour
1¹/₂	cups reduced-sodium vegetable broth
1	can (15 ounces) black beans, rinsed, drained
1	can (13¹/₄ ounces) baby lima beans, rinsed, drained
1	can (16 ounces) tomato wedges, undrained
³/₄	teaspoon dried sage leaves
	Salt and pepper, to taste

Per Serving
Calories: 209
% Calories from fat: 21
Protein (g): 7.7
Carbohydrates (g): 39.2
Fat (g): 5.5
Saturated fat (g): 0.7
Cholesterol (mg): 0
Sodium (mg): 493
Exchanges
Milk: 0.0
Veg.: 1.0
Fruit: 0.0
Bread: 2.0
Meat: 0.0
Fat: 1.0

1. Saute onion, potato, sweet potato, bell pepper, and garlic in oil in large saucepan 5 minutes; stir in flour and cook 1 to 2 minutes longer. Add remaining ingredients, except salt and pepper, to saucepan; heat to boiling. Reduce heat and simmer, covered, until potatoes are tender, 15 to 20 minutes. Season to taste with salt and pepper.

WHEAT BERRY AND LENTIL STEW WITH CARAWAY DUMPLINGS

Wheat berries have a wonderful, nutty texture. They can be readily purchased at health food stores; barley or another grain can be substituted.

6 servings (about 1¹/₂ cups each)

1   cup wheat berries
    Vegetable cooking spray
2   medium onions, chopped
¹/₂ cup chopped celery
4   cloves garlic, minced
1   teaspoon dried savory leaves
3   cups reduced-sodium vegetable broth
2   pounds russet potatoes, unpeeled, cubed
2   medium carrots, sliced
1¹/₂ cups dried lentils
    Salt and pepper, to taste
    Caraway Dumplings (recipe follows)

Per Serving
Calories: 578
% Calories from fat: 8
Protein (gm): 24.3
Carbohydrate (gm): 111.9
Fat (gm): 5.4
Saturated fat (gm): 1
Cholesterol (mg): 0.4
Sodium (mg): 389
Exchanges
Milk: 0.0
Veg.: 0.0
Fruit: 0.0
Bread: 7.0
Meat: 1.0
Fat: 0.5

1. Cover wheat berries with 2 to 3 inches water in saucepan; let stand overnight. Heat to boiling; reduce heat and simmer, covered, until wheat berries are tender, 45 to 55 minutes. Drain.

2. Spray large saucepan with cooking spray; heat over medium heat until hot. Saute onions, celery, garlic, and savory until onions are tender, 3 to 5 minutes. Add broth, potatoes, carrots, and lentils and heat to boiling; reduce heat and simmer, covered, until vegetables are just tender, 10 to 15 minutes. Stir in wheat berries. Season to taste with salt and pepper.

3. Spoon dumpling mixture into 6 mounds on top of stew; cook, uncovered, 5 minutes. Cook, covered, until dumplings are dry, 5 to 10 minutes longer.

Caraway Dumplings

makes 6 dumplings

1/2 cup all-purpose flour
1/2 cup whole wheat flour
2 teaspoons baking powder
1 tablespoon caraway seeds
1/4 teaspoon salt
2 tablespoons margarine
1/2 cup fat-free milk

1. Combine flours, baking powder, caraway seeds, and salt in medium bowl; cut in margarine until mixture resembles coarse crumbs. Stir in milk, mixing just until combined.

LENTIL AND VEGETABLE STEW

This lentil stew is flavored with chili peppers, ginger, and LOTS of garlic. It's very spicy; adjust the seasoning according to your taste, but remember that the flavors will mellow as the stew simmers.

8 servings

Vegetable cooking spray
3 large onions, sliced
1/2 cup dried lentils
1/2 pound frozen peas
1/2 pound carrots, chopped
1/2 pound green beans, chopped
3 large tomatoes, chopped
6 chili peppers, crushed into a paste, *or* 2 teaspoons cayenne pepper
1 piece gingerroot (2-inch)
10 cloves garlic
6 whole cloves
1 stick cinnamon (4-inch)
6 cardamom pods, crushed
1 teaspoon ground turmeric

Per Serving
Calories: 380
% Calories from fat: 2
Protein (gm): 14.4
Carbohydrate (gm): 79.7
Fat (gm): 1
Saturated fat (gm): 0.2
Cholesterol (mg): 0
Sodium (mg): 55
Exchanges
Milk: 0.0
Veg.: 4.0
Fruit: 0.0
Bread: 4.0
Meat: 0.0
Fat: 0.0

3 sprigs fresh, *or* $1/2$ teaspoon dried, mint leaves, crushed

1 cup warm water

6 medium potatoes, chopped

2 cups couscous, cooked, warm

Low-fat plain yogurt, as garnish

1. Spray large saucepan with cooking spray and heat over medium heat until hot. Saute onions until golden brown. Remove $1/3$ of onions and reserve for garnish. Add remaining ingredients, except potatoes, couscous, and yogurt; heat to boiling. Reduce heat and simmer, covered, 20 minutes.

2. Add potatoes and simmer 20 to 30 minutes or until potatoes are tender and water is absorbed. Serve over couscous; garnish with reserved onions and dollops of yogurt.

BEAN-THICKENED VEGETABLE STEW

Pureed beans provide the perfect thickening for this stew.

6 servings (about 1¼ cups each)

Vegetable cooking spray

3 carrots, sliced

1 medium onion, chopped

3 cloves garlic, minced

$1^3/4$ cups Basic Vegetable Stock (see p.10), *or* vegetable broth

2 cups chopped tomatoes

$1^1/2$ cups sliced mushrooms

1 yellow summer squash, sliced

1 can (15 ounces) black beans, rinsed, drained

1 can (15 ounces) navy beans, rinsed, drained, pureed

1 cup frozen peas

$3/4$ teaspoon dried thyme leaves

$1/2$ teaspoon dried oregano leaves

2 bay leaves

Salt and pepper, to taste

4 cups cooked noodles, warm

Green onions and tops, chopped, as garnish

Per Serving
Calories: 348
% Calories from fat: **5**
Protein (g): 18.3
Carbohydrates (g): 71.8
Fat (g): 1.9
Saturated fat (g): 0.2
Cholesterol (mg): 0
Sodium (mg): 589
Exchanges
Milk: 0.0
Veg.: 2.0
Fruit: 0.0
Bread: 4.0
Meat: 0.0
Fat: 0.0

1. Spray large saucepan with cooking spray; heat over medium heat until hot. Saute carrots, onion, and garlic until tender, about 5 minutes.

2. Stir in Basic Vegetable Stock, tomatoes, mushrooms, squash, black beans, navy bean puree, peas, and herbs; heat to boiling. Reduce heat and simmer, uncovered, until vegetables are tender, 10 to 15 minutes. Discard bay leaves; season to taste with salt and pepper.

3. Spoon stew over noodles in shallow bowls; sprinkle with green onions.

BEAN AND SQUASH STEW

Stews don't have to be long-cooked to be good—this delicious stew is simmered to savory goodness in less than 30 minutes. Serve with Garlic Bread (see p. 795).

6 servings (about 1¼ cups each)

Italian-flavored olive oil cooking spray
1½ cups chopped onions
1½ cups coarsely chopped green bell peppers
2 teaspoons minced roasted garlic
1 tablespoon flour
2 cups cubed, peeled butternut, *or* acorn, squash (½-inch cubes)
2 cans (16 ounces each) reduced-sodium diced tomatoes, undrained
1 can (15 ounces) red kidney beans, rinsed, drained
1 can (13¼ ounces) baby lima beans, rinsed, drained
½-¾ teaspoon Italian seasoning
Salt and pepper, to taste

Per Serving
Calories: 239
% Calories from fat: 5
Protein (g): 14
Carbohydrates (g): 50.5
Fat (g): 1.4
Saturated fat (g): 0.2
Cholesterol (mg): 0
Sodium (mg): 160
Exchanges
Milk: 0.0
Veg.: 3.0
Fruit: 0.0
Bread: 2.0
Meat: 0.5
Fat: 0.0

1. Spray large saucepan with cooking spray; heat over medium heat until hot. Saute onions, bell peppers, and garlic until tender, about 8 minutes. Stir in flour; cook 1 minute longer.

2. Add remaining ingredients, except salt and pepper, to saucepan; heat to boiling. Reduce heat and simmer 10 to 15 minutes. Season to taste with salt and pepper.

LENTIL STEW WITH SPICED COUSCOUS

This stew will keep in the refrigerator up to one week; it also freezes well.

6 servings

Per Serving
Calories: 420
% Calories from fat: **9**
Protein (gm): **24**
Carbohydrate (gm): **74**
Fat (gm): **4.1**
Saturated fat (gm): **0.6**
Cholesterol (mg): 0
Sodium (mg): **355**
Exchanges
Milk: 0.0
Veg.: 3.0
Fruit: 0.0
Bread: 4.0
Meat: 0.0
Fat: 1.0

1 cup chopped onion
1 cup chopped red, *or* green, bell pepper
1 cup chopped celery
1 cup cubed carrots
1 teaspoon minced garlic
1 tablespoon olive oil
2 cups dried lentils
1 can (14¹/₂ ounces) diced tomatoes, undrained
2 cups reduced-sodium vegetable broth
1¹/₂ cups water
1 teaspoon dried oregano leaves
¹/₂ teaspoon ground turmeric
Salt and pepper, to taste
Spiced Couscous (recipe follows)

1. Saute onion, bell pepper, celery, carrots, and garlic in oil in large saucepan until lightly browned, about 10 minutes. Stir in remaining ingredients, except salt, pepper, and Spiced Couscous; heat to boiling. Reduce heat and simmer, covered, until lentils are tender, about 40 minutes. Season to taste with salt and pepper; serve over Spiced Couscous.

Spiced Couscous

makes 3 cups

¹/₃ cup sliced green onions and tops
1 clove garlic, minced
¹/₄ teaspoon crushed red pepper
¹/₂ teaspoon ground turmeric
1 teaspoon olive oil
1²/₃ cups reduced-sodium vegetable broth, *or* water
1 cup couscous

1. Saute green onions, garlic, red pepper, and turmeric in oil in medium saucepan until tender, about 3 minutes. Stir in broth; heat to boiling. Stir in couscous; remove from heat and let stand, covered, 5 minutes or until broth is absorbed.

HEARTY BEAN STEW WITH GREENS

Focaccia (see p. 788) and fresh fruit would go beautifully with this stew.

6 servings

<table>
<tr><td>

$^1/_2$ cup dried garbanzo beans
$^1/_2$ cup dried kidney beans
2 quarts water
1 medium onion, sliced
$1^1/_2$ teaspoons instant vegetable bouillon granules
2 cloves garlic, minced
2 medium potatoes, peeled, cooked, mashed
2 medium carrots, julienned
2 small zucchini, sliced thin
$^1/_2$ cup elbow macaroni
$^1/_4$ cup quick-cooking oats
$^1/_4$ cup lemon juice
1 cup sliced spinach leaves
1 cup sliced watercress
Salt and pepper, to taste
Lemon slices, as garnish

</td><td>

Per Serving
Calories: 230
% Calories from fat: 7
Protein (gm): 10.6
Carbohydrate (gm): 44.6
Fat (gm): 1.7
Saturated fat (gm): 0.2
Cholesterol (mg): 0
Sodium (mg): 279
Exchanges
Milk: 0.0
Veg.: 3.0
Fruit: 0.0
Bread: 2.0
Meat: 0.0
Fat: 0.0

</td></tr>
</table>

1. Cover beans with 2 inches water in Dutch oven; heat to boiling. Boil 2 minutes. Remove from heat and let stand, covered, about 1 hour and drain.

2. Return beans to Dutch oven. Add 2 quarts water, onion, bouillon, and garlic; heat to boiling. Reduce heat and simmer, covered, until beans are tender, about 1 hour, adding potatoes, carrots, zucchini, macaroni, and oats into bean mixture during last 15 minutes.

3. Add lemon juice, spinach, and watercress; simmer until spinach and watercress are wilted, about 1 minute. Season to taste with salt and pepper; garnish with lemon slices.

SWEET BEAN STEW WITH DUMPLINGS

This vegetable stew is a sweet, chili-flavored treat; delicious with or without the Spicy Cheddar Dumplings.

8 servings

Vegetable cooking spray
2 cups diced red, *or* green, bell peppers
1¹/₂ cups chopped onions
2 teaspoons minced garlic
1 teaspoon cumin seeds
2 cups cubed, peeled sweet potatoes
1¹/₂ cups cubed zucchini
3 cans (15 ounces each) pinto beans, rinsed, drained
2 cans (14¹/₂ ounces each) chili-seasoned diced tomatoes, undrained
1¹/₂ cups apple cider, *or* apple juice
¹/₂ cup raisins
2 teaspoons chili powder
¹/₂ teaspoon ground cinnamon
Salt and pepper, to taste
Spicy Cheddar Dumplings (recipe follows)

Per Serving
Calories: 371
% Calories from fat: 15
Protein (gm): 13.6
Carbohydrate (gm): 69.8
Fat (gm): 6.4
Saturated fat (gm): 1.7
Cholesterol (mg): 4
Sodium (mg): 717
Exchanges
Milk: 0.0
Veg.: 2.0
Fruit: 0.0
Bread: 4.0
Meat: 0.0
Fat: 1.0

1. Spray large saucepan with cooking spray; heat over medium heat until hot. Saute bell peppers, onions, garlic, and cumin seeds until tender, about 8 minutes. Stir in remaining ingredients, except salt, pepper, and Spicy Cheddar Dumplings; heat to boiling. Reduce heat and simmer, covered, until potatoes are almost tender, about 15 minutes. Season to taste with salt and pepper.

2. Spoon Spicy Cheddar Dumpling mixture into 8 mounds on top of stew; cook, uncovered, 5 minutes. Cook, covered, until dumplings are dry, 5 to 10 minutes longer.

Spicy Cheddar Dumplings

makes 8 dumplings

- $1/2$ cup yellow cornmeal
- $1/2$ cup all-purpose flour
- 1 teaspoon baking powder
- $1/2$ teaspoon crushed red pepper
- 2 tablespoons margarine
- $1/4$ cup (1 ounce) shredded sharp Cheddar cheese
- 2 tablespoons whole-kernel corn
- $1/2$ cup fat-free milk

1. Combine cornmeal, flour, baking powder, and red pepper in medium bowl. Cut in margarine until mixture resembles coarse crumbs. Stir in cheese and corn; stir in milk, mixing just until blended.

BLACK BEAN AND SPINACH STEW

The chilies and gingerroot in this heartily spiced dish can be decreased if less hotness is desired.

8 servings

- 1 cup chopped onion
- 1 large red bell pepper, chopped
- 1 large zucchini, cubed
- 2 jalapeño chilies, finely chopped
- 1 tablespoon chopped gingerroot
- 2 teaspoons minced garlic
- 1 tablespoon vegetable oil
- 2-3 teaspoons chili powder
- 1 teaspoon ground cumin
- $1/2$ teaspoon cayenne pepper
- 3 cans (15 ounces each) black beans, rinsed, drained
- 1 can (15 ounces) diced tomatoes, undrained
- 3 cups sliced spinach leaves
  Salt, to taste
- 4 cups cooked rice, warm

Per Serving
Calories: 237
% Calories from fat: 11
Protein (gm): 10.2
Carbohydrate (gm): 53.8
Fat (gm): 3.6
Saturated fat (gm): 0.3
Cholesterol (mg): 0
Sodium (mg): 789
Exchanges
Milk: 0.0
Veg.: 1.0
Fruit: 0.0
Bread: 3.0
Meat: 0.0
Fat: 0.0

1. Saute onion, bell pepper, zucchini, jalapeño chilies, ginger-root, and garlic in oil in large saucepan 8 minutes. Stir in chili powder, cumin, and cayenne pepper; cook 1 to 2 minutes longer.

2. Stir in beans and tomatoes and liquid, and heat to boiling. Reduce heat and simmer, covered, 10 minutes; uncover and cook until mixture is desired thickness, about 5 minutes. Stir in spinach; cook until wilted, about 1 minute. Season to taste with salt; serve with rice.

EASY CREOLE SKILLET STEW

Easy to make, and fast too—dinner can be on the table in less than 30 minutes! Serve over rice, if desired.

4 servings

Vegetable cooking spray
1 package (8 ounces) all-vegetable protein sausage links
1 cup chopped onion
2 cloves garlic, minced
2 cups fresh, *or* frozen, whole-kernel corn
1 medium zucchini, sliced
2 cans (14¹/₂ ounces each) reduced-sodium stewed tomatoes
2 tablespoons flour
¹/₄ cup water
Salt and pepper, to taste
2 green onions and tops, sliced

Per Serving
Calories: 245
% Calories from fat: 19
Protein (g): 14.9
Carbohydrates (g): 38.7
Fat (g): 5.7
Saturated fat (g): 0.9
Cholesterol (mg): 0
Sodium (mg): 392
Exchanges
Milk: 0.0
Veg.: 2.5
Fruit: 0.0
Bread: 1.0
Meat: 2.0
Fat: 0.0

1. Spray large skillet with cooking spray; heat over medium heat until hot. Cook protein links over medium heat until browned, about 8 minutes, turning occasionally. Remove from skillet and reserve.

2. Add onion and garlic to skillet; saute until tender, about 5 minutes. Stir in corn, zucchini, and tomatoes; heat to boiling. Reduce heat and simmer, uncovered, 15 minutes. Heat mixture to boiling. Mix flour and water; stir into boiling mixture. Boil, stirring constantly, until thickened, about 1 minute.

3. Return sausages to skillet mixture; cook over medium heat 2 to 3 minutes longer. Season to taste with salt and pepper. Spoon into bowls to serve; sprinkle with green onions.

SOUTHERN STEW WITH DUMPLINGS

Corn, okra, and lima beans simmer in this home-style stew.

6 servings

1^1/$_2$ cups sliced carrots

1^1/$_2$ cups sliced celery

  2 cups reduced-sodium vegetable broth

  2 teaspoons very-low-sodium Worcestershire sauce

 ^{1}/$_2$ teaspoon dried oregano leaves

 ^{1}/$_2$ teaspoon dried thyme leaves

  1 package (10 ounces) frozen lima beans

  1 package (10 ounces) frozen whole-kernel corn

  1 package (10 ounces) frozen sliced okra

    Salt and pepper, to taste

    Herb Dumplings (see p. 680)

Per Serving
Calories: 254
% Calories from fat: 18
Protein (gm): 8.1
Carbohydrate (gm): 45.5
Fat (gm): 5.2
Saturated fat (gm): 1.2
Cholesterol (mg): 0.4
Sodium (mg): 435
Exchanges
Milk: 0.0
Veg.: 3.0
Fruit: 0.0
Bread: 2.0
Meat: 0.0
Fat: 1.0

1. Combine carrots, celery, broth, Worcestershire, oregano, and thyme in large saucepan; heat to boiling. Reduce heat and simmer, covered, 5 minutes. Stir in beans, corn, and okra. Simmer, covered, until carrots and celery are almost tender, about 10 minutes. Season to taste with salt and pepper.

2. Spoon Herb Dumpling mixture into 6 mounds on top of stew; cook, uncovered, 5 minutes. Cook, covered, until dumplings are dry, 5 to 10 minutes longer.

SOUTHERN VEGETABLE STEW

Team this Southern favorite with Garlic Bread (see p. 795).

4 servings (about 1³/₄ cups each)

Vegetable cooking spray

1/4 cup sliced green onions and tops

1 medium green bell pepper, coarsely chopped

1 medium red bell pepper, coarsely chopped

4 cloves garlic, minced

2 cups Canned Vegetable Stock (see p. 11), *or* vegetable broth

1 can (14¹/₂ ounces) reduced-sodium diced tomatoes, undrained

8 ounces pearl onions, peeled

2 teaspoons paprika

1 small eggplant, peeled, cut into 1-inch pieces

2 cups coarsely shredded carrots

1 medium zucchini, cut into ¾-inch pieces

4 ounces fresh, *or* frozen, thawed, okra, sliced ¹/₂ inch thick

1¹/₂ teaspoons coarse-grain mustard

Red pepper sauce, to taste

Salt and pepper, to taste

Parsley, minced, as garnish

Per Serving
Calories: 170
% Calories from fat: 8
Protein (g): 5.7
Carbohydrates (g): 34.4
Fat (g): 1.6
Saturated fat (g): 0.2
Cholesterol (mg): 0
Sodium (mg): 94
Exchanges
Milk: 0.0
Veg.: 6.0
Fruit: 0.0
Bread: 0.0
Meat: 0.0
Fat: 0.0

1. Spray large saucepan with cooking spray; heat over medium heat until hot. Saute green onions, bell peppers, and garlic until softened, about 4 minutes. Add stock, tomatoes and liquid, pearl onions, and paprika; heat to boiling. Reduce heat and simmer 10 minutes or until onions are tender.

2. Spray large skillet with cooking spray; heat over medium heat until hot. Saute eggplant, carrots, zucchini, and okra until slightly softened, about 5 minutes; add to saucepan. Stir in mustard and simmer until vegetables are tender, about 5 minutes. Season to taste with red pepper sauce, salt, and pepper.

3. Spoon stew into serving bowls; sprinkle with parsley.

HOT 'N SPICY BEAN AND VEGETABLE STEW

Make this stew as fiery as you like with serrano or other hot chilies!

6 servings (about 1¹/₂ cups each)

Olive oil cooking spray
1¹/₂ cups chopped onions
2-4 teaspoons minced serrano chilies
2-3 teaspoons minced garlic
1 tablespoon flour
1¹/₂ teaspoons dried oregano leaves
³/₄ teaspoon ground cinnamon
¹/₂ teaspoon ground cloves
1 bay leaf
2 cans (16 ounces each) reduced-sodium diced tomatoes, undrained
1¹/₂ cups Basic Vegetable Stock (see p. 10), *or* water
1 tablespoon red wine vinegar
4 medium carrots, sliced
4 medium red potatoes, unpeeled, cubed
1 can (15 ounces) black beans, rinsed, drained
1 can (15 ounces) pinto beans, rinsed, drained
Salt and pepper, to taste

Per Serving
Calories: 284
% Calories from fat: 5
Protein (g): 15.4
Carbohydrates (g): 60.8
Fat (g): 2
Saturated fat (g): 0.1
Cholesterol (mg): 0
Sodium (mg): 527
Exchanges
Milk: 0.0
Veg.: 3.0
Fruit: 0.0
Bread: 3.0
Meat: 0.0
Fat: 0.0

1. Spray Dutch oven or large saucepan with cooking spray; heat over medium heat until hot. Saute onions, chilies, and garlic 5 minutes; stir in flour and seasonings and cook 1 to 2 minutes longer.

2. Add remaining ingredients, except salt and pepper; heat to boiling. Reduce heat and simmer, covered, until vegetables are tender and stew thickened, 15 to 20 minutes. Discard bay leaf; season to taste with salt and pepper.

TOFU AND VEGETABLE STEW

As with most stews, vegetables in this dish can vary according to season and availability; tempeh can be substituted for the tofu.

4 servings (about 1³/₄ cups each)

Vegetable cooking spray
1 medium onion, sliced
¹/₂ cup sliced celery
3 cloves garlic, minced
4 cups Rich Mushroom Stock (see p. 17), *or* vegetable broth
2 cups sliced, peeled red potatoes
6 medium carrots, sliced
1 bay leaf
1 teaspoon ground cumin
¹/₄-¹/₂ teaspoon dried thyme leaves
¹/₈ teaspoon ground cloves
1 package (10 ounces) frozen chopped spinach
1 package (10¹/₂ ounces) firm light tofu, *or* tempeh, cut into ¹/₂-inch cubes
¹/₄ cup minced parsley
Salt and pepper, to taste

Per Serving
Calories: 239
% Calories from fat: 8
Protein (g): 11.1
Carbohydrates (g): 43.8
Fat (g): 2.3
Saturated fat (g): 0.2
Cholesterol (mg): 0
Sodium (mg): 182
Exchanges
Milk: 0.0
Veg.: 4.0
Fruit: 0.0
Bread: 1.5
Meat: 0.5
Fat: 0.0

1. Spray large saucepan with cooking spray; heat over medium heat until hot. Saute onion, celery, and garlic until softened, about 4 minutes.

2. Add Rich Mushroom Stock, potatoes, carrots, bay leaf, cumin, thyme, and cloves to saucepan; heat to boiling. Reduce heat and simmer, covered, until vegetables are tender, about 20 minutes. Add spinach and simmer 2 to 3 minutes. Add tofu and parsley and cook until heated through, about 4 minutes. Discard bay leaf; season to taste with salt and pepper.

TEX-MEX VEGETABLE STEW

Poblano chilies range from mild to very hot in flavor, so taste a tiny bit before using. If the chili is very hot, you may want to substitute some sweet green bell pepper.

6 servings (about 1½ ¹/₂cups each)

Vegetable cooking spray
1 medium red onion, chopped
1 poblano chili, seeded, chopped
3 cloves garlic, minced
3 cans (10 ounces each) tomatoes with chilies, undrained
12 small new potatoes, cut into halves
4 medium carrots, cut into 1-inch pieces
3 ears corn, cut into 2-inch pieces
1 cup Canned Vegetable Stock (see p. 11), *or* vegetable broth
2 tablespoons balsamic vinegar
1 tablespoon chili powder
2 teaspoons ground cumin
¹/₂ teaspoon dried oregano leaves
³/₄ teaspoon ground pepper
1 can (15 ounces) black beans, rinsed, drained
2 cups frozen peas, thawed
Salt, to taste
¹/₂ cup finely chopped cilantro

Per Serving
Calories: 423
% Calories from fat: 5
Protein (g): 16.7
Carbohydrates (g): 92.5
Fat (g): 2.4
Saturated fat (g): 0.2
Cholesterol (mg): 0
Sodium (mg): 793
Exchanges
Milk: 0.0
Veg.: 3.0
Fruit: 0.0
Bread: 5.0
Meat: 0.0
Fat: 0.0

1. Spray large saucepan with cooking spray; heat over medium heat until hot. Saute onion, chili, and garlic until softened, about 4 minutes.

2. Add tomatoes and liquid, potatoes, carrots, corn, Canned Vegetable Stock, vinegar, chili powder, cumin, oregano, and pepper; heat to boiling. Reduce heat and simmer, uncovered, 30 minutes or until vegetables are tender.

3. Stir in beans and peas; cook until peas are tender, about 5 minutes. Season to taste with salt. Serve stew in bowls; sprinkle with cilantro.

MEXI-BEANS 'N GREENS STEW

Four cans (15 ounces each) pinto beans, rinsed and drained, can be substituted for the dried beans; omit Step 1 in recipe.

8 servings

2 cups dried pinto beans
1 medium onion, coarsely chopped
1 medium poblano chili, chopped
1 medium red bell pepper, chopped
4 cloves garlic, minced
1 tablespoon finely chopped gingerroot
2 serrano chilies, finely chopped
2 tablespoons olive oil
2-3 teaspoons chili powder
2 teaspoons dried oregano leaves
1 teaspoon ground cumin
1/2 teaspoon cayenne pepper
3 cups water
1 can (15 ounces) diced tomatoes, undrained
2 cups coarsely chopped turnip, *or* mustard, greens
Salt, to taste
Cilantro, finely chopped, as garnish

Per Serving
Calories: 228
% Calories from fat: 16
Protein (g): 11.7
Carbohydrates (g): 37.9
Fat (g): 4.4
Saturated fat (g): 0.6
Cholesterol (mg): 0
Sodium (mg): 233
Exchanges
Milk: 0.0
Veg.: 2.0
Fruit: 0.0
Bread: 2.0
Meat: 0.0
Fat: 1.0

1. Cover beans with 2 inches water in large saucepan; heat to boiling and boil, uncovered, 2 minutes. Remove from heat and let stand, covered, 1 hour; drain.

2. Saute onion, poblano chili, bell pepper, garlic, gingerroot, and serrano chilies in oil in large saucepan until tender, 8 to 10 minutes. Stir in chili powder, herbs, and cayenne pepper; cook 1 to 2 minutes longer.

3. Add 3 cups water and sauteed vegetables to beans; heat to boiling. Reduce heat and simmer, covered, until beans are tender, 1 to 1¹/4 hours, adding water if necessary. Stir in tomatoes and liquid and turnip greens; simmer, uncovered, until mixture is desired thickness, 15 to 30 minutes. Season to taste with salt. Spoon into bowls; sprinkle generously with cilantro.

MEXICAN ANCHO CHILI STEW

This stew has lots of delicious sauce, so serve with crusty warm rolls or warm tortillas. Vary the amount of ancho chilies to taste.

4 servings (about 1¹/₃ cups each)

4-6 ancho chilies, stems, seeds, and veins discarded

2 cups boiling water

4 medium tomatoes, cut into wedges
Vegetable cooking spray

6-8 Mexican-style all-vegetable "burgers," crumbled (18–24 ounces)

1 large onion, chopped

2 cloves garlic, minced

1 teaspoon minced serrano, *or* jalapeño, chili

1 teaspoon dried oregano leaves

1 teaspoon cumin seeds, crushed

2 tablespoons flour
Salt and pepper, to taste

Per Serving
Calories: 275
% Calories from fat: **13**
Protein (g): 11.9
Carbohydrates (g): 50.9
Fat (g): 4.3
Saturated fat (g): 0.1
Cholesterol (mg): 0
Sodium (mg): 735
Exchanges
Milk: 0.0
Veg.: 2.0
Fruit: 0.0
Bread: 2.5
Meat: 0.5
Fat: 0.5

1. Place ancho chilies in bowl; pour boiling water over. Let stand until chilies are softened, about 10 minutes. Process chilies, with water and tomatoes, in food processor or blender until smooth.

2. Spray large saucepan with cooking spray; heat over medium heat until hot. Cook crumbled "burgers," onion, garlic, serrano chili, and herbs until onion is tender, about 5 minutes. Stir in flour; cook over medium heat 1 to 2 minutes more.

3. Add chili and tomato mixture to saucepan; heat to boiling. Reduce heat and simmer, covered, 15 to 20 minutes. Season to taste with salt and pepper.

MEXICAN-STYLE VEGETABLE STEW

A winter vegetable offering with a Mexican flair, spooned over strands of spaghetti squash. Serve with warm squares of Green Chili Cornbread (see p. 803).

4 servings (about 1⅓ cups each)

1 medium spaghetti squash, halved, seeded
  Vegetable cooking spray
2 medium russet potatoes, cut into 1-inch pieces
1 medium onion, chopped
1 large carrot, cut into ½-inch slices
1 cup cubed rutabaga (1-inch)
½ cup chopped green bell pepper
2 cloves garlic, minced
1 tablespoon flour
1½ cups Basic Vegetable Stock (see p. 10), *or* vegetable broth
1 can (14½ ounces) diced tomatoes and chilies, undrained
  Salt and pepper, to taste
  Cilantro, finely chopped, as garnish

Per Serving
Calories: 166
% Calories from fat: 6
Protein (g): 5.3
Carbohydrates (g): 37.3
Fat (g): 1.1
Saturated fat (g): 0.2
Cholesterol (mg): 0
Sodium (mg): 437
Exchanges
Milk: 0.0
Veg.: 2.5
Fruit: 0.0
Bread: 1.5
Meat: 0.0
Fat: 0.0

1. Place squash halves, cut sides down, in baking pan; add ½ inch water. Bake, covered, at 350 degrees until tender, 30 to 40 minutes. Using fork, scrape squash to separate into strands.

2. Spray large skillet with cooking spray; heat over medium heat until hot. Add vegetables, including garlic, and spray with cooking spray; saute until lightly browned, 8 to 10 minutes. Stir in flour; cook 1 minute longer.

3. Add Basic Vegetable Stock and tomatoes with liquid; heat to boiling. Reduce heat and simmer, covered, until vegetables are tender, about 15 minutes. Season to taste with salt and pepper.

4. Spoon spaghetti squash onto serving plates; spoon vegetables over. Sprinkle with cilantro.

COLOMBIAN-STYLE VEGETABLE STEW

This delicious stew is a comfort food, especially on a cold night. Be sure to add the cilantro; it's an important flavor element.

6 servings

Per Serving
Calories: 503
% Calories from fat: 14
Protein (g): 15.8
Carbohydrates (g): 93
Fat (g): 8.1
Saturated fat (g): 0.8
Cholesterol (mg): 0
Sodium (mg): 757
Exchanges
Milk: 0.0
Veg.: 4.0
Fruit: 0.0
Bread: 4.5
Meat: 0.0
Fat: 1.5

- 4 garlic cloves, minced
- 1¹/₄ cups chopped onions
- 2 tablespoons canola oil
- 2 cans (16 ounces each) reduced-sodium whole tomatoes, undrained, coarsely chopped
- 6 small baking potatoes, peeled, cubed
- 6 carrots, cut into 1-inch pieces
- 6 ribs celery, cut into 1¹/₂-inch pieces
- 6 ears corn, cut into 1¹/₂-inch pieces
- 2 cups boiling water
- 2 vegetable bouillon cubes
- 1 cup dry white wine
- 2 bay leaves
- 1¹/₂ tablespoons white wine vinegar
- 1 teaspoon dried cumin
- ³/₄ teaspoon dried oregano leaves
- 1 can (15 ounces) chickpeas, rinsed, drained
- 2 cups frozen peas
- ³/₄ cup chopped cilantro
- Salt and pepper, to taste

1. Saute garlic and onions in oil in large saucepan until onion is tender. Add remaining ingredients, except chickpeas, peas, cilantro, salt, and pepper; heat to boiling. Reduce heat and simmer, uncovered, until vegetables are tender and sauce is thickened, about 40 minutes.

2. Add chickpeas and peas to saucepan and simmer 5 to 10 minutes or until peas are tender. Stir in cilantro; discard bay leaves. Season to taste with salt and pepper.

ARGENTINEAN STEW IN A PUMPKIN SHELL

We took the meat out of this stew that's traditionally served in a pumpkin shell. Meatless, we think it's much more delicious and beautiful.

12 servings

5 garlic cloves, minced

2 cups coarsely chopped red onions

1 large green bell pepper, chopped

3 tablespoons canola oil

1 quart boiling water

4 vegetable bouillon cubes

2 cups dry white wine

2 cans (16 ounces each) whole tomatoes, undrained, coarsely chopped

2 tablespoons brown sugar

2 tablespoons white wine vinegar

2 bay leaves

1 teaspoon dried oregano leaves

5 cups cubed, peeled boiling potatoes

5 cups cubed, peeled sweet potatoes

5 cups cubed, peeled butternut squash

8 ears corn, cut into 1 1/2-inch pieces

1 pound zucchini, cut into 3/4-inch slices

10 peaches, pitted, halved

Salt and pepper, to taste

Pumpkin Shell (recipe follows)

Per Serving
Calories: 420
% Calories from fat: 16
Protein (g): 8
Carbohydrates (g): 82
Fat (g): 7.5
Saturated fat (g): 0.7
Cholesterol (mg): 0
Sodium (mg): 769
Exchanges
Milk: 0.0
Veg.: 2.0
Fruit: 0.5
Bread: 4.0
Meat: 0.0
Fat: 1.5

1. Saute garlic, onions, and bell pepper in oil in large saucepan until onion is tender. Add remaining ingredients, except corn, zucchini, peaches, salt, pepper, and Pumpkin Shell; heat to boiling. Reduce heat and simmer, uncovered, 30 minutes or until vegetables are tender. Add corn, zucchini, and peaches; simmer 10 minutes or until all ingredients are tender. Discard bay leaves; season to taste with salt and pepper.

2. Spoon stew into Pumpkin Shell; bake at 375 degrees 10 minutes.

Pumpkin Shell

   1 firm pumpkin, 10–12 pounds, washed well
  1/4 cup margarine, melted
  1/3 cup sugar

1. Cut a 7-inch-diameter circle in top of pumpkin; remove fiber and seeds. Brush margarine inside shell and lid; sprinkle with sugar. Place pumpkin on greased cookie sheet; bake at 375 degrees until pumpkin is almost tender but still holds it shape, 30 to 45 minutes. Invert pumpkin to drain liquid; place on cookie sheet.

ROMANIAN STEW WITH RED WINE AND GRAPES

Make this stew, known as Ghiveciu, with the same good red wine you serve with it.

6 servings

   4 cups peeled, cubed potatoes
   4 cups peeled, cubed eggplant
   2 cups coarsely chopped cauliflower florets
2 1/2 cups coarsely chopped cabbage
2 1/2 cups peeled, cubed celery root
1 1/2 cups cut green beans
1 1/2 cups halved baby carrots
   1 tablespoon minced garlic
   2 large red onions, coarsely chopped
   2 large red bell peppers, coarsely chopped
  1/4 cup margarine, divided
  1/4 cup coarsely chopped parsley
  3/4 teaspoon dried thyme leaves
  1/2 teaspoon dried marjoram leaves
   Salt and pepper, to taste
   1 cup water
   1 cup dry red wine, *or* vegetable broth
  1/4 cup tomato paste

Per Serving
Calories: 339
% Calories from fat: 12
Protein (g): 8.2
Carbohydrates (g): 64.8
Fat (g): 4.9
Saturated fat (g): 0.9
Cholesterol (mg): 0
Sodium (mg): 657
Exchanges
Milk: 0.0
Veg.: 4.0
Fruit: 0.5
Bread: 2.5
Meat: 0.0
Fat: 1.0

2 tablespoons molasses
1 bay leaf
2 large tomatoes, peeled, seeded, coarsely chopped
1 cup seedless green grapes
$^1/_2$ cup frozen peas

1. Steam potatoes, eggplant, cauliflower, cabbage, celery root, green beans, and carrots, or cook in 2 inches simmering water, until almost tender.

2. Saute garlic, onions, and bell peppers in 2 tablespoons margarine in saucepan until onion is tender. Add parsley, thyme, and marjoram.

3. Arrange vegetables in large casserole, alternating layers of steamed and sauteed vegetables, ending with sauteed vegetables, and sprinkling layers lightly with salt and pepper.

4. Heat water, wine, tomato paste, molasses, bay leaf, and remaining 2 tablespoons margarine to boiling in small saucepan; pour over vegetables. Cover casserole and bake at 350 degrees 45 minutes. Add tomatoes, grapes, and peas; cover and bake 30 minutes longer. Discard bay leaf.

RAVIOLI AND VEGETABLE STEW WITH BASIL

Love ravioli? In the mood for a stew? This dish offers both, and it's packed with fresh vegetables—squash, tomatoes, carrots, and escarole, too.

4 servings

2 cans (14 ounces each) reduced-sodium vegetable broth
2 carrots, cut into thin 2-inch-long strips
1$^1/_4$ cups chopped yellow summer squash
3 plum tomatoes, coarsely chopped
1 package (20 ounces) frozen small cheese ravioli
$^1/_2$ teaspoon crushed red pepper
2 cups torn escarole
$^1/_2$ cup chopped basil
Salt and pepper, to taste

Per Serving
Calories: 331
% Calories from fat: 19
Protein (g): 16.5
Carbohydrates (g): 51.8
Fat (g): 7.2
Saturated fat (g): 3.9
Cholesterol (mg): 38.6
Sodium (mg): 416
Exchanges
Milk: 0.0
Veg.: 4.0
Fruit: 0.0
Bread: 2.0
Meat: 0.0
Fat: 1.5

1. Combine broth and carrots in large saucepan. Heat to boiling; reduce heat and simmer, covered, until carrots are tender, about 10 minutes. Add squash, tomatoes, and ravioli; simmer until squash is tender and ravioli are al dente, about 10 minutes.

2. Stir in crushed red pepper, escarole, and basil; simmer 1 minute longer. Season to taste with salt and pepper.

ITALIAN BEAN AND PASTA STEW

This traditional dish, known as Pasta e Fagioli, is a cross between a soup and a stew—thick, rich, and flavorful.

5-6 servings

1 large onion, chopped
1 large garlic clove, minced
2 teaspoons olive oil
3¹/₂ cups reduced-sodium vegetable broth
1 large carrot, finely chopped
1 rib celery, finely chopped
1 can (14¹/₂ ounces) Italian tomatoes, undrained, chopped
2¹/₂ cups cooked cannellini beans, *or* 1 can (19 ounces) cannellini *or* Great Northern beans, drained
¹/₂ teaspoon dried oregano leaves
¹/₂ teaspoon dried basil leaves
3 ounces elbow macaroni, cooked
Salt and pepper, to taste
Grated Parmesan cheese, as garnish

Per Serving
Calories: 271
% Calories from fat: 9
Protein (gm): 12.3
Carbohydrate (gm): 49.3
Fat (gm): 2.8
Saturated fat (gm): 0.5
Cholesterol (mg): 0
Sodium (mg): 249
Exchanges
Milk: 0.0
Veg.: 2.0
Fruit: 0.0
Bread: 3.0
Meat: 0.0
Fat: 0.0

1. Saute onion and garlic in oil in large saucepan until tender, about 5 minutes. Add remaining ingredients, except macaroni, salt, pepper, and Parmesan cheese. Simmer, covered, until vegetables are tender, about 20 minutes. Add macaroni and simmer 2 to 3 minutes; season to taste with salt and pepper. Sprinkle with Parmesan cheese.

ITALIAN BEAN STEW

Cannellini beans are a favorite Italian bean, but almost any dried bean can be used in this easy recipe. Use 4 cans (15 ounces each) cannellini or other white beans if you don't have time to cook the dry beans.

8 servings

1 medium onion, chopped
1¹/₂ cups diced zucchini
¹/₂ cup finely chopped sun-dried tomatoes (not in oil)
1 garlic clove, minced
1 tablespoon olive oil
1³/₄ cups dried white cannellini, *or* Great Northern, beans, cooked
1 can (14¹/₂ ounces) reduced-sodium stewed tomatoes, undrained
1 can (8 ounces) reduced-sodium tomato sauce
1¹/₂ teaspoons dried basil leaves
1 teaspoon dried oregano leaves
Salt and pepper, to taste

Per Serving
Calories: 143
% Calories from fat: 14
Protein (g): 8.2
Carbohydrates (g): 24.1
Fat (g): 2.4
Saturated fat (g): 0.4
Cholesterol (mg): 0
Sodium (mg): 84
Exchanges
Milk: 0.0
Veg.: 2.0
Fruit: 0.0
Bread: 1.0
Meat: 0.0
Fat: 0.5

1. Saute onion, zucchini, sun-dried tomatoes, and garlic in oil in large saucepan 5 minutes; add remaining ingredients, except salt and pepper. Heat to boiling; reduce heat and simmer, covered, until vegetables are tender, about 8 minutes. Season to taste with salt and pepper.

CHICKPEA AND ROASTED PEPPERS STEW WITH CREAMY POLENTA

Polenta makes a nice change from pasta; this version is especially easy because it is made in the microwave.

5 servings

1 medium onion, chopped
1 garlic clove, minced
2 teaspoons olive oil
1 can (15 ounces) chickpeas, rinsed, drained
1 can (15 ounces) reduced-sodium tomato sauce
1 can (14¹/₂ ounces) reduced-sodium stewed tomatoes
1 jar (7 ounces) roasted red peppers, drained, chopped
1 medium zucchini, chopped
1 teaspoon Italian seasoning
Salt and pepper, to taste
Creamy Polenta (recipe follows)

Per Serving
Calories: 352
% Calories from fat: **13**
Protein (g): 13.7
Carbohydrates (g): 64.8
Fat (g): 5.3
Saturated fat (g): 1
Cholesterol (mg): 2
Sodium (mg): 689
Exchanges
Milk: 0.0
Veg.: 4.0
Fruit: 0.0
Bread: 3.0
Meat: 0.0
Fat: 1.0

1. Saute onion and garlic in oil in large saucepan until tender. Add remaining ingredients, except salt, pepper, and Creamy Polenta, and heat to boiling. Reduce heat and simmer, covered, until vegetables are tender, about 15 minutes. Season to taste with salt and pepper. Serve over Creamy Polenta.

Creamy Polenta

1¹/₃ cups yellow cornmeal
1 tablespoon sugar
¹/₂ teaspoon salt, optional
3¹/₄ cups water
1 cup 1% low-fat milk
1 medium onion, diced
¹/₄ cup grated Parmesan cheese

1. Combine all ingredients, except Parmesan cheese, in 3-quart, microwave-safe casserole and cook on High 8 to 9 minutes, stirring twice during cooking time. Whisk in cheese, cover, and cook on High 4 to 5 minutes longer. Let stand 3 minutes.

THREE-BEAN STEW WITH POLENTA

Use any kind of canned or cooked dried beans that you like; one 15-ounce can of drained beans yields 1¹/₂ cups beans. Many flavors of prepared polenta are now available in the produce department and can be substituted for the Polenta used in this recipe.

6 servings (about 1 cup each)

1 cup chopped onion
¹/₂ cup chopped red, *or* green, bell pepper
1-2 tablespoons olive oil
1 tablespoon flour
1 can (15 ounces) black-eyed peas, rinsed, drained
1 can (15 ounces) black beans, rinsed, drained
1 can (15 ounces) red beans, rinsed, drained
1 can (14¹/₂ ounces) reduced-sodium diced tomatoes, undrained
1 tablespoon minced roasted garlic
³/₄ teaspoon dried sage leaves
¹/₂ teaspoon dried rosemary leaves
1 cup reduced-sodium vegetable broth
Salt and pepper, to taste
Polenta (see p. 811)

Per Serving
Calories: 267
% Calories from fat: 13
Protein (g): 12.5
Carbohydrates (g): 52.2
Fat (g): 4.2
Saturated fat (g): 0.6
Cholesterol (mg): 0
Sodium (mg): 590
Exchanges
Milk: 0.0
Veg.: 1.0
Fruit: 0.0
Bread: 3.0
Meat: 0.0
Fat: 0.5

1. Saute onion and bell pepper in oil in large saucepan until tender, about 5 minutes. Stir in flour; cook 1 minute longer.

2. Add beans, tomatoes and liquid, garlic, herbs, and broth to saucepan; heat to boiling. Reduce heat and simmer, covered, 10 minutes. Season to taste with salt and pepper.

3. Spoon Polenta into shallow bowls; spoon stew over.

ROASTED RATATOUILLE STEW

Roasting vegetables intensifies their natural flavor and sweetness. Serve this full-flavored stew with warm, crusty French bread.

6 servings (about 2 cups each)

Olive oil cooking spray

8 ounces new potatoes, unpeeled, quartered

4 baby eggplant, unpeeled, cut into 1-inch cubes

3 cups sliced red, *or* green, cabbage

2 medium yellow summer squash, *or* zucchini, sliced

2 cups cauliflower florets

2 cups halved green beans

2 medium green bell peppers, cut into 1-inch pieces

2 medium onions, sliced

3 cloves garlic, minced

3/4-1 teaspoon Italian seasoning

1 cup Mediterranean Vegetable Stock (see p. 15), *or* vegetable broth

1 cup dry red wine, *or* Mediterranean Vegetable Stock

1/4 cup reduced-sodium tomato paste

2 tablespoons balsamic vinegar

1 1/2 tablespoons brown sugar

2 medium tomatoes, cut into wedges

Salt and pepper, to taste

Per Serving
Calories: 197
% Calories from fat: 5
Protein (g): 5.7
Carbohydrates (g): 38.4
Fat (g): 1.2
Saturated fat (g): 0.2
Cholesterol (mg): 0
Sodium (mg): 64
Exchanges
Milk: 0.0
Veg.: 5.0
Fruit: 0.0
Bread: 1.0
Meat: 0.0
Fat: 0.0

1. Spray 2 aluminum-foil-lined jelly roll pans with cooking spray. Arrange vegetables in single layer on pans. Generously spray vegetables with cooking spray; sprinkle with Italian seasoning.

2. Roast vegetables at 475 degrees 15 to 20 minutes or until beginning to brown, stirring occasionally.

3. Heat Mediterranean Vegetable Stock, wine, tomato paste, vinegar, and sugar to boiling in small saucepan; pour over vegetables. Add tomatoes to pans.

4. Reduce oven temperature to 350 degrees and bake, covered, 20 to 30 minutes or until vegetables are tender. Season to taste with salt and pepper.

RATATOUILLE WITH FETA AIOLI

Feta, a Greek cheese, imparts a welcome zing to this Mediterranean gem that's brimming with eggplant, tomatoes, and zucchini. For crunch, serve Garlic Croutons (see p. 785).

4 servings

2 medium onions, sliced
1 medium eggplant, peeled, cubed
2 teaspoons olive oil
1 can (28 ounces) whole tomatoes, undrained, coarsely chopped
2 small zucchini, halved, thinly sliced
1 yellow bell pepper, thinly sliced
3 teaspoons minced garlic
2 teaspoons Italian seasoning
   Salt and pepper, to taste
   Feta Aioli (recipe follows)

Per Serving
Calories: 164
% Calories from fat: 15
Protein (gm): 6.7
Carbohydrate (gm): 31.7
Fat (gm): 3.1
Saturated fat (gm): 0.5
Cholesterol (mg): 0
Sodium (mg): 522
Exchanges
Milk: 0.0
Veg.: 3.0
Fruit: 0.0
Bread: 1.0
Meat: 0.0
Fat: 0.5

1. Saute onions and eggplant in oil in Dutch oven until onions are tender. Add remaining ingredients, except salt, pepper, and Feta Aioli, and heat to boiling. Reduce heat and simmer, covered, until vegetables are tender, about 20 minutes. Season to taste with salt and pepper; serve with Feta Aioli.

Feta Aioli

makes about 1/2 cup

1/4 cup (1 ounce) crumbled fat-free feta cheese
1/4 cup fat-free mayonnaise
2-3 cloves garlic, minced

1. Process all ingredients in food processor until smooth.

CURRIED MEDITERRANEAN STEW WITH COUSCOUS

Couscous, a staple in Mediterranean countries, is one of the fastest, easiest grains to cook. Serve this stew with a selection of condiments so it can be enjoyed with a variety of flavor accents.

4 servings (about 1¹/₂ cups each)

   8 ounces fresh, *or* frozen, thawed, whole okra

   1 cup chopped onion

   1 teaspoon minced garlic

   2 tablespoons vegetable oil

   1 cup frozen, *or* canned, drained, whole-kernel corn

   1 cup sliced mushrooms

   2 medium carrots, sliced

1¹/₂ teaspoons curry powder

   1 cup reduced-sodium vegetable broth

  ²/₃ cup couscous

   1 medium tomato, chopped

    Salt and pepper, to taste

    Condiments: reduced-fat plain yogurt, chopped cucumber, chopped peanuts, raisins (not included in nutritional data)

Per Serving
Calories: 280
% Calories from fat: 24
Protein (g): 7.9
Carbohydrates (g): 47.8
Fat (g): 7.7
Saturated fat (g): 1
Cholesterol (mg): 0
Sodium (mg): 46
Exchanges
Milk: 0.0
Veg.: 3.0
Fruit: 0.0
Bread: 2.0
Meat: 0.0
Fat: 1.5

1. Saute okra, onion, and garlic in oil in large saucepan 5 minutes. Stir in corn, mushrooms, carrots, and curry powder; cook 2 minutes.

2. Add broth to saucepan and heat to boiling; reduce heat and simmer, covered, until vegetables are tender, 8 to 10 minutes. Stir in couscous (discard spice packet) and tomato. Remove from heat and let stand, covered, until couscous is tender and broth absorbed, about 5 minutes. Season to taste with salt and pepper.

3. Spoon couscous mixture into serving bowl; serve with condiments.

EGGPLANT AND BEAN CURRY STEW

The flavorful curry seasoning is created by making a simple paste of onion, garlic, and herbs.

4 servings (about 1 cup each)

2 medium red potatoes, peeled, cut into ³/₄-inch cubes
1 tablespoon olive oil
1 small eggplant, unpeeled, cut into ³/₄-inch cubes
¹/₂ medium onion, chopped
1 teaspoon minced garlic
1 teaspoon ground coriander
¹/₂ teaspoon ground cumin
¹/₄ teaspoon crushed red pepper
¹/₈ teaspoon ground turmeric
¹/₂ cup plus 1 tablespoon water, divided
1 can (16 ounces) reduced-sodium whole tomatoes, undrained, coarsely chopped
1 can (15 ounces) garbanzo beans, rinsed, drained
Salt and pepper, to taste
¹/₄ cup finely chopped cilantro

Per Serving
Calories: 242
% Calories from fat: 21
Protein (g): 8.2
Carbohydrates (g): 41.8
Fat (g): 6
Saturated fat (g): 0.8
Cholesterol (mg): 0
Sodium (mg): 446
Exchanges
Milk: 0.0
Veg.: 2.0
Fruit: 0.0
Bread: 2.0
Meat: 0.0
Fat: 1.0

1. Saute potatoes in oil in large saucepan until browned; remove and reserve. Add eggplant to saucepan; cook over medium to medium-low heat until lightly browned, stirring frequently. Remove eggplant and reserve.

2. Process onion, garlic, herbs, and 1 tablespoon water in food processor until a smooth paste. Add to saucepan and cook over medium-low heat 3 to 4 minutes, stirring frequently to prevent burning. Add reserved potatoes and eggplant, tomatoes with liquid, beans, and remaining ¹/₂ cup water to saucepan; heat to boiling. Reduce heat and simmer, covered, until eggplant is tender, 20 to 25 minutes. Season to taste with salt and pepper; stir in cilantro.

CURRIED SOYBEAN AND POTATO STEW

The curry seasoning in this recipe is a combination of 4 aromatic spices. Any white bean, such as garbanzo, navy, Great Northern, or cannellini, can be substituted for the soybeans.

4 servings (about 1 cup each)

Garlic-flavored vegetable cooking spray
- 1 cup chopped onion
- 1 medium red bell pepper, chopped
- 2 teaspoons minced garlic
- 1 jalapeño chili, finely chopped
- 2 teaspoons ground turmeric
- 1 teaspoon ground cumin
- 1/2 teaspoon ground coriander
- 1/4 teaspoon ground ginger
- 4 medium russet potatoes, peeled, cubed
- 2 1/2 cups cooked dried soybeans, *or* canned soybeans, rinsed, drained
- 1 medium tart cooking apple, peeled, cored, cubed
- 1 cup water
- 2 teaspoons lemon juice
- 2 tablespoons finely chopped cilantro
  Salt and pepper, to taste

Per Serving
Calories: 368
% Calories from fat: **24**
Protein (g): 22
Carbohydrates (g): **52.7**
Fat (g): 10.4
Saturated fat (g): **1.5**
Cholesterol (mg): 0
Sodium (mg): 28
Exchanges
Milk: 0.0
Veg.: 2.0
Fruit: 0.0
Bread: 2.5
Meat: 1.5
Fat: 1.0

1. Spray large saucepan with cooking spray; heat over medium heat until hot. Saute onion, bell pepper, garlic, and jalapeño chili until tender, about 5 minutes. Stir in spices; cook over medium-low heat 1 to 2 minutes, stirring constantly so spices do not burn.

2. Add potatoes to saucepan; cook 5 minutes, stirring frequently. Add soybeans, apple, and water; heat to boiling. Reduce heat and simmer, covered, 20 minutes. Simmer, uncovered, until almost dry, 5 to 10 minutes longer. Stir in lemon juice and cilantro; season to taste with salt and pepper.

CURRIED VEGETABLE STEW

A variety of spices and herbs are combined to make the fragrant curry that seasons this dish.

4 servings

Vegetable cooking spray
1/2 cup chopped onion
2 cloves garlic
1 large head cauliflower, cut into florets
2 medium potatoes, peeled, cut into 1/2-inch cubes
2 large carrots, cut into 1/2-inch slices
1 1/2 cups Canned Vegetable Stock (see p. 11), *or* vegetable broth
3/4 teaspoon ground turmeric
1/4 teaspoon dry mustard
1/4 teaspoon ground cumin
1/4 teaspoon ground coriander
1 tablespoon flour
2 tablespoons cold water
1 large tomato, chopped
2 tablespoons finely chopped parsley
1-2 tablespoons lemon juice
Salt, cayenne, and black pepper, to taste

Per Serving
Calories: 81
% Calories from fat: 6
Protein (g): 3.7
Carbohydrates (g): 15.8
Fat (g): 0.6
Saturated fat (g): 0
Cholesterol (mg): 0
Sodium (mg): 57.2
Exchanges
Milk: 0.0
Veg.: 2.0
Fruit: 0.0
Bread: 1.0
Meat: 1.5
Fat: 0.0

1. Spray large saucepan with cooking spray; heat over medium heat until hot. Saute onion and garlic 3 to 4 minutes. Add cauliflower, potatoes, carrots, Canned Vegetable Stock, and herbs to saucepan; heat to boiling. Reduce heat and simmer, covered, until vegetables are tender, 10 to 15 minutes.

2. Heat vegetable mixture to boiling. Mix flour and water; stir into boiling mixture. Cook, stirring constantly, until thickened, about 1 minute. Stir in tomato, parsley, and lemon juice; simmer 2 to 3 minutes longer. Season to taste with salt, cayenne, and black pepper.

VEGETABLE TAJINE

From the Moroccan cuisine, tajines are traditionally cooked in earthenware pots. Serve with couscous and Pita Breads (see p. 787)

6 servings (about 1¹/₄ cups each)

Vegetable cooking spray
1 medium onion, chopped
1 rib celery, sliced
1-2 teaspoons minced gingerroot
1 teaspoon minced garlic
1 cinnamon stick
2 teaspoons paprika
2 teaspoons ground cumin
2 teaspoons ground coriander
1¹/₂ teaspoons black pepper
2 cans (14¹/₂ ounces each) reduced-sodium diced tomatoes, undrained
1 can (16 ounces) garbanzo beans, rinsed, drained
1 cup chopped yellow winter squash (butternut *or* acorn)
1 cup chopped turnip, *or* rutabaga
1 large carrot, sliced
1¹/₂ cups whole green beans, ends trimmed
1 cup pitted prunes
¹/₄ cup pitted small black olives
¹/₂ cup Basic Vegetable Stock (see p. 10), *or* orange juice
Salt and pepper, to taste
4¹/₂ cups cooked couscous, warm
Parsley, minced, as garnish

Per Serving
Calories: 386
% Calories from fat: **10**
Protein (g): 12.5
Carbohydrates (g): **78.7**
Fat (g): 4.6
Saturated fat (g): 0.6
Cholesterol (mg): 0
Sodium (mg): 540
Exchanges
Milk: 0.0
Veg.: 3.0
Fruit: 1.0
Bread: 3.0
Meat: 0.0
Fat: 1.0

1. Spray Dutch oven with cooking spray; heat over medium heat until hot. Saute onion, celery, gingerroot, and garlic until onion is tender. Stir in spices; cook 1 minute longer.

2. Add remaining ingredients, except salt and pepper, couscous, and parsley, to Dutch oven. Bake, covered, at 350 degrees until vegetables are tender, 20 to 30 minutes. Season to taste with salt and pepper. Serve over couscous in bowls; sprinkle with parsley.

VEGETABLE STEW MARENGO

A delicious dish that picks up the colors and flavors of the Mediterranean.

4 servings

1 package (10¹/₂ ounces) light tofu, cut into scant 1-inch cubes
2 tablespoons olive oil
2 medium onions, cut into wedges
2 medium zucchini, cubed
1 cup small mushrooms
1 teaspoon minced garlic
1 tablespoon flour
1 can (14¹/₂ ounces) diced tomatoes, undrained
³/₄ cup vegetable broth
1 strip orange rind (3 x 1 inch)
¹/₂ teaspoon dried thyme leaves
¹/₂ teaspoon dried oregano leaves
   Salt and pepper, to taste
3 cups cooked couscous, *or* rice, warm

Per Serving
Calories: 349
% Calories from fat: 27
Protein (g): 16.7
Carbohydrates (g): 48.4
Fat (g): 10.8
Saturated fat (g): 1
Cholesterol (mg): 0
Sodium (mg): 608
Exchanges
Milk: 0.0
Veg.: 3.0
Fruit: 0.0
Bread: 2.0
Meat: 1.0
Fat: 1.5

1. Cook tofu in oil in large saucepan over medium heat until browned on all sides, about 5 minutes. Remove from pan and reserve.

2. Add onions, zucchini, mushrooms, and garlic to saucepan; saute 5 minutes. Stir in flour and cook 1 to 2 minutes longer. Add tomatoes and liquid, broth, orange rind, herbs, and reserved tofu; heat to boiling. Reduce heat and simmer, covered, until vegetables are tender, 10 to 15 minutes. Season to taste with salt and pepper. Serve mixture over couscous in shallow bowls.

SEVEN-VEGETABLE STEW WITH COUSCOUS

A Moroccan favorite that will please family or guests.

12 servings

8 ounces dried chickpeas
2 large onions, sliced
3 garlic cloves, minced
2 teaspoons ground cinnamon
1 teaspoon paprika
1/2 teaspoon ground ginger
1/2 teaspoon crushed saffron threads
1 pound carrots, chopped
1 medium cabbage, cut into 8 wedges
2 medium eggplant, cubed
1 pound small potatoes
1 pound turnips, cubed
1 pound green beans, cut
1 pound pumpkin, peeled, cubed
4 tomatoes, quartered
1 package (10 ounces) frozen artichoke hearts
1 cup raisins
Large bunch parsley, chopped
Salt and cayenne pepper, to taste
3 cups couscous, cooked, warm

Per Serving
Calories: 495
% Calories from fat: 11
Protein (gm): 17.6
Carbohydrate (gm): 97.5
Fat (gm): 6.4
Saturated fat (gm): 1.7
Cholesterol (mg): 0
Sodium (mg): 295
Exchanges
Milk: 0.0
Veg.: 6.0
Fruit: 0.0
Bread: 5.0
Meat: 0.0
Fat: 1.0

1. Cover chickpeas with 2 inches water in large Dutch oven; heat to boiling. Boil 2 minutes; let stand, covered, 1 hour and drain.

2. Cover chickpeas with water. Add onion, garlic, and spices; heat to boiling. Reduce heat and simmer, covered, 1 hour. Add remaining ingredients, except salt, cayenne pepper, and couscous, and simmer until vegetables are tender, about 30 minutes. Season to taste with salt and cayenne pepper.

3. Spoon couscous onto serving platter and shape into mound with well in center. Place vegetables in center and serve.

AFRICAN SWEET POTATO STEW

A spicy garlic paste seasons this delicious dish; it could also be served with Turmeric Rice (see p. 575).

6 servings

Vegetable cooking spray
1 cup sliced onion
Garlic Seasoning Paste (recipe follows)
2 pounds sweet potatoes, peeled, cubed
2 cans (15 ounces each) chickpeas, rinsed, drained
1 package (10 ounces) frozen, *or* 1¹/₂ cups fresh, sliced okra
1 can (28 ounces) whole tomatoes, undrained, chopped
1¹/₂ cups reduced-sodium vegetable broth
Salt and pepper, to taste
Hot pepper sauce, to taste
3 cups cooked couscous, warm

Per Serving
Calories: 517
% Calories from fat: 8
Protein (gm): 15.7
Carbohydrate (gm): 104.8
Fat (gm): 4.9
Saturated fat (gm): 0.6
Cholesterol (mg): 0
Sodium (mg): 544
Exchanges
Milk: 0.0
Veg.: 0.0
Fruit: 0.0
Bread: 7.0
Meat: 0.0
Fat: 0.5

1. Spray large saucepan with cooking spray; heat over medium heat until hot. Saute onion until tender, about 5 minutes; stir in Garlic Seasoning Paste and cook 1 minute. Stir in remaining ingredients, except salt, pepper, hot pepper sauce, and couscous; heat to boiling. Reduce heat and simmer, covered, 15 minutes.

2. Uncover and simmer until vegetables are tender and sauce has thickened, about 10 minutes. Season to taste with salt, pepper, and hot pepper sauce. Serve over couscous.

Garlic Seasoning Paste

6 cloves garlic
2 slices gingerroot
2 teaspoons paprika
2 teaspoons cumin seeds
¹/₂ teaspoon ground cinnamon
1 tablespoon olive oil

1. Process all ingredients in blender or food processor until smooth.

INDIAN BEAN AND VEGETABLE STEW

This stew is an easy version of the classic khichuri, an Indian bean and grain dish.

4 servings

1 can (15 ounces) adzuki, *or* red beans, rinsed, drained

1/2 cup uncooked basmati, *or* long-grain, rice

2 cans (14 1/2 ounces each) reduced-sodium vegetable broth

1 teaspoon ground cumin

1 teaspoon minced gingerroot

1/4 teaspoon ground turmeric

1 small jalapeño chili, minced

3 carrots, thinly sliced

2 cups cut wax beans

4 plum tomatoes, chopped
   Salt and pepper, to taste

1/4 cup toasted sunflower seeds

Per Serving
Calories: 496
% Calories from fat: **9**
Protein (gm): 10.9
Carbohydrate (gm): 101.1
Fat (gm): 5.1
Saturated fat (gm): 0.6
Cholesterol (mg): 0
Sodium (mg): 276
Exchanges
Milk: 0.0
Veg.: 1.0
Fruit: 0.0
Bread: 6.0
Meat: 0.0
Fat: 1.0

1. Combine all ingredients, except tomatoes, salt, pepper, and sunflower seeds, in large saucepan; heat to boiling. Reduce heat and simmer, covered, until vegetables and rice are tender, about 20 minutes. Add tomatoes and cook 2 minutes; season to taste with salt and pepper. Sprinkle each serving with sunflower seeds.

COCONUT-SQUASH STEW

Unsweetened coconut milk gives this Asian-inspired stew its subtle coconut flavor.

8 servings

1½ cups chopped onions
1½ cups sliced carrots
1 cup chopped celery
1-2 serrano, *or* jalapeño, chilies, chopped
1 tablespoon minced garlic
2 teaspoons minced gingerroot
1 tablespoon vegetable oil
6 cups cubed, peeled butternut, *or* acorn, squash
2 cans (15 ounces each) chickpeas, rinsed, drained
1 can (14½ ounces) diced tomatoes, undrained
1 can (14 ounces) light coconut milk
3-4 tablespoons reduced-sodium soy sauce
3-4 tablespoons lime juice
Salt, to taste
3-4 tablespoons chopped cilantro
4 cups cooked rice, warm

Per Serving
Calories: 344
% Calories from fat: 15
Protein (gm): 10.2
Carbohydrate (gm): 64.5
Fat (gm): 5.8
Saturated fat (gm): 0.4
Cholesterol (mg): 0
Sodium (mg): 647
Exchanges
Milk: 0.0
Veg.: 1.0
Fruit: 0.0
Bread: 4.0
Meat: 0.0
Fat: 1.0

1. Saute onions, carrots, celery, serrano chili, garlic, and gingerroot in oil in large saucepan until lightly browned, about 10 minutes. Add remaining ingredients, except salt, cilantro, and rice; heat to boiling. Reduce heat and simmer, covered, until squash is tender, about 25 minutes. Season to taste with salt; stir in cilantro. Serve over rice.

VIETNAMESE CURRIED VEGETABLE AND COCONUT STEW

Rice stick noodles, made with rice flour, can be round or flat in shape. Angel hair pasta can be substituted.

6 servings (about 1¹/₂ cups each)

Vegetable cooking spray
2 cups frozen stir-fry pepper blend
2 tablespoons minced gingerroot
1 tablespoon minced garlic
3-4 tablespoons curry powder
3¹/₂ cups vegetable broth
3 cups reduced-fat coconut milk
1 tablespoon grated lime rind
1 teaspoon oriental chili paste
1 cup broccoli florets
1 cup cubed, peeled, seeded acorn, **or** butternut, squash
¹/₂ package (8-ounce size) rice stick noodles
¹/₄ cup all-purpose flour
¹/₄ cup cold water
¹/₄ cup lime juice
Salt, to taste
Finely chopped cilantro, as garnish

Per Serving
Calories: 218
% Calories from fat: 28
Protein (g): 4.1
Carbohydrates (g): 37.1
Fat (g): 7.2
Saturated fat (g): 0.1
Cholesterol (mg): 0
Sodium (mg): 627
Exchanges
Milk: 0.0
Veg.: 1.0
Fruit: 0.0
Bread: 2.0
Meat: 0.0
Fat: 1.0

1. Spray large saucepan with cooking spray; heat over medium heat until hot. Saute pepper blend, gingerroot, and garlic 5 minutes. Stir in curry powder and cook 1 minute longer.

2. Add broth, coconut milk, lime rind, and chili paste to saucepan; heat to boiling. Add broccoli and squash; reduce heat and simmer, covered, until vegetables are tender, about 15 minutes.

3. While stew is cooking, place noodles in large bowl; pour cold water over to cover. Let stand until noodles are separate and soft, about 5 minutes. Stir noodles into 4 quarts boiling water in large saucepan. Reduce heat and simmer, uncovered, until tender, about 5 minutes; drain.

4. Heat stew to boiling. Mix flour, cold water, and lime juice; stir into boiling stew. Boil, stirring constantly, until thickened, about 1 minute. Season to taste with salt. Serve stew over noodles in shallow bowls; sprinkle generously with cilantro.

FOURTEEN

Quick-and-Easy Stews

EASY BEEF STEW

Add a green vegetable and dinner rolls, and you have a simple and delicious dinner.

6 servings

16 ounces beef round steak, cubed (^{1}/$_2$-inch)
2 tablespoons vegetable oil
1 pound mushrooms, thinly sliced
^{1}/$_4$ cup chopped onion
1 clove garlic, minced
2 cups reduced-sodium fat-free beef broth
1 tablespoon Italian seasoning
1^1/$_2$ tablespoons cornstarch
1 cup white wine, *or* beef broth
Salt and pepper, to taste
4 cups cooked wide noodles, warm

Per Serving
Calories: 331
% Calories from fat: 24
Protein (gm): 22.6
Carbohydrate (gm): 33.3
Fat (gm): 8.9
Saturated fat (gm): 1.6
Cholesterol (mg): 71.8
Sodium (mg): 100
Exchanges
Milk: 0.0
Veg.: 1.0
Fruit: 0.0
Bread: 2.0
Meat: 2.0
Fat: 1.0

1. Cook beef in oil in large skillet until brown on all sides, about 8 minutes. Add mushrooms, onion, and garlic and saute 5 minutes. Stir in beef broth and Italian seasoning; heat to boiling. Reduce heat and simmer, covered, until beef is tender, about 30 minutes.

2. Heat stew to boiling; stir in combined cornstarch and wine. Simmer until thickened, about 3 minutes. Season to taste with salt and pepper; serve over noodles.

CUBED STEAK STEW

Beef cubed steaks are quick-cooking and make it possible to have beef stew in less than 45 minutes.

6 servings

1½ pounds lean beef cubed steaks, cut into
    2 x ½-inch strips
  3 tablespoons flour
 ½ teaspoon garlic powder
  1 tablespoon vegetable oil
  1 large onion, thinly sliced
  1 can (14½ ounces) diced tomatoes with
    Italian herbs, undrained
  1 can (8 ounces) reduced-sodium tomato
    sauce
  4 medium potatoes, cubed
  1 package (10 ounces) frozen peas and
    carrots
    Salt and pepper, to taste

Per Serving
Calories: 307
% Calories from fat: 19
Protein (gm): 26.6
Carbohydrate (gm): 35.5
Fat (gm): 6.3
Saturated fat (gm): 1.6
Cholesterol (mg): 55
Sodium (mg): 372
Exchanges
Milk: 0.0
Veg.: 1.0
Fruit: 0.0
Bread: 2.0
Meat: 2.5
Fat: 0.0

1. Coat beef with combined flour and garlic powder; cook in oil in large skillet over medium-high heat until browned, about 10 minutes. Add onion, tomatoes and liquid, and tomato sauce; heat to boiling. Reduce heat and simmer, uncovered, until meat is tender, about 30 minutes, adding potatoes and peas and carrots during last 10 minutes cooking time. Season to taste with salt and pepper.

TERIYAKI BEEF AND BROCCOLI STEW

The flavors of this tantalizing stew remind me of a favorite rapid-fire stir-fry. And like a stir-fry, this stew is a complete meal in itself.

4 servings

12 ounces beef round steak, fat trimmed, cut into thin strips

1 onion, cut into thin wedges

2 teaspoons olive oil

1¹/₂ cups fat-free beef broth

2 tablespoons low-sodium teriyaki sauce

1 tablespoon minced gingerroot

2 carrots, thinly sliced

2 cups small broccoli florets

8 ounces Chinese wheat noodles, cooked, warm

Per Serving
Calories: 332
% Calories from fat: 25
Protein (gm): 26
Carbohydrate (gm): 44.4
Fat (gm): 10.3
Saturated fat (gm): 1.7
Cholesterol (mg): 45.6
Sodium (mg): 1081
Exchanges
Milk: 0.0
Veg.: 1.0
Fruit: 0.0
Bread: 2.0
Meat: 3.0
Fat: 0.0

1. Saute beef and onion in oil in Dutch oven until meat is lightly browned, 5 to 8 minutes. Add broth, teriyaki sauce, and gingerroot; heat to boiling. Reduce heat and simmer, covered, until beef is tender, about 30 minutes, adding carrots and broccoli during last 10 minutes. Spoon over noodles and toss.

LIGHT BEEF STROGANOFF

Make the sauce for this dish ahead of time if you like. Then the stew goes together in no time!

4 servings

¹/₂ cup chopped onion

¹/₄ cup dried shallots

1 clove garlic, minced

1 tablespoon margarine

3 tablespoons flour

¹/₂ cup fat-free milk

³/₄ cup chicken broth

Vegetable cooking spray

1¹/₂ pounds lean beef round steak, fat trimmed, sliced into thin strips

Per Serving
Calories: 291
% Calories from fat: 28
Protein (gm): 37.6
Carbohydrate (gm): 13.6
Fat (gm): 8.6
Saturated fat (gm): 2.6
Cholesterol (mg): 84
Sodium (mg): 194
Exchanges
Milk: 0.0
Veg.: 1.0
Fruit: 0.0
Bread: 0.5
Meat: 4.0
Fat: 0.0

8 ounces mushrooms, sliced
1 cup fat-free plain yogurt
1/4 cup minced chives
   Salt and pepper, to taste

1. Saute onion, shallots, and garlic in margarine in medium saucepan until tender, about 5 minutes. Sprinkle with flour and cook 1 minute longer. Add milk and chicken broth; heat to boiling, stirring constantly.

2. Spray large skillet with cooking spray; heat over medium heat until hot. Saute beef and mushrooms until meat is browned. Add sauce and simmer, covered, until meat is tender, about 15 minutes. Stir in yogurt and chives and cook until heated through. Season to taste with salt and pepper.

QUICK BEEF GOULASH

In Hungary, this paprika-seasoned stew is called "gulyas," and it's often served with dollops of sour cream. This fast version includes beef, mushrooms, tomatoes, onion, and cabbage.

4 servings

12 ounces boneless beef round steak, fat trimmed, cut into 1/2-inch cubes
1 teaspoon olive oil
3 large onions, cut into thin wedges
1 cup chopped portobello mushrooms
1 can (15 ounces) diced tomatoes, undrained
1 tablespoon paprika
1 teaspoon unsweetened cocoa
2 cups coarsely sliced cabbage
1 tablespoon caraway seeds
   Salt and pepper, to taste
8 ounces medium egg noodles, cooked, warm

Per Serving
Calories: 407
% Calories from fat: 17
Protein (g): 29.9
Carbohydrates (g): 55.2
Fat (g): 7.7
Saturated fat (g): 2
Cholesterol (mg): 90.9
Sodium (mg): 473
Exchanges
Milk: 0.0
Veg.: 2.0
Fruit: 0.0
Bread: 3.0
Meat: 2.0
Fat: 0.5

1. Saute beef in oil in large saucepan until well browned, about 5 minutes; add onions and mushrooms and saute 5 minutes longer. Add tomatoes and liquid, paprika, and cocoa and heat to boiling; reduce heat and simmer, covered, until meat is tender, about 25 minutes.

2. Stir in cabbage and caraway seeds; cook 5 minutes longer. Season to taste with salt and pepper. Serve over noodles.

PAPRIKA-SIRLOIN STEW WITH SOUR CREAM

Imagine tender beef, Italian green beans, and red potatoes cloaked in a heavenly paprika-spiked sour cream sauce. And suppose that such a dinner could be ready to eat in about 30 minutes. Daydream no more—here's the real meal!

4 servings

1 cup reduced-sodium fat-free beef broth
2 cups Italian flat green beans
3/4 pound red potatoes, cut into 1/2-inch cubes
2 bay leaves
   Vegetable cooking spray
1 pound boneless beef sirloin steak, fat trimmed, cut into very thin 1-inch-long strips
1 cup pearl onions, peeled
1 can (15 ounces) diced tomatoes, undrained
1 tablespoon paprika
1/2 cup fat-free sour cream
   Salt and pepper, to taste

Per Serving
Calories: 286
% Calories from fat: 17
Protein (g): 27.4
Carbohydrates (g): 32.9
Fat (g): 5.4
Saturated fat (g): 2
Cholesterol (mg): 59.5
Sodium (mg): 768
Exchanges
Milk: 0.0
Veg.: 0.0
Fruit: 0.0
Bread: 2.0
Meat: 3.0
Fat: 0.0

1. Heat beef broth, beans, potatoes, and bay leaves to boiling in large saucepan; reduce heat and simmer, covered, until vegetables are tender, about 10 minutes.

2. Spray large skillet with cooking spray; heat over medium heat until hot. Saute beef and onions until lightly browned, about 8 minutes; stir into vegetable mixture. Stir in tomatoes and liquid and paprika. Simmer, uncovered, 5 minutes or until slightly thickened. Stir in sour cream; season to taste with salt and pepper.

BEEF AND VEGETABLE STEW STROGANOFF

Fat-free half-and-half and sour cream contribute wonderful rich flavor and creamy texture.

8 servings

1¹/2 pounds lean ground beef

2 medium onions, thinly sliced

12 ounces mixed wild mushrooms (shiitake, oyster, enoki, *or* cremini), sliced

2 cloves garlic, minced

¹/4 cup dry red wine, *or* beef broth

12 ounces broccoli florets and sliced stalks

1 cup fat-free half-and-half, *or* fat-free milk

2 tablespoons flour

1¹/2 teaspoons Dijon-style mustard

1 cup fat-free sour cream

¹/2 teaspoon dried dill weed

Salt and white pepper, to taste

16 ounces no-yolk noodles, cooked, warm

Per Serving
Calories: 467
% Calories from fat: **22**
Protein (g): 27.7
Carbohydrates (g): **61.5**
Fat (g): 11.3
Saturated fat (g): **4.1**
Cholesterol (mg): **52.9**
Sodium (mg): **468**
Exchanges
Milk: 0.0
Veg.: 3.0
Fruit: 0.0
Bread: 3.0
Meat: 2.0
Fat: 1.0

1. Cook ground beef in large skillet until browned, about 10 minutes; drain well. Add onions, mushrooms, and garlic to skillet and saute until softened, about 5 minutes. Add wine and broccoli; heat to boiling. Reduce heat and simmer, covered, until broccoli is tender, 8 to 10 minutes.

2. Mix half-and-half, flour, and mustard; stir into skillet. Heat to boiling; boil, stirring constantly, until thickened, about 1 minute. Reduce heat to low; stir in sour cream and dill weed and cook 1 to 2 minutes longer. Season to taste with salt and white pepper. Serve over noodles.

GREEK LENTIL STEW

Lentils and beef are combined with fresh vegetables for flavor contrast. This is the perfect way to use leftover roast beef or lamb.

6 servings (about 1¹/₂ cups each)

Vegetable cooking spray
1 cup chopped onion
1 cup chopped green bell pepper
2 teaspoons minced garlic
2 cups cubed Idaho potatoes
1 cup dried lentils, washed and sorted
1 can (15 ounces) reduced-sodium diced tomatoes, undrained
3 cups reduced-sodium fat-free beef broth
1 teaspoon dried oregano leaves
1 teaspoon dried mint leaves
¹/₂ teaspoon ground turmeric
¹/₂ teaspoon ground coriander
12 ounces cooked beef eye of round, fat trimmed, cubed
1 medium zucchini, sliced
¹/₂ pound green beans, trimmed
Salt and pepper, to taste

Per Serving
Calories: 302
% Calories from fat: **7**
Protein (g): 25.5
Carbohydrates (g): **46.7**
Fat (g): 2.6
Saturated fat (g): 0.8
Cholesterol (mg): 27.5
Sodium (mg): 122
Exchanges
Milk: 0.0
Veg.: 3.0
Fruit: 0.0
Bread: 2.0
Meat: 1.5
Fat: 0.0

1. Spray large saucepan with cooking spray; heat over medium heat until hot. Saute onion, bell pepper, and garlic until tender, about 5 minutes. Add potatoes, lentils, tomatoes and liquid, broth, and herbs; heat to boiling. Reduce heat and simmer, covered, 15 minutes.

2. Add cooked beef, zucchini, and green beans; simmer, uncovered, until lentils and vegetables are tender and stew is thickened, 10 to 15 minutes. Season to taste with salt and pepper.

VEAL STEW WITH SAGE

Sage and dry white wine give this stew an Italian flair!

6 servings

Vegetable cooking spray

1¼ pounds lean veal leg, fat trimmed, cubed (½-inch)

¾ cup chopped onion

3 carrots, sliced

2 ribs celery, sliced

2 cloves garlic, chopped

½ teaspoon dried sage leaves

¼ teaspoon dried thyme leaves

1½ cups reduced-sodium fat-free chicken broth

½ cup dry white wine

Salt and pepper, to taste

12 ounces egg noodles, cooked, warm

Per Serving
Calories: 389
% Calories from fat: 14
Protein (gm): 35.2
Carbohydrate (gm): 43.3
Fat (gm): 5.9
Saturated fat (gm): 1.8
Cholesterol (mg): 144.3
Sodium (mg): 126
Exchanges
Milk: 0.0
Veg.: 0.0
Fruit: 0.0
Bread: 3.0
Meat: 3.0
Fat: 0.0

1. Spray large skillet with cooking spray; heat over medium heat until hot. Cook veal until lightly browned, about 5 minutes; remove and reserve. Saute onion, carrots, celery, and garlic until lightly browned, about 5 minutes.

2. Stir in reserved veal and remaining ingredients, except salt, pepper, and noodles; heat to boiling. Reduce heat and simmer, covered, until veal is cooked, about 30 minutes. Season to taste with salt and pepper; serve over noodles.

VEAL STEW MARSALA

Marsala wine flavors this easy stew. It tastes wonderful served over rice or pasta.

4 servings

16	ounces lean veal leg, fat trimmed, cubed
1	teaspoon olive oil
2	cups sliced mushrooms
2	cloves garlic, minced
1/3	cup reduced-sodium fat-free chicken broth
1/3	cup dry Marsala wine
1/2	teaspoon dried rosemary leaves, crushed
1/4	teaspoon Spike
1	teaspoon cornstarch
1	tablespoon water
	Salt and pepper, to taste

Per Serving
Calories: 213
% Calories from fat: 24
Protein (gm): 32.4
Carbohydrate (gm): 3.2
Fat (gm): 5.6
Saturated fat (gm): 1.8
Cholesterol (mg): 114.4
Sodium (mg): 74
Exchanges
Milk: 0.0
Veg.: 1.0
Fruit: 0.0
Bread: 0.0
Meat: 3.0
Fat: 0.0

1. Saute veal in oil in large skillet until browned, about 8 minutes; stir in mushrooms and garlic and saute until tender, about 5 minutes. Stir in chicken broth, Marsala, rosemary, and Spike; heat to boiling. Reduce heat and simmer until meat is tender, about 20 minutes.

2. Heat stew to boiling; stir in combined cornstarch and water. Boil, stirring, until thickened, 1 to 2 minutes. Season to taste with salt and pepper.

VEAL AND VEGETABLE STEW PAPRIKASH

Your preference of hot or sweet paprika can be used in this recipe. Serve over any flat pasta or rice.

6 servings

Vegetable cooking spray
1¼ pounds veal scaloppini, cut into 1-inch pieces
3 cups packaged coleslaw mix
1 cup chopped onion
1 medium zucchini, sliced
1½ cups sliced mushrooms
1 medium tomato, chopped
¼ cup all-purpose flour
1 tablespoon paprika
1 cup chicken broth
½-¾ cup reduced-fat sour cream
Salt and pepper, to taste
12 ounces egg noodles, cooked, warm

Per Serving
Calories: 419
% Calories from fat: 20
Protein (g): 33.5
Carbohydrates (g): 49.8
Fat (g): 9.1
Saturated fat (g): 3.2
Cholesterol (mg): 138.5
Sodium (mg): 264
Exchanges
Milk: 0.0
Veg.: 2.0
Fruit: 0.0
Bread: 3.0
Meat: 3.0
Fat: 0.0

1. Spray large skillet with cooking spray; heat over medium heat until hot. Cook veal until browned, 3 to 5 minutes; add vegetables and combined flour, paprika, and broth. Heat to boiling; reduce heat and simmer, covered, until veal is cooked and vegetables are tender, about 10 minutes. Stir in sour cream; season to taste with salt and pepper. Serve over noodles.

VEAL STEW WITH WINE

Chicken broth can replace the wine, if you prefer. Serve over rice or pasta, with a green salad.

6 servings

Vegetable cooking spray
1 large onion, chopped
1 large garlic clove, minced
1¹/2 pounds lean veal, fat trimmed, cut into strips
¹/4 cup water
¹/2 cup tomato sauce
1 cup dry white wine
1 teaspoon Spike
¹/4 teaspoon black pepper

Per Serving
Calories: 256
% Calories from fat: 31
Protein (g): 32.5
Carbohydrates (g): 4.3
Fat (g): 8.5
Saturated fat (g): 3.1
Cholesterol (mg): 128.1
Sodium (mg): 243
Exchanges
Milk: 0.0
Veg.: 1.0
Fruit: 0.0
Bread: 0.0
Meat: 4.0
Fat: 0.0

1. Spray large skillet with cooking spray; heat over medium heat until hot. Saute onion, garlic, and veal until evenly browned, about 10 minutes. Add remaining ingredients and heat to boiling; reduce heat and simmer, covered, until veal is tender, about 30 minutes.

PORK AND SQUASH RAGOUT

Stews don't have to be long-cooked to be good—this stew simmers to savory goodness in less than 30 minutes. Serve with Garlic Bread (see p. 795).

6 servings (about 1¹/4 cups each)

Olive oil cooking spray
1 pound pork tenderloin, cubed
1¹/2 cups chopped onions
1¹/2 cups coarsely chopped green bell peppers
2 teaspoons minced roasted garlic
1 tablespoon flour
2 cups cubed, peeled butternut, *or* acorn, squash (¹/2-inch cubes)
2 cans (16 ounces each) reduced-sodium diced tomatoes, undrained

Per Serving
Calories: 241
% Calories from fat: 12
Protein (g): 22.5
Carbohydrates (g): 32.8
Fat (g): 3.3
Saturated fat (g): 1
Cholesterol (mg): 43.8
Sodium (mg): 223
Exchanges
Milk: 0.0
Veg.: 0.0
Fruit: 0.0
Bread: 2.0
Meat: 2.0
Fat: 0.0

1 can (15 ounces) red kidney beans,
   rinsed, drained
$1/2$-$3/4$ teaspoon Italian seasoning
   Salt and pepper, to taste

1. Spray large saucepan with cooking spray; heat over medium heat until hot. Add pork and cook until browned, 8 to 10 minutes; remove from skillet. Add onions, bell peppers, and garlic to skillet and saute until tender, about 8 minutes. Stir in flour; cook 1 minute longer.

2. Add pork and remaining ingredients, except salt and pepper; heat to boiling. Reduce heat and simmer, covered, 10 to 15 minutes. Season to taste with salt and pepper.

PORK STEWED WITH PEPPERS AND ZUCCHINI

Flavorful pork tenderloin is low in saturated fat and cooks very quickly.

4 servings

1 pound pork tenderloin, fat trimmed, cut into strips
2 teaspoons olive oil
1 large onion, chopped
1 garlic clove, minced
1 can (15 ounces) reduced-sodium tomato sauce
2 cups frozen stir-fry pepper blend
$1^1/2$ cups thinly sliced zucchini
3 tablespoons dry sherry, *or* fat-free chicken broth
$3/4$ teaspoon dried basil leaves
$3/4$ teaspoon dried thyme leaves
1 bay leaf
   Salt and pepper, to taste
$2^1/2$ cups fusilli, cooked, warm

Per Serving
Calories: 480
% Calories from fat: 15
Protein (g): 34.8
Carbohydrates (g): 63.9
Fat (g): 7.8
Saturated fat (g): 1.9
Cholesterol (mg): 65.4
Sodium (mg): 91
Exchanges
Milk: 0.0
Veg.: 4.0
Fruit: 0.0
Bread: 3.0
Meat: 3.0
Fat: 0.0

1. Cook pork in oil in large skillet until browned, about 5 minutes; remove from skillet and reserve. Add onion and garlic to skillet and saute until tender, about 5 minutes. Add reserved pork and remaining ingredients, except salt, pepper, and fusilli; heat to boiling. Reduce heat and simmer, covered, until meat is tender, about 15 minutes. Discard bay leaf; season to taste with salt and pepper. Serve over fusilli.

ROSEMARY PORK AND WHITE BEAN STEW

An elegant and flavorful stew, with Tuscan flavors.

6 servings

1½ pounds pork tenderloin, fat trimmed, cubed

2 cloves garlic, minced

2 teaspoons olive oil

1 tablespoon flour

1 can (14½ ounces) reduced-sodium diced tomatoes, undrained

1 can (14 ounces) artichoke hearts, rinsed, drained, quartered

1 can (15 ounces) cannellini, *or* navy, beans, rinsed, drained

²/₃ cup reduced-sodium fat-free chicken broth

2 teaspoons dried rosemary leaves

2 teaspoons grated orange rind

Salt and pepper, to taste

Per Serving
Calories: 254
% Calories from fat: 22
Protein (gm): 29.3
Carbohydrate (gm): 18.7
Fat (gm): 5.9
Saturated fat (gm): 1.6
Cholesterol (mg): 65.7
Sodium (mg): 341
Exchanges
Milk: 0.0
Veg.: 1.0
Fruit: 0.0
Bread: 1.0
Meat: 3.0
Fat: 0.0

1. Saute pork and garlic in oil in large saucepan until lightly browned, about 8 minutes; sprinkle with flour and cook 1 minute longer.

2. Stir in remaining ingredients, except salt and pepper; heat to boiling. Reduce heat and simmer, covered, until pork is cooked, about 15 minutes. Season to taste with salt and pepper.

PEPPERED PORK AND WINE STEW

Medallions of pork tenderloin are coated with crushed peppercorns, then simmered in a flavorful sauce—it's perfect served with rice.

4 servings

Olive oil cooking spray

16 ounces pork tenderloin, fat trimmed, cut into 1/2-inch slices

2 teaspoons crushed peppercorns

1 onion, finely chopped

1/4 cup chopped red bell pepper

1 clove garlic, minced

1 1/2 cups reduced-sodium fat-free beef broth

1/2 cup dry white wine, *or* reduced-sodium fat-free beef broth

1/4 cup all-purpose flour

1 tablespoon red wine vinegar

Salt and pepper, to taste

1/4 cup minced chives

Per Serving
Calories: 214
% Calories from fat: 18
Protein (gm): 26.9
Carbohydrate (gm): 11
Fat (gm): 4.2
Saturated fat (gm): 1.4
Cholesterol (mg): 65.7
Sodium (mg): 110
Exchanges
Milk: 0.0
Veg.: 2.0
Fruit: 0.0
Bread: 0.0
Meat: 3.0
Fat: 0.0

1. Spray large skillet with cooking spray; heat over medium heat until hot. Sprinkle pork slices with crushed peppercorns, pressing into surface of meat; add meat to skillet and cook until browned, 2 to 3 minutes on each side. Remove from skillet and reserve.

2. Add onion, bell pepper, and garlic to skillet and cook until tender, about 5 minutes. Add broth; heat to boiling. Return pork to skillet; reduce heat and simmer until pork is tender, about 15 minutes.

3. Heat stew to boiling; stir in combined wine, flour, and vinegar. Boil, stirring, until thickened, 1 to 2 minutes. Season to taste with salt and pepper. Sprinkle with chives.

AUSTRIAN PORK STEW WITH APPLES AND CRANBERRY SAUCE

This is a delicious and unusual recipe that features a tangy medley of lean pork, fruit, and thyme.

4-5 servings

16 ounces boneless pork loin, fat trimmed, cut into 1/4-inch strips

1/2 teaspoon dried thyme leaves

2 teaspoons margarine

1 cup chopped onion

2 large tart apples, peeled, cored, thinly sliced

1 can (16 ounces) whole-berry cranberry sauce

1 tablespoon Worcestershire sauce

1 tablespoon apple cider vinegar

2 tablespoons brown sugar

Salt and pepper, to taste

8-10 ounces reduced-fat egg noodles, cooked, warm

Per Serving
Calories: 460
% Calories from fat: 17
Protein (g): 19
Carbohydrates (g): 79
Fat (g): 8.5
Saturated fat (g): 2.4
Cholesterol (mg): 77
Sodium (mg): 123
Exchanges
Milk: 0.0
Veg.: 0.0
Fruit: 3.0
Bread: 2.0
Meat: 2.0
Fat: 0.5

1. Sprinkle pork with thyme; cook pork in margarine in Dutch oven until browned, about 5 minutes. Add remaining ingredients, except salt, pepper, and noodles; heat to boiling. Reduce heat and simmer, covered, 25 minutes or until pork is tender. Season to taste with salt and pepper; serve over noodles.

ORANGE PORK RAGOUT

Orange juice and cloves give this easy dish a rich flavor.

4-5 servings

16 ounces pork loin, fat trimmed, cut into thin strips

2 teaspoons olive oil

3 cups frozen stir-fry pepper blend

1 1/2 cups orange juice

2 teaspoons sugar

1 teaspoon dried thyme leaves

1/4 teaspoon ground cloves

Salt and pepper, to taste

1 1/4 cups uncooked white rice, cooked, warm

Per Serving
Calories: 428
% Calories from fat: **23**
Protein (g): 25.5
Carbohydrates (g): **57.3**
Fat (g): 10.8
Saturated fat (g): **3.1**
Cholesterol (mg): **42.4**
Sodium (mg): 50
Exchanges
Milk: 0.0
Veg.: 2.0
Fruit: 0.5
Bread: 2.5
Meat: 3.0
Fat: 0.0

1. Saute pork in oil in large skillet until lightly browned, about 5 minutes; remove and reserve. Add pepper blend to skillet and saute until tender, about 5 minutes. Add reserved pork and remaining ingredients, except salt, pepper, and rice, and heat to boiling. Reduce heat and simmer, covered, 10 minutes. Remove lid and simmer until pork is cooked and sauce thickened, about 10 minutes longer. Season to taste with salt and pepper; serve over rice.

BARBECUE PORK STEW

Barbecue sauce and apple cider are the flavor secrets in this quick-and-easy-stew.

4 servings

Vegetable cooking spray

16 ounces pork tenderloin, cubed (3/4-inch)

1 medium onion, coarsely chopped

1 large tart cooking apple, peeled, cored, coarsely chopped

1 teaspoon crushed caraway seeds

1 1/2 cups apple cider, *or* apple, juice, divided

Per Serving
Calories: 521
% Calories from fat: 8
Protein (gm): 34
Carbohydrate (gm): **82.9**
Fat (gm): 5
Saturated fat (gm): 1.4
Cholesterol (mg): 65.7
Sodium (mg): 444
Exchanges
Milk: 0.0
Veg.: 1.0
Fruit: 2.0
Bread: 3.0
Meat: 3.0
Fat: 0.0

    1/2 cup honey-mustard barbecue sauce
      2 tablespoons cornstarch
      4 cups thinly sliced cabbage
         Salt and pepper, to taste
      8 ounces no-yolk broad noodles, cooked,
         warm

1. Spray large saucepan with cooking spray; saute pork 1 minute. Add onion, apple, and caraway seeds and saute 2 to 3 minutes longer.

2. Add 1 cup apple cider and heat to boiling; reduce heat and simmer 5 minutes. Mix remaining 1/2 cup apple juice, barbecue sauce, and cornstarch; add to saucepan and heat to boiling. Boil, stirring, until thickened.

3. Stir in cabbage; simmer, covered, until cabbage and pork are tender, about 10 to 15 minutes. Season to taste with salt and pepper. Serve over noodles.

CHICKEN STEW AND DUMPLINGS

This stew can be quickly put together, using convenient canned and frozen ingredients.

4 servings

    2-3 pounds skinless chicken breasts and
         thighs
      2 tablespoons margarine
    1/2 cup water
      1 cup sliced onion
      1 teaspoon Spike
      1 can (10³/₄ ounces) reduced-sodium,
         reduced-fat condensed cream of
         chicken soup
  1¹/₄ plus 1/3 cups fat-free milk, divided
      1 package (10 ounces) frozen mixed
         vegetables
         Salt and pepper, to taste
      1 cup reduced-fat baking mix

Per Serving
Calories: 453
% Calories from fat: 30
Protein (gm): 33.2
Carbohydrate (gm): 46.1
Fat (gm): 15
Saturated fat (gm): 3.9
Cholesterol (mg): 83.5
Sodium (mg): 853
Exchanges
Milk: 0.0
Veg.: 0.0
Fruit: 0.0
Bread: 3.0
Meat: 4.0
Fat: 0.5

1. Cook chicken in margarine in Dutch oven until browned on all sides, about 10 minutes. Add water, onion, and Spike; heat to boiling. Reduce heat and simmer, covered, 30 minutes.

2. Stir in soup, 1¹/₄ cups milk, and vegetables; heat to boiling. Reduce heat and simmer, covered, 10 minutes, stirring occasionally. Season to taste with salt and pepper.

3. Heat stew to boiling. Combine baking mix and remaining ¹/₃ cup milk in small bowl; spoon over stew into 4 mounds. Simmer, uncovered, 10 minutes. Cover and simmer until dumplings are dry, about 10 minutes.

SPEEDY CHICKEN AND RAVIOLI STEW

Use any favorite flavor of refrigerated fresh ravioli in this quick and nutritious bean stew.

4 servings

Vegetable cooking spray
1 pound chicken tenders, cut into ¹/₂-inch pieces
³/₄ cup chopped onion
4 teaspoons minced garlic
2 cans (15 ounces each) kidney beans, rinsed, drained
1 can (14¹/₂ ounces) reduced-sodium diced tomatoes, undrained
¹/₂ teaspoon dried thyme leaves
1 package (9 ounces) fresh sun-dried tomato ravioli, cooked, warm
Salt and pepper, to taste

Per Serving
Calories: 410
% Calories from fat: 12
Protein (gm): 39.1
Carbohydrate (gm): 53.3
Fat (gm): 5.7
Saturated fat (gm): 2.4
Cholesterol (mg): 63.5
Sodium (mg): 984
Exchanges
Milk: 0.0
Veg.: 1.0
Fruit: 0.0
Bread: 3.0
Meat: 3.0
Fat: 0.0

1. Spray large skillet with cooking spray; heat over medium heat until hot. Cook chicken, onion, and garlic until browned, 5 to 8 minutes. Stir in beans, tomatoes and liquid, and thyme; heat to boiling. Reduce heat and simmer, uncovered, until chicken is cooked, about 5 minutes. Stir in ravioli and cook 2 to 3 minutes longer. Season to taste with salt and pepper.

ALFREDO CHICKEN STEW

A wonderfully creamy, low-fat Alfredo sauce makes this stew especially good.

4 servings

1 pound boneless, skinless chicken breast, cubed

3 tablespoons margarine

1/4 cup sliced green onions and tops

1 teaspoon minced garlic

1/4 cup all-purpose flour

1 teaspoon dried basil leaves

2 1/2 cups fat-free milk

4 ounces small asparagus, cut into 1 1/2-inch pieces

1/2 cup frozen tiny peas

1/3-1/2 cup shredded Parmesan cheese

Salt and pepper, to taste

8 ounces fettuccine, cooked, warm

Per Serving
Calories: 507
% Calories from fat: 29
Protein (gm): 42
Carbohydrate (gm): 47.7
Fat (gm): 16
Saturated fat (gm): 4
Cholesterol (mg): 87
Sodium (mg): 394
Exchanges
Milk: 0.5
Veg.: 2.0
Fruit: 0.0
Bread: 2.0
Meat: 4.0
Fat: 0.5

1. Saute chicken in margarine in large saucepan until lightly browned, about 5 minutes; add green onions and garlic and saute 3 minutes longer. Stir in flour and basil and cook 1 minute longer; stir in milk and heat to boiling, stirring until thickened, about 1 minute.

2. Stir in asparagus and peas; reduce heat and simmer, covered, until chicken and asparagus are cooked, about 10 minutes. Stir in cheese, stirring until melted; season to taste with salt and pepper. Serve over fettuccine.

QUICK CHICKEN AND VEGETABLE STEW

Pureed beans provide a perfect thickening for the stew, and canned vegetables make it extra quick.

6 servings (about 1 cup each)

Vegetable cooking spray
1 pound chicken tenders, cut into
1/2-inch pieces
3 carrots, sliced
3/4 cup chopped onion
2 teaspoons minced garlic
1 can (15 ounces) navy beans, rinsed, drained
2 cups reduced-sodium fat-free chicken broth, divided
1 can (16 ounces) Italian-style zucchini with mushrooms in tomato sauce
1 can (15 ounces) black beans, rinsed, drained
1 cup frozen peas
1 1/2 teaspoons Italian seasoning
Salt and pepper, to taste
8 ounces egg noodles, cooked, warm

Per Serving
Calories: 434
% Calories from fat: **9**
Protein (g): 35.5
Carbohydrates (g): 63.3
Fat (g): 4.5
Saturated fat (g): 1
Cholesterol (mg): 78.6
Sodium (mg): 809
Exchanges
Milk: 0.0
Veg.: 1.0
Fruit: 0.0
Bread: 4.0
Meat: 2.0
Fat: 0.0

1. Spray large saucepan with cooking spray; heat over medium heat until hot. Saute chicken, carrots, onion, and garlic until chicken is browned, about 8 minutes. Puree navy beans with half the broth in blender; add to chicken and vegetables in saucepan. Add remaining broth, zucchini, black beans, peas, and Italian seasoning.

2. Heat to boiling. Reduce heat and simmer, uncovered, until vegetables are tender, about 10 minutes. Season to taste with salt and pepper. Spoon stew over noodles in shallow bowls.

CHICKEN STEW PAPRIKASH

Using chicken breast tenders helps speed preparation.

4 servings

   1 pound chicken breast tenders, cut into thin strips

   2 medium onions, finely chopped

   2 cloves garlic, minced

   1 tablespoon canola oil

   1 medium green bell pepper, chopped

   1 cup sliced mushrooms

   1 can (14^1/$_2$ ounces) stewed tomatoes, undrained

2^1/$_2$-3 teaspoons paprika

   1 teaspoon poppy seeds

^{1}/$_4$-^{1}/$_2$ cup reduced-fat sour cream

     Salt and pepper, to taste

   4 cups cooked no-yolk noodles, warm

Per Serving
Calories: 468
% Calories from fat: 17
Protein (gm): 38
Carbohydrate (gm): 58.1
Fat (gm): 8.9
Saturated fat (gm): 2.2
Cholesterol (mg): 74
Sodium (mg): 331
Exchanges
Milk: 0.0
Veg.: 3.0
Fruit: 0.0
Bread: 3.0
Meat: 3.0
Fat: 0.0

1. Saute chicken, onions, and garlic in oil in large saucepan until chicken is browned, about 5 minutes. Add bell pepper and mushrooms and saute 5 minutes longer.

2. Add tomatoes and liquid, paprika, and poppy seeds and heat to boiling; reduce heat and simmer, covered, until chicken is tender, about 15 minutes. Reduce heat to low and stir in sour cream; simmer 1 to 2 minutes longer. Season to taste with salt and pepper. Serve over noodles.

KASHMIR CHICKEN STEW

This hearty stew is flavored with sweet Middle Eastern spices and an accent of raisins.

6 servings

1¹/₂ cups chopped onions
³/₄ cup chopped red bell pepper
2 teaspoons minced garlic
¹/₄ teaspoon crushed red pepper
2 tablespoons vegetable oil
12 ounces boneless, skinless chicken breast, cut into 1-inch pieces
1 teaspoon ground cumin
1 teaspoon ground cinnamon
2 cans (15 ounces each) navy beans, rinsed, drained
1 can (14¹/₂ ounces) Italian-style stewed tomatoes, undrained
¹/₃ cup raisins
Salt and pepper, to taste
4 cups cooked couscous, warm

Per Serving
Calories: 470
% Calories from fat: 13
Protein (gm): 29.3
Carbohydrate (gm): 72.9
Fat (gm): 7
Saturated fat (gm): 1.2
Cholesterol (mg): 34.5
Sodium (mg): 614
Exchanges
Milk: 0.0
Veg.: 2.0
Fruit: 0.0
Bread: 4.0
Meat: 2.0
Fat: 0.0

1. Saute onions, bell pepper, garlic, and red pepper in oil in large saucepan 2 to 3 minutes. Add chicken, cumin, and cinnamon; cook over medium-high heat until chicken is lightly browned, about 5 minutes.

2. Add remaining ingredients, except salt, pepper, and couscous; heat to boiling. Reduce heat and simmer, covered, 10 minutes. Season to taste with salt and pepper; serve over couscous.

CREAMY CHICKEN CURRY STEW

Apple and raisins flavor this delicious curry. This stew could also be made with turkey or seafood.

4 servings

1 small tart apple, unpeeled, cubed
1/2 cup chopped onion
1 clove garlic, minced
1 teaspoon curry powder
1/4 teaspoon ground ginger
2 teaspoons vegetable oil
3 tablespoons flour
1 cup reduced-sodium fat-free chicken broth
3/4 cup fat-free half-and-half, *or* fat-free milk
1 1/2 cups cubed cooked chicken
1/4 cup raisins
Salt and pepper, to taste
3 cups cooked rice, warm

Per Serving
Calories: 419
% Calories from fat: 20
Protein (g): 23.5
Carbohydrates (g): 58.1
Fat (g): 9.2
Saturated fat (g): 2.1
Cholesterol (mg): 43.5
Sodium (mg): 132
Exchanges
Milk: 0.0
Veg.: 0.0
Fruit: 1.0
Bread: 3.0
Meat: 2.0
Fat: 0.5

1. Saute apple, onion, garlic, curry powder, and ginger in oil in large skillet until tender, about 5 minutes. Stir in flour; cook 1 to 2 minutes longer.

2. Stir in broth and half-and-half; heat to boiling, stirring until thickened, about 3 minutes. Stir in chicken and raisins; cook 2 to 3 minutes longer. Season to taste with salt and pepper; serve over rice.

CRANBERRY CHICKEN STEW

Apples, cranberry sauce, and raisins blend with vinegar to make a wonderfully sweet and tangy stew.

4-5 servings

Vegetable cooking spray
1 cup chopped onion
2 tart apples, thinly sliced
1 cup jellied cranberry sauce
1/2 cup dark raisins
1 tablespoon apple cider vinegar
1 tablespoon brown sugar
2-3 large skinless chicken breast halves, cut into bite-sized pieces
1 teaspoon dried thyme leaves
Salt and pepper, to taste
10 ounces no-yolk egg noodles, cooked, warm

Per Serving
Calories: 549
% Calories from fat: 8
Protein (gm): 43
Carbohydrate (gm): 89
Fat (gm): 4.9
Saturated fat (gm): 1.2
Cholesterol (mg): 91
Sodium (mg): 548
Exchanges
Milk: 0.0
Veg.: 0.5
Fruit: 3.0
Bread: 2.5
Meat: 3.0
Fat: 0.0

1. Spray large saucepan with cooking spray; heat over medium heat until hot. Saute onion 5 minutes; stir in remaining ingredients, except salt, pepper, and noodles. Heat to boiling; reduce heat and simmer, covered, until chicken is cooked, about 15 minutes. Season to taste with salt and pepper; serve over noodles.

CHICKEN STEW PROVENÇAL

Bursting with garlic and herb flavors, this stew is reminiscent of dishes from southern France's Provence region. Serve in shallow bowls with warm crusty French bread.

4 servings

1 pound boneless, skinless chicken breasts, cut into 3/4-inch pieces
4 teaspoons minced garlic
2 teaspoons olive oil
1 can (28 ounces) whole tomatoes, undrained, coarsely chopped
4 medium potatoes, peeled, thinly sliced
1 cup dry white wine
1 1/2 teaspoons herbes de Provence
Salt and pepper, to taste
Finely chopped basil, as garnish

Per Serving
Calories: 352
% Calories from fat: 14
Protein (gm): 29.6
Carbohydrate (gm): 37.2
Fat (gm): 5.6
Saturated fat (gm): 1.2
Cholesterol (mg): 69
Sodium (mg): 364
Exchanges
Milk: 0.0
Veg.: 2.0
Fruit: 0.0
Bread: 2.0
Meat: 3.0
Fat: 0.0

1. Saute chicken and garlic in oil in large saucepan until chicken is browned, about 5 minutes. Add remaining ingredients, except salt, pepper, and basil; heat to boiling. Reduce heat and simmer, covered, 20 minutes or until chicken is cooked and potatoes are tender. Season to taste with salt and pepper; sprinkle each serving generously with basil.

SWEET POTATO CHICKEN STEW

This chili-seasoned stew is made easy with canned sweet potatoes.

4 servings

1 pound boneless, skinless chicken breast, cut into 1-inch cubes

1/4 cup all-purpose flour

1 teaspoon chili powder

1/2 teaspoon garlic powder

2 tablespoons margarine

1 1/2 cups reduced-sodium fat-free chicken broth

1 large green bell pepper, thinly sliced

1 can (17 ounces) sweet potatoes, drained, cut into halves

Salt and pepper, to taste

Per Serving
Calories: 342
% Calories from fat: 24
Protein (gm): 30.7
Carbohydrate (gm): 33.3
Fat (gm): 9
Saturated fat (gm): 2
Cholesterol (mg): 69
Sodium (mg): 261
Exchanges
Milk: 0.0
Veg.: 0.0
Fruit: 0.0
Bread: 2.0
Meat: 3.0
Fat: 0.5

1. Coat chicken with combined flour, chili powder, and garlic powder; cook in margarine in large skillet over medium-high heat until browned, about 5 minutes.

2. Stir in broth and bell pepper; heat to boiling. Reduce heat and simmer, uncovered, until chicken is cooked, about 15 minutes, adding sweet potatoes during last 5 minutes. Season to taste with salt and pepper.

CHICKEN GUMBO

A quick gumbo that can't be beat!

4 servings

  1 pound cooked chicken breast, cubed

2¹/₂ cups reduced-sodium fat-free chicken broth

  1 cup chopped onion

  2 cloves garlic, minced

  1 can (14¹/₂ ounces) stewed tomatoes, undrained

  8 ounces small okra, tops trimmed

¹/₄ cup chopped red, *or* green, bell pepper

  1 teaspoon dried basil leaves

  1 teaspoon dried thyme leaves

¹/₄ teaspoon crushed red pepper

    Salt and pepper, to taste

  3 cups cooked rice, warm

Per Serving
Calories: 424
% Calories from fat: 11
Protein (gm): 42.5
Carbohydrate (gm): 49.8
Fat (gm): 5.2
Saturated fat (gm): 1.4
Cholesterol (mg): 87.5
Sodium (mg): 413
Exchanges
Milk: 0.0
Veg.: 1.0
Fruit: 0.0
Bread: 3.0
Meat: 3.0
Fat: 0.0

1. Combine all ingredients, except salt, pepper, and rice, in large saucepan; heat to boiling. Reduce heat and simmer, covered, until okra is tender, about 15 minutes; season to taste with salt and pepper. Serve over rice.

LEMON CHICKEN STEW

Fresh lemon juice and jalapeño chili boost the flavor in this very quick stew.

6 servings

  1 pound boneless, skinless chicken breast, cubed

  1 jalapeño chili, minced

  2 cloves garlic, minced

  2 teaspoons olive oil

  2 cans (14¹/₂ ounces each) diced tomatoes, undrained

  2 cups fresh, *or* frozen, broccoli florets

¹/₄-¹/₃ cup lemon juice

Per Serving
Calories: 310
% Calories from fat: 17
Protein (gm): 26.2
Carbohydrate (gm): 38.2
Fat (gm): 5.8
Saturated fat (gm): 1.5
Cholesterol (mg): 109.8
Sodium (mg): 783
Exchanges
Milk: 0.0
Veg.: 2.0
Fruit: 0.0
Bread: 2.0
Meat: 2.0
Fat: 0.0

1   teaspoon instant chicken bouillon
    crystals
$^1/_4$ cup finely chopped fresh, *or* 2 tea-
    spoons dried, basil leaves
    Salt and pepper, to taste
12 ounces angel hair pasta, cooked, warm
    Shredded Parmesan cheese, as garnish ·

1. Saute chicken, jalapeño chili, and garlic in oil in large saucepan until lightly browned, about 5 minutes. Stir in tomatoes and
liquid, broccoli, lemon juice, and bouillon crystals; heat to boiling. Reduce heat and simmer, uncovered, until chicken and broccoli are cooked, about 10 minutes.

2. Stir in basil; season to taste with salt and pepper. Serve over
pasta; sprinkle with Parmesan cheese.

EL PASO CHICKEN STEW

*Serve this stew over rice, sprinkled with tortilla chips and cheese, or with
Green Chili Cornbread (see p. 803).*

4 servings

16 ounces boneless, skinless chicken
    breast, cubed
$^1/_2$ package (1.25-ounce size) reduced-
    sodium taco seasoning mix, divided
1   tablespoon vegetable oil
2   cans (14$^1/_2$ ounces each) Mexican-style
    stewed tomatoes, undrained
1   can (15 ounces) pinto beans, rinsed,
    drained
1   package (10 ounces) frozen cut green
    beans
1   package (10 ounces) frozen whole-
    kernel corn
    Salt and pepper, to taste

Per Serving
Calories: 407
% Calories from fat: 16
Protein (gm): 34.9
Carbohydrate (gm): 51.1
Fat (gm): 7.6
Saturated fat (gm): 1.5
Cholesterol (mg): 69
Sodium (mg): 862
Exchanges
Milk: 0.0
Veg.: 1.0
Fruit: 0.0
Bread: 3.0
Meat: 3.0
Fat: 0.0

1. Coat chicken with half the taco seasoning mix. Saute chicken in oil in large skillet until lightly browned, about 5 minutes. Stir in remaining taco seasoning mix and remaining ingredients, except salt and pepper; heat to boiling. Reduce heat and simmer, uncovered, until chicken is cooked and vegetables are tender, about 10 minutes. Season to taste with salt and pepper.

PICNIC CHICKEN STEW

Canned baked beans combine with chicken in a stew with flavors of a summer barbecue.

8 servings

12	ounces boneless, skinless chicken breast, cubed
1	large onion, chopped
1	red bell pepper, chopped
2	cloves garlic, minced
1	tablespoon vegetable oil
2	cans (15 ounces each) baked beans, *or* pork and beans
1	can (15 ounces) garbanzo beans, rinsed, drained
1	can (14¹/₂ ounces) reduced-sodium diced tomatoes, undrained
2	teaspoons chili powder
¹/₂	teaspoon dried thyme leaves
	Salt and pepper, to taste

Per Serving
Calories: 251
% Calories from fat: 14
Protein (gm): 18.1
Carbohydrate (gm): 39.1
Fat (gm): 4.1
Saturated fat (gm): 0.8
Cholesterol (mg): 25.9
Sodium (mg): 616
Exchanges
Milk: 0.0
Veg.: 2.0
Fruit: 0.0
Bread: 2.0
Meat: 1.0
Fat: 0.0

1. Saute chicken, onion, bell pepper, and garlic in oil in large saucepan until lightly browned, about 8 minutes. Stir in remaining ingredients, except salt and pepper; heat to boiling. Reduce heat and simmer, uncovered, until thickened, about 8 minutes.

ISLAND STEW, SWEET-AND-SOUR

Sweet-and-sour flavors team with chicken, pineapple, and beans for this island-inspired dish—delicious with jasmine rice or couscous.

6 servings (about 1¹/₄ cups each)

1¹/₂   pounds chicken tenders
  1   tablespoon vegetable oil
  3   cups frozen stir-fry pepper blend
  2   teaspoons minced garlic
  2   teaspoons minced gingerroot
1-2   jalapeño chilies, finely chopped
  3   cups reduced-sodium fat-free chicken broth
  1   can (20 ounces) pineapple chunks in juice, drained, juice reserved
  2   tablespoons light brown sugar
2-3   teaspoons curry powder
2-3   tablespoons apple cider vinegar
  2   tablespoons cornstarch
  1   can (15 ounces) black beans, rinsed, drained

Per Serving
Calories: 288
% Calories from fat: 12
Protein (g): 29.7
Carbohydrates (g): 34.7
Fat (g): 3.9
Saturated fat (g): 0.3
Cholesterol (mg): 48.2
Sodium (mg): 537
Exchanges
Milk: 0.0
Veg.: 1.0
Fruit: 0.5
Bread: 1.0
Meat: 3.0
Fat: 0.0

1.   Cook chicken in oil in large skillet over medium heat until browned, about 8 minutes. Remove from skillet.

2.   Add pepper blend, garlic, gingerroot, and jalapeño chilies to skillet; saute 5 minutes. Stir in broth, pineapple, sugar, curry powder, vinegar, and chicken; heat to boiling. Reduce heat and simmer, uncovered, 5 minutes.

3.   Heat mixture to boiling. Mix cornstarch and reserved pineapple juice; stir into boiling mixture. Boil, stirring frequently, until mixture is thickened, about 1 minute. Stir in beans; cook over medium heat 2 to 3 minutes longer.

COCONUT CHICKEN STEW

This spicy Indonesian-influenced stew is enhanced with the unique flavor of coconut milk. Coconut milk is available in the oriental section of large supermarkets.

6 servings

1¹/₂ pounds boneless, skinless chicken breast, cubed

¹/₄ cup sliced green onions and tops

1 clove garlic, minced

2 teaspoons minced gingerroot

2 teaspoons vegetable oil

2 cups frozen stir-fry vegetables

1 can (15 ounces) red beans, rinsed, drained

1 cup light unsweetened reduced-fat coconut milk

1 cup reduced-sodium fat-free chicken broth

1 tablespoon cornstarch

2 tablespoons lime juice

Salt and cayenne pepper, to taste

4 cups cooked rice, warm

Finely chopped cilantro, as garnish

Per Serving
Calories: 404
% Calories from fat: 15
Protein (gm): 35.1
Carbohydrate (gm): 48
Fat (gm): 7
Saturated fat (gm): 1.1
Cholesterol (mg): 69
Sodium (mg): 333
Exchanges
Milk: 0.0
Veg.: 1.0
Fruit: 0.0
Bread: 3.0
Meat: 3.0
Fat: 0.0

1. Saute chicken, green onions, garlic, and gingerroot in oil in large skillet until lightly browned, about 5 minutes. Stir in stir-fry vegetables, beans, coconut milk, and broth; heat to boiling. Reduce heat and simmer, uncovered, until chicken is cooked, about 10 minutes.

2. Heat stew to boiling; stir in combined cornstarch and lime juice. Boil until thickened, about 1 minute; season to taste with salt and cayenne pepper. Serve over rice; sprinkle generously with cilantro.

LUAU CHICKEN STEW

Pineapple juice gives this stew its special sweet-sour flavor.

6 servings

1¹/₂ pounds boneless, skinless chicken
      breast, cubed
 ¹/₄ cup all-purpose flour
  1 tablespoon vegetable oil
  8 ounces mushrooms, sliced
  2 medium carrots, diagonally sliced
  1 small red onion, thinly sliced
  1 clove garlic, minced
  1 cup reduced-sodium fat-free chicken
      broth
 ¹/₂ cup unsweetened pineapple juice
2-3 tablespoons rice, *or* cider, vinegar
2-3 tablespoons reduced-sodium soy sauce
  1 large tomato, cut into thin wedges
  1 cup frozen peas
    Salt and pepper, to taste
  4 cups cooked rice, warm

Per Serving
Calories: 381
% Calories from fat: 14
Protein (gm): 32.9
Carbohydrate (gm): 47.1
Fat (gm): 5.9
Saturated fat (gm): 1.3
Cholesterol (mg): 69
Sodium (mg): 301
Exchanges
Milk: 0.0
Veg.: 0.0
Fruit: 0.0
Bread: 3.0
Meat: 3.0
Fat: 0.0

1. Coat chicken with flour; cook in oil in large skillet over medium heat until browned, about 8 minutes. Add mushrooms, carrots, onion, and garlic and saute 5 minutes.

2. Stir in broth, pineapple juice, vinegar, and soy sauce; heat to boiling. Reduce heat and simmer, uncovered, until chicken is cooked and sauce has thickened, about 10 minutes.

3. Stir in tomato and peas; cook 3 to 4 minutes longer. Season to taste with salt and pepper; serve over rice.

ISLAND CHICKEN STEW

The combination of sauce ingredients gives this chicken dish a wonderful flavor.

5-6 servings

Vegetable cooking spray
1 large onion, finely chopped
1 large green bell pepper, chopped
5-6 medium skinless chicken breast halves, cut into bite-sized pieces
1 can (8 ounces) crushed pineapple, undrained
3/4 cup fat-free beef broth
2 tablespoons reduced-sodium soy sauce
1 tablespoon brown sugar
2 teaspoons rice vinegar
1/2 teaspoon ground ginger
1/4 teaspoon black pepper
1/4 cup dry sherry, *or* fat-free beef broth
1 tablespoon flour
Salt, to taste
1 1/3 cups uncooked rice, cooked, warm

Per Serving
Calories: 421
% Calories from fat: 11
Protein (g): 43
Carbohydrates (g): 45
Fat (g): 4.9
Saturated fat (g): 1.4
Cholesterol (mg): 107
Sodium (mg): 277
Exchanges
Milk: 0.0
Veg.: 0.5
Fruit: 0.5
Bread: 2.0
Meat: 4.5
Fat: 0.0

1. Spray large saucepan with cooking spray; heat over medium heat until hot. Saute onion and bell pepper 5 minutes; stir in remaining ingredients, except dry sherry, flour, salt, and rice; heat to boiling. Reduce heat and simmer 15 minutes.

2. Heat stew to boiling; stir in combined sherry and flour. Boil, stirring, until thickened, about 1 minute. Season to taste with salt. Serve over rice.

HOME-STYLE TURKEY STEW

Here's a "thymely" stew that's loaded with tasty vegetables and ready to serve in less than 30 minutes.

4 servings

12 ounces boneless, skinless turkey breast, cut into ³/₄-inch cubes
2 medium onions, cut into thin wedges
4 ounces mushrooms, halved
2 teaspoons olive oil
2 carrots, sliced
2 potatoes, cut into ³/₄-inch cubes
1 can (14¹/₂ ounces) reduced-sodium fat-free chicken broth
³/₄ teaspoon celery seeds
1¹/₄ teaspoons dried thyme leaves
1 cup frozen peas
Salt and pepper, to taste

Per Serving
Calories: 246
% Calories from fat: 16
Protein (g): 22.1
Carbohydrates (g): 29.8
Fat (g): 4.4
Saturated fat (g): 0.9
Cholesterol (mg): 33.5
Sodium (mg): 158
Exchanges
Milk: 0.0
Veg.: 2.0
Fruit: 0.0
Bread: 1.0
Meat: 2.0
Fat: 0.0

1. Saute turkey, onions, and mushrooms in oil in large saucepan until onions are tender, about 8 minutes. Add remaining ingredients, except peas, salt, and pepper, and heat to boiling. Reduce heat and simmer, covered, until turkey and vegetables are tender, about 15 minutes.

2. Stir in peas; cook 3 to 4 minutes. Season to taste with salt and pepper.

TURKEY STEW CACCIATORE

Turkey cutlets are cut into bite-sized pieces to make a very easy, quick-cooking cacciatore-style skillet meal.

4 servings

- ³/₄ cup sliced mushrooms
- ³/₄ cup cubed zucchini
- 2 tablespoons olive oil
- 16 ounces turkey breast cutlets, cut into 2-inch pieces
- 2 tablespoons flour
- ³/₄ teaspoon dried oregano leaves
- 1 can (14 ounces) stewed tomatoes, undrained
- ¹/₃ cup water
  Salt and pepper, to taste
- 4 cups cooked pasta, *or* rice, warm

Per Serving
Calories: 579
% Calories from fat: 16
Protein (gm): 32.4
Carbohydrate (gm): 87.7
Fat (gm): 10.6
Saturated fat (gm): 1.8
Cholesterol (mg): 44.7
Sodium (mg): 265
Exchanges
Milk: 0.0
Veg.: 3.0
Fruit: 0.0
Bread: 4.0
Meat: 3.0
Fat: 1.0

1. Saute mushrooms and zucchini in oil in large skillet until lightly browned, about 5 minutes. Coat turkey pieces with combined flour and oregano; add to skillet with any remaining flour mixture. Cook until turkey just begins to brown, about 5 minutes.

2. Stir in tomatoes and liquid and water; heat to boiling. Reduce heat and simmer, covered, until turkey is cooked and mixture is slightly thickened, about 10 minutes. Season to taste with salt and pepper; serve over pasta.

SWEET-SOUR TURKEY STEW

This colorful dish is a perfect way to use leftover turkey, pork, or chicken.

4 servings

1¹/2 cups frozen pepper stir-fry blend

1-2 teaspoons dark sesame oil

1 can (8 ounces) pineapple tidbits, packed in juice, undrained

¹/3 cup packed light brown sugar

¹/3 cup cider vinegar

2 tablespoons cornstarch

1 package (10 ounces) frozen cut green beans

1¹/2 cups cubed cooked turkey

1 cup cubed tomato

1-2 tablespoons reduced-sodium soy sauce

Salt and pepper, to taste

2 cups cooked rice, warm

Per Serving
Calories: 359
% Calories from fat: 8
Protein (gm): 20.5
Carbohydrate (gm): 63
Fat (gm): 3.4
Saturated fat (gm): 0.8
Cholesterol (mg): 36.2
Sodium (mg): 192
Exchanges
Milk: 0.0
Veg.: 2.0
Fruit: 1.0
Bread: 2.0
Meat: 2.0
Fat: 0.0

1. Saute stir-fry pepper blend in oil in large skillet until tender, about 5 minutes. Drain pineapple, reserving ¹/3 cup juice. Combine juice, brown sugar, vinegar, and cornstarch in small bowl; stir into skillet. Stir in beans; heat to boiling. Reduce heat and simmer, uncovered, until beans are tender, about 5 minutes. Stir in pineapple, turkey, tomato, and soy sauce; simmer until hot. Season to taste with salt and pepper; serve over rice.

ITALIAN SAUSAGE STEW WITH HOT PEPPERS

Friends say this stew reminds them of a sassy hot sausage and peppers sandwich. I think you'll agree!

4 servings

Vegetable cooking spray

12-16 ounces reduced-sodium, reduced-fat Italian sausage, cut into 1-inch pieces

2 onions, cut into thin wedges

1 tablespoon chopped garlic

1 jalapeño chili, thinly sliced

2 cups reduced-sodium fat-free chicken broth

1 can (15 ounces) reduced-sodium diced tomatoes, undrained

1 zucchini, halved lengthwise, cut into 1/2-inch slices

4 ounces rigatoni

1 1/2 teaspoons Italian seasoning

1/2 teaspoon crushed red pepper

Salt and pepper, to taste

1/4 cup (1 ounce) shredded Parmesan cheese

Per Serving
Calories: 317
% Calories from fat: 16
Protein (gm): 24.8
Carbohydrate (gm): 43.1
Fat (gm): 5.8
Saturated fat (gm): 2.2
Cholesterol (mg): 43.6
Sodium (mg): 738
Exchanges
Milk: 0.0
Veg.: 2.0
Fruit: 0.0
Bread: 2.0
Meat: 2.0
Fat: 0.0

1. Spray large saucepan with cooking spray; heat over medium heat until hot. Saute sausage, onions, garlic, and jalapeño chili until sausage is lightly browned, about 5 minutes. Add remaining ingredients, except salt, pepper, and Parmesan cheese, and heat to boiling. Reduce heat and simmer, covered, until pasta is al dente, 10 to 12 minutes. Season to taste with salt and pepper; sprinkle each serving with 1 tablespoon cheese.

ITALIAN-STYLE BEAN AND VEGETABLE STEW WITH POLENTA

This colorful mélange can also be served over pasta, rice, or squares of warm cornbread.

6 servings (about 1¼ cups each)

12 ounces Italian-style turkey sausage, casings removed

1½ cups chopped onions

1½ cups portobello mushrooms

4 cloves garlic, minced

2 tablespoons olive oil

2 cups broccoli florets and sliced stems

1 cup sliced yellow summer squash

1 can (15 ounces) garbanzo beans, rinsed, drained

1 can (15 ounces) red kidney beans, rinsed, drained

1 can (14½ ounces) reduced-sodium whole tomatoes, undrained, coarsely chopped

1 teaspoon dried basil leaves

½ teaspoon dried oregano leaves

¼ teaspoon dried thyme leaves

¼-½ teaspoon crushed red pepper
Salt and pepper, to taste

1 package (16 ounces) prepared Italian-herb polenta

Per Serving
Calories: 380
% Calories from fat: 27
Protein (gm): 21.7
Carbohydrate (gm): 49.6
Fat (gm): 11.9
Saturated fat (gm): 2.5
Cholesterol (mg): 30.4
Sodium (mg): 833
Exchanges
Milk: 0.0
Veg.: 3.0
Fruit: 0.0
Bread: 3.0
Meat: 1.0
Fat: 1.0

1. Saute sausage, onions, mushrooms, and garlic in oil in large saucepan until onions are tender, about 10 minutes; drain excess fat. Add broccoli and squash; cook, covered, over medium heat 5 minutes.

2. Stir in beans, tomatoes with liquid, herbs, and crushed red pepper; heat to boiling. Reduce heat and simmer, covered, until broccoli is tender, 5 to 8 minutes. Season to taste with salt and pepper.

3. Heat polenta according to package directions; serve stew over polenta.

CREOLE SAUSAGE AND CORN STEW

Breakfast sausage comes to dinner! Use any lean sausage you like, or even all-vegetable sausage links.

4 servings

12-16	ounces reduced-fat spicy, *or* regular, pork sausage links, cut into 1-inch pieces
1	cup chopped onion
¹/₂	cup chopped green bell pepper
2	tablespoons flour
2	cups frozen, *or* fresh, whole-kernel corn
1	can (28 ounces) reduced-sodium diced tomatoes with roasted garlic, undrained
¹/₂	teaspoon dried thyme leaves
	Salt and pepper, to taste

Per Serving
Calories: 254
% Calories from fat: **14**
Protein (gm): 18.8
Carbohydrate (gm): 41
Fat (gm): 4.2
Saturated fat (gm): **1.3**
Cholesterol (mg): **39.7**
Sodium (mg): **570**
Exchanges
Milk: 0.0
Veg.: 0.0
Fruit: 0.0
Bread: 2.0
Meat: 2.0
Fat: 0.0

1. Cook sausage in large skillet until well browned; pour off all but 1 tablespoon fat. Add onion and bell pepper and saute until tender, about 5 minutes; stir in flour and cook 1 to 2 minutes longer.

2. Stir in corn, tomatoes and liquid, and thyme; heat to boiling. Reduce heat and simmer, uncovered, until thickened, about 8 minutes. Season to taste with salt and pepper.

BLACK BEAN AND OKRA GUMBO

Lightly spiked with chili powder, the gumbo is delicious served over Roasted Chili Cornbread (see p. 804).

8 servings (about 1¹/₃ cups each)

	Vegetable cooking spray
8-12	ounces reduced-sodium smoked turkey sausage, sliced
2	cups coarsely chopped onions
2	cups sliced carrots
1	cup chopped green bell pepper
1	cup chopped red bell pepper
4	teaspoons chili powder
1	teaspoon gumbo file powder

Per Serving
Calories: 288
% Calories from fat: **11**
Protein (g): 15.4
Carbohydrates (g): 56.8
Fat (g): 4.1
Saturated fat (g): 0.9
Cholesterol (mg): 17.7
Sodium (mg): 713
Exchanges
Milk: 0.0
Veg.: 2.0
Fruit: 0.0
Bread: 3.0
Meat: 0.0
Fat: 0.5

3 cups reduced-sodium fat-free chicken broth

2 cans (15¹/₂ ounces each) black beans, rinsed, drained

2 cups fresh, *or* frozen, cut okra
Salt and pepper, to taste

5 cups cooked rice, warm

1. Spray large skillet with cooking spray; heat over medium heat until hot. Add sausage, onions, carrots, and bell peppers and cook, covered, over medium heat until lightly browned, 5 to 8 minutes. Stir in chili powder and file powder; cook 2 to 3 minutes longer.

2. Add broth, beans, and okra; heat to boiling. Reduce heat and simmer, uncovered, until vegetables are tender and broth thickened, 8 to 10 minutes. Season to taste with salt and pepper.

3. Serve stew over rice in shallow bowls.

SAUSAGE, POTATO, AND BELL PEPPER STEW

An easy skillet stew, with the vibrant colors of bell peppers.

4 servings

Vegetable cooking spray

3 cups thinly sliced mixed red, green, and yellow bell peppers

1 cup thinly sliced onion

4 ounces reduced-sodium, reduced-fat smoked turkey sausage, thinly sliced

1 tablespoon flour

5 cups thinly sliced red potatoes

¹/₂ cup quartered sun-dried tomatoes (not in oil)

³/₄ cup reduced-sodium fat-free chicken broth

1 teaspoon dried thyme leaves

1 teaspoon dried marjoram leaves
Salt and pepper, to taste

Per Serving
Calories: 255
% Calories from fat: 10
Protein (g): 12.6
Carbohydrates (g): 48.8
Fat (g): 3.1
Saturated fat (g): 0.6
Cholesterol (mg): 18
Sodium (mg): 450
Exchanges
Milk: 0.0
Veg.: 3.0
Fruit: 0.0
Bread: 2.0
Meat: 0.5
Fat: 0.0

1. Spray large skillet with cooking spray; heat over medium heat until hot. Saute bell peppers, onion, and sausage until peppers are crisp-tender, 8 to 10 minutes; sprinkle with flour and cook 1 minute longer.

2. Add remaining ingredients, except salt and pepper, and heat to boiling; reduce heat and simmer, covered, until vegetables are tender, about 15 minutes. Season to taste with salt and pepper.

SMOKY GARBANZO BEAN STEW

Smoked turkey sausage gives this stew lots of flavor; the beans and vegetables make it extra-nutritious. Great with Herbed-Garlic Breadsticks (see p. 787)!

6 servings

8 ounces reduced-fat smoked turkey sausage, sliced
1 tablespoon olive oil
1 large onion, chopped
1 green bell pepper, chopped
2 medium zucchini, sliced
2 cloves garlic, minced
1 can (28 ounces) reduced-sodium tomatoes, undrained, chopped
2 cans (15 ounces each) garbanzo beans, rinsed, drained
1¹/₂ cups fresh, *or* frozen, cut green beans
2 teaspoons dried oregano leaves
Salt and pepper, to taste

Per Serving
Calories: 298
% Calories from fat: 17
Protein (gm): 15.9
Carbohydrate (gm): 48.9
Fat (gm): 5.8
Saturated fat (gm): 1.1
Cholesterol (mg): 17.6
Sodium (mg): 556
Exchanges
Milk: 0.0
Veg.: 1.0
Fruit: 0.0
Bread: 2.0
Meat: 1.0
Fat: 0.5

1. Cook sausage in oil in large saucepan over medium-high heat until browned, about 4 minutes. Add onion, bell pepper, zucchini, and garlic; cook over medium heat until vegetables are lightly browned, about 5 minutes.

2. Add remaining ingredients, except salt and pepper; heat to boiling. Reduce heat and simmer, uncovered, until vegetables are tender, about 10 minutes. Season to taste with salt and pepper.

QUICK PEPPERONI, VEGETABLE, AND PASTA STEW

Pepperoni is a high-fat ingredient, but fortunately, it is so flavorful that a small amount goes a long way.

4 servings

1 large onion, coarsely chopped
$1/2$ cup coarsely chopped red bell pepper
2 large garlic cloves, minced
3 ounces pepperoni, sliced, coarsely diced
$1^1/2$ teaspoons olive oil
$1/3$ cup reduced-sodium fat-free chicken broth
1 can ($14^1/2$ ounces) reduced-sodium Italian tomatoes, undrained, chopped
$3/4$ teaspoon dried oregano leaves
$3/4$ teaspoon dried marjoram leaves
3 cups small broccoli florets
$1^1/3$ cups dry macaroni, cooked
$1^1/2$ tablespoons grated Parmesan cheese
   Salt and pepper, to taste

Per Serving
Calories: 390
% Calories from fat: 30
Protein (g): 16.2
Carbohydrates (g): 53.5
Fat (g): 13.3
Saturated fat (g): 4.3
Cholesterol (mg): 1.9
Sodium (mg): 538
Exchanges
Milk: 0.0
Veg.: 3.0
Fruit: 0.0
Bread: 2.5
Meat: 1.0
Fat: 2.0

1. Saute onion, bell pepper, garlic, and pepperoni in oil in large saucepan until onion is tender, about 8 minutes. Add remaining ingredients, except macaroni, Parmesan cheese, salt, and pepper; heat to boiling. Reduce heat and simmer, covered, 15 minutes; add pasta and Parmesan cheese and simmer 2 to 3 minutes longer. Season to taste with salt and pepper.

BEAN AND CANADIAN BACON STEW WITH PASTA

Because Canadian bacon comes from the pork loin, it's low in fat. Happily, it's also very flavorful, so a little bit can add a wonderful smoked-meat taste to recipes such as this hearty dish.

6-7 servings

1 large onion, finely chopped
1 large garlic clove, minced
2 teaspoons olive oil
1 can (15 ounces) tomato sauce
3/4 cup fat-free beef broth
2 1/2 cups cooked Great Northern beans, *or* 1 can (19 ounces) white kidney beans, drained
1/2 large green bell pepper, diced
1/2 large red bell pepper, diced
1 teaspoon dried thyme leaves
1/2 teaspoon dried basil leaves
1/4 teaspoon dry mustard
1 bay leaf
6 ounces Canadian bacon, fat trimmed, cut into strips
1/4 cup non-fat ricotta cheese
Salt and pepper, to taste
1 1/2 cups fusilli, cooked, warm

Per Serving
Calories: 255
% Calories from fat: 15
Protein (g): 17
Carbohydrates (g): 39
Fat (g): 4.3
Saturated fat (g): 1
Cholesterol (mg): 15
Sodium (mg): 787
Exchanges
Milk: 0.0
Veg.: 1.0
Fruit: 0.0
Bread: 2.0
Meat: 1.5
Fat: 0.0

1. Saute onion and garlic in oil in Dutch oven until onion is tender. Add remaining ingredients, except Canadian bacon, ricotta, salt, pepper, and fusilli; heat to boiling. Reduce heat and simmer, covered, 10 minutes.

2. Add Canadian bacon and simmer 10 minutes longer. Remove from heat and stir in ricotta. Discard bay leaf; season to taste with salt and pepper. Serve over pasta.

CORNED BEEF AND RED CABBAGE STEW

Don't wait until St. Patrick's Day to enjoy this luck-of-the-Irish stew. It's fast. It's easy. It's delicious.

4 servings

Per Serving
Calories: 259
% Calories from fat: 29
Protein (g): 13.6
Carbohydrates (g): 34.1
Fat (g): 8.5
Saturated fat (g): 2.8
Cholesterol (mg): 42.3
Sodium (mg): 646
Exchanges
Milk: 0.0
Veg.: 1.0
Fruit: 0.0
Bread: 2.0
Meat: 1.0
Fat: 1.0

8-12 ounces cooked lean corned beef, cut into $1/2$-inch cubes
   6 medium red potatoes, cut into $1/2$-inch cubes
$1^1/2$ cups sliced carrots
   1 cup cubed, peeled turnips
   1 can ($14^1/2$ ounces) reduced-sodium fat-free chicken broth, divided
   1 tablespoon apple cider vinegar
   1 teaspoon pickling spice
   1 pound cabbage, coarsely sliced
$1^1/2$ tablespoons flour
   Salt and pepper, to taste

1. Combine corned beef, potatoes, carrots, turnips, $1^1/4$ cups broth, vinegar, and pickling spice in large saucepan. Heat to boiling; reduce heat and simmer, covered, 12 minutes.

2. Add cabbage; simmer until vegetables are tender, about 5 minutes. Heat stew to boiling; stir in combined remaining $1/2$ cup broth and flour. Boil, stirring, until thickened, about 1 minute. Season to taste with salt and pepper.

GERMAN-STYLE STEW

This is the perfect combination of ingredients for a delicious, Old-World meal. Serve with Hearty Vegetable-Rye Bread (see p. 796).

5-6 servings

2 cups fresh sauerkraut
2 large apples, thinly sliced
1 large onion, thinly sliced
2 cups thinly sliced, peeled potatoes
1½ cups cubed, peeled rutabaga
6 ounces reduced-sodium ham steak, cut into small pieces
1 tablespoon flour
2 bay leaves
1 cup apple cider
1½ tablespoons brown sugar
Salt and pepper, to taste

Per Serving
Calories: 242
% Calories from fat: 6
Protein (g): 5
Carbohydrates (g): 55
Fat (g): 1.6
Saturated fat (g): 0.1
Cholesterol (mg): 0
Sodium (mg): 684
Exchanges
Milk: 0.0
Veg.: 1.5
Fruit: 1.5
Bread: 1.5
Meat: 0.0
Fat: 0.0

1. Combine all ingredients, except salt and pepper, in large saucepan; heat to boiling. Reduce heat and simmer, covered, until vegetables are tender, about 20 minutes. Discard bay leaves; season to taste with salt and pepper.

ONE-STEP HAM AND BEAN STEW

Making a stew doesn't get much easier than this! Use any beans you like, and get that can opener working!

6 servings

6 ounces reduced-sodium lean ham, fat trimmed, diced
1 can (15 ounces) black beans, rinsed, drained
1 can (15 ounces) pinto beans, rinsed, drained
1 can (15 ounces) navy beans, rinsed, drained
1 can (14½ ounces each) reduced-sodium fat-free beef broth

Per Serving
Calories: 296
% Calories from fat: 9
Protein (gm): 20.6
Carbohydrate (gm): 54.4
Fat (gm): 3.3
Saturated fat (gm): 0.8
Cholesterol (mg): 13.5
Sodium (mg): 922
Exchanges
Milk: 0.0
Veg.: 1.0
Fruit: 0.0
Bread: 3.0
Meat: 1.0
Fat: 0.0

1 can (28 ounces) reduced-sodium diced
   tomatoes, undrained
¹/₃ cup quick-cooking barley
1 large onion, chopped
2 cloves garlic, minced
1 tablespoon chili powder
2 teaspoons dried oregano leaves
¹/₂ teaspoon crushed red pepper
   Salt and pepper, to taste

1. Combine all ingredients, except salt and pepper, in large saucepan; heat to boiling. Reduce heat and simmer, covered, 20 minutes. Season to taste with salt and pepper.

SOUTHERN STEWED BLACK-EYED PEAS, CHICKPEAS, AND HAM

This hearty stew can be made in 20 minutes with pantry staples. Serve with warm biscuits or cornbread.

6 servings (about 1¹/₄ cups each)

10 ounces reduced-sodium ham, cubed
1¹/₂ cups chopped onions
1 teaspoon minced garlic
1 tablespoon olive oil
1 can (28 ounces) reduced-sodium diced
   tomatoes, undrained
1 can (15¹/₂ ounces) chickpeas, rinsed,
   drained
1 can (15¹/₂ ounces) black-eyed peas,
   rinsed, drained
1 package (10 ounces) frozen spinach
2 cups fresh, *or* frozen, okra, cut into 1-
   inch pieces
1 teaspoon dried marjoram leaves
³/₄ teaspoon dried thyme leaves
¹/₄ teaspoon hot pepper sauce
   Salt and pepper, to taste

Per Serving
Calories: 282
% Calories from fat: 16
Protein (g): 18.9
Carbohydrates (g): 42.8
Fat (g): 5.2
Saturated fat (g): 1
Cholesterol (mg): 21.9
Sodium (mg): 776
Exchanges
Milk: 0.0
Veg.: 3.0
Fruit: 0.0
Bread: 2.0
Meat: 1.0
Fat: 0.0

1. Saute ham, onions, and garlic in oil in large saucepan until onions are tender, about 5 minutes. Stir in remaining ingredients, except salt and pepper; heat to boiling. Reduce heat and simmer, covered, until okra is tender, about 10 minutes. Season to taste with salt and pepper.

BUTTER BEANS, MOSTACCIOLI, AND HAM STEW

This extra-easy bean and pasta stew has three great things going for it— it's fast to prepare, has a subtle anchovy flavor, and is delightfully rich tasting, thanks to Romano cheese.

4 servings

1¹/₂ cups frozen, thawed, small butter beans
   2 cans (14 ounces each) reduced-sodium fat-free chicken broth
   4 ounces mostaccioli
   4 ounces lean reduced-sodium ham, diced
 ¹/₂ can (2-ounce size) anchovies, rinsed, drained, mashed
   2 teaspoons minced garlic
   1 small mild chili, chopped
 ¹/₂ cup sliced scallions
 ¹/₄ cup grated Romano cheese
     Salt and pepper, to taste

Per Serving
Calories: 289
% Calories from fat: 16
Protein (g): 23.5
Carbohydrates (g): 36
Fat (g): 4.9
Saturated fat (g): 2
Cholesterol (mg): 28.4
Sodium (mg): 783
Exchanges
Milk: 0.0
Veg.: 0.0
Fruit: 0.0
Bread: 2.5
Meat: 2.0
Fat: 0.0

1. Combine all ingredients, except Romano cheese, salt, and pepper in large saucepan. Heat to boiling; reduce heat and simmer, covered, until pasta is tender, about 10 minutes. Stir in cheese; season to taste with salt and pepper.

HAM AND PEPPER STEW WITH POLENTA

This microwave method not only speeds cooking but also helps eliminate lumps and the constant stirring necessary when polenta is made on the stovetop.

5-6 servings

1 medium onion, chopped

1 garlic clove, minced

2 teaspoons olive oil

1 can (14¹/₂ ounces) reduced-sodium diced tomatoes, undrained

1 can (15 ounces) reduced-sodium tomato sauce

8 ounces reduced-sodium ham steak, cooked, cut into bite-sized pieces

1¹/₂ cups chopped mixed green, red, and yellow bell peppers

1 bay leaf

1¹/₂ teaspoons Italian seasoning
Salt and pepper, to taste
Microwave Polenta (see p. 618)

1 tablespoon grated Parmesan cheese

Per Serving
Calories: 247
% Calories from fat: 17
Protein (g): 9.1
Carbohydrates (g): 44.1
Fat (g): 4.8
Saturated fat (g): 0.6
Cholesterol (mg): 1.7
Sodium (mg): 261
Exchanges
Milk: 0.0
Veg.: 3.0
Fruit: 0.0
Bread: 2.0
Meat: 0.0
Fat: 0.5

1. Saute onion and garlic in oil in large saucepan until onion is tender, about 5 minutes. Add remaining ingredients, except salt, pepper, Microwave Polenta, and Parmesan cheese; heat to boiling. Reduce heat and simmer, uncovered, 15 minutes or until vegetables are tender. Discard bay leaf; season to taste with salt and pepper.

2. Serve over Microwave Polenta; sprinkle with cheese.

FRESH TWO-BEAN STEW WITH ROSEMARY

This stew of green and wax beans has a fresh flavor that is perfectly complemented with rosemary.

4 servings

2 slices turkey bacon
1¹/₄ cups chopped red onions
2 teaspoons minced garlic
¹/₂ pound Roma green beans, halved
¹/₂ pound wax beans, halved
1 can (28 ounces) crushed tomatoes with basil, undrained
2 large red potatoes, unpeeled, cut into ¹/₂-inch cubes
1 teaspoon dried rosemary leaves
Salt and pepper, to taste

Per Serving
Calories: 199
% Calories from fat: 8
Protein (gm): 8.3
Carbohydrate (gm): 38.7
Fat (gm): 1.9
Saturated fat (gm): 0.6
Cholesterol (mg): 4.5
Sodium (mg): 605
Exchanges
Milk: 0.0
Veg.: 1.0
Fruit: 0.0
Bread: 2.0
Meat: 0.0
Fat: 0.5

1. Cook bacon in large skillet until crisp; transfer to paper-towel-lined plate and reserve. Saute onions and garlic in fat remaining in skillet until tender, about 5 minutes.

2. Add reserved bacon and remaining ingredients, except salt and pepper; heat to boiling. Reduce heat and simmer, covered, until vegetables are tender, about 20 minutes. Season to taste with salt and pepper.

QUICK TOMATO-VEGETABLE STEW

This recipe is very flexible. Although it calls for zucchini and cauliflower, you can substitute any desired vegetable.

4 servings

4 ounces Canadian bacon, cut into thin strips
1 medium onion, chopped
2 garlic cloves, minced
2 teaspoons olive oil
1 can (14¹/₂ ounces) reduced-sodium stewed tomatoes, undrained
1 cup sliced zucchini
1 cup small cauliflower florets
1-2 teaspoons Italian seasoning
Salt and pepper, to taste
8 ounces penne, cooked, warm

Per Serving
Calories: 325
% Calories from fat: 16
Protein (g): 15.2
Carbohydrates (g): 53.7
Fat (g): 5.6
Saturated fat (g): 1.2
Cholesterol (mg): 13.5
Sodium (mg): 380
Exchanges
Milk: 0.0
Veg.: 2.0
Fruit: 0.0
Bread: 3.0
Meat: 1.0
Fat: 0.0

1. Saute bacon, onion, and garlic in oil in large saucepan until onion is tender, about 5 minutes. Add remaining ingredients, except salt, pepper, and penne; heat to boiling. Reduce heat and simmer until vegetables are tender, 8 to 10 minutes. Season to taste with salt and pepper; serve over penne.

FRESH VEGETABLE STEW

Use any vegetables on hand for this quick veggie stew.

4 servings

4	green onions and tops, sliced
3	tomatoes, chopped
2	small carrots, sliced
2	small turnips, peeled, sliced
1/2	pound green beans, halved
8	frozen, *or* canned, artichoke hearts
8	small new potatoes
4	ounces lean smoked ham, cut into thin strips
2	cups reduced-sodium fat-free chicken broth, divided
1/2	teaspoon dried marjoram leaves
1/4	teaspoon dried thyme leaves
1	cup frozen peas
8	asparagus spears, cut into 2-inch pieces
1 1/2	tablespoons flour
	Salt and pepper, to taste
3	cups cooked rice, warm

Per Serving
Calories: 471
% Calories from fat: 5
Protein (gm): 23.1
Carbohydrate (gm): 89.9
Fat (gm): 2.9
Saturated fat (gm): 0.8
Cholesterol (mg): 15.6
Sodium (mg): 701
Exchanges
Milk: 0.0
Veg.: 5.0
Fruit: 0.0
Bread: 4.0
Meat: 1.0
Fat: 0.0

1. Combine green onions, tomatoes, carrots, turnips, green beans, artichoke hearts, potatoes, ham, 1 1/2 cups chicken broth, and herbs in large saucepan; heat to boiling. Reduce heat and simmer, covered, until vegetables are tender, about 15 minutes, adding peas and asparagus during last 5 minutes of cooking time.

2. Heat stew to boiling; stir in combined remaining 1/2 cup broth and flour. Boil, stirring, until stew is thickened, 1 to 2 minutes. Season to taste with salt and pepper; serve over rice.

VEGETABLE STEW WITH CHEESE TORTELLINI

Serve this simple vegetable stew over your favorite flavor tortellini.

4 servings

4 small green, *or* yellow, zucchini, cubed

1 green bell pepper, chopped

1 cup sliced mushrooms

1/2 cup finely chopped onion

1 can (14 ounces) stewed tomatoes, undrained

1 can (14 1/2 ounces) reduced-sodium vegetable broth, *or* reduced-sodium fat-free chicken broth

1/4 teaspoon allspice

1/2 teaspoon dried chervil leaves

1/2 teaspoon dried basil leaves

Salt and pepper, to taste

1 package (9 ounces) cheese tortellini, cooked, warm

Per Serving
Calories: 276
% Calories from fat: 15
Protein (gm): 13.4
Carbohydrate (gm): 47.3
Fat (gm): 5
Saturated fat (gm): 2
Cholesterol (mg): 33.9
Sodium (mg): 511
Exchanges
Milk: 0.0
Veg.: 3.0
Fruit: 0.0
Bread: 2.0
Meat: 0.0
Fat: 1.0

1. Combine all ingredients, except salt, pepper, and tortellini, in large saucepan; heat to boiling. Reduce heat and simmer, covered, 15 minutes. Season to taste with salt and pepper; serve over tortellini.

CREOLE FISH STEW

Rich flavors, quick and easy preparation—who could ask for more?

4 servings

2 cups chopped onions

1 cup chopped green bell pepper

1 cup chopped celery

2 teaspoons minced garlic

1/2 teaspoon dried thyme leaves

1/4 teaspoon crushed red pepper

2 teaspoons olive oil

1 can (28 ounces) reduced-sodium diced tomatoes, undrained

Per Serving
Calories: 378
% Calories from fat: 10
Protein (gm): 28
Carbohydrate (gm): 56.1
Fat (gm): 4.1
Saturated fat (gm): 0.7
Cholesterol (mg): 48.6
Sodium (mg): 385
Exchanges
Milk: 0.0
Veg.: 1.0
Fruit: 0.0
Bread: 3.0
Meat: 3.0
Fat: 0.0

   ¹/₄ cup dry white wine, *or* fat-free chicken
      broth
   1 pound cod fillets, cubed
   2 tablespoons reduced-sodium soy sauce
   1 tablespoon paprika
   2 bay leaves
      Salt and pepper, to taste
   3 cups cooked rice, warm

1. Saute onions, bell pepper, celery, garlic, thyme, and red pepper in oil in large saucepan until tender and lightly browned,
about 10 minutes.

2. Stir in remaining ingredients, except salt, pepper, and rice;
heat to boiling. Reduce heat and simmer, covered, until fish
flakes with a fork, about 10 minutes. Discard bay leaves; season
to taste with salt and pepper; serve with rice.

CAJUN SHRIMP, CORN, AND BEAN STEW

*A milk-based shrimp stew with a spicy tang! Serve this stew with crusty
bread or over rice.*

4 servings

   1 medium onion, chopped
   1 jalapeño chili, minced
   2 cloves garlic, minced
   1 teaspoon dried thyme leaves
   ¹/₂ teaspoon dried oregano leaves
   1 tablespoon margarine
   2 tablespoons flour
   2 cups fat-free milk
   1 cup frozen, *or* fresh, broccoli florets
   1 cup frozen cream-style corn
   1 can (15 ounces) red beans, rinsed,
      drained
   12 ounces shrimp, peeled, deveined
      Salt, to taste
      Hot pepper sauce, to taste

Per Serving
Calories: 311
% Calories from fat: 14
Protein (gm): 26.4
Carbohydrate (gm): 42.3
Fat (gm): 4.8
Saturated fat (gm): 1
Cholesterol (mg): 132.2
Sodium (mg): 677
Exchanges
Milk: 0.0
Veg.: 2.0
Fruit: 0.0
Bread: 2.0
Meat: 2.0
Fat: 0.0

1. Saute onion, jalapeño, garlic, and herbs in margarine in large saucepan until tender, about 5 minutes. Stir in flour; cook 1 minute longer. Stir in milk and heat to boiling, stirring until thickened, 1 to 2 minutes.

2. Stir in vegetables and heat to boiling; reduce heat and simmer 10 minutes. Add shrimp and simmer until shrimp are pink and cooked, about 5 minutes longer. Season to taste with salt and hot pepper sauce.

SHRIMP AND VEGETABLE STEW

The use of small vegetables which need no chopping or slicing speeds preparation time.

4 servings

1 cup baby carrots
1 cup frozen whole-kernel corn
1 cup small Brussels sprouts
1 medium onion, cut into thin wedges
1 can (14¹/₂ ounces) stewed tomatoes, undrained
4 ounces reduced-sodium, reduced-fat smoked sausage, cut into ¹/₄-inch slices
1 teaspoon chili powder
12 ounces peeled, deveined medium shrimp
Salt and pepper, to taste
3 cups cooked rice, warm

Per Serving
Calories: 361
% Calories from fat: 7
Protein (gm): 25.6
Carbohydrate (gm): 59.6
Fat (gm): 2.8
Saturated fat (gm): 0.8
Cholesterol (mg): 143.2
Sodium (mg): 594
Exchanges
Milk: 0.0
Veg.: 3.0
Fruit: 0.0
Bread: 3.0
Meat: 1.0
Fat: 0.0

1. Combine all ingredients, except shrimp, salt, pepper, and rice, in large saucepan; heat to boiling. Reduce heat and simmer until vegetables are tender, about 15 minutes, adding shrimp during last 5 minutes cooking time. Season to taste with salt and pepper; serve over rice.

THAI-STYLE SHRIMP STEW

This lovely dish gets its fabulous flavor from shrimp, bok choy, scallions, and Chinese chili sauce.

4 servings

2 cups reduced-sodium fat-free chicken broth

1/4 cup rice wine vinegar

2 tablespoons Chinese chili sauce with garlic

16 ounces peeled, deveined medium shrimp

2 cups chopped bok choy

1 medium red bell pepper, sliced

1 cup sliced scallions

4 ounces bean threads, *or* cellophane noodles, cut into 2-inch lengths and soaked in hot water 10 minutes

1 cup fresh, *or* canned, rinsed, drained, bean sprouts

Reduced-sodium soy sauce, to taste

Salt and pepper, to taste

Per Serving
Calories: 236
% Calories from fat: 5
Protein (gm): 23.7
Carbohydrate (gm): 31.2
Fat (gm): 1.2
Saturated fat (gm): 0.3
Cholesterol (mg): 173.3
Sodium (mg): 395
Exchanges
Milk: 0.0
Veg.: 3.0
Fruit: 0.0
Bread: 1.0
Meat: 1.5
Fat: 0.0

1. Combine all ingredients except bean threads, bean sprouts, soy sauce, salt, and pepper; heat to boiling. Reduce heat and simmer, covered, until shrimp are cooked and pink, 5 to 8 minutes. Stir in bean threads and bean sprouts; simmer, uncovered, 2 minutes longer. Season to taste with soy sauce, salt, and pepper. Serve in shallow bowls.

FIFTEEN

Breads

AND

Accompaniments

CROUTONS

Croutons can brighten a soup, add crunch to a stew. Make in advance and store in an airtight container for up to 2 weeks, or freeze until needed.

12 servings (about ¼ cup each)

3 cups cubed firm, *or* day-old, French, *or* Italian, bread (¹/₂-³/₄-inch cubes)
Butter-flavored, *or* olive oil, cooking spray

Per Serving
Calories: 20
% Calories from fat: 13
Protein (g): 0.6
Carbohydrates (g): 3.7
Fat (g): 0.3
Saturated fat (g): 0.1
Cholesterol (mg): 0
Sodium (mg): 39
Exchanges
Milk: 0.0
Veg.: 0.0
Fruit: 0.0
Bread: 0.0
Meat: 0.0
Fat: 0.0

1. Spray bread cubes generously with cooking spray; arrange in single layer on jelly roll pan. Bake at 375 degrees until browned, 8 to 10 minutes, stirring occasionally. Cool; store in airtight container.

Variations: (Bake all as above)

Italian-Style Croutons—Spray bread cubes with olive oil cooking spray; sprinkle generously with combined 1 teaspoon garlic powder and 1 teaspoon Italian seasoning. Bake as above.

Sourdough Croutons—Spray sourdough bread cubes with cooking spray and sprinkle with 2 teaspoons bouquet garni. Bake as above.

Parmesan Croutons—Spray bread cubes with cooking spray and sprinkle with 1 to 2 tablespoons grated fat-free Parmesan cheese. Bake as above.

Rye-Caraway Croutons—Spray rye bread cubes with cooking spray, and sprinkle with 2 teaspoons crushed caraway seeds. Bake as above.

Sesame Croutons—Spray bread cubes with cooking spray and sprinkle with 2 to 3 teaspoons sesame seeds. Bake as above.

Herb Croutons—Spray multi-grain or whole wheat bread cubes with cooking spray and sprinkle with 2 teaspoons dried herb or herb combinations, such as basil, tarragon, oregano, savory, rosemary, etc. Bake as above.

Garlic Croutons—Spray whole wheat or white bread with olive oil cooking spray and sprinkle generously with garlic powder.

Chili Croutons—Spray bread cubes with cooking spray and sprinkle lightly with chili powder and ground cumin.

TOMATO-BASIL BRUSCHETTA

In Italy I learned to love bruschetta. This version is a tasty accompaniment for almost any soup.

12 servings (about 3 slices each)

1 loaf (13 ounces) unsliced Italian bread
1 tablespoon olive oil
1½ tablespoons reduced-sodium fat-free chicken, *or* vegetable, broth
1½ tablespoons red wine vinegar
1 teaspoon minced garlic
1 teaspoon dried basil leaves
⅓ cup grated Parmesan cheese
2 medium tomatoes, thinly sliced
Salt, to taste
12 fresh basil leaves

Per Serving
Calories: 109
% Calories from fat: 24
Protein (gm): 3.9
Carbohydrate (gm): 16.6
Fat (gm): 2.9
Saturated fat (gm): 0.8
Cholesterol (mg): 1.7
Sodium (mg): 224
Exchanges
Milk: 0.0
Veg.: 0.0
Fruit: 0.0
Bread: 1.0
Meat: 0.0
Fat: 0.5

1. Discard ends of bread. Cut remainder of bread into ¾-inch slices; arrange on large cookie sheet.

2. Combine oil, broth, vinegar, garlic, and dried basil; spread mixture evenly over bread slices and sprinkle with Parmesan cheese.

3. Bake at 375 degrees until bread is lightly browned, 10 to 15 minutes. Top each bread slice with a tomato slice and sprinkle lightly with salt. Garnish with basil.

BRUSCHETTA

These simple-to-make Italian garlic toasts are perfect for serving with any kind of savory appetizer spread.

12 servings (1 slice each)

½ loaf French bread (8-ounce size, about 8 inches long)
Olive oil cooking spray
1 clove garlic, cut in half

Per Serving
Calories: 26
% Calories from fat: 10
Protein (gm): 0.8
Carbohydrate (gm): 5
Fat (gm): 0.3
Saturated fat (gm): 0
Cholesterol (mg): 0
Sodium (mg): 107

1. Cut bread into 12 slices; spray both sides of bread lightly with cooking spray. Broil on cookie sheet 4 inches from heat source until browned, 2 to 3 minutes on each side.

Exchanges
Milk: 0.0
Veg.: 0.0
Fruit: 0.0
Bread: 0.5
Meat: 0.0
Fat: 0.0

2. Rub top sides of bread slices with cut sides of garlic.

SESAME BREADSTICKS

Made with food processor ease, these breadsticks are the perfect accompaniment to your favorite soup or stew!

12 servings (1 each)

$2^1/_3$-$2^3/_4$ cups all-purpose white flour, divided
1 package rapid-rising dry yeast
1 cup water
$1^1/_2$ tablespoons olive oil, divided
$3/_4$ teaspoon salt
3 tablespoons sesame seeds
Sea salt for garnish, optional

Per Serving
Calories: 117
% Calories from fat: 23
Protein (g): 3.3
Carbohydrates (g): 19
Fat (g): 3
Saturated fat (g): 0.4
Cholesterol (mg): 0
Sodium (mg): 135
Exchanges
Milk: 0.0
Veg.: 0.0
Fruit: 0.0
Bread: 1.0
Meat: 0.0
Fat: 1.0

1. Process $1^1/_3$ cups white flour and yeast in food processor fitted with steel blade until mixed well.

2. Combine water, 1 tablespoon oil, and salt in a saucepan. Heat until boiling. Add liquid to running food processor; add 1 cup flour and process until incorporated. Dough should form a firm ball; add more flour if necessary.

3. Transfer dough to greased bowl. Lightly brush top of dough with $1/_2$ of remaining olive oil. Let rise, covered, in warm place until doubled in size, about 45 minutes. Punch down dough.

4. Shape dough into twelve 10-inch sticks and arrange on greased baking sheets; brush with remaining oil and sprinkle with sesame seeds and sea salt.

5. Bake at 425 degrees until browned, about 15 minutes.

HERBED-GARLIC BREADSTICKS

Hot, hip, trendy—garlic breadsticks like these come together in no time flat. And no one need know they're made with purchased frozen dough!

8 servings (1 each)

Olive oil cooking spray
1 tablespoon yellow cornmeal
8 frozen yeast dough rolls, thawed
1/2 teaspoon garlic powder
1/2 teaspoon dried marjoram leaves

Per Serving
Calories: 80
% Calories from fat: 17
Protein (gm): 2.2
Carbohydrate (gm): 14.3
Fat (gm): 1.5
Saturated fat (gm): 0.3
Cholesterol (mg): 1.4
Sodium (mg): 137
Exchanges
Milk: 0.0
Veg.: 0.0
Fruit: 0.0
Bread: 1.0
Meat: 0.0
Fat: 0.0

1. Spray cookie sheet with cooking spray; sprinkle evenly with cornmeal.

2. Stretch and roll each yeast ball into a 12-inch stick; place on baking sheet and press ends to the baking sheet. Spray with cooking spray; sprinkle with garlic and marjoram. Let stand, loosely covered, in warm place until doubled in size, about 30 minutes.

3. Bake at 425 degrees until golden, about 10 minutes.

PITA BREADS

Also called Syrian bread and pocket breads, pitas can be eaten plain or split and filled to make sandwiches to serve with soups. The breads freeze well, so make lots!

12 servings (1 each)

1 package active dry yeast
1 1/3 cups warm water (110-115 degrees)
1/4 teaspoon sugar
1 1/2 tablespoons olive oil
3-4 cups all-purpose flour
1 teaspoon salt

Per Serving
Calories: 131
% Calories from fat: 14
Protein (g): 3.5
Carbohydrates (g): 24.2
Fat (g): 2
Saturated fat (g): 0.3
Cholesterol (mg): 0
Sodium (mg): 178
Exchanges
Milk: 0.0
Veg.: 0.0
Fruit: 0.0
Bread: 2.0
Meat: 0.0
Fat: 0.0

1. Combine yeast, water, and sugar in large bowl; let stand 5 minutes. Add oil, 3 cups flour, and salt, mixing until smooth. Mix in enough remaining 1 cup flour to make smooth dough.

2. Knead dough on floured surface until smooth and elastic, about 5 minutes. Place dough in greased bowl; let stand, covered, in warm place until doubled in size, about 1 hour. Punch dough down.

3. Shape dough into 12 balls; let stand, loosely covered, 30 minutes (dough will not double in size). Roll balls of dough on floured surface into rounds 5 to 6 inches in diameter. Place rounds, 2 to 3 inches apart, on cookie sheets; let stand 30 minutes.

4. Bake breads, 1 pan at a time, at 500 degrees until breads are puffed and brown, 3 to 5 minutes. Cool on wire racks.

FOCACCIA

This delicious Italian bread can be frozen, so bake extra to have on hand.

2 focaccia (10 servings each)

5¹/₂ cups bread flour, divided
1 package fast-rising yeast
1 teaspoon sugar
1 teaspoon salt
1³/₄ cups very hot water (125-130 degrees)
    Olive oil cooking spray
¹/₄ cup grated Parmesan cheese

Per Serving
Calories: 139
% Calories from fat: 5
Protein (g): 5.2
Carbohydrates (g): 28.2
Fat (g): 0.8
Saturated fat (g): 0.2
Cholesterol (mg): 1
Sodium (mg): 131
Exchanges
Milk: 0.0
Veg.: 0.0
Fruit: 0.0
Bread: 2.0
Meat: 0.0
Fat: 0.0

1. Combine 4 cups flour, yeast, sugar, and salt in large mixing bowl. Add water, mixing until smooth. Mix in enough remaining 1¹/₂ cups flour to make soft dough.

2. Knead dough on floured surface until dough is smooth and elastic, about 5 minutes. Place dough in greased bowl; turn greased side up and let rise, covered, in warm place until doubled in size, about 1 hour. Punch dough down.

3. Divide dough into halves. Roll 1 piece dough on floured surface to fit jelly roll pan, 15 x 10 inches. Grease pan lightly; ease dough into pan. Repeat with remaining dough. Let dough rise until doubled in size, 45 to 60 minutes.

4. Make 1/4-inch-deep indentations with fingers to "dimple" the dough; spray lightly with cooking spray and sprinkle with Parmesan cheese.

5. Bake focaccia at 425 degrees until browned, about 30 minutes. Cool in pans on wire racks. Serve warm, or at room temperature.

Variation:
Leek and Onion Foccacia—Make bread as above through Step 4, except do not sprinkle with cheese. Combine 1/2 cup each thinly sliced leek (white part only), sliced yellow onion, sliced red onion, and 1 tablespoon olive oil; spread over dough and sprinkle with cheese. Bake as above.

TOMATO-BASIL FOCACCIA

Win rave reviews when you serve this flavorful bread accompaniment. Refrigerated dough cuts prep time to practically nothing.

9 servings (1 each)

Olive oil cooking spray
1 tablespoon yellow cornmeal
1 package (10 ounces) refrigerated pizza crust
2 plum tomatoes, thinly sliced
2 teaspoons minced garlic
10 basil leaves, minced

Per Serving
Calories: 90
% Calories from fat: **12**
Protein (gm): 3
Carbohydrate (gm): **16.8**
Fat (gm): 1.2
Saturated fat (gm): 0.2
Cholesterol (mg): 0
Sodium (mg): 176
Exchanges
Milk: 0.0
Veg.: 0.0
Fruit: 0.0
Bread: 1.0
Meat: 0.0
Fat: 0.0

1. Spray a perforated pizza pan with cooking spray; sprinkle with cornmeal.

2. Gently stretch dough into 12-inch circle. Spray top of dough lightly with cooking spray. Arrange tomatoes on dough; sprinkle with garlic and basil.

3. Let rise, loosely covered, in warm place until doubled in size, about 30 minutes.

4. Bake at 425 degrees until golden brown, 10 to 12 minutes.

INDIVIDUAL OLIVE FOCACCIAS

Thinly sliced stuffed olives and caramelized onion rings top personal-sized focaccias—perfect to serve with soup!

8 servings (1 each)

Vegetable cooking spray
1 tablespoon yellow cornmeal
8 frozen yeast-dough rolls, thawed
1 large onion, thinly sliced
1 teaspoon olive oil
1 teaspoon sugar
8 pimiento-stuffed green olives, thinly sliced
1/2 teaspoon poppy seeds

Per Serving
Calories: 99
% Calories from fat: 24
Protein (gm): 2.5
Carbohydrate (gm): 16.4
Fat (gm): 2.6
Saturated fat (gm): 0.5
Cholesterol (mg): 1.4
Sodium (mg): 216
Exchanges
Milk: 0.0
Veg.: 0.0
Fruit: 0.0
Bread: 1.0
Meat: 0.0
Fat: 0.5

1. Spray a cookie sheet with cooking spray; sprinkle with cornmeal.

2. Gently stretch each roll into a 4-inch circle; spray lightly with cooking spray.

3. Saute onion in oil in large skillet 2 to 3 minutes; sprinkle with sugar and saute until onions are golden, 8 to 10 minutes longer. Arrange onions and olives on bread rounds; sprinkle with poppy seeds.

4. Let rise, loosely covered, in warm place until doubled in size, about 30 minutes.

5. Bake at 425 degrees until golden brown, 9 to 11 minutes.

SPINACH-MUSHROOM FLATBREAD

This attractive bread is made in a freeform shape and topped with spinach and Parmesan cheese. The bread can be made in advance and reheated at 300 degrees, loosely wrapped in aluminum foil, 15 to 20 minutes.

1 loaf (12 servings)

3-3½ cups all-purpose flour, divided
1½ cups whole wheat flour
2 tablespoons sugar
1½ teaspoons dried rosemary leaves, crushed
½ teaspoon dried thyme leaves
½ teaspoon salt
1 package fast-rising yeast
2 cups very hot water (125-130 degrees)
Olive oil cooking spray
¼ cup sliced onion
3 cloves garlic, minced
2 cups torn spinach leaves
1 cup sliced cremini, *or* white, mushrooms
¼ cup (2 ounces) shredded reduced-fat mozzarella cheese
2-3 tablespoons grated fat-free Parmesan cheese

Per Serving
Calories: 190
% Calories from fat: 5
Protein (g): 7
Carbohydrates (g): 38.8
Fat (g): 1
Saturated fat (g): 0.4
Cholesterol (mg): 1.3
Sodium (mg): 123
Exchanges
Milk: 0.0
Veg.: 0.0
Fruit: 0.0
Bread: 2.5
Meat: 0.0
Fat: 0.0

1. Combine 2½ cups all-purpose flour, whole wheat flour, sugar, herbs, salt, and yeast in large mixing bowl; add hot water, mixing until smooth. Mix in enough remaining 1 cup all-purpose flour to make soft dough.

2. Knead dough on floured surface until smooth and elastic, about 5 minutes. Place dough in greased bowl; let rise, loosely covered, in warm place until doubled in size, 30 to 45 minutes. Punch dough down.

3. Pat dough on floured surface into a round. Pull the edges of the dough into a freeform shape, about 10 x 14 inches. Transfer dough to greased cookie sheet and let stand 20 minutes (dough will rise but will not double in size). Bake bread at 350 degrees until golden, about 20 minutes.

4. While bread is baking, spray medium skillet with cooking spray; heat over medium heat until hot. Saute onion and garlic until tender, 3 to 4 minutes. Add spinach and mushrooms; cook, covered, over medium to medium-low heat until spinach is wilted, about 5 minutes. Cook, uncovered, until mushrooms are tender, about 5 minutes.

5. Arrange spinach mixture over top of bread; sprinkle with cheeses. Continue baking until spinach mixture is hot and cheese melted, 5 to 10 minutes. Remove from cookie sheet and cool on wire rack.

OLIVE FLATBREAD CRISPS

Served warm from the oven, these food-processor fast flatbread wedges are wonderful with soups.

24 servings (1 each)

2¹/₄-2¹/₂ cups all-purpose flour, divided
    1 package (¹/₄ ounce) fast-rising dry yeast
  ³/₄ cup water
1¹/₂ tablespoons olive oil, divided
  ³/₄ teaspoon salt
  ¹/₂ cup pitted, chopped green olives
    1 tablespoon grated Parmesan cheese

Per Serving
Calories: 56
% Calories from fat: 23
Protein (g): 1.5
Carbohydrates (g): 9.1
Fat (g): 1.4
Saturated fat (g): 0.2
Cholesterol (mg): 0.2
Sodium (mg): 145
Exchanges
Milk: 0.0
Veg.: 0.0
Fruit: 0.0
Bread: 0.5
Meat: 0.0
Fat: 0.5

1. Process 1¹/₄ cups flour and yeast in food processor fitted with steel blade until mixed well.

2. Combine water, 1 tablespoon oil, and salt in saucepan. Heat over medium-high heat, stirring until salt dissolves. Add to food processor; add 1 cup flour and process until incorporated. Dough should form a firm ball; add more flour, if necessary.

3. Transfer dough to greased bowl. Lightly brush top of dough with half of remaining olive oil. Let rise, covered, in warm place until doubled in size, about 25 minutes. Punch down dough.

4. Sprinkle dough with olives, and knead until incorporated. Shape dough into a round on lightly floured work surface; brush dough with remaining olive oil.

5. Bake on greased baking sheet at 450 degrees until bread is nicely browned, about 15 minutes. Cut into 24 wedges, sprinkle with Parmesan cheese, and bake until cheese melts, 2 to 3 minutes.

EASY HERB LAVOSH

A quick, easy, delicious accent for soups and stews.

6 servings

1 whole wheat, *or* plain, crisp lavosh (15 inches)
Vegetable cooking spray
1/2-3/4 teaspoon dried herb leaves (see Tip below)

Per Serving
Calories: 132
% Calories from fat: 3
Protein (g): 5
Carbohydrates (g): 29.2
Fat (g): 0.6
Saturated fat (g): 0.1
Cholesterol (mg): 0
Sodium (mg): 1
Exchanges
Milk: 0.0
Veg.: 0.0
Fruit: 0.0
Bread: 2.0
Meat: 0.0
Fat: 0.0

1. Spray top of lavosh generously with cooking spray and sprinkle with herbs. Bake on a cookie sheet or piece of aluminum foil at 350 degrees until browned, 4 to 6 minutes (watch carefully as lavosh can burn easily).

Tip: Use any dried herb leaves you want, or a mix of herbs, such as Italian seasoning, bouquet garni, or creole seasoning.

Variation:
Caraway-Dill Lavosh—Make recipe as above, substituting 1¹/2 teaspoons caraway seeds and ³/4 teaspoon dried dill weed for the dried herb leaves.

WHOLE WHEAT LAVOSH

A flat cracker bread that is perfect to serve with soups and stews.

6 servings (1 each)

1/2 cup warm fat-free milk (110-115 degrees)
1 package active dry yeast
2 1/3 cups whole wheat flour
1 cup all-purpose flour
1/2 teaspoon salt
1 egg white
1 tablespoon water

Per Serving
Calories: 186
% Calories from fat: 4
Protein (g): 7.7
Carbohydrates (g): 38.5
Fat (g): 0.8
Saturated fat (g): 0.2
Cholesterol (mg): 0.3
Sodium (mg): 150
Exchanges
Milk: 0.0
Veg.: 0.0
Fruit: 0.0
Bread: 2.5
Meat: 0.0
Fat:0.0

1. Mix milk and yeast in large bowl; let stand 5 minutes. Mix in whole wheat flour, 1/2 cup all-purpose flour, and salt; mix in enough remaining 1/2 cup all-purpose flour to make a smooth dough. Let stand, covered, 15 to 20 minutes.

2. Divide dough into 6 equal pieces. Roll each piece on lightly floured surface into a 3 to 4-inch round; place on greased cookie sheet. Beat egg white and water; brush over tops of dough.

3. Bake lavosh at 425 degrees until crisp and browned, 5 to 8 minutes, turning lavosh halfway through baking time. (Lavosh will become crisper upon cooling, so do not overbake.) Cool on wire rack.

GARLIC BREAD

Select a good quality French or Italian loaf for this aromatic bread, or use a sourdough bread for an interesting flavor variation.

4 servings

4 thick slices French, *or* Italian, bread
Olive oil cooking spray
2 cloves garlic, cut into halves

Per Serving
Calories: 71
% Calories from fat: 10
Protein (g): 2.3
Carbohydrates (g): 13.5
Fat (g): 0.8
Saturated fat (g): 0.2
Cholesterol (mg): 0
Sodium (mg): 152
Exchanges
Milk: 0.0
Veg.: 0.0
Fruit: 0.0
Bread: 1.0
Meat: 0.0
Fat: 0.0

1. Spray both sides of bread generously with cooking spray. Broil on cookie sheet 4 inches from heat source until browned, about 1 minute on each side.

2. Rub both sides of hot toast with cut sides of garlic. Omit garlic cloves.

Variation:
Parmesan Garlic Bread—Combine 2 tablespoons grated Parmesan cheese and 1 teaspoon minced garlic. Spray bread with cooking spray as above and spread top of each slice with cheese mixture. Broil as above, or wrap loosely in aluminum foil and bake at 350 degrees until warm, about 5 minutes.

HEARTY VEGETABLE-RYE BREAD

Cauliflower adds a subtle flavor to this aromatic rye loaf.

1 loaf (10 servings)

1 package active dry yeast
1/3 cup warm water (110-115 degrees)
1 teaspoon sugar
1 cup pureed cooked cauliflower
1 tablespoon margarine, melted
1 tablespoon light molasses
1 tablespoon spicy brown mustard
2¹/₂-3 cups all-purpose flour, divided
1 cup rye flour
1/2 teaspoon salt
1¹/₂ teaspoons caraway seeds, crushed, divided
1¹/₂ teaspoons fennel seeds, crushed, divided
1 teaspoon dried dill weed
1 egg white, beaten

Per Serving
Calories: 177
% Calories from fat: 9
Protein (g): 5.3
Carbohydrates (g): 34.8
Fat (g): 1.9
Saturated fat (g): 0.3
Cholesterol (mg): 0
Sodium (mg): 149
Exchanges
Milk: 0.0
Veg.: 0.0
Fruit: 0.0
Bread: 2.0
Meat: 0.0
Fat: 0.5

1. Mix yeast, water, and sugar in large bowl; let stand 5 minutes. Mix in cauliflower, margarine, molasses, and mustard. Mix in 2 cups all-purpose flour, rye flour, salt, 1 teaspoon caraway seeds, 1 teaspoon fennel seeds, and dill weed. Mix in enough remaining 1 cup all-purpose flour to make smooth dough.

2. Knead dough on floured surface until smooth and elastic, about 5 minutes. Place dough in greased bowl; let stand, covered, in warm place until doubled in size, about 1 hour. Punch dough down.

3. Shape dough into long or round loaf on greased cookie sheet. Let rise, loosely covered, until doubled in size, 45 to 60 minutes. Slash top of loaf with sharp knife; brush with egg white and sprinkle with remaining 1/2 teaspoon caraway seeds and 1/2 teaspoon fennel seeds.

4. Bake at 350 degrees until bread is golden and sounds hollow when tapped, 40 to 50 minutes. Cool on wire rack.

ROASTED RED PEPPER BREAD

Bake in freeform long or round loaves, or in pans. For convenience, use jarred fire-roasted red peppers.

2 loaves (8 servings each)

2¼-2¾   cups all-purpose flour
     ³/₄   cup whole wheat flour
     ¹/₄   cup grated fat-free Parmesan cheese
     1   teaspoon Italian seasoning
     ¹/₂   teaspoon salt
     1   package fast-rising active dry yeast
  1¹/₄   cups very hot water (125-130 degrees)
     1   tablespoon olive oil
     4   ounces reduced-fat mozzarella cheese, cut into ¹/₂-inch cubes
     ¹/₂   cup coarsely chopped roasted red pepper
     1   egg white, beaten
     2   teaspoons water
       Italian seasoning

Per Serving
Calories: 119
% Calories from fat: 16
Protein (g): 5.6
Carbohydrates (g): 19
Fat (g): 2.2
Saturated fat (g): 0.9
Cholesterol (mg): 3.8
Sodium (mg): 133
Exchanges
Milk: 0.0
Veg.: 0.0
Fruit: 0.0
Bread: 1.5
Meat: 0.0
Fat: 0.5

1. Combine 2¹/₄ cups all-purpose flour, whole wheat flour, Parmesan cheese, Italian seasoning, salt, and yeast in large bowl; add water and oil, mixing until smooth. Mix in mozzarella cheese and red pepper; mix in enough remaining ¹/₂ cup all-purpose flour to make smooth dough.

2. Knead dough on floured surface until smooth and elastic, about 5 minutes. Place dough in greased bowl; let rise, covered, in warm place until doubled in size, about 30 minutes. Punch dough down.

3. Divide dough into 2 equal pieces. Shape each into loaf and place in greased 9 x 5-inch loaf pan, or shape into round or long loaves on greased cookie sheets. Let stand, covered, until doubled in size, about 30 minutes.

4. Slash top of loaves with sharp knife. Mix egg white and water; brush over dough and sprinkle with Italian seasoning. Bake at 375 degrees until loaves are golden and sound hollow when tapped, 35 to 40 minutes. Remove from pans and cool on wire racks.

LIMA BEAN WHEAT BREAD

Any kind of pureed beans can be used in this moist, dense bread.

3 loaves (10 servings each)

2	packages active dry yeast
1/2	cup warm water (110-115 degrees)
1	cup cooked dried lima beans, *or* canned lima beans, rinsed, drained
1	cup water
2	cups fat-free milk
4-6	tablespoons margarine, melted
1/3	cup sugar
4 1/2-5 1/2	cups all-purpose flour
1 1/2	cups whole wheat flour
1 1/2	teaspoons salt
	Fat-free milk

Per Serving
Calories: 125
% Calories from fat: **13**
Protein (g): 4
Carbohydrates (g): **23.2**
Fat (g): 1.9
Saturated fat (g): 0.4
Cholesterol (mg): 0.3
Sodium (mg): 133

Exchanges
Milk: 0.0
Veg.: 0.0
Fruit: 0.0
Bread: 1.5
Meat: 0.0
Fat: 0.5

1. Mix yeast and warm water in small bowl; let stand 5 minutes. Process beans and 1 cup water in food processor or blender until smooth. Mix bean puree, 2 cups milk, margarine, and sugar in large bowl; mix in yeast mixture, 4 1/2 cups all-purpose flour, whole wheat flour, and salt. Mix in enough remaining 1 cup all-purpose flour to make soft dough.

2. Knead dough on floured surface until smooth and elastic, about 5 minutes. Place dough in greased bowl and let rise, covered, in warm place until doubled in size, about 1 hour. Punch dough down.

3. Divide dough into 3 equal pieces. Shape each piece into oval loaf on greased cookie sheet. Let rise, loosely covered, until doubled in size, about 45 minutes.

4. Brush loaves with milk. Bake until loaves are golden and sound hollow when tapped, about 1 hour. Transfer to wire racks and cool.

Variation:
White Bean Rye Bread—Make recipe as above, substituting Great Northern or navy beans for the lima beans, and rye flour for the whole wheat flour. Add 1 1/2 teaspoons lightly crushed caraway seeds to the dough; sprinkle loaves lightly with additional seeds before baking.

SWEET POTATO BRAIDS

Canned pumpkin can be substituted for the sweet potatoes, if desired.

2 loaves (12 servings each)

2 packages active dry yeast
1/4 cup warm fat-free milk (110-115 degrees)
1 cup mashed cooked sweet potatoes
1³/4 cups fat-free milk
1/4 cup vegetable oil
1 egg
4 cups all-purpose flour
2 cups whole wheat flour
1 teaspoon salt

Per Serving
Calories: 156
% Calories from fat: 17
Protein (g): 4.9
Carbohydrates (g): 27.7
Fat (g): 2.9
Saturated fat (g): 0.5
Cholesterol (mg): 9.2
Sodium (mg): 105
Exchanges
Milk: 0.0
Veg.: 0.0
Fruit: 0.0
Bread: 2.0
Meat: 0.0
Fat: 0.5

1. Mix yeast and warm milk in large bowl; let stand 5 minutes. Stir in sweet potatoes, milk, oil, and egg; add 3 cups all-purpose flour, whole wheat flour, and salt, mixing until smooth. Mix in enough remaining 1 cup all-purpose flour to make smooth dough.

2. Knead dough on floured surface until smooth and elastic, about 5 minutes. Place dough in bowl; let rise, covered, in warm place until doubled in size, about 1 hour. Punch down dough.

3. Divide dough into 2 equal halves; divide each half into thirds. Roll pieces of dough into strips, 12 inches long. Braid 3 strips; fold ends under and place on greased cookie sheet. Repeat with remaining dough strips. Let rise, loosely covered, until doubled in size, 30 to 45 minutes.

4. Bake until breads are golden and sound hollow when tapped, 45 to 55 minutes. Transfer to wire racks and cool.

MULTI-GRAIN BATTER BREAD

Batter breads are quick and easy to make, requiring no kneading and only one rise.

2 loaves (16 servings each)

3¼ cups all-purpose flour
1 cup whole wheat flour
¼ cup soy flour, *or* quick-cooking oats
¾ cup quick-cooking oats
¼ cup sugar
½ teaspoon salt
2 packages fast-rising yeast
1 cup cooked brown rice
2¼ cups very hot fat-free milk (125-130 degrees)
2 tablespoons vegetable oil

Per Serving
Calories: 97
% Calories from fat: 13
Protein (g): 3.5
Carbohydrates (g): 17.9
Fat (g): 1.4
Saturated fat (g): 0.2
Cholesterol (mg): 0.3
Sodium (mg): 43
Exchanges
Milk: 0.0
Veg.: 0.0
Fruit: 0.0
Bread: 1.0
Meat: 0.0
Fat: 0.5

1. Combine flours, oats, sugar, salt, and yeast in large bowl; stir in rice. Add milk and oil, mixing until smooth. Spoon batter into 2 greased 8½ x 4½-inch bread pans; let stand, loosely covered, until doubled in size, about 30 minutes.

2. Bake bread at 375 degrees until loaves are browned and sound hollow when tapped, 35 to 40 minutes. Remove from pans and cool on wire racks.

PEASANT BREAD

Six grains and ground nuts are combined in this hearty, dense-textured, country-style bread. Wonderful toasted too!

2 small loaves (8 servings each)

2 packages active dry yeast
½ cup warm water (110-115 degrees)
1¼ cups whole wheat flour
½ cup millet
½ cup cracked wheat
½ cup yellow cornmeal
½ cup bulgur wheat
½ cup quick-cooking oats

Per Serving
Calories: 197
% Calories from fat: 22
Protein (g): 5.4
Carbohydrates (g): 34.2
Fat (g): 5
Saturated fat (g): 0.6
Cholesterol (mg): 0
Sodium (mg): 137
Exchanges
Milk: 0.0
Veg.: 0.0
Fruit: 0.0
Bread: 2.0
Meat: 0.0
Fat: 1.0

^{1}/2 cup ground pecans
1 teaspoon salt
1^1/4 cups lukewarm water
^{1}/4 cup honey
2 tablespoons vegetable oil
1-2 cups unbleached all-purpose flour

1. Mix yeast and ^{1}/2 cup warm water in small bowl; let stand 5 minutes. Mix whole wheat flour, millet, cracked wheat, cornmeal, bulgur, oats, pecans, and salt in large bowl; stir in yeast mixture, 1^1/4 cups water, honey, and oil. Mix in enough all-purpose flour to make dough easy to handle.

2. Knead dough on floured surface until smooth and elastic, about 5 minutes (dough will be heavy and difficult to handle). Place bread in greased bowl; let rise, covered, in warm place until doubled in size, about 1^1/2 hours. Punch down dough.

3. Divide dough in half; shape into 2 round loaves on greased baking sheet. Let stand, loosely covered, until doubled in size, about 1^1/2 hours.

4. Bake bread at 350 degrees until loaves are deep golden brown and sound hollow when tapped, about 40 minutes. Transfer to wire racks to cool.

POTATO BREAD

Breads made with mashed potatoes are very moist and retain their freshness well. This dough can be conveniently made in advance and refrigerated up to 5 days.

2 loaves (16 servings each)

1 package active dry yeast
1^1/2 cups warm water (110-115 degrees)
2 tablespoons sugar
3 tablespoons margarine, softened
2 eggs
1 cup mashed potatoes, lukewarm
6-6^1/2 cups all-purpose flour
1 . cup whole wheat flour
1 teaspoon salt
Fat-free milk

Per Serving
Calories: 121
% Calories from fat: **13**
Protein (g): 3.6
Carbohydrates (g): **22.7**
Fat (g): 1.7
Saturated fat (g): 0.4
Cholesterol (mg): 13.4
Sodium (mg): 103
Exchanges
Milk: 0.0
Veg.: 0.0
Fruit: 0.0
Bread: 1.5
Meat: 0.0
Fat: 0.5

1. Mix yeast and warm water in large bowl; let stand 5 minutes. Mix in sugar, margarine, eggs, and mashed potatoes. Mix in 5^1/$_2$ cups all-purpose flour, whole wheat flour, and salt; mix in enough remaining 1 cup all-purpose flour to make smooth dough.

2. Knead dough on floured surface until smooth and elastic, about 5 minutes. Place dough in greased bowl; let rise, covered, in warm place until doubled in size, 1 to 1^1/$_2$ hours. Punch down dough.

3. Divide dough into 2 equal pieces; shape into loaves and place in greased 9 x 5-inch loaf pans. Let stand, loosely covered, until doubled in size, about 45 minutes.

4. Brush tops of loaves with milk. Bake at 375 degrees until loaves are golden and sound hollow when tapped, about 45 minutes. Remove from pans and cool on wire racks.

THREE-GRAIN MOLASSES BREAD

Molasses and brown sugar give this hearty-textured quick bread a special flavor.

1 loaf (12 servings)

1 cup all-purpose flour	
1 cup whole wheat flour	
1 cup yellow cornmeal	
1 teaspoon baking soda	
^{1}/$_2$ teaspoon salt	
1^1/$_2$ cups water	
^{1}/$_2$ cup light molasses	
^{1}/$_2$ cup packed light brown sugar	
3 tablespoons vegetable oil	

Per Serving
Calories: 155
% Calories from fat: 17
Protein (g): 2.5
Carbohydrates (g): 30.5
Fat (g): 3
Saturated fat (g): 0.4
Cholesterol (mg): 0
Sodium (mg): 153
Exchanges
Milk: 0.0
Veg.: 0.0
Fruit: 0.0
Bread: 2.0
Meat: 0.0
Fat: 0.5

1. Mix all ingredients in large bowl. Pour batter into greased 9 x 5-inch loaf pan.

2. Bake bread at 350 degrees until wooden pick comes out clean, about 1 hour. Remove bread from pan and cool on wire rack.

BREAD MACHINE CORNBREAD

Here's an easy machine bread that's a perfect go-with for chilies, chowders, or stews. To add a little nip in each bite, add 2 teaspoons crushed red pepper along with the salt and sugar.

12 servings

1 cup water
1 tablespoon canola oil
1 tablespoon fat-free dry milk crystals
1/2 teaspoon salt
1 tablespoon sugar
2 1/2 cups bread flour
1/2 cup yellow cornmeal
2 teaspoons bread machine yeast

Per Serving
Calories: 136
% Calories from fat: 11
Protein (gm): 4.2
Carbohydrate (gm): 26.4
Fat (gm): 1.6
Saturated fat (gm): 0.1
Cholesterol (mg): 0.1
Sodium (mg): 102
Exchanges
Milk: 0.0
Veg.: 0.0
Fruit: 0.0
Bread: 2.0
Meat: 0.0
Fat: 0.0

1. Place ingredients in bread machine pan in order given in ingredient list. Program machine for basic white bread; press start.
2. When bread has finished baking, remove it from pan. Cool on wire rack.

GREEN CHILI CORNBREAD

If using mild canned chilies, consider adding a teaspoon or so of minced jalapeño chili for a piquant accent. Serve this flavorful cornbread warm.

9 servings

Vegetable cooking spray
1/4 cup chopped red bell pepper
2 cloves garlic, minced
1/2 teaspoon cumin seeds, crushed
1 1/4 cups yellow cornmeal
3/4 cup all-purpose flour
2 teaspoons baking powder
1/2 teaspoon baking soda
1 teaspoon sugar
1/2 teaspoon salt
1 1/4 cups buttermilk

Per Serving
Calories: 184
% Calories from fat: 29
Protein (g): 5.6
Carbohydrates (g): 27.6
Fat (g): 6.1
Saturated fat (g): 1.3
Cholesterol (mg): 24.9
Sodium (mg): 562
Exchanges
Milk: 0.0
Veg.: 0.0
Fruit: 0.0
Bread: 2.0
Meat: 0.0
Fat: 1.0

$^1/_2$ cup canned cream-style corn

1 can (4 ounces) chopped hot, *or* mild, green chilies, drained

1 egg

2 egg whites

$3^1/_2$ tablespoons margarine, melted

1. Spray a small skillet with cooking spray; heat over medium heat until hot. Saute red bell pepper, garlic, and cumin seeds until pepper is tender, 2 to 3 minutes.

2. Combine cornmeal, flour, baking powder, baking soda, sugar, and salt in large bowl. Add buttermilk, bell pepper mixture, and remaining ingredients; mix until smooth. Spread batter in greased 8-inch-square baking pan.

3. Bake at 425 degrees until cornbread is golden, about 30 minutes. Cool in pan on wire rack.

ROASTED CHILI CORNBREAD

Roasted chilies and corn cut from the cob make this a cornbread to remember!

9 servings

2 ears corn, in the husks

Mesquite-flavored vegetable cooking spray

1 small red bell pepper, halved

1 small poblano chili, halved

1 jalapeño chili, halved

3 green onions, white parts only

$^1/_2$ teaspoon ground cumin

$^1/_2$ teaspoon dried oregano leaves

$1^1/_2$ cups all-purpose flour

$^1/_2$ cup plus 1 tablespoon yellow cornmeal

3 tablespoons light brown sugar

$2^3/_4$ teaspoons baking powder

$^1/_2$-$^3/_4$ teaspoon salt

2 eggs

1 cup buttermilk

3 tablespoons minced cilantro

Per Serving
Calories: 169
% Calories from fat: 10
Protein (gm): 5.8
Carbohydrate (gm): 32.5
Fat (gm): 2
Saturated fat (gm): 0.6
Cholesterol (mg): 48.1
Sodium (mg): 328
Exchanges
Milk: 0.0
Veg.: 0.0
Fruit: 0.0
Bread: 2.0
Meat: 0.0
Fat: 0.5

1. Soak corn in water to cover for 30 minutes; drain.

2. Spray aluminum foil-lined jelly roll pan with cooking spray; arrange vegetables in single layer on pan, with corn to the outside. Spray vegetables, except corn, generously with cooking spray; sprinkle vegetables, except corn, with cumin and oregano.

3. Roast vegetables at 425 degrees until browned and tender, about 40 minutes. Let stand until corn is cool enough to handle. Remove and discard corn husks; cut corn kernels off cobs. Chop remaining vegetables into 1/4-inch pieces.

4. Combine flour, 1/2 cup cornmeal, brown sugar, baking powder, and salt in large bowl. Whisk eggs into buttermilk; add to flour mixture, stirring just until combined. Stir in vegetables and cilantro.

5. Grease 8-inch baking pan and sprinkle with the remaining 1 tablespoon cornmeal; pour batter into pan. Bake at 350 degrees until cornbread is browned and toothpick comes out clean, 35 to 40 minutes. Cool on wire rack; serve warm.

JALAPEÑO CORNBREAD

The secret to the moistness in this spicy cornbread is pureed white beans.

9 servings

1/4	green bell pepper, chopped
1-2	teaspoons minced jalapeño chili
2	cloves garlic, minced
3/4	teaspoon dried oregano leaves
1/2	teaspoon ground cumin
1/4-1/2	teaspoon crushed red pepper
1/4	cup margarine
1 1/3	cups all-purpose flour
2/3	cup yellow cornmeal
1	tablespoon sugar
2	teaspoons baking powder
1/2	teaspoon baking soda
1/2	teaspoon salt
1	cup canned Great Northern beans, rinsed, drained, divided
1	cup buttermilk
2	eggs
1/4	cup canned cream-style corn

Per Serving
Calories: 202
% Calories from fat: 30
Protein (gm): 6.6
Carbohydrate (gm): 29.8
Fat (gm): 7
Saturated fat (gm): 1.6
Cholesterol (mg): 48.1
Sodium (mg): 508
Exchanges
Milk: 0.0
Veg.: 0.0
Fruit: 0.0
Bread: 2.0
Meat: 0.0
Fat: 1.5

1. Saute bell pepper, jalapeño chili, garlic, oregano, cumin, and crushed red pepper in margarine in small skillet until tender, about 5 minutes; cool.

2. Combine flour, cornmeal, sugar, baking powder, baking soda, and salt in large bowl.

3. Process $2/3$ cup beans in food processor until smooth; add buttermilk, eggs, and corn and process, using pulse technique, until smooth. Add to flour mixture, mixing just until ingredients are blended; fold in remaining $1/3$ cup beans and pepper mixture.

4. Pour batter into greased 8- or 9- inch-square pan. Bake at 425 degrees until cornbread is browned and toothpick inserted in center comes out clean, about 40 minutes. Cut into squares.

DILL-CREAM CHEESE BISCUITS

Fresh dill puts plenty of herbal pizzazz into these tender biscuits. And because they're a drop rather than a rolled biscuit, they're fast to make.

12 servings (1 each)

2	cups unbleached all-purpose flour
3	teaspoons baking powder
$1/4$	teaspoon salt
$2^1/2$	tablespoons cold margarine, cut into pieces
$2^1/2$	tablespoons fat-free cream cheese
2	tablespoons finely chopped fresh, *or* 2 teaspoons dried, dill weed
$3/4$	cup fat-free milk

Per Serving
Calories: 106
% Calories from fat: 22
Protein (gm): 3.2
Carbohydrate (gm): 17.1
Fat (gm): 2.6
Saturated fat (gm): 0.5
Cholesterol (mg): 0.5
Sodium (mg): 224
Exchanges
Milk: 0.0
Veg.: 0.0
Fruit: 0.0
Bread: 1.0
Meat: 0.0
Fat: 0.5

1. Combine flour, baking powder, and salt in medium bowl. Cut in margarine and cream cheese until mixture resembles coarse crumbs. Mix in dill; mix in milk with fork until ingredients are just combined.

2. Drop biscuits by tablespoons onto greased cookie sheet. Bake at 450 degrees until lightly browned, 10 to 12 minutes.

WHEAT BISCUITS WITH POPPY SEEDS

These slightly nutty-tasting biscuits will complement any recipe in this book.

12 servings (1 each)

1¹/2 cups unbleached all-purpose flour
¹/2 cup whole wheat flour
3 teaspoons baking powder
¹/4 teaspoon salt
1 tablespoon poppy seeds
3 tablespoons cold margarine, cut into pieces
³/4 cup fat-free milk

Per Serving
Calories: 109
% Calories from fat: 28
Protein (gm): 3
Carbohydrate (gm): 16.8
Fat (gm): 3.4
Saturated fat (gm): 0.7
Cholesterol (mg): 0.3
Sodium (mg): 212
Exchanges
Milk: 0.0
Veg.: 0.0
Fruit: 0.0
Bread: 1.0
Meat: 0.0
Fat: 0.5

1. Combine flours, baking powder, salt, and poppy seeds in medium bowl. Cut in margarine until flour mixture resembles coarse crumbs. Mix in milk with fork until ingredients are just combined.

2. Drop biscuits by tablespoons onto greased cookie sheet. Bake at 450 degrees until lightly browned, 10 to 12 minutes.

QUICK SELF-RISING BISCUITS

Two cups all-purpose flour can be substituted for the self-rising flour; add 3 teaspoons baking powder and 1/2 teaspoon salt.

18 servings (1 each)

2 cups self-rising flour
1 tablespoon vegetable shortening
³/4-1 cup fat-free milk
1 tablespoon margarine, melted

Per Serving
Calories: 65
% Calories from fat: 21
Protein (g): 1.7
Carbohydrates (g): 10.8
Fat (g): 1.4
Saturated fat (g): 0.3
Cholesterol (mg): 0.2
Sodium (mg): 189
Exchanges
Milk: 0.0
Veg.: 0.0
Fruit: 0.0
Bread: 1.0
Meat: 0.0
Fat: 0.0

1. Measure flour into medium bowl; cut in shortening until mixture resembles coarse crumbs. Stir enough milk into flour mixture to make a soft dough. Roll dough on floured surface to 1/2 inch thickness; cut with 2-inch biscuit cutter.

2. Place biscuits in greased 13 x 9-inch baking pan; brush with melted margarine. Bake at 425 degrees until golden, about 15 minutes.

Variations:
Chive Biscuits—Mix 3 tablespoons snipped fresh, *or* dried, chives into biscuit dough.

Parmesan Biscuits—Brush biscuits with melted margarine as above; sprinkle with 2 tablespoons grated fat-free Parmesan cheese.

SWEET POTATO BISCUITS

Sweet potatoes offer moistness and a delicate sweetness to these biscuits.

18 servings (1 each)

3/4 cup mashed cooked sweet potatoes	
3-4 tablespoons margarine, melted	
2/3 cup fat-free milk	
1 3/4-2 cups all-purpose flour	
4 teaspoons baking powder	
1 tablespoon brown sugar	
1/2 teaspoon salt	
Fat-free milk	
Ground nutmeg, as garnish	

Per Serving
Calories: 82
% Calories from fat: 23
Protein (g): 1.8
Carbohydrates (g): 14
Fat (g): 2.1
Saturated fat (g): 0.4
Cholesterol (mg): 0.1
Sodium (mg): 161
Exchanges
Milk: 0.0
Veg.: 0.0
Fruit: 0.0
Bread: 1.0
Meat: 0.0
Fat: 0.5

1. Mix sweet potatoes and margarine in medium bowl; stir in 2/3 cup milk. Mix in 1 3/4 cups flour, baking powder, brown sugar, and salt. Mix in remaining 1/4 cup flour if dough is too sticky to handle easily.

2. Knead dough on floured surface 5 to 6 times. Roll on floured surface to 1/2 inch thickness; cut with 2-inch biscuit cutter and place close together on greased baking sheet. Brush biscuits lightly with milk and sprinkle lightly with nutmeg.

3. Bake biscuits at 425 degrees until golden, 12 to 15 minutes.

Variation:
Herbed Mashed Potato Biscuits—Make recipe as above, substituting mashed Idaho potatoes for the sweet potatoes; add 1 teaspoon bouquet garni or Italian seasoning to the dough. Bake as above.

VINEGAR BISCUITS

Every cook, no doubt, has her or his version of this old-fashioned biscuit recipe.

12 servings (1 each)

³/4 cup fat-free milk

¹/4 cup cider vinegar

2 cups all-purpose flour

1¹/2 teaspoons baking soda

1 teaspoon cream of tartar

¹/2 teaspoon salt

3 tablespoons vegetable shortening, melted

Per Serving
Calories: 109
% Calories from fat: 27
Protein (g): 2.7
Carbohydrates (g): 17.1
Fat (g): 3.2
Saturated fat (g): 0.8
Cholesterol (mg): 0.3
Sodium (mg): 255
Exchanges
Milk: 0.0
Veg.: 0.0
Fruit: 0.0
Bread: 1.0
Meat: 0.0
Fat: 0.5

1. Mix milk and vinegar in glass measure; let stand 3 to 4 minutes. Combine flour, baking soda, cream of tartar, and salt in medium bowl; add milk mixture and shortening, mixing until blended.

2. Knead dough on generously floured surface 1 to 2 minutes. Pat dough into ¹/2 inch thickness; cut with 3-inch biscuit cutter. Bake on greased cookie sheet at 425 degrees until golden, 10 to 12 minutes.

WILD RICE MUFFINS

Wild rice adds crunchy texture and a nutritional boost to these hearty muffins.

12 servings (1 each)

1/2 cup uncooked wild rice
2 cups water
1 teaspoon salt, divided
1 cup fat-free milk
4 tablespoons margarine, melted
1 egg, beaten
2 egg whites
1 cup all-purpose flour
1/2 cup whole wheat flour
3 tablespoons baking powder
1 tablespoon sugar

Per Serving
Calories: 136
% Calories from fat: 30
Protein (g): 4.6
Carbohydrates (g): 19.4
Fat (g): 4.5
Saturated fat (g): 0.9
Cholesterol (mg): 18.1
Sodium (mg): 494
Exchanges
Milk: 0.0
Veg.: 0.0
Fruit: 0.0
Bread: 1.5
Meat: 0.0
Fat: 0.5

1. Heat wild rice, water, and 1/2 teaspoon salt to boiling in small saucepan; reduce heat and simmer, covered, until rice is tender, 45 to 50 minutes. Drain, if necessary, and cool.

2. Mix milk, margarine, egg, egg whites, and cooked rice in large bowl. Add combined all-purpose and whole wheat flour, baking powder, sugar, and remaining 1/2 teaspoon salt, mixing just until dry ingredients are moistened.

3. Spoon batter into 12 greased muffin cups. Bake at 400 degrees until muffins are browned, 20 to 25 minutes. Remove from pans and cool on wire racks.

POLENTA

This basic recipe can be varied to your taste by adding sauteed onion and garlic, cheese, herbs, etc. Note the variations below.

6 servings (about 1 cup each)

3 cups water
³/₄ cup yellow cornmeal
    Salt and pepper, to taste

Per Serving
Calories: 55
% Calories from fat: 9
Protein (g): 1.2
Carbohydrates (g): 11.7
Fat (g): 0.5
Saturated fat (g): 0.1
Cholesterol (mg): 0
Sodium (mg): 5
Exchanges
Milk: 0.0
Veg.: 0.0
Fruit: 0.0
Bread: 1.0
Meat: 0.0
Fat: 0.0

1. Heat water to boiling in medium saucepan; gradually stir in cornmeal. Cook over medium to medium-low heat, stirring constantly, until polenta thickens enough to hold its shape but is still soft, 5 to 8 minutes. Season to taste with salt and pepper.

Variations:

Blue Cheese Polenta—Stir ¹/₂ cup (2 ounces) crumbled blue cheese, *or* other blue-veined cheese, into the cooked polenta.

Goat Cheese Polenta—Stir ¹/₄ to ¹/₂ cup (1 to 2 ounces) crumbled goat cheese into the cooked polenta.

Garlic Polenta—Saute ¹/₄ cup finely chopped onion and 4 to 6 cloves minced garlic in 1 tablespoon olive oil in medium saucepan; add water, as above, and complete recipe.

Roasted Pepper-Goat Cheese Polenta—Gently stir ¹/₄ to ¹/₂ cup crumbled goat cheese and ¹/₃ cup coarsely chopped roasted red pepper into the cooked polenta.

HERBED POLENTA

Gently seasoned with onions, garlic, and basil, this polenta can be served immediately after cooking, or cooled and cooked as the recipe directs.

4-6 servings

Olive oil cooking spray

2 green onions and tops, sliced

1 clove garlic, minced

1 teaspoon dried basil leaves

2¹/2 cups reduced-sodium vegetable, *or* chicken, broth

³/4 cup yellow cornmeal

¹/2 teaspoon salt

Per Serving
Calories: 124
% Calories from fat: 9
Protein (g): 2.5
Carbohydrates (g): 22.4
Fat (g): 1.3
Saturated fat (g): 0.2
Cholesterol (mg): 0
Sodium (mg): 309
Exchanges
Milk: 0.0
Veg.: 0.0
Fruit: 0.0
Bread: 1.5
Meat: 0.0
Fat: 0.5

1. Spray large saucepan with cooking spray; heat over medium heat until hot. Saute onions, garlic, and basil until tender, about 5 minutes. Add broth and heat to boiling; gradually stir in cornmeal and salt. Cook over low heat, stirring constantly, until thickened, about 10 minutes.

2. Pour polenta into lightly greased 8-inch cake pan; cool to room temperature. Refrigerate, lightly covered, until polenta is firm, 3 to 4 hours.

3. Spray large skillet with cooking spray; heat over medium heat until hot. Cut polenta into wedges; cook in skillet over medium heat until browned, 3 to 4 minutes on each side.

SPINACH PESTO

This robust pesto will enhance the flavor of many soups and stews.

4 servings (about 2 tablespoons each)

  1 cup loosely packed fresh spinach

  3 tablespoons finely chopped fresh, *or* 1 tablespoon dried, basil leaves

1-2 cloves garlic

  1 tablespoon grated Parmesan cheese

  2 tablespoons olive oil

1-2 teaspoons lemon juice

     Salt and pepper, to taste

Per Serving
Calories: 68
% Calories from fat: 86
Protein (g): 1
Carbohydrates (g): 1.4
Fat (g): 6.8
Saturated fat (g): 0.9
Cholesterol (mg): 0
Sodium (mg): 22
Exchanges
Milk: 0.0
Veg.: 0.0
Fruit: 0.0
Bread: 0.0
Meat: 0.0
Fat: 1.5

1. Process all ingredients, except lemon juice, salt, and pepper, in food processor or blender until smooth. Season with lemon juice, salt, and pepper.

2. Let stand 2 to 3 hours for flavors to blend, or refrigerate until serving time. Serve at room temperature.

Variations:

Spinach-Cilantro Pesto—Make recipe as above, adding 1/4 cup packed cilantro leaves, 2 cloves garlic, and 1/4 to 1/2 teaspoon ground cumin; substitute lime juice for the lemon juice.

Cilantro Pesto—Make recipe as above, using 1/2 cup spinach and 1 1/2 cups packed cilantro and adding 3 tablespoons pine nuts or walnuts; omit basil.

SUN-DRIED TOMATO PESTO

Use yellow or red sun-dried tomatoes in this flavorful pesto.

4 servings (about 2 tablespoons each)

> $^1/_2$ cup sun-dried tomatoes (not in oil)
> $^1/_2$ cup boiling water
> $^1/_2$ cup packed basil leaves
> 2 cloves garlic
> 3 tablespoons olive oil
> 2 tablespoons grated fat-free Parmesan cheese
> Salt and pepper, to taste

Per Serving
Calories: 118
% Calories from fat: 75
Protein (g): 2.2
Carbohydrates (g): 5.5
Fat (g): 10.4
Saturated fat (g): 1.4
Cholesterol (mg): 0
Sodium (mg): 164
Exchanges
Milk: 0.0
Veg.: 0.0
Fruit: 0.0
Bread: 0.5
Meat: 0.0
Fat: 2.0

1. Soak tomatoes in boiling water in bowl until softened, about 10 minutes. Drain, reserving liquid.

2. Process tomatoes, basil, garlic, oil, and cheese in food processor or blender, adding enough reserved liquid to make a smooth, spoonable mixture. Season to taste with salt and pepper.

3. Let stand 2 to 3 hours for flavors to blend, or refrigerate until serving time. Serve at room temperature.

FENNEL PESTO

This pesto is especially good with vegetarian soups and stews.

6 servings (about $^1/_4$ cup each)

> 1 tablespoon fennel seeds
> Hot water
> 1 cup chopped fennel bulb, *or* celery
> $^1/_2$ cup loosely packed parsley
> 2 cloves garlic
> 14 walnut halves (about 1 ounce)
> 3 tablespoons water
> 1 tablespoon olive oil
> $^1/_4$ cup grated Parmesan cheese
> Salt and pepper, to taste

Per Serving
Calories: 71
% Calories from fat: 61
Protein (g): 2.6
Carbohydrates (g): 4.6
Fat (g): 5
Saturated fat (g): 0.6
Cholesterol (mg): 0
Sodium (mg): 42
Exchanges
Milk: 0.0
Veg.: 1.0
Fruit: 0.0
Bread: 0.0
Meat: 0.0
Fat: 1.0

1. Place fennel seeds in small bowl; pour hot water over to cover. Let stand 10 minutes; drain.

2. Process fennel, fennel seeds, parsley, and garlic in food processor or blender until finely chopped. Add walnuts, 3 tablespoons water, and oil; process until walnuts are finely chopped. Stir in Parmesan cheese; season to taste with salt and pepper.

3. Let stand 2 to 3 hours for flavors to blend, or refrigerate until serving time. Serve at room temperature.

RED PEPPER PESTO

Make this pesto with jarred roasted peppers, or make your own, following Step 1 in the recipe for Roasted Red Pepper Sauce (see p. 213).

4 servings (about 2 tablespoons each)

1 cup roasted red peppers
1 cup packed fresh basil
2 cloves garlic
1/4 cup grated Parmesan cheese
1 teaspoon sugar
1 teaspoon balsamic vinegar
3 tablespoons olive oil
Salt and pepper, to taste

Per Serving
Calories: 124
% Calories from fat: 71
Protein (g): 2.7
Carbohydrates (g): 6.8
Fat (g): 10.3
Saturated fat (g): 1.4
Cholesterol (mg): 0
Sodium (mg): 46
Exchanges
Milk: 0.0
Veg.: 1.0
Fruit: 0.0
Bread: 0.0
Meat: 0.0
Fat: 2.0

1. Process all ingredients, except salt and pepper, in food processor or blender until smooth. Season to taste with salt and pepper.

2. Let stand 2 to 3 hours for flavors to blend, or refrigerate until serving time. Serve at room temperature.

MINTED PESTO

The refreshing flavor of this pesto is especially good with lamb stews.

8 servings (about 2 tablespoons each)

1 cup packed mint leaves
1/2 cup packed parsley sprigs
2 cloves garlic, minced
2 tablespoons grated fat-free Parmesan cheese
2 tablespoons walnut pieces
2-3 tablespoons olive oil
2-3 tablespoons water
Salt and pepper, to taste

Per Serving
Calories: 51
% Calories from fat: 78
Protein (g): 1.2
Carbohydrates (g): 1.7
Fat (g): 4.6
Saturated fat (g): 0.5
Cholesterol (mg): 0
Sodium (mg): 15
Exchanges
Milk: 0.0
Veg.: 0.0
Fruit: 0.0
Bread: 0.0
Meat: 0.0
Fat: 1.0

1. Process all ingredients, except water, salt, and pepper, in food processor or blender until smooth. Stir in enough water to make a spoonable mixture; season to taste with salt and pepper. Serve at room temperature.

Variation:
Mixed Herb Pesto—Make recipe as above, substituting fresh basil for the mint, and adding 1/4 cup packed oregano leaves. Season to taste with lemon juice.

ROASTED SWEET PEPPER RELISH

Stir this intensely flavored relish into any soup or stew to enhance flavors.

8 servings (about 3 tablespoons each)

4 large red bell peppers, cut into halves
2 teaspoons sugar

Per Serving
Calories: 14
% Calories from fat: 4
Protein (gm): 0.3
Carbohydrate (gm): 3.4
Fat (gm): 0.1
Saturated fat (gm): 0
Cholesterol (mg): 0
Sodium (mg): 1
Exchanges
Milk: 0.0
Veg.: 0.0
Fruit: 0.0
Bread: 0.0
Meat: 0.0
Fat: 0.0

1. Place peppers, skin sides up, on a broiler pan. Broil 4 to 6 inches from heat source until skins are blistered and blackened. Place peppers in plastic bag for 5 minutes; remove skins.

2. Finely chop peppers; stir in sugar. Refrigerate until ready to use.

INDEX